TRUSTWORTHY MEN

Trustworthy Men

HOW INEQUALITY AND FAITH
MADE THE MEDIEVAL CHURCH

Ian Forrest

PRINCETON UNIVERSITY PRESS

PRINCETON & OXFORD

Published by Princeton University Press,
41 William Street, Princeton, New Jersey 08540

In the United Kingdom: Princeton University Press,
6 Oxford Street, Woodstock, Oxfordshire OX20 1TR

press.princeton.edu

Jacket image: James le Palmer, *Omne Bonum*, c. 1360–1375. F. 141r of Royal MS 6 E VI/1.
© The British Library Board

ISBN 978-0-691-18060-1

Library of Congress Control Number: 2017962588

British Library Cataloging-in-Publication Data is available

This book has been composed in Miller

Printed on acid-free paper. ∞

Printed in the United States of America

10 9 8 7 6 5 4 3 2 1

For Rees

CONTENTS

Figures

Tables

ACKNOWLEDGEMENTS

THIS BOOK HAS EMERGED from many years of enjoyment and struggle. The rewards of time spent in archives, or thinking, talking, and writing about history are immeasurable, but there's no point pretending that academic life is straightforward or easy. Frequently it's anything but. This makes the help and sustained fellowship of some wonderful people all the more valuable and worthy of celebration.

Helen Brockett has always believed in me, and has never shown any doubt that this book would see the light of day. At several crucial points from grant applications to the publication proposal, she has made me make sense. I couldn't have done it without her. Our son Adam came up with the title that a different publisher, and younger readers, may have preferred: *Trustworthy Men and Where to Find Them*. The book itself could not have been written without the inspiration and encouragement of two very special friends: Sethina Watson and John Arnold. At a number of decisive moments they made it all seem so clear and worthwhile. I trusted in their discernment and was right to do so.

I have been lucky in finding dedicated and skilled people to help with the tasks that were beyond me. The historian of enclosure in nineteenth-century Spain, Fran Beltran, worked as my research assistant, helping to produce the statistical analysis in Chapter 6. Mike Athanson, map librarian and geo-spatial data specialist in the Bodleian Library, produced the map of Lincolnshire in Chapter 7. My doctoral student Lesley MacGregor was the ideal editorial assistant during the final stages of writing. Ben Tate at Princeton's Europe office has been attentive and encouraging every step of the way, while Jenny Wolkowicki has been extremely helpful as production editor and Joseph Dahm's close attention to the text was much appreciated. Many archivists and librarians provided an impeccably professional service, giving me access to the raw materials that tell us about trustworthy men and their social contexts. In particular I would like to single out Richard Samways for his assistance with the archives of the earl of Shaftesbury, Paul Dryburgh for helping me to decipher place names in the archiepiscopal registers held at the Borthwick Institute, and Mark Forrest of the Dorset Heritage Centre who was generous enough to share with me his database of manorial debt transactions. For many years Rosalind Caird, formerly of Hereford Cathedral Library, has been a constant source of encouragement, while it has been a pleasure to spend time searching for and poring over visitation records with Chris Whittick. I would also like to note my gratitude to the Warden and Fellows of All Souls College for giving me three years of precious research time in 2003–6 during which the first, and very different, version of the present book was imagined. The award of a research fellowship by the Leverhulme Trust in 2011–12, and the provision of a year's sabbatical leave by the Oxford History Faculty and the Provost and Fellows of Oriel College in 2012–13 enabled me to complete most of the necessary research and some of the writing.

I have benefitted from discussions about trust, inequality, information, and the medieval church with a huge number of people, but most notably Frances Andrews, Merridee Bailey, Paul Brand, Chris Briggs, Oli Brown, David Charles, Teresa Dillon, Andy Fleming, Anne Haour, Susan Hurley, Paul Hyams, Tom Johnson, Annette Kehnel, Sara Lipton, Ian McLean, Shannon McSheffrey, Steve Mileson, Avner Offer, Gervase Rosser, John Sabapathy, Phillipp Schofield, Dan Smail, Alice Taylor, Claire Taylor, and Chris Wickham. I hope I've done justice to the ideas they shared with me. In addition my students Anna Boeles Rowland and Jenn Depold brought to my attention some invaluable findings from their own work on marriage litigation records and late medieval sermons respectively. It was a pleasure to be able to develop ideas in conversation with seminar participants in Cambridge, Mannheim, Nottingham, Oxford, Reading, Sheffield, and St Andrews, besides which my greatest intellectual stimulation and companionship came in three settings. The first was a conference on the study of medieval and early modern belief organised by Lucy Sackville, which occurred at a point when I naïvely thought that studying trust did not particularly involve thinking about belief: how wrong can you be? The second is my long-running involvement with the Medieval Economic and Social History seminar in Oxford which has opened my eyes to the depth and interest of historical research in these fields, to the subjective human experience of broad economic trends, and to the importance of having a question when writing history. Many of the seminar regulars have given me food for thought over the years, but none has been more influential than Ros Faith, for whose friendship and tough interrogations I am forever grateful. The third context is the Social Church Workshop (funded initially by the Higher Education Institute and the Fell Fund of Oxford University Press), which Sethina Watson and I set up in 2006, and which met regularly until 2015. Conversations with the workshop participants, including (besides those already mentioned) Anthony Bale, Lucy Donkin, Sarah Hamilton, Bronach Kane, Nick Karn, Rob Lutton, Catherine Rider, Simon Yarrow, and many others, taught me that the history of religion and the church *had* to be a social history if it were to make any sense at all. We also had a good time.

Teresa Morgan, Chris Wickham, and John Arnold kindly read the entire book in draft, delivering a sustained critique that has improved the presentation of my arguments no end. In Teresa I was lucky enough to have a college colleague working on very similar themes, and whose work on trust in the Roman Empire and early Christianity is truly inspiring. Alongside their comments, a further anonymous reviewer for the press gave advice that helped immeasurably as the book took its final form. Some of the ideas presented here appeared in different forms in *Past & Present* (2013) and *Studies in Church History* (2016); I would also like to thank the editors of those publications, especially Lyndal Roper and Frances Andrews, for their advice, and for permission to reuse material from those articles.

I owe each of these friends and colleagues a great deal, but for the past fifteen years I have been striving to repay a greater debt owed to my doctoral supervisors Miri Rubin and Rees Davies, for the investment of time and care that they made in me. It has taken this long for me fully to appreciate their wisdom and example. I hope Miri will see something of her influence in this book, and I wish I could have discussed it with Rees. From its inception, this book has always been for him.

TRUSTWORTHY MEN

IN 1328 THE VICAR of St Breock, a parish just outside Wadebridge in Cornwall, received a letter from his bishop, John Grandisson. For a parish priest this would not have been an especially common occurrence, and its arrival may have unnerved him. A letter from the bishop meant that something was afoot: perhaps some sought-for favour had been granted or, as was the case in this instance, unwelcome trouble was brewing. The letter had been written at Clyst, one of the bishop's residences, and was dated 22 June. It read:

> On behalf of some of your parishioners who have sent us an irritable petition intimating that you, against the custom long observed in the said parish regarding the payment of mortuaries, have rashly and without cause molested and unsettled them: not wishing to fail in the defence of the rights of these parishioners, our tenants, we order and exhort you to desist from all molestation, introducing no novelty until we shall be fully informed about the matter by some trustworthy men unsuspected by either party. Otherwise, we are not able to lie, we shall use whatever lawful ways and means we may to ensure that the injury done to them by you is stopped, and corrected according to the exigencies of the law.[1]

The vicar of St Breock cannot have remained unruffled by this threatening message. Bishop Grandisson was a powerful man, not only in the church, but also among the landed elite of the West Country and of the kingdom.[2] His appointment as bishop had taken place only the previous August, and this angry fulmination arrived in St Breock even before he had been enthroned in Exeter cathedral. The unfortunate vicar's existence was about to be disrupted by a bishop making a statement about episcopal power.

We know about the message because Grandisson, following the common practice of most English bishops since the middle of the thirteenth century, made copies of all his outgoing correspondence in a register. Bishops' registers are full of similar letters, taking an interest in the conduct and income of the local clergy, haranguing them, insisting that they change their ways: this was the daily grind of administering a diocese. There was a certain amount of idealism in play, with grand references to ancient customs, rights, and the law, but the bishop was also acting in his own interests. He was the lord of a manor within the parish of St Breock, benefitting from his control of some of the land and labour there, and the parishioners had complained to him in this dual capacity. What was the substance of their grievance? The vicar appears to have been collecting 'mortuaries' from the parishioners, which were payments to the parish church from the goods of deceased relatives, ostensibly in lieu of tithes unpaid during life. It was normal for these payments to be made to the rector of a church, the priest who possessed the 'benefice' or living, but St Breock was served by a vicar, in other words a deputy (from the Latin *vice*). The rector had been given leave of absence to study, and his deputy was almost certainly trying to make his salary go further by claiming the mortuaries.[3] It is hard to say exactly why the parishioners were upset, but most likely they feared being asked to pay twice (to the rector as well as the vicar), or even three times (to their lord the bishop as well, in the form of a 'heriot' or secular death duty). Although England in 1328 was recovering from the famines that had struck between 1315 and 1322, and the 'great pestilence' was twenty years away, clergy and peasantry alike were always keen to protect their means of subsistence.

Grandisson for his part rarely did things by halves, and the rumbling menace of this letter is rather typical. It exudes the self-assurance of power with its evocation of the force of the law, the rights of his tenants, and the ancient customs of the parish. It is also a missive acutely aware of the impact it seeks to make, namely the arrival of awesome secular and spiritual power in the small world of a Cornish parish. And yet its actual substance reveals a very different power dynamic. The bishop was not able to act in as summary and decisive a fashion as his rhetoric implies he might have wished. He had heard a complaint and he feared his interests might be compromised, but he did not know the local context, and he had not heard all sides of the story. Instead he had to postpone his pursuit of the 'exigencies of the law' until he had heard from 'some trustworthy men unsuspected by either party'. Who were these people? What did they do? Why did bishops need them?

The answers to these questions will unfold in many directions in this book, until they have extended so far as to demonstrate the need for a complete reconceptualization of the medieval church. In short, the 'trustworthy men' (in Latin *viri fidedigni*, literally 'men worthy of faith') were predominantly lay (that is to say nonclerical) witnesses and jurors who made the medieval church what it was between about 1200 and about 1500. In 1200 the adjective *fidedignum* was already an old word, used in the first millennium to refer to the gospels and their authors, some saints, and other holy men, and in the eleventh and twelfth centuries to refer to living informants by historians and collectors of miracle stories. But it did not yet form part of the discourse of church administration, and was notably absent from the vocabulary of Gratian, the twelfth century's most influential legal writer.[4]

Some clues as to their role and importance are contained in Grandisson's letter, and much of the evidence on which the ensuing interpretation is based comes from thousands of similar documents recorded in the registers of scores of bishops from across England between the thirteenth and the fifteenth centuries. The challenges of governing a church are revealed in Grandisson's language. We can perceive a tension between 'long observed' custom and the 'novelties' brought about by trying to make a living. At first glance custom is being praised and novelty denigrated, but a bishop's role and intellectual formation suggest something more ambiguous. He would have seen himself as both the guardian of a stable and well-ordered creation, and as the reformer of a fallen humanity and the builder of a church. Grandisson's recorded deeds show him adopting both personae. The power that bishops wielded in pursuit of these conceptual contradictions was both spiritual and temporal, deriving from their status within a hierarchy and their possession of frequently enormous landed wealth. But this did not mean they could act alone, and it was both in order to promote reform and to arrest change that bishops sought out allies in the parishes. They could not operate without such knowledge of local realities as only the locals could provide. And that is the dynamic that I shall explore in this book. It was a relationship that made the church.

The importance of the relationship between 'trustworthy men' or *viri fidedigni*, on the one hand, and bishops, on the other, is further indicated by the pattern of communication implied in Grandisson's letter. In it we see that parishioners petitioned the bishop and he responded by writing to the offending priest, saying that information would be gathered from 'trustworthy men', and that action would follow. There would also have been a report from this panel of adjudicators, and other stages of consultation and documentation, which survive less often, may have been undertaken. We can begin to see that governing a church was not simply a question of how forcefully a bishop could proclaim his authority. Even an expression as forceful as this letter had to acknowledge the gulf that separated the bishop from his subjects, and his reliance upon judgements other than his own. Furthermore, the requirement that his informants should be not only trustworthy but also 'unsuspected' hints at a nagging doubt about involving laypeople in the business of rule. These are all themes whose significance I will explore in the coming pages. Reading such letters at face value might encourage a view that the late medieval church was composed of institutions at two very different and separate levels: the diocese and the parish. But as this brief dissection of just one example has shown, to do so would be to miss the real location of institutional dynamism, which was in the communication and interaction between the two.

The institutional history of the medieval church has become something of a poor relation within the wider historical discipline in recent decades, despite, or perhaps because of, its importance to the origins of professional historiography in so many European countries. My purpose in this book is not to make a plea for the restoration of the sort of ecclesiastical history that dominated the nineteenth and twentieth centuries. The legacy of that tradition, in describing organizational structures and the emergence of offices and record-keeping procedures, as well as in editing documents, retains enormous value in its own right, but its potential to inform the history of a living social world is limited.[5] The medieval church has been much described, but its existence and character little analysed.[6]

In reaction to the traditions of ecclesiastical history the past forty years have seen historians turn in droves to the study of lived religion as a changing, dynamic, varied, and above all human phenomenon. Influenced by the anthropology of religion and often conducted across the divisions between formal academic disciplines, this movement in historiography has sought to understand religious experience in terms of gender, age, status, language community, devotional preference, identification with particular saints or cults, and a host of subtle individual negotiations of the boundaries between heresy and orthodoxy. In this movement the subjectivity of experience has been a touchstone for authenticity, and the individual Christian—rather than 'the church' as an institution—has become the primary focus of enquiry.[7] During this time the practice of ecclesiastical history has continued, but it has not responded as much as it might to the questions and methods that characterize the history of religion. As a result the 'institutional church' tends to feature most often as a backdrop to the stage upon which more exciting historical questions are addressed. But this need not be so. A wholly new set of questions can be asked of the 'institutional church' if we just change our perspective, and thinking about that letter to the vicar of St Breock in 1328 has shown us what some of these might be.

What I propose here is a new sort of institutional history, one that could be summed up in the phrase 'a social church'.[8] This is a history that treats as inseparable the influence of actions and phenomena usually studied disjointedly as religious, social, cultural, political, economic, and institutional history; it is a history in which the impact and effects of institutional action are essential to explanations of its nature and meaning. As well as being an amalgam of clergy, bishops, law, and formal institutions, the church was simultaneously an identity, something to which people felt they belonged, and an endlessly shifting constellation of real relationships: their belief, belonging, and identity experienced in relation to specific people. Because the church meant all these things, it makes little sense for historians to study the institutions, the identity, the belief, the belonging, and their socioeconomic situation as if they were not all mutually constitutive. The starting point for analysis, suggested by the example from early fourteenth-century Cornwall, is the observation that in deciding upon obligations arising from membership of a parish and the passage from life to death, neither the parishioners nor the bishop possessed the capacity to effect change on their own. Each appealed to the other for assistance, making plain their symbiosis and mutual historical development. We might say that both the character of life in the parish and the bishop's government of his diocese were formed by the interaction between the two. The clergy, though they were often central to the lives of parishes and the work of dioceses, found themselves caught in the middle of this alliance between bishops and 'trustworthy men'. Thinking of parishes and bishops as part of a 'social church' therefore necessitates a more expansive definition of 'institutions', seeing them more as the sum of multiple actions and habits of thought rather than simply as organizational structures. It is an approach heavily influenced by the sociology of interaction, which sees repeated patterns of human connection as the building blocks of all social phenomena, by the so-called 'new institutional economics', which interprets individual transactions as constitutive of (and not just reactions to) the 'rules of the game', and by feminist history writing, which sees patriarchy as a dispersed and adaptable institution without any single definitive location.[9] The ways in which this scholarship has affected my thinking will become apparent in the following chapters.

I will pursue this new history of the church by putting the 'trustworthy men' centre stage as the vector for communication between bishops and parishes, the site where processes of mutual formation affected both institutions. There will be two distinct, and yet closely connected, strands to my investigation. First, to take a cue from the keyword itself, the *fidedigni*: trustworthy people or people worthy of faith. What was the faith, the *fides*, of which they were worthy? What relation did it have to the faith that all Christians were supposed to have in God? What did it owe to legal conceptions of good faith, or feudal ideas about fidelity? How was it connected with the con*fide*nce essential to the conduct of everyday life? Why was this name used, especially when other terms were available to describe local collaborators with governmental power, as we shall see in Chapter 4? What were its connotations, and what meanings of faith—such a ubiquitous and malleable word in medieval culture—did it incorporate? Second, bearing in mind the distinction that Bishop Grandisson was careful to make between 'some . . . parishioners' and 'some trustworthy men', how did the act of discrimination inherent in trusting affect both parish society and the bishop's government of his diocese? Calling some people trustworthy was a choice with real social consequences. Who could be trustworthy in the bishop's eyes? Because the trustworthy men were living people, and not just a figure of speech, such questions have to do with material inequality, and I will ask how a bishop's attributions of trustworthiness (and by implication untrustworthiness) intersected with the multiple existing inequalities of life. Did the concept and the sociology of the 'trustworthy men' merely echo constructions of gender difference and the facts of social stratification, or did they in turn affect those fundamental aspects of life? The faith that made the church was the trust placed in these men; the inequality that made the church was the social status that enabled them to be trusted.

It is fair to say that beyond a community of specialist scholars the medieval church has not enjoyed the academic attention that its interest and importance merits. To some extent this is because it is church history, but the fact of it being medieval history has also played a part. Medieval history is so often assumed to be irrelevant to broader historical concerns. Yet, as a phenomenon in global history, the medieval church is of considerable significance, being the complex institutional expression of a major world religion at a crucial time. It is worthy of study in its own right, but also as something amenable to comparison with other religious institutions or other governing systems. Indeed, by engaging critically with the massive and varied scholarly literature on trust in disciplines as diverse as economics and the philosophy of science, I hope that study of the medieval church can not only be enriched in itself, but also make a contribution to other fields of enquiry. Indeed a medievalist's perspective on the study of trust immediately disrupts a whole series of complacent assumptions about 'modernity' that have come to dominate thinking in the social sciences, and by coupling the study of trust with the interrogation of inequality, it is also possible to confound some of the more developmental and celebratory accounts of 'Western' history.

In order to reframe this study of the medieval church, each of the four parts of the book begins with a short introduction situating the discussion within the scholarly literature on trust, inequality, and a number of related topics. The chapters in Part I examine three components in the late medieval culture of trust, namely belief in God (Chapter 1), trust and promises (Chapter 2), and faith as an element in personal identity and reputation (Chapter 3). All of these fed into the contemporary meaning of *fides*; they had their distinct histories and implications, but they also overlapped with one another in conscious and unconscious ways. Part II identifies the trustworthy men, beginning with their emergence as a feature of ecclesiastical rhetoric in the twelfth and thirteenth centuries (Chapter 4), and the impressions that bishops had of them as collaborators with episcopal power (Chapter 5), before looking in detail at the identities, social status, and economic position of named trustworthy men (Chapter 6). The conclusions of these chapters then contribute to a discussion of faith and inequality in the parish in Part III, looking first at the ways in which trustworthy men could and could not be said to have represented their communities (Chapter 7). Inequality is revealed as fundamental to the church's reliance upon so-called trustworthy men, and I show (in Chapter 8) how the impact of this was felt differently in changing conditions between about 1250 and about 1500, in the varied landscapes of England and the wider British Isles. Discussion of faith and inequality is concluded with an intimate history of life lived alongside the trustworthy men (Chapter 9), where the social capital accrued from collaborating with bishops is shown to have been a major contributor to enduring, and worsening, social inequalities. In Part IV the relationship between parish and diocese is looked at in detail from the bishop's perspective, describing the ways in which bishops thought about knowledge and testimony when dealing with hundreds of people they did not know and of whose motives they were suspicious (Chapter 10), before examining three areas in which the trustworthy men made the power of bishops what it was. These are the management of financial transactions of various kinds (Chapter 11), coping with change in the material world (Chapter 12), and probing relationships through subtle judgements about character, intentions, and belief (Chapter 13). In all of this we will see bishops gaining power by commodifying social relations for their institutional benefit. This leads to a discussion of the role of information and trust in shaping the late medieval church (Chapter 14).

Finally, before launching into the enquiry proper, it is worth pointing out what I am *not* doing in this book. In arguing that the church was made by faith and inequality, the two principal attributes of the 'trustworthy men', I may risk giving the impression that I am resuscitating two corpses of historical prejudice. One is that the medieval centuries were an 'age of faith', a naïve view of the period as a time of unquestioning faith, which has been inflected as credulity or piety depending on the writer's point of view. This position was attacked in the 1970s by historians who argued that Christianity was never more than a thin veneer of elite culture prior to the sixteenth century, and in some cases beyond. However, that revisionism was equally condescending towards the majority, who were cast as the bearers of folkloric traditions, their capacity for engaging with cognitive belief implicitly denied.[10] In opposition to both these approaches, I assume that faith was such a pervasive and multifarious concept affecting so many areas of life, that there was no-one who did not experience it and think with it in some fashion, but also that no two people had precisely the same conception of faith. Faith certainly made the church, but not in the way you might think. Equally, the European Middle Ages, and especially the medieval church, are frequently bywords for intolerance and ideological control, so my assertion that inequality also made the church could be mistaken for a rather totalitarian view of ecclesiastical power.[11] On the contrary, feeling like a member of the church did not depend upon the coercive power of bishops or inquisitors, and one of the leading arguments of this book is that ideas about belonging and belief were formed at every location within the 'social church', though especially where people of different social and cultural backgrounds had to negotiate one another's divergent perspectives and relative power.

PART I

Late Medieval
Cultures of Trust

TRUST IS A RICH SUBJECT for academic study, offering insight into the nature of human social experience, the subjectivity of individual lives, the conduct of politics, collective action, exchange and value, and a host of other related topics. There is an extensive scholarly literature across many disciplines, exploring numerous aspects of trust in perceptive and provocative ways. And yet the study of trust in specific times and places is rare. Much philosophical and social science work is either ahistorical, in searching for universal or fundamental features of human society, or unhistorical, obsessed with differentiating 'modernity' from what came before. Much of this will be questioned here as I clear the way for a study of the culture of trust in Europe, particularly England, between the thirteenth and the fifteenth centuries: the world of the 'trustworthy men' or *fidedigni*. The chapters in Part I explore the character of the *fides*/faith of which those men were said to be worthy.

For many writers in the social sciences the very idea of trust in the Middle Ages would seem problematic. This is because the study of cooperation, solidarity, and related forms of interaction has been very strongly influenced by the idea of a transition to modernity. Within this, trust (defined as a conscious decision to rely upon another person or entity without the possibility of knowing for certain whether that reliance is well-founded) has been seen as unnecessary or simple in premodern societies, and necessary only in so-called modern conditions of uncertainty and impersonal relations. The study of trust has predominantly taken place within this framework, under the influence of a number of significant thinkers. The idea of a transition from direct forms of interaction in medieval community (*Gemeinschaft*) to indirect forms in modern society (*Gesellschaft*) was principally developed by Ferdinand Tönnies, but then elaborated by Max Weber for whom communal relations were affective while modern social relations were rational. Émile Durkheim then established an axiom of sociology in identifying a difference between the 'mechanical solidarity' of simple societies where life was lived face-to-face and cooperation was automatic, and the 'organic solidarity' of complex societies where it was necessary to learn how and when to trust someone who was not part of one's immediate social group. Karl Polanyi later characterized this as a shift from a world in which social interaction involved many roles simultaneously (neighbour, co-worker, relative, co-parishioner, creditor and so on), to one in which the economic roles are separated from the social; in modern times a borrower is just a borrower, and not also a friend or neighbour.[1] For each of these influential writers, trust emerged as a distinct concept only when it became necessary. And it was not necessary until modern social conditions made it so. Theorists of trust have largely accepted this framework. For example Adam Seligman has written that in premodern forms of social organization 'the recognition of our essential identity . . . may well have been sufficient for the provision of social solidarity', while Jan Philipp Reemtsma has argued that the shift from medieval to modern was a transition from fixed to fluid relationships and from universal to individual values that involved 'a transformation of trust as a means of social cohesion'.[2] Meanwhile Barbara Misztal is representative of a widely held view in saying that 'trust becomes a more urgent and central concern in today's contingent, uncertain and global conditions'.[3] Such broad-brush accounts of Western history over the past six hundred years or so have come in for a great deal of criticism, some of it—unsurprisingly—from medieval historians who can see that it rests on a caricature of societies that do not resemble a supposed present-day norm.[4] With reference to Durkheim's sociology, even a historian of the twentieth century such as Geoffrey Hosking is moved to point out that there was never 'a golden age of trust' when reliance and assurance were automatic, adding that such a view rests upon 'historical ignorance'.[5] Others have noted that thinking with 'modernity' can also be excruciatingly blinkered in its geographical and cultural-linguistic vision.[6]

One particular element in the historical simplifications of the 'modernization' literature, which has to be dealt with at the outset, is that during the Middle Ages people were credulous and possessed of a blind faith. They supposedly relied upon God instead of working out how to trust one another. Seligman in particular has argued that with the fracturing of the Western church at the Reformation, faith 'could no longer be supported by the armature of a transcendent God nor could it provide the nexus for interpersonal relations. What took its place was . . . a search for trust'.[7] If modern life is uncertain, so the argument goes, medieval life revolved around certainties, and religious faith is imagined to have obviated the need for trust.[8] This is an unhistorical view that needs to be corrected. While certainty was indeed a very important feature of the way that trust was conceptualized in medieval societies, equally important, even fundamental, was uncertainty, which functioned in ways that a superficial knowledge of the period cannot reveal. Similarly, faith in God was crucial to the ways in which trust between people, and between people and institutions, was experienced and articulated. It is therefore a travesty to say that identity was collective, solidarity automatic, faith in God sufficient for all agreements, and trust unnecessary in the Middle Ages.

Present-minded fallacies about the credulity of Christian belief in the Middle Ages will be tackled head-on in Chapter 1, while Chapter 2 will address the lingering assumption that the premodern world was noninstitutional, focusing on the key issue of promises and promise keeping. Promises have received a good deal of attention from writers on trust, often featuring in the supposed transition from a world guaranteed by 'mechanical' trust in persons, to one underpinned by a reasoned trust in legal contracts. As a herald of modernity, this tends to be treated as something of a moveable feast by historians, who have seen it occurring on the cusp of whatever period they specialize in. For Richard Firth Green, working mainly with literary texts, the late fourteenth century witnessed a 'gradual erosion of the faith once placed in the truth of human beings' and 'a widespread loss of faith in the word of trusted neighbours'.[9] However, as I will show, this is far too simplistic. Working with different material and a different chronology Craig Muldrew's *Economy of Obligation* explores the links between household economies and the expansion of the market in sixteenth- and seventeenth-century England, arguing that a change in contract law meant that the quantity and value of interpersonal credit were much greater in the sixteenth than in the fifteenth century, and that the challenge of this precipitated the creation of the Bank of England in 1694, and joint stock companies around the same time.[10] There is no reason to question the broad truth of this interpretation, but Muldrew also suggests that the sixteenth century saw the replacement of medieval honesty with legal enforcement, and of faithfulness to God with trust between contracting individuals.[11] This is more problematic and, again as I will show, there was no simple replacement of 'medieval' community with 'modern' legal rights.

Besides those who see a transformation of trust with the onset of 'modernity', there are also many writers who offer prescriptions for a good society that pay no attention to cultural or historical difference.[12] In works that reject history altogether in favour of supposed universal norms, contract and interpersonal trust are still assumed to be mutually exclusive. Some social scientists have argued that contracts emerge when trust will not suffice; others, making a similar point from a different perspective, say that the sanctions inherent in contract law make trust redundant.[13] What is more, this has led some to propose *as a universal rule* that when humans signal trust we are merely offering 'false commitment signals', whilst all the time secretly calculating how best to protect our interests.[14] Rather than follow such approaches any further I will instead pursue Charles Tilly's assertion that trust is 'a historical product rather than a phenomenon whose variation we can explain without reference to history', and accept the need for detailed empirical study in order to appreciate the cultural specificity of late medieval talk about trust in the realms of theology, law and agreements, and identity and emotion, the subjects respectively of Chapters 1 to 3.[15] In the welcome words of the philosopher Bernard Williams, 'at a certain point philosophy needs to make way for history'.[16] In taking up this invitation we have to jettison some of the baggage that comes with thinking about modernity or universal values, while retaining the capacity to think with some of the useful insights and questions that arise from that literature.[17] In historical terms, this boils down to two things: first, asking how necessary institutions are to promise making and promise keeping in particular situations, which will be the subject of Chapter 2, and second, considering how we should treat trust in terms of sincerity and emotional authenticity, a neglected topic that will occupy us in Chapter 3. On the one hand institutions might be seen as inimical to the social practices of trust, a point vividly captured in Gellner's quip that 'anarchy engenders trust and government destroys it', while on the other, they might be seen as essential to it, as in

Hosking's recent assessment of the operation of trust in the Middle Ages: 'the institutions of the Christian church were crucial in giving people what sense of security they managed to achieve'.[18] While it is hard to disagree that the church was important to late medieval cultures of trust—given how central the language of *fides* was, with all its connotations of belief—to suggest that there was no security, no trust, without the church and that it was, in addition, thin on the ground, is far too reductive.

The persistence of a binary separation between trust and contract is perhaps a product of the contrary ways in which we habitually talk about trust: on the one hand as the assurance felt in meaningful relationships, on the other as a means to overcome the uncertainty of dealing with strangers. But these two forms of trust can be found side by side in all times and places, and it can be hard to disentangle them.[19] A number of historians, working on subjects as diverse as ancient Greece and Rome and seventeenth-century science, have made great strides in delineating some specific cultures of trust, and in what follows I will draw on their findings and examples.[20] Trust has particularly featured in a number of studies focussed on guilds, credit, networks, and contract enforcement, and some of these have branched out to look at the wider cultural discourses surrounding trust.[21] Epistemological issues arising in medieval thought have also generated some interesting insights into related concepts such as doubt and probable knowledge.[22]

Over the ensuing three chapters I will make a case for the trust cultures of the European Middle Ages being complex and not at all reducible to 'blind faith' or 'mechanical solidarity'. This will pave the way for a detailed investigation of the phenomenon of the 'trustworthy men' in episcopal governance. Each chapter of Part I explores a different sense of *fides* that was in its own way important to episcopal evocations of the trustworthy men. Chapter 1 examines belief in God in broad European terms, and highlights the assumption that faith was necessary wherever reason and direct sense perception failed, that it pertained to a fixed and certain object, but that one had to be circumspect in one's relationship to it. Chapter 2 highlights the reliance of interpersonal trust/*fides* upon an act of voluntary discrimination, upon clear symbolic communication, and upon knowledge of a person's sanctioning community, introducing more material specific to the English context with which the bulk of the ensuing analysis is concerned. Chapter 3 shows how faith, in several distinct yet related spheres, was a powerful constituent in personal identity and experience, something that should be counted among the major drivers of individual action in the later Middle Ages. The discussion in later parts of the book will demonstrate how these historically specific understandings of *fides* were essential to the alliance upon which the English church was built: that between bishops and the trustworthy men.

CHAPTER ONE

Theology

BELIEF IN GOD

Faith attains to what is above one's reach, it perceives what is unknown, grasps what is beyond measure.

—*FASCICULUS MORUM*

BELIEF IN GOD is probably what springs to mind most readily when one thinks of faith in the Middle Ages. The concept of faith is indeed central to Christian societies, although it cannot be said to be a constant in their histories, and belief in God is only one aspect of religious faith. Nor, it must be said, has its importance been much examined by historians. Faith has meant different things in different times and places, and has always been both intellectually complex and a subjective experience. Faith can describe an attitude towards God, a relationship to the church or to other Christians, a quality or possession of individuals, a set of propositions or dogma concerning God, and even the Christian religion itself. Furthermore, the medieval Christian concept of faith or trust was influenced by pre-Christian Roman and Greek, as well as Jewish, cultures. These influences persisted in legal thought, which will be examined in Chapter 2, but also in the literary inheritance from the ancient world— including the Hebrew and Greek scriptures—as well as more generally in the complex linguistic history of trust words in the oral and written languages of Europe.[1]

Faith is too important a subject for our understanding of history in the 'medieval' centuries to be left to academic theologians and philosophers. Historians should pay more attention to a concept that was ubiquitous in everyday life. Religious faith was promoted as a leading value in structuring relationships with other people, in ways that were distinct, though not entirely separate, from the operation of *fides* in legal agreements and interpersonal promises (the subject of Chapter 2) and in the emotional expression of identity and reputation (the subject of Chapter 3). Sometimes the terms of such relationships of faith were equitable, such as the feeling of mutual trust or good faith binding members of the 'community of the faithful', and sometimes more hierarchical, imposing obligations and reinforcing power within the church. There was no clear separation between the cultures of religious and secular faith in the Middle Ages. Rather, I will examine some of the ways in which belief in God was rationalized in terms familiar from legal agreements and ordinary friendships, where the bonds of 'the faith' were very much social bonds. Equally, in Chapters 2 and 3, I will show what interpersonal trust owed to concepts of religious belief.

But asking questions about faith as belief is tricky. In all contexts, whatever the weight of legal expectation or power relationships, faith and trust are subjective and ambiguous. The subjectivity, as the anthropologist Rodney Needham once pointed out, makes faith difficult to study. It is an interior process whose essence is hard for another person to grasp, and it is not fully captured in what anthropologists used to call 'collective representations': shared cultural expressions associated with a defined group.[2] Needham was thinking about the difficulty of enquiry into the beliefs of living people, but historians face the added challenge of being unable even to hear the speech and observe the actions of their subjects. While it is important to be clear what we, as historians, cannot do—we cannot experience what long-dead people felt—we can recover what was written, and somewhat less directly said, about faith. Because language is best treated as a component of social life, rather than simply a reflection of it, social historians can and should make it the focus of their study. In this light it is rather strange that the nature of faith and trust—belief itself—has not been at all prominent in the work of medieval social historians, or even among historians of the church. Among the former a range of related themes have been studied, such as lordship, solidarity, credit, and voluntary associations, while among the latter the leading question has been how successfully the church taught the laity the 'articles of the faith'.[3] Conversely a social history of the medieval church has much to gain from looking at what was said about faith.

But neither is medieval talk and writing about faith a simple object of study. Ambiguity and contestation haunt every utterance and written expression. But, arguably, it is this very uncertainty that makes it so necessary to examine faith as a social and historical phenomenon. This point was put very eloquently in 1981 by the philosopher Michel de Certeau who, writing in response to a volume of essays on medieval church history, argued that belief is an attitude towards the unknown 'other' and the unknown future. It implies an epistemological and cognitive deficiency—one trusts because one cannot be certain—and this makes trusting susceptible to the play of powerful interests. That is to say, for all that belief or faith is a cognitive act, it is also always necessarily a social act as well. Although, as we shall see, medieval theologians were unanimous in saying that faith was in fact certain because God was certain, de Certeau makes a shrewd observation. For most people living in the thirteenth to fifteenth centuries the demand that Christians should have faith meant accepting the word of an institution—the church—or striving for something that was difficult to attain. Faith therefore involved personal and social struggles, and, as we shall see, it created inequalities or asymmetries of knowledge.[4] In this chapter I will begin to look at the language of faith, belief, and trust as it was used in the later Middle Ages, with some glances back at the indelible influences of St Augustine of Hippo (AD 354–430) and St Paul (ca. AD 5–ca. 65). As well as seeking to understand what was meant by faith in God, I will be looking for signs of what relationships and what structures of power were implied and sustained by this language.

The language of faith and its related concepts has a broad and complex history. In both English and Latin the noun faith/*fides* corresponds most closely to the verb to believe/*credere*, rather than having its own verbal form along the lines of '*fidere*'.[5] 'Belief' could sometimes mean the same as faith, in the sense of the attitude one might hold towards certain propositions or beings. In order to hear this sense we might listen to one of the carefully scripted renunciations of heresy that some unfortunate men and women had to make in late medieval England: for example, in 1457 Robert Sparke had to promise not to give 'faith, credence, consent, and belief' to the words of heretical preachers.[6] In this formulation consent clearly implied a close relationship between trust and obedience to authority, while credence is an Anglicization of the Latin *credentia*, synonymous with both faith and belief. I will return to the many other senses of faith not encompassed by 'belief' later in this chapter, and in the two that follow.

But we may begin with belief, or rather its more common verbal form: *credo*, I believe. This was an utterance familiar from the Creed, that 'vast subject contained in such few words', as Augustine put it, which all Christians were supposed to learn by heart as children and repeat regularly as adults.[7] The fourteenth-century English author of a handbook for parish priests, John Mirk, advised that two or three times a year every curate should preach to his flock on the subject of the Creed along with the Lord's Prayer and the Ave Maria, to promote their recitation and explain their meaning. How often the mouths of Christians must have murmured:

I be-leue in oure holy dryȝt
Fader of heuen, god almyȝt,
Þat all thyne made & wroȝt,
Heuene and erþe & alle of noȝt.
On Ihesu Cryst I be-leue also,
Hys only sone and no mo . . .[8]

The loosely rhythmic sound of a faith recited during Mass or at the baptism of a child, in the company of family and neighbours, was held together by the down beat of that repeated 'I believe' (in God, in Christ, in the Holy Ghost, in the Eucharist and in God's promise of salvation). 'I believe' may have been a ritual utterance as much as it was an expression of emotion or understanding, but what meaning might it have had? What was it that people believed *in*? What did faith and *the* faith ('the fey' in Mirk's Middle English) mean to Christians?

These are questions that could take us on a journey through all of medieval culture, but we can retain our focus by remaining with the Creed, a recurring affirmation of imagined community.[9] Recitation of the Creed, or academic reflection upon it, could address both 'the faith' as contained in the articles of faith, and faith as a mode of knowing and experience. The distinction of these two meanings of *fides* was crucial to medieval debate, though it had first been clarified in an influential formulation of St Augustine. He had written of the difference between that faith in which we believe (*fides quae creditur*) and the faith by which we believe (*fides qua creditur*), while stressing their conceptual connection.[10] Despite its continuing importance, by the later Middle Ages if not before, Augustine's integration of *fides quae* and *fides qua* was unravelling. It came to be, for the most part, only theologians who discussed the operation of faith in detail, while pastoral writers addressing ordinary Christians tended to ignore this and focus upon the articles of faith. This bifurcation means that even when considering the meaning of belief in God, we also have to pay attention to the inequalities that shaped everyday experience of it.

Faith in an Unseen God: Scholastic Theology and the Fides Qua

In discussing the faith *by which* we believe, Augustine, and his successors between 1100 and 1500, were exploring the cognition and capability of a fallen humanity. Upon Adam and Eve's expulsion from the Garden of Eden they and their descendants had lost the capacity for direct sight and understanding of God, having chosen instead to acquire knowledge of the physical world. The consequence for humanity was an occluded vision of the divine; men and women were destined to see God but 'through a glass, darkly' (1 Corinthians 13.12). Faith, for Augustine, was the condition of knowledge in which humanity must try to approach God before such time as they would see him 'as if face to face' once more. This knowledge, as memorably articulated by the monastic theologian Hugh of St Victor (ca. 1096–1141), was 'a kind of certainty of the mind in things absent, established beyond opinion and short of knowledge'.[11] This is a definition of faith that we shall encounter again and again, resonating through many different contexts and uses during the course of this book.

There was merit in believing something unseen, like Noah who built the ark 'having received an answer concerning those things which as yet were not seen' (Hebrews 11.7).[12] In the thirteenth-century *Ordinary Gloss* to the Bible it was explained that Noah believed the word of God and did not heed the world. He had faith in that which he could not see, partially making good Adam's fault.[13] Medieval Europeans heard this moral again and again through the story of John the Baptist's supposed doubt towards the divinity of Christ. In Matthew's gospel the imprisoned Baptist was said to have sent some of his friends to ask Jesus whether he was 'the one who is to come' or whether they should continue to wait for another Messiah (Matthew 11.2). This verse came to be hotly debated in the Middle Ages because it seemed to imply that John doubted Christ, which would be tricky to explain. However, it was eventually interpreted as a lesson in believing in unseen things: the challenge and very essence of faith. John's friends were the ones who doubted, and so the Baptist had sent them to Jesus to see him in the flesh. In medieval tradition they returned from their journey only to be rebuked by John for their lack of faith in things they had not seen for themselves.[14] The particular association between faith and the apprehension of unseen things, and the greater merit in believing something unseen as opposed to something seen, became touchstones of systematic theology.[15] For the English chronicler and pastoral writer Ranulph Higden (d. 1364) faith related to 'things not apparent in either the past, the present, or the future', while the Franciscan author of the *Fasciculus Morum* explained that 'faith attains to what is above one's reach, it perceives what is unknown, grasps what is beyond measure'.[16] The unseen quality of God was closely related to the deficiencies of human cognition arising from the Fall. For Hugh of St Victor God 'can only be believed, not at all comprehended', while Bernard of Clairvaux (1090–1153) wrote that faith is 'a sort of voluntary and certain foretaste of truth not yet apparent'.[17] Thomas Aquinas, a century later, wrote that God is the most important nonapparent thing there is, and so faith pertains especially to him.[18]

In humanity's fallen state, reason by itself was generally thought incapable of leading someone to an understanding of God. But in the monasteries, cathedral schools, and universities of Europe between 1100 and 1500 reason was a core value, and its relationship to faith therefore came to dominate scholastic theology. Anselm of Bec (1033–1109), later archbishop of Canterbury, had asserted an inextricable link between faith and reason. Indeed the subtitle of his *Prosologion* was 'faith seeking understanding'. In it he wrote that knowledge of God requires that faith is supported by reason. In this formulation neither faith nor reason was sufficient on its own, and Anselm was clear that he believed in order that he might understand God, rather than seeking to understand as a precondition to believing.[19] Despite the disagreements between scholastic thinkers, there was a great deal of common ground in their ideas about faith. Peter Abelard (1079–1142) thought that rather more could be achieved by reason alone, but even he acknowledged the importance of faith.[20] Hugh of St Victor distinguished between 'the faith', which could be apprehended by reason alone, and the nature and existence of God, which were ineffable and required a leap of faith. This was a view repeated in the standard teaching text of medieval theology, the *Sentences* of Peter Lombard (ca. 1096–1164), through whose influence it became a salient feature of the intellectual landscape.[21] It was still, nevertheless, capable of being seen from different perspectives. In the thirteenth century Aquinas mounted a defence of reason's positive role, while William Ockham (ca. 1285–1347) separated faith and reason into discrete spheres of knowledge.[22] After Ockham theology took a more reflective approach to God's revelation, with prominent voices—among them Jean Gerson and the Council of Constance—setting limits on the application of Aristotelian logic to the highest truths about God. Gabriel Biel (ca. 1415–95) for instance believed that there was a line beyond which the faith acquired by reason could not reach, where 'infused faith' from God was required.[23] Throughout all of these twists and turns in the relative importance of reason and faith, the grace of God—Biel's 'infused faith'—was consistently deemed necessary to understanding the truths he had revealed in the Bible and in creation. Faith was said to 'proceed from inner hearing', and God was thought to be already known in the minimal sense that a person must have a concept of God before they could believe in him.[24] So faith was never seen as a purely cognitive act, entirely willed by the believer, but the person in receipt of grace would be able to attain faith, and perhaps thereby understanding.

This faith was almost always described as certain. Even though Hugh of St Victor thought that faith fell short of knowledge, he nonetheless regarded it as definite. Faith was certain because its object—God—was eternal and fixed. This position was arrived at partly in response to the perceived challenge of Aristotelian natural science. William of Auvergne (ca. 1180–1249), for instance, argued that faith possessed greater certainty than science because the object of faith (God) was fixed while the object of scientific enquiry (the world) was contingent upon God's creation.[25] Aquinas and Bonaventure, though they represent divergent theological traditions as the leading minds of the Dominican and Franciscan orders respectively, were at one in making this very same point.[26] While the logic of the contention that faith could be certain because God was certain may be judged deficient, the aesthetic symmetry of the proposition gave it a strong hold on theological reasoning. Baldwin of Ford (ca. 1125–90) illustrates this well, with his statement of the case for the certainty of faith achieved by an accumulation of synonyms: 'because we trust (*fidimus*) in God and believe in God through faith, and since God is truth . . . the same faith should be underpinned with such great certainty, such great firmness of undoubting assent'.[27] Trust, belief, faith, truth, certainty, firmness, lack of doubt, and assent: these were the keywords of Christian faith in God between 1100 and 1500.

Faith in the Church:
Pastoral Theology and the Fides Quae

As it developed in the twelfth and thirteenth centuries, however, scholastic theology diverged significantly from the practical texts designed to teach the laity, what is often called pastoral theology. Whereas academic theology devoted a great deal of attention to the faith by which we believe (Augustine's *fides qua*), debates about reason, understanding, and knowledge were side issues in most pastoral theology, which instead focussed on Augustine's *fides quae*, the faith in which Christians were supposed to believe.

This sense of 'the faith' was embodied in the 'articles of the faith', contained in the Creed. There have been many creeds in the history of Christianity, and in the Middle Ages there was no 'official' text. The most widely promulgated version, though, was known as the Apostles' Creed, consisting of fourteen articles: one (for mnemonic purposes) supposedly instigated by each of the twelve apostles and two by Christ. There were not really fourteen separate propositions, and the division into 'articles' varied somewhat between different versions, but the essence consisted of belief in the three persons of the Trinity—God the father, Christ the son, the Holy Spirit—that these persons are one and three simultaneously (like water, ice, and snow as John Mirk put it);[28] belief in the humanity and divinity of Christ; and belief in the church, the communion of saints, the resurrection of the body, the forgiveness of sins, and everlasting life. The fourteenth-century English canon lawyer John Acton extolled the Creed's simplicity, a quality that made it a core element in the education and pastoral care of Christians throughout the later Middle Ages.[29] Godparents were enjoined, to take an example from a late thirteenth-century sermon, 'here bileue cunnen', that is to know their belief, and accept their duty.[30] Another influential proclamation of faith was that which introduced the first decree of the Fourth Lateran Council, formulated in 1215 under the papal leadership of Innocent III: 'We firmly believe and simply confess that there is only one true God, eternal and immeasurable, almighty, unchangeable, incomprehensible and ineffable, Father, Son and Holy Spirit, three persons but one absolutely simple essence, substance or nature'.[31] In 1234 this decree, with its characterization of the *fides qua* limited to firmness and simplicity, became the opening canon—*questio* 1, *titulus* 1, *capitulum* 1—of Gregory IX's collection of canon law known as the *Decretals*, and in that guise hugely influential for the church's engagement with lay Christians.

In their mission to laymen and laywomen, priests and preachers were armed with homely metaphors and a simplified theology. For example, in one exposition of the theological virtues charity was said to be bread because it is the most essential food, faith to be bread plus the fish that comes from the water of baptism, and hope to be bread and the egg that people hope will hatch into a bird. Tellingly, the ways to faith listed in another (and perhaps typical) thirteenth-century sermon skirt around any kind of cognitive belief: the believer must acknowledge God as lord, love him, stand in awe of him, honour him, and praise him.[32] There is no mention of belief, faith, understanding, or knowledge. Instead of teaching laypeople how to have faith in God, pastoral texts placed greater emphasis upon loving God. Between about 1250 and 1500 love was the action or attitude over which Christians were thought to have the most personal control, and when medieval theologians (and possibly St Paul too) talked about the importance of 'works' what they usually meant was acting with love or 'in charity'.[33] Indeed, in *The Vision of Piers Plowman*, love, in the guise of the Good Samaritan or the *Lex Christi*, comes to the aid of a man left wounded by robbers, while Faith and Hope run away, unable to stomach the tasks necessary to help this poor wretch.[34] Love, and not faith, was also the defining social virtue in pastoral works like the *Quinque verba*, which enjoined its readers to love their neighbours, rather than to trust them.[35]

This is not to say that the nature and operation of faith were entirely absent from texts aimed at the laity, just that there was more exhortation than explanation. For instance the influential Dominican author of a *Summa* for confessors, John of Freiburg (d. 1314), wrote that faith was necessary for belief in the doctrine of the Trinity; Ranulph Higden argued that the Eucharist was incomprehensible without faith; Thomas Spofford (ca. 1370–1456), bishop of Hereford, said that just as the bat and the owl cannot look at the sun, 'so the teachings of Christ have to be believed and not subjected to reason'.[36] A possible exception to this general tendency is Robert Grosseteste (ca. 1170–1253). He was concerned about infidelity, defined quite carefully as an indiscriminate belief in the wrong thing, and about possible 'superfluity' of faith in people who could not believe unless shown tangible proofs. The unfaithful person would appear to be incredulous and hard of heart, he wrote, while the ideal faith was shown by believing that which should be believed, and not believing that which should not be. Another potential pitfall was scrupulosity, which he defined as a sceptical refusal to believe anything.[37] Grosseteste, however, wrote in Latin and for a highly learned audience.

John Mirk, a fourteenth-century Augustinian canon who wrote in English and was more in touch with the realities of pastoral care, gave no explanation of the faith *by which* people were meant to believe, nor any acknowledgement that this might be something that could raise psychological difficulties. Only his question to be asked of the dying man—'Art þow fayn (*satisfied*) . . . þat þow dyest in crysten fay?'—suggests anything of the intellectual and emotional challenge presented by belief.[38] Such texts expected their readers to cultivate an implicit faith, and this was not best promoted by endlessly casting it up as a subject for reflection. Most practical texts for a mass lay audience were content to say that faith is 'a fundement of religioun wiþ out the which hit is inpossible to qweme (*know*) god'.[39] As Bishop Peter Quinel's short treatise written for parish priests in Exeter diocese in 1287 explains:

> Since perhaps they [the laity] cannot know everything that they ought to believe, people who are unlearned should be taught to keep their hearts fixed and steadfast; in other words, they should believe what the church believes and perform Christian acts.[40]

It was by worshipping God in church that the majority of Christians were imagined acting out their faith. They were the faithful, their 'faith . . . known and devotion noted' by God as they congregated in church.[41] This simple faith meant saying and doing, a combination that Ranulph Higden explained by referring to a popular, yet false, etymology for the Latin *fides*. This word, he said, derives from the Latin phrase *fiant dicta*: 'let words be made'.[42] In the minds of many clerics, the laity were thus expected to speak and act their faith, while cognition was far less important: the declaration of the Creed was what gave it meaning (Romans 10.10), and its proclamation to one's neighbours made it strong.[43] The recitation should be firm and simple, unfeigned and steadfast, direct and not obscure, with no extraneous words.[44] People were to 'trowe withouten fayntyse' (believe without pretence) and 'trowe with hert stedefast'; nothing 'ought to be stronger in a man than his faith'.[45] As the Psalmist put it 'they that trust in the Lord (*confidunt in Domino*) are like mount Sion, which cannot be moved but abides forever' (Psalms 125.1). Sermon authors variously called faith 'a substancyal grownde þat berythe all vp' and something that should be held 'firmly and surely' (*firmo et rato*).[46] In the Middle English of the Wycliffite translation of the Bible, St Paul's advice to the Colossians was to 'dwellen in the feith, foundid, and stable, and vnmouable (*unmoveable*)'.[47] The obverse of this stability was the instability of the sea, a common metaphor for doubt and uncertainty.[48] Christians were enjoined to have faith in God, in his truthfulness and unchanging endurance, despite his being unseen and—apart from by exceptionally holy or learned people—unknowable.

Asymmetries of Faith

A firm faith was protection against doubt, error, and heresy. From the twelfth century onwards this defensiveness was central to how church writers thought about society.[49] Muslims, Jews, and pagans regularly cropped up in theological and pastoral treatises as the enemies of the Christian faith (wherever they were located geographically), though Muslims and Jews were sometimes treated as 'the faithful' of another (wrong) faith. But within Christendom, within 'the faith', defensive lines were also drawn that created significant asymmetries of belief, faith, and trust. The most divisive of these was between those thought capable of understanding the mysteries of the faith, and those whose lot was merely to trust and remain obedient. Christian faith was unequal at its heart. Even at the birth of the pastoral revolution, Hugh of St Victor had referred somewhat condescendingly to the limited capacity of the 'simple minded in Holy Church' who, unable to raise their own minds to the mysteries of the faith, had to rely upon the greater intellect of 'the more perfect knowers and believers' by which he meant men like himself.[50] For Peter Lombard Christians 'of lesser ability' posed a serious challenge to the church: what was the nature of their faith and how could it be strengthened? The answer, repeated in commentaries upon Lombard's *Sentences* and in many works of pastoral theology, was that the simple believer had not a different faith, just a different manner of believing. Or, put another way, the simple had less capacity for intellectual faith, though not a lesser spiritual faith. In a metaphor that quickly became popular, the clergy were described as oxen leading the plough, while the people were merely asses grazing alongside them.[51] Another common stereotype, in which mental simplicity was gendered female, was the *vetula* or 'little old woman' whose simple belief was strong, but whose obedience harboured a suggestibility that made her susceptible to heresy.[52] Such condescension was habitual: for instance, in Vienna the theologian Henry of Langenstein (1325–97) told his students of the 'imprudence of rustics and artisans' who attempted to meddle in matters they did not understand, while in England an early fifteenth-century Benedictine sermon author advised his audience not to involve themselves 'too much in matters of faith'.[53]

This attitude was dominant, but its articulation was increasingly made in response to claims from clerics and laypeople who aspired towards a more inclusive Christian experience of both the *fides qua* and the *fides quae*.[54] In England, and elsewhere in Europe, the largely Latin pastoral literature of the thirteenth century was augmented in the fourteenth and fifteenth by translations into vernacular languages, and original compositions in a variety of genres, designed for clerical and lay readers, including women, who aspired to cultivate their practice and capacity in the *fides qua*, the faith *by which* they were to believe.[55] For example in the *Speculum vitae*, written sometime between 1350 and 1375, the difference between things seen 'in hert gastly' (in the heart spiritually) in this life, and the sight of God that would be enjoyed by the blessed in heaven where 'als es proued' (all is proven), is carefully described for an English-reading audience:

> For alle þat comes to þat place
> Sal se him þare face to face
> And þat sight es þair souerayne blisse.[56]

The *Speculum* is arranged not only according to the traditional pattern—the teaching of the Decalogue, the Creed, the seven deadly sins, and so on—but also as an epistemological journey that the believer has embarked upon. From the 'gift of knowing' the believer might pass to the 'gift of understanding' which is likened to the sun clearing 'þe myrkenes þat lettes þe day / And þe mystes of þe mornynge'.[57] The concepts come from academic theology, but the language is more poetic and used to describe an active journey, progressing through more and more advanced ways of identifying, knowing, and understanding faith. Churchmen were torn between encouraging such lay intellectual ambition and maintaining the boundary between oxen and asses, learned and unlearned. They were worried about the dangers of a little learning, and a flood of doubt.[58] This ambiguous attitude towards the laity in academic theology and the higher reaches of the church is something that we shall find echoed in bishops' attempts to obtain testimony from the 'trustworthy men'.

It was sometimes said that doubt was a fertile state of mind, so long as it was passing and led ultimately to a firmer faith. It was also a necessary companion to free will.[59] Something of this was frequently articulated in telling the story of Christ's disciple Thomas, who doubted the resurrection until he had seen and touched the wounds of the crucifixion. This was not always—as it might have been—interpreted as an outright condemnation of doubting. It was in fact described as a valuable sign by which Christians were brought to belief. Thomas was also praised for staying in fellowship with the other disciples despite his disbelief, and for his eventual journey from doubt to belief. While he perceived Christ as a man, he believed in him as God: that is, as an unseen reality.[60] Thomas's doubt was, however, undeniably a weakness to be explained away, and pastoral writers advised priests and believers alike on how to fortify souls against it. Doubt was thought to be a moral and psychological failing arising from the sin of sloth. It was 'lethargy about spiritual goods from which a person fails to delight in God or sing God's praises'.[61] If unchecked, doubt—loss of faith—could make someone personally dubious and unreliable in all sorts of ways.[62] It might also lead to heresy: Aquinas certainly thought so.[63] Historians have disagreed about the prevalence of truly atheistic doubt about the existence of God. Recently Dorothea Weltecke has taken the view that atheism was a straw man set up by theologians as a vehicle for teaching doctrine. Conversely, John Arnold has argued that in heresy trials across late medieval Europe we find examples of scepticism expressed in terms of a refusal to believe in that which could not be seen. Doubt of this kind was stubbornly at odds with what we have seen to be the central pillar of Christian faith in this era: belief in an unseen God.[64]

Trusting People: The Relationships of Faith

Given the disquiet in the church about unguided lay understanding, doubt, error, heresy, and human cognition in general, it is hardly surprising that laypeople were not simply told to find their own faith in God. Indeed, it was the church in which laymen and laywomen were bidden to trust. A stable faith in God was to be achieved by obedience to his earthly representatives. The church was said to be the embodiment of God's word, the visible evidence of God's truth, built on foundations of faith; the simple should believe or trust in what the church taught.[65] The reason why the Christian church of the later Middle Ages was able—despite challenges—to maintain a hierarchy of knowledge was, ultimately, because of the way belief was constructed and preached by churchmen. They put a great deal of effort into arguing that no-one could gainsay the church about something that was unseen, be it God or the future. The people were told that they simply had to trust. Dissenters could always be portrayed as trusting only themselves and being out of communion with the church, while for those who did trust the church, their doing so perpetuated the power it had over their lives, which in turn preserved the reason they had to trust it in the first place. Faith or trust had a lot to do with power, and it was a cultural component of many of the inequalities of medieval life, as I will demonstrate in the ensuing chapters. While much of the language of faith suggested unity and equality, its use frequently supported intellectual hierarchies and coercive boundaries of belonging. In the course of this book I will uncover many layers of the relationship between faith or trust and the inequalities of wealth, gender, and status.

However, for ordinary Christians belief was far from simply being a matter of trusting in God, having faith in the church, and being obedient to authority. Though it was certainly the dominant strand of opinion in texts emanating from the church hierarchy, to accept this as the whole story would mean falling into the unhistorical view of the Middle Ages peddled in much of the political science and economics literature on trust that was criticized in the introduction to Part I of this book. Christians in fact used the lexicon of faith in forming relationships with one another, both on an individual and on a collective basis, and these usages fed directly into the way that they conceived of their faith in God.[66] Augustine was once again a powerful influence upon later centuries. In arguing against the sceptical position that belief or knowledge in 'things absent' was impossible, Augustine demonstrated that, on the contrary, much that we take on trust is invisible. He cited the existence of our own minds, our trust in another person, and that person's trust in us as socially significant examples:

> For the truth is that from your heart you trust a heart other than your own . . . with your mind you can see your own trust, but the trust of your friend cannot be the object of your love if no such mutual trust is found in you, a trust which enables you to believe something you cannot actually see in your friend.

Friendship, he wrote, is possible only if faith is kept between people. If we insist on visible signs of trustworthiness we will be misled, because these can be feigned, so we should act in 'good faith' even where evidence of trustworthiness is lacking. When we entrust ourselves to a friend we are putting our faith in him or her without any evidence that our faith is merited.

> If trust of this kind were to disappear from human affairs, how could anyone escape being aware of the confusion and appalling upheaval which would follow?

Warming to his theme of social collapse in the absence of trust, Augustine continued:

> The consequence of our refusal to believe what we cannot see is that human relationships are thrown into chaos, and the foundations are utterly swept away by our failure to trust the goodwill of people.

The point of this implicit theory of mind and explicit social ethic of trust was to set up an analogy between interpersonal trust and faith in God:

> If therefore human society itself could not endure because of our refusal to believe what we cannot see ... how much more credence ought to be given to those divine matters which remain unseen.[67]

This idea formed by an African bishop would shape the history of Europe in fundamental ways. Augustine's inspiration echoed through many later medieval texts, such as Johannes Balbus's influential thirteenth-century encyclopaedia, where faith in the faith of another human was said to bring the hearts of friends together, and faith in the faith of God was said to be necessary for arriving at a personal belief in the articles of faith.[68] There was a clear and compelling analogy in this way of thinking, but also a very strong implication that the trust felt between friends was an element of the act of believing in God. Significantly, this suggested the possibility of a degree of lay agency, or control over a faith that was theirs to give.

However, despite Augustine's compelling evocation of interpersonal trust as comparable with trust in God, this was something with which many medieval writers felt uncomfortable. As Abraham is made to say in *Piers Plowman*, man is in the devil's power and only Christ's sacrifice can free him: no material 'wed' (symbolic pledge object) or 'borrow' (personal surety or guarantor) can acquit the debt of original sin, a judgement that makes a stark distinction between human and divine promises.[69] This was an echo of what many Old and New Testament authors had repeatedly insisted: that only God, not human beings or material goods, was a proper object of trust.[70] Victory in war was said to come from trust in God, not in arms, and the only weapon that Christians needed in their own daily battles was faith in God.[71] In a popular late medieval story from the collection known as the *Gesta romanorum*, a hasty and worldly king of Hungary was told that in order to cross a river he would need a bridge, but—as the moral gloss explained to readers—the material bridge was only a metaphor: 'as hit is hard to passe a depe water withoute a brig, So hit is hard to be saved withoute feith. But ther be many of vs that woll rathir put her lyf & trust in to the help of the world þan to the help of god'.[72] It is notable that the moral of this tale, to 'trust not the world', was itself a proverbial and ubiquitous phrase.[73]

And yet none of these attempts to claim faith as unique to the relationship between God and humanity could achieve a clear demarcation of conceptual territory. The importance of all sorts of 'faith words' to many spheres of human relations was indelible, and their meanings frequently overlapped with the connotations of faith in God, expanding the range of the *fides* lexicon, and making it possible for new usages to appear, as we shall see during the course of this book. When religious faith was described in terms of human relationships, this went beyond analogy, and many theologians, canon lawyers, and authors of pastoral texts accepted and even embraced the interpenetration of ideas. Belief in God and a properly Christian bearing towards others therefore became integral to concepts of good faith in agreements (despite the pre-Christian origins of this in Roman law), of Christians being 'the faithful', and of Christianity being 'the faith'.

This interpenetration of secular *fides* and more religious concepts was commonplace, and while *fides* in law and agreements will be discussed in much more depth in Chapter 2, it is worth foreshadowing some of that material here in order to emphasize its importance in forming the concept of belief in God. For example, medieval canon lawyers understood faith to mean contracts, promises, debts, securities, equity, and 'good faith' in general as well as religious belief, a collection of meanings that ultimately derived from Roman law. Ranulph Higden and William Paull were the English pastoral writers most deeply influenced by this legal tradition. Higden wrote that faith was one of the three comforts of marriage, along with children and the sacrament. It was also the 'fidelity or covenant that must be observed even by an enemy', that is, a binding agreement, treaty or contract.[74] Paull similarly explained faithfulness in a practical vein. Priests should be like 'good and faithful stewards' towards the laypeople in their care, and tithes should be paid faithfully to them in return.[75] Boiling things right down, the canon lawyer William Lyndwood (ca. 1375–1446) said that *fides* simply meant sufficient evidence or proof, particularly, commenting on anti-heresy legislation, with regards to proof of a preacher's orthodoxy.[76]

All of these uses of 'faith' were connected with inter-human relationships, usually involving the placement of trust and a degree of uncertainty about future action and the truth of information, but none of them were wholly 'secular'. As in canon 1 of the Fourth Lateran Council, which said that people find favour with God by 'right faith and good actions', or canon 21, which required 'all the faithful of either sex' to confess their sins 'faithfully' at least once a year, or canon 41, which decreed that no secular law was valid unless it was compatible with good faith, there was always a deep connection between loyalty to the church and belief in God.[77] The faith that formed part of a relationship was never utterly distinct from religious faith. We see this particularly clearly in a further paradigm for acting 'in faith', which had been established by the anonymous first-century author of the letter to the Hebrews, who described first Abraham following God's instruction to sacrifice his son, and then the actions of Isaac, Jacob, Joseph, Moses, and the entire body of Israelite refugees from Egypt, all acting 'faithfully' on divine instruction without fully understanding what it was they were being told to do (Hebrews 11.17–33). This was a pattern of action and explanation that resounded through the biographies of saints, written from antiquity right through the Middle Ages, in order to convert, teach, and sustain the people. For example, in the eleventh-century *Passion of Sainte Foy* the bishop of Agen, who had built a church in honour of this 'St Faith', was suddenly filled with doubt as to whether he should disturb her bones. Was this the proper way to treat a saint? 'Faith' herself intervened to answer his question: the bishop was made to realize that he 'should not unfaithfully neglect what he had faithfully believed'.[78] His loyalty and duty to a particular saint was inseparable from his belief as a Christian. There were differences in emphasis, of course, with faith as belief implying certainty in the face of ignorance, and faith as action resting more on the courage of conviction, but the common ground between these ways of thinking about *fides* is also plain to see.

The binding contract that did most to link medieval Christian faith with the legal senses of *fides* was baptism. But this was a problematic area. How could promises of faith, made on behalf of an infant by his or her godparents, be binding upon that child in later life? One canon lawyer to propose a solution was Laurence of Spain (ca. 1180–1248), who wrote that baptism created freedom from original sin rather than a contract to be kept. Being free and 'in the faith' as an adult, the Christian was then capable of exercising his or her free will to remain faithful or not. Laurence did, however, talk about godparents as if they were the guarantors—*fideiussores*—of a pledge or a debt (for which see Chapter 2). Just as the *fideiussores* were answerable for a debt if the principal debtor failed to pay, godparents were responsible for their godchild's adherence to *the faith*.[79] This was not a perfect solution. Laurence thought that the faith promised by godparents and 'the faith' joined by the baptized child could be isolated from one another, but it is difficult to imagine a child's sponsors standing beside a font thinking that their renunciation of Satan was more of an 'objective legal obligation', in Elisabeth Vodola's words, than it was a transfer of their Christian faith to the infant.[80] After all, the ceremony was intended for the salvation of the soul of the child and during it the godparents were more than once required to recite the *credo*. Faith in the sense of belief was central to this ceremony of relationship forming, or belonging.

The thing that the baptized infant joined, as well as being called the church or the body of Christ, was sometimes referred to as 'the faithful'—a group of people—and sometimes as 'the faith'—a more capacious term whose meaning encompassed the group, the institution, a set of beliefs, and a shared situation relative to God and to history. In this the Christian sense of faith in the later Middle Ages was distinctly different from that which prevailed in biblical times when faith most often meant belonging. The Hebrew term *'emunah* and its Greek equivalent *pistis*—which may both be translated as trust, confidence, faith, or hope—often involved the forging of new relationships between God and the Jews.[81] While Old Testament relationships of faith were configured around covenant, protection, and promises from God, the four gospels introduced a stronger element of obedience within hierarchy. Even the disciples were, at this early date, rebuked for their repeated lack of faith in Christ.[82] And in the Pauline epistles to nascent churches *pistis* involved the creation of relationships and the formation of community from disparate social elements. The 'promise' of Christ was not exclusive to any one people, and so Paul paid great attention to mutual trust as well as individual belief.[83] Teresa Morgan has recently argued that for St Paul faith was 'neither a body of beliefs nor a function of the heart or mind, but a relationship which creates community'.[84]

Although the later medieval concept of faith was more capacious, this sense of a relationship and a community was nevertheless central. St Paul's assertion that the believer who recognizes he is 'of' Christ must also recognize that 'so are we also' found an echo in Augustine's dictum that individual faith was properly so-called if it was a catholic (that is to say universal) faith. This in turn fed into Peter Lombard's formulation that the faith by which we believe is the same in all believers.[85] Community and belief were twin concepts, part of a single understanding of faith. For example, in 1224, when Archbishop Walter Gray of York had the bones of St Wilfrid moved to a new casement in Ripon Minster, the skull was left on public view so it would 'strengthen *the faith* of *the faithful* and increase their devotion'.[86] More or less all medieval writers subscribed to this unity of belief, action, and belonging. The rare exceptions can be taken to prove the rule. For John Wyclif (d. 1384) 'the faithful' was not a term that could be used to describe the church on earth, since 'it is impossible for someone to sin without being deficient in faith'. Acting wrongly meant being incapable of true faith and that in turn meant not being counted among 'the faithful', which for Wyclif was synonymous with the elect.[87] But most theologians used the language of faith in a more integrated way, which reminds us that *fides* was simultaneously a social and a religious concept.

For the institutional and pastoral history of the church in the later Middle Ages there was no more influential expression of this integration of meanings than that inscribed within the first canon of the Fourth Lateran Council in 1215: 'There is indeed one universal church of the faithful, outside of which nobody at all is saved'.[88] Despite a forceful argument made by Berndt Hamm to the effect that love, and not faith, was at the 'normative centre' of late medieval Christianity, faith in the sense of belonging was clearly fundamental.[89]

The church was conceived of as a community of *the faithful* after all, not of *the loving* or of *the hopeful*. Faith comprised the relationship of Christians to one another, their identity as a group, their collective relationship to God, and the ethic of constancy in behaviour and belief that derived from the legal sense of equity.[90]

But as we have seen, faith as belief could rely upon hierarchies and inequality as well as equity and inclusion. To what extent was this also true of faith as Christian belonging? For as much as it was a phrase that evoked a sense of unity and timelessness, referring to Christians as 'the faithful' was a common way of putting shared identity to work in the service of the particular spiritual or political imperatives of the moment, an instrumentalism that flowed through many articulations of *fides* in the later Middle Ages, as we shall see with bishops' references to *viri fidedigni* or trustworthy men. 'The faithful' was always used to clarify boundaries as well as to invoke belonging, and the 'community of the faithful' could be a moral façade for national chauvinism, evoked in times of foreign attack: this danger to 'our community of the faithful'.[91] The most frequent occurrence of this particular phrase however was in excommunication: forbidding someone from having any dealings with Christians and from entering churches. For example, a charter granted to Thorney Abbey by the bishop of Lincoln around 1150, giving it the right to hold a market at Yaxley, was addressed to the earl and sheriff of Huntingdon and 'all faithful French and English people of Huntingdonshire'. Anyone who disrupted the market would suffer the wrath of the bishop and be excluded from 'the community of the faithful'.[92] Similarly, when an Augustinian canon called Robert Wetwang ran away from his convent in 1292, his excommunication was described as 'segregation from the community of the faithful'.[93] The boundaries of belonging could also be negotiated by those who voluntarily sought exclusion for spiritual reasons, but this is a reversal that serves only to reinforce how thoroughly integrated the social and theological notions of *fides* were. In 1418, for example, Margaret Shipster was locked into a cell as an anchorite (a female hermit) 'away from the community of the faithful' in a house beside St Peter's parish church in Hereford.[94] Although she was walled up in the middle of a bustling cathedral city beside the marketplace, Margaret's was a spiritual exclusion, voluntarily undertaken: she had eschewed one form of community with the faith, but entered into another.

Although such language invoked universal values and forms of belonging, even when it was drawing boundaries around 'the faith', the people who might think of themselves as 'the faithful' did not all experience faith, belief, and trust in identical ways, with anchorites such as Margaret Shipster being a case in point. Indeed, much of the best recent historical writing on medieval religion seeks to demonstrate the sheer variety in the experience of faith. To speak of an 'age of faith' or 'medieval belief' is therefore to overgeneralize and flatten out the variety and the political character of this malleable concept *fides*. Late medieval people may have been members of a church that made universal claims upon their loyalty, but the faith that they professed, possessed, gave, and made with one another was shaped by the conditions in which they lived, whether these were material, social, or emotional. This was true of belief in God and of faith in the church, which were always individual as well as collective experiences. But it was also true of those other parallel, and no less important, discourses of *fides* having to do with promises and agreements on the one hand, and reputation and identity on the other, which we have found woven into the cloth of belief in God. The particular character and social meaning of those uses of *fides* will be more fully explored in the following two chapters.

❦

There was some circularity to medieval conceptions of faith as belief. You can be certain about something that is certain, but you cannot be certain about uncertain things. There was not—nor has there ever been—any empirical means of escaping such circular reasoning, but this, a medieval theologian might have said, is simply the nature of faith. This problem should alert us to the importance of power relations in the act of trust.[95] As historians we can ask how language and ideas served and perpetuated inequalities, and how those same inequalities perpetuated such language and ideas. From this survey of the ways in which faith was discussed and deployed in later medieval theology and pastoral writing we can observe several pervasive senses of the term. First, faith traversed hierarchies and obstacles: it was a means to approach an understanding of things that exist in the present but are unseen or beyond the grasp of pure reason; it was something that presented an intellectual challenge to the 'simple', a moment of risk that could usher in doubt, error, and heresy, and was therefore best mediated by an authoritative individual or institution. Second, and in some ways counter to this, faith everywhere described bonds between people, or between people and God or the church; it denoted safety and surety, and could constitute certain knowledge if its object were certain. There are paradoxes here, and these are what made faith capable of being used in a great number of different ways. It held certainty and uncertainty in the balance.

CHAPTER TWO

Law and Agreements

A WORLD MADE FROM PROMISES

IN THE FIRST CHAPTER I showed how belief in God was inseparable from, and in some respects relied upon, the culture of *fides* inherited from Roman law, particularly the concept of good faith. St Augustine's analogy between belief in an unseen God and trust in the good intentions of other people made precisely this link, and did so in such a way as to emphasize the momentous importance of both attitudes. Augustine's theology was steeped in Roman legal culture and his own acute observations of the social world of late antiquity. Without belief in God humanity was doomed, but equally, without good faith between people 'how could anyone escape . . . the confusion and appalling upheaval which would follow?'[1] It has sometimes been assumed, most recently by Geoffrey Hosking as discussed in the introduction to Part I, that this secular trust, good faith between people, was upheld in the Middle Ages only by the presence of the church.[2] But as we have seen in the previous chapter, even the huge institutional prejudice against lay capacity for faith (as belief) could not occlude the vitality of faith talk in general or individual belief in particular. When we turn to trust between persons, we find that the everyday 'practices of social trust', as the philosopher Jan Philipp Reemtsma has called them, 'constitute the most fundamental parameters of a society', an observation that is as true when applied to the European Middle Ages as it is in relation to the present day.[3] Such practices often involved the church, but even in the institutional settings one would think were under the tightest ecclesiastical control, namely the church courts, we find to the contrary that ideas and talk about trust bubbled up from the tumult of social interaction as much as they were imposed from above. Understanding such fundamentals of faith will be essential to perceiving the significance of what bishops were asking when, as will be discussed in Parts II to IV of this book, they came looking for *fidedigni*: trustworthy men.

The Roman law concept of good faith meant equity: honouring the spirit as well as the letter of obligations, especially in sales, exchanges, hire agreements, partnerships, guardianship, loans, pledges, and the partition of estates and common property. Good faith was also a reasonable defence in law if the facts upon which one had acted turned out to be incorrect.[4] These understandings of faith were repeatedly put to use in legal and administrative documents in late medieval England, where, in common with the rest of Latin Christendom, the categories and forms of argumentation of Roman law underpinned canon law, the law of the church. Through the influence of canon lawyers, as well as a broader stream of jurisprudential thought, Roman ideas about *fides* as equity, proof, and promise also affected the English Common Law.[5] This influence lay behind assertions of faith in a variety of contexts. People made wills with 'complete faith' that their wishes would be carried out (even though hope would arguably have been a more appropriate attitude); they promised to stand by agreements in good faith and wondered whether other people had spoken in good faith; at the conclusion of a dispute the rival parties might hope that they could in future be 'ful and faithfull frendes for all maner maters and querelles from hens bakward' (*all manner of quarrels from hence backwards*); judges looked for men whose faith, in the sense of truthfulness, was undoubted.[6]

As we turn from the culture of faith as belief in God to faith as promise and agreement we find ourselves leaving behind one body of scholarship to engage with another, primarily in legal and economic history. It is notable that communication between these subfields of medieval history has been minimal, except perhaps regarding ecclesiastical attitudes towards usury and trade with non-Christians, with the result that connections between faith as belief and faith as equity have not been thoroughly explored. This has impoverished our understanding of both areas. In this chapter I will show how the *fides* that structured promises and agreements owed a great deal to the faith in which Christians lived and through which they thought about God. At the same time it will become apparent that this other discourse of faith had its own existence and deep roots in pervasive social institutions and widespread habits of thought. In order to understand the phenomenon of the trustworthy men, *both* ways of talking about faith need to be taken into account.

Focussing on law and agreements also means working with a very different body of sources from the theological treatises, pastoral texts, and legal compendia used in Chapter 1. The study of agreements is capable of encompassing a much wider swathe of the population than the study of belief. We are able to use the records of the courts, primarily the church courts, but also to a lesser extent the common-law and municipal courts, to see the language of *fides* in action. Although the people of late medieval England did not habitually conduct all their relationships under the glare of judges and lawyers, they did frequently make use of the law to manage difficult or high-stakes moments in their lives, besides thinking with legal concepts even when they had no intention of going to law.[7] I will focus on the enforcement of promises before the law. In promises, trust and the law were locked in a firm, but uncomfortable, embrace. At every turn the legal enforcement of obligations and rights was underpinned by trust: trust in witnesses, trust in written documents, trust in memory, and trust in the courts themselves. While there could be no law without trust, in this chapter I will question Hosking's assumption that there was no surety in the Middle Ages beyond that which derived from the church's institutional power. Could the trust inherent in promises concerning debt, marriage, and a number of other related issues exist without the law?

I will attempt to answer this question by establishing the balance between two possible motivations for promising: to create trust in the sense of a positive fellow feeling, empathy, even altruism, or to enforce the pattern of the other person's future behaviour by way of formal and informal sanctions and incentives. This dichotomy will soon be exposed as hopelessly simplistic, but as a tool to think with it can aid understanding of the nature of *fides* in our period. What is more, such binary thinking occupies so prominent a place in the historiography and social science literature that it is necessary to address it directly. As we have seen, narratives of modernization have often postulated a transition from the automatic solidarity and unquestioning trust of the imagined village, to the eventual breaking of social bonds and the placement of trust in institutions.[8] In the more abstract scholarship trust has been said to be incompatible with the presence of legal or extralegal sanctions, and some have argued that we should not describe as trust what is 'really' calculation and coercion.[9] While scholars of the medieval and early modern past have been more subtle in their approaches to questions of trust, the idea of a transition from trust in persons to trust in institutions is tenacious, whether in Green's articulation of a shift in the meaning of *troth* from one's 'word' or reputation to the more abstract 'truth', or in Muldrew's posited replacement of medieval honesty and faithfulness to God with legal enforcement and trust between contracting individuals.[10] Steven Justice's extrapolation of communal solidarity and mutual obligation from the use of the words *troth* and *trewthe* by the English rebels of 1381 is another case in point, although he examines a culture fixed at a single point in time and does not make arguments about modernization. While Justice identifies an important rhetorical sense of these words, which both translate the Latin *fides*, showing how important it was for peasants to be 'in good faith' with one another, this was very much a matter of local politics in which individuals paid close attention to the quality of their own and each other's 'trewthe' at the same time as experiencing it as a communal bond.[11] The present chapter will show that there was no simple replacement of 'medieval' community with 'modern' legal rights in our period, instead asking where in articulations of *fides*, *troth*, and *trewthe* the balance lay between attempts to create a community-based good faith and attempts to enforce obligations through a system of legal rights. For practical purposes this boils down to a question about language and gestures: what did people think they were doing when they 'gave their faith'?

Promises in Law and in Life

We must begin by recognizing that there was a great deal of faith or trust talk around, and an array of social practices more or less explicitly geared towards the communication of promises. In what follows I will look at some fifteenth-century private letters and other evidence, but for the most part the sources comprise depositions made in the church courts or at visitations (a bishop's or an archdeacon's tour of his jurisdiction), where promises made in 'good faith', or accompanied by the giving or 'making' of faith, were taken very seriously. While litigation immediately highlights the importance of sanctions and the law, the stories that plaintiffs, defendants, and witnesses told about broken promises reveal a more complicated picture.[12]

Litigation on promises was far from being limited to the church courts. Cases of debt and other obligations were common in manorial and borough courts, where the language of faith was occasionally mentioned as a feature of transactions.[13] In the common-law courts, this question was far from simple because—in contrast to the rest of Europe—there was no catchall action for litigation on promises until the sixteenth century. Rather peculiarly, the common law considered sale to be the simultaneous exchange of goods for payment, which ignored the reality of promises for future delivery, deferred payment, and the provision of services over a period of time: elsewhere sale was seen as an agreement imposing obligations and entailing credit. The English abnormality necessitated a series of legal fictions in order to enable disappointed buyers and sellers, creditors and debtors, to litigate on broken promises.[14] The three principal routes to redress were the actions of covenant, debt, and *assumpsit*, though each was unsatisfactory in some way, driving many litigants to use the church courts, where the language of faith was heavy with significance and consequences.[15]

Although in strict legal terms the English church courts did not provide a remedy for underlying obligations—that is the obligation to pay the debt, to perform the task, or whatever—the canonical principle that satisfaction or restitution was a necessary preliminary to penance meant that in practice successful plaintiffs could expect the enforcement of a debt or obligation. Given a need for written agreements and the imposition of a forty-shilling minimum value threshold for common-law cases, it is no surprise that actions for debt under the category of 'breach of faith' comprised the single biggest group of cases in the English church courts by the mid-fifteenth century.[16] For example, when she failed to pay him back the money he had lent her around 1471, John Child of South Mimms in Hertfordshire must have wondered what sort of a bargain he had made with Margery Faust, but he alleged 'breach of faith' and she settled to repay the money.[17] In permitting litigation on debt the English church courts were unusual in European ecclesiastical perspective, and plaintiffs were attracted by the seriousness with which promises made 'by faith' were treated. Promises, wrote the canonist Hostiensis, should always be kept, unless they were contrary to the law, against good morality, or fraudulent (by which he meant impossible to honour).[18] This expectation that promise keeping was simply a duty for Christians, and not something that required the involvement of the courts is, perhaps somewhat paradoxically, amply illustrated in legal records, where disputes that end up in court are shown to have had origins in a different world of noninstitutional good faith. When, for example, the receiver of Southwell in Nottinghamshire said in 1315 that he would pay the reeve there five marks 'in good faith and without a tally', the seriousness of the agreement was enhanced, and not diminished, by the lack of an official record, and it was the breach of the receiver's faith upon which the subsequent action for recovery was based.[19] In addition to an economic culture of trust, much else in medieval society was negotiated with talk about faith and *troth*. As James Coleman has astutely observed, 'in many situations involving the placement of trust . . . the parties involved cannot use [contracts], often because there is no agreed value attached to the things the trustor gives up'.[20] Contracts cannot apprehend value or 'goods' that are not easily measurable, but—as I will show in what follows—expressions of faith and trust could be used to heighten promises so that they were more than mere transactions.

The canon law action for breach of faith was capable of being turned to the enforcement of all kinds of promises, whether based on a written contract or not. In the sphere of economic relationships the biggest single category comprised actions for the recovery or recognition of a debt. Credit and debt actually encompass a multitude of relationships, and this is reflected in the variety of the cases, some of which may seem unusual to modern eyes. In economic systems where neighbourly reciprocity is an important social obligation, tools, labour, and produce may be lent without much formality, or an expectation of recompense. In such historical circumstances real value could well lie in the longevity of relations, and not necessarily in the satisfaction of a one-time debt.[21] Often debtors promised to repay the loan in instalments, and an appearance in court simply elicited a further promise to repay the loan at a later date, even if the defendant was left thinking to him- or herself—as John Paston did in a letter of 1477—'I knowe nott yitt the meanes possible that I myght paye . . . by thatt daye'.[22]

Aside from loans of money a great deal of late medieval credit took the form of advanced purchase sales and credit sales. In an advanced purchase sale the price was agreed and paid before the delivery of the goods or the performance of the service. This was the norm in the wholesale trades, but also familiar in smaller transactions.[23] In Kent in 1455 Robert Gyland was said to have promised 'by his faith' to deliver two cows to John Lightfoot, having been paid for them already.[24] Around 1480 three parishioners (possibly the church-wardens) of Barking in Essex accused Richard Laverock of breaking faith by failing to build a new porch for their church despite having been paid forty shillings in advance.[25] Smaller transactions, such as for clothes made to order, could also become the subject of breach of faith litigation.[26] Some of the larger advance purchase agreements concerned land and houses. These were proba-bly a form of gage (as in mortgage): property surrendered as security for other loans. Around 1480, for example, Alice Bassett broke faith with John Dyer 'for sellyng of an howse' in London, and Alice Curle did the same in respect of John Fordom.[27] By contrast, a credit sale involved the transfer of goods in ex-change for a promise to pay the price at an agreed later date. Given the scarcity of coin in the medieval economy, relative to the volume of transactions, this mode of sale was both ubiquitous and completely normal.[28] But this is not to say it was without its problems. Because the church courts permitted litigation on promises without written agreements, the transaction was often between neighbours, involving goods of a low value. Whatever the circumstances, there was ample scope for misunderstanding, forgetfulness, or intentional default. A husband and wife were accused of refusing to pay four shillings for a gold brooch; a man promised to pay for goods his wife had ordered from a baker; a friar failed to pay for the bespoke book he had commissioned.[29] Around 1485 the London brewer John Byland supplied a firkin of 'thre halpenny ale' to Richard Reynold on credit for his son's wedding, but Reynold had failed to pay. In court the purchaser promised that he would now pay in full by an agreed date, or he would pay in kind, giving Byland one 'finderkyn' of penny ale and one 'finderkyn' of good beer.[30]

A range of other economic promises could be treated as breaches of faith. While in common law, agreements to enter into someone's employment were hard to assess, the church courts were content to hear them.[31] All trades, even the clergy, seem to have used the courts for this purpose. In 1418 for example the vicar of Givendale near Pickering in North Yorkshire sued Robert Norton for the breach of his promise, which had been 'made with faith and an oath', to serve as a parish chaplain.[32] It was also relatively common for employers to sue employees for breach of faith if they failed to complete an agreed term of service. The case of a London servant, Elizabeth Scherborn, is typical in that we cannot tell why she did not complete 'her service for a hole yere' around 1485, but occasionally we do know more: Robert Thoroughgoode, for example, walked out of his position, 'breaking faith', after his employer's wife accused him of stealing a candlestick.[33] Apprenticeships could also be subject to litiga-tion, especially surrounding their termination. In the late 1470s William Colet wanted to offer employment to William Bishop, but Bishop was apprenticed to another master. So Colet secured the agreement of Bishop's master, Richard Rycher, to release his apprentice from his service a year early. When this did not happen Colet claimed that Rycher had broken faith with him.[34]

Breach of faith was also widely used to hold the executors of wills to their obligations, a coercive sanction that we shall see, in Chapter 11, being taken up at the bishop's command by *viri fidedigni* or trustworthy men. The obligations of executors may or may not have been incurred with an express promise to faithfully perform their duty, but litigants and the courts seem to have been happy with the procedure in either event.[35] For example, when a testator's daughter was cited for breach of faith at Tideswell in Derbyshire in 1347, we may assume that the case was brought by a disgruntled beneficiary of the will, but no actual promise was alleged.[36] Conversely, at other times executors did make express promises. At Hartlebury in Worcestershire Edith Bayly had to pay a fee and promise to faithfully execute her late husband's will in 1406.[37] John Scharpe gave his faith to the warden of West Ham church (Essex) around 1480 that he would hand over money set aside to pay for masses for the souls of some other parishioners.[38] Executors might also use the courts to elicit and to enforce promises of good faith from people who owed money to the estate of the deceased;[39] a creditor could be asked to give faith that he would not hold the executors liable for the deceased's debts;[40] even in the absence of a will, assertions of good faith could be required in order to establish that no unlawful deathbed transfer of property had taken place.[41]

Many financial obligations could be incurred as a result of simple residency in a parish, membership of a guild or fraternity, or tenancy of a particular holding. Although these circumstances rarely involved express promises on the part of the liable person, actions for breach of faith were sometimes used to claim payment, strongly suggesting that implied promises or the simple obligations incurred by belonging were treated just as seriously.[42] One particular class of implied promise was the obligation for executors of wills to make restitution for unpaid tithes and mortuary payments, in which case breach of faith seems to relate to the faith that parishioners were expected to have towards their church.[43] But there is also a class of action in which people were called to court simply for 'withholding' money from a church or guild, and then required to make an express promise and an offer of good faith concerning future payment.[44] For example, Thomas Owersuell of Emneth in Norfolk was accused of withholding a mortuary owing on his late mother's estate around 1460. He promised—by his faith—to reach an agreement with the churchwardens that took account of his being a pauper. Here it seems that his good faith also stood surety for his claim to poverty.[45]

Marriage litigation could, by implication, be seen as a special—and massive—category of *fidei laesio* (breach of faith) all on its own. Almost all marriage cases involved a claim that one or the other party had failed to abide by a faithful promise, or that a marriage should be dissolved because promises had not been made in good faith. This will be fleshed out in the following section where I discuss the words exchanged in betrothals, but it is worth noting that marriage suits could also very occasionally be treated explicitly as actions for breach of faith.[46] Breach of faith was also invoked to deal with cruelty, neglect, and desertion within families, and the kin and neighbours of the offending party (usually the husband) were frequently drafted in as collective guarantors of his future good faith. Sometimes a monetary bond for future good behaviour would be lodged with a court or the bishop, which would be forfeited if the man in question repeated his offence.[47] Something very similar took place in the manorial courts where pledges were sometimes used as a means of holding a bad husband to his promise of treating his wife better in future.[48] A variation on this could see *fideiussores* or guarantors agreeing to pay a fine if an offender returned to his bad old ways. In a case from early thirteenth-century Yorkshire Hugh of Berwick was thus bound over, having promised to 'treat his wife with due marital affection, so far as was in his power'.[49]

In all of these actions taking place under the auspices of canon law in church courts, faith was clearly a concept capacious enough to mean several different things. In common with the usages surveyed in Chapter 1, there are implications of a bond between two people arising from an express or implied promise, a bond between an individual and a group, a bond made before— and perhaps with—God, and the trust put at risk by an unknown future or the unseen intentions of another person. It is also possible to discern hints of a theme whose importance to the history of trustworthy men and the church will become more and more apparent as this book proceeds, namely the discrimination inherent to the act of trust. Since it was *particular* bonds of faith that were broken, the implication is that faith entailed decisions to trust this person rather than that one. There is also a strong undercurrent of compulsion, or at least limited options, causing people to make promises because they had to, and not necessarily because they wanted to. This being so, as the argument unfolds further I want to draw attention to the possibility that bonds of trust among the people might reinforce hierarchical relationships, however available and seemingly inclusive the lexicon may have been. In thinking about the importance of a discriminating trust for our study of trustworthy men, it is worth drawing a distinction between the faith in God surveyed in the last chapter, and the faith in people dealt with here: while in the former case deficient faith could slide into doubt and error, it was no heresy to trust one person rather than another, even though the breach of a faithful promise was considered actionable in the church courts. As we shall see, to the habitual distrust of the laity by churchmen was added a willingness to discriminate and trust some people rather than others.

Heightened Formality and Public Words

The communication of faith and trust was something that in theory everyone knew how to do. And yet it was perilous: easy to get wrong, likely to be misinterpreted, with potentially critical results for individuals and relationships.

In London around 1468 Christopher Balton was in the bishop's consistory court recalling a betrothal he had seen. There had been an exchange of consent, a mutual giving of faith, and a kiss between a man called Richard Colyn and a woman called Joan Deyndo. Now though another man, Robert Arwam, had come forward, saying that he and Deyndo had earlier agreed to marry one another. He claimed there was a prior contract that would invalidate the betrothal between her and Colyn. Other witnesses said much the same as Balton, adding that they had all been invited to a tavern called 'le George' where they ate and drank with Colyn and Deyndo for about an hour, but they were doubtful whether this constituted a contract to marry.[50] As with all the stories told by witnesses in marriage litigation we are in no position to judge the truth of the matter, but the way that things were remembered and presented by the protagonists is the thing of real interest. Consent, formal words of faith, and a kiss seem pretty certain indicators of a betrothal, but there were doubts: perhaps, with Arwam's prior claim on Joan Deyndo preying on their minds, some witnesses began to question whether the eating and drinking they had thought was a formal ritual had in fact been so.[51]

What this circumspection shows is that there was a continuum of words, gestures, and rituals surrounding promises and faith. Life, it seems, was full of implied agreements and tacit expressions of faith: how could it have been otherwise? There were many words and actions that implied promises, but not all of them were easily actionable in court. What I want to do here is to describe the ways in which people constructed moments of heightened formality to make binding promises using the lexicon of faith, careful gestures, and witnesses. This will then shed more light on the question of how reliant trusting was upon the institutional power of the church courts, and begin to delineate the social practices of trust upon which bishops wished to draw when they identified trustworthy men in the parishes.

For the sake of clarity it is useful to begin with a model of the various registers of speech associated with promises, before delving into the actual words used. In the course of daily life and conversation everyone would have been continuously and unconsciously, or perhaps with some dim awareness, processing all sorts of linguistic and gestural indications of intentions, promises, trust, and trustworthiness. This complex and continuous stream of communication is not, of course, recoverable by the historian, but it seems sensible to remember its existence as we discuss the evidence. With that evidence it is *just about* possible to see, emerging from the cultural morass of unconscious signalling, something of the range of conscious utterances by which people communicated their intentions and accepted obligations. At the far end of the spectrum from unconscious signalling, there was a finely tuned vocabulary of promising associated with aspects of contract actionable in law. In a number of circumstances people seem to have crafted promises so carefully that their 'web of symbolic acts and gestures' would be understood not only to advertise an agreement, but also to constitute the agreement itself and anticipate future legal enforcement.[52] Between uninhibited communication and legal speech there was a further category: when circumstances demanded it people could adopt a heightened formality, choosing words that would be understood as intentional recitations of meaningful words rather than mere chitchat, and gestures that appeared choreographed and considered. This heightened formality had to borrow from the everyday language of intentions in order to seem sincere, but also from the precise vocabulary of the law in order to protect against future disagreement.

The bulk of our evidence about trust among the people concerns such public words, and it comes from litigation on marriage and debt, where many plaintiffs, defendants, and witnesses claimed that words and gestures had been misconstrued. Because there were several registers of promising in speech it was possible to present particular words or occasions as having had more or less meaning than they might have had for the other party. It was also possible to wilfully misrepresent what had been well understood at the time in order to renege on an agreement. The uncertainty of words, particularly in terms of which register they fell within on a specific occasion, was sometimes emphasized by the poet Geoffrey Chaucer, who particularly relished referring to the existence of promises without actually allowing them to appear as reported speech.[53] This artful narrative device seems intended to resonate with an audience for whom such uncertainty was familiar.

However, there was also a widespread idea that promises were all alike to God, following Hostiensis's comments cited above, which would reduce the importance of register. Oaths were in many quarters seen as unnecessary at best and sinful at worst, since swearing could not make false declarations true nor could it cause things widely doubted to command universal assent. Matthew's gospel recounts Christ's suspicion of oaths, proclaimed in the Sermon on the Mount. Instead of swearing you should simply say 'yes' or 'no' and live by your utterances. Do what you say you will do. Swearing an oath by the hairs of your head cannot turn them from black into white.[54] The second commandment of God to the Israelites had been not to take the Lord's name in vain. Besides being a warning against casual blaspheming, this text was glossed by some commentators as an injunction to avoid swearing oaths 'for nothing', rashly, or excessively upon God, holy books, the limbs of Christ, and so on.[55] There were only two circumstances in which oaths were acceptable, and neither was without risk. Baptism entailed promises, made by godparents as proxies or *fideiussores*, which brought the child into the faith. But these promises were oaths before God that if broken could be construed as heresy. In adult life a Christian might also be called upon by the church to swear an oath. This was permissible in defence of 'law and reputation, the faith, and God's honour' or when danger threatened or truth was imperilled. But, nonetheless, oaths heightened the risk to the swearer and raised the stakes of one's promises.[56] These strictures against oaths held even when the deponent told the truth. Someone who was too ready to swear an oath was actively disbelieved and could be considered *ipso facto* (that is 'automatically') excommunicated.[57] Going one step further and failing to tell the truth having sworn an oath fell under the eighth commandment against bearing false witness. This was perjury, a crime punishable under canon law and a capacious net to catch the unwary speaker. Although a common definition was 'a lie strengthened by an oath', a perjurer could also be anyone 'who should in any way speak or depose against the instruction of his conscience . . . under whatever cloak or show of words': that is, without an oath necessarily having been sworn.[58] Those who swore oaths other than 'for rightwysnes in declaring of trouthe' did not escape perjury either.[59]

Despite these warnings oaths were commonly used in forming binding promises, but the 'naked agreement' or *nudum pactum* comprising mere words, was frequently 'clothed' with formal words, rituals, and symbolic tokens so that they would be more amenable to memory and thereby to legal enforcement.[60] And yet in the course of their lives people were making all sorts of promises with 'bare words'. Canon lawyers shared the Roman idea that a promise without evidence could not be enforced, and yet as ethicists they could not escape the gospel injunction to keep promises: all promises.[61] This was keenly observed by Maitland: 'if, not merely a binding contract to marry, but an indissoluble marriage can be constituted without any formalities, it would be ridiculous to demand more than consenting words in the case of other agreements'.[62] Ridiculous, maybe, but it was a question that troubled the church courts. Litigants and witnesses frequently spoke of promises that they considered binding, even if they could not be upheld in law. They followed, or pretended to follow, the biblical ethic and they valued the moral precept. For example a marriage suit of 1457 records words of consent that a witness believed constituted a contract of marriage, even though others called it into question because they did not conform to the usual pattern: 'I will have you to my husbonde and such promes'.[63] Crucially there is no 'faith' component to this contested utterance, indicating that some promising and some trust was informal.[64] The rituals of giving faith were not always observed, or they were not always accorded the significance that the ensuing lawsuits placed upon them. In 1420 John Coly and Stephen Webbe were witnesses in a breach of faith case. They recalled John Tadewell and Richard Wennyston discussing arrangements for the repayment of a loan: there was a surety, but—they were clear about this—no words of faith between the two men.[65] They were happy to rely on their witnesses, until, that is, trust broke down and they ended up in court. But still the case reveals a world of trust without words of faith or oaths. Much, or indeed most, of life must have worked this way. Quite a lot of the breach of faith business in church courts concerned low-value loans of goods for temporary use or reciprocal exchange between neighbours.[66] Though they ended up in court, there is often no mention of any formalities having attended the original promises in such cases.

Despite informality being commonplace in promising, the judicial evidence also supports the view that most people recognized a distinction between ordinary moral and legally enforceable obligations. A disputed advance purchase sale in London in 1470 for example pitted the word of one witness—who recalled a formal promise of faith (*fide sua media promisit*), a physical gesture amounting to a promise (*fidem corpore*), and even the presence of a *fideiussor*—against that of another who said the parties had agreed merely 'with bare words, without giving faith' (*nudo verbo et non . . . fidei dationem*).[67] This was not a denial that the agreement had ever taken place, but an attempt to claim that there was nothing the court could do about it, and it rested upon the second witness's belief that without words of faith there was no case to answer.[68] In 1383 the rector of Huggate in Yorkshire, Thomas Etton, tried to back out of an arbitrated judgement that he owed the previous rector eighty marks, by saying that he had never, either by his faith or by swearing an oath touching a gospel book, promised to abide by the settlement. Etton believed that having not given faith, nor sworn an oath, meant that he was not bound by the agreement. But his opponents thought otherwise. For them the fact that there had already been arbitration meant that he was bound whether the words were 'naked according to the law' or not.[69] The reality of a distinction between the ordinary language of obligations and legally binding speech is vividly brought home by a terse entry in a London commissary court act book. In March 1493 a note relating to the dispute between John March and Thomas Comyngham was altered, presumably by the scribe, but perhaps at the insistence of one of the parties: the word *fides* was crossed out and replaced with the English 'promise', indicating that promises without faith were treated as inferior by some people.[70] *Fides* could of course mean promise, but it was always stronger and more formal than the naked word.[71] The formality that talk of *fides* brought to a person's word is also of huge importance in understanding why bishops wanted to align themselves with the *fidedigni* of a parish, rather than with informants described in any other way.

Promises, it seems, were one thing, while giving faith was different. It was more formal and it brought a relationship definitively within the purview of the law. Giving faith was not, however, always the same thing as swearing an oath. Legal historians have tended to assume that faith and oaths amounted to the same thing, discussing breach of faith as if it always pertained to oaths and translating *fidem dari* or *fide dati* as the swearing of an oath.[72] Admittedly this category of action was sometimes called 'breach of faith and perjury', but even though they were both actionable in the same way, the *juramentum* was distinguished from giving faith.[73] Maitland recognized this.[74] As we have seen, oaths were highly problematic in theology and canon law. The gospels urged people not to swear but to live by their words and do their duty; oaths were proscribed during Lent; being too ready to swear could lessen a person's credibility and even lead to excommunication.

Oaths were frequently differentiated from faith by litigants and witnesses, as when Alice Chamberlain 'bound herself by her faith *and* swore an oath' (*per fidem suam se astrinxit et iuravit*) to pay Thomas Lyster seven shillings in 1402.[75] It is true that faith and oaths *could* be wrapped up in the same illocution—'by way of faith and under oath' (*fide media sub iuramento*)—and courts sometimes made little distinction between them.[76] When Hugh Dunlord promised to work for William Port in 1452 and take a widow of William's household as his wife in return for some land and a horse, the main witness could recall only that William, for his part, had either given faith *or* sworn an oath.[77] But these were statements that reflected the indifference of the court as to the legal distinction between faith and oath: the same action applied so long as there was *some kind* of formal promise. At other times the courts reflected the popular view that oaths were more stringent and more perilous than giving faith, as when William Bude was required to swear an oath to William Alyn, having already broken faith with him over a small debt.[78] While oaths were promises in a formal register, giving faith was an intermediate form of public speech.

This explains the lengths to which people went to ensure that their formal utterances could be distinguished from day-to-day speech. Ritual and a recitation were necessary. When, around 1511, William Erle wanted to be certain whether Agnes Colson would indeed marry him, he said to her:

> I pray yow shew me your mynde how ye be disposed tomewarde for some of my compeny saith un to me that ye bot triffil (*trifle*) with me and will not performe that thyng that yow have promised me here before.

Agnes then took William by the hand and said 'by my faithe and trowthe here I Agnes take yow William to my husbond'.[79] He required a formal recitation from her—a performance and a promise—and she knew that this meant public words that would be recognized as such.[80]

Words and Gestures

The Erle and Colson example reveals some of the actual words and gestures used to heighten the formality of promises and turn a moral duty into an enforceable obligation. Matrimonial litigation, from the thirteenth century to the sixteenth, furnishes us with many examples of the words most commonly used to preface a promise of marriage: 'I give you my faith' (*do tibi fidem meam*).[81] This hit just the right level of heightened formality for the manifold purposes of interpersonal sincerity, the satisfaction of the two families, and the unspeakable, latent prospect of future litigation. Saying 'I give you my faith' meant my promise, my word, or even something of myself. But it also harboured meanings rooted in public commitments: *I commit myself to standing by my obligation and I am prepared to be held to it*. It was also an expression of trust in the other person (an implicit affirmation of Augustine's insistence on the need for trust in the formation of relationships), and acceptance of potential sanctions in the event of default.

Giving faith had to be consensual and reciprocal, otherwise there was no contract. In a fascinating case from Norwich in 1506 we get a glimpse of how two people might edge towards and then away from the exchange of faith that loomed over certain social circumstances. Katherine Fydill brought a suit for breach of faith against William Pye, alleging that he had promised to marry her. But the event that she presented as a betrothal does appear to have been rather one-sided. Pye had been invited to her house, and Fydill had also made sure there was a witness present. The witness said to Pye, 'Sir, me semeth ye were to be at home here', to which Fydill added, 'I trust in tyme to cum he shall be at hoom'. Pye was not moved: 'Dame, ye woit (*know*) what I have said to you. I am the same man that I was'.[82] His refusal was clear enough, but it also seems that her failure to use any formal words of betrothal sprang from her knowledge that they would not have been reciprocated.

In financial transactions or the acceptance of a debt people did not say 'I give you my faith'; they promised to do something 'by my faith'.[83] This illocution is closer to the dubious oaths ('by God's bones' and so on) that made market traders so mistrusted by moral writers, but this particular formulation, which bound a person to his or her own integrity and did not make any claim on God's supposed intervention, was acceptable to the church. These words could be augmented in various ways, by saying 'by my faith I will pay you faithfully' for example, but the essential element seems to have been the reference to 'my faith'.[84] Faith is sometimes treated as a personal quality that may be 'given' without being lost, sometimes as a new bond 'made' between two people, and sometimes as a 'pledge' held by the recipient. This latter sense conveyed a willingness to be called on one's promises: you have my faith in your possession, and therefore the right to demand that it is redeemed. This allowed plaintiffs to demand that defendants honour *their* contract and *their* faith.[85]

So far I have translated the *fides* of the Latin sources with the words 'faith' or 'promise', but court scribes were often themselves translating from English into Latin and so we cannot always be certain what vernacular words the litigants and witnesses actually uttered, either in court or in the conversations that lay behind the legal actions.[86] 'Promise' was indeed a vernacular term in common usage, as in John Osbern's 1451 letter to John Paston, which referred not only to plain promises, but also to his 'very true promise' and his 'gift and promise'.[87] Fourteenth- and fifteenth-century poets had their protagonists use a wider variety of words when they promised, depending on the register they were trying to adopt. Verbs such as 'sweren' (to swear), 'plighten' (to pledge), 'wedden' (to bind or pledge), and 'behesten' (to promise or command) were common, and may be evidence of an even richer repertoire of words and phrases in everyday life that could imply promises and intentions without such overt commitments being made.[88]

During betrothals the vernacular form of *do tibi fidem meam* was often 'I plight thee my troth', while in financial transactions the usual exclamation was 'Yes by my faith', 'Yee for fathe', or something of that sort.[89] Sometimes the language of the marketplace seeped into betrothals, as in Richard Higham's words to Joan Kyppynge in Kent in 1456:

> I Richard tak the Johan to my wyffe from this day forward be myn faith
> yif holi church wull hit favyre.[90]

The English 'troth' conveyed all the subtle meanings of faith and the two words were sometimes found together as synonyms.[91] However, scribes were also capable of translating troth as *veritas* (truth) as well as *fides* (faith), even within the same legal proceedings, supporting Green's contention that troth was acquiring a sense of objective fact in the later Middle Ages.[92] However, as this example shows, it is not correct to argue that truth was replacing faith: both existed side by side.

When words were recited in a formal register they were also, almost always, accompanied by ritual gestures. Documentary historians must try particularly hard to understand the importance of physical deportment and behaviour since gestures formed a corporeal language in late medieval England, interwoven with spoken words. It was not uncommon for the words of a betrothal to refer to the accompanying gestures, in phrases such as 'yea by my fayth & trew hand', while other obligations might be undertaken with a 'physical promise' of faith.[93] The hand was hugely important in advertising the public nature of undertakings to casual bystanders and primed witnesses alike.

Like words, gestures could also be misinterpreted, but understandably people thought that they knew insincerity when they saw it. Around 1470 a Londoner called William Rate told the story of how he had been forced into a betrothal with a publican's daughter. In his version of events he had innocently gone for a drink in John Wells' tavern when Wells had pulled a knife on him and accused him of raping his daughter Agnes. Rate claimed he had fled the house, chased down the street by Agnes's mother who was shouting 'Holde the thef', before being grabbed by some passers-by and dragged back into the house to be told that if he did not marry Agnes they would either lead him to his grave, or haul him before the mayor and aldermen so that through shame and despair he would relent. Rate told the court how he had gone through the motions because he feared both the threatened violence and the shame. A witness said that whereas Agnes had pledged her faith and kissed William

Rate, Rate himself had merely proffered the customary words and then 'swiftly and rudely' (*incontinenti*) withdrawn his hand. The words indicated consent, but the witnesses drew attention to the importance of bearing, manner, and gesture in determining whether someone had offered their faith willingly and freely, or not.[94]

There were proper ways of doing things, without which words and actions might appear insincere or even shocking, whatever the intention had been. In the commercial sphere particular hand gestures were even becoming essential elements of a sale or bargain, and not just additional markers or mnemonics for the benefit of witnesses. A sale was not a sale unless the proper rituals had been undertaken.[95] The centrality of gestures to late medieval law and society, and in particular to the transaction of faith—as we shall see—means that we should not treat them lightly. In this respect, as in so many others, the period should not be seen as a staging post on some grand developmental historical journey away from a sacral towards a modern rationality. The gestures of faith were not the denuded remnants of some ancient ceremonial culture.[96] They were meaningful in their own time as part of an interlocking culture of words, actions, assumptions, and expectations.

In the records of the church courts we find four principal hand gestures associated with faith: the *immixtio manuum* as a sign of submission, the raised hand as a sign of an oath, the slap as a sign of a deal or bargain, and the clasp as the sign of a new partnership. There were other physical signs of good faith, such as the kiss and the judicial oath taken hand-on-Bible, but the hands are mentioned more often and in more contexts, suggesting that it was here that visual understandings of faith were concentrated.[97]

Giving homage was the characteristic gesture of feudal society, involving the *immixtio manuum* or conjoining of hands: the vassal would place his palms together and offer them to his lord, who would in turn clasp his hands around those of the vassal. Marc Bloch called this 'a plain symbol of submission'.[98] The *fides* that a vassal offered with these gestures was his fealty or loyalty, which will be discussed a little further in Chapter 4, and it denoted an asymmetric relationship: the inferior party was often said to have 'put his faith into the hands' of the superior party.[99] The faith exchanged in the more socially widespread and commonplace gestures of betrothal and the marketplace denoted a putative equality. On the basis of these differences Maitland distinguished between *fides facta* and homage, but there is evidence to suggest that some exchanges of faith outside 'feudal' relations also involved the submissive *immixtio manuum*.[100] Typically these were agreements to abide by the decision of arbitrators. As third parties to disputes and agreements, arbitrators, who will be discussed in more detail in due course, received the submission of the principal parties as faith 'placed in their hands'.[101] They were not lords, and no permanent relationship was brought into being, but the act itself was clearly modelled on that of homage.

A gesture signifying greater independence than *immixtio manuum* was the raised hand of the sworn oath. The thirteenth-century legal treatise known as Bracton enjoined jurors swearing to tell the truth to stand all together with their hands lifted up.[102] This was a gesture regularly represented in narrative poetry in order to set the scene and make the reader complicit in the action. The pilgrims' host in Chaucer's *Canterbury Tales* asks the company to 'Hoold up youre hondes, withouten moore speche' before they embark on their journey, and in the prose romance *Lancelot* a group of knights hold up their right hands and swear by the saint of a nearby church.[103] The raised hand was rarely associated with giving faith in daily life, but in one example from Canterbury diocese in 1410 someone swearing an oath 'by my faith' also raised his right hand.[104]

References to the faith given or offered in debt contracts or sales are extremely terse, and witnesses almost never describe the nature of the physical gesture that accompanied it. We can be fairly sure, however, that it was not a handshake as we understand it today. This is what some legal historians have assumed, but it is an anachronism without basis in the records of litigation on debt. Equally, John Burrow finds no evidence in literary texts to suggest that handshakes were a feature of late medieval life.[105] If not a handshake, then what kind of gesture was it that sealed the deal? The most likely would seem to be some sort of slap. Paul Hyams has pointed to an aphorism of the twelfth-century Roman law commentator Azo, who derived a very vivid false etymology for *pactum*. Azo explained that *pactum* derived from the 'striking of hands (*percussione palmarum*) used to make a sign of inviolable faith'. Although etymologically unsound, it seems likely that Azo called to mind a familiar gesture. As Hyams points out, it cannot be construed as a gentlemanly handshake, and may have been more of a high-five.[106] In the very recent past a highly performative vertical slap onto the other person's out-held palm was common in British agricultural and equestrian markets.[107] The slap is certainly the most visible and audible form of hand gesture, and this would argue for it being particularly suited to the marketplace, where the security of a deal depended on it being witnessed. Traders would literally 'strike' a bargain. Naturally it was not the only practice, and many regional and chronological variants must be hidden beneath the silence of the sources.[108]

James Davis has recently argued that small transactions undertaken without written contracts were 'workable only when a sufficient level of trust had been created between participants', and that by this trust 'transaction costs were lowered and future alliances could be created'.[109] Although the need for trust in trade has become a truism of economic sociology, it is debateable whether genuine trust could be created between traders and customers in a busy marketplace; such judgements are likely to have involved hasty stereotyping of an unfamiliar merchant or reliance upon assumptions about people based on secondhand knowledge of them and their families. Creating meaningful fellow feeling based on knowledge and a lasting relationship may not often have been possible. Another model is necessary. Gestures and symbols were made in public, possibly before a group of trusted acquaintances for whom every other trader was him- or herself a witness in turn. The hand-slap was thus a gesture signifying heightened formality, performed so as to be witnessed. As well as signifying a deal, it created a memory that could be useful in any future dispute.

Much of this must also have been true of the customary gestures involved in betrothals, although these could be choreographed more easily than most marketplace deals. Troth plighted 'in the hand' is referred to explicitly in the 'Franklin's Tale' and the 'Wife of Bath's Tale'; John Lydgate's *Pilgrimage of the Life of Man* (1426) describes trothplight being confirmed 'hand in hand ybounde faste'; John Gower referred to 'trowthe in honde' in his *Confessio Amantis*; Thomas Malory described a couple being 'honde-faste and wedded'.[110] These were very clearly attempts to impart verisimilitude to literary depictions of a familiar homemade ritual. Indeed witnesses in marriage litigation frequently described a declaration of faith accompanied by clasped right hands.[111] What is more, so-called *fede* rings and brooches have been found in several parts of the country upon which clasped hands complete a gilt copper or gold circlet, confirming that this was the gesture most commonly associated with the faith exchanged in betrothal.[112] One particular case heard in the London consistory in 1470 presented a detailed description of the ritual: man and woman stood side by side; she placed her right arm across the back of his shoulders and he raised his right hand to hold hers; after a few words had been said she then raised her left hand in front of her and, extending one finger, accepted a ring and asked whether it was given out of love; the woman said she wished it to last until death, reciting 'I shall never have husbond but you and þerto y plyght the my trouth a fore God'; taking her left hand the man replied in the same terms, and they kissed.[113]

Taking stock of all the evidence for the hand gestures that accompanied words of faith, it is possible to offer a hypothesis about the symbolic language that connected them all, but also made different gestures more suitable to certain circumstances. It seems as though the gestures in which the hands of two people were bound together—namely the handclasp of betrothal and the *immixtio manuum* of submission—signified the beginning of a new relationship, something that formed a lasting bond between two people. These were quite distinct situations, the one involving equals and the other not, but both gestures signified the hoped-for longevity, even permanence, of the bond. By contrast, those gestures in which there was only the briefest contact, or none at all—namely the slap of the marketplace and the raised hand of the oath—related to promises on a single issue and did not constitute a permanent bond. There are of course exceptions to this, such as the individual oath taken hand-on-book that accompanied a religious vow, but as a general model it works for most cases in the English church courts.

Homemade Rituals

All promises in the register of heightened formality involved a personal pledge of integrity, trust vested in the other party, and knowledge of duties and sanctions implied by their public character. The extent to which the public element could be choreographed must have depended upon the possibilities of the moment, but it also varied between types of promise, as we have seen. All homemade rituals, however, included some or all of the following elements in addition to words and gestures of faith: a carefully chosen place or position, the exchange of gifts, ritual eating or drinking, and the presence of witnesses who would—ideally—see and hear what happened and make it the common talk of the parish.

Betrothals often took place in the more public rooms of a house, where witnesses could be invited in, but other venues were popular too.[114] Taverns provided the much-valued public space on some occasions, ecclesiastical disapproval notwithstanding, though some people did opt for a ceremony in church.[115] On one remarkable occasion in Lichfield around 1460 a couple who had been reported at a visitation for fornication produced witnesses who were able to say that they had pledged their faith to one another in the very church where the visitation tribunal was being held.[116] Memories of public faith do not come stronger than that. Equally, faith given to repay a debt in the public forum of the London guildhall, which we see in one late fifteenth-century case, must also have been extremely difficult to wriggle out of.[117] The gifts accompanying betrothals included but were by no means limited to rings. Purses, rosaries, symbolic coins, veils, handkerchiefs, and many other more unusual items besides were all exchanged.[118] Material tokens accompanying sales were important both as 'a symbolic confirmation of the obligation' and for imposing 'future fidelity to the obligation'.[119] Such pledged objects, or the 'wed', could be interpreted as the material equivalent of *fides*: a thing pledged could be redeemed by its recipient. In the late medieval marketplace, buyers and debtors handed over 'earnest money' or a 'God's penny' upon the agreement of a bargain. Like a hand slap, this token was treated as creating a binding contract and a dissatisfied merchant could sue in the borough courts on this basis if he had not been paid or not received the goods, or if a deadline for payment had passed. Whereas the earnest penny created an obligation, the simple transfer of goods or money—without the symbolic token—did not always create an obligation to pay or deliver.[120] Public festivities following a betrothal were regularly recalled by witnesses in such a way as to suggest that they were meaningful parts of the ritual itself, as well as effective ways to fix an event in social memory. Ritual drinking might take place in the cemetery, a private house or a tavern, and it was also a common element of deals done in the marketplace.[121] Ideally all of this would have meant that invited witnesses, bystanders, and gate crashers would see and hear what happened and remember it if the need arose in time to come.

Public memories depended on good witnesses who could attest to having been present and seen and heard what happened.[122] A less good witness was one who had seen but not heard the exchange of faith.[123] Even less desirable was having to rely upon people who had not seen or heard what had happened and who could only attest warily to the 'common *fama*' (for discussion of *fama* see Chapter 10) or to knowledge derived from trustworthy persons.[124] They had every reason to be wary because much was at stake in terms of family fortunes, neighbourhood relations, and individual emotions. In financial transactions as in betrothals the ritual of giving faith was made credible by the preparations, the guests, the 'earnest money', the drinking, and the open and public manner in which everyone had conducted themselves. Giving one's faith had to be public to be credible, and it had to be done freely, or else it was meaningless. Alleged coercion lay behind many marriage suits in the church courts, and witnesses must have spoken fully aware that their description of the event would be picked over for what it revealed about sincerity and consent.[125] This was made necessary by the fact that faith was up for grabs. Sincerity and consent were matters about which it was possible to be wrong. In a dramatic difference of opinion in Yorkshire in 1287 Alice Sterling and Hamo of Caveringham not only disagreed about the facts; their interpretations of what faith meant were poles apart. Alice claimed she had given her faith to Hamo three times in different people's houses, and that they had afterwards had sex. Hamo admitted only one of these acts of betrothal (saying nothing about the sex), adding that in any case he had agreed to marriage only on condition that Alice pay him three marks so he could 'go to Rome'. He needed papal dispensation from a contract of marriage he had made twenty years before with another woman. For Alice faith was strengthened when repeated, and their marriage was confirmed by their having sex. But Hamo was happy to admit that his faith had been given on a false promise: the thing he offered Alice was neither logically nor morally possible.[126]

The custom and choreography surrounding promises raised the stakes, elevating talk about intentions and duties from the realms of ordinary conversation to the heightened formality of public undertakings. Trust was inherent in all this talk of faith because of the expectation that fellow Christians would heed the gospel, as well as natural justice, and live by their words. But these were also promises made in the knowledge that one could be called upon to honour them, either by the exertion of moral pressure, the application of communal sanctions, or the imposition of a legal judgement. The people of late medieval England inhabited a sophisticated and highly complex culture of giving faith, which would prove valuable to bishops seeking information on trust from the parishes under their governance.

The Social Institutions of Faith

The historian of crime and punishment James Given has written that in medieval England 'the most effective means of settling disputes were informal'. He goes on to say that 'the mediation of friends, relatives, and neighbours was undoubtedly far more effective than the activities of royal and manorial courts'.[127] While there is a great deal of truth in this statement, it does set up something of a false dichotomy between formal and informal means of dispute resolution. As we have seen in the heightened formality that accompanied much promising, there was a broad spectrum of behaviour that fell short of oaths and written contracts but amounted to a great deal more than casual undertakings. In thinking about whether promises sought to create trust or impose sanctions, it is important to bear in mind that trust without the courts is not the same thing as trust without institutions. In fact a situation of pure trust is hard to imagine: it was always affected by some social institution such as family obligation, neighbourhood expectation, or parish custom. As the economist Paul Seabright has put it, 'even when third-party enforcement mechanisms (such as the courts) do play a role in strengthening the web of trust, reciprocity is the glue that makes these mechanisms credible'.[128]

Sometimes giving faith was a conscious tactic to keep agreements out of court, but the oversight of the law could still be necessary. In a 1467 defamation suit Joan Coke appeared without the compurgators she had been told to produce (for discussion of compurgation, see Chapter 13), saying that she had come to an agreement with a man she was accused of defaming; she promised 'by her faith' that she would pay his costs. Her informal agreement was guaranteed by her much more formal promise. Even more explicitly, around 1485 John Reynold made faith with John Holwey for a debt of six shillings eight pence on condition that he would not be prosecuted.[129] Out of court, however, the parties to a dispute were not free to do as they liked. People suspected of breaking faith risked being suspended from their parish church, which had all sorts of serious social consequences, and direct action could be taken against them.[130] In 1378 John Castre, a vicar's servant, was caught in bed with an unmarried woman. He promised to marry her, but under a barrage of threats and violence.[131] His case is a salutary reminder that where the documentary record emphasizes agreement, affection, arbitration, and love, we should not be seduced into thinking that community forms of dispute resolution were intrinsically fairer and less coercive than legal judgements.[132] The opposite could be true: all kinds of belonging harboured an immanent potential for coercion.

The most prevalent social institution mediating this mixed-up world of trust and coercion was pledging. We have already seen how one's faith or a symbolic object could be given as a pledge, but a third-party guarantor could also be described by this noun. In the records of church administration and justice a pledge was known as a *fideiussor* (pl. *fideiussores*), literally 'one who commands faith in others', a word that derived from Roman law and seems to have had a strong association with financial liability.[133] The *fideiussor*, in a classification of intermediaries devised by James Coleman, could be either an *advisor* trusted by both parties, a *guarantor* trusted by two parties who do not trust each other, or an *entrepreneur* who mediates transactions between multiple trustors and trustees.[134] But where they acted as guarantors this does not necessarily mean that the principal party was distrusted: pledging was normal and not the sign of a dysfunctional relationship. Like words of faith and pledge tokens, to act as a personal pledge was to be ready to stand by one's promises. But more than that, it was a social institution by which real sanctions and solutions could be effected. Rooted in reciprocity, it was nevertheless often required by courts, bridging the theoretical gap between personal relationships of trust and institutionally backed guarantees of future behaviour. The major categories of obligation for which pledges were provided were the payment of debts, the payment of fines, appearance in court, and the performance of labour services.[135]

In the church courts we mainly find cases of pledging for debt, for the payment of fines, and for appearance in court.[136] Chris Briggs and Mark Koyama have recently argued that pledging for debts in the manor courts meant that strangers, the poor, and people living in other jurisdictions could obtain access to credit that would not otherwise have been available to them. A pledge could be sued by the lender if the principal borrower did not pay; the pledge could then sue the borrower to reclaim the sum he had lost by acting as his guarantor.[137] We see the church courts being used in much the same way, but with greater emphasis upon the breach of faith entailed in a broken promise. Ecclesiastical judges could order a *fideiussor* to pay;[138] they usually did pay;[139] and the pledge might then indeed recoup the money from the original borrower.[140] Seeking to avoid risk, some pledges wanted written expressions of good faith from lenders that they would be quit of their obligations when the borrower paid up.[141] Others assumed significant liabilities that suggest they either had a more bullish attitude to risk, or calculated that the costs of not pledging would be greater than the costs of becoming liable. If one refused to back one's peers, how could one expect to find sureties oneself in the future? In an extreme example of such cost-benefit reasoning from 1237, the abbot of Bordesley actually had to pay sixty marks to the bishop of Worcester for which he had been the *fideiussor* on behalf of Albreda de Camville.[142] Whether he had trusted Albreda or not, the abbot was surely bound by ties of reciprocity that made it impossible for him to refuse his services if he wanted to remain a credible, and creditworthy, member of local landed society. The same calculations shaped life at every social level, and in Chapters 6 and 7 below we will find that parish representatives known as trustworthy men were very often those whose wealth made them good for their obligations, showing how episcopal attributions of trustworthiness relied upon the social politics of trust.

Much of the literature on trust and debt in modern economics and political science indeed places great emphasis on the need for the 'trustor' and 'trustee' to be independent agents, unbeholden to others and good for their financial obligations.[143] In the medieval period this was a salient issue where corporate groups, such as monasteries, were concerned about the liability ensuing from reckless individual lending and pledging by their members.[144] It is also possible that independence and personal means were significant factors behind decision making in credit markets, but it is equally plausible that a rather different conception of trust, risk, and liability was at work: that trust was located within groups or networks as well as within individuals. This is in line with the emerging literature on microcredit as well as finding an echo in the mutual faith that could define communities in certain circumstances.[145] Because pledging for debts, at all social levels, typically cast the same person in the three roles of lender, borrower, and pledge over time, or even simultaneously, it created a web of crosscutting transactions and relationships that could plausibly be described as 'group lending'.[146] For example, in 1414 Hamo atte Stapul, who was the farmer of the rectory at Waltham in Kent, acted as *fideiussor* for some rent that Richard Huet owed to John Baldwin. But Huet believed that he was owed money from the estate of John Pope, for whom Baldwin was the executor. There were several relationships and obligations at work in this case: Baldwin hoped that Atte Stapul would put pressure on Huet to pay, but Huet exerted moral pressure on Baldwin by saying that if only he would expedite the execution of Pope's will, then there would be no need for his *fideiussor* to step in.[147] Since pledges were also sometimes provided by executors unsure of their ability to make all the payments expected by the beneficiaries of a will, there may well have been symmetry in the obligations and incentives in the Huet-Baldwin case.[148] No single promise was purely a matter of trust between one lender and one borrower. Many people in a local area were implicated in what were mutually dependent obligations. For this reason Briggs and Koyama have characterized pledges, borrowers, and lenders as 'a small insurance network'.[149] This may well be too formal, but it is certainly true that in such contexts faith was not merely given by the borrower to the lender, with onlookers as witnesses; all interested parties—which might mean the whole community or the whole network—wanted to be reassured that a new obligation was underwritten by faith.

These characterizations stress the collective web of interlocking obligations, incentives, and sanctions that made pledging a successful and ubiquitous social institution, but we do need to be careful not to confuse collective with 'communal', which seems at times to creep into Steven Justice's account of the 'trewthe' that bound the rebels of 1381 to one another. Edwin DeWindt, in this vein, has argued that since most pledging was done by people outside the family before 1348 yet kept within the family after the plague, there must have been a decline of community and a privatization of trust (though he did not put it in quite those terms) over that period.[150] Martin Pimsler, Dave Postles, and Maryanne Kowaleski have countered DeWindt's interpretation of the evidence, showing that much pledging outside the family was in fact done for money by professional pledges, and at the lord's behest and so was not 'communal'.[151] We encounter a professional pledge in an ecclesiastical case in 1492, where he was suing for breach of faith over the nonpayment of his twelve-shilling fee.[152] And the overbearing influence of lordship upon pledging is amply demonstrated by the conditions under which the tenants of Sedbergh entered into new tenancy agreements with their lord during the reign of Edward IV. The formula was written out for a transfer of land to Hugh Fawcett:

> If þai let vex aranese or noy anny man for that caus þat shall tak þe said tenur or anny parcell ther of of þe said lord or of his heires that then he sall forfett to the said lord & to his heires XLs and þat it shall be ledful to þe said lord & his heires to dystreyn the said hew and his Borowes by all thar godis for the said XLs to it be fully payed and content.[153]

The pledges were liable for a hefty sum if Hugh did not keep to the terms of his tenancy. Since much of the village would have been bound by similar crisscrossing liabilities, as was the case with pledging for debt, personal pledging might be seen as not so much a matter of the trust between individuals as a means by which the lord incentivized collective peacekeeping and good order. The social mechanism at work here is the pledge's assumption that the principal would not want to be seen by his or her neighbours as a person who could not fulfil his or her own obligations. And the lord's trust arises from his knowledge of the sanctioning community in which his tenants and their pledges are embedded, not from information about their personal probity.[154] But nor was this simply 'communal' trust: it was the product of multiple personal ties of obligation. The culture of faith in late medieval villages and towns was striated with the influence of power in many crosscutting directions.

Such anticipation of how sanctions would be avoided by other people was a core element of the late medieval social order. There was a 'continuous interplay between litigation and extra-judicial manoeuvring and negotiation' at all social levels and in all jurisdictions.[155] An important part of this was arbitration; more formal than mediation by friends, it involved the *submission* of the disputing parties to abide by the decision of their chosen arbitrator, who might be an advisor, guarantor, or entrepreneur according to Coleman's classification. In common with homage to lords, the arbitrator received the faith of the disputants 'into his hands', and if the arbitration failed it was usually said that the defaulting party had broken faith with the arbitrator, not with the other party.[156] Arbitration became more visible in the royal courts in the late fourteenth century when it was made enforceable at common law, at which time we also find it in the church courts.[157] The primary aim was to create 'love' between disputing parties, in the sense of forming a binding but nonjudicial settlement that was both consensual and public. The parties were free to choose their arbitrator, making it a more bespoke form of dispute resolution than going to law. If the two sides could not agree on an arbitrator, they would each choose an equal number to form a panel.[158] But having chosen their arbitrators they were bound by a moral duty to respect the ensuing judgement or 'award' (*laudo*), and despite talk of faith, the parties would typically agree to conditional bonds payable if they failed to abide by the arbitration.[159]

A case from Norfolk in 1477 illustrates this very well. Edmund Roray, the vicar of Elm and Emneth, and his parishioner, Robert Bunch, had long been arguing over tithes that Robert allegedly owed. So they agreed to appoint the vicar and parish chaplain of nearby Wisbech in Cambridgeshire as arbitrators. They obligated themselves with faith offered (*fide prestita*) to abide by their arbitration on pain of a forty-shilling fine. The arbitrators decided that although Robert owed Edmund twenty shillings, the debt could be written off if he paid three shillings six pence for oil and four shillings for tithes. Edmund pardoned the rest of the debt 'in order to nourish love' (*ad amorem nutrendum*) between them.[160] This was evidently a compromise arrangement. As Clanchy perceptively notes, love was the means of dispute settlement best suited to antagonists for whom an ongoing relationship was vital. It risked less.[161] For a priest and one of his parishioners the maintenance of good faith was at a premium on both sides if 'the faith' were not to suffer. Note though how it depended upon submission and the threat of sanctions. Accepting undertakings based on faith created obligations and expectations, something that the institutional church found enormously valuable in its dealings with 'trustworthy men'.

On the other hand, despite the frequent presence of hierarchical power relations, arbitration was 'a force for peace-making and social harmony', and sometimes even a means to strengthen local networks in the face of intervention by higher authorities.[162] At all social levels it relied on there being parity between the parties submitting to a *laudo*, otherwise the dictates of power would always outweigh the incentives for peace.[163] But equally the arbitrators had to be sufficiently superior to both parties to ensure they would be respected, and that no humiliation would be involved in the act of submission. At Chalfont St Peter in Buckinghamshire, for example, two parishioners 'promised their faith' to the archdeacon's commissary court in 1511, saying that they would abide by the arbitration of honest persons impartially chosen as arbitrators, namely Thomas White, Adam Splen, William Burton, and John Tochyn.[164] Of these four Tochyn and Burton are otherwise unrecorded, but White and Splen are identifiable as leading figures in the parish. White worked as a fuller and was a pillar of the village community. He owed suit of court; he was a member of the homage of the manor; he had been an affeeror of the court, setting the level of fines paid; his family members were active in the local land market. By 1519 White was no longer part of the homage, but was still called upon to deliver forfeited lands into the hands of the lord. In 1522 his goods were assessed at three pounds in the muster certificate for Buckingham-shire. Splen was a man of considerable local wealth. His goods were valued at twenty pounds in 1522, and he was a major creditor in the village, taking gages of property as security for loans.[165] Arbitration by a group of leading parishioners could involve compromise and lateral trust, but it was also fortified by the facts of social hierarchy. This is not to say that hierarchy was inherently beneficial, just that it was a fact of life that had to be worked around. The status that allowed these arbitrators to mediate the faith of their community was one of the most significant elements in the culture of trust surrounding law and agreements, and when bishops came looking for men worthy of *fides*, to give them information and do their bidding, they drew deeply upon such social institutions and the inequalities that sustained them.[166]

Of all social forms in the Middle Ages, that in which people most strove to reject hierarchy and live by charity was the guild,[167] but even its boundaries were policed with recourse to the law, and by evoking the collective sanctions of the group against the individual. We can see this in the practice of new members giving faith: they did so with two or more existing guildsmen or women standing by them as pledges, and their faith was received by the guild as a whole.[168] But if members broke the collective ordinances then action might be taken against them in the church courts, as for example when the guild of All Saints in Sedgeford, Norfolk, sued Margery Chosell and Margaret Hammond for breach of faith in 1429. Membership of what Rosser has described as a community consciously founded upon trust did not protect Chosell from the force of the law, and Hammond could escape prosecution only because she denied being a sister of the guild in the first place.[169] Here the artificiality of any distinction between trust and contract, solidarity and the law, is fatally revealed. Even in a guild solidarity was perpetuated not only by trust among the members, but also by social institutions such as the obligation and shame arising from pledging new members, and even—if push came to shove—by using the force of the law to police the boundaries of the ethical community. It seems that everywhere we find trust and faith articulated in the formation of social bonds, there is some form of coercive potential or legal sanction lurking very close by, a point well worth remembering for its resonance in episcopal reliance upon trustworthy men.

The Courts and the Enforcement of Promises

The closeness of the relationship between trust and the law is demonstrated by the fact that men and women frequently gave faith to the courts as institutions, promising to pay fines or to ensure that litigants and witnesses appeared at a hearing. In January 1470, for example, Henry Smith and his wife were reported in Lichfield for permitting fornication in their house. They were sentenced to be whipped around the chapel in the marketplace, and they also promised 'by way of faith' to pay a fine of twenty-two pence.[170] Litigants elsewhere entered into horizontal pledge agreements, confirmed by faith, that their friends and relatives would produce witnesses in court.[171] Thomasina Plumerden of Holmbury in Surrey was reported for fornication with Thomas West in 1454. She did not appear when cited and was given a second chance. When this too had come and gone, John Plumerden, perhaps her father or brother, 'promised faith' on her behalf saying he would pay six shillings if she did not appear at a third hearing.[172] Somewhat more formal roles are suggested by the use of churchwardens to cite offenders to the bishop of Winchester's visitation in 1517, but they too 'made faith' to the visitor that they had done as he asked.[173]

In some courts there was a custom to allow offenders to make faith and pay a reduced fine. Their promises and good faith were recognition that the normal strictures of the law were being relaxed, but on the say-so of a court. Offenders at Hartlebury in Worcestershire were often permitted to make faith to pay a smaller fine than that initially levied. For example, on 20 March 1402 William Jena was reported for fornication. He was fined two shillings but made faith for twelve pence. Presumably there was a conditional element to this arrangement, with the remission being subject to his future good behaviour. An unusual variation occasionally occurs. Hugh de Ghonthalf fornicated with Agnes Corage and was reported on 29 October 1402. They were both cited, but she did not appear and so was suspended from the church. Hugh did appear, and he admitted the crime. He made faith for two shillings, which is explained as twelve pence on his own part and twelve pence for Agnes, to be paid on the feast of the Purification of the Blessed Virgin Mary.[174] Here we see an institution not only creating the opportunity for offenders to assert their trustworthiness and good faith, but also requiring them to guarantee the same for another person altogether. As trust relationships go, this is very far from being free contracting or altruistic reciprocity. Instead it is an instance of personal promises of good faith being permitted at the discretion of authority, which is in some manner similar to the way that we shall see trustworthy men summoned into being by bishops, commodifying an element of social life and making it serviceable to institutions (for discussion of which see Chapter 5).

The power of institutions and lords to demand expressions of faith from subordinates was an inescapable fact of life, but there were other planes on which trust circulated in the late Middle Ages. We need to take care in identifying them because our evidence comes from judicial proceedings that must skew our perspective to some degree, giving us a clear view of dysfunctional relationships while obscuring the majority of successful ones. What the courts reveal is, nonetheless, suggestive of strong self-sustaining lateral trust relations among the people but which sometimes relied upon the law. As discussed above, the heightened formality of many public words and gestures was intended both to create strong bonds of trust and to prepare the way for future litigation, should the need have arisen. To take just one example from the church courts, the case between Laurence Ashford of Lydd in Kent and Henry atte Crouche of Norwich around 1412 illustrates how the creation of trust could loom large in exchanges of faith, but equally how giving faith was prudent preparation for potential legal action. In 1410 the two men had met in Ashford's house in Kent to discuss the terms of payment for some charcoal or firewood (*focalia*) that Ashford had delivered to Atte Crouche in Norfolk. Ashford claimed that Atte Crouche 'had given his faith and by his faith undertaken' to pay him a forty-pence instalment of the five-shilling price by a certain date, but had not done so.[175] Clearly a story about merchants giving guarantees of good faith to seal a deal was thought credible enough to present in court. These were merchants operating over long distances, presumably involving freight transport by barge down the Thames or Medway and around the coast of East Anglia. Their preferred mode of dealing was to 'trust trust', as Gambetta puts it, and giving faith was their way of managing this aspect of their relationship. But when trust failed, faith also made their agreement cognisable in the church courts.[176] It is possible that they chose an ecclesiastical tribunal precisely because the original deal had not been made in writing; if it had been, the merchants could have settled their case in the royal courts, which conducted a lot of business on wholesale-trade debt recovery.[177]

The phrasing of breach of faith actions nonetheless suggests that many agreements were made with one eye on future legal enforcement: plaintiffs sought payment 'on account of the faith' made by the defendant.[178] This seems to have been true even of those cases where formal arbitration had been pursued as an alternative to litigation. For a last-resort breach of faith action to be successful, the preceding arbitration, if not the original contract, had to have been confirmed with an exchange of faith.[179] Many varieties of breach of faith can be read as failures of neighbourly agreements, especially those in which someone had reneged on a faithful promise not to take legal action,[180] had failed to stand surety,[181] or had failed to appoint arbitrators.[182] But litigation on promises could also be a collusive fiction, entered into by both parties on the understanding that costs would be shared and no damages sought. This provided borrowers with an opportunity to give faith, perhaps where such a ritual had *not* accompanied the original bargain.[183] In effect, litigants might have been using church court proceedings as an unofficial archive of their agreements. Such 'recognizances' for debts were only available for sums above forty shillings in the central common-law courts, but there may well have been an appetite for them in lower-value cases too.[184]

The relationship between courts and the interpersonal or network enforcement of agreements was two-way. Difficult cases of failed arbitration or refusals of mediation may have come before the ecclesiastical judges, but the courts could also encourage litigants into an out-of-court settlement, once again facilitated by promises made with faith. For instance, sometime between 1460 and 1463 John Merydew had defamed Robert Digby in Wisbech, saying in a malicious spirit that Robert profited by 'le brybury' and that he had sold a gallon of beer in his house for four pence. Both men appeared in court and promised 'by faith pledged in the hand of the official' (*fide huic inde prestita in manu officialis*) to abide by the judgement of two impartially chosen arbitrators. They also agreed to submit to a conditional penalty of twenty pounds if they shirked their obligations.[185] The role of the court in this settlement is very interesting. The two men gave faith to the official of the court, but really they were making promises to the arbitrators and to each other about their intentions. They were able to trust one another because they each knew that the other believed in the capacity of the courts to issue fines and penances.

The arbitration in the Merydew-Digby case suggests the ecclesiastical judges could be sensitive to how best their powers might be used. Sometimes judgement was precisely *not* what was needed. On one occasion in 1434 even a carefully choreographed inquest of 'trustworthy men', looking into the division of tithes between Fulwell chapel and Mixbury parish church in Oxfordshire, failed because the bishop's judgement did not command the respect of the disputing parties. While they continued to wrangle, the parishioners took it upon themselves to bring the parties to a consensual agreement and bind them to abide by the bishop's decision so that the cure of souls was not affected in either church.[186] Without consensual local arbitration this particular judgement would have failed, utterly. This must have been true in many of the cases described in this book. Bishops could not govern by authoritative pronouncement alone, and so, as I will demonstrate in Parts II to IV, they fed greedily upon the social practices of *fides* described here in order to give their judgements local traction.

{≈≈≈≈W≈≈≈≈}

For those who could afford the court fees and the legal advice, church courts were a popular venue for the settlement of disputes, but they were only one small part of how peace and order were achieved. There was a world of promising based on person-to-person expressions of good faith or troth, and although we catch glimpses of it, we can only guess at its extent and variety: contrary to Hosking's assertion, people did not need the church to define trustworthiness on their behalf. Because the majority of my evidence comes by necessity from judicial sources, it also delineates a sphere of heightened formality, conscious gestures, and homemade rituals all geared towards creating trust between people, but with an eye on the possibility of future litigation. At one level the canon law action on breach of faith was an extension of the social practices of trust, which themselves involved sanctions and institutional mediation even if they never came to court. But at another level the courts made deliberate interventions in the wider culture of trust to resolve cases, permitting expressions of faith as a way for defendants to avoid fines or penances, and as a means for the court to augment its own authority. There was, therefore, some commodification of trust by church institutions. This is a theme that will be developed at length in the remainder of this book, though most particularly in Part IV, where the cultural and institutional system of trust and faith and how it served bishops will be pieced together. At this point in the argument it is merely necessary to note that almost all of the articulations of trust dealt with in the present chapter were person-to-person utterances, and not the communal bonds described by Steven Justice. Those were certainly real, but medieval trust was more complex than that. As we shall see it was the ability of *individuals* to claim *fides* not only on behalf of their communities, but also over and above their fellow parishioners that was incorporated into episcopal reliance upon trustworthy men. Bishops drew as much upon the divisions inherent within relationships of *fides* as upon the unity.

However, although the interpenetration of law and social practice defined a great deal of the late medieval talk about faith, there was much that was not apprehended by the courts, and has not been adequately acknowledged by theorists of trust. It is time to think about trust as a feeling.

CHAPTER THREE

Identity and Emotion

FAITH IN THE HEART

THE THIRD CULTURE of late medieval trust that we must grasp in order to understand the meaning and role of the trustworthy men is one that might at first seem somewhat removed from the worlds of theology and law: the trust that was felt as an emotion. As a subjective personal feeling and possession, with physiological and cognitive components as well as culturally specific expressions, the importance of trust to people of any station in life is at one level easy for the historian to grasp. We recognise this experience of trust, especially when we encounter it in a writer of such subtlety and perception as St Augustine. To reprise for a third time his momentous analogy between trust and belief:

> For the truth is that from your heart you trust a heart other than your own . . . with your mind you can see your own trust, but the trust of your friend cannot be the object of your love if no such mutual trust is found in you, a trust which enables you to believe something you cannot actually see in your friend.[1]

Trust here is a matter of the heart, of love, mutuality, and friendship. In many respects this seems a world away from the business of credit and debt relations, or obedience to the church, certainly far removed from the calculation and risk management that has most interested economics and political science. Indeed Karen Jones's philosophical work stands out in the more theoretical scholarship for its treatment of trust as an attitude of goodwill that is to a certain degree independent of justification or evidence.[2] But looked at another way it seems remarkable that such feelings have not been more prominent in social science approaches, especially given Luhmann's influential assertion not only that trusting is a *substitute* for calculation, but that being trusted involves paying attention to one's own image and the expectations of others.

Indeed among social scientists, even the advocates of cost-benefit calculation will occasionally concede that 'reputational information is valued', while recognizing that it is 'ambiguous and open to many readings'.[3] As we shall see in this chapter, feelings of self-worth and the protection of reputation were often expressed using the language of faith and trust in late medieval England, and when people did this, it is notable that they were also frequently drawing upon the discourses of belief in God and trust in institutions, even while they staked out a thoroughly personal realm of experience. Indeed, if it were not already apparent enough from the foregoing chapters, it is worth reminding ourselves that both religious faith and promises of even the most formal kind were themselves fundamentally subjective.

So, following Dorothea Weltecke's liberating advice for historians to extricate themselves from the instrumental and institutional thinking of much research on trust, I will look again at the evidence from witness depositions in the church courts, besides gentry letters and literary texts, to tease out this neglected aspect.[4] Doing so means that I shall need to steer carefully around that easy recognition of fellow feeling stimulated by Augustine's words on friendship, for this could lead us away from, rather than towards, a better understanding of late medieval culture. We should not assume that feelings of trust were always expressed in ways we would understand today, nor that familiar metaphors retain their meaning across the centuries. Instead we have to reconstruct the distinctive ways in which trust, faith, and belief were expressed and felt in the thirteenth, fourteenth, and fifteenth centuries by chasing metaphors through different genres of text and giving them some social context. I say 'expressed and felt' advisedly, since nothing is to be gained from adopting the position that we can never study or perceive emotions in another person, let alone in history, and that we are doomed to study only cultural representations of emotion.[5] This seems to me an especially barren interpretative position, based on the scholarly self-flagellation of knowing that much of the world is unknowable. Taking that unknowability as a given, the account of trust as an emotion that I present here proceeds on the assumption that even though we may never *truly* know how this or that person in the past *really* felt, they certainly did feel something, and their expressions of their feelings were meaningful to them in some way.

In terms of my wider purpose of investigating the meaning and role of the 'trustworthy men' in episcopal governance, emotion and identity (for all that they spiral out into worlds of subjectivity beyond the ken of bishops or historians) nonetheless formed the basis of trust as a useful and significant social value, something upon which the representatives of the institutional church drew in order to build confidence in their own authority (a subject introduced in Chapters 4 and 5, and elaborated at length in Chapters 11 to 14). Study of emotion and identity also highlights some important features of the way in which speech, deeds, and sincerity were connected, which can help inform the discussion of the practical epistemology of trust in Chapter 10. In a nutshell it was accepted that truth, words, and deeds could diverge from one another, but it was also widely assumed that they should not diverge too much. Trust recognizes uncertainty as well as providing a remedy for it.

Some brief illustrations will provide us with an entry point into the discussion. The personal and subjective is often vividly to the fore in the public presentation of the self that we find in marriage litigation. At one level this is because marriages could be made privately and without any public ritual. Private contracts were sometimes said to be the resort of the dishonest suitor, even of rapists, and this is certainly true, but they also—so far as we can tell—established lasting marriages on many occasions. In a 1317 case of suspected cohabitation without marriage, heard at a visitation of Tarvin in Cheshire, William Rode and Emma Pymme admitted giving faith to each other, but when questioned they said that they did not propose to do anything more about it.[6] In their eyes they were married by that private promise. But even in the more choreographed rituals of betrothal that often came before the church courts the personal was a necessary component of the public face of trust, since genuine *fides* was thought to involve affection. For some people faith could be so personal that to speak of it was painful; it was intimately connected to feelings of self-worth. *Is this person's faith in me justified? Do I really have sufficient faith to give another?* Around 1470 in London witnesses in the marriage suit between Agnes Twetynge and Robert Tryse recalled hearing Robert give his faith in the following way:

> I give you this my faith by way of accepting you as my wife.

In reply Agnes was recalled to have said:

> You are stupid (*stultus*) to give your faith as you have, but you have my faith to this.[7]

She felt her liking unworthy of his faith. Others might find that presenting a public face of dislike could have consequences for the faith in which they were held. For example, in a late fifteenth-century defamation case John Nayns was said to have asked Margaret Hert why she had recently reproached his wife. In reply Margaret hurled abuse at John, saying:

> I defye the ballyd (*bald*) horeson. I shall chastyse thee and that yonge hor thy wyf.

Two of the witnesses to this exchange said that until Margaret had purged *herself* of being a whore, they would have 'less faith in her and little liking' for her.[8] Giving faith could be personal in many ways. Its trust might be felt as a comfort and a reassurance, but when it foundered, was withdrawn, or was broken it could induce what Reemtsma memorably characterizes as 'transcendental homelessness' and 'metaphysical tailspins'.[9] With social life so deeply indebted to a public value that was also an element of personal identity, is it any wonder that faith should have such momentous potential to destabilize?

Faith in the Heart

Because most of the evidence in the previous chapter came from court cases in which defective or broken promises were argued over and contested, I emphasised the need for promises to reflect public and formal undertakings. We encountered marriages in which the interests of the wider family were paramount and business deals made with an eye on future enforcement or sanction. But people receiving promises also craved sincerity and signs of reciprocated desire in the person making the promise.

From time to time the evidence reveals something that we can assume to have been a common occurrence: people expecting mutual promises to be more than outward words and gestures. Let us take the case of Thomas Brabourn of Faversham and Joan More of Milton—possibly Milton Regis near Sittingbourne—in Kent, in which the manner of giving faith in a betrothal became central to later litigation. Thomas Brabourn denied he was betrothed to Joan More, and his witnesses set out to prove it. They claimed that on the occasion in 1418 when she thought they had exchanged solemn promises, Thomas had not in fact offered his free and willing consent. In their recollections the witnesses put words into Joan's mouth that make her seem to acknowledge the defective character of the words exchanged. Thomas, they said, had indeed offered his hand to Joan, but something about his gestures, about the way he offered his hand, had made Joan unhappy. She reproved him, explaining that 'faith is not in your hand but in your heart'. Joan, for her part, cried out that she would not offer herself to another man before Thomas came to the church door, and that if 'by her faith', Thomas could in return promise not to have another woman for the rest of his life, they would be married.[10] Whereas Joan's promises had been made with an enthusiasm that the witnesses could not deny, they cast doubt on the reality of Thomas's intentions, undermining her claim that they were truly betrothed.

Quite apart from the fact that we will never know who actually said what, the reported speech in this case is very interesting. The witnesses appear to have agreed that Joan's words, although recorded in Latin, were—in the vernacular—'*troth* is not in your hand but in your heart', a deduction strongly suggested by the scribe's indecision as to how to translate the particular word: in one deposition he uses *fides* and in another *veritas*, both of which were acceptable translations of 'troth' at this time, as Richard Firth Green has shown. While *fides* embodied the senses of personal submission, fellowship, and trust found in the English word, *veritas* suggests the presence of other possible meanings: an objective truth that was missing from Thomas's performance.[11] Whether it was so consciously intended by the witness, the scribe's rendition of troth as 'truth' had the effect of making her seem to admit that something was wrong. But what was the contemporary resonance of Joan's alleged contrast between faith in the heart and in the hand? Most straightforwardly, her words seem to draw attention to the difficulty of knowing whether physical gestures could truly signify personal intentions and convey a sound knowledge of future action: there was always a possibility that the hand would fail to convince. But was the denigration of the hand a valorisation of passionate commitment: did her words constitute what Barbara Rosenwein has called an 'emotional script'?[12] Considering this means questioning whether the heart was thought to be the source of feeling as—colloquially at least—it is today, or whether we are in danger of reading her words with present-day assumptions in mind. As ever with questions of cultural history there are things that connect us to our past but also things that make the rift more difficult to cross. The heart could indeed be thought of as the place where several emotions, among them love, joy, distress, pity, and woe, were experienced, but this does not mean that a reference to the heart in the fifteenth century meant exactly what it would today.[13] Crucially, we no longer see the heart having any role in cognition or sensory perception, yet these were integral to how it was thought about in the late Middle Ages. This is significant because Joan More's words may have been as much about cognition as they were about emotion. Specifically *faith* in the heart could refer not only to love, desire, and commitment directed towards another, but also to a purposeful intention to trust him or her. Clearly these meanings were also related to the way that emotion and cognition combined in the idea of faith in God, surveyed in Chapter 1: believers were to move beyond where reason could take them and submit themselves to faith, but they were to do so willingly. Faith in God was a conscious act. Whatever the object of the faith that came from the heart, the act of faith—Augustine's *fides qua creditur*—was thought to combine feeling and emotion with cognition, sense perception, and intention.

Joan More was far from being alone in speaking of the faith or troth that made marriages as if it came from the heart, and this must be what made her alleged words credible to the court. For example, Margery Brews wrote to her 'Valentine', the younger John Paston, in February 1477, persuading him with expressions of heartfelt hope and trust of her concern for his welfare and of her desire to see him:

> And yf ye command me to keep me true wherever I go, I wyse (*counsel*) I will do all my might you to love, and never no mo. And yf my Friends say that I do amiss thei schal not me let (*prevent*) so for to do. *Myne herte me bydds evermore to love yowe* truly over all ertheley thing, and yf thei be never so wroth, I tryst it schall be better in tyme commyng.[14]

For Margery the heart was the wellspring of both intention and feeling. She was bidden by her heart to act, but she also writes of her conscious intention and the mental effort involved in overcoming objections, while trust is used as a synonym for hope in a better future. These are themes that are commonplace in letters, poetry, and marriage litigation, and therefore clearly an important element in popular understandings of trust and faith.

To take a further example, certain anonymous verses in a miscellaneous fifteenth-century manuscript used 'heart' as a synonym for lover or dear one and 'trusting' as the active emotional verb:

> My own dear heart I greet you well
> Even as it is my mind
> In your love trusting for to dwell,
> And loving you to find
> Wherefore old love to renew,
> Now to you writ I,
> Therein trusting to continue
> Until that I shall die.[15]

Love and trust are things in which a person may 'dwell', echoing some of the ways in which faith or trust in God was understood as refuge or repose, as we saw in Chapter 1. The love that needs renewing betrays its own fragility, but the familiar desire for endurance until death, which we find in the medieval marriage liturgy and even in the legal records, is here given a more lyrical air. Similar discourses of the heart pervade another set of verses written in the later fifteenth century, this time by an anonymous female author (or a female authorial persona) and addressed to an absent lover. The author imagines her lover's reception of her poem, which she describes as a bill—in the sense of a petition—a bill that is written on her heart, and which

> I commit, and all my whole service
> Into your hands, demean it as you list (*think of it however you wish*).[16]

Eric Jager has drawn attention to the many close connections between medieval physiological theories about the heart and the practice of writing, which demonstrate how familiar this image of the heart as a petition or poem would have been. Christ's name could be found written on the heart, and in troubadour lyrics love could pierce the heart; in manuscript illuminations a depiction of a lover might include an image of his beloved's face upon his heart.[17] The anonymous verses continue with a vow that the author has no more 'franchise' with the petition—it is no longer hers to control:

> Of it, I keep to have no more franchise
> Than I heartless surely me wist (*would be*),
> Saving only that it may be as [I] trist,
> And to you true, as ever was heart, and plain,
> Till cruel Death depart it up on twain.

In the form of a petition or letter, allegorized as her heart, the author's poem was committed into her lover's hands, an image that resonates with the placement of faith into the hand in public undertakings. But it goes deeper than that. As Jager argues, the image of the heart as a book conveyed a sense of true feelings: possibly secret, certainly sincere, and capable of being opened up and read. This is because the 'book of the heart' was a synonym for conscience and the reckoning of judgement day, thereby combining the quality of faith with self-knowledge, or emotion with cognition.[18] In the verses under consideration, the gift of the poem or petition is indeed private, and once it has been delivered the author acknowledges she can do nothing to affect her lover's reading of it; she must trust, otherwise she would be heartless, and hope that its meaning is as true and plain 'as ever was heart'. If she cannot be with him 'till cruel death breaks her heart', then at least her poem, and the heart on which it was written, can.[19]

If in poetry promises made by, and written upon, the heart were thought to convey the sincere intentions of lovers, what of the hand in the same genre? We saw in the last chapter how poets could represent handclasps and betrothals for the sake of verisimilitude, but they also reflected upon the fallibility of promises where the hand and the heart were not in agreement, precisely the situation which Joan More supposedly perceived in Thomas Brabourn's approximation of a betrothal. In the verses just quoted, the petition merely passes through the hands, on its way to the heart. Such a contrast between the hands and the heart was also used by Chaucer in 'The Franklin's Tale' to imply a disparity between sincere and insincere promises. The heroine of this tale, Dorigen, made two pledges of her troth, the first to her husband Averagus and the second to her suitor Aurelius, whose affections she enjoys but does not take seriously. Dorigen performs an insincere but perfectly credible trothplight made 'in the hand' to the infatuated Aurelius, which is meant to be unfavourably compared with her earlier—sincere—promise to her husband, made from her heart:

> I wole be youre humble trewe wyf–
> Have heer my trouthe—til that myn herte breste (*bursts*).[20]

Chaucer understood the distinction between formally binding promises and the heartfelt sincerity that many people, including the Joan More portrayed in that Canterbury court case, craved. It was not that faith in the hand was not binding: far from it. The pleasure of the tale arises from the fact that the reader knows Dorigen is being too free with formalities, treating them as meaningless signs. Chaucer's Dorigen is certainly presented as flighty and her defective promise to Aurelius is meant to be an example of female failure in the public sphere, despite her apparent sincerity, at least with her husband.[21] Belief in the primacy of the heart over the hand may have been associated with foolish pride and negatively gendered female, an allusion also perhaps being made by the witnesses' representation of Joan More.

Nevertheless faith in the heart was clearly part of the accepted and expected script for betrothals. It denoted sincerity and consent for both women and men.[22] For example, around 1470 a case was heard before the London consistory to establish whether there was a true marriage between Margaret Dawdele and Martin Partriche. Martin said that he had asked whether Margaret could find it in her heart to have him as her husband, and he claimed that she had replied:

> Yf ye may fynde in your hert to have me to your wyffe by my trouth and by þe feth of my body þer is not þat man alyve þat y wale have be fore you.[23]

As well as implying sexual fidelity and companionship, the 'faith of my body' seems also to deepen the explicit association between the faith or troth that Dawdele was offering, and the movement of the heart that she sought from Partriche.[24] Poets, and people crafting narratives of disappointing or unfulfilled promises for legal purposes, agreed that although the gestures of the hand were really only outward intimations of the inner feeling and sincerity that made promises genuine, one without the other was sure to lead to trouble.

The personal sincerity and affection conveyed by the conjunction of trust and the heart was not limited to the relationship between lovers or spouses. In fact, as Philippa Maddern so memorably put it, 'even the trust involved in mundane business affairs could be represented in terms of almost Chaucerian romance'.[25] Principally what the trope denoted was a desire to express the deepness and sincerity of one's feelings. For example, in Richard Calle's 1469 letter to his wife, Margery Paston, he assured her of his concern for her mother's health:

> For by my trowthe ther is no gentilwoman on lyve (*alive*) that my herte tendreth more then it dothe her, nor is lother (*more loathe*) to displese, savyng only your person.[26]

Calle invoked his troth to match the claim that concern for his mother-in-law was sincere and heartfelt. In a letter of 1476 that Elizabeth Stonor wrote to her cousin William, she used similar constructions in order express her desire to be with a sick relative:

> Also, gentyll Cosyn, I understonde that my brother and yowris is sore seke of the poxes: wherfore I am right hevy and sory of your beyng there, ffor the eyre (*air*) of poxe is ffull contagious and namely to them than ben nye of blode (*related by blood*). Wherfore I wolde praye you, gentyll Cosyn, that 3e wolde come hedyr (*hither*), and yif hit wolde plese you so to doo, &c. And yif that hit lyke you not so to doo, Gentill Cosyn, lettith me have hedyr some horsis I pray you, and that I may come to you, ffor in good faith I can fynde hit in my herte to put my

self in jubardy (*jeopardy*) there as ye be, and shall do whilst my lyffe endureth to the plesure of God and yours.[27]

Several elements of this effusion of concern are shared with the language of romantic love and betrothal. Emotion and sincerity lie behind Elizabeth's desire to be with her sick brother; desire springs from the heart and is enveloped in her 'good faith'; faith and desire will endure until (her own) death. There is also a resemblance between the risk to her health that Elizabeth Stonor proposed to take for faith and the risks contemplated by couples on the verge of betrothal. Faith, as we have seen already in relation to belief in God, and as we shall soon see with the work of the trustworthy men, was always closely associated with uncertainty: with its acknowledgement and its remedy.

In a similar situation Margaret Paston composed a letter to her husband John in 1443 communicating her concern for his health in terms of 'troth' and the heart:

By my troth I had never so heavy a season as I had from the time that I wist (*learned*) of your sickness, till I wist of your amending, and yet my heart is in no great ease, nor nought shall be, till I weet (*know*) that ye be very whole.[28]

Like the heart that would burst with love, or remain faithful unto death, Margaret expresses her care as an uncontrollable swelling of emotion. But we should remember that the heart was the source of sincere intentions as well as passion and affect, and so Margaret Paston's concern may also have sprung from uncertainty about the future, and her thoughts about what might happen.

It was well-known that trusting involved taking risks, and that to achieve 'the heart's ease' a degree of uncertainty had to be accepted.[29] In 1461 a friend wrote to John Paston in an attempt to persuade him to take the advice of certain men even though he was not well-disposed towards them. In order to do so he would have to overcome his misgivings and be advised to:

make Heu Fen and Tomas Grene on your consel, if ye can fyne in yow herte. For I dare sey, as I her (*hear*) and understonde, that they how (*owe*) yow ryth good well (*will*) and servyse.[30]

In this example it is not passion and feeling that John Paston is told to find in his heart: he is directed to look there for the reason and good sense that would overcome his dislike for Fen and Grene, making plain the heart's connection with cognition and intention.

The heart was also commonly described as the location of an individual's faith in God.[31] For example in the Wycliffite translation of the Book of Daniel, where Susan is falsely accused of adultery, it is said that 'the hert of hir was havynge trist in the Lord', while Daniel himself is elsewhere said to have borne

God in his heart.[32] One early fifteenth-century sermon author characterized faith as a necklace that the Christian should wear close to the heart, explaining that the belief necessary for justification came from the heart:

> Faith is not wholly in beautiful words, belief does not hang completely on the tip of the tongue. Faith does not produce fruit unless it is rooted in the heart.[33]

This did not quite mean that faith originated in the human heart, just that that is where it was formed. This is repeatedly made clear in a fifteenth-century English translation of an earlier Latin work for monks and nuns—*The Doctrine of the Hert*—which advised its readers to prepare their hearts for God. They would not initiate this all by themselves, for as they went through the successive processes of opening, keeping, stabilizing, giving, lifting up, and punishing their hearts, God would enter into them with the gifts of fear, intelligence, pity, strength, counsel, understanding, and wisdom that would enable them to move their hearts. The spiritual work of the heart was thus a willed and voluntary motion, but one made possible by God, stimulated by conscious actions, and stirred by emotion.[34] The role of the will in moving the heart is also assumed in another fifteenth-century mystical treatise—*The Chastising of God's Children*—in which an imagined reader questioning his or her faith is advised that 'in eche doute and drede euermore a man shulde cast his herte to god wiþ a sad trust'. Casting, or directing, the heart towards God with trust was then immediately glossed by the author with an injunction to 'cast þi þouȝt (*thought*) in god'.[35] Trust is thereby acknowledged as an emotional abandonment of the will, submitting one's own clouded reason to God's perfect knowledge, but it is also said to have a cognitive element. One had to intend this trust, to think, and to willingly submit. The inner workings of cognition and emotion could be differentiated from the outward actions that fulfilled one's faith by—tellingly—a contrast between the heart and the hand. In 'The Man of Law's Tale' Chaucer writes of Custance, his heroine, that:

> Hir herte is verray chambre of hoolynesse,
> Hir hand, ministre of fredam for almesse (*alms*).[36]

In this couplet a distinction between the inward formation of faith and the active charity that expressed it is made clear. It is, nevertheless, a distinction between two conjoined parts of a whole, sometimes articulated as the mutual reinforcement of the active and the contemplative forms of religious life. Intention and action must go together: one without the other speaks of insincerity.

Trust that came from the heart was also a step along the path to virtue. In the ethical treatise known as *Jacob's Well* the trust that 'settyth a mannys herte faste in goodnes' seems to have implied confidence in one's own capacity for goodness as much as faith in God.[37] The two were undoubtedly connected.

The heart could waver, and the pure will was a force that might, on occasion, be able to fortify its trust in God. In the English translation of Thomas of Kempen's *Imitatio Christi*, made around 1500, a wavering heart caused by insufficient trust in God became a cause of temptation:

> The begynnyng of all temptacions is *inconstance of herte & litel trust in god*, for as a ship wiþoute gouernaunce is stired hiderwarde & þiderwarde wiþ þe wawes (*waves*), so a man þat is remysse & holdiþ not stedfastly his purpos is dyuersely (*diversely*) tempted.[38]

For Kempen and his translator the heart was the source of the fortitude needed to face a changeable world, a quality of trust we shall encounter later on, in Chapter 12, in inquests that arrested the mutability of decaying buildings and changing land use. If the will could not strengthen the heart, help had to come from a more reliable source. In the devotional text *The Orchard of Syon*, written around 1425, God explains the purpose of the Holy Spirit in just this way:

> The mercy of þe holy goost certifiede and made siker þis trewe doctrine, and *strengþide þe hertis and þe soulis of hise disciplis to triste* up þis soþfastnes and to schewe þis wey, that is to seye, þe doctryn of Crist.[39]

If Christ's disciples experienced doubt, their hearts were stirred by the Holy Spirit to trust in the ultimate truth ('soþfastnes') and the abiding path that was Christ's teaching. There was a circulation of motive and action in this causal scheme, with the heart at its centre.[40] The individual believer had it in his or her power to arouse the heart by 'piercing' it with pious emotions such as pity and anguish, or by using some material stimulus that would make it receptive to God.[41] For example in 'The Second Nun's Tale' Chaucer tells the story of the conversion of Tiburce in which roses and lilies stand for chastity and belief. Tiburce reflects upon the material and spiritual experience of the two flowers:

> For though I hadde hem in *myne handes* two,
> The savour myghte in me no depper go.
> The sweete smel that in *myn herte* I fynde
> Hath chaunged me al in another kynde (*has changed my nature altogether*).[42]

Like the circulation of love and trust that we encountered with the petition written on the heart, a faith merely held in the hands cannot enter into the identity and inner experience of a person, but a richer form of sensory experience, felt in the heart—namely the entry of God's grace—can change the believer in a meaningful way.[43] Like trust and love for another human being, faith in God could be written—and read—in a 'book of relygyon of the herte', which although corporeal was inscribed more deeply than paper or parchment or a shallow faith held only in the hands.[44]

The sincerity of intention conveyed by references to the heart is usually, understandably, missing from the administrative documents that will form the majority of my evidence in the ensuing parts of this book. But the range of texts across which the value of sincerity was associated with faith or troth indicates that this is something we should listen for carefully when we come to examine the provision of testimony in inquests (principally in Chapter 10). An expectation or purpose to speak the truth as far as one saw it, and to do so in the knowledge that one might be called to answer for it—in other words not to speak casually—was indicated by a reference to *fides*.

The Eyes of the Heart

One of the principal ways in which the distinction between deeply felt bodily experiences were differentiated from mere gestures without significance was in the common injunction to see with the 'eyes of the heart' rather than the eyes of the flesh. This pairing is a distinct echo and parallel discourse to the distinction between faith in the heart and faith in the hand, and an encapsulation of the need for belief to move beyond what could be proven by sensory perception alone: 'blessid ben thei, that seyn not, and han bileued' (*blessed are they who see not and have believed*).[45]

The eyes of the heart constituted a favoured metaphor in the letters of Augustine of Hippo, from where it was received into the broad river of later medieval thought. In a letter to the Donatists, attempting to persuade them that they were all Abraham's children and as much the recipients of God's promises as anyone, Augustine enjoined them to 'lift up the eyes of your hearts and consider the whole extent of the earth'.[46] The eyes of the flesh permitted them to see only material things, and not God's truth. He explained this at much greater length in a long letter to the rich Roman Christian, Paulina. She had asked him: can we see God with our corporeal eyes? Augustine's answer was that we see some things with our bodily eyes (*corporalibus oculis*), such as the sun; others we see with our mind's gaze (*mentis aspectu*), such as life, will, and knowledge. He seems to mean something like 'reason', and indeed some high medieval theologians would later speak of the 'eye of reason', although Augustine's theory of sensory and spiritual perception was capable of being interpreted in a number of different ways.[47] God, however, can be seen only with faith, which is the eye of the heart (*oculus cordis*). The heart had to be 'clean' to see God and the eyes of the heart must be 'enlightened'.[48]

Augustine was, as we have seen repeatedly, ever keen to draw analogies between faith in God and faith in other people, and one of his most arresting thought experiments occurs in a sermon dated to 417. He asks his audience to imagine choosing between two slaves, one beautiful but faithless, one ugly and faithful. The eyes of the heart would choose the latter, he wrote, showing how the perception of personal trustworthiness was achieved by the same means as a true perception of God.[49] Perhaps the most famous Augustinian use of the phrase 'eyes of the heart' though was made in the influential letter correcting his fellow theologian Jerome. The subject of Jerome's error—in Augustine's eyes—was his view that St Paul had told prudent lies in his letter to the Galatians (Galatians 2.11–14) concerning St Peter's apparent advocacy of circumcision and other Jewish practices. Paul wrote that Peter had deviated from the faith in doing this, and he reproved him. For Jerome this was difficult to take. How could Peter, one of the apostles, have deviated from the faith? His solution was that Paul had lied in order not to encourage gentile Christians to adopt Jewish customs. There was an uncomfortable problem here. One could believe either that Peter did not deviate from the faith and that Paul had lied, or that Peter had indeed deviated and Paul had not lied. Jerome preferred the former and excused Paul's lie; Augustine preferred the latter and explained that Peter showed his virtue by submitting to Paul's fraternal correction.[50] Writing to Jerome about their disagreement, Augustine explained:

> I do not say this as asking you *to regain the eyes of your heart*—may you never lose them!—but that you turn them back, strong and watchful, from that deceitful averted glance which prevented you from noticing what disadvantages would arise if once it could be believed that the writer of the Sacred Books could lawfully and justly lie in any part of his work.[51]

If Paul had lied, Augustine argues, this would set all scripture in doubt, which was unacceptable. In asking Jerome to recover the eyes of his heart, Augustine was urging him to have faith in the gospels, however challenging they proved to reason. The eyes of the heart saw with the faith that was necessary to overcome both mental doubt and the imperfection of the senses. In the later Middle Ages, this was an imperfection particularly associated with Jewish error, though as much for the purpose of educating Christians as for demonising Jews.[52] Having faith in the gospels might be challenging, but, as we shall see in the following chapter, Christians were told that their authors were supreme exemplars of trustworthiness.

Although medieval theologians were content to see Christian faith as a repudiation of Jewish ritual, they were somewhat less comfortable in accommodating the soul-body distinction to advances in natural philosophy. Here the heart was seen as integral to sensory perception, making the concept of the spiritual eyes of the heart less obviously distinct from pure bodily experience and lending the discourse on the eyes of the heart a more metaphorical tone. In *De sensu* and *De partibus animalium* Aristotle had argued that the heart was the seat of all perception; every sense imprinted information onto the heart.[53] This idea was a commonplace of first-century Greek culture, transmitted to the later medieval West by St Paul's letters, Augustine, and his interpreters as well as via the Arabic philosophers. In 1 Corinthians 2.9, for instance, Paul seems to say that the heart is the vessel that receives visual and auditory sensations: 'What the eye has not seen nor the ear heard has not been realized in the heart of man'. There were notable developments of the parallel between optical theory and the operation of faith in the work of Anselm of Canterbury, who wrote that 'just as the golden light shines on the eyes of the body, so does the light of faith on the eyes of the heart', and Hugh of St Victor, who said that while the eye of the flesh perceived the physical world and the eyes of reason perceived abstract things, the eye of contemplation was necessary to see God.[54] By the later Middle Ages the connections between faith and an Augustinian inner vision were commonplace, and frequently alluded to. The heart received the impression of sight in a similar manner to its reception of emotions like love and anger: an 'impure eye is the messenger of an impure heart'.[55]

Having moved some distance from the defective promises in marriage litigation, where faith in the hand was scorned if it did not accord with a deeper faith in the heart, it is nevertheless possible to close the circle and perceive the ways in which these various discourses of the heart might have influenced one another. A key clue is to be found in a late fifteenth-century religious text called *The Treatise of Hope*, in which Augustine's influential analogy between human trust and religious faith is developed in yet another way: the text instructs its reader that she should believe in her own heart and its movements if she desires to have faith in God. Human fear or dread is described as 'a mystrust of the herte which makith a man dredefull to trust God'.[56] If one does not trust one's heart, one cannot trust God. A lack of attention to inner perception and reason could have momentous consequences for the individual. For Joan More, reproving not St Jerome but her lacklustre lover in late medieval Kent, the contrast between faith in the hand and faith in the heart was thus a powerful turn of phrase drawing upon multiple associations of the heart with accurate perception, receptiveness to God, sincerity, deep emotion, and conscious intentional action. The witnesses' statements made her seem indignant at his empty gestures, a reminder that their transaction was a betrothal and not some one-shilling sale in Sittingbourne marketplace. Such moments called for feeling, passion, sincerity, and open-hearted promises, but also for an intentional leap of faith, for Thomas Brabourn could never have received Joan's troth unless he had also abandoned himself to the trust in his heart.

Losing Faith, Losing Reputation

Faith was a personal possession in many ways. In addition to the manner of its being given—to another person, from the heart, with feeling and sincere intention—the people of late medieval England spent a great deal of time and energy ensuring that the faith that other people had in them was not diminished. The *fides* that people maintained and defended is a slippery concept to define: it was at once a quality of the relationship between two specific people—a trust that could be bestowed and withdrawn by either party—and a description of the respect in which a person was held by various groups. Much of this book will be taken up with discussion of a very particular, though monumentally important, instance of the latter: the trust that was vested in parish elites by bishops and other churchmen. But every individual possessed (or wished to possess) *fides*, not just the so-called trustworthy men, this universal concept of reputation or respectability consisting in the opinion in which an individual was held by other people. This was widely described in the period as *fama* or fame, a term derived from Roman law that became hugely important in the canon law on witnesses, evidence, and inquests, and will be discussed at greater length in Chapter 10. This form of *fides* was inherently social even as it was intimately personal. One's ability to function in society was determined not by one's own character and behaviour alone, but by how one appeared to others, a phenomenon over which the individual had minimal control, and which depended not only on multiple individual opinions, but also upon the formation of shared attitudes towards a person. In defending the faith that was their inner wealth and outward currency, people had to consider the complex play of rumour, gossip, and defamation.

Reputation was arguably the most valuable possession of most adult men and women in the later Middle Ages.[57] At some level it underpinned the ability of people at all economic levels to make a living and function as members of society, so when it was threatened people tried to take action. When for example the rector of West Horsley in Surrey was deemed 'careless of his reputation' (*fame sue prodigus*) in 1328, his bishop took a stern interest.[58] Most of our historical knowledge of reputation arises from those moments when people felt that it had come under attack from gossip and rumour—which were hard but not impossible to counter in law—and specific insults, which were more actionable as defamation in the church courts and slander in manorial, and latterly, royal jurisdictions too.[59] Of course court proceedings capture only those moments in life when reputation had actively been attacked and a satisfactory resolution had not been reached by other means; they were, moreover, not entirely without risk for the litigants, who might find themselves accused of the very offence for which they had been defamed, or regretting that legal action had not repaired their reputation.[60] As David Good has observed, once challenged information on reputation could become 'ambiguous and open to many readings'.[61] As we shall see, a damaged reputation could lead swiftly to a diminution of trust and the loss of public credibility.

Legal records tell us about the insults that people felt to be so dangerous that they had to be countered in court. These covered a wide range of embarrassing slurs, imputations of crime, and condensed narratives of shame.[62] The harm that insults could cause was sometimes referred to explicitly. In 1317 Richard Dounleghe complained to the bishop of Winchester that some people were putting it about that he was a thief in prison, and this, he protested, had harmed his reputation.[63] In late fifteenth-century London when John Patrick called Margaret Moure a brothel keeper (*pronuba*) and prostitute (*meretrix*), Margaret explained to the commissary court what effect this had had on her husband. Finding it impossible to uphold a position amongst his peers and neighbours, the insults had caused him 'to witdraw hym owt of þe town'.[64] Whatever their subject matter such defamations before the church courts were often public words uttered with some intention to harm a person's reputation for trustworthiness, a reputation that can be said to consist of socially formed assessments of adherence to accepted norms based on observations of bearing and behaviour, memories of past actions and words, and expectations about future conduct. By pointing out how such assessments were 'socially formed' I wish to draw attention to the slipperiness and unpredictability of changes to reputation: rumour and falsehood lay beyond the power of the individual to control, while trustworthiness was, as we shall see throughout this book, something that was *attributed to* people rather being a purely innate characteristic.

Reputation also shares with trust the quality of being a form of knowledge held in the absence of information to the contrary.[65] As such it can be susceptible to all manner of unsettling stories. Around 1471 for example the London commissary court heard that Clement Wilks had broken faith with John Dawson for a debt of forty shillings. Denying this, Wilks had retaliated by spreading rumours about Dawson and his wife being 'strong thieves', rumours that they reported as defamation.[66] Similar tit-for-tat insult and rumour mongering was at play in 1512 when the rector of Attleborough in Norfolk said that the master of a nearby college had damaged the trust that the patron of his church had in him, complaining that 'through yor synystre informacyon (*sinister information*) thei be not contented with me'. Moreover the rector reportedly retaliated by telling his parishioners, from the pulpit, that all the brethren of the college were liars, flatterers, and tale-tellers.[67] These were social strategies designed to affect reputations for good faith, with court action playing an important role in pursuing as well as resolving the dispute. Following the rector's pulpit outburst both sides may have felt their reputations for good faith had been reduced.

Reputation or *fama* was worth defending so far as it affected one's ability to inspire confidence in others concerning all manner of public undertakings. Naturally, given the huge inequalities of late medieval culture (discussed at length in Chapters 6 to 9), not to mention the differential capacities of individual human beings in any historical moment, this had different implications for different people. The double standard, by which men were judged largely according to ideals of financial responsibility and women largely for sexual propriety, was one of the most important structures in the politics of talk, and it long outlasted the Middle Ages. It does not explain all insults—for example, men were often the targets of sexual insults directed at their wives or daughters—but it was fundamental to gendering the defence of reputation and the parameters within which 'faith' could wither, an element in the culture of trust that would be enthusiastically adopted and reinforced by the church in its dealings with trustworthy *men*. Examples of this gendered distinction in reputation are legion and have been much recounted and commented upon by historians.[68] Here I will give just a few examples. For women a reputation for sexual propriety meant not having sex before marriage, which was a rebellion against paternal authority, and not committing adultery once married, which was a rebellion against a husband's authority. Women who gained a reputation for either could find that they were deemed unruly in other areas of life. In one extreme case we find a woman calculating that it would be better to live in an unwanted or even illegal marriage than to lose her reputation for chastity. Joan Harries entered into a contract to marry William Taylor in 1502 despite, she said, being betrothed to Richard Doget. She said she had breached her precontract with Doget 'out of fear of losing her virginity' to Taylor, perhaps fearing that he would rape her and leave her unmarriageable.[69] Her willingness to be known as a promise breaker if it meant retaining her reputation as a chaste woman tells us something about the hierarchy of values underpinning female faith and reputation. Men were much more effectively attacked as financially irresponsible: as a 'false creditor' or for using false weights and measures, for example.[70] Their sexual behaviour had to be especially heinous, and unmanly, for it to create problems for their credibility.[71]

Defamation cases also sometimes reveal faith—as a personal quality and possession—under attack rather more directly. When John Scheffe was called a false and lying man who had committed perjury in the London Guildhall, his accuser wanted to deny him the very credibility upon which life in public depended.[72] A direct assault on credibility could also be a retaliatory strategy. In 1310 Florence and John Ede, and their daughter Matilda, were supposedly going around Kelvedon in Hampshire telling a peculiar defamatory story about three members of the Croke family. The Edes were meant to have claimed that the Crokes were prostitutes and the children of prostitutes, but the Crokes launched a complaint of defamation aimed squarely at the credibility of the Ede family. The Crokes' retaliatory claim was that the Edes had said that it was the ghost of the rector of Kelvedon who, walking after his death, had spread the rumours about their family. This detail can only have been intended to make the Edes' insult look farfetched, and thereby to reverse its reputational damage.[73] Quite apart from achieving legal redress, it was possible to emerge from a defamation suit looking very silly.

Besides gender, another common thread in attacks upon good faith was to play upon the cultural differences of geography and ethnicity. In late fourteenth-century London, northerners, Flemings, and Scots, as well as migrants from closer to town, were the butt of jokes for Langland and Chaucer, as well as a source of suspicion amongst the people.[74] Calling someone a 'Scot' was an adjectival intensifier used to increase imputations of untrustworthiness based on other insults. It was a slur that drew upon deep cultural roots. In 1299 Edward I had written to Bishop Halton of Carlisle rehearsing the 'perfidy' of the rebellious Scots who would be punished with the help of God, ordering the bishop, 'considering the faith and love' in which he held the king, to be ready with his men to join the royal army at Carlisle.[75] The faith words here are all about loyalty or 'fealty', collapsing faith in God and loyalty to the king into a single virtue, one which the Scots by implication lacked. Scottish perfidy was proverbial in the militaristic climate of the late thirteenth century. According to Rees Davies 'the Church's social morality became thereby, as it were, the ethical wing of English civility'.[76] This was so prominent a feature of English culture that in the late fourteenth century John Wyclif could explain the journey from doubt and fear to faith and hope by allegorizing Scotland as the place where we 'struggle with faith', from whence we might hope to return to be 'perpetually rewarded by grace for the passion of our trials in the heaven of England'.[77]

And Scottishness was still the epitome of untrustworthy foreignness in fifteenth- and sixteenth-century England, both near the border and much farther south. For example in 1496 James Wilson, living in Scarborough, had to produce three witnesses to the fact that he came from County Durham and was not a Scot, in order to escape detention in the town stocks. The bishop of Durham even wrote a letter asserting the 'indubitable faith' that he had in Wilson's Englishness.[78] In London 'Scottish whore' was a favourite insult bespeaking mistrust of outsiders even at the heart of the English realm.[79] The illocutionary purpose of these Scottish insults was to claim that someone was not of the community: a stranger outwith those bonds of obligation and reciprocity that enabled others to trust him or her. This is brought home in three particularly vivid examples: one from London and two from Norwich. In the parish of St James Garlickhythe Agnes Dodge was said to have defamed Matilda Clerk, calling her 'Thefe, Skottyssh quene and vnthryft', which are all ways of implying untrustworthiness. 'Queen' meant whore or concubine, while 'unthrift' meant disrespectable. But Agnes Dodge did not stop there. She reached a crescendo in proclaiming:

> I defye the suche as thu art; ther ys no man knoweth from whense thow cam.[80]

Being a stranger evidently meant being hard to trust. If no-one knows where you come from, how can you be held to account? Agnes Dodge was not alone in equating suspicious, untrustworthy strangeness with Scottishness. Citizens of Norwich in the early sixteenth century did the same. In 1520 William Wilson supposedly said of Richard Holme 'I cannot see but an outalion (*outlier/outsider*)', going on to make a comparison familiar to expressions of xenophobia across the centuries: 'an horeson Scotte hath more privilege and liberties in the town than an Englishman'. Nearby, and a few years later, William Barn claimed that John Bealis had called him 'an outlandishe knave and a scotishe knave' in the bishop of Ely's secular court.[81] The person without roots, or without a known group around him or her, risked being seen as 'outlandish', an 'outlier'. The individual was harder to trust because it was unclear how communal sanctions could be brought to bear upon him or her. In what must be the ultimate outsider insult, a woman living at Trowse Newton in Norfolk claimed in 1428 that the son of one of her neighbours was in fact the child of a woodwose, a semi-human wild thing of myth and folktale.[82] People who had to defend their reputation *as human* might find it very hard indeed to be trusted, wherever they turned. There was no faith, no trust, in someone who did not belong. In the chapters that follow we shall see how bishops played upon this theme of belonging to make certain parishioners answerable, upon their faith, for the answers to questions posed in inquests and visitations.

Insults of all kinds were ways of limiting other people's freedom of action, by denying them the support of all but their most loyal friends. In the street or marketplace such words could be damaging, but it was possible to take remedial action to repair one's reputation. In the courtroom attempts to undermine trustworthiness were harder to counter, and more immediately consequential. Let us look at one detailed example of this. Katherine Stevyns was on the receiving end of a devious and calculated attempt to undermine her credibility in 1470. She had been betrothed to Richard Hardy sometime in the past, but had gone on to marry Robert Mortimer. When Mortimer's father discovered her prior contract he sent word that unless Katherine confessed—which would result in an annulment—he would press for a separation, which would have removed Katherine from her home and left her unable to remarry. Katherine's defence would depend on denying the earlier betrothal, but there were witnesses, and it was the foolishness of her attempt to disprove them that was then used to call her own trustworthiness into question. It is an unusual and convoluted rigmarole of a story.

One of Mortimer's witnesses, John Brown, explained to the court how he had been loitering in the street one day when he had seen Katherine Stevyns going into the house of Thomas and Agnes Grove. Now, the Groves—so the witness said—were notorious brothel keepers, paupers, and beggars. Trustworthy men said so. Perplexed as to what business Katherine could have with them, he peeped in at their window and overheard their conversation. Katherine, he claimed, was trying to bribe them to undermine the testimony of the witnesses she knew would come forward to attest to her earlier betrothal to Richard Hardy. She supposedly said to the disreputable Thomas and Agnes:

You never deceived me before this time. Now, because of the unique trust and confidence (*singularem fiduciam et confidenciam*) which I have in you, do me this thing . . . the father of Robert Mortimer now comes to the city and he intends to prosecute a divorce between me and Robert unless I confess, so this is what I want: when you are examined before the official of London about that which concerns you, say that to find three witnesses I gave John Brown a scarf and twelve pence, and my nurse another scarf and twelve pence, and another woman . . . another scarf and twelve pence to depose that I contracted marriage with Richard Hardy. And if you do this for me I will give you both twelve pence immediately, and if you come to the close called Pardonchurch Lane near St Paul's church there Master Thomas Chopyng will pay you for your labours, as much as you like.

Then John Brown heard the Groves agree to the proposition and take her bribe. Katherine does not seem to have considered what motive the court would imagine she could have had for bribing people to say she had been betrothed, but there it is. People do stupid things when they are under pressure.[83] The one piece of reasonable calculation on her part was that the Groves were so disreputable that the court would believe their malice, if not her own. The story is pretty odd in itself, but the great interest of the case is the way that John Brown chose to present his testimony. Of course, the discrepancies and idiocies in Katherine's strategy were of John's making, as he was the one telling her story and putting words into her mouth. He had a threefold task to perform: to discredit the Groves, to discredit Katherine, and to rescue his own reputation having been implicated in the Groves' suborned testimony. The first task was easy. He told the court that the Groves were poor, vile, beggars, and brothel keepers. Katherine was undone by the substance of his testimony, but further damned by the trust that she put in the Groves. If she trusted them, was her judgement sound? They were so clearly untrustworthy, unlike the men who spoke of their reputation. In peppering his testimony with the language of trust, John Brown was attempting to draw an implicit contrast between the people whose word should be believed, and those who should be disregarded.[84] Battles over reputation could require effort on all sides.

People often talked about reputation explicitly in terms of trust. In Huntingdonshire in 1271 Adam atte Bury claimed that the testimony of a witness speaking against him in a marriage suit was 'not to be trusted' (*non est fides adhibenda*) because she was of ill fame, suspect life and opinion, and under a criminal charge of theft. What is more, she was a pauper.[85] Quite a bit of this was the formulaic talk of church court advocates, and it persisted over time, as the following examples from the records of the London commissary court between 1467 and 1476 show. Joan Kynge said she would place less trust (*minorem fidem*) in Joan Thorness unless Thorness was proved innocent of charges against her; Thomas Hay was given less credence (*fidem*) by his neighbours after he had been defamed; many men had said that they would trust

Robert Fauconer less (*adhibuerunt et adhibebunt minorem fidem*) until he was cleared of unspecified allegations; having been defamed of theft, Henry Fuller of East Ham was distrusted by his fellow parishioners.[86]

The church court examiners were especially interested in the transmission of information, taking pains to discover who had been the originator of a rumour, asking exactly what had been promised and in what terms, and recording testimony about how reputation and *fama* spread within neighbourhoods and parishes. Who had heard what from whom was their stock-in-trade. Around the same time as the Stevyns case, the London consistory court heard about the alleged defamation of Margaret Jennyng. James Janson was claimed to have called Margaret a 'stronge hoor, a gallid (*rancorous*) hoor, and a stronge bawd'. The witnesses explained how the substance of this street insult had been spread about the town. The first witness had—at some unspecified later point in time—heard two men called Langley and Norrys talking about the affair in the George Tavern. One had said to the other that he would place less trust in Margaret (*minorem fidem dederit eidem*) now than before hearing those words. A second witness said that he had heard many of his neighbours, particularly the wives of the men from the tavern—Langley and Norrys—talking about Margaret, saying that they too now had 'less confidence' (*minorem confidenciam*) in her. A third witness said that she had heard the wife of the first witness saying that she would 'never wish to trust' Margaret (*nunquam confidere voluit*) in the future.[87] Trust in Margaret Jennyng had been damaged by James Janson's insults because people thought there was no smoke without fire. Men talked about it in taverns, husbands and wives discussed it at home, women talked about it amongst themselves, and it was overheard as gossip by the three witnesses. In the case and—one suspects—in life as well, each distrustful utterance reinforced the last, turning insult into rumour and rumour into fact. This trajectory from rumour to fact, or from *fama* to truth, is something that arose not only in the course of ordinary life, but in the interaction between parish representatives (the trustworthy men) and bishops. As we shall see in Chapter 10, once it was given the imprimatur of episcopal record, the reports of *fidedigni* could become hard to question. The ebb and flow of *fides* at every social level was determined more by social processes than by objective truth. Margaret Jennyng went to court because she *had* to counter the talk of the town. If she did not—so she argued through these witness testimonies—she would face a disreputable future.

Transcendental Homelessness and Metaphysical Tailspins

As Margaret Jennyng began to hear about the erosion of trust in her, did she feel alone in the world? It is impossible to say. But we do know that loss of trust was widely associated with isolation: both physical isolation from friends and family or from familiar shores, and emotional isolation from the certainties of the future and from the world around oneself. This existential unease and uncertainty is exactly what Reemtsma means by that feeling of 'transcendental homelessness', which fills the void left by a diminished trust.[88] As a facet of personal identity, *fides* was a fragile and porous thing.

Being able to trust without too much calculation was part of feeling at ease with the world. The faith-talk of betrothals—however contrived or coerced it may have been in some sad cases—took place between individuals and families who had come to know one another, and the witnesses were frequently friends or neighbours. In the marketplace traders and buyers might take more risks, but among the throng of strangers they would have seen people they knew and perhaps called them together to witness bargains struck with a hand slap. Further afield, many travellers felt cut off from their familiar friends and feared the risks they had to take. As Kathryn Reyerson has put it, 'how merchants coped abroad was a harbinger of their business success or failure'.[89] Heeding St Paul's injunction to trust to the power of God and not to have faith in the wisdom of men, merchants, itinerant workers, and pilgrims may have experienced the homelessness of the stranger as often as the excitement of encounter. Perhaps they wondered whom they could trust, if anyone at all. In 1407 a number of merchants from York, calling themselves trustworthy, complained about the dishonesty and duplicity of some merchants (or pirates as the complaint would have it) from Gdansk who had taken possession of their goods.[90] Calling upon the resonance of popular sayings which referred to 'trusted land, uncertain sea' (*fida terra, infidum mare*), their binary view of the world pitted the 'home' community of the York guildhall against the perilous Baltic domain of 'away'.[91] Much more could be said about trust in the lives of merchants: losing one's goods while overseas threw merchants upon the uncertain mercy and efficacy of foreign courts. But if these institutions failed them, it could be hard to find legal redress at all.[92] For our purposes these few illustrations serve to emphasize one important fact: that trust between people was entirely conditional, unlike the faith that Christians were supposed to have in God. This is worth remembering when we come to explore the trust that bishops placed in lay informants. Although churchmen couched this relationship in terms of *fides*, their faith was very much of the conditional sort that defined interpersonal trust.

The other condition of vanished trust evoked by Reemtsma is the 'metaphysical tailspin': the feeling of shock and disorientation that follows on the heels of some calamitous event. In medieval literature the blows from which trust could least recover were betrayal and bereavement. Both entailed the loss of someone close: 'Let every man take heed of his neighbour, and let him not trust in any brother of his: for every brother will utterly supplant, and every friend will walk deceitfully' (Jeremiah 9.4). Thomas Wyatt's poem to his faithless lover, 'What Should I Say?', begins with a direct correlation between these losses of betrayal and death.

> What should I say,
> Since faith is dead,
> And truth away
> From you is fled?[93]

This is typical of the connections that had regularly been made between those two catastrophes over the preceding three centuries.

Having a future was a crucial facet of trustworthiness, as we shall see in our examination of the traits desirable in trustworthy men (discussed in Chapter 5), but it was not only an important element in calculative trust. Faith in the future—in longevity, continuance, stability, and familiarity—was, and is, the fundamental underpinning of emotional confidence. When the future becomes suddenly uncertain, confidence can evaporate just as quickly, leaving people in a tailspin of insecurity. Because we lack the means to capture these moments in the lives of real late medieval people, we have to turn to the stylized narrative devices of literature, but we do so on the assumption that texts worked upon their readers by seeming real, even as they were spinning some fantastical yarn. Romances made especial use of sudden uncertainty as a means of exposing the underlying emotional tissue of a relationship. In Thomas Malory's *Morte d'Arthur*, for example, the narrative climax of the king's death becomes an existential vanishing point seen through the eyes of Bedevere. Once his loyal knight has finally thrown the sword Excalibur into the lake Arthur foresees the effect that his death will have:

> 'Comforte thyselff', seyde the kynge, 'and do as well as thou mayste, for in me ys no truste for to truste in. For I muste into the vale of Avalon to hele me of my grevous wounde'.[94]

Dying, Arthur has no future. There is no trust within him, and thus no-one can any longer trust in him. This double perspective on trust reflects the duality of faith as both a personal and an attributed quality, something central to our investigation of the 'trustworthy men'. But it is Lancelot, who was not present at the crucial moment, who experiences the most visceral shock on learning of Arthur's death: 'Alas! Who may truste thys world?'[95] Bedevere threw away the sword and was prepared for loss, but Lancelot was not, and his confidence in the future evaporates.

Dramatic loss is a recurrent narrative device. In the tale of the Roman emperor Theodosius and his three daughters, retailed in the popular *Gesta romanorum*, Theodosius decides to test his daughters' loyalty by pretending to be destitute and throwing himself on their mercy. When his eldest daughter rebuffs him he cries 'Alas! alas! all my trust was in her; for she said she lovidd me more than her self, and þerfore I avauncedd (*advanced*) her so hye'.[96] His assumptions were shattered in a moment. Similarly vertiginous feelings overtake Chaucer's Troilus when, in a dream, he sees his lover in a boar's embrace. Her bestial betrayal shocks him:

> My lady bryght, Criseyde, hath me bytrayed,
> In whom I trusted most of ony wight (*soul*) . . .
> O trust, O feyth, O depe asseuraunce![97]

His exclamation, like that of Lancelot above, seems intended to evoke a usually unexamined trust in the continuation of the world upon which our visions of reality are built.[98] Confidence is about things that can be taken for granted, a fact that is true not only for the individual but also for institutions (for which see Chapters 5 and 14), but when our assumptions falter the absence of trust or faith is far more alarming to the ordinary person than it is to a bishop calculating the strength of his information. While bishops could cope with occasional deceit because the risks to their knowledge were spread over a wide field of political action, individuals were more exposed.[99]

The one 'record' source in which we get a glimpse of these 'metaphysical tailspins' is the occasional breach of faith case in the church courts where the usual language was rejected in favour of something stronger. The characteristic Latin term for a breach of faith was the *fidei laesio*, while sometimes an offender was said to have 'broken' faith (*fregit fidem*), but in two notable cases from London in the 1480s telling interventions were made in the judicial record. Edward Westbey was owed thirty shillings by Thomas Castell and thirteen shillings four pence by John Denby and he brought an action for breach of faith. In both cases the scribe recorded the debtor's offence as *fregit fidem* in the usual way, but this was subsequently scored through and replaced by the much more disturbing *violavit fidem*.[100] Why was the record altered in this way? It made no substantial difference to the suit. Violations of faith were dealt with in just the same way as breaches of faith, so far as we can tell, in church courts at Canterbury and Norwich as well as in London.[101] Occasionally the sentence in a breach of faith case might refer to the guilty party as a 'violator of your [own] faith'.[102] Since it was all the same to the court how exactly the offence was described, we might assume that the excision of *fregit* and its replacement with *violavit* in Westbey's case was a reflection of his own preference. He did not feel that 'breach' adequately reflected what had happened to him.

'Violation' is most commonly used in a legal context in Sabbath-breach cases—the violation of the Sabbath—which was sometimes pointedly the failure to receive the Eucharist. As such, violation may have evoked a rejection of the most central symbol, and certainty, of medieval Christianity, a betrayal of the symbolic order that made society possible. If promises are not kept, how can trust exist, to paraphrase Augustine? Theorists in a number of academic fields have noted that human beings base much, or even most, of their daily lives on an assumed and unexamined trust: the kind of trust that militates against calculation, that is based on feeling at home and confident in things being what they appear to be. For example, the unwitting subjects of an experiment in which researchers professed not to trust a word that was said to them experienced 'bewilderment to the point that some of them even began to doubt their own sanity'.[103] 'Alas!' as the poets (and perhaps a research ethics committee) would say.

Emotion and Obligation

Trust could be an emotion, and distrust too. The writers of episcopal letters knew this, and they milked it for all it was worth. It was 'not without a certain *bitterness of mind*' that Lewis Charlton the bishop of Hereford informed a subordinate of the 'recent report of trustworthy persons' that confessions had been heard by unsuitable people. The destabilization of his faith in the lower clergy caused his brow to furrow in bitterness, and recovery of the proper order of things began only with an assuredly trustworthy report.[104] This emotional language was, of course, designed to impose obligations on the recipients of this and other similar letters. At the interpersonal level, as we have seen, faith was something that could bind a person to his or her obligations. People bound themselves by their faith (*fide media se astrinxit*).[105] There was an emotional aspect to this alongside the calculation of future sanctions.

Because giving faith was a real personal commitment it could be used cynically to create feelings of obligation that were not, in fact, likely to be reciprocated. The classic case was the offer of faith and promises by men trying to get women to have sex with them, in situations where the precise level of coercion is impossible to recover. In 1347, for example, Alice Pleyneys from Wellingore in Lincolnshire had an experience of this kind with someone called Simon Piers. According to her version of events, he had said to her: 'I will take you as my wife as soon as I am in a position to take a wife, if you will let me have sex with you, and to this I give you my faith'.[106]

Women were frequently warned about such ruses. Richard Whitford's *Werke for Housholders*, written around 1537, explained that

> for many men whan they can not obteyn theyr vnclene desyre of the woman wyl promyse marryage, & thervpon make a contracte promyse, & gyve fayth & trouth.[107]

Robert Mannyng of Brunne also criticised men who

> bygyle a womman wyþ wordes / To ȝyue (*give*) here trouþe but lyghtly / For no þyng but to lygge (*lie*) here by.[108]

Alice Pleyneys did indeed give her faith in return. She and Simon Piers had sex, and a child was born, but Simon claimed there had been no contract to marry, whatever Alice might say about the matter. Alice most likely brought this case because she wanted respectability for her child, and perhaps even Simon as a husband. Even so, she makes him seem so nasty in his highly conditional promise of marriage in return for sex—now!—that one suspects part of her purpose may have been to bring him to court simply to humiliate him and to recover a little of her own *fides* in the process. Her account of his faith talk and his alleged bad faith may have been intended to undermine his masculinity as someone whose word was worthless.

The social practices and words of trust that coursed through narratives of self-definition in letters, poetry, romance, religious literature, and court cases had much in common with the trust that built the institutional church, which will be the subject of the remainder of this book. Nevertheless, before we enter the world of the trustworthy men, it is important that we note the differences between interpersonal and institutional trust. For one thing the *fides* that people exchanged with one another, found within themselves, and attributed to others was an intensely personal quality and sentiment: part emotion, part cognition, having conscious and unconscious aspects to it. It was bound up with feelings of self-worth, closely tied to a life history, written on the heart, and offered up at moments of deep significance. This intimacy was made even more poignant by the fact that faith mediated the junction between the self and society, meaning that individuals had little control over how they were perceived. They were vulnerable to the impressions of others, and although it was a strong social bond, faith could be quickly diminished by human and natural events. *Fides* in the personal and social realm was in this sense much more conditional than belief in God was supposed to be. It could turn to distrust without any hint of heresy, and it was based on discrimination and preferences (trusting this person rather than that one, trusting more, trusting less) that would have been out of place in the expression of a monotheistic faith. However, despite these differences, in what follows we shall see churchmen making profitable use of the dense and complex webs of interlocking trust relationships and language within late medieval society. In their identification of trustworthy men bishops turned the ability of some people to acquire a greater reputation for faith (what some have called social capital) to their own advantage.

PART II

Identifying the
Trustworthy Men

THE THREE CULTURES of *fides* surveyed in the preceding chapters each had its own dynamic and history, while being intimately linked to the others by shared concepts and language. Each was also fundamental to social experience in the later Middle Ages. The focus of the present book is, however, trained on a very particular element in the *fides* lexicon: the identification by bishops of certain parishioners as 'trustworthy men' or *viri fidedigni*. Trustworthy men represented their parishes during inquests and when the bishop toured his diocese in a periodic 'visitation'. They provided bishops with information and a route into local power structures. As churchmen, bishops used the language of *fides* conscious of its evocation of strong belief and of the faith that bound Christians to one another, to the faith as a body of doctrine, and to the faith as a church founded on authority. This *fides* negotiated uncertainty, while being the route towards knowledge of a certain, though unseen, entity. As power-holders in the world, however, churchmen were also steeped in the traditions of Roman and canon law, where *fides* meant proof, promise, contract, and equity. This form of *fides* likewise navigated doubt, but in the realm of human rather than divine relationships, where trust was often conditional, and discrimination between the trustworthy and the untrustworthy was legitimate. Bishops were also people, a point that is worth remembering as we delve into the institutional history of the church, and there is no reason to question their awareness of the ways in which *fides* and its vernacular analogues structured individual identity and reputation. One of my salient arguments here is that episcopal governance through trustworthy men commodified personal and social *fides*: bishops benefitted, so too did the trustworthy men, but whether such institutional predation upon the fundamental relations of society could be neutral in its impact is a question that will be addressed in Part III.

The chapters in Part II identify the trustworthy men. First, in Chapter 4, I discuss the emergence of *fidedignus* as a term to describe lay witnesses and jurors, and the conceptual debt that this owed to the cultures of trust discussed in Part I. Then, in Chapter 5, I elaborate the ethical and political profile of the trustworthy men from the perspective of the bishops who made use of them: what did bishops want to see in their trustworthy men? Chapter 6 takes lists of named trustworthy men and examines these individuals in as much detail as the evidence will permit, to flesh out their social and economic characteristics. Altogether this will give us a picture of who the trustworthy men were.

The wider scholarly discussion of trust has to be used in more creative ways than was necessary in Part I, because social scientists have had remarkably little to say about institutions trusting the people. This is despite the idea of a shift from trust in people to trust in institutions being an important component of the modernization narrative discussed in the introduction to Part I. Niklas Luhmann wrote that the conditions under which personal trust developed—face-to-face familiarity and undifferentiated social structure—are diminished in modern societies and so trust must rest on other bases. The advent of modernity, according to him, involved a shift towards 'systems trust', meaning trust in institutions, but also in such abstract concepts as truth, love, power, and money.[1] The elaboration of office-holding and the emergence of the institutional role of the *fidedignus* in twelfth-century Europe suggest that the chronology of Luhmann's transition to modernity may be incorrect, or chimerical. In fact it is hard to find a society without any institutions or systems for communicating beyond the immediacy of the face-to-face. The medieval period in European history was certainly awash with such things, from the church itself to social institutions such as arbitration or pledging, as we saw in Chapter 2. A more realistic account of trust in world history would have to accept that changes in the object of trust are decidedly nonlinear, with shifts towards and away from trust in institutions and individuals, depending on a variety of circumstances. For example, Teresa Morgan has recently observed that in the first century BC, political and social upheavals precipitated a retreat from trust in institutions towards a preference for relying on friendships.[2] Indeed, the reality of such reversals in the modernization narrative is further borne out by the widespread idea that since the late twentieth century, 'modern' societies have experienced a crisis of trust in institutions, brought about by phenomena as diverse as the hollowing out of civil society under both communism and capitalism, public mistrust of politicians, and the implosion of financial institutions in 2008.[3]

There is, by contrast, very little scholarly discussion of trust travelling in the opposite direction: how and when do institutions trust the people? A minor theme in some work on the growth of states is whether governments trust people to pay taxes and how this is connected to public trust that governments will spend their taxes responsibly.[4] Otherwise the economics of banking and insurance are configured in terms of aggregate risk, not trust in particular people. The present investigation of 'trustworthy men' as collaborators in church government therefore shifts the study of trust into an unfamiliar area, which has been little theorised, even, as we shall see in Chapters 10 and 14, by those who have thought hard about trust and epistemology.

Nevertheless we can profitably draw upon ideas from the social sciences about another facet of trust, which will prove central to the way I wish to interpret institutional attitudes towards the trustworthy men, namely the reliance of public trusting upon symbolic roles rather than innate virtues. In order to be able to trust, when knowledge about genuine trustworthiness is hard to come by, people can either adopt, or be cast in, symbolic roles. Frequently these model the relationships of family and friendship bonds, and people can place great weight upon them.[5] There are many medieval examples of friendship or brotherhood being performed in stylized and controlled ways that substituted for 'real' familiarity and affinity.[6] The question is then whether someone competently fulfils certain expectations of the symbolic role, and not whether the individual is innately honest or sincere.[7] Despite Augustine's warning against reliance on the visible signs of trustworthiness, the qualities of all sorts of jurors, as I suggest in Chapter 4, could indeed be treated as a mutually convenient fiction by rulers and locals alike. Who the witness or juror is ceases to matter, but what *sort* of person he or she is, or what the individual represents in cultural or social terms, matters a great deal.[8] In the following chapters I will discuss how roles and interests (as opposed to honesty) provided sufficient guarantees of the testimony provided by trustworthy men. Chapter 5 describes the symbolic role from the bishop's perspective, while Chapter 6 asks what social and economic characteristics helped real trustworthy men to live up to the symbolic role.

The investigation of these social and economic characteristics builds upon the observation made already, that trusting involves discrimination between the potential objects of trust available to a person or institution. When the person being trusted is not known to the person trusting, discrimination must be based on stereotyped visible clues about trustworthiness. The symbolic role, I will argue, was based upon the intersection of myriad inequalities structuring late medieval life, which allowed bishops to roughly match the qualities they were looking for in trustworthy men.

Before proceeding with the identification of the trustworthy men, it is necessary to make two further points, about geography and language. While, as will be shown in Chapter 4, the lexicon of trustworthiness was known and used across Latin Europe, the present study focuses on England, where the concept was applied with particular frequency and vigour in relation to inquests and visitations. The reasons for this demand further investigation by specialists in other regions, but one possibility is that the identification of *viri fidedigni* substituted for the sorts of village government that were common in many parts of Southern Europe but absent from England, which had manorial institutions from the twelfth and thirteenth centuries, and parish bodies from the mid-fourteenth century, but nothing like the Italian or Provençal commune.[9]

Because the study focuses on England and, as is already apparent, a great deal of legal and literary material in Middle English will be involved, it is also worth making a point about translation. Besides being the Middle English term that came to encompass both the general faith and individual hope discussed in Chapter 1, trust is also important as a modern English translation of *fides*, particularly one emphasizing the sense of 'good faith' present in secular affairs and interpersonal relationships. I therefore propose to translate *viri fidedigni* as 'trustworthy men' and not the more literal 'faith-worthy men', which is rather unwieldy.[10] While there was a great deal of common ground between the concepts of faith in God and trust in other people, 'trustworthy men' better suggests the differences between these two cognitive acts. Placing trust in people was much more risky and questionable than placing faith in God. Real insecurity about whether God could be trusted was a minority fear, limited to certain nominalist theologians of the fourteenth and fifteenth centuries, and quickly faced down as too serious a challenge to the fabric of Christianity. But doubts about the trustworthiness of people were ever-present.

CHAPTER FOUR

The Emergence of the
Trustworthy Men

AMONGST ALL THE VARIANTS on the Latin *fides* that described attitudes towards God, the church, and other people, the word that stands out as crucial to an understanding of the social and institutional history of the medieval church is *fidedignus*, the trustworthy man. This figure emerged in the church's administrative and legal documents in the late twelfth century, and was commonplace by the late thirteenth. Obviously there were plenty of trustworthy, and untrustworthy, men and women around before the twelfth and thirteenth centuries. But this is not a history of trustworthiness per se. It is a history of people being called trustworthy by the church, primarily in England, and that is something that has its own chronology. How and why this term became so common can be understood only in a broad context though. In this chapter I will first sketch some changes affecting both secular and ecclesiastical government in Western Europe in the crucial period, and then trace the appearance of 'trustworthy men' in church rhetoric, looking at the history of the phrase and indicating the broad lineaments of its function and meaning. In the chapters that then follow, it will be picked apart and turned over in a quest to understand how the church took shape in England as an institutional and social body in the later Middle Ages.

Rulers Contemplate the People, 1100–1300

In these two centuries the rulers of Europe—kings, aristocrats, and churchmen—achieved what one historian has described as an 'intensification of government and . . . penetration of society by governmental power' so great that few areas of life were unaffected.[1] They claimed to offer justice to all within their territories, they established the principle of taxation and the practices of fiscal management, and they celebrated ideologies of personal authority and the public good. How did they do all this? The complexities and challenges of rule in this period were considerable. Rulers were members of powerful dynasties that sought to pursue their own private interests, which are not simply reducible to state-building; their institutional resources were—in 1100—relatively limited; they shared the landscape of power with other aristocratic dynasties; other institutions—notably churches—owned land and possessed governing authority; the wider population did not necessarily see themselves as subject to anyone except their immediate lord, if that. In explanation Bob Moore, quoted above, argues that the territories of kings, churches, and aristocrats were coming to be governed by a technocracy of literate clerics who cultivated a professional identity and ethos, while Michael Clanchy has placed greater emphasis upon the developing technology of records and archival practices themselves, together with new attitudes to writing and authority.[2] Other historians describe the growth of government as a process by which a tax-raising state was bolted onto the 'feudal' or patron-client relationships that kings had with their vassals. This in turn has been said to have rested upon demographic growth and the expansion of arable cultivation and trade.[3] In truth all these developments were related, and several of them have been studied in concert. However, the issue of the separation of church history from social and political history—raised in the introduction—has affected this synthesis, impoverishing histories of both the church and of politics. Making a departure from the usual focus of church histories, I will argue that the key relationship to understand is that between the bishop and the parish, that the currency of that relationship was information, and that its vector was the trustworthy man. It is in order to set the scene for this that we must begin by placing the government of the church in the context of changes to government more generally, for the church was not merely a spiritual institution affected by these trends, but a conglomeration of governing institutions which, in their own right, contributed to the changing face of power and authority.

The competing authorities, power-holders, and institutions of the high medieval period presented a challenge to those kings and princes who sought to be recognized as overlords or 'sovereign'. It proved impossible for kings to grow their governing institutions without giving the warrior, church, and landholding elites some access to the benefits of rule, either in the form of office-holding or the possession of quasi-public 'franchises' of royal power. Even so, officials acting on the king's behalf were always liable to antagonize powerful people, who might dispute certain royal prerogatives or property, and as the holders of franchises themselves royal officials were equally among those capable of being provoked by governmental power. Many powers in the land might simultaneously be victims and perpetrators of corruption in the service of the king. In order to promote stability (as well as their own interests) rulers found it helpful to provide opportunities for complaints about all this to be heard and officials to be disciplined. The main means by which they did so was to use inquests: investigations of an allegation, rumour, or a putative fact, carried out by some middle- or high-ranking official, calling upon the testimony of local people. Two of the most celebrated examples of this were Henry II of England's 'Inquest of Sheriffs' in 1170, and Louis IX of France's *enquêtes* into misconduct by his officers between 1247 and 1269, which contributed enormously to the strengthening of Angevin and Capetian rule, respectively.[4] The inquest was popular, however, not for this single reason, but because it was amenable to many different situations: inquests were widely replacing ordeals and trial by battle as the means by which criminal justice was served; they were also used in civil litigation over things like ownership and use, and to gather information about taxable wealth, as well as allowing rulers to pursue their rights and monitor their officials. In these ways they underpinned the most important elements of government and social order. In the regions of eleventh-century Europe where the institutions of public authority were most active, namely Anglo-Saxon England, Byzantium, and those areas of Sicily and Spain under Arabic rule, inquests of this kind had deep roots, but in the twelfth and thirteenth centuries they were harnessed to the growing ambitions of princely power, used much more systematically, and in many more regions.[5] In Castile, for example, the inquest (known as a *pesquisa*) was codified in King Alfonso's *Siete Partidas* code of 1252, although it drew on older practices.[6]

The history of governing institutions in this period has recently become more sophisticated than ever before, with older, more descriptive histories of bureaucratization giving way to subtle accounts of the interplay between office and status, and of the importance of accountability. In the older mode, the motivation behind Henry II of England's innovations in justice and administration was assumed to have been an objective desire to tackle crime and disorder, thought to be on the rise in the aftermath of civil war.[7] His aims were purportedly rational justice, equity, and efficiency. This way of writing administrative history was much in thrall to nineteenth- and twentieth-century notions of progressive institutional evolution and it made medieval rulers look curiously un-medieval. By contrast, for Tom Bisson government grew because the exercise of private lordship by princes elicited so many complaints about the behaviour of its agents. In responding to criticisms of oppressive lordship and 'authorized . . . tyranny' a bureaucracy of accountability developed, creating a public realm almost by default. There were signs of this throughout the twelfth century, but it became sustained only in the thirteenth when oaths of personal fidelity more regularly came to resemble oaths of office.[8] Formalising expectations as office-holding transformed the problem of whom to trust from a matter of personal loyalty into a question about conformity to a pattern of permissible behaviour: or, we might say, a symbolic role. It was one way in which princes tried to ensure fidelity to their rule.[9] Advancing some of the same themes as Bisson, John Sabapathy takes a 'view from the middle' in order to understand how office-holding functioned, describing the practices, attitudes, and relationships that made bailiffs, stewards, *podestà*, and other officials involved in inquests the lynchpins of a more governed society.[10] The glue that held such systems together, so far as that was the case, was the prospect of these men being held to account: making the individual fulfil the role. Rulers made the most of demands for accountability, and, in Bisson's words, they 'feasted on the violence their peoples suffered' because they were praised for suppressing it.[11]

Explanations for the growth of government such as these, seeing institutions as the product of political needs and cultural attitudes, seem much more satisfying than those that focus on the internal elaboration of bureaucracy. And yet one feature—arguably the fundamental feature—of government by inquest barely features in the current historical writing on the subject. That is the involvement of the wider public in providing testimony before a ruler's investigations.[12] This is notable by its omission from Bisson's otherwise compelling analysis. There, nonelites are mostly present only as the field upon which elites act, whether it is as victims of aristocratic violence or beneficiaries of public authorities. For him the growth of government involved the replacement of unreliable feudal (personal) relationships with administrative routines and public justice. But besides the accommodation of old warrior and landholding classes to newer clerical elites and governing institutions, the most ubiquitous relationship of the emerging new world was that between the thousands of predominantly peasant witnesses and jurors and the officials who conducted inquests.

The 'public' was newly prominent in governing ideology as well as in the practice of inquests, and we see this in the importance that rulers placed upon new legal and theological discourses celebrating their purpose and usefulness.[13] In the twelfth and thirteenth centuries scholastic notions of the common good or public benefit, which had been mooted in the eleventh century, came to be applied to many things that concerned rulers, such as taxation, crime, service in war, hierarchy, obedience, and the vexed question of dispensation from legal norms in special circumstances (the rules governing exemption from the rules).[14] Canon and civil (Roman) lawyers were beginning to apply the idea that it is 'in the interests of the community (or city) that crime should not go unpunished' as justification for public judicial authority. Inquisition into heresy, pioneered as a legal instrument in the late twelfth century and codified by Pope Gregory IX in the 1230s, allowed a judge to control investigatory procedures from start to finish: making the accusation, conducting the examination, arriving at a judgement, and issuing the sentence. In the Italian cities the punishment of crime was increasingly a matter for a judge, acting in an inquisitorial capacity, and less often reliant upon individual plaintiffs.[15]

This entailed something of a shift in legal mentality, from punishment as vengeance and restitution, to punishment as deterrence and the maintenance of order. Commentators on legal procedure argued that an *inquisitio* not only furthered the public interest, but more easily discovered the truth than a trial based on an accusation.[16]

Alongside this valorization of the 'public good', rulers increasingly had an elevated sense of their own power and position, and this became entrenched in legal thinking about authority. The monarchical will of the 'prince' (in effect any ruler in secular or ecclesiastical office) was thought reason enough to justify an act of dominance.[17] The ideology of government in this period can therefore be described as public utility animated by personal authority, two principles that came together with perhaps their greatest potency in the inquest. For example in the 1190s Philip II of France began to introduce his proclamations with the grand assertion that 'it is the royal office to provide for the needs of subjects in every way and to prefer the public to its private utility'. Bisson cites this as the 'most spectacular normative record of its kind' and a symptom of the growing tendency to justify power in terms of government rather than mere domination.[18] In a classic example of the way in which inquests served this combination of public ideology and practical rulership, King James I of Aragon launched an *inquisició* in 1267 into counterfeiters of coinage, a key prerogative claimed for sovereign power.[19]

Just as in the realm of scholastic theology, the questions of what could be known, and how, were becoming a defining feature of the age. The rising ambitions of rulers and their institutions encouraged a view that the world could be not only governed, but known, and every situation in which ambition crystallized into action involved attempts to know the physical and social world. Even though some currents of doubt and anxiety affected theology (discussed in Chapter 1) and law (discussed in Chapter 2, as well as at greater length in Chapter 10) there was great confidence in the capacity of human knowledge to serve practical ends.[20] The question—for medieval rulers and modern historians—is this: whose knowledge was trustworthy enough to inspire confidence? Contemplated as a whole, the masses were inscrutable and unmanageable, but since most problems of government and justice pertained to individual people, places, and communities, an ideology of local knowledge developed around the various sorts of *inquisitio*, which constituted a major cultural shift, and reflected the intensification of older Carolingian and Anglo-Saxon forms of government by inquest. One thirteenth-century canon lawyer commented that 'knowledge of local facts is presumed to come from the locality', a seemingly banal truism that encapsulates a pervasive idea: that although authority and judgement came from above, the knowledge necessary for government and justice came from below.[21] 'Who may know from afar?' St Augustine had asked in a sermon later popular among canon lawyers.[22]

In order to get close to the things in need of correction 'the inquisitor should descend to the place . . . [in question] and make inquiry there, because there he will be better able to inquire'.[23]

When he was able to survey 'the place', there were several ways in which the inquisitor, *enquêteur*, bailiff, or sheriff might acquire local testimony. Some legal historians have sought to sharpen the difference between them, and certainly there are meaningful procedural and political distinctions to be made, but there was also a general family resemblance between all forms of inquiry based upon local knowledge. The basic theoretical distinctions are between witnesses in litigation (produced by the parties and examined individually), witnesses in canonical inquisition (summoned by the judge and examined individually), arbitrators in a brokered settlement (produced by the parties and arriving at a collective judgement), and jurors in an inquest (summoned by the judge and providing collective testimony). In reality, there was a great deal of cross-fertilization, the 'ideal types' often blurred into one another, and they were not exclusive to particular jurisdictions. It is not true, for instance, that jury-based systems were entirely separate from witness-based systems.[24] As well as the distinction between plural individual and collective testimony, legal historians have sometimes stressed a difference between the provision of testimony (proof or evidence) and of judgement (definitively settling a case), and also troubled themselves over whether testimony was given freely or coerced.[25] These distinctions are likewise not always discernible in practice.

One of the key features of this variety and permeability was a shared vocabulary with which to describe the witnesses or jurors. As inquests occurred more often, and made greater demands upon witnesses, a specialised vocabulary emerged. In contrast to the rather bland descriptions of the Domesday jurors of England in 1086, to take one major example, as the 'men of the hundred' or the 'men who are sworn', inquests of the twelfth and especially thirteenth century used terms that were more evocative of the moral, political, and legal values that rulers wanted to associate with their exercise of power.[26] This lexicon describing the symbolic role of the local collaborator with power was so frequently deployed that it must have been a major force in shaping conceptions of authority and government, and yet it has been seldom studied in its own right. This is of course unsurprising given that the indispensability of local intermediaries to state, church, noble, and seigneurial power is only just beginning to be recognised by historians.

There were four broad and nonexclusive categories of term: *boni homines, fideles, probi homines,* and *legali* or *legitimi homines*. Each makes use of an adjectival noun that could stand alone: *bonus*, meaning a good, virtuous, worthy, respectable, admissible, proficient, innocent, or serviceable person; *fidelis*, meaning someone faithful, constant, sworn, trustworthy, reliable, a loyal subject or vassal; *probus*, meaning a person of upright character, a righteous, honest, or law-worthy man, a person of ability or status, and more abstractly a proof; *legalis*, meaning a law-worthy or loyal man, someone with legal rights; *legitimus*, meaning someone who is legitimate, law-worthy, or genuine.[27] The first is the least specific and most malleable in terms of its implied status and associated values, but perhaps for this reason it was commonplace across Europe from the Roman period onwards as a designation for notables, witnesses, and local representatives.[28] *Boni homines* were often the witnesses to documents recording gifts, sales, and leases; they could be witnesses in litigation and even sit alongside judges, and in parts of Italy and Catalonia they seem to have been particularly associated with the valuation of lands and goods in legal disputes.[29] By the twelfth century in northern Italy this was the name given to elite men in towns who might be the agents of lords or the representatives of communes, depending on local political circumstances; either way it was a relatively formal designation indicating some military, political, and bureaucratic functions.[30] Less formal, perhaps, but no less meaningful, was its use in twelfth- and thirteenth-century Languedoc as a courteous and respectful form of address for wealthy landowning men within a village.[31] When rulers sought local collaborators it was no wonder they sometimes invoked the native prestige of the term, as in the call for 'men of good testimony' (*viros . . . boni testimonii*) to make tax assessments in the Ile-de-France in 1186, or Alexander II of Scotland's demand for the testimony of 'good and loyal men' in a general inquest in 1244 (*bonorum et fidelium hominium*).[32]

Already we can see how miscellaneous such language could be, with *fidelis* being used alongside *bonus*, for example. The concept of fidelity itself was very broad, encompassing both allegiance to a specific person and the more general character trait of reliability, and it resonated with a host of other *fides*-based terms for witnesses or law-worthy persons common to Roman law and feudal traditions. In particular Roman writers made use of the term *fidus*, which meant simply trustworthy, but this was not much used in later centuries. Otherwise, in the Roman and post-Roman West fidelity denoted a range of personal relationships: the qualities of a good slave, a good friend, the committed servant of the emperor or the public, and the troops loyal to a commander who trusted them in return.[33] In early and high medieval Europe fidelity also came to describe the state entered into by a vassal upon taking an oath to his lord or king; the *fidelis* was thereby a loyal subject, a follower who provided counsel and assistance; to act with fidelity was to behave as one ought towards one's lord. Some oaths of fidelity might be given in return for a fief, but others were more general promises of loyalty.[34] Despite the implied reciprocity of such relationships and oaths there was, as Benveniste shrewdly observed, an inherent inequality to giving or bestowing one's faith. It created a bond based on obedience and the constraint of action.[35] In both its feudal and its Roman forms fidelity was highly personal, and this sense was evoked even when used of anonymous inquest jurors. Such faith-based terms of approbation also echoed the equity (*fides*) that ancient writers and medieval lawyers felt should characterize witness testimony and the conduct of trustees (*fiduciarii*), and which 'guarantors' or sponsors (*fideiussores*) embodied when they pledged to stand surety for a fine or act as godparents.[36] Even more significantly, they also evoked the *fides* that was understood as good faith or sincere intention, expressed in Middle English as *troth* or *trewthe*, and familiar to almost everyone from the language of everyday life and the formation of formal and informal promises, as discussed in Chapters 2 and 3.

The term *probus* came to prominence somewhat later as an alternative to *bonus*, which arguably had too many shades of meaning; *probus* was also less weighed down with connotations of personal service than *fidelis*. It conveyed a sense that someone was worthy of consideration by the law, or capable of acting and speaking in a legal context. This meant that it was more exclusively tied to the exercise of public and representative functions. Across Western Europe from the early thirteenth century it was usual for communal delegations to courts or assemblies to be described in this way, such as the *probi homines* from towns and villages in the Agenais who attended the general court of the county, those responding to inquests conducted by the count of Anjou in the twelfth and thirteenth centuries, and the representatives of towns at the general court of Daroca, Aragon, in 1228. In some areas of Languedoc this term had replaced *boni homines*, and was more closely tied to communal representation as opposed to personal status.[37] Similarly in Scotland the Ayrshire formulary, a compilation of thirteenth-century documents made in the 1310s, seems to be part of a comparable shift, noting a brieve for an inquest to be carried out by sheriffs with the aid of 'upright and loyal men of the country' (*probos et fideles homines patrie*).[38] *Probi homines* seems to have corresponded to various versions of the vernacular *prudeshommes* (with additional overtones of prudence) used especially by urban elites across the same territories.[39] In England the twenty-four arbiters of disputes in Leicester were sometimes known as 'prudishomes'; in Southampton twelve 'proddeshomes' were a precursor of the guild merchant; in Norwich the 'prudeshomes' of the early fourteenth century comprised the twenty-four electors of the city bailiffs.[40]

But most explicit in connecting the qualities of local jurors to the sovereign claims of legal authority were the terms deriving from *legalis* and *legitimus*. These were prominent in the legislative programmes of the Angevin and Capetian monarchs in the second half of the twelfth century, first in Henry II of England's introduction of regular local juries for the prosecution of crime in his Assize of Clarendon in 1166. The Assize provided for inquiries in every county and hundred based upon the sworn reports of twelve of the 'more lawworthy men' (*legaliores homines*) from the hundred and four from each vill. They were to report robbers, murderers, thieves, and their receivers. Philip Augustus then pioneered the inquest in France in 1190, taking testimony in some cases from individual witnesses and in others from a panel of 'lawworthy men of the land' (*legitimos homines terre*).[41] In thirteenth-century

England the phrase 'free and law-worthy men' (*liberi et legali homines*) was commonly used to describe the non-knightly jurors before the hearings of itinerant justices (the 'eyre'), and it appears frequently in the legal treatise known as Bracton.[42] A sure sign of its ubiquity comes from those instances when it was amplified for effect, as in the claim that the witnesses in a Sussex lawsuit of 1253 were the 'wiser and *more* law-worthy' (*discrecioribus et legalioribus*) men of the neighbourhood.[43]

The differences between these various phrases were for the most part subtle and slight, and there were many ways in which they could be combined to express the qualities desired in local collaborators with judicial and governmental power: people who adequately fulfilled the symbolic role of providing reliable and trustworthy testimony. For example in Henry III's England inquest jurors were almost always described as *probi et legales homines*, and the same term was also used for the juries set up to hear disputes over assessments of taxable wealth in 1225.[44] Similarly Edward I's 1279 inquiries into administrative 'hundreds' empanelled juries of twelve *probi et legales homines*.[45] Such terminology is clearly a wishful projection of social qualities onto the local men upon whom rulers were coming to rely. But it is also the way in which these local representatives were eager to be described. Whether the jurors were in fact 'upright', 'loyal', or just plain 'good' is not a question to which historians can provide an objective answer, but this is not the point. Social qualities of this sort were a mutually convenient fiction, or a symbolic role, that allowed the business of control and profit to go on under the guise of public utility, consultation, and consensus.

In this ever more governed world, particularly in England where the intensity of royal rule was arguably greater than anywhere else in the Latin West, how did churchmen choose to describe the laymen providing information and judgements in inquests? In the twelfth century they generally chose between three options. The first available option was to use the language of virtue and probity, in common with many lay rulers. For example in the 1150s the bishop of Lincoln confirmed the patronage of North Witham church after consulting 'many men of good reputation as witnesses' (*testes quam plurimos bone opinionis viros*); around 1213 the bishop of Winchester sought the testimony of 'good and prudent men' (*bonorum et prudentum virorum*) about the proposed new site of St Thomas's hospital in Southwark, the old buildings having been destroyed by fire.[46] Such terms persisted as a minor strand in ecclesiastical documentation, right through the medieval period and beyond, but many bishops preferred to reserve what was perceived as a secular language for dealings with the administration of their temporal estates.[47] When seeking answers to questions about their spiritual responsibilities bishops placed an understandable premium on the lexicon of *fides*, the second option available to them. This was not only because it resonated with concepts of faith in God and 'the faith' as the church or community of believers, as in the description of Christians as *fideles*, faithful persons, but also because the language of faith was so deeply ingrained in how people had—for centuries—conducted significant relationships, formed agreements, and made promises, in the ways I described in Chapter 2. Of course the term *fidelis* was also ubiquitous in describing the sworn loyalty of feudal relationships. Thus, when applied to the jurors giving information on matters that affected the church, *fides*-based terms carried several layers of meaning. For example an instruction of around 1180 for the chaplain and two or three 'from among the faithful of the parish' (*parrochianorum fidelium*) of Teynham in Kent to use the tithes from newly cultivated land to purchase vestments and books, 'the faithful' may be interpreted as sworn (for the purpose) or loyal (to the chaplain), but they were surely primarily faithful in the sense of being members of 'the faith'.[48] This was, however, a rather undiscriminating term. All Christians were expected to be faithful in the sense of being obedient to the pronouncements of the church, trusting of God, sincere in their promises, careful in their participation in a register of speech that conveyed heightened formality, and protective of their own personal *fides*, as discussed above in the chapters of Part I. How then could a superior 'law-worthiness' be signified? It was possible to speak of 'the oath of the *more* faithful tenants' of a church, but this seemed to compromise the universal connotations of Christian faithfulness, relying more on the sense of *fides* as loyalty.[49] If 'the faithful' were too undifferentiated, then the *fideles* of Roman and feudal law were too individuated, being men who had a personal sworn relationship to their lord. There was also, apparently, no appetite to adopt the Classical Latin term *fidus*, which meant simply trustworthy or reliable. The third option was one that certainly seems to have been in the air during the Fourth Lateran Council in 1215, a moment when questions of the membership, law, and doctrine of the church were being reconfigured in significant ways. The term most commonly used for witnesses or jurors in the decrees of the council was 'suitable' (*idoneus*): in respect of the detection of heretics, the discovery of faults in the clergy and laity, and of witness testimony in general.[50] But this did not enter general use, a fact that may be explained by its strong association with men of some status within the church, namely teachers of grammar and theology, preachers, confessors, scribes, and officials.[51] In the emerging world of government by inquest such connotations may not have best captured the qualities desired in thousands of unknown lay collaborators.

The remarkable thing is that despite, or perhaps because of, their increasing use and availability in secular discourses of power, all these options were either consciously rejected or gradually fell into desuetude in the ecclesiastical context, in favour of a far less common and in some ways entirely new term: the *fidedignus* or trustworthy man. In the second half of the twelfth century, we find a small number of examples of this word in the acts of English bishops, England being notably precocious in comparative terms. In common with usage in several continental bishops' chanceries, *fidedignus* sometimes described a passive witness to a judgement or a grant, but particularly in England it characterised men who provided information or judgement to an inquest or visitation.[52] This last sense of *fidedignus* was an innovation, adopted with particular vigour in England during the century and a half from 1150, and less prevalent in other regions of Latin Europe.[53] Its use tells us that even though English churchmen participated in a very broad movement to augment institutional power, encompassing not only their counterparts elsewhere in Europe but also secular rulers making use of inquests, they were searching for a new and specifically ecclesiastical language with which to achieve it.[54]

The Prehistory of a Concept

Where did this term *fidedignus* come from, and what cultural baggage did it carry? Before the twelfth century, trustworthiness was emphatically not associated with lay testimony and inquests. In late antique and early medieval Christian texts the adjectival phrase *fide dignum* was used fairly frequently to refer to someone or something that was a trustworthy witness to God's truth. Fundamentally this meant the word of God embodied in scripture. Thus for Augustine trustworthiness was a matter of authority and it was the authority of scripture that counted for most, being more trustworthy than a single human voice. This was so despite—or in some cases because of—its unusual admixture of divine clarity and mystery.[55] That the word of God was *fide dignum* was simply assumed by many authors.[56] Theodoret of Cyrus (393–466) and Bede (672–735) praised the gospel authors as trustworthy witnesses. The latter's commentary on the Acts of the Apostles was, furthermore, prefaced by a letter to Bishop Acca of Hexham in which Bede explained that Luke's gospel was probably the most trustworthy account of the Acts available to the church (*fide dignus haberetur in ecclesia*). It was Luke's great faith (*fides*) that made him worthy of belief (*fide dignum*) in this way.[57] As well as the gospel writers themselves, the apostles more generally were often credited with being trustworthy carriers of the word of God. For example Stephen's and Barnabus's credentials included their being 'full of faith' (Acts 6.5, 11.24), while Paul wrote of the gospel being 'committed to my trust' (1 Timothy 1.11). These early Christians thought of themselves as witnesses to the truth, and it was this concept of witnessing that came to dominate medieval discussions of trustworthiness.[58] The twelfth-century Ordinary Gloss to the Bible returned repeatedly to the theme of an eternal truth whose witnesses spoke on God's behalf and which could not be silenced. For Hugh of St Victor and Peter Lombard the authority and trustworthiness of patriarchs and apostles was carried forward in time by the saints of the church, whose example to Christians was a proof worthy of faith (*fide digna*). The saints were, as Augustine had written, the 'faithful people' whose acts of witness illuminated the darkness.[59]

But beyond the gospel writers, apostles, and early saints, problems naturally arose in deciding who was a trustworthy bearer or witness of the word. Augustine was fairly circumspect, warning that prophecies were 'most worthy of faith' when repeated in reputable sources, and other writers made censorious comments on the dangers of treating schismatic clerics and 'slanderers' as *fide dignum*.[60] On the other hand some writers, such as Hrabanus Maurus (ca. 780–856) and Hervé of Bourgdieu (d. 1150), could sound a very optimistic note, arguing that since the word of God was itself faithful and worthy of being accepted by everyone, anyone who uttered it truly could be esteemed *fide dignum*.[61] But there was plenty of room for doubt over who spoke 'truly'. In keeping with the condescension towards lay understanding discussed in Chapter 1, Peter the Venerable (1092–1156) worried about the 'opinions of the common people' concerning authoritative texts, which, he wrote, 'are not to be accepted without certain and trustworthy authorities'. While the common people might not be trustworthy for these purposes, by the twelfth and thirteenth centuries the 'common opinion of the doctors of the church' was being treated as *fide dignum*.[62] In both these contexts trustworthiness was invoked in an attempt to establish consensus, recognising the potential for disagreement in the interpretation of scripture.[63] Other writers used 'trustworthy' to describe with greater certitude arguments that were 'manifest', consonant with reason, or capable of being proven, while Hincmar of Laon (d. 879) found assurance in the determinations of church councils that were *fide dignum* in the sense of being authentic.[64]

Debates over the interpretation of scripture acknowledged only reluctantly the possibility that human testimony could be *fide dignum*, but in history writing it was much more common to defend the trustworthiness of living informants.[65] Although Bede famously preferred the classical rhetoric of *communis opinio* to establish the reliability of his sources, Cassiodorus initiated the use of the noun *fidedignus* in relation to people as well as texts and testimony in the abstract.[66] By the twelfth century it was common for historians to gather testimony from *viri fide dignis*.[67] This was how the compilers of miracle collections also described their witnesses. For example, in his quest to verify miracle stories in the region surrounding his abbey at Cluny, Peter the Venerable said that he had sought written corroboration from several trustworthy men.[68] The writing of history and saints' lives involved overcoming problems of knowledge that had been gathered at one remove. Other people's testimony was crucial.

At some level bishops and their staff in the twelfth century were likely to have been aware of these usages in theology, historiography, and miracle collecting, alongside their wider familiarity with the valences and resonances of the *fides* lexicon as it related to law and agreements, and identity and emotion (as discussed in Chapters 2 and 3). Something *fide dignum* was authentic, it came from God, and it was mediated by a witness whose credibility was guaranteed by their status: someone who could be described as *fide dig-nus*. The crucial additional element here, the thing that was not so promi-nent in the universal discourses of *fides* in which all manner of people could participate, was the importance of status. Someone *fidedignum* had to be of an appropriate status. Before the explosion of inquests and lay testimony in church government during the thirteenth century, it was mainly members of religious orders who lived up to these criteria and were labelled trustworthy informants. For example a letter from Peter the Venerable to Pope Eugenius written around 1145 reported what the abbot had heard from trustworthy men about the character of the archbishop of Besançon. In another letter of 1149 he praised the opinion of 'many religious, wise, and trustworthy clerics and monks'.[69] With a similar idea in mind Pope Alexander III wrote to Bishop Jocelin of Salisbury around 1174 requiring him to send to Rome four or five trustworthy and honest religious men of his diocese—that is monks—to swear that the bishop-elect of Bath and Wells had not been involved in the murder of Thomas Becket.[70] Alexander's letter had but few precursors, with just a handful of earlier papal letters citing *fidedigni* as a source of information.[71]

Although *fidedignum* was seeping into papal correspondence around the year 1200, the evidence points away from its more widespread adoption being the result of influence from above. While it is likely that papal letters gave *some* stimulus, and while we do find two relevant early uses in the canons of the Fourth Lateran Council, its popularity derived more from its resonance with individual bishops and its concrete applicability as a meaningful way to describe the qualities sought in lay witnesses, jurors, and informants, than from any learned innovation among canon and civil lawyers. Largely this is an argument constructed from a series of telling absences.

The first absence is the lack of interest shown by canon lawyers in an early use of the phrase in Justinian's *Codex* of AD 534, in a prohibition on the clergy playing dice or attending the games, which included provisions for inquiry to be made into any suspicions. The inquiries were to omit nothing in their quest for the truth, taking testimony from *testes fide dignos*, which here seems to mean something like 'witnesses worthy of belief', that is people whose word would carry weight in court.[72] The silence among canonists is deafening. Text-books, commentaries, and procedural writings of the late twelfth and early thirteenth centuries were all equally indifferent to the availability of this term, even though it was occasionally used in local documents besides the theo-logical and historiographical contexts described above. Remarkably neither the historic canons nor the authorial comments in the hugely influential mid-twelfth-century compendium known as the *Decretum* of Gratian mention the *fidedignus*.[73] The closest its author (or authors) came to coining such a term was in arguing that the faith, worth, character, and dignity of witnesses should be assessed and that any witness who changed his testimony and reneged on his oath (*fidem*) should not be heard.[74] This absence is striking, given the

learning and influence of Gratian. The renowned late twelfth-century commentator on civil law procedure, Pillius, also preferred other ways of describing the qualities of witnesses. Poor witnesses were only to be admitted, he
wrote, if their *fides* (in the senses we have explored in Chapter 2) could be
attested as well as their abilities: they would have to be of 'good fame, reputation and faith'. But there is no mention of their being 'trustworthy'. Among
the canonists neither Bernard of Pavia's influential *Summa de matrimonio*
written in the 1170s, nor his *Summa decretalium* of around 1195 contained the
phrase. Instead he referred to 'men of good reputation' (*bonae famae viri*) or
'faithful persons' (*fideles*). Another influential procedural tract, written by Tancred around 1216, similarly refers to the ideal witness as a person of good fame
and describes the perfect notary as a 'faithful man'.[75] Such works did often
place in suggestively close proximity an interesting pair of injunctions: first,
that no trust (*fides*) ought to be placed in disqualified or unreliable witnesses,
and second, that the more worthy (*dignior*) witness should be believed.[76] But
the negative meaning of the first and the positive connotation of the second
seem to have stood in the way of their conjunction as a single word or phrase
in legal commentaries.

When the phrase did appear in relation to monastic elections and matrimonial lawsuits in two canons of the Fourth Lateran Council it was not,
therefore, the product of learned discussion, but rather a useful neologism
picked up from provincial examples. As we have seen, some English bishops
and abbots were using *fidedignus* in practical documents relating to inquests
and witnesses, and, in addition, the statutes made for Canterbury diocese in
1213 or 1214 by Archbishop Stephen Langton identified 'trustworthy men' as
those best placed to guard the money raised by alms collectors in parishes.[77]
The influence seems to have been 'upwards' from local experience rather than
'downwards' from papal or conciliar models. Canon 24 of the Lateran council legislated for monks recognised as *fide digni* to canvass the opinions of
their brethren in the event of a contested election to the abbacy of their house.
Canon 52 was concerned with matrimonial litigation arising from the council's new definition of consanguinity (marriage to within four rather than the
seven degrees of relation). It recognized that defining degrees of relation was
likely to be a contentious matter, and so permitted some weight to be given to
hearsay evidence, so long as it came from 'substantial persons who merit trust'
(*personae graves . . . quibus fides merito*). These should be neither infamous
nor suspect but trustworthy (*fide dignis*) and beyond objection. Both canons
were soon incorporated into Pope Gregory IX's collection of decretal letters,
and thereby widely disseminated across Latin Christendom over the ensuing
decades.[78] The canons of the council, and the *Decretals*, stimulated a huge
amount of learned reflection among canonists, but again none of the major
commentaries made any remark on this novel term. It passed unnoticed. Nor
did the important canonist Johannes Teutonicus use or discuss the term *fide*

dignus in his treatment of witnesses and marriage law in his gloss of the *Compilatio tertia* written around the same time. The *Ordinary Gloss* on Gregory's *Decretals* (complete by about 1260), described people meriting trust as 'men of good reputation held in high regard, and older men', citing several texts referring to the wisdom of age. The phrase *fide dignis* attracted no comment.[79] But it did begin to creep into papal decrees, and the trickle of local documents using the term in relation to witnesses, especially in England, continued to grow. As a term particularly associated with *churchmen's* use of inquests, it is remarkable how infrequently scribes in royal or civic service employed it, even though legal learning was permeable across the jurisdictions.[80] One can assume only that the weight of theological tradition, surveyed here, and the strong association with personal Christian faith (discussed in Chapters 1 and 3) militated against its adoption by secular authorities. Two early thirteenth-century examples from opposite ends of the church hierarchy may serve to illustrate these beginnings: an undated letter of Honorius II (1216–27) contrasted testimony taken from criminals with that acquired from 'trustworthy witnesses', while in 1224 a land dispute between the abbot of Chertsey and the rector of Cobham in Surrey was settled by the bishop of Winchester consulting the relevant documents and hearing 'trustworthy witnesses'.[81]

As the thirteenth century wore on, the *fidedignus* became entrenched as a figure in the English church's administration of financial relationships, material interests, and justice. For the most part this meant participation in inquests and visitations (a specialised subcategory of inquest), but the word was also used in rhetorical justifications for executive action by popes and bishops. It was a term known across the Latin West, but for the sake of gaining some sense of its social and institutional effects and meaning, the analysis that follows will focus on the English experience. The role played by trustworthy men in various activities of English bishops is partly to be explained by the constellation of meanings and associations of the word *fidedignum*, together with some of the resonances made by generations of thinking about the operation of *fides* itself (as seen in Chapters 1 to 3). While theologians of the twelfth century and earlier may have been shocked by the idea that low-status laymen could be lauded as trustworthy after the manner of the apostles and saints, this did not prevent some of the same thinking about trust and knowledge being applied to them, while being modulated by some of the senses of *fides* more prevalent in the conditional practices of promising and contracting (for which see Chapter 2). Churchmen were now not only in the business of knowing God, they had to know the people, the land, and the law too. In worldly as in divine affairs human cognition had its limits, but collective judgement was better than individual opinion. The practice and implications of episcopal governance through trustworthy men will be extensively treated in Part IV of the present book. The settlement of disputes by inquest relied upon finding truth, which was elusive and unseen, as was God (for which see Chapter 1).

But unlike the quest for knowledge of God—who was certain—the search for knowledge about the material and social world meant accepting a greater degree of uncertainty, although as we shall see, the results of that search could still be presented as if stable and enduring. Some of God's certitude must have entered his creation, after all.

{≈≈≈≈≈≈}

Finally a note of caution should be sounded. Just because churchmen now wanted to trust the laity as witnesses and jurors did not mean an end to suspicion, condescension, and hostility towards them, as shown already in Chapter 1's discussion of fifteenth-century scepticism regarding lay interpretation of scripture. More generally, the culture of the thirteenth, fourteenth, and fifteenth centuries was saturated with disdain for what peasants represented, both in their real bodies and in literary parody: lowliness, subordination, and dirt.[82] In their expositions of biblical proverbs churchmen repeatedly returned to the difficulty entailed in trusting the common people. For example the words of Bildad the Shuhite in the Book of Job concerning people who do not heed God—that 'their folly shall not please them, and their trust shall be like a spider's web'—was in the thirteenth century treated as a comment on the fragility of trust and the dangers of gullibility.[83] Representations of Adam as a false juror who broke the agreement of his charter with God tended to cast all of humanity as inherently untrustworthy.[84] But even more significantly, the extensive effort by written and spoken word to justify the trust placed in lay witnesses is evidence of a latent distrust and institutional unease with this dictate of necessity. Such discursive struggle is apparent in Thomas Cobham's justification for his investigation of abuses at Llanthony Priory (Monmouthshire) in 1325: 'Public discredit . . . is not created without cause, and there is something in the popular saying *vox populi, vox dei*'. But the voice of the people was not synonymous with the voice of God. However proverbial it became, this Latin tag was thought dangerous in its invocation of the clamour of the streets, the mob.[85] When Bernard of Angers heard about the cult of St Faith in Conques he was sceptical: 'Partly because it seemed to be *common people* who promulgated these miracles and partly because they were regarded as new and unusual, we put no faith in them'. According to him there could be no faith in the common people.[86] From Bernard's cynicism in the eleventh century, distrust of the people was ever-present. The problem, as the fifteenth-century English poet George Ashby put it, was that one could not completely trust the commonality: 'thai be ever wavering in variance', a weakness that put at risk the stability of their judgements.[87] Perhaps aware of just how fragile and conditional trust could be in everyday life (for which see Chapter 3), late medieval writers were wary of placing too much importance upon it. However, such expressions of distrust were not necessarily inimical to the idea of lay

informants, and in fact could be seen as an important ingredient in their authority. For without the persistence of generalized distrust, churchmen would
not have been spurred to coin a phrase that made claims for the special trustworthiness of a select few.[88]

The foregoing exploration of the intellectual inheritance of *fides* and the
fidedignus gives us some insight into what the trustworthy men meant to
bishops, and into the astonishing novelty that they represented. In order to
overcome their habitual distrust of the laity, and to address the exigencies of
institutional growth and a more intensively governed society, bishops had to
take a word hitherto reserved for the gospel writers and the saints and make
it fit for application to many thousands of peasant informants. However, so
far as our understanding of the bishop's perspective goes, the story told here is
only half an explanation. The full meaning of the concept can be grasped only
through a detailed examination of how it was deployed in the day-to-day documentation of episcopal governance, where the scholarly legacy was perhaps less
important than immediate circumstances and familiar examples. Chapter 5
adopts the bishop's perspective on who the trustworthy men *should have been*,
while Chapter 6 looks at who in fact they were.

CHAPTER FIVE

Bishops Describe Trustworthiness

BECAUSE THE FIGURE of the trustworthy man emerged into church legal and administrative discourse over a long period of time, and because it was an adaptation and repurposing of a long-familiar word, there was no single moment at which it was defined. As we saw in Chapter 4, the major commentaries in the canon law tradition ignored the words *fidedignus* and *fidedignum*, not considering them in need of any explanation. There was also no standard papal or conciliar decree that set out exactly what a trustworthy man was: the word instead acquired its meaning from its context and use over time. And yet it is notable how much agreement there was among bishops as to what a *fidedignus* was and what they were for. In this chapter I gather together the statements made by bishops on the qualities looked for in trustworthy men, before, in the next chapter, looking at how those qualities were realised in the social profile of real live trustworthy men.

Already we have seen how the scope of being trustworthy (*fidedignum*) expanded in the twelfth century from the gospel writers and the saints to witnesses informing historians and compilers of miracles, and then to the jurors and witnesses in church inquests. In the course of this shift certain elements were clearly jettisoned. The trustworthy man in an inquest could not be called close to God in the way the apostles were close to Christ, but the change here was in the subject matter, rather than in the nature of their knowledge. The trustworthy man was still expected to be a reliable source of information, someone with access to the truth, and a person who represented a degree of certainty. Of course the trust placed in a human witness could not be certain in the sense that belief in God should have been certain, because humans were thought fallible and inconsistent in contrast to God's constancy and endurance; as Augustine said, it is possible to be certain about something that is certain. But even if in human affairs the object of faith was less certain, bishops nonetheless expected trustworthy men to exhibit signs of constancy, suggesting that the trust placed in them was not completely divergent from the faith with which Christians were supposed to approach God. Faith in human witnesses also echoed the importance of accepting incomplete knowledge, and the acknowledgement of risk. This was not the risk of heresy, but the risk of factual and legal error, and the person taking the risk was the bishop rather than the ordinary Christian, and so faith was still—though in a different sense—being mediated by an authoritative institution. The language of faith was, as we shall see, very much the tool of bishops.

In moving information from the laity to the church hierarchy, *fides* formed bonds across a hierarchical divide, suggesting that the feudal sense of loyalty and service was also present in the way trustworthy men were conceived, even though the term *fidelis* had been rejected as too redolent of personal service and obligation. The trustworthy men had no personal ties to the bishops whose governance their actions supported. On the contrary, the *fides* with which they provided information was more akin to the faith given in formal promising or when acting as a personal pledge (discussed in Chapter 2) in the sense of guaranteeing the truth of what they said, with all the attendant expectations of sincerity and obligation that we encountered in Chapter 3. However, trustworthy men, as we shall see in Chapter 7 and throughout Part IV, gave faith on behalf of their parishes rather than as private individuals, but despite this representative function, they should not be seen as mouthpieces for a shared communal 'trewthe' of the sort described by Steven Justice (for discussion of which see Chapter 2). The *fides* of which bishops deemed them worthy brought to trustworthy men a good deal of personal capital or status that emphasized their value over and above the majority of their fellows. In Chapters 6 to 9 the inequality that this stimulated will be explored in detail.

What Made a Trustworthy Man?

Given the absence of a definitive description in canon law, the qualities bishops looked for in trustworthy men were largely those they looked for in witnesses, to whom canonists had devoted more attention given their importance in judicial procedure, as we saw in Chapter 4. Although inquests and visitations were not, strictly speaking, courts, they were parts of a sprawling judicial-pastoral-administrative system in which canon law was of huge importance, even though the commentary tradition gave most emphasis to the judicial aspect. The integration of the pastoral and administrative work of bishops into the judicial system can be illustrated by the fact that information provided by trustworthy men was frequently tested in court at a later date, while inquests might be ordered as part of judicial proceedings. It was therefore advisable for the trustworthy men to be presented as if they met the standards of witnesses in the courts, though there were limits to the resemblance between them. For example, witnesses could be disqualified if they were found to be unfree, but trustworthy men did not usually need to be free. On the other hand women were legally capable of giving testimony to courts in some circumstances but were hardly ever numbered among the trustworthy for inquest purposes.[1] Only in suits for the annulment of marriage on grounds of male impotence were 'matrons held in good opinion, trustworthy and skilled in nuptial matters' specified in canon law.[2] The few circumstances in which real female witnesses were described as *fidedigna* will be discussed in Chapter 6, while the impact of distrust of women will be explored in Chapter 9. Another difference between canonical witnesses and trustworthy men was that the latter usually gave a collective opinion and were not accountable as individuals for the truth of their word (for which see Chapter 10). Occasionally the records are explicit about the expectation that inquest testimony might be tried in court, which we can take to be indicative of a much more broadly held assumption. A 1309 inquiry into an elite marriage in Hampshire was to be conducted through 'trustworthy men who would overcome all exceptions', and at Melton Mowbray in 1434 the poverty of the vicar was to be investigated through trustworthy men 'who are not susceptible to exceptions'.[3] In these rare instances it looks as though they were expected to be free men.

We know about the qualities desired in witnesses because judicial procedure permitted litigants to object to those produced by the other party. The professed aim of these objections, or 'exceptions' as they were known, was to eliminate the testimony of witnesses who might be biased or generally inadequate in some way. The example of a Leicestershire case from around 1270 illustrates this very well. Two clergymen, Thomas Nevill and Robert Picheford, each claimed to be the rightful rector of Houghton, and their dispute reached the provincial court of appeal in London having begun in the bishop of Lincoln's diocesan courts. Nevill's legal representative prepared a list of questions that he wanted the court examiners to put to Picheford's witnesses. Were they infamous or perjurers, were they excommunicates or had they been condemned or convicted for any evil or crime (in the church or royal courts)? Were they serfs, servants, or members of Picheford's household? Were they friends of Picheford or, conversely, enemies of Nevill? Were they more inclined to favour or oppose one party or the other? Had they been 'instructed', or had they colluded with other witnesses in deciding their testimony? Had they been paid to testify? This list of possible objections covers most of those frequently considered by the church courts. Serfs and criminals, including perjurers and excommunicates, could not testify, and a host of disqualifications arose from relationships that might prejudice the testimony. Ultimately the court felt that more weight could be placed on Picheford's witnesses since they were more consistent with one another, they had better knowledge of the parties to the suit, and more were from Houghton, the place in question. The examiners concluded that 'more trust may be placed in them (*maior fides sit eis adhibenda*) than in the witnesses produced by the other party'.[4]

Some objections rested on facts (however hard they were to establish) such as being a criminal, or of unfree status. These immediately disqualified a witness. An undated (but probably fifteenth-century) petition to the court of Chancery summed up the categories of inadmissible witnesses in suggestive language: thieves, common women (which meant prostitutes), and 'other mysdoers' were described as 'peple withe oute consience' who 'mowe not of reson be vndirstoden worthi of trouthe nor to bere witnesse of trouthe in any cause wher ryght ys to be enquered'.[5] We know that Chancery petitions were often framed by lawyers who were aware of the influence of canon law concepts on the court, which was overseen by the Chancellor, who was often a bishop. In this light it seems likely that 'worthy of troth' was a literal English rendering of *fidedignum*, intended to trigger associations with the men trusted by bishops.[6] Other objections were less absolute and were intended to influence the judge's impressionistic evaluation. Arguing that someone was likely to be biased because of friendship, kinship, age, gender, wealth, or mental capacity all fell into this category. For example in 1510 a female witness in a breach of faith case was said to be 'poor and a simpleton', dependent on the parishioners for food, drink, and clothing: she had also supposedly been coached in what to say. Another was said to be a little girl 'of no consequence' who had given evidence in fear of her mother.[7] These assertions were not easily proven, but they show us what sort of thing was considered likely to sway opinion against a witness. In contrast to these negative qualities, consistency, proximity to the events in question, and the rather nebulous 'better knowledge' emerge as the positive characteristics of witnesses.[8]

In squabbles over the admissibility of witnesses, wider social attitudes were thus entwined with legal precepts. Not only were social facts brought to bear, the quality of the deponent's voice and the manner in which they delivered their testimony were open to scrutiny. Aristotle had argued that trust in another person should derive from the manner of his speech rather than resting upon prior knowledge of his character, a perfect illustration of the value of the symbolic role if ever there was one. In the later thirteenth century the philosophers William of Moerbeke and Giles of Rome bent their interpretation of Aristotle to reach the opposite conclusion: that trust should arise from knowledge of character.[9] In considering witness testimony late medieval judges in fact followed Aristotle (though it is doubtful whether many would have read him, or indeed encountered William or Giles) in looking to outward signs that made the witness credible: whether they competently and plausibly fulfilled the symbolic role of witness. Sometimes the court examiners who took down witnesses' depositions made notes—meant for the judge's attention—on their credibility. The legal historian Richard Helmholz has highlighted a case from Canterbury in 1291 where an examiner recorded that a particular witness spoke 'in a vacillating fashion, and also gave the cause of his knowledge as if he were suborned'; another at York in 1364 suggested that less trust should be placed in a witness whose accent shifted from southern to northern English and even 'the manner of Scotsmen speaking the English language'.[10] In London around 1470 Mariona Phypp was questioned about the betrothal of Agnes Chambyrlayn and John Holder. Witnesses thought she had spoken 'intemperately' and none gave much credence to her protestations of good faith. When asked about the betrothal she was recalled to have said:

> By my feith and by my trouth and so helpe me god atte holy dome (*doom*), I knowe of none nor y was not privy therto and yt wole y swere upon all the bokes in London.

Another witness remembered that she had offered to swear on all the books in England, not just London; yet another thought she had promised to swear before all the judges in England. The point is that they all believed she had gone over the top. Testimony could be made to appear worthless if it was inconsistent or immoderate. This was a tactic especially favoured when discrediting female witnesses.[11] Revealingly, the courts did not pursue the impossible standard of the perfect witness, preferring rather to assess how they measured up to the components of the symbolic role under attack from the lawyers' exceptions.

The essence of such exceptions was a slur upon the 'constancy' of a witness, and this was the key characteristic of the symbolic role of trustworthy men. Although in the courts this was a concept that could be applied to women, it was nonetheless strongly gendered masculine, helping it to become an important component in the construction of the trustworthy male juror, the *fidedignus*.[12] Trustworthy men were expected to be 'honest, respectable men who would not commit perjury for love or money or out of malice', and they were called upon to 'report fully and truly what they know, putting aside all intemperate feelings'; they might even be expected to swear that they had not been swayed in such a way.[13] Nor should they be liable to be led astray by the many temptations of the world. When, for example, the people of Herefordshire began worshipping at an unofficial holy well in Turnaston parish in 1410, the bishop claimed that he had heard about it from 'many trustworthy people'. These were the men and women who had *not* been influenced by the bad example of others, but were upright and constant in their sense of responsibility to the church.[14]

Constancy also required a certain level of confidence, even audacity, and this was often reflected in the instructions that bishops sent to their subordinates for holding inquests and visitations. When the sub-dean of Salisbury replied to his bishop's instructions for an upcoming visitation in 1394 he reported that he had cited 'twelve men of good repute from each city parish who were the more familiar with the customary visitation articles and who *would dare* to tell the truth'.[15] The bishop of Durham was looking for similar qualities among the visitation representatives of Gainford in 1432, who were to be 'faithful men of good fame who would know *and be prepared to speak* the truth about the customary articles of visitation, especially concerning disputes and controversies'.[16]

In line with the canonical principle that knowledge of the locality should come from the locality (discussed in Chapter 4), mandates for inquests frequently used the language of neighbours and neighbourhood, asking for those 'living closest' (*viciniores*) to be selected.[17] In 1283 the official of the archdeacon of Worcester was told to cite 'three, four, or more trustworthy parishioners of every parish, through whom the truth of things may be better investigated', and in 1322 the archdeacon of Stafford received a similar order for the citations of 'three or four who are the more trustworthy of the parishioners and the better informed about the state of the churches, chapels, rectors, vicars, and priests, as well as the state of the parishioners'.[18] Talk of neighbours was generally considerably more inclusive than references to 'the trustworthy', but it could on occasion be deployed as an ideological term. When his visitation party was attacked in Yeovil in 1349 the bishop of Bath and Wells described the offenders as 'sons of perdition, forming the community of the said town'. Fortunately for him, he was rescued by 'neighbours, devout sons of the church'. This is an interesting comparison. 'Neighbours' emerges from the bishop's letter as an even more positive piece of moral social description than 'community'. To be a neighbour was to be a devout son of the church, not a son of perdition.[19]

On occasion more defined qualifications were needed, especially when the information that was sought involved a degree of technical knowledge. This was most obviously the case with building repairs. For example, a survey of the episcopal manors in Bath and Wells diocese in 1310 was to be carried out with 'skilled men' and 'competent witnesses', while at Skillington in Lincolnshire in 1338 Simon son of Thomas and Stephen the clerk were described as 'good men, trained [or capable] (*boni sunt et habiles*) in the preservation of the church goods and fabric'. They were made 'reeves of the church'.[20] Once, when an inquest into the state of a house belonging to Southwell Minster in Nottinghamshire did not produce satisfactory results, the chapter were told to do it all again, though this time with 'more expert men', above suspicion, who would inspect the place with their own eyes. It sounds as though someone had been cutting corners and pulling figures out of the air.[21]

In addition to such qualitative provisions the value of the trustworthy men was sometimes counted in numerical terms, just like Picheford's witnesses above. A priest called John Dagenhale had been reported for adultery in Salisbury diocese around 1320, and he was required to purge himself (to swear an oath of innocence attested by a set number of 'compurgators') with ten fellow priests of the neighbourhood. When Dagenhale protested that ten such priests could not be found the bishop offered to reduce the number first to eight, then to six, and finally to four priests and four trustworthy laymen. But Dagenhale was clearly out of favour in his parish of Childrey and he could not find anyone to help him. His request to purge *himself* was batted away as absurd, but he was permitted to distribute bread to the poor instead of doing public penance in front of his enemies.[22] The gradual reduction in the number of compurgators suggests an assumption that four trustworthy laymen were equal to two priests. This sort of calculation is extremely rare though. More often a bishop would demand a 'suitable number' of trustworthy men, leaving it up to his representative to decide what this was. In visitations the norm was between three and eight, depending on the size of the parish, but there are some indications that the common-law jury could be the model for church inquests, giving us a few examples of twelve trustworthy men.[23] The institutional mind also occasionally thought about knowledge in terms of quantity—'the most information'—in order to arm itself against objections and to recover ground perceived to have been lost through ignorance.[24]

Whether quantified or not trustworthiness as understood within medieval church administration was an attributed characteristic and a symbolic role. It might be desirable that local informants were honest and reliable, but being thought of as such was quite enough. This seems to be the thrust of Archbishop Corbridge of York's description of visitation representatives in 1304: they were to be 'truthful, well-thought of, and of good reputation' (*veredici, bone opinionis et fame*).[25] What he was really looking for was some sense that his informants were people whose word would not be questioned. This quality—of being difficult to disagree with, for whatever reason—lay at the heart of the symbolic role played by trustworthy men in episcopal governance. In a similar vein, Archbishop Melton of York wanted men whom 'reliable opinion considered best'.[26] Quite what 'best' meant in this context is a little unclear, though there is no explicit reason for us to connect it with virtue. Sometimes the instruction was to inquire through 'trustworthy and well-known' (*famosos*) men or the 'better-known' (*famosiores*) people of a place, which suggests a reliance on public prominence, power, and position as proxies for the far less discernible qualities of truthfulness and honesty.[27] In adapting the canonical requirement for witnesses to be 'constant', bishops described the trustworthy men in such a way as to conflate this characteristic with social position, or social capital as anthropologists call it. Irrefutable witnesses offered the church something invaluable. They could guarantee stable information, and help to ensure that a case did not repeatedly return to court (for discussion of which see Chapter 10). Exactly how this aspect of the symbolic role was realized in the composition of actual juries of trustworthy men will be examined in detail in Chapters 6 and 7.

Controlling the Symbolic Role

On 8 August 1287 the chapter of York Minster petitioned Archbishop Romeyn to absolve some citizens of York who, they said, had rebelled against the liberties of the church. This was a rather passive-aggressive way of saying that the citizens had done something the chapter did not like and that the archbishop's forgiveness (so they believed) was needed. But this was not Romeyn's view of the matter. These citizens, he replied, had in fact come at his own request to aid him against servants of the dean of York; servants who had been overstepping the dean's rights of visitation and patronage within the city, encroaching on the archbishop's jurisdiction. The church of York was riven by competing factions and interests—dean and chapter on one side, archbishop on the other—and this was played out in competition over the language of trust. If they really insisted, Romeyn told the chapter haughtily, he could prove his version of events by the testimony of trustworthy persons.[28] What he meant was *don't you dare make me justify myself*. Romeyn was also responding to the chapter's opening gambit, which had been to tar the archbishop's supporters with the brush of rebellion. Were the citizens of York who assisted the archbishop to be counted among the trustworthy, or the rebellious? This question was not, nor is it now, an issue of whether the citizens of York were truly honest or genuinely unruly. For this was a battle over the power to control the symbolic role of trustworthiness: the power to make normative judgements about moral categories.[29] Romeyn may be judged to have landed the knockout rhetorical blow in this instance. His retort was based on the knowledge that the invocation of trustworthy witnesses would strengthen his case.

The stakes were high in this exchange because the language of trustworthiness was liable to reversals of polarity. A number of striking examples support this point, but in order to appreciate what they are telling us we have to understand that it was much more important for bishops to defend the integrity of the symbolic role than it was to preserve the position of a particular group of men. It was not at all unusual for a group of trustworthy men to find that if they behaved in some undesirable way, or if the exigencies of the moment changed, they could find the attribution withdrawn. This was the prerogative of bishops. It was *their* language. It was possible, for example, to say in 1272 that witnesses in a suit before the court of Canterbury were 'uninformed laymen' in whom no trust could be placed, or, as in a case from 1372 that trustworthy witnesses were mere 'bystanders' (*circumstantibus fidedignis*).[30] This casual dismissiveness was the flipside of institutional necessity. As human beings trustworthy men were seen by bishops to be expendable in a way that the information they provided was not. For example, in 1298 the men representing Dover during a metropolitan visitation were all excommunicated for nonattendance. The archbishop referred to them as 'men whom we had believed to be trustworthy' (*nonnullos intelleximus fidedignos*). In this case we can perceive that the symbolism guaranteeing public trust in episcopal judgements was secure so long as everyone played their proper role, but there was no way to construe absenteeism as trustworthiness, and so the trustworthy men of Dover became untrustworthy.[31] The same thing happened in 1405 in different circumstances. The vicar general of Hereford (the bishop's deputy) explained how the purgation of Roger Coly, a cleric accused of theft, should proceed: Coly's crime had supposedly been reported by trustworthy men, but if his purgation was successful these same people—now called 'those defamers'—were to be excommunicated.[32] This was an extreme course of action—in Chapter 10 we shall see how the soliciting of trustworthy testimony generally reduced the risks faced by witnesses—but it serves to demonstrate how, under a bishop's control, moral categories could be reassigned in the blink of an eye.

If information proved unreliable, or if a judgement did not stand the test of time, the people behind it must have been untrustworthy all along. Conversely, stability of information was proof that one's informants had been trustworthy from the start. During Bishop Waltham's visitation of Salisbury diocese in 1394 there were a number of moments when the initial reports of 'trustworthy' parish representatives were contradicted or superseded by evidence heard on the day. At Berwick St James and Barford St Martin in Wiltshire 'the parishioners' were said not to make offerings to their churches on their dedication days, so the visitor demanded that 'four or five of the *more trustworthy*' be cited to answer the charge and see to it that offerings were made in future. 'The parishioners' must be shorthand for the trustworthy representatives, and because they were at fault some 'more trustworthy' men were required. Similarly at South Newton 'the parishioners' had failed to provide the clergy with a processional cope and 'four of the more trustworthy' were to be cited.[33] Contradiction negated the trust placed in the first set of parish representatives, who may be said to have failed in their fulfilment of the symbolic role (we will never know whether or not they were truly trustworthy), and so another group was needed.

When the record provides us with the names of the trustworthy and the 'more trustworthy' we can speculate further as to the visitor's understanding of trustworthiness. In Amesbury the formal parish representatives were John Madyngton, Thomas Spaldyng, John Harold, John Carre, John Danvere, and John Croucheston. The 'more trustworthy' men were an entirely different group: John Tanner, Hugh Towker, Robert Lytman, Henry Dible, William Maryons, and John Hobbys. Of the second group Tanner, Towker, Dible, and Lytman, together with another man called William Baker, had themselves been reported by the first group for winnowing grain in the churchyard, casting up a cloud of dust that got into the eyes of the parishioners walking to church. They had been made to promise not to winnow antisocially again on pain of a fine of half a mark, and were sentenced to be beaten three times around the church. While these men must have had sufficient social position to be credible as 'trustworthy men' they seem to have composed a faction within the town's elite who were not above being chastised themselves. Perhaps the original group of trustworthy men had bridled at being superseded—and implicitly deemed untrustworthy—and reacted by lashing out at their rivals.[34] Meanwhile in Gillingham in Dorset a different situation obtained. Here the trustworthy and 'more trustworthy' groups overlapped a little. Nicholas Benet, Robert Archer, Richard Cresben, John de Wyke, William Wodye, and William Squibbe were named as the parish's representatives, but a group of 'more trustworthy' men comprising Matthew Vynyng, John Boglee, Walter Taylor, and John Parker, but also Squibbe and Wodye from the first group, were called to answer specific charges. Here there was no clear-cut faction suggesting that the visitor was satisfied that a few changes to the personnel would restore faith in the symbolic role that was being performed.[35]

The men who were replaced in these Wiltshire and Dorset visitations were sidelined rather quietly so far as the written record goes. There was no need to denigrate them or publicly call their probity into question as had happened in York in 1287 or Dover in 1298. Although bishops needed local knowledge in order to carry out many of the functions of diocesan government, the attributions of trustworthiness with which they validated that knowledge were, for the most part, theirs to make. When push came to shove bishops were powerful enough to be able to decide whose version of the truth was more likely to command consensus and achieve stability and durability. And because their institutional power was based on many attributions of trustworthiness, not just one, bishops could afford to make mistakes some of the time. Discovering that one group of 'trustworthy men' had failed to provide durable information did not substantially damage the institution of episcopal power. It merely prompted a reassertion of the symbolic role of the trustworthy men, just with different actual men involved. In this sense medieval bishops were rather like banks: they placed trust in many people without truly knowing how often their trust was misplaced. Default or malfeasance in a single case did not dent the power of the institution in the long run.[36] Medieval bishops were also cushioned from the effects of misplaced trust by the fact that they possessed the means to make public declarations about trustworthiness.

The boundaries of trustworthiness were sometimes policed with greater severity in order to demonstrate the extent of the bishop's power to define them. This was done by drawing upon the dichotomies of neighbours and strangers, orthodox and heretical. An example from the fight against lollardy in the late fourteenth century gives us a flavour of the highly symbolic reasoning employed. On 17 November 1389 William Smith, Roger Dexter, and Alice Dexter of Leicester were reconciled to the church. They had been convicted of heresy but now recanted. The seriousness of the crime and its social ramifications demanded that some ceremony and symbolism accompany their readmission to the church, and this was outlined in the documentation produced by Archbishop Courtenay's visitation. The preamble to his document cast lollardy as the revival of an ancient, primordial evil in the shape of a ravaging wolf preying upon the human heart 'which is known to be fickle in the faith'. The penitent heretics were said to have been discovered through the 'repugnant notoriety of the facts' and by the statements of the 'trustworthy and upright men of Leicester' who had been examined by the archbishop. At one level this text contrasted the infidelity of heretics with the fidelity, or staunch reliability, of the trustworthy witnesses. But since this was a record of penitents returning to the church, the target of its polemic was somewhat more comprehensive. The constancy of the trustworthy man was in fact being juxtaposed with the inherent suggestibility of the human heart (something we encountered in Chapter 3), which was fickle in the faith. This was a universal weakness. Those trustworthy burgesses of Leicester were supposedly the sort of people who were not so fickle: in their constancy they were not susceptible to the temptations of the ancient enemy.[37]

A similar implication was broadcast by Bishop Grandisson of Exeter a generation before Wycliffism had emerged to shake the English church. Grandisson had himself been a pupil of Jacques Fournier, the Paris theologian who had become bishop of Pamiers and a renowned inquisitor, before eventually being made Pope Benedict XII.[38] In 1354 Grandisson was alarmed to uncover heresy in his own diocese, and he was swift to act against it. Although we know next to nothing about the substance of the case, we do have the bishop's written instruction for his official to deal with Ralph Tremur, whose heresy he had heard about from trustworthy persons. Tremur's words were said to have led astray the simple, the untaught, those ignorant of theology, and those prone to heresy. As in Courtenay's formulation Grandisson made his contrast between trustworthiness and heresy stretch much further than the suspected individual. Heresy was dangerous because it arose from a weakness of the will that was especially prevalent among the simple, the untaught, and the ignorant. The bishop was referring to the laity as a whole in this sweeping aside, in terms that recall the words of the theologians I presented in Chapter 1, but it tacitly exempted his trustworthy informants.[39] A bishop's power was arguably at its apogee when dealing with heresy—the greatest threat to the church and a crime reserved for episcopal attention—and so such rhetoric served simultaneously to emphasize his control over the more positive symbolic role of the trustworthy man.

Was This Just a Hollow Rhetoric?

Given how consciously bishops elevated the symbolic role above the personal virtues of the trustworthy man, we should ask whether they were at all sincere in their use of the lexicon. When we read between the lines of the sources, episcopal reliance upon a symbolic role within an ideological structure potentially reveals a gaping absence at the centre of talk about trustworthiness. First we must acknowledge how normal it was for bishops to use trustworthy men in the service of their own interests. In 1321, for example, Bishop Sandale of Winchester used an inquest of trustworthy men to investigate dilapidations on his own estates (in Chapter 12 we will see that it was more normal for bishops to initiate inquests into the condition of other clerics' properties); in 1353 Archbishop Thoresby of York investigated a complaint from a clerk of his household in the same way; in 1409 Bishop Rede of Chichester wrote of how shocked he was to discover from trustworthy men that his own deer park had been raided; in 1477 Bishop Grey of Ely gave thanks for the 'trustworthy reports' he had heard about the character of his own kinsman John Grey; around 1480 the commissary court of the bishop of London appealed to trustworthy witnesses in its defence of one of its own officers who had been accused of adultery.[40]

Self-serving behaviour in institutions is perhaps to be expected, and is not necessarily at odds with sincerity, but trustworthiness was also invoked in circumstances where we can justifiably expect bishops to have known that it was nonsense. Inquests in support of papal dispensations to marry or to divorce constitute prime examples. A typical case might involve a bishop writing to the papal curia explaining that he had received the testimony of trustworthy persons confirming that the couple in question had married in ignorance of the fact that they were related to one another within the prohibited degrees of affinity or consanguinity.[41] Such investigations and conclusions are not, at face value, difficult to believe. But on closer inspection they are shot through with hypocrisy, touching all concerned. For example in 1344 William and Juliana Elys from Martley beside the river Teme on the edge of Worcester diocese had petitioned the pope to permit them to remain married and have their children counted as legitimate, following their discovery that William's mother had been Juliana's godmother at her confirmation by the bishop. This counted as 'spiritual incest' and made the marriage invalid. Trustworthy men, speaking under oath, told Bishop Bransford that these facts were true—both the prohibited relationship and the recent date of its discovery—and so he went ahead with the process for a dispensation, effectively permission to remain married despite the impediment.[42] However, it is simply implausible that William, Juliana, William's mother, their entire families, and the community that would later provide well-informed trustworthy testimony had all been ignorant of the crucial fact at the time of their marriage. They may have been unaware that god-parenthood constituted a prohibited relationship and an impediment to marriage, but this was a question of law, not of fact. Everyone concerned must have agreed to agree that they had not known about the god-parenthood until sometime after the marriage. It is easy to imagine the course of events in outline: William and Juliana wanted to marry, or their families were set on the idea; this was a small community and it was decided to brush aside the issue of god-parenthood; after the marriage some threat of legal action, perhaps from a potential rival heir, arose, making a papal dispensation seem like sensible insurance against the possible future disinheritance of the couple's children.

The concerns of the two families are easy to reconstruct, but why were the bishop and the pope prepared to believe such a clear fiction? Did this not do irreparable damage to the notion of trustworthiness? The local trustworthy men had not, presumably, made much of a fuss about common spiritual parenthood when the banns were being read. We have to conclude that such men could only be called trustworthy in the sense of doing what was expected of them. They did so twice. First they kept quiet, and later they spoke up: what more could they do? Their testimony was called into being by the bishop, and his action was required because the politics of marriage among the landed classes demanded it. Inheritance had to be protected as well as the sanctity of marriage. We have to conclude that for their bishop, it was more important to sustain marriage and the legitimacy of children (as well as to preserve relations with landed society) than it was to stand by the values of truth and honesty. This was not necessarily hypocrisy, just politics.[43]

Values are always clashing, in any society, but the language of trustworthiness could also serve as new clothes for naked power. At one level the massive extension of governance in the thirteenth century had brought large numbers of local people into new positions of responsibility. But the aim of this activity had always been to protect traditional forms of authority, which sometimes meant that the rhetoric of trustworthiness rang hollow. For example around 1230 William Percy had built a mill at Guisborough in the North Riding and tried to force his tenants to use it by holding their cattle and dray-horses to ransom. Percy was a powerful baron and one of the young King Henry III's major supporters. Archbishop Walter Gray made Percy promise to return the animals but added that if he could prove 'lawfully and by trustworthy witnesses' that the people of Guisborough were obliged to use his mill then the archbishop would enforce it. His tenants were in an invidious position: they received their draught animals back, but can have been under no illusions that such a powerful man would sooner or later find 'trustworthy' men to back his claim against them.[44] The secular nobility were learning this game of trustworthiness quickly, but they sometimes gave the whole thing away. In 1268 the bishop of Exeter complained about the treatment of Bodmin Priory at the hands of bailiffs working for Richard of Cornwall, here called by his putative title 'King of the Romans'. Richard's son, Henry of Almain, admitted the truth of the bishop's allegations, and promised that he would impose a 'suitable fine' on the wayward bailiffs and launch an inquiry to be conducted by himself or 'other trustworthy and prudent men above suspicion, acting at his command'.[45] In this appropriation of church rhetoric by a powerful aristocrat a dreadful tension is revealed between the exercise of authority and the pursuit of legitimacy through the language of impartiality. How could 'trustworthy and prudent men above suspicion' be found amongst those acting at the earl's command? The potential for abuse was compounded by the pressures upon trustworthy men to say what the powerful wanted to hear. At Kingston, Cambridgeshire, in 1458 trustworthy men told the bishop of Ely that the patronage of their church lay with King's College, but in 1462 the same men reported to their lord's court that he, and not the college, was the true patron of the church.[46] In such cases trustworthiness seems to have meant little more than being 'yes men'.

The story of Alice Kirkbride brings the suspicion of insincerity right to a bishop's door. Talk about trustworthy men could sometimes conceal a failure to act. Bishops could be particularly unwilling to move against powerful gentry families, taking to an extreme the kid-glove handling that was commonplace and to some extent expected. On 4 July 1340 Alice Kirkbride had appeared before Bishop Kirkby of Carlisle to make a complaint about her husband and to ask to be legally separated from him. Where divorce was not possible (that is where there was no legal impediment to marriage) separation permitted spouses to live apart while preventing their remarriage, and it was generally allowed only in cases of 'excessive' cruelty.[47] Alice had first been the wife of Walter Kirkbride, a local lord of relatively limited means. When he died in 1337 she said she had been persuaded to marry Thomas Lengleys. She and Thomas had given faith to one another and, she said, had loved each other equally, but he soon became violent and she came to believe that she had been wrong to marry him. She determined to try to escape. When the violence had become intolerable, Alice said, she had gone to Carlisle to live with an 'honest matron' and from there she had sued for a formal separation. Some people who thought they should stand by Alice spoke out about what he had done to her: cutting off her hair and some of her skin, hitting her so hard when she was pregnant that the child died, and breaking another of her children's backs.

We know about this domestic violence, however, only because Thomas called the denunciations slander and began a defamation case against the witnesses. As was the way with these things, this swung the force of canon law behind him as a plaintiff. Although Bishop Kirkby inquired into the truth of the so-called defamation through 'trustworthy persons', there was to be no rescue of Alice through the solidarity and conscience of the community. She had by now repeated the allegations herself, but for reasons that we will never know, she changed her story, coming to the bishop with her sister to confess that the accusations were false. This sad, but all too familiar, story might have ended there had not the court of York, which was the court of appeal for the northern province of the English church, deemed Bishop Kirkby to have worsened her situation by delaying justice and, in April 1342, ordered him to render it swiftly.[48]

The report of the case in Kirkby's register is perfunctory, and the rebuke he received following the success of Alice's appeal in York makes the invocation of 'trustworthy persons' look like a pretty pathetic fig leaf for inaction rather than the arrow for truth that it was meant to be.[49] The trustworthy, if they ever really existed in this case, appear only so as to allow the bishop to wash his hands of the matter. One might suppose that such uses of trustworthy rhetoric diminished its credibility: it was supposed to create a feeling that truth had been reached and that no-one could have done more. Had Alice heard it at any stage she would surely have been unimpressed, to say the least (*trustworthy men!?*). And indeed, the priorities of bishops were not always well-aligned with the best interests of their people, a fact that is brought home by comparing Alice's experience with that of a prize hunting bird a few years later. When Sir William Lengleys, kinsman of the wife-beating Thomas Lengleys, lost his falcon, he prevailed upon the bishop of Carlisle to have proclamations for its return made in all the churches of the city. The bishop even offered to excommunicate anyone harbouring this no-doubt magnificent bird.[50] But because, as I have already suggested, a bishop's power was akin to that of a bank, he could lose a certain amount of political capital in one ill-judged transaction, without incurring a fatal collapse of public trust in the judgements he provided. The value of trustworthy men lay primarily in their capacity to fulfil a symbolic role in the service of episcopal power.

⟨⟶⟶⟩⟨⟶⟶⟩

Trustworthiness was, from the institutional point of view, all about creating an impression of consensus and impartiality. It was a characteristic attributed to real people, but its strength derived from the integrity of the symbolic role (it was difficult to disagree about the solicitation of trustworthy testimony), and not from the integrity of any one person to whom trustworthiness was attributed. Bishops understood that they were not seeking the most honest or virtuous collaborators from among their parishioners. Asked what a trustworthy man was, a late medieval bishop might have answered that it was someone whose standing in his community was a guarantee of the information he provided. It was a man who could not be gainsaid. It was a man who knew what was required of him.

CHAPTER SIX

Very Local Elites

IN THE SPRING of 1444 six men trudged at the head of a procession in the shadow of Dent parish church in North Yorkshire. They were barefooted, wearing just their undershirts, each carrying a candle. The clergy were in their vestments, accompanied by the dean of Kendal and Lonsdale, and the banners of the parish hung from poles. The first penitent was John Hogeson, who was flogged while walking nine times around the church. Then came Richard and William Pereson, flogged four times around the church, and finally William Leke and two members of the Syggiswick family, John and Gilbert, each flogged three times around the church. The men from Dent had been sentenced to this humiliation by the vicar-general of York for their parts in an exchange of insults and blows the previous year. Because they had brawled in the churchyard at Dent, and because blood had been spilled, the cemetery would have to be reconsecrated and an example set. Such things worked through shame, spectacle, and memory.[1] The archdeacon of Richmond and the vicar-general in York wanted the locals to remember what had brought them to this moment, and to create memories of dishonour that would mould future behaviour. Local attitudes and relationships shaped the unfolding events too.

A delegation of indigenous trustworthy men had reported to York: the fight had started, they said, when William Leke insulted Adam Pereson in the churchyard, perhaps as they came out of church. Robert Syggiswick pulled a knife on Pereson, who retaliated in kind. The two families waded in and bystanders got caught up in the confusion. Richard Pereson and William Pereson junior attacked Gilbert Syggiswick with sticks. John son of Robert Hogeson hit George Mason, spilling his blood on consecrated ground. John Syggiswick uttered more malicious words but, reportedly, did not assault anyone. It must have been hard to assign responsibility within the small crowd involved in this affray. Nonetheless there are some striking inconsistencies between the account of the trustworthy men and the decisions of the vicar-general. Robert Syggiswick, who drew a knife, did not do penance while Gilbert Syggiswick, who is mentioned only as the victim of an attack, did. Some of the dynamics of these events, and the contours of local politics and society, begin to emerge if we examine the status of the participants and the relationships between them, subjects that will be examined in detail throughout this chapter.

The 'trustworthy men of Dent' who had investigated on behalf of the archdeacon were John Coupestake, John Mason of Myers, William Couestake of Alanhous, Henry Hogeson, Christopher of Burton, Nicholas Garnet, John Welan, John Fauzet, Richard of Lounde, William Trotter, William of Stokdale, and Richard Hogeson senior. Six of them can be identified in the estate records of the Fitzhugh family who were lords of Dent and Sedbergh (besides several other Yorkshire and Westmorland manors). In addition we can use these records to say something about the men involved in the fight, and how the whole community was affected by it.[2]

Those we can identify formed a clear local elite, involved in the management of the Fitzhugh estates as bailiffs and rent collectors, and conspicuous for their peasant wealth and standing. They must have dominated the inquiry. John Mason had been lord Fitzhugh's rent collector in Dent in 1422 and 1425; he was related to one of the victims in the fight: George Mason. Richard of Lound was a bailiff of the Fitzhugh manorial court at Dent in 1422 and 1424–25 alongside his kinsman Robert, while William and Henry of Lound were also bailiffs in 1439–40. Office-holding was in the blood. William Trotter was one of the lord's rent collectors in 1422, and he sat in the middle-rank of rent-paying tenants in Dent in 1425; a relative called John Trotter was part of a landholding consortium in 1438–39 which included three of the other 'trustworthy men' from this case. John Welan was rent collector for all the northern Fitzhugh manors between 1437 and 1440, and a relative of his called Richard had also been the collector. Richard Hogeson senior was clearly part of a prominent local peasant family: he was renting a newly enclosed pasture from the lord in 1437–38 and 1439–40, and in 1451 he was a juror in the inquest into the patronage of Sedbergh church along with two other Hogesons, several esquires, and the local clergy; Roger Hogeson, the father of one of the brawlers, was bailiff of the court at Dent in 1437–38, and as we have seen another relative, Henry Hogeson, also served as a trustworthy man of the inquest. The livelihoods of Welan and Hogeson were also entwined with each other, and with that of John Fauzet, who together held land in Dent in the late 1430s.[3]

John Fauzet, the sixth identifiable trustworthy man, was a substantial peasant landholder in Sedbergh and Dent, and a member of another dominant local family. In 1457 the Fauzets (or 'Fawsids'), including John, made up a high proportion of lord Fitzhugh's tenants at Sedbergh, and by 1469 landholding and the manor court there were dominated by the family. Though they often broke the by-laws and were fined small amounts, they also regularly provided manorial officers from the 1420s to the 1460s. They served as affeerors setting the fines levied by the court, as rent collectors filing accounts with the lord, and even on one occasion as the bailiff of the whole wapentake. They were clearly making the most of their opportunities wherever they could. In 1469 they held seven out of eighteen customary tenures in Sedbergh, almost all bunched at the top of the scale in terms of rental value, and out of thirty-six pledges providing surety for men and women entering into tenancies, thirty-one were Fauzets. John himself was a pledge (or 'borowe') six times.[4]

Three of the men who did penance for their parts in the churchyard brawl—John Hogeson, and John and Gilbert Syggiswick—therefore seem to have been junior members of prominent local families. George Mason, one of the victims, was also related to a leading member of Dent Dale peasant society. There was a relatively small circle of dominant office-holders in this community and their lives interlocked as tenants, office-holders, parishioners, and neighbours. They could not, it seems, tolerate the involvement of their relatives in such unseemly happenings. Local office-holding depended upon respectability, and sometimes the only way this could be protected was to deal harshly with the faults closest to home.[5] The position of trustworthy men was such that they could not always, though surely they often did, cover up for their kin.

The action taken by the trustworthy men of Dent was intended to secure their own position and to repair the equilibrium of life, and it is clear that they were defined by several of the inequalities that divided late medieval society. The first of these is the most obvious: they were 'trustworthy'. But to what extent did this depend upon or contribute to any of the other inequalities of late medieval life? Was it related to inequalities that involved attributions of worth based on gender, age, or family? How was it connected to the unequal possession of income, wealth, and the opportunities to acquire them? These questions are all clearly linked, not least because the variables concerned affected one another, but they also need to be given separate consideration. None of them was simple, even those that were practically inescapable, such as gender. In tracing the social and economic profile of those who served on inquests and at visitation as trustworthy men, this chapter gauges how the qualities imagined by bishops were realised in practice. For the most part the trustworthy men were drawn from very local elites comprising the wealthier, more substantial, peasants, but the presence of lower-status *fidedigni* is also notable, and the balance between them will figure in the discussion.[6]

Sometimes the things bishops said about the trustworthy men hint at a broadly representative ideal. For example in 1536 the bishop of Hereford sent out an order for parish representatives to be summoned to attend his visitation, indicating that they might come from the whole breadth of the parish (*multitudine*) or a limited section (*paucitatem*); they might merely be the inhabitants or people of a parish, so long as they were trustworthy men (*fide dignos*).[7] The bishop's order allowed for all eventualities, but what was the normal profile of a trustworthy man? Was he 'old and rich' (*senum et divitum*), as a document of 1349 would have it, or was a wider cross section of the parish capable of acting in this symbolic role?[8] As we shall see, despite the inclusion of some poor men amongst the trustworthy, this did not mean they were perfectly representative of their parishes. Moreover, being reliant upon trustworthiness made the church dependent upon inequality, an argument whose foundations will be laid here and developed in Chapters 7 to 9.

There is wide recognition amongst social and economic historians that peasant society in the later Middle Ages was stratified in complex ways, and the existence of very local elites has been noted in many different regions. These were men who held more land than their neighbours, or were engaged in longer-distance trade, or who dominated formal and informal local offices.[9] As our knowledge increases with more and more case studies, historians have begun to understand just how important apparently small distinctions in wealth and status were in structuring society. Accordingly my aim here is to say something as precise as possible about the social status of trustworthy men in relation to their fellow parishioners. When it comes to office-holding many studies of medieval and early modern English villages have been content with impressionistic assessments of status, and have made little of the inequality upon which it rested, often making use of the curious sixteenth-century phrase 'the middling sort'. It is hard to deny the expediency of a contemporary term of such latitude, but its usefulness depends entirely on the scale at which one views society. Wealthy merchants and the county gentry are 'middling' in relation to the nobility and the peasantry, but if the category includes yeomen and artisans as well, as it often does, then its analytical utility must be in doubt.[10] We have to make an effort to be more precise if we are to understand how the sociology of the trustworthy affected their capacity to fulfil the symbolic role demarcated by churchmen. The crucial scale for our analysis must be the individual parish, where a small number of 'the faithful' were designated *fidedigni* from time to time. How did this designation intersect with the multiple inequalities that structured late medieval life?

Although most references to trustworthy men do not permit their identification, we are fortunate in that a substantial minority of visitation returns and certifications of inquests named the men through whom an investigation had been conducted, and sometimes included other details such as their ages, legal status, occupations, administrative experience, and family connections. Gender is of course apparent from names. When and where these lists coincide with manorial documents and the records of royal taxation, it is possible to find out more about trustworthy men and move beyond single measures of status which, as Amartya Sen writes, can provide only a 'quasi-ordering' of social distinctions.[11] Some simple statistical tests will permit the comparison of different groups of trustworthy men according to how they stood in relation to the rest of the parish that they represented. This will help build up a picture of the trustworthy men as very local elites whose profile varied from place to place.

Gender, Age, and Legal Status

There are few explicit references to trustworthy women serving on inquest or visitation juries: institutional trustworthiness was systematically gendered male. This was despite the acknowledged capacity of women to make promises upon their faith, and to see faith as an essential aspect of their identity and experience, as we saw in Chapters 2 and 3, while the ability of women to act as witnesses in court (see Chapter 5) did not translate into this other symbolic role. The institutional exclusion of women from inquest and visitation panels does, however, point to public promises being heavily gendered in practice, something whose implications will be discussed at length in Chapter 9 where the experience of living face-to-face with the trustworthy men will be described. I have been able to find only a handful of instances in which women were described with the adjective *fidedigna*, and only one of these comes from a routine inquest: a late thirteenth-century inquiry into the life and character of an aspiring rector, in which Matilda Houlyng 'appeared as a proxy for her husband Robert' along with five clerics and five trustworthy men.[12] This suggests that Robert was a regular witness, substituted by Matilda when he was unavailable. The other few instances confirm how exceptional women's trustworthiness was to the institutional mind. Two female witnesses to the posthumous miracles of Simon de Montfort, erstwhile leader of the baronial revolt against Henry III, were described as *fidedignae* by the monks of Evesham in the 1260s. Alice of Canterbury had appealed to Simon for aid after her four-year-old son was badly injured in a fire, while 'a certain trustworthy lady' attributed the miraculous recovery of a prize peacock to his intercession.[13] These two women were witnesses only to their own experience, not to the collective or communal truth that trustworthy *men* were expected to report, a limitation that we see in some of the other, rare, cases. In 1466 one of King Edward IV's household servants went to court to prove that he was betrothed to Alice Walle; she denied this and was required to purge herself with 'six trustworthy women who had the fullest knowledge of her actions in this matter'. In 1477 Agnes Goode of Hartlebury in Worcestershire purged herself with 'honest and trustworthy women of her neighbourhood', of the charge that she had three illegitimate children with a butcher from Worcester.[14] This tendency for women to be allowed to testify only to the experience of their own bodies, either as victims of rape or as eyewitnesses, was common to many medieval jurisdictions.[15]

The fact of female unsuitability is brought crushingly home in the remarkable example of an inquest at Withernsea on the Yorkshire coast in 1444, when eighty-six parishioners were questioned, of whom just two were women: even at their most inclusive church inquests excluded women.[16] The root cause of this discrimination was the sad fact that women could be gainsaid too easily. The information they provided, except in a few special areas of expertise, was unlikely to be reliable because it could be contradicted with ease.[17] Of course, institutional pragmatism on this issue was also one of the main reasons for the persistence of prejudice against women in representative roles in the first place: misogyny in the social realm and misogyny in the institutional realm were therefore causally connected, each reinforcing the other.

Even so, trustworthiness could not be claimed by all men. One of the principal limiting factors seems to have been age, with a premium placed on long memories. Of course memory was a craft practised by everyone, but the recovery of local knowledge and custom was a specific realm of expertise dominated by the older male inhabitants of a place.[18] Sometimes bishops spelled out their preference for older informants, echoing St Paul's praise for elders who were 'sober, chaste, prudent, and sound in faith' (Titus 2.2). In the case of the church of Burford, Shropshire, in 1326 for example, where three rectors each in possession of a 'portion' of the rectory could not agree on who had responsibility for the care of souls, the bishop of Hereford summoned an inquest of the interested parties, some clergy from neighbouring churches, and the *older* inhabitants of the parish as well as other trustworthy sworn men. By specifying the participation of the older inhabitants the bishop sought to avoid any claim that new duties were being imposed through wilful ignorance of past practice.[19] Similarly, a complicated patronage case from Northumberland in 1436 was to be investigated by 'vicars and other suitable chaplains together with such trustworthy and older secular men who better know the truth of the matter'.[20]

References to older witnesses are couched in terms that suggest that they came forward and identified themselves as such without any special prompting by the bishop. In 1272, or thereabouts, the archbishop of York was sent responses from some 'elder neighbours' who had been questioned in a synod about the rights of patronage and means of support for a rector and vicar in Gargrave.[21] In 1313 Master John from Sedgefield in County Durham was trying to dispel rumours that the woman he lived with was his lover and not his sister, as he claimed. Master John's version was eventually established as true through the testimony of trustworthy, especially older, men in his place of birth. John and Agnes were said to be known throughout the neighbourhood as brother and sister.[22] In 1442 the parishioners of Holy Trinity in Exeter had said that 'according to their elders, in whom they trusted', their church had never been polluted by bloodshed or sexual activity. In 1511 John Wellis from Wanstead (then in Essex) referred to 'the older and more senior people in his parish, some of whom had since died, and whose words he trusted to contain the truth'.[23] Longevity and respect for elders (even if grudging) spoke to the constancy that bishops desired in trustworthy men, even if the traditions they confirmed were in fact rather more malleable.[24]

But how old was old? This is more of a vexed question than it might at first appear. There were various assumptions about aging that may have influenced bishops' thinking. Depending on context and purpose schematic divisions of the life course placed the onset of old age anywhere between thirty-five and seventy-two.[25] In cases where informants gave their age we can see what 'older' meant to the people who had to interpret bishops' orders. The 1442 inquest into the status of Holy Trinity church in Exeter, referred to above, began with a question about the ages of the witnesses and the duration of their residence in the parish. The first witness was unusually precise about his age—seventy-six—but he counted his time in the parish at a nice round forty years. All the other witnesses gave their ages in round numbers: fifty, forty, seventy, forty, and eighty.[26] The propensity to give round numbers was often compounded by age inflation. Trustworthy witnesses inquiring into the building of a private chapel at Soulbury, Buckinghamshire, in 1303 supposedly numbered one man aged forty 'or more', six men aged sixty or more, two men aged eighty or more, and two aged one hundred or more.[27] How much credence should we give to these figures?

In his study of 'proof of age' juries between 1377 and 1414 Joel Rosenthal found that only 5 percent of jurors were less than forty-five years old.[28] The largest cohort (46 percent) was aged between fifty-five and fifty-nine. Although the age structure of medieval populations is difficult to establish, the data on age at death acquired from burial archaeology prompt caution about accepting such documentary claims of age. It is difficult for osteologists to establish age at death from skeletal remains beyond the age of about forty-six years, but even so it is striking that the analysis of remains from medieval parish churchyards and hospital cemeteries suggests that only 9 percent of people died beyond that age.[29] This does not mean that no-one could have reached the age of eighty or one hundred, but we should be wary. It seems unlikely that a single village could produce six sexagenarians, two octogenarians, and two centenarians. If Rosenthal's figures represent real ages then it would seem that the vast majority of his jurors (95 percent) were drawn from the oldest 10 percent of the population. This could of course have been accurate, but ages were reckoned in relative rather than absolute terms and there was a strong cultural association between elder status and social credibility. We should therefore probably assume a degree of age inflation generally.

As we saw in the previous chapter men were able to litigate or serve as witnesses in the common-law and church courts only if they were legally free. But when it came to representing their parishes in visitations and inquests legal status did not matter.[30] In fact, when bishops wanted witnesses to local conditions they could not have excluded men who were not free because some of the most substantial peasants, in all regions, could in some sense be said to be 'unfree'. In the broad swathe of 'champion' countryside stretching from the Dorset coast through the midlands and into northeastern England, character-ized by open fields, arable cultivation, nucleated villages, and strong manorial lordship, there were many places where in 1300 as much as three-fifths of the peasant tenants were unfree, though this changed over the next two hundred years, as we shall see in Chapter 8.[31]

A complicating factor is that it was often hard to tell exactly where indi-viduals sat along the hazy spectrum of legal status. Though the common law had, from the late thirteenth century, framed such questions in black-and-white terms, the reality was always more shaded. Lawsuits that hinged upon someone's status as a villein (thereby barring them from a variety of activities) reveal huge disagreement over exactly what facts of tenure, birth, or custom were indicators of freedom and unfreedom. Labour services and customary payments made to a lord created a presumption of villeinage in some regions but not in others, and the differences could be very local indeed.[32] An exam-ination of the manor court rolls from those places for which we have named trustworthy men provides some clear-cut evidence, but also a good deal that is more equivocal. For example the visitation representatives of Chalbury in Dorset in 1394 included a man called Richard Wiltshire who held customary land 'at the lord's will'. This is a phrase that indicates villein status in most circumstances. But Richard disputed his liability for some of the payments and services arising from this, and as one of the richest men in the village he would strain most definitions of unfree. John Smith, another of the Chalbury representatives, paid some minor tolls and fees to the lord, and even owed labour services in return for one three-acre plot of land, all of which would suggest unfree status, but a manorial court roll explicitly names him among the free tenants.[33]

One class of estates where the canon law preference for free witnesses would have been impossible to meet were those of the major abbeys and other wealthy churchmen, which imposed villeinage more stringently and retained it longer than many of their secular counterparts. The manors belonging to the bishops of Winchester are a case in point. Most of the tenants were classed as villeins, the lord's administration was strong, and demesne cultivation de-pended heavily on labour services. When in 1310 there was a dispute over the apportionment of tithes between the churches of Marwell and Twyford, both of them Winchester manors in Hampshire, Bishop Woodlock ordered an in-quest through trustworthy men. Most of the fifteen who were called can be shown to have been villeins, though they were drawn from across the spec-trum of rural wealth. From the prosperous Walter Bole and William le Sedare to the notably land-poor Henry Coke and John le Long, these trustworthy men were liable for labour services and paid the customary marriage and death duties ('merchet' and 'heriot') to their lord.[34]

Family and Occupation

Local positions of responsibility sometimes ran in families. Although the elites of medieval villages were never reproduced entirely along dynastic lines, the repetition of surnames among trustworthy men and other jurors over time indicates that family was important in qualifying someone to represent their community. It is possible here to draw upon a large body of historical research into the patterns of office-holding in medieval English villages based on the records of manorial courts. There are many historians for whom the appearance of multiple members of the same family in important local roles is evidence of an elite, or even an oligarchy, dominating village affairs over long periods of time.[35] But on the other hand there are those who see a much more meritocratic social environment in the same evidence; one based on communal values and either a sense of egalitarianism or the acceptance of a natural order.[36] The precise balance between these alternative interpretations will be considered in the following chapter, but there is certainly evidence to ponder when it comes to trustworthy men. For example Henry atte Thorne and his son John were both visitation representatives for Clyst Honiton in Devon in 1381.[37] Robert and William Taylor both served at Wimborne St Giles in Dorset in 1394.[38] At Blandford Forum in the same year, Thomas and Richard Helier were visitation representatives; Thomas was also the bailiff of the manor court, while Richard was one of its chief pledges.[39] The Pauntley family of Culmington in Shropshire provided parish representatives in 1347 and 1475, litigating against the rector in the earlier case and staffing an inquest into patronage in the latter. The Ballard family of Hartlebury, Worcestershire, provided visitation representatives repeatedly throughout the fifteenth century.[40] Longevity in a place was an important constituent of trustworthiness, the antithesis of the vagrancy that was associated with untrustworthiness in the Old Testament: 'Who will trust him that has no resting-place, who lodges wherever the night takes him, and as a robber . . . lurches from place to place?'[41] Physical stability across generations contributed to the constancy that bishops and judges ascribed to the ideal witness.

Very occasionally there are suggestions that the characteristics associated with trustworthiness—respectability, prosperity, long-standing residence, incontrovertibility—were acknowledged in surnames. There are of course plenty of medieval surnames that derive from specific offices like reeve, bailiff, and constable, but Thomas Prudomme, a parish representative at Culmstock in Devon in 1301, and Adam Triewe or Trowe at Twyford, Hampshire, in 1310 may have been members of families who had once established a more general reputation as creditable and suitable for service in such roles, whether designated as a *prudhomme* (for which see Chapter 4) or simply 'true'.[42] There certainly seems to have been an expectation that certain families would always be represented in some places. For example at Friesthorpe in Lincolnshire almost every semiannual inquest between 1337 and 1349 included Thomas Francis, but in the autumn of 1345, when he did not serve, he was replaced by someone described as Thomas Francis junior; in nearby Glentham the two Adam Walshes, senior and junior, served together three times; and in Scredington Peter Merchant and his son John took turns to serve.[43] One can imagine these families and others like them insisting on their rights, and, conversely, feeling the sting of ignominy if they fell from favour with the other leading families.

If family was an important facet of institutional trustworthiness, it would seem that occupation was not. A 1328 letter from the bishop of Exeter making an implicit contrast between trustworthy men and others 'indecently' running alehouses in the 'search for filthy profit' (*turpis lucri questus*) does not signal any wider exclusion of merchants and traders from the role, despite the pervasive moral condemnation of profit and commerce in sermons.[44] The majority of trustworthy men whose occupation we know were engaged in agricultural production, and from the size of their operations we can deduce that some were engaged in marketing considerable volumes of grain, wool, or livestock. We also have some direct evidence that merchants could act as parish representatives, such as a group of clothiers at Salisbury in 1394 or William Potter the 'mercer' at Blandford Forum in the same year.[45] It is harder to discover much about the extent of involvement in minor craft trades, but we know that a lot of trustworthy men were reported for breaching the assize of ale, indicating that brewing was common as an additional source of income. We also have occasional direct evidence of craft employment: at Norwich in 1303 the trustworthy included two glovers and a tailor, while at Blandford Forum in 1394 two had been listed as artisans in the 1381 poll tax lists.[46] As we saw in Chapter 5, bishops sometimes demanded men with the expertise necessary to assess the extent and cost of buildings repairs during inquests into liability for maintaining churches and rectories. When for example we read that the trustworthy men of Nymet Tracy in Devon who gathered in 1447 to inspect the rectory buildings included two labourers, two carpenters, and a thatcher, it is clear that trades expertise—rather than status—was what was valued. A similar case from Lanteglos-by-Camelford in Cornwall the same year called upon the testimony of three stonemasons and a roofer as well as other trustworthy men.[47] Given that a substantial minority of our trustworthy men were, as we shall see, too poor or unimportant to appear in manorial or tax records, it is likely that trustworthiness did not exclude those who worked for wages, just as it did not exclude those who worked for profit.

Office-Holding

One of the salient characteristics of trustworthy men was that they were frequently local office-holders. At one level this is unremarkable. There were many offices connected with manorial and village administration, some more formal than others (being a trustworthy man seems to have lain at the less formal end of the spectrum, without ongoing responsibilities between the moments when their services were called upon). Someone had to perform all these tasks, and so it is not surprising that on occasion this was a person who went on to represent his parish as a trustworthy man. However, as we saw in the case of 1440s Dent Dale above, groups of trustworthy men could be dominated by such local office-holders. There we found bailiffs (day-to-day management), affeerors (setting fines), and pledges (providing guarantees of other people's behaviour) in the manor court, as well as rent collectors working across several manors and a bailiff of a whole wapentake. To a great extent this was a common feature of inquests, from the late thirteenth century to the late fifteenth.[48]

A wood ward headed a list of trustworthy men in Maplederwell, Hampshire, in 1314, attesting to the patronage of a chantry chapel and the qualifications of its priest. He said that he had seen a charter made by Ela, the daughter of the earl of Salisbury (the previous lord of Maplederwell), sometime between 1272 and 1297. Along with other parishioners he had heard it read out in English, and he remembered its contents.[49] This glimpse of a sturdy local office-holder speaking up for local memory is not unique. 'Walter the steward' was one of the visitation representatives for Wingham in Kent in 1294; he may well have been Walter of Basing, bailiff of the archbishop's estate in the 1270s and styled Walter Seneschal in the 1280s.[50]

William Abbay was one of the most important men in Shapwick, Dorset, over a period of almost thirty years: in the early 1380s he had leased the whole manor from the lord of Shapwick, and in 1397 he was the lord's hayward, agent, and receiver; it was in 1394 that he was a leading figure on the panel of trustworthy men representing Shapwick before Bishop Waltham's visitation, and during Henry IV's reign Abbay also regularly served as a presentment juror in the manor court. He would have been responsible for reporting the offences of his neighbours and, crucially, deciding what was worth reporting in the first place. The manorial and hundred court rolls also show that he was active as a creditor and guarantor of other people's debts. One entry in 1410 suggests he had bought up the lord's debts in order to manage them himself, presumably at a profit. The last we hear of him is as the lessee of a fishery on the river Stour in 1417. An entry in the court rolls for 1412 records that Abbay breached the assize of ale, which meant in practice that he was paying a licence to sell ale in greater measures than strictly allowed. He was not alone in this, but the identities of the other 'offenders' are revealing: they were the current lessee of the manorial demesne lands, the reeve, and the constable of the village. Abbay was well-connected within the bounds of his parish: a big fish in a small pond. As such he was certainly more influential than his fellow parish representatives in 1394, of whom two, John Bayly and Walter Rede, occasionally acted as jurors for the assizes or the manorial court, but were otherwise known only for being debtors.[51]

When a group of habitual local office-holders acted together as trustworthy men, the effect of their double status could be considerable. The men who served on the inquest into the patronage of Kingston parish church (Cambridgeshire) in 1458 were drawn from four different places: Cambridge, Kingston, Caldecote, and Toft. The men from Cambridge and Caldecote are difficult to identify in the surviving sources, but most of the men of Kingston and Toft were tenants of the manor of Kingston St George, where the Chamberlain family were lords. Records of the manor and 'leet' court from the 1460s show a group of trustworthy men dominated by manorial presentment jurors with significant local responsibilities.[52] Richard Madingley, Thomas Ward, Robert Ward, Thomas Borley, and William Adam were all presentment jurors in Kingston St George throughout the 1460s. Thomas and Robert Ward were on occasion affeerors, while Thomas Borlay was an ale-taster, responsible for regulating the sale of beer. It is notable that the trustworthy men from Toft were in a slightly lower league. They were never presentment jurors or manorial officers, and we hear about them only as the owners of stray animals. The jurors of Kingston dominated the leet court, while the men of Toft were merely subject to its authority. Since they rarely provided jurors, it is unlikely the men from Toft could have made their voices heard when they acted alongside their overbearing counterparts as trustworthy men in 1458.[53]

However, office-holding and trustworthiness were double-edged. The potential for this is suggested by the presence in a group of Norwich trustworthy men, adjudicating a tithe dispute in 1303, of the intriguingly named William le Ponderaticer.[54] This is a scribe's French rendition of the English 'ponder': the man responsible for keeping the town's weights and measures. Local offices such as this brought power and prestige, but also subjected men to higher-than-usual levels of public scrutiny.[55] Weighing goods and money in the market and weighing the truth in a lawsuit could easily see one fall foul of wider opinion, and bishops may have welcomed the involvement of men who had a position to maintain, thinking that they would not wish to fall foul of either the local community or the church authorities: but then again, perhaps such men were primarily useful because they could easily beat down the flames of gossip and command local opinion.

Trustworthy men also participated in the lowest rungs of royal government, serving as sub-taxers responsible for assessing their neighbours' tax liability, which brought great local power: they could decide the levels at which taxpayers were assessed and who would be exempt because of poverty, opening up opportunities for favours and petty corruption as well as the risk of tension and conflict. At Buckland in Buckinghamshire the visitation representatives in 1338 included two men who had been sub-taxers in 1332.[56] Of the men who represented the Lincolnshire parishes of Strubby, Friesthorpe, Glentham,

Hainton, and Searby between 1337 and 1349 a total of fourteen served as sub-taxers in 1340.[57] Two men each from Ide and Clyst Honiton in Devon who were visitation representatives in 1381 had acted as sub-taxers in assessing the 1377 poll tax.[58] The concentration of manorial, royal, and parochial offices in the hands of a few men was a recurring fact of life. It benefitted those men who could perform ambidextrously across various jurisdictions, enjoying a degree of access to power sources beyond the village. From the perspective of institutions, office-holding made the *fidedigni* hard to contradict, and this, as we shall see, was a key component of pragmatic trusting. It could affect what the trustworthy men said, either because they were sensitive to their position in local society or, equally, because they possessed enormous sway amongst their neighbours. This is a theme to which we shall return in the following chapter, and throughout Part IV.

Landholding

Landholding was a major component of status in the period we are examining, even amongst the peasantry, and although it can only be a proxy measure for a person's wealth and standing, it is a very good place to start. A complete analysis of the landholding of trustworthy men in relation to the rest of their parish is not possible, at least not directly. It is impossible to find every person mentioned in a list of trustworthy men in manorial records, because there was often more than one manor within a given parish, and the peasants most often mentioned in court rolls were the villein tenants of a lord. So even where some records survive they rarely present the whole picture.[59] And then if there were landless trustworthy men they would not show up in any manorial or taxation records. Nevertheless, our information on landholding is extremely valuable and cannot be ignored. Some strong impressions do emerge, which will be tested by further analyses of rents and taxes as additional proxy assessments of wealth and standing.

Foremost among the impressions derived from the records of landholding is the range in the resources possessed by trustworthy men. A perhaps surprising number of smallholders are attested. The fifteen trustworthy men who formed the inquest into the allocation of tithes at Twyford, Hampshire, in 1310 referred to above included John le Long and Henry Coke. Coke seems to have possessed only a messuage (a house and garden) and four acres, which was a very small plot by the standards of the time. John le Long's holdings were even more modest, comprising a single acre that was subdivided among his sons after his death around 1312. For macroeconomic historians such holdings have become, in aggregate, an illustration of population pressure and declining living standards at the start of the great European famine.[60] As individuals, Coke and Le Long must have made a living from wage labour on the lands of some of their better-off neighbours. Among these they might have looked to two other men of the 1310 inquest: Walter Bole and William le Sedare. These major tenants each held at least two virgates of arable land, that is, about sixty acres or more, on which they must have employed wage labour.[61]

The presence of men from opposite ends of the peasant landholding spectrum in one inquest does not, on its own, demonstrate that trustworthiness was blind to distinctions of wealth, but it is striking nonetheless. However, while it was not uncommon for a few of the poorest to serve as trustworthy men, it was unusual for the most substantial tenants to be routinely excluded. Although canon lawyers and churchmen did not, as we saw in Chapter 5, say very much about poverty disqualifying witnesses, this was a prevalent opinion among English common lawyers, which is likely to have influenced local determinations of fitness to serve.[62]

In another area of 'champion' England a generation earlier, around 1280, signs of the agricultural intensification that would lead to population pressure in the 1310s were beginning to show. The managers of Peterborough Abbey's estates in Northamptonshire were taking advantage of rising wool prices by leasing out their arable land and buying up meadow and pasture suitable for sheep from their richer tenants. One of these men was Richard son of Stephen from Irthlingborough, a wealthy farmer in possession of at least six and a half virgates of land (about two hundred acres), who sold some of this to the abbey in the 1280s. In the 1301 lay subsidy (the prevalent form of royal taxation) Richard was estimated to have goods and an agricultural surplus worth almost two pounds. One hundred and twenty-nine householders in Irthlingborough were assessed as having less taxable wealth than he did, only seven as having more. He was an important tenant of the abbey, and active in the local land market. Richard was subletting small parcels of land to his neighbours and receiving some rents by the hand of the abbey's reeve. Getting the monastic administration to work for him in this way meant that Richard was the sort of man who could not be ignored when there were questions to answer about local matters. In 1281 the bishop of Lincoln wanted to know about the character and suitability of an Irthlingborough man whom the monks were promoting as their candidate for the benefice of nearby Clopton. They interviewed seven trustworthy men, beginning with Richard. The other witnesses fell into line and merely confirmed his statement. This was a man who could not be disregarded: he embodied constancy in Irthlingborough.[63]

Status and landholding had a strong relationship, but one heavily determined by regional differences. Wingham was the archbishop of Canterbury's largest estate in Kent and the administrative centre of one of the seven bailiwicks into which his estates were divided between 1292 and 1295. This rearrangement of administrative units had been presaged by the conduct of an extensive survey in 1283–85 which sought to itemize the often minute payments and services owed to the lord archbishop. The estate covered about twenty square miles and encompassed many scattered settlements where the archbishop's property and rights were tangled up with those of many other lords and freeholders. In 1286 Wingham had also become a collegiate church. The incoming provost and canons were given some lands and income from tithes and granted a large degree of autonomy from ordinary episcopal power. But this led to complaints, and a visitation was launched in 1294 while the archbishopric was vacant. The visitation roll records the names of twenty-six lay parish representatives for the various settlements, and we can learn something about the landholding of twelve of them from the 1283–85 survey.[64]

The representatives of the churches around Wingham came from the elite of free tenants. Some enjoyed a status that elsewhere in England would be called gentility.[65] In Kent, where commerce was more developed and the population more dense than in some other regions, the lower and middle bands of peasant wealth were filled with those families holding five to ten, and ten to fifteen acres of land, respectively.[66] Of our twelve identifiable lay parishioners, most sit comfortably above these categories, while circumstances suggest that the two who fall into the middle band in fact punched above their weight. Paul of Snakestone, acting on behalf of Ash church, had total recorded holdings of about nine acres in 1283–85, but these comprised numerous minute portions and sub-tenancies, suggesting one of the 'individual histories of enterprise' associated with rising families in the region.[67] Richard of Deane, acting for Wingham church, does not appear in the estate survey in his own right, but his son John, who was the reeve in 1273–74, is said to have held twelve and three-quarter acres. However, Richard's possession of an eighth of a knight's fee in Deane puts him in a different bracket to others with similar resources, obliging him to attend the county court: a burden to be sure, but also an opportunity for building status.[68]

No identifiable parish visitation representatives from Wingham came from the lower band of Kentish landholding. This does not exclude the possibility of involvement from that group since fourteen of the men could not be identified. Some of these may have been smallholders or even landless men. However, it is equally likely that many of the fourteen unidentifiable men had landholdings outside the archbishop's lands. Like Richard Deane the obligation to attend the county court also fell upon those tenants holding the peculiarly Kentish title 'shireman'; men who have been called 'knights in embryo'.[69] There were four such families in Overland, of whom two, the Bridges and the Cooks, provided visitation representatives in 1294.[70] Holding shireland is likely to have raised their profile above that of their equals in wealth, making them not only important tenants but also men known and recognized in local administrative circles. The other lay representatives can either be identified in their own right as substantial peasant tenants, or as members of significant local families.[71]

These three case studies from the decades either side of 1300—in Hampshire, Northamptonshire, and Kent—show trustworthy men being drawn disproportionately from the wealthier strata of peasant landholders, though with the involvement of some men of considerably more meagre resources. This was a social world undergoing rapid changes, which will be itemized and placed in longer-term perspective in Chapter 8, principally the notable widening of the gap between the wealthiest and the poorest peasant families.[72] The trustworthy men therefore, at this point in time, possessed greater wealth in land than the majority of the families they would have called neighbours. On the strength of their landholdings quite a few were nudging the edges of the next, higher, social bracket, asserting their right to be counted among the gentry.

Rent

Whereas snapshots of landholding are necessarily impressionistic, if suggestive, a consideration of rent permits us to make some more precise comparisons between the trustworthy men and their neighbours, from which some extremely interesting variations begin to emerge. Certain caveats still need to be borne in mind, but considered alongside all the other available variables, rent is an important part of the picture. As we move from isolated pieces of evidence to a more quantitative consideration of status, the picture that has begun to emerge—a preponderance of the more substantial men of the parish alongside occasional involvement from more humble *fidedigni*—will become more certain, and we will begin to see how the social parameters of trustworthy status varied from place to place. The main interpretative principle to remember is that rent can be only a proxy value for wealth and status, and our findings here must be viewed in the round alongside landholding and tax liability. Three rentals survive from times and places that can be matched to named groups of trustworthy men. The earliest is from Blyth in Nottinghamshire in 1273, eight years before a group of trustworthy men were gathered to inquire into the endowment of their vicar. The next comes from the Hampshire village of Southwick in 1396, seventeen years after trustworthy men had been asked to approve the purgation of a chaplain for theft. The time-lag does not seem to have affected the usefulness of the rental data very much—ten out of the thirteen jurors were still alive—but we can also augment it with information from manorial court rolls and accounts, and some charters. The third is a 1390 rental for Woodlands manor in the Dorset parish of Horton-with-Knowlton, which was visited by Bishop Waltham in 1394.[73]

The main benefits of rentals are that they record a larger number of tenants than any other documentary source, and they permit comparison according to a single criterion: rent paid to a lord. They do, however, record only the tenants of one particular manor, and in many parishes this excludes a proportion of the population. Furthermore rent was an item of peasant expenditure and cannot always be a reliable guide to relative income levels.[74] While we need to be cautious about comparisons between the rents paid they can be meaningful nevertheless. We are comparing like with like: there is no reason to suspect that trustworthy men were any more likely than their neighbours to have taken on properties whose rents they could barely afford. We can also use quantitative methods to mitigate any temptation to read too much into impressionistic assessments of the sources, establishing the statistical correlation between rent paid and trustworthy status, expressed as a Spearman rank correlation coefficient ranging from –1 to +1.[75] This tests the null hypothesis that *there is no relationship between the level of rent paid and the attribution of trustworthy status*: a situation that would suggest an even, or random, distribution of responsibility amongst all rent-paying tenants. If the coefficient is 0 the null hypothesis is proven. If the result is between 0 and +1, we can say that as wealth increased the likelihood of being a trustworthy man increased. If the result is between –1 and 0 we can say that as wealth decreased the likelihood of being a trustworthy man increased. In this way it is possible to see whether attributions of trustworthiness tended to be associated with those who paid higher rents, with those who paid lower rents, or whether there was no association between rents and trustworthy status.[76] Given the small absolute numbers of trustworthy men in each place there is a risk that the results of the correlation would not be statistically significant. Therefore a probability (*P*) test has been carried out for each result to assess the likelihood that it could be due to chance. A *P*-value of 0.10 indicates a 10 percent likelihood that the result is due to chance. This probability or lower has been taken to indicate statistical significance. We can also look at the data in another way, to confirm our findings. Comparing the mean rent paid by all tenants listed in each rental with the mean rent paid by the trustworthy men gives us a sense of whether the trustworthy paid roughly average rents, or whether they fell above or below the average.

In addition to this a 'Gini index' of inequality has been calculated for each parish based on the distribution of rents across the population of the manor.[77] The higher the index value, the more unequal was the distribution of rent. The Gini index allows us to compare the rental structure of the three manors, and to say not only whether the trustworthy men paid above or below average rents, but whether they did so in a place that was more or less unequal in the rents paid by different tenants.[78] Further to this we can contextualize each place within its region, using the measures of regional wealth in Bruce Campbell's and Ken Bartley's atlas of lay lordship, land, and wealth in the half-century before the Black Death. Although our case studies fall somewhat earlier and later than this period, their figures help us to compare the three parishes with one another.[79]

The calculation of rank correlation coefficients for rent and trustworthy status immediately demonstrates a clear difference between Southwick and the other two places. In Blyth and Horton there was a similar likelihood that higher rents were related to the attribution of trustworthy status (coefficients of 0.32 and 0.31). Both results are statistically significant with *P*-values of 0.01

Table 1. Rental values and trustworthy status

	Spearman coefficient (P-value) whole sample	Spearman coefficient (P-value) excluding outliers	Mean rent of all tenants (pence)	Mean rent of trustworthy men (pence)	Gini index of rent inequality	Wealth of vill in 1334	Regional wealth
Blyth 1281	0.11 (0.38)	0.32 (0.01)	27.28	42.5	49.31	£98 9s 0.75d	High £.p.t. Low £.p.m. Low t.p.m.
Southwick 1379	0.04 (0.64)	0.04 (0.64)	59.98	65.14	44.35	£43 6s 10d	High £.p.t. Low £.p.m. Low t.p.m.
Horton 1394	0.31 (0.02)	0.31 (0.02)	70.5	204.5	39.71	£40 10s	Low £.p.t. Low £.p.m. High t.p.m.

Note: £.p.t. = regional mean wealth per taxpayer; £.p.m. = landed wealth per square mile; t.p.m. = number of taxpayers per square mile.

(Blyth excluding outlier) and 0.02 (Horton). On the strength of these correlations we can therefore propose that in Blyth and Horton trustworthiness was associated with the payment of higher rents. At Blyth there were seven men on the inquest: William Person, John of Blyth, and John le Fuster were identified in the 1273 rental as paying among the largest sums; Adam of Greasbrough is not named but twenty years later his son was named in another rental; Gilbert son of Stephen is hard to pin down, but his family seems to have been significant in the local area, with a trader called Thomas FitzStephen (son of Stephen) of Blyth taking large sums of credit in the 1290s from Peter de Sarts, a major figure in regional mercantile networks; Adam Aldan and one illegible name cannot be described in any meaningful way.[80] At Horton there were four visitation representatives: John Abbot, Richard Hert, John Colyns and John Donet. Donet cannot be identified in the rental or court rolls relating to Woodlands manor and was probably a tenant elsewhere. Abbot and Hert appear in the Woodlands rental paying massive rents of eleven shillings ten pence and twenty-two shillings three pence, respectively, which explains the striking difference between the mean rent of trustworthy men and that of all tenants. They both held at least one and a half virgates (probably more than forty-five acres) of land, confirming their status as major tenants. While Colyns was not named as a tenant in 1390, the reeve's accounts for 1396–97 show him paying for exemption from labour services, suggesting that he was at least comfortably well-off.[81]

The correlation between higher rents and trustworthy status in late thirteenth-century Blyth and late fourteenth-century Horton occurred in two rather different sets of economic circumstances. Although both places were associated with sheep rearing, Blyth was a thriving market centre with links to regional and international wool traders, where mean taxpayer wealth was high and rents—although inequitably distributed—were comparatively modest. The trustworthy men were bunched in the second rank of rent payers, with only six men paying more. They were among the better-off. At Horton the trustworthy men were the very highest rent payers, as confirmed by the massive difference between their mean rent when compared to that of all tenants. This could be explained by the fact that Horton was a poorer vill where individual prosperity was limited by rents much higher than at Blyth. This may have meant that status went hand-in-hand with the occupation of high-rental properties in Horton to a greater extent than in Blyth.

Differences between Horton and Blyth were, however, minimal when those two places are compared to Southwick. Here there was almost no correlation (0.04) between rent and trustworthy status, with the seven identifiable trustworthy men (out of an inquest of thirteen) spread fairly evenly across a wider spectrum than we saw at Horton or even Blyth. Andrew Hurt and Richard Prat paid sixteen pence, yet there were nineteen tenants paying less than them; Nicholas Grym paid thirteen shillings, yet there were twelve tenants paying more than him. In Southwick trustworthy men did not pay the very highest rents, but nor did they pay the very lowest. The lack of distinction based on rents is emphasized by the similarity of the mean rent paid by all tenants and by the trustworthy men.[82] There is admittedly a tendency for the rental to under-record rents at the lower end.[83] However, even if we assume an incomplete picture of the rent they paid, the distribution at Southwick is still much wider than that at Horton or Blyth. While the P-value for Southwick is very weak (0.64), this is not a problem for our interpretation since a near-random distribution is most likely to be achieved by chance. Here trustworthy status was in no way linked to the rental values of property.

What were the features of Southwick's social structure that made the relationship between rent and trustworthy status so different to that in Blyth and Horton? Southwick was under the lordship of a religious house, like parts of Blyth, and the inequality of its rental distribution was midway between that of Blyth and Horton. The difference must lie elsewhere. It is the landscape and settlement pattern of Southwick that contrast most sharply with north Nottinghamshire and mid-Dorset, whose open fields and nucleated villages were quite unlike this part of Hampshire. Southwick was a more dispersed settlement of discrete steadings within a wood-pasture landscape dominated by dairy, stock, and grazing.[84] This did not make it poor. Wealth per taxpayer was high and the parish was very close to the major sea ports of Portchester, Fareham, and Portsea. The landscape and settlement pattern did, however, make it less likely that economic inequalities would be concurrent with political inequalities. Living in dispersed steadings with an economy based on stock rearing may have promoted a degree of independence among the tenants. The dispersal of the inquest across the range of rents paid suggests a system of assigning responsibility based on where people lived, and not on how important they were as tenants.[85]

Tax Liability: The Lay Subsidies

The relationship between attributions of trustworthiness and economic inequality is somewhat clearer if we turn to the records of royal taxation. While tax is less problematic than rent as an indicator of wealth, its records are far from perfect for our purposes, and once again we should remind ourselves that it is only a proxy for wealth and status. Nevertheless, because the findings on tax liability point in the same general direction as those for landholding and rent, we can be fairly confident about the overall picture. The lay subsidies of the early fourteenth century and the poll taxes levied between 1377 and 1381 provide more matches with lists of trustworthy men than did rentals. The lay subsidies, known as 'fractional taxes' (taking a tenth, fifteenth, or twentieth of the assessed goods of householders), have hitherto mainly been used by economic historians plotting the geographical distribution of wealth across England.[86] Analyses of the distribution of wealth within single communities are less common, and the studies to date highlight several methodological considerations that we need to bear in mind.[87] First, the subsidies provide us with evidence of local impressions of wealth, rather than wealth itself, although these are still valuable relative assessments. Second, the wealthiest inhabitants were very often under-assessed, for a variety of reasons.[88] Third, householders whose moveable goods were valued at less than ten shillings in the countryside or six shillings in the towns were completely exempt, removing between half and two-thirds of households from liability for tax altogether.[89] And finally, among those remaining householders who were subject to the assessment only moveable wealth was counted, excluding the market or rental value of land, credit, stocks of coin, personal or household goods, foodstuffs, and the craft tools deemed necessary to support the taxpayer's family. This meant that in most rural areas only larger stock animals such as horses, cattle, sheep, and pigs, plus grains and other crops were commonly assessed, reflecting the amount of produce a person had available for the market: his or her surplus.[90] What the lay subsidies provide, therefore, is a reasonable if rough measure of how local sub-taxers thought marketable surplus was distributed amongst the mid- to higher-band households in their communities. We can measure the extent to which the trustworthy men conformed to or deviated from that distribution.

There are five lists of trustworthy men from the early fourteenth century that can be cross-referenced with assessments for lay subsidies. From Fiskerton in Lincolnshire in 1302 we have one of the few early visitation documents to name trustworthy men. These names can be cross-referenced to the assessment

for a subsidy of a twentieth in 1327.[91] At Eaton Bray in Bedfordshire in 1307
the bishop of Lincoln requested information concerning the character of a
local cleric. The six trustworthy men of Eaton can be cross-referenced with
the assessment for a subsidy of a twenty-fifth in 1309, where five can be identified.[92] In Warwickshire in 1330 the eleven trustworthy men of Snitterfield
were required to value the endowment of their vicarage. Perhaps because of
chronological proximity nine out of the eleven jurors can be identified in the
assessment for a fifteenth in 1332.[93] Henstridge in Somerset had the dedication of its church and cemetery in 1332 witnessed by twelve trustworthy men,
of whom nine can be identified in the assessment for a twentieth in 1327.[94]
The final case study linked to the subsidies is Wellingore in Lincolnshire where
seventeen out of thirty-three *inquisitores* who represented the parish at visitations between 1337 and 1349 can be identified from the assessments for the
fifteenth in 1332.[95] The relationship of trustworthy status to tax liability has
been calculated in much the same way as for the rental data. A Spearman rank
correlation coefficient establishes the strength of the relationship between
the two variables (tax liability and trustworthy status), and we can also compare the mean values of tax assessed for all taxpayers and for the trustworthy
men.[96] Since all the case studies come from the first half of the fourteenth
century, we have the opportunity to make meaningful comparisons between
average taxpayer wealth in the vill and in its wider region, as calculated by
Campbell and Bartley.[97]

Looking at the rank coefficients we can say that at Eaton Bray, Snitterfield, and Wellingore there was no relationship between taxable wealth and
trustworthy status. This is true whether or not we include the outlying highest taxpayer in each place. Trustworthy men were drawn from all sections of
the taxpaying population, and the mean tax paid by the trustworthy was actually less than the mean for all taxpayers. In each of these three places the
tax burden, as expressed in the Gini indices, was distributed with about the
same degree of inequality, whether the taxpayers were individually relatively
wealthy (as in Snitterfield and Wellingore) or relatively poor (Eaton Bray).
However, there were two distinctive regimes of local representation operating
in these three places. In Eaton Bray and Snitterfield almost all the trustworthy
men are identifiable as taxpayers. This means that while trustworthy status
was widely distributed amongst taxpayers, it was also nearly confined to that
group. We should remember that payers of the lay subsidies were heads of
household, and that somewhere between half and two-thirds of households
fell below the tax threshold. These two parishes can only, therefore, be said
to have been inclusive in a very limited sort of way: if you were a taxpaying
male head of household you stood a good chance of serving as a trustworthy
man. Wellingore looks to be a different story. Here we can only identify seventeen out of thirty-three trustworthy men, and while some may have been
assessed as taxpayers in other vills, the rest may have been drawn from below

Table 2. Lay subsidy assessments and trustworthy status

	Spearman coefficient (P-value) whole sample	Spearman coefficient (P-value) excluding outliers	Mean tax liability: all taxpayers (to nearest penny)	Mean tax liability: trustworthy men (to nearest penny)	Mean assessed wealth per taxpayer 1327–34	Gini index of tax inequality	Wealth of vill in 1334	Regional wealth
Fiskerton 1302	0.42 (0.02)	0.42 (0.02)	22	32	£2.1 (high)	23.20	£65 11s 3d	High £.p.t. High £.p.m. High t.p.m.
Eaton Bray 1307	−0.06 (0.63)	−0.03 (0.63)	25	19	£1.6 (low)	32.77	£124 13s 1.5d	High £.p.t. High £.p.m. High t.p.m.
Snitterfield 1330	−0.11 (0.53)	0.05 (0.79)	35	22	£2.1 (high)	28.45	£65 3s 9d	High £.p.t. High £.p.m. High t.p.m.
Henstridge 1332	0.23 (0.10)	0.23 (0.10)	11	11	£1.3 (very low)	32.89	£67 10s	Low £.p.t. High £.p.m. High t.p.m.
Wellingore 1337–49	−0.02 (0.90)	−0.05 (0.76)	33	31	£2 (high)	33.58	£90	High £.p.t. High £.p.m. High t.p.m.

Note: £.p.t. = regional mean wealth per taxpayer; £.p.m. = landed wealth per taxpayer; t.p.m. = number of taxpayers per square mile. The coefficient for Fiskerton was calculated using three close relatives (one brother, one son, and one widow) of trustworthy men as analogues. At Eaton Bray and Snitterfield the lords of the manors have been excluded as outliers. The mean total assessed wealth per taxpayer is based on the average tax burden for 1327, 1332, and 1334 (where all three are available) divided by the number of taxpayers in 1327/1332. Values from 'very high' to 'very low' are given according to the Campbell and Bartley classifications to permit comparison with the values for the local region.

the taxable threshold. This, in conjunction with the wide distribution of trust-worthy status *amongst* taxpayers, suggests the possibility that in Wellingore the trustworthy men were less easily distinguishable from their neighbours than was the case in Eaton or Snitterfield.[98]

Fiskerton and Henstridge were, however, at the opposite end of the spectrum from Wellingore. Here the rank coefficients indicate a positive relationship between the possession of higher value moveable goods or marketable surplus and the institutional attribution of trustworthiness. The relationship was stronger at Fiskerton (coefficient of 0.42) than Henstridge (coefficient of 0.23), and the result was also more statistically significant at Fiskerton than Henstridge (probability value of 0.02 as opposed to 0.10). In Fiskerton, and to a lesser extent in Henstridge, a man was more likely to enjoy trustworthy status if he possessed greater taxable wealth. In Henstridge the trustworthy were bunched in the second rank of taxpayers: those paying between ten and eighteen pence. There were no trustworthy men in the upper band between twenty-two pence and four shillings. So we can say that the likelihood of being a trustworthy man in Henstridge increased in line with taxable wealth *up to a point*, beyond which it became less likely. Glancing at Campbell and Bartley's figures for regional wealth, it is notable that while wealth per taxpayer was very low here, landed wealth was high, suggesting a sharp distinction between peasant and gentry society. However, if trustworthiness had an upper social limit in Henstridge it was marked by the Toomer family, who certainly seem to have straddled that divide. Although Thomas and Richard Toomer, both of whom acted as trustworthy men, paid only the mean contribution of ten pence towards the lay subsidy, they came from a family which held a minor estate from Henstridge manor from about 1302 onwards. They had also created a deer park in their corner of the parish. At the time of its consecration in 1332 one aisle of the parish church was named after the family.[99] Their local influence far outstretched their tax assessment in 1327, which presumably means their wealth was held in forms exempted from the subsidy: coin, credit, and rents.

The mean wealth of trustworthy men in Fiskerton was much more emphatically that of the leading families. Their contributions to the lay subsidy averaged at thirty-two pence as opposed to twenty-two pence for all taxpayers; the highest taxpayer, Richard Granger, was a trustworthy man, while the second and third taxpayers, Robert le Sees and Margery 'wife of Theobald', may stand as proxies for their close relatives who were trustworthy men. What is curious is that although the tax burden was distributed much more equitably in Fiskerton than in the other four parishes being examined here, this did not equate to an equitable distribution of trustworthy status, a disjuncture that raises the possibility that where wealth alone did not provide emphatic social differentiation, then social capital or political status—in the shape of office-holding and institutional trustworthiness—could fill the void. The trustworthy men of Fiskerton were indeed important to the administration of

Peterborough Abbey's estates in the region. Two were involved at the level of the manor: Richard le Sees was a manorial presentment juror, confirming the extent of other tenants' holdings in an account roll dated 1300–1301; John the wood ward was employed to manage the abbey's woodland resources and to prevent their abuse by other villagers. From the abbey's point of view, Fiskerton was most important as a hub for collecting and packing wool from its Lincolnshire manors, and the Le Sees family had a role in this wider venture as well. Robert le Sees, who in 1301 was the second wealthiest man in the village (after Richard Granger), was also the servant of Bernard of Castor, bailiff of the five northern manors of the Peterborough estate. As his servant, Robert le Sees was paid to travel to Peterborough on several occasions, and he may have accompanied Bernard on other journeys to Boston and Lincoln, making the Le Sees name well-known in local administrative and trading circles.[100]

The evidence of the lay subsidies points to there being a range of relationships that trustworthy status could have with the possession of moveable goods and a marketable surplus, although in all cases it tends to confirm a general association of the trustworthy with household wealth. In some places (Eaton Bray and Snitterfield) there was a broad dispersion of institutional trusting across the taxpaying population. But we must remember that taxpayers constituted only between one-third and half of all householders. In other places (Fiskerton and Henstridge) trustworthy status was more closely correlated with higher wealth, though this could happen in different ways. At Wellingore the data are most difficult to interpret. Here we can only just identify a majority of the trustworthy men amongst the taxpayers. The others may have come from much poorer sections of the parish. I will return to Wellingore in Chapter 7 because the peculiar nature of our evidence there permits us to delve much further into the question of who represented the parish.

Tax Liability: The Poll Taxes

Long-harboured doubts about the profitability of the subsidies, coupled with the collapse in the revenues of landholders during the extraordinarily good harvest of 1376, created incentives for Parliament to try to shift the burden of taxation firmly down the social scale.[101] The tax granted in 1377 was a levy of four pence (or one groat) on every layman or laywoman over fourteen years of age except for 'true and genuine beggars'. This has become known as the first poll tax. Its records are useless for our purposes since everyone paid the same amount. But in 1379 and 1380 two grants were made that sought to assess everyone's wealth 'according to his estate and degree and according to his property, lands, rents, possessions, goods, and chattels'. Even though these are known as the second and third poll taxes, they were graduated—each in its own way—making them useful to an analysis of economic inequality.[102] There has, however, been very little historical use of these taxes for the investigation of social structure. Much more attention has been given to their potential to shed light on total population, national wealth, and broad structural features of settlement and the economy.[103]

In 1379 payments were fixed on a scale ranging from the maximum ten marks paid by the dukes of Lancaster and Brittany right down to householders assessed at four pence. There were many points in between with, for example, leading merchants paying twenty shillings, 'sufficient merchants' thirteen shillings four pence, and lesser merchants lumped in with artisans paying between six shillings eight pence and six pence.[104] Assessments for 1379 survive for Blandford Forum in Dorset, from where we have a list of visitation representatives in 1394. In 1380 a further experiment was attempted. One shilling was due from every man and woman over fifteen years of age, but the burden could be distributed however the local taxers chose, provided that 'the rich should help the poor' and that no-one should pay more than twenty shillings or less than four pence.[105] Assessments for 1380 survive for two other Dorset parishes visited by Bishop Waltham in 1394: Stour Provost and Sutton Waldron.[106] In addition to the widespread evasion that seems to have occurred in 1380–81, the evidence from Stour Provost and Sutton Waldron suggests that some householders who would have paid under the provisions of 1379 were purposefully exempted. The average burden in Stour Provost was 21.6 pence rather than the stipulated one shilling (12 pence), while in Sutton Waldron it was 19.2 pence. It may be that the local sub-taxers were trying to replicate the distribution of taxation usually seen in subsidies, or, as Carolyn Fenwick puts it, to 'strike a balance between the desire not to aggravate their fellow villagers, on whom they depended, and the need to satisfy the Crown'.[107] In many regions commissioners were sent in to reassess, fearing that the returns were fraudulent, but we do not have this evidence for Dorset.[108]

All three case studies come in this instance from a single region with many common features. The lowlands of mid-Dorset were dotted with settlements that practised a mixed agriculture, although there was a strong regional specialism in sheep rearing. The nucleated villages were set in a landscape dotted with many isolated farmsteads. All three parishes were predominantly under secular lordship. Blandford was part of the Duchy of Lancaster; Stour Provost was at this time a royal manor, while the lord of Sutton Waldron was the knight Laurence of St Martin.[109] The principal distinction that can be drawn is that between Blandford and the other two places. Blandford was a market town with more than double the taxpaying population of either Stour Provost or Sutton Waldron. While in these two more rural parishes there was no statistically significant relationship between trustworthy status and taxable wealth (in Stour Provost a coefficient of 0.08 with probability of 0.68; in Sutton Waldron a coefficient of −0.02 with probability of 0.90), in small-town Blandford

Table 3. Poll tax assessments and trustworthy status

	Spearman coefficient (P-value)	Mean tax liability to nearest penny	Mean tax liability of trustworthy men to nearest penny	Gini index of tax inequality	Regional wealth 1327–34
Blandford Forum	0.43 (0.0004)	7	16	16.39	Low £.p.t. High £.p.m. High t.p.m.
Stour Provost	0.08 (0.68)	22	24	12.84	Low £.p.t. Low £.p.m. High t.p.m.
Sutton Waldron	−0.02 (0.90)	22	24	29.44	Low £.p.t. Low £.p.m. High t.p.m.

Note: £.p.t. = regional mean wealth per taxpayer; £.p.m. = landed wealth per square mile; t.p.m. = number of taxpayers per square mile.

attributed trustworthiness was strongly related to taxable wealth (coefficient: 0.43, probability: 0.0004). What was it about these places that made them so different?

Being a small market town, Blandford had a higher population and there was also a concentration of landed wealth not seen in the other two places. The Gini indices measuring the degree of inequality in the distribution of the tax burden are of little help given the relatively flat structure of the poll taxes, despite the experimentation with graduated levies. We can, however, glean a little more information from manorial records. Nothing survives for Sutton Waldron, but there appears to be a notable difference between the visitation representatives of Blandford Forum and Stour Provost.

At Blandford Forum the trustworthy men were dominant in the manor court. Richard Helier and John Towker were pledges in 1390; Towker, described as an artisan in the 1380 poll tax returns, was also a creditor who used the court to pursue various claims of debt. Walter Potter, a merchant, and Thomas Helier, an artisan, were together elected as bailiffs of the manor in 1391. Thomas Gogayn cannot be identified in the poll tax returns, but does appear in the court roll in breach of the assize of ale. While this suggests no more than a minimal level of commercial activity, one Henry Gogan was amongst the highest taxpayers in 1380, in the same bracket as the merchant Potter.[110] By contrast at Stour Provost, the most proximate court roll, dating from 1404, names only one of the four trustworthy men: Robert Vryng was a customary tenant. Later rolls, from 1425 and 1428, identify two others, Robert Symmer and Robert Metherew, as presentment jurors, but as a group these trustworthy men do not seem to be in quite the same league as those of Blandford. Robert Symmer only paid a median rent in 1425 for example, and relatives of three of the four men crop up transacting tiny parcels of land or paying minuscule rents.[111]

The evidence from poll tax returns tells us that trustworthy status may have been more closely connected with higher taxable wealth in larger settlements where there was more commercial activity.

{⸎⸎⸎⸎⸎}

In this chapter I have traced the relationship between the discrimination involved in institutional attributions of trustworthiness and some of the key factors differentiating people from one another in late medieval society. As we saw in the previous chapter, what bishops were doing when they talked about trustworthiness was describing a symbolic role, not accurately identifying the most honest or virtuous people in the parishes. They certainly valued constancy and reliability, and they needed people who could convincingly present themselves as the representatives of their communities. These attributes of the symbolic role were, it seems, met by the distinctive social profile of the trustworthy men. Most strikingly, they were men: women could not, apart from in quite specific exceptional circumstances, be trustworthy in the eyes of the church, despite their *fides* being as much a component of their identity and reputation as any man's (as we saw in Chapter 3), and despite their being expected to have faith (in the sense of belief in God) and to give faith (in promising). The value of the symbolic role was primarily sustained by excluding women. I will return to the experience of this exclusion in Chapter 9. This did not leave all men equally capable of fulfilling the symbolic role however. There was a clear preference for elders, although given the limiting facts of demographic history these cannot always have formed the parade of septuagenarians that sometimes presented itself to a court or a bishop. So far so predictable, but when it comes to legal status we find ecclesiastical trustworthiness diverging from the dominant normative categories of public life. Freedom and unfreedom played no part in determining who could be a trustworthy man.

Some of the most important ways in which this society was ordered and categorized did not constitute clear dichotomies. Instead they were features in an instinctively known political landscape that many people could have navigated in the dark. Which families could not be ignored? Which occupations implied respectability? At what point did an individual's history of office-holding make him impossible to disregard? The evidence presented in this chapter has at least strongly suggested that there were families who dominated from year to year and over the generations because of who they were, a phenomenon that will be investigated further in the following chapter. There does not seem to have been any moral or cultural bar to the participation of merchants, peasant cultivators, or wage labourers in the building trades, but given the age and gender constraints there are many occupations that would never have been represented amongst groups of trustworthy men, such as spinners (generally women) or servants. Office-holding in the manor, the vill, and the parish was perhaps the surest route towards unassailable trustworthy status. The men who represented their neighbours in a number of different settings were naturally the ones to step forward or to be sought out when reliable local testimony was needed. They looked convincing as representatives of the symbolic role that bishops had in mind for them.

It would be a simplification of the evidence to say that wealth and trustworthy status went hand in hand. Society was ordered in more complex ways than that. My examination of landholding identifies some trustworthy men who controlled very little land, which is extremely interesting, but repeatedly we see that men with extensive landholdings were hard to ignore. Their dominance could also have been adaptive. Research on various regions has shown that wealthier peasant families tended to have more children, and that their resources meant they were able to form new, independent households at a younger age than their poorer neighbours, giving them longer to establish themselves in local hierarchies. Since being a householder was a precondition for many local positions of responsibility, over the long term trustworthiness may have selected in favour of wealth.[112] While this is hard to verify, other aspects of inequality entrenched over time will be examined in Chapter 7.

Turning from qualitative, and necessarily impressionistic, evidence to the statistics derived from rentals and tax assessments, we found that the co-presence of poorer and wealthier trustworthy men varied from place to place. The evidence from rentals showed that higher rents correlated with an increased likelihood of holding trustworthy status, except in places where a dispersed settlement pattern and the economic dominance of wealthy peasant producers militated against oligarchy. Similarly, tax assessments showed that trustworthiness was generally limited to taxpaying householders. This meant it was concentrated in the upper half or third of householders, and sometimes in an even more exclusive group. There were circumstances across England and across the period between 1281 (our earliest quantitative case study) and 1394 (our latest) where trustworthiness was attributed to men located on the indeterminate border between substantial peasants and the gentry, or to men slightly below the wealthiest stratum of village society. In making this observation we would also do well to recall the way in which the term *fidedignus* echoed that of the *fideiussor*: the guarantor who required sufficient wealth to back up his promises with payment if the need arose (for discussion of whom see Chapters 2 and 4). On the other hand, in one of our case study parishes— Wellingore in Lincolnshire—it appears that trustworthiness was attributed to a very wide range of men indeed. The great benefit of the statistical approach pursued in the second part of this chapter is that it permits us to introduce some sense of topographical variation into the discussion of parish elites. We can move away from the blandness of 'the middling sort' and see something of the different social profiles that trustworthy men could form against the horizon of our evidence.

The differences emerging here, and to be developed in the following chapter, cannot however be elevated into definitive categories sufficient to encompass all experiences. They function instead as indications of the range of likely experiences in late medieval English parishes. Peasant society was riven by all sorts of inequalities which, because of the episcopal desire for incontrovertibility, predetermined who could step forward as a trustworthy man. Being male, older, and the head of a household were major components of this, and where there were more significant preexisting inequalities of wealth, those too were important to the profile of trustworthy men. However, attributing trustworthiness was also an intervention in the sociology of the parish. It introduced another inequality, another route to status. Very local elites were defined by gender, age, family, and wealth, but also by the relationships that they formed with authority.

PART III

Trustworthiness and Inequality in the Parish

THE TRUSTWORTHY MEN, these very local elites, were principally the representatives of parishes, and it is to the parish that we now turn. More often than not distinguished from their fellow parishioners by landholding and wealth, perhaps quite often by age, and always by definition male, they were certainly *of* the parish, but in what sense could they speak *for* it? Bishops approached them for information and assistance with all sorts of matters relating to the parish, and to the church in local society more generally. The nature of this engagement will be thoroughly investigated in Part IV, but before we can properly understand the way in which these men, and the symbolic role performed by them, contributed to the development of episcopal governance we need a better understanding of how attributed trustworthiness affected the social parish.

We may begin by picking up the threads of the last chapter, in which we saw that being called trustworthy by bishops frequently aligned with other modes of differentiation in late medieval society, namely gender, age, status, and wealth. As well as this positive correlation (with its caveats duly noted) we have also seen that the ecclesiastical decision to trust one set of people was predicated upon the disqualification of others, notably women, from consideration. We might say that institutional trusting depended upon and sustained multiple inequalities. When it comes to discussion of inequality and equality, the primary issue, as formulated by Amartya Sen, is 'equality of what'?[1] People can be roughly equal in one regard while being wildly unequal in another. It is also generally agreed that different 'axes of inequality', whether economic, political, or social, must be considered together: they might overlap with, reinforce, or completely bypass one another. Certain forms of differentiation or prejudice, particularly those relating to gender and either race or class, seem always to be found together.[2] In this light we can appreciate, for example, how the status of the trustworthy men was never solely about gender, but rather always about gender in conjunction with age, wealth, or being a taxpaying head of household. In other words, patriarchy is maintained by the way that markers of status combine with one another. In the following three chapters I will explain, based upon the evidence of inquests and visitations, as well as the wider documentation of life in the late medieval English parish, how the concept of the *fidedignus* itself became a marker of status: another vector for inequality that intersected with those that were expounded in Chapter 6.

Many authors have assumed that being trusted confers 'social capital' upon individuals, and that trusting relationships have a similar beneficial effect upon groups of people.[3] Social capital expresses the nature and quality of someone's connections within society, and how these can reinforce advantages or, conversely, how the lack of them can reinforce disadvantage. The idea that there is social advantage in being someone who is habitually trusted, or in being part of a group within which trust is easily established, is certainly borne out by the evidence relating to the 'trustworthy men' of late medieval

England.[4] Having seen how the social profile of the trustworthy man echoed existing inequalities, we may now observe that if being a trustworthy man conferred social capital, it is likely to have done so at the expense of others: it was an active, and potentially negative, force in society.

A second widespread assumption in the literature on trust is that trusting arises most easily between social equals, and that trust promotes equality.[5] However, trust between equals may also depend upon mistrust of those people not considered equals, which has often led to marginalization of women, the poor, and people categorized as ethnic minorities. This is what Sheilagh Ogilvie calls the 'dark side' of social capital, and Geoffrey Hawthorn 'the viciousness . . . inherent in virtue'.[6] Historians have indeed been readier than social scientists to acknowledge the association between trust and inequality, whether in the 'geometric' equality of ancient Greece whereby greater trust was placed in 'greater' men, the unequal reciprocity expressed by *fides* in Imperial Rome, or the patron-client or lord-vassal relationships of early medieval Europe and elsewhere.[7] Here, however, I am at pains to illuminate a particular relationship between trusting and inequality: one that is more systemic, going beyond the relationship between two unequal—though trusting—parties, and extending to the entire socioeconomic and ideological structure of society. The trust that the institutional church placed in select local men was a major component in the inequalities of life, and the church in turn depended upon the existence of those inequalities in order to identify trustworthy men. After all, it was a symbolic role. The trustworthiness of the trustworthy men was established by a combination of institutional rhetoric and their possession of a certain status in local society.

Having seen in Part I how vibrant and participatory were the cultures of trust during our period (in spite of the huge ideological power accruing to the church and the law) it is possible to resist a bowdlerization of the 'Middle Ages' as *crushingly* patriarchal and unequal, certainly not in contrast to any self-congratulatory fantasy of a progressive modernity. Yes, the late medieval social environment was riven by deep and growing inequalities that suppressed the social and political participation of women and the poor in significant ways, but this does not mean that no-one but the socially privileged had meaningful agency in their own lives, as we have seen with the examples of women giving and receiving credit 'in good faith' in Chapter 2. However, it does mean that the ability to act in public roles, and to gain social capital thereby, was greater for some than for others. At times this may have felt crushingly oppressive to those excluded or on the receiving end, but for much of the time, as in most societies in world history, inequality was simply a fact of life to which one had to accommodate one's choices. In the following chapters I therefore seek to disclose the relationship between inequality and institutional power that was particular to the thirteenth, fourteenth, and fifteenth centuries.

CHAPTER SEVEN

Representing the Community?

WHILE THE KEYHOLE CASE STUDIES of Chapter 6 have produced valuable insights into the political life of parishes, we must also recognize their limitations. As single moments they do not show us how very local elites interacted with their parishes over time, something which is essential to understanding how trustworthiness was underpinned by different regimes of inequality, and how it contributed to those other inequalities.[1] Charles Tilly has argued that if a relatively closed group or network manages to hoard opportunities over time, this can have the cumulative effect of enhancing the very exclusivity that allowed it to dominate in the first place, thus deepening inequalities.[2] While it is hard to find historical examples with such clear beginnings and end points as exist in theoretical models, Tilly's observation prompts the question of whether the inequalities of single moments, identified in the last chapter, were likely to have been repeated over time. It also suggests an explanation—albeit one that is almost impossible to confirm absolutely and finally—that serving as a trustworthy man not only relied upon preexisting inequalities, but also contributed further to them, making them persist over years and generations.

The initial focus of this chapter will be on the evidence for a collection of parishes in Lincolnshire under the jurisdiction of the dean and chapter of Lincoln Cathedral, where visitation representatives are named in the records for twelve successive years, a very rare occurrence indeed. This will allow us not only to see whether and how the social capital and inequalities of trustworthiness were reproduced over time, but also to take a clearer view of the question of representation, something that will then be pursued through detailed examples drawn from a wide range of circumstances across England, and across the thirteenth, fourteenth, and fifteenth centuries. Then, in Chapter 8, I will address change across that period, and comparative regional variations in the scope for parishes to be represented by 'trustworthy men'. Here I address the crux of the matter: trustworthy men were called upon to represent their parishes, but did they, and could they? As Chris Dyer has written, the distribution of local office-holding raised men's status and 'gave them advantages in their everyday lives', including the capacity to use their 'small-scale powers . . . to help their friends, and . . . discriminate against those who were not'.[3] Did the trustworthy men hoard opportunities and use their power in such a way? How exactly did they represent their communities?

Historians Debate Parish Leadership

Insofar as they have discussed it at all historians have tended to see parish leadership and representation as principally a question about churchwardens. Perhaps this is because churchwardens' accounts are such rich sources, but it is important to recognize that they are not the only ones available to us, and there is much to be gained by broadening the discussion. A number of historians have argued that churchwardens were the leading figures in their parishes, the 'chief executives' enjoying 'effective headship', but Clive Burgess has notably taken issue with this, characterizing them as mere 'caretakers' or 'foremen'.[4] Neither portrayal tells the whole story: churchwardens bore much responsibility, but they were certainly not executive leaders. They were identified by the terms proctor (suggesting a legal representative function), church reeve or receiver (hinting at the collection of money on behalf of an authority figure), master of the fabric (pointing to a specific responsibility for the physical church building), or the Greek derivation *iconomus*, which, echoing monastic terminology, has overtones of stewardship, perhaps of funds and livestock.[5]

Burgess's argument, which usefully opens up the field, is that these functions were delegated to churchwardens by more powerful groups within the parish. He uses the early sixteenth-century accounts of St Andrew Hubbard in London to demonstrate that there was a group of auditors or assessors who regularly heard the wardens' accounts, and the records of All Saints' in Bristol and St Mary-at-Hill in London to show them taking orders, not taking the initiative. That was the responsibility of those described as the 'council' or 'masters' of the parish. Being churchwarden was, so Burgess argues, 'a rung on the ladder *en route* to a position among the parish governors'.[6] Although Burgess's examples come from large parishes in cities, the evidence for hierarchies of office is ubiquitous. A variety of sources speak, for example, of *majores* or 'elders' in parishes across the country, echoing the valorization of age discussed in Chapter 6. At Tanfield and Lamesley in County Durham in 1312 four or six elders from both vills were cited to say why they should not contribute to the expenses of the church of Chester-le-Street.[7] Elsewhere in the north of England the term 'kirkmaster' was commonly used to denote the more executive role.[8] At Hainton, Lincolnshire, in 1336 the 'elders of the parish' gave evidence about how the tithe on milk was customarily collected, and elsewhere in that county we find references to the 'thrifty' men of the parish.[9] In Devon there was an especially strong custom of parishes having an executive group of governors or trustees. Hartland had its 'four men' and a larger group of twenty-four 'governors', Ashburton its 'eight men', and Morebath a group of three, four, or five men 'that have the churche stock yn governansse'. This terminology, which echoed that of urban government, extended well into the fifteenth and sixteenth centuries.[10] Whatever the language of particular places or regions, there were clearly other men who were superior to the churchwardens: they would serve for longer and therefore comprised a smaller group of the adult male population than the men who might be wardens from time to time; they may also have been expected to be wealthy enough to carry the parish through hard times.[11]

Using visitation records—a source neglected by almost all historians interested in churchwarden's accounts—the people we have come to know as trustworthy men can be identified with those variously called masters, governors, elders, the thrifty, and so on.[12] Before the later fifteenth century, and in many places long after, parishes were represented at visitation by *fidedigni* who were clearly differentiated from the churchwardens (however described).[13] The records show churchwardens and trustworthy men (or their analogues) conducting distinct aspects of the parish's business at visitation, with the churchwardens almost always acting in an inferior and strictly limited capacity. In late thirteenth-century Herefordshire, Rutland, and Kent wardens reported the nonpayment of various ecclesiastical dues and looked after the material interests of their church, but the trustworthy men or sometimes simply 'the parishioners' reported the faults and offences of the clergy and laity.[14] There are also instances from the thirteenth, fourteenth, and fifteenth centuries of churchwardens being disciplined or criticized by clearly superior parishioners.[15] In the later fifteenth century there seems to have been a gradual improvement in the status of churchwardens as the accumulation of parish property brought greater prominence to the men who controlled it.[16] In the deanery of Wisbech between 1458 and 1484 visitation presentments were still being made by *inquisitores* who were differentiated from *iconomi*, but the latter were sometimes drawn from the ranks of the former.[17] In the Worcestershire parish of Hartlebury the late fifteenth century saw close associations between the parish representatives—called trustworthy or 'upright' (*probi*) men—and the wardens of the church, of its chantry dedicated to St Mary, and of its fabric fund known as 'le chetul'. Men variously served as wardens whilst simultaneously trustworthy men, before becoming trustworthy men, and having already served as trustworthy men. Here being a warden was not simply a rung on the ladder to higher status within the parish.[18] By the early sixteenth-century wardens were playing a more central role in visitation, a novel situation that has been read backwards anachronistically into the late medieval period: in the diocese of Winchester, for example, churchwardens became responsible for citing offenders to appear before the visitor, working closely with the archdeacon's summoner.[19]

Discussion of parish representation has also been hampered by a tendency to read certain highly rhetorical documents as straightforward representations of social reality, especially where churchwardens are concerned. Here is a fairly typical entry of 1474 from the Hartlebury court book, a document that fascinatingly combines some of the features of both visitation records and churchwardens' accounts:

> First, twelve upright, honest, and trustworthy men appeared in the name of all the parishioners there and, on behalf of all the other parishioners and by their will, chose the wardens of the said church for the coming year.
> *In primis xij probi honesti et fidedigni viri nomine omnium parochianorum ibidem comparuerunt et elegerunt vice omnium aliorum parochianorum et de eorum voluntate in Iconomos dicte ecclesie per anno sequentibus.*[20]

As with all documentation of late medieval social relations, such records are imbued with a normative view of the world that goes beyond description. If read uncritically they could be taken to show that parish government proceeded in a consensual and representative way, with 'broad participation' in the selection of parish officers.[21] Although it is recognized in some quarters that the late medieval parish was formed not by mechanical solidarity, but by a combination of communal feeling and the pursuit of sectional advantage, there is scope for a great deal more investigation of the complexity of this subject.[22] Ellen Rentz's recent work on the parish in late medieval literary texts in particular throws into relief the extent to which evocations of community and consensus are metaphorical, idealized, imagined, and normative.[23] When it comes to the selection of churchwardens Beat Kümin sees 'no reason to doubt such "all inclusive" formulations', but I think we should be wary. For one thing instinctive mental associations may well have linked 'the parish' with the heads of household who contributed to parish funds and served as wardens, rather than with all its inhabitants.[24] At Hartlebury even the consensual lustre fades in places, with references to wardens chosen 'by the consent of the whole inquest' (*de consensu totius inquisicionem*) rather than 'of the parish', a slippage that calls into question similar rhetoric elsewhere, for example the 'majority' of parishioners of St Helen's in York who presented a chantry priest in 1468, the 'three parts and more of the parishioners', or 'whole community' of St Saviour's York who did the same in 1490 and 1498.[25] It was equally common for comparable formulations to refer openly to the 'better parishioners' or those 'more worthy by status and rank'.[26] In Kümin's pioneering work there is certainly recognition of the importance of the 'leading parishioners' and yet for him the parish was principally defined by 'communal action', 'shared values', and a 'sovereign assembly'.[27] As I argued in the introduction to Part I of this book, these are interpretations that ultimately derive from a narrative of modernization in which the medieval past is characterized by an unrealistic vision of communal solidarity, far removed from the complicated interplay of real inequalities with both egalitarian and hierarchical principles. As we shall see in what follows, communal identity and shared values were more likely to be impressions left upon the evidence by the activities of parish elites, than to have been the whole reality of social experience.

Parish Elites over Time

Twice a year between 1337 and 1349 a judge (known as the provost) appointed by the dean and chapter of Lincoln visited twelve Lincolnshire parishes owned by the 'common fund' of the cathedral. He was received in each place by an inquest of local men who reported moral and spiritual infractions and presented wills for probate. These parishes constituted a jurisdictional 'peculiar' outside the bishop's control and the proceedings of their visitation were recorded in a single court book.[28] This furnishes us with the rare opportunity to follow the trustworthy men of several parishes over time. They are, in ascending order of population, Skillington, Scredington, Hainton, Searby, Strubby, Wellingore, and Glentham. Good corroborative data survive in the form of assessments for the lay subsidies in these parishes, and for some of the analysis I will add Friesthorpe to the list, although here the supporting evidence is less good.

For comparative purposes the parishes are very interesting. They are scattered around the lowlands, scarps, heaths, and wolds of Lincolnshire; they differ in size, wealth, and market integration; and they exhibit some distinctive forms of parish representation.

Each parish was represented by an inquest of between four and six men, and the provost held his chapter twice a year in each place. Unfortunately we do not have an unbroken set of records for any single parish, but we do have the names of between 28 (Searby) and 109 (Friesthorpe) of the post-holding trustworthy men, known locally as *inquisitores*, over the twelve-year period.[29] Using the data from lay subsidy assessments I will begin by providing reasoned estimates of the proportion of householders who served on the inquest over twelve years. This will give us a baseline sense of how inclusive or participatory the representation of each parish was. I will then present an analysis of the frequency with which individual trustworthy men served in order to ascertain what inequalities *within the elite* may be hidden by the total figures. This seems a worthwhile approach because some individuals stand out among the *inquisitores*—even on an impressionistic reading of the evidence—as being more involved than others. Their frequent, almost ubiquitous service is likely to have made them extremely powerful within their communities. For example in Friesthorpe John Stures acted thirteen times and Thomas Francis sixteen times, out of a total of twenty-one occasions when they had the opportunity to serve. They were also both sub-taxers for the vill in 1340, suggesting an

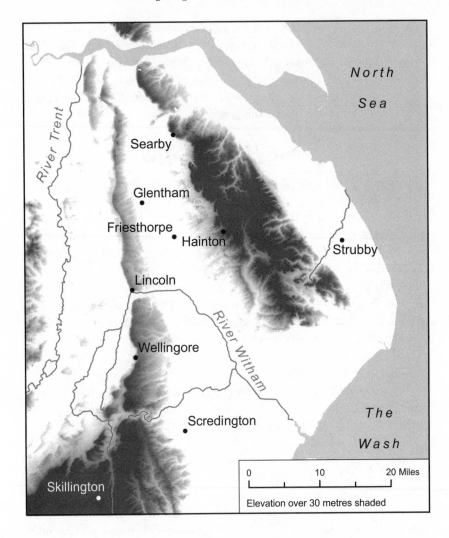

importance that extended to all areas of local life.[30] Another such dominant individual was Adam Walsh of Glentham: he served on nine of a possible eleven occasions.[31] They, and a few others, were dominant in determining what was reported as the business of the parish over a twelve year period.

How did people like them fit into the social hierarchies of their communities? I shall begin by discussing what proportion of the parish had an opportunity to serve on the inquest *at all*. Figures 1 to 3 illustrate reasoned estimates for the proportion of the population in each parish who served on an inquest between 1337 and 1349. Establishing the proportion of each parish that served on the inquest begins by comparing the number of *inquisitores* with the number of taxpayers. Using some standard multipliers proposed by historical demographers we can then extrapolate from the size of the taxpaying population

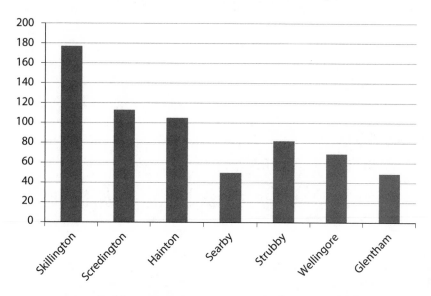

FIGURE 1. Parish representatives as a percentage of taxpaying population
Note: Skillington 177%, Scredington 113%, Hainton 105%, Searby 50%, Strubby 82%,
Wellingore 69%, Glentham 49%. Parishes arranged from smallest to largest population.

to the number of households in each parish and, more tentatively, to the total population. Both of these estimates can then be compared with the number of men serving on inquests.[32]

Figure 1 shows the number of *inquisitores* as a percentage of the taxpaying population in each parish.[33] In the three parishes with the smallest taxpaying population—Skillington, Scredington, and Hainton—the *inquisitores* amount to more than 100 percent of the taxpaying population. This means either that service on the inquest regularly extended beyond the taxpayers to include other parishioners, or that with such a small population the taxpayers each served more than once. In the larger settlements, there were fewer opportunities to serve on the inquest than there were taxpaying heads of household, and so the *inquisitores* as a percentage of the taxpaying population falls below 100 percent. However, as we saw in Chapter 6, the lay subsidies left between half and two-thirds of households unassessed and unrecorded, meaning that we have to think beyond this first tranche of information.

When historians have claimed some sort of inclusivity for the late medieval parish they have sometimes done so without qualification. A more cautious position has been to argue that the household and not the individual was the basic unit of social life. It was only as householders that women could serve as churchwardens, for example, and parochial levies to pay for the upkeep of the church were imposed upon households rather than individuals. Figure 2 shows the number of *inquisitores* as a percentage of the estimated number of

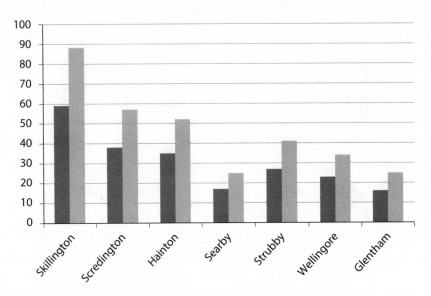

FIGURE 2. Parish representatives as a percentage of estimated
number of households: lower and upper estimates
Note: Skillington 59–88%, Scredington 38–57%, Hainton 35–52%,
Searby 17–25%, Strubby 27–41%, Wellingore 23–34%, Glentham 16–25%.
Parishes arranged from smallest to largest population.

householders. The figures presented here cast doubt on the assumption that parish responsibility and privilege were divided equally *amongst householders*. This is clear from the fact that even in the smaller parishes where the number of *inquisitores* exceeded the number of taxpayers, not all householders were able to play a part in the representation of the parish. It is possible that in Skillington almost all the households within the parish took their turn on the inquest, but the lower estimate for the number of households would suggest participation was limited to about 60 percent of households. In Searby and Glentham only between 16 percent and 25 percent of households could have participated. Clearly the situation could vary a great deal from place to place.

Figure 3 pours even more cold water on any notion of general or widespread inclusivity. This chart shows the number of men serving on inquests as a percentage of the total estimated population.[34] Even in Skillington, the parish with the smallest total population, and where a majority of the taxpayers may have served on the inquest at one time or another, the proportion of the whole parish who had this opportunity was limited to between 13 percent and 20 percent. In Searby and Glentham only between 4 percent and 6 percent of the total population served on the inquest. The figures lying behind these proportions must obviously be treated with some caution as they are derived from estimates, which are in turn based upon assumptions about tax

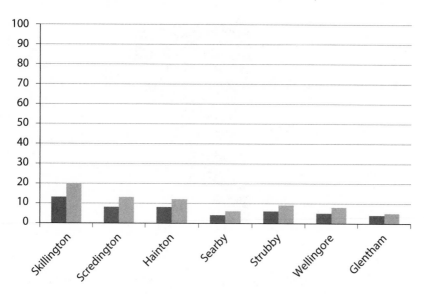

FIGURE 3. Parish representatives as a percentage of estimated
population: lower and upper estimates
Note: Skillington 13–20%, Scredington 8–13%, Hainton 8–12%,
Searby 4–6%, Strubby 6–9%, Wellingore 5–8%, Glentham 4–5%.
Parishes arranged from smallest to largest population.

paying and household size. It is possible that one or more of our parishes was seriously anomalous on one of these counts, though no reason has been found to indicate that this was the case. It might also be countered that the total population included women and children as well as adult men and that it is unfair to judge medieval social institutions by present-day standards. While the exclusion of women from many areas of public life in the Middle Ages was commonplace and seldom remarked upon by contemporaries, that does not mean that we should not comment on it, seek to explain it, or ask how it affected the lives of people in the parish. The invisible structures of everyday life are, after all, arguably the most important ones. Many adult men—servants, labourers, youths, and grandfathers—were also excluded from householder privileges and responsibilities, and their absence from the public life of the parish is likewise obscured by the tendency to treat householders as if they alone constituted 'the parish'.

The Structure of Parish Elites

In Chapter 6 we saw that trustworthy status correlated to higher wealth (measured by the proxy values of rent and tax) to some degree, especially in regions

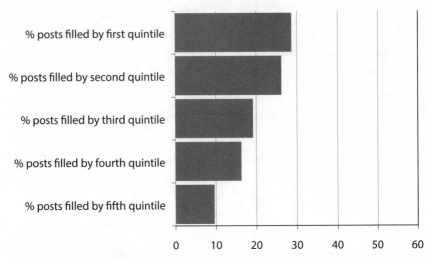

FIGURE 4. Frequency of service amongst the parish representatives of Skillington.

of commercial agriculture with pronounced economic inequality. Now we have seen that over a twelve-year period a group of Lincolnshire parishes were represented by between 16 and 88 percent of householders, or between just 4 and 20 percent of the total population. Despite bringing large numbers of male peasant householders into the lower rungs of ecclesiastical government, we clearly need to resist the temptation to accept the assumptions of many parish historians. The quality of our data allows one further piece of analysis, which is to investigate whether trustworthy men were all equal—amongst themselves—or whether there were further inequalities structuring these very local elites. Figures 4 to 11 depict the distribution of the frequency of service amongst the men of the inquest in our group of parishes. They illustrate political inequalities *within* the elite. These charts were produced by dividing the *inquisitores* into five bands or quintiles depending on frequency of service.[35] The first quintile therefore includes those who acted most often, while the fifth quintile is made up of those who acted least often. In a situation of perfectly rotating service there would be no difference between these bands: each quintile of *inquisitores* would fill 20 percent of the available posts over the twelve years. The parish that comes closest to this distribution is Skillington (Figure 4), where the first quintile of *inquisitores* filled 29 percent of the posts, the second 26 percent, the third 19 percent, the fourth 16 percent, and the fifth just under 10 percent. It looks as though Skillington was a place where the parish elite was relatively flat within itself. If you were a member of this group you could expect to serve your turn.

All the other parishes for which this exercise has been completed show a markedly different distribution of service on inquests (Figures 5–11), emphasizing how unusual Skillington was. In Friesthorpe, for example (Figure 11),

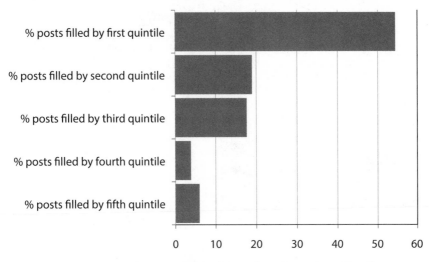

FIGURE 5. Frequency of service amongst the parish representatives of Scredington.

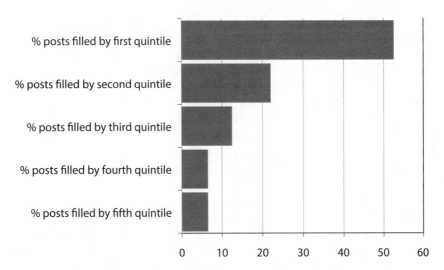

FIGURE 6. Frequency of service amongst the parish representatives of Hainton.

the first quintile of *inquisitores* filled 49 percent of the posts, the second 24 percent, the third 16 percent, the fourth 7 percent, and the fifth just under 4 percent. This was an oligarchy made up of just four men who served sixteen, fifteen, thirteen, and twelve times, respectively. We must question therefore just how much of an impact the other fifteen trustworthy men of Friesthorpe could have hoped to make. In Glentham (Figure 10) the first quintile filled 52 percent of posts and the second 16 percent, while the third, fourth, and fifth

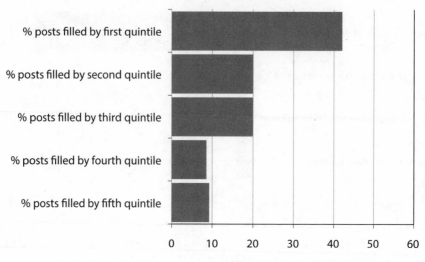

FIGURE 7. Frequency of service amongst the parish representatives of Searby.

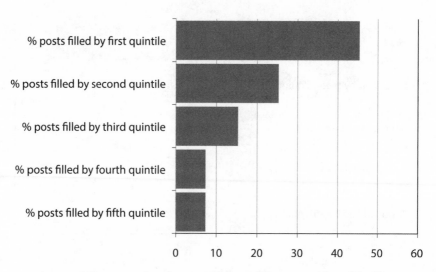

FIGURE 8. Frequency of service amongst the parish representatives of Strubby.

quintiles filled just under 11 percent each. One man served nine times, while twenty-three men served just once.[36] We must conclude that even when a large number of men serve as *inquisitores* in relation to the number of opportunities over twelve years (a task for which they were presumably thought qualified), this does not indicate a flat elite where each suitable man could expect to serve his turn with any regularity. Where we have comparable evidence from elsewhere in the country, similar basic patterns present themselves. For example, in some

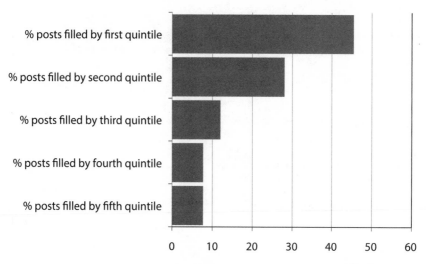

FIGURE 9. Frequency of service amongst the parish representatives of Wellingore.

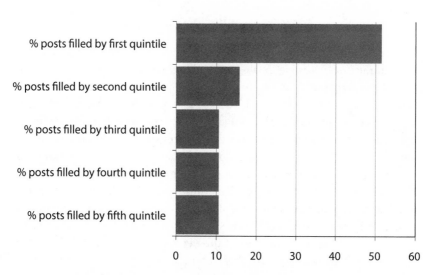

FIGURE 10. Frequency of service amongst the parish representatives of Glentham.

of the Devon parishes under the jurisdiction of Exeter cathedral we have records of two or three successive visitations in the early fourteenth century. At Culmstock there were eight synodal witnesses or jurors in 1301 and nine in 1303; three men served on both occasions. At Norton there were five jurors in 1301 and twenty in 1303; four men served on both occasions. Finally, at Salcombe, there were eight 'parishioners' in 1301, fifteen in 1303, and fourteen in 1307; two men served on all three occasions and eleven served twice.[37]

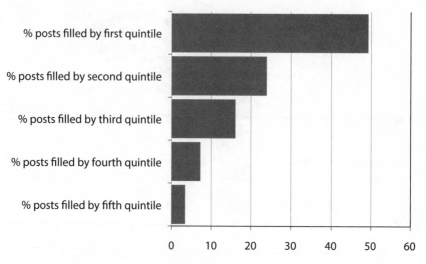

FIGURE 11. Frequency of service amongst the parish representatives of Friesthorpe.

Regimes of Representation

Differences between the Lincolnshire parishes can be used to describe and explain the range possible in late medieval regimes of parish representation. The characteristics for which they will be compared are those contained in Table 4. The nature of the local landscape and its agriculture and settlement patterns was of fundamental, if not always determinative, importance to the social lives of late medieval parishioners. The underlying potential and limitations of agriculture and the nucleation or dispersal of settlements did much to shape the geographical distribution of wealth at a number of scales, from the broad region to the parish or village. Varieties of lordship could affect the balance of economic power and the nature of local authority, and the wealth of the parish was also affected by its size, location, and resources. The wealth of each parish has been taken from the 1334 lay subsidy returns.[38] For the most part our parishes were roughly coterminous with the vills used in royal administration, the exceptions being Strubby, which also included the hamlet of Woodthorpe, and Searby, which included the settlements of Owmby and Grasby in addition to the main village. Knowing the size of the taxpaying population and the assessed wealth of parishes means that we can calculate the mean 'wealth' of individual taxpayers in each place.[39] This figure can be compared to the wealth of individual *inquisitores*, where they can be identified. As in Chapter 6, the mean wealth of taxpayers in each vill can be used in conjunction with Campbell and Bartley's calculations of *regional* mean wealth per taxpayer, regional landed wealth, and the density of taxpayers per mile. All this information helps to contextualize the characteristics of local office-holding and parish representation as seen in the dean and chapter's visitation book.[40]

Table 4. Comparing the parishes subject to the Dean and Chapter of Lincoln, 1337–49

Parish	Landscape, agriculture, settlement	Lordship	Taxable value in 1334	Taxpaying population in 1327/1332	Mean assessed wealth per taxpayer 1327, 1332, 1334	Measures of microregional wealth	Inequality of tax burden (Gini index)	Inequality amongst the men of the inquest (Gini index)	Men of inquest as percentage of all householders
Wellingore	Scarp parish (limestone heath and clay vale); nucleated settlements	St Catherine's Priory, Linc.; Temple Bruer Hospitallers	£90	45	£2 (high)	High £.p.t. High £.p.m. High t.p.m.	33.58	38.08	23–34%
Skillington	Limestone heath; mixed farming; nucleated settlements	Thomas de Sancto Laudo	£41 18s	13	£3.2 (very high)	High £.p.t. Low £.p.m. High t.p.m.	44.95	19.24	59–88%
Scredington	Clay or marl lowlands (floodplain); mixed farming; nucleated settlements	William Latimer	£65 14s 8.25d	15	£4.4 (very high)	Very high £.p.t. Very high £.p.m. Very high t.p.m.	30.61	45.32	38–57%
Hainton	Chalk wolds; mixed farming; nucleated settlements	D&C Lincoln	£55 17s 6d	22	£2.5 (very high)	Low £.p.t. Low £.p.m. High t.p.m.	43.15	43.00	35–52%

Table 4. (*continued*)

Parish	Landscape, agriculture, settlement	Lordship	Taxable value in 1334	Taxpaying population in 1327/1332	Mean assessed wealth per taxpayer 1327, 1332, 1334	Measures of microregional wealth	Inequality of tax burden (Gini index)	Inequality amongst the men of the inquest (Gini index)	Men of inquest as percentage of all householders
Searby	Scarp parish; mixed farming with sheep specialism; nucleated settlements	D&C Lincoln	£31 5s	25	£1.3 (very low)	Low £.p.t. Low £.p.m. High t.p.m.	33.53	31.08	17–25%
Strubby	Chalk/flint lowlands; medium to high density of dispersed settlements	Duchy of Lancaster and Bardney Abbey	£51 2s 6d	33	£1.5 (low)	Low £.p.t. High £.p.m. High t.p.m.	34.81	37.36	27–41%
Glentham	Clay or marl lowlands; mixed farming, open fields; nucleated settlements	D&C Lincoln	£135 11s 3d	65	£2.1 (high)	Low £.p.t. High £.p.m. High t.p.m.	38.10	35.12	16–25%
Friesthorpe	Chalk/flint lowlands; nucleated settlements	D&C Lincoln	–	–	–	Low £.p.t. Low £.p.m. High t.p.m.	–	–	–

Note: £.p.t. = regional mean wealth per taxpayer; £.p.m. = landed wealth per square mile; t.p.m. = number of taxpayers per square mile.

I will begin with Wellingore, the parish that in Chapter 6 seemed to be an example of broad-based trustworthy status, with the men of the inquest drawn from across the spectrum of the taxpaying population. The lands of Wellingore rise from the clay vale of the river Witham to the south of Lincoln, up a steep scarp and onto the limestone heath, giving it a variety of soil conditions and supporting a mixed agriculture of pastoral and arable farming. The main settlement was a nucleated village beside Ermine Street, and there appears to have been relatively little dispersed settlement beyond this. Lordship was shared between St Catherine's Priory just outside Lincoln and the Hospitallers of Temple Bruer. Wellingore was the second wealthiest parish of the seven, with the second largest taxpaying population. Mean individual wealth was high, in common with the surrounding region; landed wealth was also high in the area. Economic inequality amongst the taxpayers was not very pronounced, and so we could characterize Wellingore as a parish where substantial peasant producers lived side by side with some very successful lords and major landholders. Given its size it is not surprising that participation in the inquest was limited to between 23 and 34 percent of householders. This starts to make the picture of inclusivity sketched in Chapter 6 look decidedly shaky. But we can go further: Wellingore had the third most unequal distribution of service amongst the trustworthy men, expressed in the Gini index. Within its trustworthy elite, a very small number dominated the business of the parish.

If we want to see what 'broad participation' might have looked like, we must turn to Skillington, the smallest of our seven parishes, situated on rolling limestone heathlands on the border between Lincolnshire and Leicestershire, an area of mixed farming and nucleated settlements. It was under the secular lordship of Thomas de Sancto Laudo in the 1330s and 1340s. Its small size—just thirteen taxpayers—partly explains its position as the second poorest parish in the sample, but we need to compare this to the mean assessed wealth of all vills in England in 1334, which was just under forty pounds, with a modal value of between fifteen and twenty pounds. At forty-one pounds eighteen shillings Skillington was, although small in its taxpaying population, just above this mean, an achievement explained by the very high mean level of wealth enjoyed by its individual taxpayers. They were richer than the inhabitants of most neighbouring villages at this date, though some were wealthier than others. Lordship in this area, however, was not so well-to-do. The *inquisitions post mortem* indicate low levels of landed wealth. Given its size the majority (between 59 and 88 percent) of householders served on the inquest at one time or another in the twelve recorded years. What is more there was great parity amongst the men of the inquest in the regularity of their service. As demonstrated by Figure 4, the frequency of service within Skillington's officeholding elite was distributed remarkably equitably. This is even more striking when set against the fact that Skillington suffered from the highest level of inequality between taxpayers, to say nothing of the resources of the population who fell below the tax threshold. This was not quite a republic of wealthy peasant landholders, but simply a place where the economic elite did not dominate parish representation. Why this was will be discussed in due course.

Scredington lies to the south of Sleaford on the edge of the fens. It was an area of mixed farming and nucleated settlements in the early fourteenth century, with a propensity to dramatic flooding. The lord was William Latimer. Although it was the second-smallest parish, Scredington was extremely wealthy because its taxpayers had the highest mean wealth of the seven parishes. It was, furthermore, surrounded by equally wealthy villages. Landed wealth was also high, and the density of the taxpaying population was very high. This area of England had one of the premier concentrations of wealth at all levels of society. This is borne out by the very low level of economic inequality amongst taxpayers. We are looking at a society made up of substantial peasant landholders living alongside wealthy lords. The size of the parish also meant that quite a high proportion (38–57 percent) of householders could expect to serve on the inquest at one time or another. In many respects Scredington looks exceedingly similar to Skillington. But one crucial fact separated them. While service on Skillington's inquest was shared fairly evenly amongst the householders despite economic inequality, the pattern in Scredington was completely different. Here the distribution of service amongst the men of the inquest was the most unequal of all seven parishes. There may have been economic parity between the householders of Scredington, but an elite nonetheless differentiated itself by exerting tight control over the representation and regulation of the parish over time.

Hainton was one of three parishes where the dean and chapter of Lincoln were simultaneously patron of the church and lord of the manor. Situated on the western edge of the Lincolnshire wolds, this was another wealthy parish based on mixed farming, with a regional specialism in sheep rearing. The mean wealth of taxpayers was very high, though not as great as in Skillington or Scredington, and Hainton was also different from those two places in that it stood out vividly against a backdrop of low wealth within its microregion, both for lords and for taxpayers as a whole. Mean wealth is, in this case, quite misleading, because Hainton was a very unequal place, with a Gini index of economic inequality similar to that of Skillington. Between a third and a half of householders took part in the inquest over time, but service was not distributed equally. Hainton shared with Scredington a very high degree of inequality amongst the men of the inquest in terms of frequency of service. This was a parish where a small economic elite also dominated the politics of the parish.

In social terms Searby was an altogether different place. A scarp parish in northern Lincolnshire, it was, like Hainton, in a sheep rearing area. But while this fact had made some men in Hainton quite well-off, the taxpayers of Searby were the poorest of the seven parishes, falling into Campbell and Bartley's 'very low' category of mean wealth. There was a good deal of parity amongst these parishioners, with a relatively low rate of inequality, and they did not have many wealthy landed neighbours. Their lord was the dean and chapter of Lincoln. Unlike any of the parishes described so far, Searby enjoyed both relatively low economic inequality amongst taxpayers, and relatively low inequality of service amongst the men of the inquest. However, this did not translate into broad-based participation in parish government because only between 17 percent and 25 percent of householders were able to serve on the inquest. If a male householder made it into the group deemed worthy to represent the parish he could expect to serve with reasonable regularity, but there was quite a low probability that he would achieve this first, necessary, step. The men of the inquest guarded their exclusivity with quite careful attention to the rotation of service within their select group. This must have left a considerable portion of roughly equal neighbouring householders excluded from the inquest.

Strubby, on the lowlands of eastern Lincolnshire about two miles from the medieval coastline, was, unlike all the other six parishes, located in an area of dispersed settlement. It was under the lordship of the Duchy of Lancaster and Bardney Abbey, in a region where landed wealth was high, but the rest of the taxpaying population possessed only 'low' mean wealth. The taxpayers of Strubby were of a kind with their neighbours. In this land of the poor householder there was a median level of economic inequality. But shared hardship did not translate into equal opportunities for householders to represent the parish and to contribute to the regulation of local society. Between 27 and 41 percent of householders could expect to serve on the inquest at one time or another, but service was concentrated unequally into the hands of a small group of regular *inquisitores* who must have dominated their fellows over the years.

Glentham stands out as the only one of the seven parishes to have had a regular market, meeting every Monday since 1278.[41] The market charter had been renewed to the lord of one local manor, William de Snartford, in 1328, but the dean and chapter of Lincoln also had a manor in the parish. The vill was inhabited by sixty-five taxpaying householders in the 1330s and, with a possible total population of between 585 and 878, it could be classed as a small town.[42] The taxpaying population enjoyed high mean wealth, though there was quite a high degree of economic inequality amongst them. Because of the high population only between 16 and 25 percent of householders could expect to serve on the inquest, and regular participation was further restricted to the first quintile of *inquisitores* who, over time, filled more than half the available posts. The peasant producers of the surrounding countryside were not wealthy, falling into Campbell and Bartley's 'low' category of mean wealth. The urban features of the parish also had a striking effect on the assessment for the tax of a twentieth on moveable goods in 1327. Of all the places surveyed in this and the preceding chapter, Glentham's assessment is divided into the greatest number of minute gradations.[43] The most common approach taken by sub-taxers elsewhere was to simplify the wealth of the people in their vill, resulting in bands assessed at round numbers—eight pence, twelve pence, two shillings, five shillings, and so on—with a few anomalous individual assessments that look like the result of some careful negotiation. In Glentham, by contrast, the liabilities assigned to the sixty-five taxpayers were divided into thirty-one bands, sometimes differentiated by a single penny. The strong impression this gives is of a parish where the precise position of men within an intuitively known economic hierarchy was enormously important, at least to those whom it affected.

Hierarchy was real, and it mattered. This has been too-little acknowledged in historians' debates about the governance of the late medieval parish. Even if there was a high degree of participation amongst male householders, the implications of this need to be understood within the context of the total exclusion of women from ecclesiastical inquests and visitation panels, and the near-total exclusion of young men, servants, and others who were not heads of households. To take a prominent example from the field of parish studies, Eamon Duffy's wonderfully evocative study of Morebath in Devon relies upon a view of the parish as broadly participatory, whatever the tensions and struggles that shaped people's lives. Duffy uses the Tudor lay subsidy rolls to show that those who held parish office at one time or another made up a majority of the taxpaying population (35 out of 55, or 64 percent). This figure is given in support of the claim that there was a 'highly self-conscious community life' in this now-famous parish where 'decision-making and accountability were dominant characteristics'.[44] But Morebath was not, on the basis of this figure, a typically, or even exceptionally, inclusive place. Historical demographers tend to assume that the Tudor lay subsidies recorded about 15 percent of the total population in any given place.[45] This would mean that Morebath's total population was in the region of 367, a figure that would significantly reduce Duffy's proffered 64 percent participation rate in parish government to something more like 10 percent.

A salient feature of parish life in Morebath, which may have encouraged Duffy to argue for its inclusive nature, was the rotation of offices, particularly that of the 'high warden', among the various households of the parish.[46] This was a parish made up of scattered hamlets and farms with barely a greater concentration of habitation in the main village, where the church was located. Rotation of offices according to its settlement pattern may have been a way to minimize social envy and maximize the flow of such emotions as would make it easy to collect money on behalf of the church. Something similar is suggested by the archbishop of York's 1306 instruction to conduct a visitation of the hospitals of St Mary Magdalen and St John in Ripon through the priests and wardens of the hospitals as well as 'eight trustworthy men *from one part of the town of Ripon*, whose opinion is to be commended above that of others, as well as the same number of trustworthy and unsuspected men *from the other part of Ripon*, through whom the states and foundations of the hospitals may better be inquired into and known'.[47] Local sensitivities about representation and inclusivity could often be felt in geographic terms. Kit French has identified the rotation of service as a churchwarden among about thirty families in Nettlecombe, Somerset, over a fifteen-year cycle. The rotation seems to have been related to landholding.[48] In this respect Morebath may have experienced rough parity amongst the men who regularly served the parish. But it is misleading to present those qualified men, drawn only from among the taxpayers, as if they constituted a majority, even amongst the householders.

In our Lincolnshire parishes rotation of service is most pronounced in Skillington. Here men acted in groups of four, to be replaced the following year with a wholly different group: for example Robert atte Church, Richard Strouston, William son of Thomas, and William Coldhill in the autumn of 1337, replaced in the summer of 1338 by John Bully, Simon son of Thomas, Robert atte Gate, and Richard Coynthorp.[49] Rotation of this kind, with very little overlap from one inquest to the next, indicates a planned and well-understood system, perhaps based on the microgeography of habitation with the parish, or on tithings or guild membership. The underlying rationale is unrecoverable, but its effects are clear and we can speculate about its implications. Regular rotation, whatever its mechanism, would have created an expectation of service; not just at some nonspecific and hoped-for point in the future, but according to a broadly predictable timetable. Service in relatively fixed groups would, moreover, have given individual *inquisitores* a shared sense of expectation. All of this would have made it harder for a small faction to dominate the inquest over time, even if they had wanted to.[50]

On occasion deviation from patterns of service hints at the tensions that everywhere must have affected parish representation.[51] In November 1345 there seems to have been some sort of crisis in the inquest at Friesthorpe, a place where service rotated amongst the leading families. For several years the families of Stures, Sembel, Jolliffe, Swalecliff, and Francis had been present on almost every inquest. Suddenly they were all gone, save that Thomas Francis was substituted by his son, Thomas Francis junior. However, the new inquest was weak and does not seem to have commanded the respect of the wider pool of suitable men. Francis junior could not control the reporting of sin and crime in the way his father had done, for, despite being on the inquest, he found himself cited for violence against Margaret Rauf, something which he admitted and for which he was flogged three times around the church. The old order returned in July 1346.[52] We have no way of knowing what caused this temporary disturbance of oligarchy, but it serves to emphasize the political importance of service on the inquest.

One place that allows us to corroborate the importance of some of the themes we have been discussing, as well as to make wider comparisons, is Hartlebury in Worcestershire. Like the Lincolnshire parishes, Hartlebury was

a peculiar jurisdiction outside the bishop's control and where an equally id-
iosyncratic form of record keeping was applied to the annual chapters and
visitations, allowing us to follow a group of parish representatives over time.
First we may observe something of the mechanism by which the trustworthy
men were selected each year from the wider pool of men qualified (in whatever
way) for such service. On 11 October 1408 eighteen parishioners were listed in
the book, of whom six were picked out by a small cross beside their name.[53]
This hints at a similar situation to that in the fourteenth-century Lincolnshire
parishes, where there was a pool of suitable men who might serve on the inquest from among whose number a few would be selected, or self-select, on
each occasion.

These general principles are borne out by a more rigorous analysis of the
frequency with which Hartlebury men served between 1475 and 1480, when
the court book records the names of the trustworthy men and the wardens of
the church and its 'services' most systematically.[54] Each year there were twelve
'parishioners' or trustworthy men, plus two or three churchwardens, and there
were usually (except in 1479 and 1480) two wardens of St Mary's chantry. In
1478 there was an additional warden given responsibility for 'le chetul', which
may have meant the chattels of the church. Altogether there were ninety-one
posts to be filled over five years. These roles were undertaken by 41 men out
of a total adult population that may have numbered between 340 and 420.[55]
Although comparison with the Lincolnshire parishes discussed above is complicated by the differences between the 1327–32 lay subsidies and those of 1524
and 1525, it is worth our consideration.

In Hartlebury around 72 percent of the taxpaying population were active
in the parish elite. When we expand the number of taxpayers, having used a
multiplier of 6.67 to reach an estimated figure for the total population, we
can say that there were around 380 adults living in Hartlebury, of whom
11 percent acted as trustworthy men in the five-year period. There was clearly
considerable selection by gender and social status. Within the pool of men
suitable for office-holding there was a further hierarchy dividing those who
served once or twice from those who served frequently, and expected to do so.
Men such as Ralph Hart of Lincomb, Richard atte Wall of Gatebridge, and
William Merston of Waresley acted with such regularity that they must have
been instrumental in deciding who else could serve and how often. There was a
steep gradient between them and the other office-holders, though not so pronounced as that which afflicted most of the Lincolnshire parishes.[56]

Hartlebury was also characterized by assiduous sensitivity to the representation of the various settlements within the parish and to the perennial
involvement of the leading families. Each record of a court session gives the
names of the hamlets of Waresley, Lincomb, Gatebridge, Titton, Torton,
Charlton, Mitton, and Hartlebury itself as toponyms, attached to the names

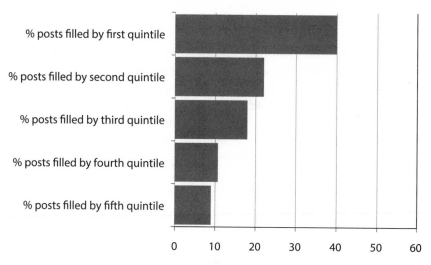

FIGURE 12. Frequency of service amongst the parish
representatives of Hartlebury, 1475–80.

of the office-holders in addition to their surnames. Moreover, certain leading
families like the Harts, Ballards, Walls, Thatchers, and Hodges were represented by at least one member at each session. This suggests a collective acceptance, among the elite, that expectations should be met if stability was to be
maintained. Many other relationships are, of course, obscured from our sight,
and the play of local politics that would have been palpable at the time without
needing explicit articulation is now almost obliterated. Late fifteenth-century
Hartlebury therefore provides another example of a small elite maintaining its
hold on the tasks of representing and regulating the parish by ensuring that all
those deemed suitable to serve got an opportunity to do so, while most power
was concentrated in the hands of a core group.

The examples discussed here have demonstrated some of the possible variation in regimes of parish representation over time. While no two places were
exactly alike, they all experienced concentrations of power based on gender,
wealth, or status.

Allegiances

But in order to understand how the trustworthy men set about using this
power, we need to piece together what evidence we can about their allegiances
and their behaviour. This is to turn from a quantitative to a qualitative analysis
of parish representation. There is no reason to imagine this could be a simple
task. Determining the allegiances of trustworthy men—with each other, their
neighbours, lords, clergy, and other institutions—is a matter of interpretation.

For example, at Kingston in Cambridgeshire, in an example we have encountered more than once already, the trustworthy men can be seen juggling the demands of the lord, the community, and their own activities: working together to bring a violent thief to court—surely a matter of public concern—but also using the court to pursue personal complaints about defamation, and feeling the wrath of the lord and their neighbours alike for allowing their animals to graze on other people's land, and for failing to maintain common resources like ditches.[57] There can be no conclusive evidence, but there are strong indications of how such relationships were structured.

It is sensible to begin with a fuller consideration of the evidence for how trustworthy men were selected. For some historians local leadership has seemed consensual, an expression of the popular will: churchwardens elected in popular assemblies and manorial office-holders 'chosen' by the community as a whole on the grounds of their skills and experience.[58] In reality it was complex, everywhere. As with the appointment of churchwardens, the language used to describe the selection of trustworthy men is not always helpful. Examples of that etymological false-friend *electus*, meaning chosen, can be found in Hereford diocese in 1363, 1385, and 1513 for example, as well as equally opaque talk of 'nomination'.[59] Bishops often assumed that their commissioned officers would personally select the men. The archbishop of York in 1287 asked his official to choose those men 'whose opinion you would rate more highly than others' (*quos ceteris preferat opinio commendata*); the bishop of Carlisle around 1340 instructed his commissary to exercise his own discretion; the archdeacon of Stow in 1364 was told it was 'his decision' who to cite from the parishes.[60] In a lawsuit of 1303 the archdeacon of Dorset was given slightly more detailed instructions: he was to cite 'trustworthy and sworn witnesses' chosen by himself, in addition to whoever the plaintiff produced. Differentiating between publicly chosen and privately produced witnesses suggests something of the ideology of the law. Trustworthiness was meant to rest upon impartiality, and while the locals were thought the best source of information, *which* locals was a decision best taken by a figure of authority.[61]

Sometimes very lowly, and local, church officers were charged with the selection of trustworthy men. At Edlingham, Northumberland, in 1430 a summoner was instructed to empanel visitation representatives. He was to see that they were of good fame and opinion, and that they were the sort of people who would better know and would speak the truth. Their trustworthiness was his to assess.[62] But the local clergy must often have been best placed to make such assessments. At Glentham in 1337 the vicar was told to lead the men 'nominated to the inquest' to inspect a piece of church land, while at Ludlow in 1536 the rural dean was given detailed instructions for the citation of trustworthy men. In both instances the phrasing suggests that these local clerics were responsible for the selection.[63] At other times, however, the risks of local selection—inscrutable bias and the loss of impartiality—sprang to the front of the institutional mind, and the local clergy were explicitly sidelined in favour of selection by 'the official himself'.[64]

All of this may, however, have been a bureaucratic fantasy. How could an official, or even a rural dean, arrive in a parish and begin making assessments of who was trustworthy and who was not? The variability in local regimes of representation, as seen in the Lincolnshire examples above, may be evidence of how inscrutable such arrangements were to a church official. The bishop's commissary, whoever he was, would have had to find a way of including those men without whom nothing could be done, and this meant finding a balance between the needs of episcopal government, the ebb and flow of social capital in the parish, and the demands of lordship. Lordship was one form of authority whose perspective was often closer to the ground than that of bishops. Lords, unlike bishops, could certainly influence the choice of trustworthy men, though this tends to be visible only when it related to an issue that aligned with the lord's own interests. On such occasions the *fidedigni* might have been closer to the *fideles* or loyal dependents of a lord, discussed in Chapter 4.

There were seven members of the inquest into the value of Blyth vicarage in 1281. We can say something about the status of six of them.[65] A more fundamental detail though, is that they were all tenants under the lordship of Blyth Priory, which controlled the vicarage, and, what is more, none of them held any land in the two other manors within the parish for which records survive.[66] Since the inquest had the potential to result in a call for the monks of the priory to increase their expenditure on the vicar's income, it may not be a coincidence that the panel was packed with the priory's tenants. As lord, the monks may have influenced the composition of the inquest in the hope that the trustworthy men would realize what side their bread was buttered. One of them, John of Blyth, was a tenant of the priory whose known activities illustrate the multiple levels at which dealings with the monks shaped local life. He was a substantial tenant with at least three separate properties rented from the priory; one of these he sublet. He regularly witnessed the land transactions of his neighbours, including some among the local gentry. By 1281 he was an old man, and he died soon after 1290. His son Simon granted one of John's properties back to the monks in return for an anniversary mass, and his widow Beatrice was at pains to remain a friend of the priory, granting them one acre of land in return for a token rent of a rose.[67] John and his fellow trustworthy men, and their families, owed the continuation of their tenancies to the good will of the priory as their lord.

In common with secular lords of the later Middle Ages, religious houses believed they had the right to influence the composition of inquests that affected their interests. Indeed they believed that this was the best way to achieve justice. Bishops meanwhile often sought to limit the exercise of this local power, or at least to be seen to limit it. In another dispute rumbling on in 1281 the bishop of Lincoln and the abbot of Peterborough were arguing over the right to present a priest to serve in Clopton church in Northamptonshire. Commenting on this dispute, the chronicler of the abbey noted caustically that the trustworthy men of the inquest had been examined without anyone seeking the assent or consulting the will of the abbot and convent. He presented this as an error of judgement by Bishop Sutton, but it may well have been intended as a snub to the convent. Perhaps the bishop preferred not to interview stooges put up by the monks to parrot their line.[68]

When inquests of trustworthy men were called to look into the patronage of churches, there were almost always powerful interests at work behind the scenes, a point discussed at greater length in Chapter 11. It could be very helpful to local lords if some of the (supposedly impartial) locals were tied to them or had a similar outlook. In 1419 for example there was an inquest into the desirability of unifying the Somerset parishes of Capland and Beercrocombe. Neither church, it was said, could support a rector from its own resources, but together they might. A local panel of trustworthy men was asked to report on the value of Capland, and to say who its rightful patron was. Eight laymen and several clerics together recommended the union of the two parishes, and they recited how the patronage of Capland had descended through the Beaupeny and Harewell families. In fact the patronage of both Capland and Beercrocombe had been in Harewell hands since 1389, so it seems likely that this union was being promoted by the present lord, Roger Harewell. Sadly, most of the trustworthy men cannot be identified. One, John Cok, described himself and his wife as 'poor people of mediocre status', surely without vested interest, but another, John Drew looks to have been closely aligned with the lord. Drew should probably be described as a yeoman. Ten years after the parish inquest Roger Harewell sold various pasture and meadows in Beercrocombe and Capland to Drew and his heirs for a single payment of twenty-two pounds thirteen shillings four pence.[69] Drew was clearly a wealthy man with connections to the lord; and it is hard to imagine him being the buyer of Harewell's land had he not given a decision favourable to his lord in 1419. By the fifteenth century there was often little to separate a struggling lord from a wealthy peasant, and we could reasonably imagine these two men sharing the influence that accrued to the richest in the village.

For the most part we should imagine that trustworthy men were identified through a combination of self-selection and the exercise of episcopal and lordly power. But self-selection did not mean the community selection that Sheri Olson has argued in respect of manorial officers. It meant selection by those who were already the acknowledged leaders of local society, for contrary to Tilly, in historical reality it is impossible to pinpoint precise moments when elite formation begins.[70] Neither was it ever entirely a done deal. Fortunes could fall as well as rise. Take for example the case of Hugh Writhel of Tarrant

Gunville in Dorset. Hugh's family had been substantial villein tenants of the manor at least since the 1370s, when John Writhel was one of just three house-holders to hold twenty-four acres of land. In the early 1390s Hugh Writhel's fortunes were on the up. He had just leased twelve acres of land with a house and garden from the reeve of the manor, and in April 1394 he was chosen to be one of the three laymen representing the parish before Bishop Waltham's visita-tion. With the right family background, good-sized landholdings, and positive relations with the manorial administrators it should be no surprise that he was inducted into the small group of trustworthy men. However, in October 1394, just six months after he had stepped into the bishop's presence as a trustwor-thy parish representative, Hugh's fortunes began to change. The court roll tells that his son, Thomas, failed to perform 'suit of court'. That is, he was obliged to appear in the manor court as a condition of his tenancy, but had not done so. This was common enough. Suitors of manorial courts often found attendance a bit of a burden when they had other pressures on their time, and Thomas's default need not have affected the family unduly, had it not continued. But by 1395 it was clear that Thomas was not just absent from court; he had fled the village. He may have been chasing a better opportunity elsewhere. If he had committed some crime it is likely to have been mentioned in the court rolls, but there is nothing there. Villein tenants were bound to their lord's manor un-less manumitted (freed), and one option open to the lord of Tarrant Gunville would have been to pursue Thomas under the terms of the Statute of Labour-ers, which had been reissued as recently as 1390.[71] But in keeping with local custom the whole homage of the court (all the suitors) were collectively fined for Thomas's absence. This fine, with its implication of collective responsibility for Thomas's return, was repeated at every court until October 1400. The pres-sure and expectation heaped upon Hugh Writhel must have been immense. In 1400 Thomas was still absent, and now Hugh failed to appear as well.

His standing in the village was in jeopardy. But then we begin to discern the beginnings of a recovery. In March 1401 Hugh was able to act as a guaran-tor to a property transaction, which would not have happened had he been unpopular with the suitors. In April the following year he was fined personally for his son's absence. Perhaps he had persuaded the court that responsibility should not lie with the whole homage. Whatever the micropolitics of his career during this period, by 1407, when he was appointed reeve, Hugh had clearly resumed his position as a trusted member of the village elite.[72] Selection by the group of already-elite leading householders gave trustworthy men a natu-ral allegiance to that group, but it could be broken.

Self-selection is also implied by the fact that local office-holders used their position to further their own interests.[73] At Blandford Forum in Dorset Walter Potter and Thomas Helier were appointed as bailiffs in 1391. They were im-mediately fined for failing to levy twenty-two shillings on the goods of one *Wil-liam* Potter on account of an unpaid debt. If William was Walter's kinsman, it is hardly surprising that Walter did not distrain (confiscate) his goods. Remarkably this abuse of power was allowed to persist, with the same bailiffs making the same refusal in 1392. Two years later Potter and Helier were parish representatives together, reporting to Bishop Waltham's visitation.[74] Given that they were capable of using manorial institutions to further their own interests we cannot be sure that they did not do the same when called to the visitation tribunal as trustworthy men. Compromises sometimes had to be made between the demands of family or self-interest and the bonds of obligation to the wider community. However, it may not be necessary to confine this question to the sphere of conscious motivations. At a deeper level, 'positions of authority . . . brought secondary economic and social advantages' whether these were actively sought or not.[75] Many things that were done consensually in the name of the community might in fact serve the interests of a narrower group, and we should not confuse collective action with egalitarian principles. In the absence of clear evidence one way or the other we should assume that trustworthy men acted sometimes for the common good and sometimes from more personal motivations. There is, moreover, some evidence that these motivations made them rather unpleasant neighbours.

The parishioners of Wimborne St Giles and Wimborne Sanctorum (or All Hallows) in Dorset seem to have been particularly unlucky in this regard. These two parishes sat within the large manor of Upwimborne Plecy, and in the 1394 visitation they had been represented by Edmund Brut (or Brit), Robert Taylour, William Taylour, Thomas Rill, Gilbert atte Mulle, Richard Symond, and William Clavill. Clavill was a wealthy man, at home among knights and lords, but this had not always been so. He had been born a bastard, the illegitimate son of another William Clavill who had died in 1373 leaving most of his land in Dorset to a distant cousin. The unfavoured son was left with the tiny estates of Ferne in Wimborne St Giles and Hyde in Tarrant Hinton. These were manors without lordship, mere parcels of land held by 'knight service' where a superior lord exercised judicial authority. But Clavill junior was dogged and calculating. He married Edith de la Hyde, a widow and the heiress of a childless family, acquiring her substantial lands in Afflington, Moreton, Hurst, Woolgarston, and Knitson. Altogether he amassed four messuages (houses with gardens and outbuildings), seven caracutes of land (of perhaps a hundred acres each), thirty-nine acres of meadow, sixty acres of pasture, sixteen acres of woodland, four hundred acres of heath or rough grazing, one mill, and rents totalling fifty shillings plus two pounds of pepper and half a pound of wax. The estimated value of his lands at his death in 1401 was fourteen pounds sixteen shillings twenty pence. This was serious money. But even so in 1393 Clavill leased the whole of nearby Woodlands manor to manage as a 'farm', for which he paid an enormous sixteen pounds twelve shillings sixteen pence. It seems likely that he funded this from the profits of subletting or perhaps through credit.[76]

Although we do not know how Clavill behaved when he represented his parish as a trustworthy man, the manorial and hundred court records of Upwimborne and Knowlton give us some evidence that enables us to imagine his demeanour. To begin with, his relationship to the lord of Upwimborne was always fractious and ill-defined. He held some land from Sir John Hamely as freehold and also some for which services were owed. But his lands were so extensive that he considered them a separate manor. On more than one occasion he was called to court to explain the terms on which he held his land, which was an attempt to get him to acknowledge who was tenant and who was lord. One of the most jealously guarded perquisites of lordship in the Middle Ages was the income from the seigniorial flour mill. Tenants were generally barred from owning their own hand-operated mills, being forced instead to bring their grain to the lord's mill, paying a fee for the service. William Clavill had so much land that this would have seemed absurd from his point of view. He already had a mill on his wife's lands, and in 1388 he decided that he needed one in Upwimborne as well, running on horse-power. This was too much for Sir John, and the two men clashed in court. That day the court also heard that Clavill had enclosed some of the lord's woodland for his own benefit, possibly to make a hunting park.[77] The erection of a horse-powered mill and the aggravated enclosure of woods may well have been Clavill's bid to advertise both his status as a putative lord and his distinction from the mass of peasant tenants.[78]

If Clavill was a thorn in Hamely's side, he was not alone. In fact, in addition to Clavill, four more of the seven men who were parish representatives for Wimborne St Giles and All Hallows were 'difficult' tenants. Gilbert atte Mulle was called upon three times in 1387 and 1388 to acknowledge the services he owed to the lord for his tenancy, and twice, in 1390 and 1403, to answer the charge of allowing his animals to graze on the lord's land.[79] Robert Taylour was late paying his rent in 1385; he was fined for grazing the lord's land in 1385 and 1386, for letting his buildings fall into disrepair in 1386 and 1388, and for damaging the lord's mill race in 1398.[80] William Taylour's buildings were in disrepair in 1382 and in 1388 he imperiously demanded that Hamely should summon to court the prioress of Amesbury, whom he claimed was denying him access to his tenancy.[81] Edmund Brut claimed in 1388 that he had only occupied the lord's land 'accidentally' and merely 'forgotten' to perform labour services, and he was still staking a claim to independence in a small way in 1415 by failing to do his duty as a suitor of Knowlton hundred court.[82] The physical state of buildings was a major concern for lords who worried about attracting future tenants, and while stray animals were an unavoidable consequence of mixed agriculture, they were a frequent bone of contention.[83]

For small lords like Sir John Hamely such men were difficult to live with, but so powerful were they in his little kingdom of Upwimborne that he could not afford to operate without their say-so. Though not quite in Clavill's league, Thomas Rill was a major tenant with at least one and a half virgates (about forty-five acres), and Gilbert atte Mulle had a flock of at least forty-six sheep. As well as being the visitation representatives for the two local parishes, some of the men we have encountered also served as tithing, manorial, and hundred jurors. Robert Taylour, William Clavill, and Gilbert atte Mulle were hundred jurors in 1382, 1383, 1398, and 1400; Richard Symond acted alongside them in 1398 and 1400, and Edmund Brit joined the group in 1400. At times we see them at work, aiding the lord's administration and managing the business of the court. In 1386 Clavill and Atte Mulle brought a case against someone unjustly 'detaining chattels', that is, keeping something that was not his to use. In 1390 Atte Mulle apparently failed in his duty as a manorial juror, unable to produce a recalcitrant villein in court. In 1399, in his capacity as a tithing juror, Robert Taylour had to confiscate the goods of a neighbour wrongfully in possession of a cottage. The year before, Robert's kinsman William Taylour, and fellow trustworthy man Edmund Brut, were also noted as tithing jurors. Robert Taylour was even the reeve in 1398.[84] Clearly these men were the stalwarts of local administration, but it is fair to say that what they desired most was their own freedom of action, not the profit of the lord.

Being antagonists of lordship might, in some circumstances, have endeared such men to their fellow villagers. Much in their behaviour and attitude indeed tells of an independence that could have been valuable when mediating between the community and institutions. But the trustworthy men of Upwimborne also excelled in antisocial behaviour. They were independent of lordship but equally unsympathetic to the rest of the village. The court rolls reveal a litany of threatening behaviour and a cavalier attitude towards the common resources of this agricultural community. William Taylour, for example, was accused of raising his dagger against a man in 1385, while Robert Taylour whom, it will be remembered, was also a juror and once the reeve, was alleged to have unlawfully taken the goods of a 'native' tenant and obstructed the road with hedging. Richard Symond and Thomas Rill had damaged the riverbank by letting their animals stray towards the water.[85]

By one crucial contemporary standard the trustworthy men of Wimborne were not trustworthy at all. It was very common for the richer members of agricultural communities at this time to be fined regularly for infringing the assize of ale. The assize was so restrictive that breaching it was unavoidable and the fines were really an early form of licensing law.[86] However, in the Upwimborne court rolls indictments in respect of the assize of ale frequently refer to buying and selling with false measures: actively deceiving customers and suppliers. Such was the medieval obsession with the honesty of trade that moral treatises inveighed against fraudulent practices, while the use of false weights and measures was outlawed by royal statutes and included by bishops in a list of offences that would incur automatic excommunication.[87]

In terms of antisocial behaviour the main offender was, perhaps unsurprisingly, William Clavill. Minor or unspecified transgressions attributed to him spatter the court records between 1382 and 1401, including a recurring failure to maintain the paths and tracks across his land.[88] Much more concerning for the parish as a whole though, was his willingness to threaten violence when he did not get his way. He was indicted for drawing his sword upon John Rill in 1388 and 1389. The issue at stake is not mentioned in the rolls, but it may well have had something to do with Clavill's use of the commons to pasture his animals. Encroachment on the commons was a perennial concern of late medieval villagers, but when the offender was a man with many hundreds of acres of his own, it was even more infuriating. The other tenants tried to stop Clavill, but even Hamely's bailiff was unable to distrain the goods that would force his appearance in court and his submission to the will of the lord and the tenants.[89]

In his aggressive stance towards Sir John Hamely and the villagers of Upwimborne, William Clavill exploited his connections with other powerful local families. He had long been an associate of the Plecy family, the former lords of the manor, and had been instrumental in facilitating the transfer of the manor upon John Hamely's marriage to Joan Plecy. Upwimborne seems to have been Joan's dowry. Joan's three uncles—John, Peter, and Robert—retained lands in the Wimborne area, and may have been aggrieved to see the manor go to her instead of to them. Peter Plecy occasionally appeared in the court rolls as a delinquent tenant alongside Clavill. What is more, when Clavill intruded his stock onto the common he claimed a right deriving from a charter granted by Sir Robert Plecy. The court, under Hamely's supervision, predictably determined that this document was of no consequence.[90] Clavill was part of a group of very powerful men—some with inherited wealth like the Plecy family, some self-made like himself—who dominated the local economy without possessing lordship as such. This group of prosperous peasants and regional gentry showed an alarming disregard for common resources, equalled only by their disdain for the authority of lords.[91] We certainly cannot assume that when representing the parish they subordinated their own interests to those of the community.

Their Behaviour as Trustworthy Men

At a very local level, trustworthy men were caught in a similar net of expectations and obligations as the rulers who retrenched their authority in the twelfth and thirteenth centuries through an ideology of serving the public good (for which see Chapter 4). They were positioned by episcopal rhetoric in the symbolic role of parish representatives, but given what we now know of their locally exclusive social status and their complex allegiances—split between their neighbours, their lords, and themselves—we cannot assume that there was any simple equation between speaking for the parish and acting for the common good. As I have already suggested, it is likely that self-interest or the perspective of the parish elite influenced their behaviour even while they gave voice to 'common' complaints and the will of 'the parishioners'. There is naturally room for disagreement, and for the identification of different forms of behaviour in different times and places. For example, Phillipp Schofield has argued, with considerable justification, that 'any excessive promotion of self-interest' on the part of elite peasants 'would fall foul of the expectations of the wider community'.[92] This is what bishops had in mind when they wrote, for example, that the trustworthiness of some parish representatives had been established 'by common judgement'.[93] On the other hand Chris Dyer's suggestion that the community 'could mean a privileged elite defending its interests' is equally plausible.[94] Where did the balance lie?

In all likelihood the balance between the pursuit of communal and individual interests depended upon the issue. There were some matters about which it is hard to imagine there being much disagreement, especially the behaviour of the clergy. All parishioners expected their clergy to be resident, celibate (or at least respectably discreet), competent in saying divine service, dutiful in giving alms, and even to offer credit to laymen when they were able.[95] When we read in visitation reports that the clergy 'do no good in the parish' the voice of common judgement rings out as clearly as we could hope it to. Similarly, protests that a rector 'does not know that which a rector ought to know' or that a chaplain 'has too much land and busies himself in secular affairs' speak of frustration arising from the long accumulation of expectation and grievance.[96] In some other matters, such as supervising the execution of wills, the reports of trustworthy men must have reflected a good deal of consensus about the social utility of visitation, even though this was a quintessentially 'private' matter. Upholding the duty of parishioners to maintain the nave of the church and especially to light it with candles may also have been widely popular in the abstract, if unpopular with particular individuals when it came to coughing up their own contribution. The evidence can indeed be very hard to read: private disputes could be couched in the language of public order, and while community expectations may have weighed upon the minds of trustworthy men concerned about their reputations, they often occupied that position precisely because they were able to define local agendas to some extent.

For example, in 1294 the brothers Stephen and John Barates of Womenswold in Kent were reported for holding back five quarters of barley that their mother had left to the work of the church. Stephen and John were probably the largest peasant landholders in the village, holding over eighty acres as co-tenants.[97] Their tithes would have been one of the most important sources of income for the parish church, making the disputed amount seem trifling by comparison. Interestingly, two of the three lay representatives of the parish were also from leading peasant families, though perhaps only half as wealthy as the Barates, raising the possibility that their report reflected competition within the elite as much as—or perhaps more than—it was an impartial application of canon law.[98] Equally, holding the wealthiest members of the community to account even for small beer may indeed have been a popular measure among the wider population, and certainly with the clergy who benefitted considerably from tithes, bequests, mortuary payments, fees for marriage ceremonies, and the provision of candles.[99] However, enforcement for the benefit of the parish clergy might have entailed alienating certain groups of parishioners, which we can see in a case from Cheshire in 1464. Here, the bishop of Coventry and Lichfield recited the complaint of 'the venerable and trustworthy men' of Prestbury that their cemetery wall was in poor repair: pigs and other animals had wandered in, dug up the bones of the dead, and fouled the ground. No doubt many parishioners agreed that something should be done about this, but the fact that payment for the repairs had to be enforced by the vicar of this enormous parish alongside the chaplains of Macclesfield, Marton, Bosley, Poynton, Adlington, Siddington, and Chelford, suggests a degree of resistance. It looks very much like a complaint of the trustworthy elite, in alliance with the vicar of Prestbury, against their scattered and distant co-parishioners.[100]

In the regulation of sexual morality the relationship between consensus and conflict begins to look particularly strained. Controlling access to sexual partners is one of the commonest ways in which power is maintained and resources distributed in all societies, and sexuality had been of interest to the church long before the late thirteenth century when it became a major issue in the regulation of parish communities.[101] But do reports of sexual immorality reflect the consensus of communities or the sectional interests of the parish representatives? One might assume a report that 'the chaplain of Overland keeps a young girl in his house', or that 'the chaplain of Womenswold keeps a certain Alice in his house' to be uncomplicated assertions of the community's desire for a celibate clergy, in line with the ideology of reform. This might, however, be to assume too much, given the presumably long tolerance such relationships had enjoyed while the episcopal gaze lay elsewhere.[102] It may have suited parish representatives to chide particular people at particular moments. For example Alan of Helles had already been under sentence of excommunication for three years when he was reported in 1294 for his long-term unmarried partnership with Sarah Malmeyns. Holding over seventy acres of land in Wingham, Kent, and enjoying the status of a shireman (for which see Chapter 6), he was powerful enough to set his own course, but his presentation before the visitor suggests a story of elite competition and personal animosity.[103]

Sometimes the reports of sexual and marital offences seem to express the collective will of the parish as a body of male householders. This is especially apparent when the record does not name female offenders, preferring to identify them by reference to their fathers or husbands. In the Kent parish of Goodnestone the trustworthy men reported that 'the wife of William Pykoche treats her husband badly'.[104] She was not named. It was the husband's position that concerned the parish representatives. Fatherhood, household management, and parish governance were intimately connected by common expectations of self-control, discipline, and stability.[105]

The impartiality of an inquest could be compromised if it was too closely tied to the parties involved, a situation that must have been rather common in small communities. This happened in 1379 at Southwick in Hampshire when a chaplain of Boarhunt called William Halpennyman was accused of theft and released by the crown to the jurisdiction of the bishop of Winchester. Halpennyman had allegedly stolen two oxen worth five shillings from Simon atte Mede, and two from John Mullebrugge. The bishop's official was told to see whether Halpennyman could purge himself, or whether there was evidence of his guilt. The official inquired at Southwick through sworn trustworthy men, supposedly those 'who had the better knowledge of the matter'. They were Valentine atte Mede, William atte Halle, William Clement, James Tayllour, Walter Knyght, Thomas Hystfelde, John atte Hulle, Andrew Hurt, Nicholas Waythe, Roger Tayllour, John Boucher, Nicholas Grym, and Richard Prat. This inquest said that the *fama* against Halpennyman was serious, not light, both before and after his incarceration, and that this *fama* arose from his own deeds. They explained that this was known among many trustworthy men who were not enemies of Halpennyman. Because of this forthright opinion the bishop could not permit Halpennyman's purgation.[106]

Southwick is an extremely well-documented medieval parish, as we have seen from the discussion of this group of trustworthy men as a case study in Chapter 6. We know enough from the rentals of Southwick Priory, plus other court rolls and charters, to be able to say that the trustworthy men of 1379 were not really likely to support poor William Halpennyman, even if he had been innocent.[107]

For one thing, his two alleged victims had been important and wealthy men. Simon atte Mede was a man with landed interests across several parishes in the area, described as an esquire in the 1381 poll tax assessments.[108] John Mullebrugge was recorded as a significantly well-off peasant tenant in Southwick as early as 1352, when he paid rents totalling one pound ten shillings, some of the highest in the village and worth a scribal 'Nota' in the margin of that rental.[109] Had William Halpennyman picked the wrong oxen to steal? Although the quantitative analysis of the Southwick inquest in Chapter 6 found no significant relationship between rent paid and trustworthy status, we also saw that the rental underrepresented some men's wealth. Indeed if we consider all the available evidence—including not only rents, but also recorded landholdings, positions of responsibility, relationships, and actions—it does look as though a powerful local clique had closed ranks against the unfortunate Halpennyman. The most striking thing about the list of trustworthy men is that it was headed by Valentine atte Mede, a member of Simon's family of at least equal standing. Simon and Valentine together had their fingers in many pies, and were linked to some of the other trustworthy men.[110]

Relationships with the priory made the Atte Mede family formidable in local society. Valentine and Simon had been the leading members of a group of feoffees who received the manors of Boarhunt Herberd and Boarhunt Herbelyn from Sir John de Boarhunt and Richard Danvers between 1361 and 1364. The feoffees held the manors in trust, with their number gradually being reduced until Simon and Valentine atte Mede were each in possession of one of the manors, which they then handed over to Southwick Priory (via Bishop Wykeham) between 1364 and 1368. This involved managing the disentanglement of lands disputed by another local knightly family. The manors had been acquired by Bishop Wykeham who wanted to establish five chantries in the priory. He had received a licence to alienate the manors in 'mortmain' (literally 'dead hand', a reference to the 1279 statute of that name which banned donations of land to the church without a licence) in 1368. Valentine atte Mede then performed the same role, alone, for the transfer of Hinton manor to the priory in 1369.[111] After it had been acquired the manor of Boarhunt Herberd was immediately farmed out, presumably to guarantee the necessary income. One of its two lessees was John Mullebrugge, the victim of Halpennyman's alleged theft of oxen.[112] Other men who acted as trustworthy jurors in 1379 had relationships with the priory around the same time. For example William Clement may have been related to John Clement, the cellarer of the priory in 1391; in 1398 John atte Hulle and William atte Hall were jurors on an inquest into the priory's possessions; William atte Hall was the local agent for Sir Robert Marchaunt in his dealings with the priory.[113]

The relationships that these trustworthy men had with the victims of the oxen theft, with each other, and with the priory, are given what is perhaps their most meaningful expression in a series of documents stretching from the 1360s to the 1390s. Over this period Nicholas Waythe, John atte Hull, John Bucher, Walter Knyght, Valentine atte Mede, Simon atte Mede, William atte Halle, and Andrew Hurt were all purchasing either 'corrodies' or stalls in church from the priory, despite this having been outlawed in 1385 by Bishop Wykeham. They were investing in the priory and expected benefits in return, in this life. Stalls in church gave their occupants status within the parish, while corrodies were an insurance or pension scheme guaranteeing an income or assisted-living arrangements for their old age. These men not only supported each other, they supported the most powerful local institution in the shape of Southwick Priory. In turn they were beneficiaries of the priory's presence and seem to have been under its protection.[114]

This all suggests that not only would they have been capable of subverting the bishop's request for an inquiry of trustworthy men, they had plenty of motive to do so, bound as they were to one another in webs of reciprocity and common action. They made sure that the poor chaplain's theft of oxen would not be swept under the carpet of compurgation. Were they trustworthy? Who is to say? They were certainly biased, and could not have seemed trustworthy to William Halpennyman. The crucial fact is that their interests as neighbours of the Mullebrugge and Atte Mede families and as clients and allies of the priory set certain parameters upon their performance as trustworthy men. Their interests lay in supporting the claims made by the victims of the original theft.

The visitation of Gillingham in Dorset in 1394 provides a different sort of example—equally striking—of such interests in action. Some of the offences reported to Bishop Waltham were the direct concerns of the trustworthy (and 'the more trustworthy') men.[115] As a group the trustworthy men reported someone for committing adultery with the wife of one of their number, Nicholas Bennet, and with the servant of another, John Parker.[116] But this was only one manifestation of a much more pervasive enactment of sectional interests in the visitation of Gillingham. The trustworthy men inhabited a social and economic world almost wholly separate from, and even opposed to, that inhabited by the people they reported to the visitor. As a group the trustworthy men were almost all well-to-do brewers, drapers, and merchants heavily involved in the local property and credit markets and in the administration of the manor court and view of frankpledge. The most prominent of their number was probably Richard Cresben, part of a wealthy family of merchants, and one of only two men (the other was an esquire) taxed above the standard four pence for the 1379 poll tax: Richard was taxed at six shillings eight pence. He was a pledge of the manor court in 1394 and a juror in 1397.[117] Other trustworthy men of the town frequently used the court to litigate on debt and the transmission of property. However, with a very few minor exceptions, the offenders reported to the visitor by these men—for adultery, fornication, failing to pay for lights in the church, and so on—were not part of the same milieu.[118] They do not appear in the records of the manorial court as pledges, jurors, creditors, lessees, or purchasers of land. Instead they are infrequently mentioned as heirs for tiny properties and parcels of land, or as petty offenders against the customs of the manor.[119] This group of parish representatives used their position to pursue their own sectional interest, making use of the opportunity afforded them by trustworthy status to entrench the very inequalities that had made them suitable for the role in the first place: landholding, wealth, office-holding, and householder masculinity. They are a perfect illustration of Tilly's model of 'opportunity hoarding', monopolizing local representative offices on the basis of their social difference, and using them to project their higher status into the future.[120]

The allegiances and behaviour of trustworthy men have been repeatedly questioned in the course of this chapter. But trustworthy men have also, in at least equal measure, been assumed to have honestly represented their parishes' interests *as they saw them*. This is a crucial caveat. What this and the preceding chapter have shown is that most trustworthy men were simply not in a position to make an objective assessment of where their parish's interests, or those of an individual parishioner, lay. Although the sociology of representation varied from place to place, there was potential for every parish to be divided between those who served as representatives and those who did not. There was further, marked, differentiation within each representative body between those who served frequently and controlled parish affairs, and those whose presence was occasional and less important.

Calling medieval villages or parishes 'communal' institutions does not adequately encompass the range of their social and political experiences. All too often communal is assumed to equate to egalitarianism, but the success of the trustworthy men in maintaining their position arose in part from the fact that hierarchy and inequality was seen as part and parcel of communal identity and action. Also, as we have seen, experiences varied from place to place. Kaleidoscopic conjunctions of population size, the wealth of the taxpayers, economic inequality, and the exclusivity of the inquest combined to create a broad spectrum of experiences in the parishes of late medieval England. Some *appear* to be inclusive while others are more clearly hierarchical. Wellingore, which in Chapter 6 was shown to conform in some ways to the broad-participation model of parish governance, was in fact distinctly exclusive in the way a minority of the population hoarded the social capital that accrued from acting as trustworthy men. Of the Lincolnshire parishes examined in detail in this chapter only Skillington conforms (and then only at first glance) to the idealized broad participation evoked in much of the existing parish scholarship. Even there though, further investigation revealed huge economic inequalities: what inclusivity existed was maintained in the face of pressures which elsewhere resulted in a drift towards oligarchy. For the men concerned there was certainly individual and collective benefit in acting as *fidedigni*. This was a form of social capital that added to the hierarchies established by gender, age, and wealth, and contributed to them in many instances. Sometimes the various inequalities of life were disaggregated from one another, and differentiation was sought by one means alone, but there was frequently a marked intersection between different forms of social capital and social exclusion. While the men of an inquest or a visitation panel may have looked upon one another as rough equals (though they were also riven by hierarchy, as we have seen), the trust placed in them did not emanate outwards into some nebulous 'generalized trust'. Rather it made the majority look untrustworthy in the eyes of authority. The boundaries were naturally porous— every elite needs to be able to replenish itself and to shed members—but the likelihood of ever being a trustworthy man depending on one's social position. Women could almost never find themselves in this public symbolic role; young poor men were excluded most of the time; middling-status male householders might be called upon once in a while. Thinking of parishes as egalitarian rather depends upon the perspective adopted by the historian.

Another dominant strand in writing on the late medieval parish has been the assumption that parishes were more similar than they were different. But we have seen here that no parish was typical. The places we have surveyed cannot be proposed as ideal types, but they do illustrate something of the range of experience, and we can identify the key variables. The most important quantitative variables were the size of the population, the number of householders, absolute levels of wealth, and the extent of economic inequality. More qualitative variables introduced further complexity. Were there factors that encouraged the rotation of offices, for example an historic tradition or a dispersed settlement pattern? How close, in economic terms, were the trustworthy men to lords? How did lords behave in relation to the parish and its institutions? How did particular men of the inquest behave? Even more ineffable are some variables that we can barely discern: local ideologies of consensus and accountability, a sense of expectation surrounding involvement and consultation, but perhaps above all the effect of contingent events upon visitations and inquests.

These factors could combine in myriad ways, and are all deserving of further study, but in the following chapter I will draw some general conclusions about how ecclesiastical trustworthiness varied across the British Isles between 1250 and 1500.

CHAPTER EIGHT

Time, Place, and the Limits
of Trustworthy Status

IN HIS INFLUENTIAL ANALYSIS, James Coleman highlights the significance that social differences and historical change have for the meaning of trust and trusting.[1] Of course he is right, and yet, as I have now noted on a number of occasions, even the most thoughtful theoretical speculation on trust and trustworthiness has given scant attention to historical context. The last two chapters have shown that bishops' placement of trust in parish elites was experienced in different ways at the local level depending upon the nature and extent of preexisting inequalities, the characteristics of settlement and landscape, as well as regional economic circumstances. Although the available evidence does not permit a comprehensive analysis, it is possible to draw together the findings so far and assess those case studies (as well as some revealing stand-alone examples) against a series of variables along two principal axes. First the social questions surrounding trustworthy men will be examined in a succession of changing economic conditions between the mid-thirteenth and the early sixteenth century. The same can then be done with some patterns of large-scale geographical variation, namely the distinctions between upland and lowland regions, between rural and urban parishes, and between England and the rest of the British Isles. This will give us a good sense of what institutional trusting meant for church authorities in different times and places, laying the foundations for the sustained analysis of an institutional church based on trust in Chapters 10 to 14. It will also permit me to reflect upon how the social meaning of elite formation and the acquisition of social capital mutated during a period of momentous change. Over the late medieval centuries, and across the British Isles, what were the limitations upon the church's institutional trusting?

In searching for the limits of trustworthiness the extent to which people were trustworthy or not in different times and places could never be a relevant question, even if it were answerable. As a symbolic role the ebb and flow of institutional trusting was determined by the dictates of governance and by social change, not by the incidence of virtue. I am seeking to establish the situations in which a piece of political language and a type of social capital were more or less important in shaping life in the parishes.

Arriving at a general model that takes account of chronological and geographical factors is a task shaped by the nature of the available evidence. The tax assessments underpinning the analyses in Chapters 6 and 7—those that identify the payments of individual taxpayers—survive only for the periods 1327–32, 1377–80, and 1522–26. The manorial records that allow us to see something of the workings of the communities in which our trustworthy men operated survive in large numbers from the century and a half between 1275 and 1425, thereafter diminishing rapidly in line with the tumbling profitability of coercive lordship; manorial records also survive far more infrequently from the north of England than from the south and midlands. Furthermore, by the early sixteenth century references to trustworthy men become rarer in bishops' registers, especially lists of named individuals. These features of the evidence base mean that there are certainly challenges in comparing the fifteenth century with the fourteenth, and lowland with upland England; when we move beyond the quantitative data we have to rely more often upon isolated cases and stand-alone sources, and upon inference from what we know of the changing social and economic environment. Nevertheless the exercise is extremely instructive and well worth the attempt.

Change Over Time: Growing Social Exclusivity

We have seen in Chapter 6 that trustworthy men were typically, though not exclusively, those who possessed larger holdings and produced a surplus to sell at markets. We have also, in Chapter 7, seen the dominance of a small number of families over time, and further evidence that suggests the importance of long-term residence and family continuity in determining who could be a trustworthy man. These elements of trustworthiness in the eyes of bishops were crucially dependent on economic conditions and upon the social characteristics of the peasant elite and their relationship with the wider community. The salient questions for consideration here are therefore: how many men fitted the bill in different periods, and how did the parameters of their identification change over the long term? I will begin in the mid-thirteenth century, and draw together an analytic narrative of growing social exclusivity in the profile of the trustworthy men.

The emergence of the trustworthy man coincided with a long period of inflation, demographic expansion, and widening inequality in the thirteenth century.[2] In many areas of the country the pressure that population growth exerted upon agricultural production and the distribution of resources occasioned a shift from two-field systems of crop rotation to three-field systems. Whether or not this constituted a vicious cycle of soil impoverishment and irredeemable human hardship, as some economic historians once argued, it was certainly a sign of great difficulties in the rural economy.[3] Lords were charging higher rents and larger entry fines (fees for taking up tenancies), exploiting the land hunger of their tenants; small holdings were being sold by poorer peasants who turned in ever larger numbers to waged labour as a way to make ends meet. Their tiny plots of land were being snapped up by peasants at the other end of the wealth spectrum: those whose holdings were already large enough to give them a marketable surplus and the necessary capital for expansion. Intense downwards pressure on the living standards of the most vulnerable therefore came hand-in-hand with enhanced opportunities for others.[4]

As we have seen in the case studies of Blyth (1281) and Fiskerton (1302) in Chapter 6, the locals most useful to the church were men whose fortunes had ridden the crest of this momentous historical wave. The interaction between social stratification and social capital can be most clearly seen at Fiskerton, where the wealthiest families simultaneously represented the parish and filled the ranks of Peterborough Abbey's estate management. In the decades around 1300 the parish elite, in the guise of trustworthy men, was socially conspicuous against the backdrop of intense economic and political inequalities.

In the fourteenth century these clear hierarchies were challenged and modified. Repeated and devastating harvest failures and terrible weather between 1315 and 1322 caused widespread malnutrition and mortality, while recovery was hampered by serious epidemics affecting livestock. The horses and oxen used to pull carts and ploughs were expensive to replace, and so fewer families found themselves in possession of a key resource that might have speeded their return to prosperity, or at least subsistence. Rising commodity prices further weakened the majority who lived at or below subsistence level: those who could not grow enough grain to feed their families could scarce afford to buy it from elsewhere. Many tried to move to places where they had heard things were better.[5] This local migration may in part explain the absence of so many of the Lincolnshire parish *inquisitores* of 1337–49 from the tax lists of 1327 and 1332: perhaps they had only recently arrived from a place where the young corn had not seemed so green. In these circumstances of widespread suffering there were nevertheless winners. Wealthier peasants and lords profited from the rising prices that impoverished others, and this widened the divisions within village society.[6]

The advent of virulent epidemic disease in 1348, usually known as the Black Death (though contemporaries simply called it 'pestilence'), further reduced the population of England from around 4.8 million to around 2.6 million.[7] Some of the economic effects of this dramatic demographic collapse cancelled one another out: falling demand for foodstuffs was offset by falling levels of production, so that prices remained reasonably stable for a generation. Others brought more immediate change, the most pronounced being the increased demand for wage labour: 'hunger for labour . . . had replaced hunger for land'.[8] This had the effect of pushing wages up, despite the repeated efforts of Parliament to rig the labour markets in favour of employers. Higher wages ate into the profits of lords and of peasants with larger holdings, and the market for waged labour encouraged new levels of geographic mobility.[9]

Although mean prosperity rose steadily amongst the survivors of pestilence, the poorer peasants—smallholders and wage labourers whose resources lay more in their own bodies than in land—became a more mobile and transient population. At the same time there was simply a smaller pool of stable resident householders from among whose ranks trustworthy men might be selected.[10] They were still there, but their absolute number was reduced and they formed a narrower group within each village. In times like these the premium upon stability and long-term residence was likely to have favoured, even more than usual, the selection of wealthier villagers in the trustworthy role. The difficulty that this presented to bishops is hinted at in an inquest launched by the bishop of Winchester in September 1370 into the number of people living in the parishes of his diocese. There had been reports that some places had been so ravaged by 'recent pestilences and epidemics' that the buildings were crumbling and the clergy could not be sustained from their revenues. The inquest was to be conducted by the bishop's official in conjunction with trustworthy men from each parish 'where they may be found'.[11] There is no apparent reason for the bishop's instruction to have included this pessimistic comment, unless there were real concerns in administrative circles that it was no longer obvious who their local informants should be.

In such circumstances it was harder to believe the results of inquests. There was a question mark hanging over the capacity for trustworthy men to properly fulfil their symbolic role. Would they die in a recurrence of plague? If they survived would they remain long in their parish? Who would guarantee local memory? When would some supposedly settled dispute rear its head again, causing more expense and trouble? If bishops were experiencing a crisis of the trust that they needed to place in local men, they had two options: accept a wider group of people as trustworthy, or reduce institutional reliance upon local knowledge. There is evidence for both reactions. At Southwick in Hampshire, just six years after the bishop of Winchester's lament, the group of trustworthy men that I have analysed in Chapters 6 and 7 were distributed widely across the entire rent-paying population. I have suggested that their relative equality was a result of the dispersed settlement pattern in this wood-pasture microregion, but it may also have had to do with the challenges of finding men of unquestionable stability and social standing. Some evidence for borough and manorial office-holding by families who had never before served in positions of responsibility also exists from this period, corroborating the suggestion, but it remains no more than that, though it is certainly an intriguing avenue for further research.[12]

Whether bishops also scaled down their reliance on local knowledge is equally hard to establish beyond doubt, but again there is some very suggestive evidence. One, perhaps subconscious, response to the difficulties of the post-plague world was for bishops to begin making more use of a particular and distinctive 'trustworthy' formula in their letters, independently of their reliance upon real-life trustworthy men. Since the middle of the thirteenth century some bishops had found it useful to refer vaguely to 'trustworthy reports' they had received about some lamentable state of affairs, or the 'hints of certain trustworthy men' about faults that required correction. As we saw in Chapter 4 this was a formula learnt from papal letters, and widely distributed across Latin Europe. Usually bishops chose these words when they had no intention of actually asking a group of trustworthy men what was going on. There may not even have been a specific report behind their concern. They simply wanted to take executive action, and this rhetorical flourish was their way of saying: *trust me, I have to act.* It was a phrase that was employed in relation to lay offences such as the nonpayment of tithes or offerings, recalcitrant contribution to parish funds, social sins, attacks on the clergy, and crimes against churches and churchyards such as holding markets or polluting holy ground through sex, animal defecation, or bloodshed. It was also used to launch action against priests, monks, and nuns whose behaviour had become scandalous or who were no longer able to fulfil their duties without assistance. Rumours of unlicensed alms collectors, confessors, schools, and preachers were frequently conveyed in this way, and denunciations of heretics often invoked the 'trustworthy reports of men with God before their eyes' as a polemical intensifier.[13]

Across the later Middle Ages references to 'trustworthy reports' are slightly more common between 1350 and 1400 than at other times.[14] What could it mean that bishops reached more often for this wholly allusive trust phrase? There are two main possibilities. It is possible that bishops were finding it harder to administer the consultation of trustworthy men, given the difficulties in clerical recruitment identified in some regions after the plague.[15] Communicating the instructions for inquests may have been problematic if the parish clergy had less collective experience and clout than their pre-plague predecessors. However, since I have established that the ranks of the long-resident peasantry, who possessed the land and produced the marketable surplus that would make them typical trustworthy men, were thinned by the plague, and given we have some evidence that bishops did worry about being able to find enough trustworthy men in the parishes, there may have been a real difficulty in actually identifying convincing performers of the symbolic role.

The exceptionally good harvest of 1376 heralded a new era of benign climate, low prices, and high real wages. There was a general rise in living standards (visible in diet, clothing and housing) but this was not shared equally across the board. Once again we see a minority of families able to expand their holdings at the expense of the poorer majority, even though that majority now contained fewer households in absolute poverty. The minority went from strength to strength as commercial farmers. Those who were selling up, by contrast, were forming a new majority class of smallholders who also toiled as labourers, craft workers, and servants.[16] In a period that used to be called the golden age of the peasantry, we in fact see 'hitherto unknown polarisations of landholding'. In these conditions, as Phillipp Schofield writes, 'unanimity of purpose could only be maintained if the wealthier members of the community were prepared to be constrained by their perceived social obligations to the poorer members'.[17] As we saw in Chapter 7, historians are divided as to whether the late medieval village was in fact defined by competition or cooperation. A compelling argument has, however, been made to the effect that both impulses were present: cooperation became more necessary for poor and middling peasants who could not live off their own land, while competition defined the behaviour of the increasingly wealthy elite who got no benefit from cooperation beyond lip service to societal norms.[18]

Much of this rings true for the Dorset parishes I analysed in Chapters 6 and 7. As lords gradually retreated from demesne cultivation men like William Clavill of Upwimborne became de facto members of the lower gentry without possessing formal lordship. In Chris Dyer's analysis, during the period between 1370 and 1410 all sorts of decisions that shaped the local economy and social relations—hiring labour, wages, cropping, the care of livestock, the repair of buildings, and many other things besides—'were being transferred from the aristocracy to entrepreneurs who came mostly from lower-class origins'.[19] The sort of men who had been called trustworthy for a century were now not only thinner on the ground, but also increasingly important as managers and employers, even as lords in all but name. So when they acted as trustworthy men they would have found themselves economically, and to some extent culturally, adrift from the interests of most of their fellow parishioners. Their social power was ramified in multiple spheres, even as their ability to understand the concerns of their neighbours was diminishing.

As the fifteenth century wore on, new economic realities set in. This was an era of chronic low profits, caused not only by the high costs of labour but also by intermittent civil war, a recurrent shortage of circulating coins, and a concomitant retraction of credit available on terms favourable to the borrower.[20] Lords may have struggled, but they had wide interests and could prosper in other ways. The likes of William Clavill, on the other hand, may well have seen their fortunes stall. This was neither a 'crisis of feudalism' nor (quite) the beginnings of agrarian capitalism, but many wealthier peasants—precisely the kind of men to whom trustworthiness was regularly attributed—seem to have been unable to pass on their holdings to the next generation. There was much more short-term instability. This was partly caused by recession limiting the price of wool, and partly by the uncertainty of living in a low-profits economy. For the time being large landholdings did not translate seamlessly into social dominance. Furthermore, civil war was not conducive to stable and continuous relationships between institutions and local communities.

These developments exposed a bishop's need for durable information to even greater risk. From time to time during the fifteenth century we can see bishops adopting a novel approach to inquests that allowed them to sidestep the problems in identifying trustworthy collaborators within peasant society. They replaced the peasants with men of unquestionable gentle status. Reports of inquests in which the bulk of the lay trustworthy men were identified as gentlemen, esquires, knights, or even nobles occurred in the dioceses of Bath and Wells in 1418, 1478, and 1490, Hereford in 1418, Exeter in 1440, York in 1443, 1451, and 1467, and Coventry and Lichfield in 1454.[21] In normal circumstances the gentry were certainly not included amongst the trustworthy of a parish, probably because they were interested parties to so many of the questions upon which the trustworthy adjudicated, as we shall see in Chapter 11. They were also rather distant from issues such as the dilapidation of buildings, the sex lives of servants, or what had happened to that missing tithe corn, making them unreliable in the matters of common concern that will be examined in Chapters 12 and 13.

Some fifteenth-century reports of inquests do not advertise the high status of their trustworthy men, but a little digging can reveal it nonetheless, suggesting it may have been a more widespread trend. One such involved a disputed chaplaincy at North Newton on the edge of the Somerset levels, where inquests were summoned to adjudicate by Bishop Bubwith in 1418 and his successor Bishop Stafford in 1425.[22] The dispute pitted local lords and lessees of manors against powerful outsiders such as the earl of March and Thomas Chaucer, the poet's son. In order to produce information that would stand up in court against the claims of the mighty men of the realm, the local men with an interest in the patronage of Newton made sure that they and their fellow Somerset gentry dominated the two inquests. The trustworthy men in 1418 included Sir John Poulet, a man marked out by his knightly status, but also Thomas Mitchell who held a great deal of land in return for 'knight service', which meant he had to provide some of the costs of arraying a knight.[23] In 1425 the dominant figure was Sir Thomas Popham, a knight of Petherton, and he was joined by John Payn of Petherton, a man with a good deal more land than most peasant tenants in the area, and William Godehyne, who was on a par with Thomas Mitchell.[24] More humble peasant elders of the parish were also involved, including John Andesey, a man whose recorded landholdings amounted to just one and a half acres, and John Godehyne, who can have done little more than get by on his five-acre plot.[25] But it was not usual for knights to participate in such inquests alongside poor peasants. Besides the presence of considerable economic and social weight, the two Newton inquests are also remarkable for the degree to which the trustworthy men knew one another and were used to acting together, largely as witnesses. The Godehynes, Thomas Mitchell, and Sir Thomas Popham, besides other trustworthy men Hugh Skathelok, John Ellis, and Robert Parle were linked in a web of local connections and obligations. They had acted together in so many ways that combining to beat back the claims of high authority was no great feat of cooperation.[26]

The trustworthy gentry were, however, a temporary phenomenon. By the last years of the fifteenth century political stability and a buoyant cloth trade were stimulating the beginnings of economic recovery, and from perhaps the second decade of the sixteenth century the population was also starting to rise. This period has been characterized as one of aspiration, social mobility, and a new optimism. Its outstanding material expression was the flowering of church architecture in the more prosperous parishes, particularly in woolproducing regions.[27] But for all this was an age of opportunity and lower absolute poverty we need to remember that opportunities (for social-climbing marriages, education, and professional service) were in fact limited to a minority of the population. For the majority this was the time when price rises began to overtake wages, wage labour became entrenched as the dominant way of life in the countryside, and inequalities widened. Below the level of the gentry, but frequently now shading into it, rural and urban communities were coming to be controlled by commercial 'farmers', clothiers, millers, and brewers.[28] In their journey from substantial villagers to commercial employers this 'dominant group of yeomen'[29] had effectively expropriated their less well-off neighbours. Land was concentrated in fewer hands; landlessness led with increasing regularity to vagrancy; charity became the salient mode of interaction between the haves and the have-nots. It was in this context that parish governance began to concentrate a little more in the hands of the churchwardens, many now managing wide property portfolios to fund chaplains, charity, and the beautification of churches.[30] It may have been their elevation that ensured parish representation was not lost forever to the gentry.

Between its first appearance in bishops' letters around 1200 and the eve of the Reformation, ecclesiastical trustworthiness appears to have been attributed to an ever-narrower group in parish society, even as the demand for their contribution to diocesan government enlarged (for which see Part IV). Although this is a general synthesis, it represents a clear trend and is corroborated by the observations of historians working in parallel fields. For instance, historians of the manor such as John Beckerman and Phillipp Schofield have noted the progressive erosion of community involvement in local decision making and peacekeeping. In 1200 the 'whole homage' of the manor could expect to be involved in decisions that affected them all, but by 1300 power had shifted significantly into the hands of the lord's officers and a presentment jury. The tithing (a group of ten men into which every adult male was expected to be sworn) was in decline as a system of mutual self-policing by 1300 and dead by 1400, while the hue and cry (communal pursuit of suspected offenders) was falling out of use from about 1350. Schofield sees the fifteenth century as a time when wealthy villagers and office-holders alone could express the 'limits of normative behaviour'.[31] Writing about an overlapping period, from 1370 to 1600, and using manorial, borough, and other local court records, Marjorie McIntosh has argued that social regulation became most pronounced in those places where economic and political power fell into the same hands, eventually—though beyond our period—feeding into the so-called reformation of manners.[32]

The Upland Limits of Institutional Trusting

Any consideration of change over time must be accompanied by attention to variation according to place. While the limitations of source availability meant that the case studies in Chapters 6 and 7 were focussed on lowland England, we did encounter some differences in the attribution of trustworthiness that were shaped by landscape and settlement. Here I will draw out those differences and supplement them with other bodies of evidence in order to focus on an intriguing question in relation to rural society: did upland parishes experience a relationship with the institution of the trustworthy men that was distinct from that in lowland parishes?

The parishes in which trustworthy status was closely correlated with higher economic standing all bore the hallmarks of classic lowland England: nucleated settlements, open fields, the supremacy of arable farming, commercial production for the market, a relatively high incidence of legal unfreedom, pronounced social stratification, and the presence of strong lordship in concert with strong communal institutions. In such places churchmen seeking reliable informants found a preexisting and self-identifying economic elite among the better-off male peasant householders, men for whom the trustworthy label was just one thread in the web of social capital that kept them in their dominant positions. The variable that seems to have been most likely to tilt some places away from such clear-cut affinities between social and economic power was the degree of settlement dispersal within a parish. Dispersed settlement (fewer villages, more isolated farmsteads) occurred in a variety of landscapes in late medieval England, as we saw in Chapters 6 and 7: late fifteenth- and early sixteenth-century Nettlecombe in Somerset and Morebath in Devon were nestled in steep-sided valleys where sheep-rearing dominated a mixed agriculture and small core settlements were surrounded by outlying farmsteads; both practised rotation of parish offices according to place of residence. At Southwick in Hampshire we found a relatively broad distribution of trustworthiness amongst the male householders in a classic wood-pasture region where livestock grazed in woods and on heaths. At Skillington on the limestone heath of Lincolnshire in the 1330s and 1340s there was strict rotation in the regime of representation, perhaps determined by very local subdivisions of parochial geography in a mixed farming economy supporting a substantial class of well-to-do peasants.

These examples are also indicative of a much broader category of landscape where trustworthiness was less important as an institutional ideology. Rough-grazing heathland of the sort found around Skillington and Southwick was present in pockets throughout late medieval England, but in the true upland areas—such as the Welsh Marches, the moors of the southwest, in Cumbria, and along the Pennine spine—its prevalence shaped society to a more pronounced degree.[33] While fertile plains and river valleys were prime grain-producing areas, and among rolling hills crops and livestock were balanced in various ways to provide for subsistence and the market, the high ground of England was suitable only for extensive stock rearing: cows and sheep. Settlement was by necessity more dispersed in these regions, and the peasantry were generally freer and poorer. Market exchange was a less important part of their lives.[34] All of this, in Angus Winchester's words, 'resulted in the creation of very different cultural landscapes'.[35] One of the distinctive economic and social features of this world was lesser transhumance or 'summering': the movement of flocks and herds away from lowlands in the summer, when these were needed for grain and fodder crops, and onto the uplands, which were in any case better-suited to grazing in the summer than the winter. This is attested in the statutes of Bishop Alexander Stavensby for Coventry and Lichfield diocese (which stretched into the upland areas of Cheshire, Staffordshire, and Derbyshire) in 1240, which instructed that 'if sheep are fed in one place in winter and in another place in summer the tithes shall be divided'.[36] Transhumance involved the seasonal movement of people as well as animals, adding to the dispersion of the population and discouraging the interventions of authority. Patterns of interaction among shepherds and drovers may have been defined by the high road inn and the smithy as much as by the parish church, while the makeshift hillside shieling demanded far less obeisance to power than living under the nose of a lord.[37]

The disparity between lowlands and highlands is something of a commonplace in history and political science. Fernand Braudel's social typology of the Mediterranean basin famously contrasted 'the mountains' with the more highly connected plains and coasts, while James Scott has developed a model of 'state' and 'non-state' spaces in Southeast Asia that maps political and social forms onto the relief geography.[38] Viewing the Islamic world from high in the Atlas mountains, Ernest Gellner pithily remarked that 'shepherds are hard to govern', by which he meant to contrast the relative ease with which institutions and cities could extract surplus from sedentary arable farmers whilst finding it much harder to subject migratory pastoralists to their rule.[39] How easy was it for late medieval bishops to penetrate the communities that lived in the upland regions of England? When they came looking for trustworthy men, what did they find?

Archbishop Melton of York went looking for trustworthy men in Wensleydale in 1323. He did not find much that would have given him confidence in his ability to exercise authority in the Dales. Two brothers from Wensley had been passed into his custody by the royal justices having been arrested for a burglary committed eighteen miles away over the fells at Conistone in Wharfedale. They had pleaded benefit of clergy, the rule whereby clerics suspected of crimes could insist on being tried before a church court. The friction that this caused between church and crown officials at every level will be more thoroughly explored in Chapters 11 to 13. Melton's first instinct was to commission an inquest through trustworthy men, but the official of Richmond and the dean of Craven could not put a panel together. This meant the archbishop had to resort to a less-than-satisfactory examination of the siblings themselves, and then to a plea made in local churches, markets, fairs, and streets for anyone with information to come forward. No-one did.[40] Wensley was a struggling parish that had suffered depredations in recent Scottish raids. The value of its church had almost halved between 1290 and 1318. Settlement was widely dispersed, the peasantry was poor, and the economy was dominated by the forests, chases, and 'vaccaries' (cattle ranches) of powerful noblemen.[41] In this country peasant society was less stratified than in the arable lowlands, and it is possible that there was neither local agreement nor institutional recognition as to who might actually comprise a social elite capable of convincingly performing the symbolic role of trustworthy men.[42]

Two other northern examples of a similar date reveal the use of alternative modes of fact-finding to the inquest of trustworthy men. In 1333 the bishop of Carlisle and the prior of that city's Augustinian convent reached an agreement about the tithes from assarts (newly cultivated land) carved out by the parishioners of Dalston from the royal forest of Inglewood. Although this was not upland country, Inglewood was sparsely populated, did not have a highly developed economy, and had suffered in Scottish raids in common with much of the north.[43] Bishop Kirkby did call for a jury of twelve trustworthy men but he also 'consulted other auguries': *insortiationibus*, from the Anglo-Norman *ensorcerer*, to bewitch, or the Latin *sortes*, meaning casting lots. Following the consultation of these auguries it was agreed that the bishop should have all tithes from currently cultivated parochial lands, and that the convent should have those from the lands in the forest beyond the bounds of Dalston, even if these were taken into cultivation at a later date.[44]

Two years later in 1335 Archbishop Melton had to explain to the monks of Coverham Abbey in Coverdale a peculiar local custom that had been omitted from the documentation when they appropriated Sedbergh church, across the hills from them on the edge of Westmorland. When the tithes were paid in kind the arrangement between the abbey and the vicar of Sedbergh was very simple: they would receive all the adult beasts, while he would receive the foals, calves, and piglets. But when some of the tithe was paid in coin, the parishioners were accustomed to decide exactly how much was owed by a process known as 'caveling'. This meant casting lots, rolling dice, or drawing straws.[45]

In these two northern parishes we see customary forms of fact-finding that elsewhere would have troubled the authorities a great deal. Consulting auguries and casting lots were defined as divination: at best dubious superstition, at times redolent of witchcraft or even heresy.[46] But here the archbishop of York and the bishop of Carlisle accepted them and explained them to uncomprehending third parties. In the Dalston example the bishop's scribe even alluded to sorcery in his choice of vocabulary. What was going on?

Casting lots to set the vicar's share when tithes were paid in coin suggests that the value of young animals fluctuated and could not be easily determined. We do not know the range of possible outcomes from 'caveling' but it seems sensible to assume that over the medium term a degree of mitigated chance looked fair to all concerned and helped to avoid conflict. The practice would not have become customary had it not produced decisions that bishops and locals alike could live with. We are not looking at examples of backwoods irrationality. There was a good deal of reason at work, both among the parishioners and in the minds of the churchmen involved, and a very similar attitude to trust and information prevailed as that which underlay inquests of trustworthy men. But in finding these accommodations between chance and formal inquiry bishops had to abandon one aspect of canon law—the condemnation of sorcery or gambling—in order to buttress another—ensuring that tithes were paid in the proper way. They had shifted the question of truth into territory hemmed about with intense doubt, and chance.

The three northern cases described here tell us much about the limitations of episcopal power in the region. Although inquests of trustworthy men could, and did, happen in Cumbria and the Pennines, they were not always conclusive and they shared legal and epistemological status with divination![47] Trustworthy men were just the job in the parishes of lowland England where polarizations of wealth and standing sifted out men who were happy to speak for their communities and whose power to enforce a local consensus was trusted by bishops. But in upland parishes social ties 'were evidently slacker' as Edward Miller and John Hatcher once put it. 'The north', they went on to say, 'with its far-ranging parishes embracing many townships, was merely one of the regions where social bonds (including ecclesiastical bonds) were weaker than they were in Midland England, where communities were less coherent, where society was more diffuse, and where peasant individualism had an ampler scope'.[48] Not all historians would agree with Miller and Hatcher's depiction of 'peasant individualism': pastoral communities may well sometimes have been defined by an aggressive communalism that took a very dim view of personal enrichment. But nevertheless this is an insightful characterization of the church in the English uplands. The only element lacking is ecclesiastical authority. And what these examples have suggested is that the power of bishops, while still being important, was felt less intensely where it was harder to form an alliance with a local peasant elite. Such a conclusion certainly echoes Braudel's broad thesis that feudal authority 'failed to catch in its toils most of the mountain regions'.[49]

The Exclusive Parish Life of Towns

In late medieval English towns parish representation and regulation consistently found its way into the hands of men who dominated civic governance and regional trade to a degree that puts the trustworthy men of even lowland rural parishes somewhat in the shade. Because urban parochial income was more often derived from rents than from ad hoc fund-raising, the financial concerns of town parishes were greater than those in the countryside, and these resources were often concentrated in the hands of churchwardens or a guild.[50]

In Chapter 6 I looked at Blandford Forum in Dorset, where the attribution of trustworthy status was strongly linked to taxable wealth. Its trustworthy men were artisans and merchants deeply involved in the functioning of the manor court, which may have functioned as a municipal government in all but name. In Chapter 7 I examined the cases of two other small towns. At Gillingham, also in Dorset, the parish representatives were brewers, drapers, and merchants heavily involved in the local property and credit markets. As at Blandford they were also crucial to the administration of the manor court and view of frankpledge. At Glentham in Lincolnshire we encountered a fairly large parochial elite, but we found it was dominated by a very small number of regular *inquisitores*; the Edwardian tax assessment was also finely gradated, suggesting an obsession with rank and position. In what follows we will look at further evidence from Newark, Leicester, Stratford, and Salisbury, all of which were more substantial places and which demonstrate the elitism of attributed trustworthiness in the towns of late medieval England.

Newark in Nottinghamshire was a thriving town in the late Middle Ages.[51] In 1200 it had been a relatively small seigniorial borough, but a new bridge over the river Trent boosted its connections to the wool-producing regions of north Nottinghamshire and southern Yorkshire and made it a major regional market.[52] But social and political life in Newark was constrained in ways that shaped the nature of its parochial elite. The parish church of St Mary Magdalene was appropriated to the Gilbertine priory of St Katherine just outside Lincoln, and as the town grew the canons of the priory were reluctant to permit the foundation of any new parish churches. Parish government was therefore concentrated into the hands of a much smaller proportion of the population than was the case in most places, and the church itself became the vehicle for the expression of elite identity. Altars and chantries funded by guilds and private donations, and served by priests who were appointed by the guildsmen, multiplied and competed for space and attention in a fashion analogous to the famous tower houses of twelfth- and thirteenth-century Tuscany.

The Corpus Christi chantry was founded in 1349 by Alan Fleming. During his lifetime Fleming, who was already prominent as a guild patron of other chantries in the parish, presented the chaplains himself, but he determined that after his death the vicar of Newark together with four 'trustworthy men of the parish' should make the appointments 'with the consent of the greater and elder part of the parish'.[53] Between 1381 and 1443 three more chantries were founded at the altar of the Holy Trinity guild. In 1381 Robert Caldwell endowed the first of these, to pray for the souls of his family and ancestors.[54] In 1402 four members of the local gentry paid twenty-two pounds to Henry IV for a licence to establish a second. The priest serving it was required to pray for the souls of Richard Scrope the archbishop of York, for all present and future members of the guild of Holy Trinity, and for the family of Thomas Ferrour, one of the founders. As with Fleming's foundation the patronage first lay with Ferrour himself, reverting to the warden of the Holy Trinity guild and six of the 'more cautious and trustworthy men' of the guild after his death.[55] In 1443 a rich draper called Henry Forster endowed a further chantry priest to serve at this altar.[56] The constant round of commemorative masses, the establishment of legal instruments for their endowment, and the regular gatherings of influential guildsmen to appoint new clergy all served to advertise the prominence and power of a small and wealthy civic elite.

In common with other seigniorial boroughs, lacking the charters of self-government enjoyed by incorporated towns, the guild of Holy Trinity functioned as a de facto civic government, with the warden and aldermen operating as an executive.[57] Various members of the regional gentry had houses and mercantile interests in the town and the guilds were their route to civic power. Even the vicar of Newark could wield influence only through membership of the Holy Trinity guild. The chantry priests reflected the status of their patrons, and from time to time they asserted their superiority over the vicar appointed by the priory.[58] But real power in Newark parish church lay with the trustworthy men of the guilds, though they might sometimes claim they were acting in accordance with the will of the 'more rational' (*sanioris*) men of the town, a judgement which—of course—lay in their own hands.[59]

Between 1361 and 1500 fifty-eight presentations of chantry priests to various altars in Newark parish church are recorded in the registers of the archbishops of York.[60] Across these fifty-eight occasions, there were 269 separate 'slots' for trustworthy men to fill as patrons, and 119 men are recorded as playing a part. While this large number may suggest broad participation, in fact the handful of men who acted as patrons on each occasion comprised a tiny fraction of the taxpaying population, which numbered 1,178 in 1377. Furthermore, although some of the guilds had female members, only men could be patrons of the chantries.[61] Guild action was dominated by the heft of a few leading inhabitants in each generation. Fifty-six men served once, thirty served twice, and twelve more served three times; seven served four times, six five times, and four six times. Four more men served repeatedly: Nicholas Kayser was a patron seven times between 1383 and 1402; Thomas Meryng served eight times between 1483 and 1500, Richard Wakefield nine times between 1400 and 1423, and John Sharp (the vicar) eleven times between 1391 and 1421.

Such men were wealthy and influential. The draper Henry Forster, who endowed a chantry in 1443, left monetary bequests of more than thirty-seven pounds in his will, not including the cows given to each of his female servants, nor the 'best horse with harness' offered to the vicar as a mortuary (a payment notionally in lieu of unpaid tithes), nor indeed the residue of his estate which was to fund the chantry.[62] Thomas Meryng, who served as a patron eight times, was styled 'esquire' and in his will of 1500 requested burial 'be twix the two pillars next the altar, as at the tyme of Esturr itt is used to sett the sepulcur of Jhesu Criste'. This was a man sure of his position in the town and in the church, and he was able to pay for it.[63] As with all small elites, oligarchy was maintained through a combination of cooperation and competition. We know that the guildsmen of Newark could not always agree who should be presented to a particular chantry. Jostling for position, they put forward rival candidates with the aim of exercising patronage in the political as well as the ecclesiastical sense. This sometimes put the bonds of ritual brotherhood under stress, and on these occasions, in accordance with their foundation documents, the archbishop stepped in to fill the vacancy.[64]

Such a pronounced concentration of urban trustworthy status in the hands of the mercantile elite is corroborated by the evidence from other towns. Timmins's research into the backgrounds of the visitation representatives for Salisbury's parishes in 1394 revealed that around three quarters of them either held or had held the offices of mayor, MP, coroner, city reeve, or deputy city bailiff. Many of them were wealthy clothiers.[65] At Bridgewater in Somerset the patronage of the chantry of the Blessed Virgin Mary was in the hands of the stewards of the merchant guild of the town, while at Lynn in Norfolk the wardens of the guild of St Anthony described themselves in 1389 as 'trost men and trewe'; in the same town a generation later the jurors in crown pleas were required to be 'fremen and laweful of the most discreet sufficient and lest suspecious persones of the toun . . . [with] londis and tenementz to the value of 100s be yere'.[66] Reports of heresy in Leicester in 1389 were investigated through 'the more trustworthy of the community of the town' (*fidedignores communitatis ville*), which meant the vicars of All Saints, St Margaret, and St Mary, as well as those 'trustworthy burgesses of the town' Geoffrey Clerk, Roger Belgrave, and Richard Burgh.[67] Clerk was a member of the guild merchant, mayor in 1392 and an MP five times between 1384 and 1394. Belgrave was an assessor of the tallage (royal tax) in 1353 and of the 1379 poll tax. He was mayor in 1364–65 and MP in 1360, 1368, 1377, and 1383. In 1362 he had lent the duke of Lancaster five pounds, in 1366 he had helped organize the building of the guildhall, and in 1378 he is recorded as a money lender. His family were so important in the area that one of the town gates was named after them.[68]

The tendency for urban trustworthy men to be much more substantial figures than those in rural parishes was exacerbated in places where lords had obstructed the construction of new parish churches despite population growth in the twelfth and thirteenth centuries. When a town—even a small one—had just one parish church the proportion of adult male householders who could act as trustworthy men was very low. Newark furnished us with one example of how this could be felt after 1348, but its effects were likely to have been more pronounced in the high-population pre-plague era. This is certainly at least suggested by the example of Stratford-upon-Avon, where since 1270 the aspirations of the mercantile elite had been expressed through the fraternity of the Holy Cross, a guild which acted as a 'shadow government'. The fraternity began to rival the parish church as the focus of worship and corporate identity in the town, and from the 1320s onwards their influence was joined to that of John Stratford, a local man who became bishop of Winchester (1323–33) and archbishop of Canterbury (1333–48). In an aisle of the parish church Stratford founded a chantry chapel dedicated to St Thomas the Martyr, whose popularity soon outstripped that of the main church. Extraordinarily, in 1336, the archbishop petitioned his friend Simon Montacute (the diocesan bishop and also the patron of the parish church) to have the revenues of the rectory ploughed into the chantry, the better to support its priests. This required an inquest of trustworthy men, which was composed of five local clerics and seven laymen. From what can be gleaned by examining other local sources, the lay trustworthy men ranged from fraternity members such as Adam Steventon employed within the bishop's temporal administration, to the archbishop's aristocratic friends such as William de Clinton (later earl of Huntingdon).[69] The closeness between the commercial community, local knightly society, civic government, and the composition of the 1336 inquest illustrates the constellation of inequalities that combined to make towns, of whatever size, politically more unequal places in which to live than the rural parishes of late medieval England. This made urban life receptive to the exercise of church government—trustworthy men were easy to find—but population size, the institutionalization of local power structures, and the breadth of the wealth spectrum combined to make parish representation a genuinely elite affair.

Across the British Isles

The close connection between marked inequalities and bishops' recurring talk about trustworthiness was a feature of church government in lowland England that stood in contrast not only to upland and northern England, but also to the dioceses in Wales, Scotland, and Ireland. Beyond the hierarchical and market-oriented regions of England, bishops across the British Isles had less opportunity for intensive engagement with local society. They were hampered by distance, terrain, and the paucity of their own resources, but they were also unable to make so many alliances with such very local elites as existed in lowland England. The trustworthy man was still a feature of episcopal rhetoric, just not one that was used with the same frequency or social impact as in lowland England.[70]

This was a social as well as an institutional difference, and despite the marked contrasts between the churches in Wales, Ireland, and Scotland, each was more different from England than they were from the other, at least in this respect. Since Edward I's conquest in 1284 the Welsh church had been a peripheral part of the ecclesiastical province of Canterbury, though its dioceses were very much less wealthy than those in England; Ireland, which had experienced piecemeal and inconclusive English invasion and colonial settlement since 1169 had an independent church hierarchy and forms of law and social organization quite different to those in most parts of England; Scotland had been an independent kingdom since the 1330s, and had had its own archbishop since the 1280s. Although the church in the wider British Isles was thus different to England in a number of ways, the absence of a developed ideology of the *fidedigni* was not a product of cultural isolation. The churches of the northern and western regions of the British Isles were extensively involved in the major currents of intellectual life flowing across Europe. Cathedrals and religious houses were centres of theological and legal learning and by the end of the fifteenth century Scotland had three universities, at St Andrews (1413), Glasgow (1451), and Aberdeen (1495). Papal letters referring to trustworthy men were regularly sent to bishops in these regions, and the more allusive 'as we have heard from trustworthy persons' phrase was also used from time to time.[71] Nor was the difference a case of deviation from a norm: England, as I have suggested in Chapter 4, was the unusual region in a European context, with several other continental churches also making less use of the rhetoric of trustworthiness. Those comparisons would be enormously instructive if developed further, but the contrast between England and the wider British Isles is especially so since the English church had a *degree* of cultural influence in each of Wales, Ireland, and Scotland.

We have a number of examples of passive witnesses being described as trustworthy: in 1220 Bishop Walter of Glasgow reached agreement with the abbot of Jedburgh about the provision of services and pastoral care in several parish churches belonging to the abbey; the two sides met in the chapel of Nesbit in Northumberland in the presence of 'many trustworthy persons'. Similarly in 1286 the patrons of the two parts of Duffus church near Lossiemouth swore an oath 'by way of corporal faith' before the bishop of Moray and 'many other trustworthy persons' to abide by an agreement over the future of the church.[72] The more active role of trustworthy men in inquests is also attested: for example, in the fourteenth and fifteenth centuries the archbishops of Armagh regularly conducted visitations at which 'trustworthy men' from the English (and occasionally the Irish) parishes were expected to appear.[73] Trustworthy men conducted inquests into the responsibilities of vicars in churches appropriated to Monmouth Priory in 1254, the lands of the countess of Douglas in 1384, defects in church fabric in South Wales in 1400 and the vacancy of Talbenny in West Pembrokeshire in 1488.[74] In 1488 an inquest into the patronage of Penbryn on the Ceredigion coast was conducted by twenty of the 'healthier trustworthy elders' of the parish, in the presence of 'the whole parish'.[75] The diocese of St David's also furnishes examples of trustworthy men supervising the collection of alms in 1259, witnessing probate of a will in 1399 and carrying out the purgation of a cleric charged with rape in 1488.[76] Clearly the concepts and practices of institutional trusting were present (more so in the anglicized parts of Ireland and South Wales than in Scotland), even if they were not widespread.

But there are also some telling lacunae in the sources. Some diocesan visitations took place in late fourteenth- and early fifteenth-century Ireland and Wales without mention of lay representation in any form, while we have no clues as to whether Scottish bishops even conducted visitations of parishes.[77] On many occasions where, in English sources, we would expect to find a mention of trustworthy men, other terms were used instead. For instance a thirteenth-century memorandum on the bounds of Campsie parish to the north of Glasgow gives no indication of how the information was collected, while another relating to the boundary between Stobo and Happrew parishes near Peebles gives a list of thirty local clerics and laymen who were witnesses, but does not describe them with any collective noun.[78] As archbishop of Armagh Milo Sweteman conducted three 'inquests through *good men*' into the vacancy of churches in 1361;[79] the diocese of Aberdeen saw inquests or arbitrations undertaken by the 'upright men' or 'upright and faithful men of the country' in 1259, 1387, and 1398;[80] another in Aberdeen itself in 1446 was described as 'ane worthy asysse of þe eldast and worthiest' men of the country and the worthiest burgesses of the town, all of whom were gentlemen.[81] Inquests in thirteenth- and fourteenth-century Moray were carried out through the inspection (*visum*) or on the advice (*consilia*) of men described as 'up-right', 'reverend and cautious', or simply 'good'.[82] In 1400 defects in the Hospitallers' church at Slebech in South Wales were to be made good under the supervision of five lay parishioners described not as trustworthy men but 'our beloved sons'. A similar case in 1402 simply required 'craftsmen', with no mention of trustworthiness.[83] Although there are clear analogues here to trustworthy men, the absence of that particular term suggests that the connections *fides* could make between promising, reputation, local hierarchy, belief, and participation in ecclesiastical governance did not shape the public culture of these regions quite so intensively as they did in lowland England.

When the phrase was used, it could also differ in crucial respects from lowland English practise. For instance in 1382 the bishop of Aberdeen orchestrated a penitent's absolution in the presence of a group of high-ranking secular and ecclesiastical lords who were all described as trustworthy: these were no sturdy peasant householders.[84] Similarly in his court of audience in 1335 the bishop of Aberdeen heard many upright and trustworthy men adjudicate on the inheritance of Duncan Tendman.[85] By comparing their names with other witness lists in the episcopal register it is clear that the trustworthy men were members of the bishop's *familia* or retinue. The limits of institutional trusting in the northeast of Scotland seem to have been drawn closely around the bishop's immediate circle. In preconquest South Wales we find a different—but equally telling—use of trustworthy language. In 1234 Bishop Elias of Llandaff concluded a dispute between Margam Abbey and the Welsh lord Rhys Goch over the mountain of Mynydd Llangeinwyr north of Bridgend. On the face of it, Elias awarded the land to Margam, but Lord Rhys was left with the vaguely defined territory 'pertaining to three houses', which would be his so long as a panel of 'trustworthy and cautious men' gave an arbitrated judgement in his favour.[86] Faced with the absolute limits of his power in the thoroughly Welsh uplands the bishop abdicated responsibility to trustworthy men whom he did not propose to summon himself and who would have acted as arbitrators on their own account, without the institutional standing of an episcopal inquest. Given Rhys Goch's independent lordship in these hilly regions the bishop's invocation of trustworthy men seems like a retreat from, and not an engagement with, local society.

The bishops of Scotland, Ireland, and Wales had local churches to supervise, disputes to adjudicate, and relationships to cultivate just like their English counterparts. But these political imperatives were more extensive than they were intensive. They arose from smaller populations across more difficult territories, and did not lead to the ongoing and repetitive links that characterized the institutional intensification of lowland England. This was most true in regions of pastoral agriculture, but also seems to have characterized the relatively prosperous arable areas of Fife, Aberdeenshire, and parts of Pembrokeshire.

Having considered change over time and variation across the landscapes of the British Isles, we can say with some confidence that bishops found it easier to identify parish representatives capable of fulfilling the symbolic role of the trustworthy man when and where economic inequality was pronounced, and society reasonably stable. This meant times and places defined by commercialization and economic growth, with all its attendant social polarization, characteristically, though not exclusively, in the lowlands of southern and midland England, especially between the mid-thirteenth and the mid-fourteenth centuries. In upland England as well as the wider British Isles, trustworthy parish elites were not so clearly delineated, and here bishops relied upon other, less intensive, forms of engagement with parish society and local religion. The aftermath of plague and the disruptions of the mid-fifteenth century also appear to have presented difficulties, even in lowland England, but they were not insurmountable: the profile of the trustworthy man simply shifted up the social scale, achieving the necessary differentiation from the mass of parish society that bishops seemed to need. This reliance upon inequality was, we should remind ourselves, occasioned by the fact that trustworthiness was a quality attributed without knowledge of character, to men who were largely self-selecting. When it was not obvious who the leading members of parish society were, it was harder to find *fidedigni* with whom to work. For the people themselves, the more bishops were able to identify and work with small elites of trustworthy men, the more unequal their parishes were likely to become, as social, economic, and political opportunities combined in the hands of fewer and fewer men.

CHAPTER NINE

Face-to-Face with the Trustworthy Men

THIS CHAPTER ADVANCES the preceding discussion to ask what it was like to live alongside those men elevated above mere faithfulness and called *fidedigni* by the church. The simple numerical fact is that while the majority of the adult population would at one time or another in their lives have had cause to consider what *fides* they possessed in the eyes of others, only a tiny proportion stood any chance of being called a trustworthy man, and fewer still acted often enough in that capacity for it to become a major part of their social selves. The reasons for some people never being considered suitable as trustworthy parish representatives can be found partly in the structural inequalities discussed in Chapters 6, 7, and 8, but these do not tell the whole story. Inequality was experienced in specific relationships between people, people whose identification as faithful Christians, creditors, neighbours, and witnesses is both something that we can take for granted, whilst also being aware of how it was determined by inequalities at every turn. Also, we have to consider *fides* and the relationship with the *fidedigni* not only as subjective individual experiences (for which see Chapter 3), but as 'inter-subjective' mutual perceptions: I scrutinize and doubt your faith, while you assume and mistake mine. This constant looping of perceptions, judgement, assumptions, respect, envy, distrust, and trust between multiple individuals was what made up the culture of *fides* in parishes, the varied landscape into which episcopal attributions of trustworthiness intruded.

Perceptions of *fides* and the *fidedigni* are also—for the most part—instinctive, and thus require sensitive handling by historians. We can probably assume that when a bishop's official or the rural dean arrived with an instruction to gather trustworthy men, there was no need for the parishioners to recapitulate the structural bases of social stratification. They would have known instantly who could not be ignored, who would be the kind of person the official would find acceptable, and whose participation was unthinkable. To the priest, the church-warden, or wealthy peasant farmer thinking about who would represent the parish, 'any number of markers served to identify people of whose moral qualities and temperaments he was vaguely aware and whose social position, wealth, and reputation he had always known in a more or less confused manner'.[1] The moment at which the trustworthy men stepped forward was the realization of such instinctive knowledge.

How then was that experienced? How did faith and attributed trustworthiness coexist? The faith placed in the trustworthy men by bishops was dependent upon a deep and variegated culture of *fides* comprising trust between people, promise keeping, belief in God, the personal troth that everyone strove for, and membership of a society imagined as the community of the faithful. The separate elements in this culture of trust—explored at length in Chapters 1 to 3—formed an interlocking set of values whose mutual reliance made them all seem true and important.[2] As the trustworthy man emerged in the rhetoric of church government during the thirteenth century (as discussed in Chapter 4), the meaning of his role was therefore supported on all sides by linguistic, conceptual, and—most importantly of all—habitual buttresses. What this means is that actual trustworthy men would have been hard to criticise or question because it had been made to seem as though they occupied a special place in the single most important cultural construct of the era: faith.

The author of Luke's gospel had drawn a bold connection between human affairs and the word of God. In the parable of the unjust steward asked to give an account of his responsibilities Christ asked his disciples: 'If you have not been faithful in the unjust mammon, who will trust you with that which is the truth?'[3] Such a direct association between right belief and correct business practice went on to have a massive impact on medieval thinking. Mercantile metaphors for belief were widespread, and this particular parable was a popular text for moralizing, as in Thomas Wimbledon's 1388 sermon asking each order of society to give a 'reckoning of their bailey'.[4] The ritual of giving faith also implied strong links between belief in God and trust in persons. Occasionally this was made explicit, as in a promise made 'by my feith and my Cristendome'. Although Maitland's explanation of such phrases—that the person giving their faith 'pawns his hope of salvation'—may be too neat in treating 'Christianity' as the conceptual equivalent of a pledged object, the link between personal *fides* and membership of the church is plain.[5] The church courts might also advertise the continuity between personal promises and collective faith in requiring pilgrimage to the diocesan mother church as penance in breach of faith cases, symbolically repairing the bond between two people by reiterating membership of the whole.[6] With such deep and insistent connections between religious belief, interpersonal trust, and confidence in the world, oneself, and the future, the parish representatives 'worthy of faith' occupied a position within a value-system that seemed natural and right, and yet, as Chapter 7 showed, this did not mean that the attitudes and interests of trustworthy men were always aligned with those of their 'merely faithful' neighbours.

There is nevertheless some evidence that the language and the concept were seen as significant, even useful, among the laity at large. Although it was principally a piece of episcopal rhetoric, allusions to *viri fidedigni* can also be found in church court depositions, usually as descriptions of other witnesses— off-stage—whose word was being relied upon to sway the judge. For example, a woman who claimed that a summoner in Hereford had tried to frame her for adultery deposed that she had only ever spoken to the man in question once, and that that had been out in the open with honest and trustworthy men present.[7] Similarly in a breach of faith suit from Scarborough in 1441 the plaintiff argued that the defendant had 'freely and often' admitted the substance of their agreement in the presence of trustworthy persons.[8] The witnesses in a 1511 tithe dispute between the rector of Wanstead and the vicar of West Ham applied the language of trustworthiness thickly and with a trowel in their depositions as to the location of a field called Pickerynge: several groups of 'honest and trustworthy persons' were referred to, sometimes the 'older and more trustworthy' and sometimes men 'whose words could be trusted to contain the truth'.[9] Such formulations appear in a number of different courts, and increasingly so towards the early sixteenth century.[10]

In cases such as these the intended effect of calling someone trustworthy was to imply they were more reliable and conveyed weightier opinion than the witnesses of the other party. It could also have hinted at the witnesses being people whom bishops would believe. Of course in some instances the words of the deposition may well have been those of an advocate who knew what would help a litigant's cause, but there is also evidence that laypeople knew of the phrase and were prepared to give it meanings all of their own. For instance in 1454 when Harry of Haldon in Kent stepped forward as a witness in a marriage suit he not only recounted being present at the ceremony in question, but asserted that this had taken place 'in the presence of trustworthy persons . . . so many he could not count them'.[11] Now at first glance this may not appear out of the ordinary. Unnamed trustworthy people are invoked in order to inspire confidence in a particular recollection, and it is made to seem as though they had been gathered for the purpose. But Harry clearly thought it was possible for a whole crowd of people—so many he could not count them—to be trustworthy. While this might have reflected the genuine esteem in which he held his neighbours, Harry's words were far removed from the discriminating and selective identification of trustworthy men by bishops, and by the witnesses in the earlier examples. Trustworthiness functioned as political rhetoric only when it was applied sparingly and in order to differentiate. In a similar case from Hampshire in 1520 the banns for a marriage were said to have been read by the rector of the church 'in the presence of many people of that parish and other trustworthy persons'.[12] By implying that those 'many people of the parish' as well as anonymous others were trustworthy, the phrase was given much more of its face-value meaning than was the case in official communications. Such people were simply reliable, to be trusted. Subtle modifications of institutional trustworthiness such as these are just one element in a varied and eclectic popular language of approbation, seen in frequent references to the thrifty, neighbourly, true, well-ordered (*bene dispositus*), and good, and the use of 'false' as a catchall condemnation for untrustworthiness.[13] However, despite some popular resistance and modification, the adoption of the 'official' concept of trustworthiness by litigants and their advocates arguably did more to heighten the status and difference of a bishop's trustworthy men than it did to undermine them.

In asking about the encounter between the merely faithful and the *fidedigni* we are, then, looking at a complex mesh of words and values that are not easily separable into local and institutional spheres. But this does not mean that everyone possessed equal power over the discourse. We are still looking at the 'relations between people's basic trust networks and rulers' strategies of rule' which, as Charles Tilly suggested, define the 'quality of public politics' in any era.[14] We are also looking at a deeply gendered discourse in which the language of trust was central to the exclusion of women from the late medieval public sphere. As Sheilagh Ogilvie has observed, it is not simply the case that trust is abused in certain malignant social situations, such as organized crime. Very much in line with what we have found in the case of the trustworthy men she argues that prejudice, discrimination, and abuse are in fact 'implied by the very characteristics that enable *any* social network to generate social capital to begin with'.[15]

To Bring the World About: Seeing Hierarchy

Firmly entrenched in the conceptual landscape of late medieval England, trustworthy men also made their presence felt in spatial and material terms. The analysis that follows takes its cues from the sociology of ecclesiastical trustworthiness established in the preceding chapters. This can be summarized by saying that across much of lowland England trustworthy status correlated with higher taxable wealth, tenancies of higher rental value, and larger landholdings (see Chapter 6 in particular). If trustworthy men were more likely to be among the wealthier inhabitants of their parishes, what effect would that have had on how they were perceived? The instinctive knowledge upon which the group self-selection of trustworthy men was founded inevitably took account of innumerable tiny pieces of information about suitability that are impossible for historians to recover. Some of these, however, may have had to do with the ways in which space was ordered and material goods distributed, according to categories and juxtapositions that would have oozed significance for people at the time, however indistinct they are to historians. Fortunately the documentary and archaeological records reveal the shadows of such things from time to time.

Some of the ways in which space was ordered and inhabited were daily reminders of status differences. Differences in status meant living within different horizons, something that is likely to have been an intuitively known marker of, and perhaps justification for, those distinctions. Given their greater-than-average economic clout, trustworthy elites were more likely to be involved in trans-local markets for produce, land, and credit than many of their less secure neighbours.[16] An example of this that is perhaps extreme, but which illustrates the point very well, is Gillingham in Dorset where, as we saw in Chapter 8, the men who acted as parish representatives were deeply implicated in the credit and land markets while those they reported at visitation were not. Such involvement meant having more links beyond a single place than did poorer parishioners, a fact that manifested itself in different patterns of movement and access to opportunities.

Credit was common in late medieval England and most of it was probably small-scale, local, and neighbourly or charitable in motivation. This world is largely unrecorded, although we get glimpses of it in manorial and church courts, as discussed in Chapter 2. A good deal of credit however—certainly that which was of higher value—connected people who did not belong to the same parish, meaning that again wealthier people operated within more distant economic horizons.[17] Something similar occurred in produce markets. Kathleen Biddick has shown that in Bedfordshire around 1300 the trade in high-value or bulk products traded over longer distances—notably sheep, oxen, and fodder crops, but also to a lesser extent wheat and malting grains—was significantly concentrated in the hands of the wealthiest peasant producers and urban traders. This produced distinctive geographies of trade determined by economic status: the poor traded locally, the rich traded regionally.[18] We have seen numerous examples of trustworthy men who embody this pattern, such as John Towker of Blandford Forum who used the town's seigniorial court to pursue his debtors in the 1390s and 1400s.[19]

Such economic connections beyond the parish were often likely to have been inextricable from the wider regional connections involved in being a parish representative. Trustworthy men travelled from their home parishes to visitation centres in order to make their reports, where they would have met and talked to other men in the same situation. Churchwardens often went to fund-raising ales in neighbouring parishes, providing opportunities for them to make comparisons with their peers there.[20] The Dorset network of William Clavill (for whom see Chapter 7) is illustrative of the webs that linked parish elites to one another, reinforcing a common outlook based on a wider frame of reference than that inhabited by some poorer parishioners. William and his wife Edith were childless, and her heir was a man called Robert Cyprian from Horton-cum-Knowlton parish. Cyprian was the wealthiest man in Woodlands manor, and had been executor and attorney for one of the Horton trustworthy men, John Abbot.[21] Being able to call upon the advice or assistance of other men considered trustworthy at a regional rather than just a parochial level gave these men a social presence that is hard to quantify but must have seemed an inescapable fact of life. We can see it at moments when wider connections were translated into valuable social capital. For example, around 1470, John Fuller, a fifty-three-year-old draper from St Albans, was called as a witness in a London marriage suit. His role was to verify the testimony and status of men who were not available, given the distance, and he did so by calling them 'trustworthy men of good fame and a proper manner of living' (*viri fidedigni bone fame et conuersacionis honeste*).[22] Being able to validate in one place information gathered in another meant that this witness was deploying the rhetoric of trustworthiness in much the same way as the bishops whose work will be analysed in Part IV.

Such differences in the geographical horizons of trustworthy men relative to poorer parishioners made structural inequalities visible on a day-to-day basis. Something similar took place even within the parish church, where one might think that the rhetoric of Christian unity—heard in sermons and the liturgy, experienced in the ritual of the mass, and imbibed from visual representations—was dominant. Working against the impact of these media, the arrangement of the nave 'manifested, and in some ways facilitated' social differences amongst parishioners.[23] At Bridgewater in the later fifteenth century, pews were bought by wealthier men who occupied town rather than mere parish offices. Meanwhile women often stood or sat on the north side of the church, associated with St Mary but also with the devil, or at the back where they would commonly have been surrounded by murals warning against the gendered-female sins of gossip and backbiting.[24] The trustworthy men of Brilley in Herefordshire asserted in 1397 that 'it has been laid down from early times' that women should not sit beyond a certain point in church, and there was a hefty customary fine of six shillings eight pence for infringements.[25] Talking in church and arguing with neighbours were offences for which women were punished more often than men in visitations and the church courts; male parish elites made judgements about the propriety of female sex workers sitting in church at all; even sharing the kiss of peace—that symbol of Christian equality—with women could be deemed scandalous.[26] Higher status was made flesh in masculine bodies, segregated from women and the poor of the parish in the very space where Christian equality before God might be expected to have been a value to which all subscribed.

In addition to spatial reminders of inequality personal material culture also contributed to the status of trustworthy men seeming part of the natural order. The material culture of people below the nobility changed in various ways during the later Middle Ages, with the main watershed for the peasantry being the Black Death, in whose wake historians have identified an increased consumption of meat and white bread, higher spending on the small luxuries of personal adornment, and larger houses.[27] Not all peasants and townspeople were equal beneficiaries of these changes. For the most part the improvements in diet, clothing, and housing were enjoyed only by the wealthier peasants and traders. What we see is more of a realignment of social groups than a general increase in the standard of living. The reactionary Statute on Diet and Apparel of 1363 stipulated the precise grades of cloth that different classes could wear and made more general comments about foodstuffs appropriate to various 'estates'. Lawmakers were frightened by the adoption of an 'excessive and outrageous' material culture that blurred the boundaries between lord and tenant, master and servant. In the same spirit commentators and satirists like the distempered Ricardian poet John Gower condemned the household servant who 'demands things for his belly like a lord'. In 'The Miller's Tale' Chaucer permitted his audience to snigger at a gullible carpenter who was a 'riche gnof': a rich 'neif' or villein.[28]

Gower was a miserable snob, but his vitriol contained a fairly precise piece of social observation. Improving material conditions were indeed beginning to blur the distinctions between the upper peasantry and the lower gentry, precisely the group from which the trustworthy men of parishes were increasingly drawn. In the thirteenth century, despite the frequently close association between wealth and trustworthy status, the average male peasant had been able to look at his parish representatives and see people who dressed more or less as he did, who ate similar foods, and who lived in similar houses. By the end of the fifteenth century it would have been a more common experience to be represented by men who—to some degree—dressed, dined, and lived like little lords.[29] This was a reconfiguration of material culture and wealth that also meant the upper peasantry had more in common with the beneficed clergy (rectors and perpetual vicars) rather than the unbeneficed (stipendiary vicars, chaplains, and others).[30] As the lord-peasant boundary became less distinct, material differences amongst the peasantry became markers of great social importance.

Another aspect of this was involvement in documentary culture: Michael Clanchy has demonstrated that by the thirteenth century many well-to-do peasants owned their own seals for use in witnessing land transactions and other recorded agreements.[31] This was the world of the trustworthy men. For instance at Goodmanham in the East Riding an inquest into the vacancy of a portion of the parish church in 1269 was conducted by the dean of Harthill and 'other trustworthy men' who all affixed their seals.[32] Similarly in 1416 eighteen of the 'trustworthy senior parishioners and neighbours' of Sturminster Marshall church in Dorset reported that the rector and not the vicar was responsible for repairs to the chancel. They all fixed their personal seals to the account of the inquest that was sent back to the bishop of Salisbury.[33] They 'spoke' the visual and material language of power.

These were not differences between free and unfree peasants, echoing the church's lack of concern for this distinction when recruiting trustworthy men (as seen in Chapters 5 and 6). Rodney Hilton's perceptive 1978 article on inequality highlighted instead disparities in the tools and equipment possessed by those families who had enough land to support themselves, and those forced to supplement their meagre cottage economy with wage labour, irrespective of legal status. The former would have likely possessed a plough and draught animals, perhaps an oxen or even a horse, while the latter worked their small plots with hand tools: the spade and the hoe. These differences, well-known and visible to everyone, could occasionally be the source of tension and resentment, as we see in the many complaints in manorial court rolls about draught animals wandering into the fields and trampling corn. For Hilton this material difference was possibly 'the basic form of stratification inherent in any peasant society in the temperate zone'.[34] Day-to-day in the village, on the roads, and in the fields everyone would be able to see these reminders of unequal material resources. Those peasants who possessed horses, even past-their-best beasts pulling carts and ploughs, stood at the lower end of an equine culture that was effectively a material lingua franca among medieval elites. Though there were obvious differences between them, knights, wealthy clerics, messengers, and officials, as well as some wealthy peasants could all recognize one another as men who did not rely upon their own feet for getting around. No muddy inclines or swollen fords would detract from their notable cleanliness, in contrast to those who walked.

Differences in clothing, food, housing, tools, and equipment were silent yet eloquent reminders of the hierarchies within medieval peasant society, at whose apex stood most of the trustworthy men. For the most part their influence on the experience of inequality was implicit, a source of instinctive knowledge, but from time to time we can glimpse the envy and suspicion that could attach to material goods. Possessions could be read as signs of a person's probity, but they were open to other interpretations. In 1492 Elizabeth Carpenter and Margery Clerke were reported to the commissary court of London for defamation. Each had made remarks about the honesty of men by raising suspicion about their possessions. Carpenter had allegedly commented on a tallow chandler, Thomas Marshall, who had recently lost some goods or money in a failed debt suit. She marvelled at how he lived and questioned how he had acquired those things he lent if not 'by falsenesse by stelyng and pikyng of his master's goods'. Without such worldly possessions, she continued, 'he colde (*could*) never bryng the worlde aboute as he dothe', meaning that he would not have been able to get his own way were he not so well-appointed; moreover his wealth was—so she claimed—ill-gotten. In a less eloquent but more direct way, Clerke was said to have defamed John Jakeman by saying that 'he hathe not one disshe to ete his mete in that he got be trowthe but by falsenesse'.[35] A reputation for 'truth' and the ability to 'bring the world about' were the highly prized assets of men occupying public roles in village and town, and it is very revealing that women trying to take them down a peg or two should do so by implying that their wealth was a sign of dishonesty rather than trustworthiness.

Women's Faith and Masculine Trustworthiness

The actions of these two late fifteenth-century defamers, fighting on the front line of masculine reputation, can be viewed as a miniature portrait of the encounter between female *fides* and masculine trustworthiness. To whatever extent women were able to deploy *fides* in forming relationships, which we saw very clearly in Chapters 2 and 3, their public role was heavily circumscribed by deep-rooted and negative constructions of the female voice, sexuality, and rationality. When churchmen came looking for trustworthy informants they were not looking for women (for which see Chapters 5 and 6). Nor were the parishes prepared to be represented by women. This was despite the ubiquitous presence of women in a number of public roles where their word—their trustworthiness—was put to the test. From fourteenth-century Cambridgeshire and late fifteenth-century London we have many examples of women borrowing money and making faith to repay their debts. The manorial and church court records made no distinction between the promises of men and women and everyone was expected to be trustworthy in the sense of being faithful or true to their word.[36] Equally, women could be creditors. In London Stephen Reygate broke faith with Isabelle Scarlet in failing to pay her six shillings eight pence; Robert Gyll broke faith with Elizabeth Incoll for failing to repay five shillings.[37]

For the most part female involvement in credit-debt relationships was limited to unmarried women, mainly widows.[38] Married women, although they controlled greater economic resources, were represented in public by their husbands. The husband was 'so much the head of the wife' that her promises could be made only through him.[39] Judith Bennett notably found that in early fourteenth-century Northamptonshire women were frequent litigators in the manor courts, but only as single women: 'marriage brought private security, but public subordination, and life as a spinster or widow brought public independence, but vulnerability'.[40] In the church courts too, as we have seen in Chapter 5, women could be witnesses, though they often faced denigrating comments based on their gender. Female witnesses were less common than male in cases heard before the archbishop's court at York in the fourteenth century, but they were more common in cases where the litigants themselves were women. By the sixteenth century, however, nearly all witnesses were male.[41] In the business of parish governance female involvement was not unthinkable. Kit French has discovered enough female churchwardens to suggest that many people would have been aware that this was a possibility. But, once again, such involvement was often limited to single heads of households, usually the widows of male churchwardens.[42]

The subordination of married women, female children, and servants to male heads of household was so fundamental a feature of medieval life that it is frequently unremarked in our sources. Only occasionally is normality described. In early fifteenth-century Devon the settlement of a dispute about parishioners going to a chapel instead of their parish church provides one such moment: every married male householder was told hear mass in the parish church on the Feast of the Assumption and pay one pence to the rector 'on behalf of himself and his family', while every unmarried householder—male or female—was to do the same and make an additional payment on the saint's day of the parish church.[43] The norm of social respectability was masculine, married, and propertied. Those who did not fit the bill could find their very time, movements, and money controlled in ways that served to emphasize and entrench the difference.

The reason why women's participation in public life was precarious and so often subordinated to that of men must be sought in the complex of mutually affirming assumptions about the capacities of women. Humoral predisposition and menstrual uncleanliness were the supposedly self-evident bodily weaknesses that underpinned persistent belief in female mental incapacities. Driven by lust, imperfection, and feebleness women were imagined to be both irrational and disobedient.[44] Small wonder then that statements on the untrustworthiness of women, their instability, inconstancy, and changeability were so prominent across a host of late medieval discourses. We should consider it one of the dominant organising concepts of social life. The impact of cultural misogyny on ideas about the trustworthiness of women can be illustrated with the words of the poet John Lydgate, writing in the first quarter of the fifteenth century. In his *Troy Book* Lydgate expresses views about women and trust that we may regard as having been axiomatic in their day:

> For who was euery ʒit so mad or wood,
> To ʒif feith or hastily credence
> To any womman, with-oute experience,
> In whom is nouther trust ne sikernesse.
> Þai ben so double & ful of brotilnesse,
> Þat it is harde in hem to assure.[45]

This was itself something of an echo of the popular song which advised men to put their trust in women only when 'whytynges do walke forestes to chase hertys . . . and goslynges hunt, the wolfe to overthrow'.[46] If female trustworthiness was as unnatural as a fish on a forest path, men's was—by implication—

natural. We also find this way of thinking in depositions made by witnesses in marriage and defamation suits in the church courts. Comments about the unfaithfulness of women were made as if statements of the obvious. In 1377 for example a priest in Wilburton, Cambridgeshire, stood up in church to read the banns for the upcoming marriage of the young John Frost to the widow Anya Brid. No sooner had the priest opened his mouth than another voice was heard to shout

> It is remarkable how fickle women can be—if she had been faithful she would have been my wife![47]

This voice belonged to John Fish, a man who claimed that he was already betrothed to Anya, which would have prevented her marriage to John Frost.

It was this manifest inconstancy that made it possible to brush aside female witnesses when they did appear in court. In 1272 Alice Dolling of Winterbourne Stoke in Wiltshire claimed that she had married William Smith. He rejected the testimony of her all-female witnesses, producing ten male witnesses who placed him four miles away in Bulford at the time of the alleged betrothal. William's witnesses were members of the parish guild of Bulford. When the court examiner asked him who was in the guild he replied 'the brothers of the gild'; asked who these brothers were he replied, in words that seamlessly melt gender into social status, 'all the better persons of the parish'. The Salisbury diocesan court found in favour of Dolling, but when Smith appealed to the Court of Canterbury in London only he and his rich male witnesses could afford to attend.[48] Smith did not need to explain the contrast between his male 'better sort' and Dolling's female witnesses. He allowed it to speak for itself. In 1374 a man and a woman were cited to the bishop of Ely's consistory court for committing spiritual incest. Isabelle Tavern was the godmother to two of Stephen Barnwell's children. He purged himself with three trustworthy men, she with eight honest women.[49] Compurgators were rarely called trustworthy men, a term that was reserved for the parish elite. Here its use, in conjunction with the disparity between the numbers of compurgators, strikes a contrast between the status of male and female witnesses. The thresholds of credibility were different for men and women.

As Jeremy Goldberg has observed, women were most often witnesses in cases affecting other women. There were certain spheres of knowledge—childbirth, virginity, sexual activity—that were seen as being within women's competency, though not exclusively so.[50] In 1311, for example, some women suspected of having sex with the monks of Selby in Yorkshire were to purge themselves with the assistance of twelve 'honest women of the parish'.[51] At Edlingham in Northumberland in 1435 Margaret Lindsay was defamed by three men of being a sorcerer who had, along with other women, used some kind of stick to bind their penises so that they could not have sex. She denied it, and swore to her innocence with five other women, after which the bishop of Durham restored her 'pristine fame'.[52] Why were women used in this case? It is possible that they were asked whether the practice was common love magic. Equally, because the men alleged a conspiracy among women, perhaps only women were thought competent to comment on things discussed out of sight of men.

Exclusively female forms of sociability are strongly suggested by other cases involving women as witnesses or compurgators. One 1469 case of fornication involving a chaplain from Boroughbridge ended with him purging himself with six honest priests and six trustworthy laymen. But the archdeacon also called for eight female parishioners to attend the purgation to make sure that it would satisfy local opinion.[53] The implication is that the female respondent's good name could only be repaired if the denials were witnessed by women. Playing a similar card in reverse, when Katherine Strong of Hampshire found herself suspected in 1520 of having married despite being contracted to another man, she took the trouble to come to court with ten named female witnesses and 'a great many other women and girls' as her compurgators.[54] Research into the workings of the parish below the level of churchwardens has brought to light the fairly widespread existence of all-female religious guilds.[55] Though the sexes were by no means segregated, there were parallel societies of women and men in medieval villages.[56] In cases such as these there was certainly a female sphere of knowledge, but in being limited by the construction of gender it was not a fully public sphere. Women could have specialist knowledge of their own world, but only male knowledge could speak for both.

For the most part female speech was excluded from the public sphere by tacit assumptions. Sometimes though there was more aggressive policing of the gendered boundary of trustworthiness, leaving women in no doubt as to their circumscribed role. A casual identification of women as prostitutes ran through the everyday language of street insults for example, and, as Ruth Mazo Karras has suggested if 'all women were sexually suspect, the treatment of commercial sex could become a tool to control all women'.[57] Sex work was also sometimes synonymous with service work in inns.[58] Reports of women for fornication or gossip sometimes overdescribed their occupations as, for example, a 'tapster working in the common street' or 'formerly a tapster' as if this explained their actions and confirmed their culpability.[59] Such easy associations informed the narrator's comment on a fictional lecherous pardoner in the pseudo-Chaucerian *Canterbury Interlude*: having held the pardoner up for ridicule the narrator then pictures him 'remembryng his foly, / That he wold trust a tapster of a comon hostry (*hostelry*), / For comenly for the most part, they been wyly echon (*each one*)'.[60] This conventional wisdom about inns also lay behind the stream of invective that Sybil Whatton aimed at John Hellg in

1470s London: he was, she said, a false knave and false churl, his wife a false tapster and a harlot and their children common prostitutes.[61]

One case from the diocesan court of Canterbury in 1412 records the use of alleged sexual behaviour and scatological imagery to disparage a female witness in ways that suggest women's voices were very easily associated with sex, pollution, dirt, and untrustworthiness. Agnes Hacchys was a witness in the matrimonial suit between William Rede and Juliana Prat of Kent. After she had given her evidence on behalf of Rede, Thomas Copyn stepped forward to speak in favour of Prat. Copyn said that Agnes Hacchys was 'reputed to be a badly behaved and poorly controlled (*inhoneste gubernatam*) woman of frivolous opinions' who within the past three years had formed relationships with several men and borne three children; she was reputed to be the 'concubine' of William Rede, the plaintiff in the suit. Copyn went on to explain that her ill fame was widespread, that he had often heard his neighbours say that she frequently left her house in search of sexual encounters, and that her reputation was well-established among the greater part of her neighbours. The next two witnesses, Thomas Strete and Robert Rikedon, confirmed Agnes Hacchys' poor reputation, and in particular recalled a night before the previous Easter when, on her way to William Rede's house, she had fallen into a ditch or cesspit (*puteo cum aquam . . . siue in stagnam*).[62]

This incident is more than a random *aide-memoire*. Scatological insinuations hit a number of targets in medieval literature, among them corporeality and fertility but also the commission of unwilling (often sexual) acts.[63] It is therefore reasonable to think that the image of Agnes emerging from the cesspit covered in filth was a story whose telling had been refined, even as its content coarsened, as it was discussed in the village. Her visual appearance seems to have acted as confirmation of her moral depravity, and her soaking may have been understood as the just-desserts of a scold, a woman speaking out of turn.[64] Besides the well-worn trope of the inconstant promiscuous woman, the imagery of these depositions recalls street insults such as 'shittyn knave' and 'shittin churle' as well as Chaucer's comment on the 'shiten shepherde', or priest who cannot be trusted, in 'The General Prologue' to the *Canterbury Tales*.[65] The whole assemblage of misogyny, scatology, and moral superiority made it *obvious* that her testimony could not be trusted, although the effort involved in rubbishing her shows that making things seem natural in fact required a lot of low-level work on behalf of masculinity. The fact that it made such a good, if cruel, story also made it memorable. Her sexual relationship with William Rede, which was presumably the substantial fact in legal terms, becomes almost incidental to this demolition of her character.

What this material serves to demonstrate is the fragility of female *fides*— not on its own terms and within its own allotted sphere—but when confronted with the idealization of a masculine trustworthiness. Men were more able to command trust and to cast doubt upon the trustworthiness of others, and women's capacity for public action was for the most part limited to a female sphere. When the lionization of some men as a trustworthy elite was added to this situation, it strengthened all cultural and political barriers to female participation in public life. The male power inherent in this relationship was brought to bear in innumerable moments of microcultural behaviour when the subordination of women in general was perpetuated through the denigration of particular women, and their particular powerlessness was deemed as natural as dominion over beasts and deference to the king. Over the late Middle Ages the position of women seems to have worsened, and given the ever-narrower social stratum from which the trustworthy men were selected, it seems likely that female exclusion from this public symbolic role was much more than simply a product of the general 'medieval' misogyny: it was a contributory factor to a worsening public position for women between 1200 and 1500.

Patriarchal Encounters between the Trustworthy and the Merely Faithful

Trustworthiness was explicitly, and tacitly, constructed as a facet of local elite masculinity in the language of ecclesiastical governance, in the practice of inquests and visitations, and in the way that these discourses were employed in interpersonal conflict. Female voices were relegated below those of men, and most male voices were sidelined in favour of an increasingly restricted elite, despite some variation according to settlement and landscape type. In this way the needs of church government and the ways in which they were met were a major component in the maintenance and modification of patriarchy over the course of the late Middle Ages. Not all men could possess the social capital that came with trustworthy status, and even though its masculine lustre might from time to time rub off on them, the majority of men experienced the patriarchal hierarchy even if they were subordinated less than women. Being a trustworthy man gave one considerable status within the community. It also thrust a man into encounters where his words, actions, and behaviour were moulded to that status. These were encounters between the *fideles* and the *fidedigni*, between the 'merely' faithful mass of Christians and the select few deemed trustworthy by the institutional church; they encapsulated and ramified social divisions, played out at the point where the paths of two contrasting lives crossed. Frequent flashpoints included the distribution of charity and the correction of misbehaviour.

Charity was a relationship that increasingly came to dominate interaction between the elites of late medieval parishes and their poorer neighbours. With trustworthy men being drawn from a narrowing demographic in the fifteenth century, their involvement in organized charity gave them a degree of economic control over their parishes in addition to their political role. As

Gervase Rosser has recently shown, late medieval charity was the enactment of a universal Christian ethic in a particular social situation: a question not of feeling charitable towards all, but of being charitable towards the people in one's immediate social group.[66] This meant that it was a virtue that could arise only in a real social relationship, where the subjectivity of both giver and receiver was of the utmost importance. Claiming to be poor meant adopting a position as powerless and in need of protection, whilst simultaneously laying claim to some of the humble virtue possessed by those choosing to live in the voluntary poverty of monastic orders. Conversely, giving alms to the needy was inscribed as an element of Christian social morality: the rich could make reparations for their sin of avarice by giving to the poor, and the poor could, in return, offer prayers for their benefactors or simply fulfil a useful function as a vehicle for the alleviation of guilt.[67] Those who presented themselves as poor or who gave money for their relief were thus opening up the potential for concrete social interaction.

Much of this took place at close quarters: either face-to-face or mediated through guilds, hospitals, almshouses, the executors of wills, the parish clergy, or other bodies representing the parish. Frequently this meant churchwardens and trustworthy men or their analogues.[68] The responsibility for priests to give alms was codified in 1281, at which point the role of trustworthy men was also institutionalized, supervising charity in parishes where the profits of the rectory estate had been farmed out.[69] Formal arrangements for regular parish-based relief, as opposed to informal expectations about token doles, were however not common before the sixteenth century.[70] But there are occasional glimpses of institutions like the 'village loan chest' of Dennington in Suffolk, financed by a local lady and kept in the parish church, with loans disbursed by 'local worthies' to the other villagers.[71] Microcredit at the parish level was often motivated by charitable concern more than immediate personal profit, and mutual assistance was the safety net of many precarious livelihoods.[72] But however it was mediated, however much motivated by Christian love or genuine feelings of obligation, and however much it was received in gratitude, the relationship at the heart of charity was inherently unequal. It is not unreasonable to assume that it felt this way too, much of the time, as the possessors of economic and social capital lined up alongside one another in decisions as to who was deserving of charity and who was not.

For example, at Casterton in Rutland in 1301 the rector, William Emp-ingham, granted some land and a modest rent from another property for the foundation of a charity. The charity was to support 'seven poor men of God and beggars of the parish' who would pray and attend church regularly. Four male lay parishioners were set up as its feoffees, and their successors were to be the 'higher-status and more rational section' (*maior et senior pars*) of the parish. In addition two 'faithful men of the community' were to be chosen as proctors to manage the funds and give an annual account to the rector or the feoffees. The recipients were to be honest men of good fame, chosen by the feoffees, but if any one of them was notably defamed he was to be replaced by someone more deserving.[73] There were several moral assumptions and expectations on both sides of this relationship, but while the beneficiaries had to meet a fairly minimal level of esteem (good fame, regular prayer) the distributors of the relief had to be the leading men of their parish. These were distinctions that emphasized the moral divide between donor and recipient. Similar assumptions were in play at Clifton Campville in Staffordshire where, in 1361, the lord and patron Richard of Stafford founded a chantry in the parish church. Besides praying for Stafford and his family the chantry priest was made responsible for distributing a token halfpenny dole once a year to two hundred poor people chosen not by him, but by the rector, chaplain, and four trustworthy men of Clifton.[74] With two hundred recipients, the job of the trustworthy men would have been more to decide who was undeserving than who was worthy of the payment. But the moral and social assumptions of the document are all the more striking for this. Stipulating two hundred recipients suggests that the vast majority of the parishioners were imagined as poor in contrast to the trustworthy few. Face-to-face with the trustworthy men, the parishioners received a powerful message about the conjunction of their economic and political inferiority.

Chris Dyer has commented that executors and supervisors of wills as well as the feoffees of proto-'trusts' would all have been drawn 'from the same group at the top of village society who would be judged to be worthy of trust'.[75] As village society became more polarized this had the effect of strengthening the alignment between economic and political inequalities, and by 1600 the sort of arrangements we have seen in Casterton and Clifton Campville had been formalized under the Poor Law, in which overseers of the poor were frequently described in the language of social superiority, reputation, and trustworthiness. They were to be substantial, circumspect, respectable, discreet, credible, and conscionable. None of the 'meaner sort who are not fitt to be trusted with the stock of the poor' were to serve.[76] This was an institutionalization of social capital and inequality that had deep roots in the late medieval politics of trustworthiness.

The other major arena in which people regularly came face-to-face not only with the trustworthy men but with the power that their institutional status brought them, was in visitations, inquests, and church court proceedings.[77] Regulating behaviour divided those people 'most in need of reformation'—the phrase ubiquitous in late medieval visitation mandates—from those who were the agents of regulation. For example, the 'trustworthy reports' received in 1389 by the bishop of Winchester about people attending markets on Sundays, 'to the profit of the Devil', were especially concerned with labourers, artisans, and servants playing games, drinking, and skulking; perhaps less so with breaking the Sabbath through trade.[78] The trustworthy men were here engaged in reporting their social and economic inferiors in terms of immoral behaviour, eliding distinctions between ethical, social, and economic differences. Each time neighbours came face-to-face in such instances of social competition and moral contestation the ideology of trustworthiness was realized, affecting the experience of the social church. A striking individual example of this concerns John Jolliffe of Friesthorpe in Lincolnshire, who was an important member of his parish elite, serving as an *inquisitor* at least seven times between 1337 and his probable death in 1349 (see Chapter 7). He was certainly one of those men without whom nothing could happen in the parish. So when in July 1342 he asked the provost of the court to cite Alice Cran for a breach of faith against him, the inequalities of institutional trustworthiness were brought to bear upon one of his neighbours. Cran was alleged to have promised to pay Jolliffe eighteen pence on a day that had by then passed. When she appeared she agreed another deadline for payment 'with the consent of both parties', indicating that she and he were present in court at the same time.[79] The terms by which this encounter was described—the trustworthy man and the faithless woman, the creditor and the debtor—made Cran and Jolliffe into exemplars of universal moral categories, which in turn made themselves felt in their particular relationship.[80] Although they were both laypeople subject to church authority, he was *institutionally* more powerful than she. This encounter, and countless others like it, served to naturalize the moral and social categories of the church.

This is not to say that the ideology of trustworthiness held complete sway over the minds of ordinary Christians. There is in fact considerable evidence of a competing social doctrine in circulation: it is important to remember that the medieval church was far from being a monolith, and there were many ways of interpreting some basic concepts. Building a reputation for trustworthiness necessarily involved a degree of social climbing, an activity widely frowned upon in criticisms of ill-gotten gains—as we have seen—and in warnings about succumbing to the sin of pride. In one English sermon of the fifteenth century, concern for reputation was said to be a sure route to feelings of pride.[81] Likewise, in John Mirk's *Instructions for Parish Priests* confessors were instructed how to elicit admissions of pride from their subjects. Clambering over one's fellows in order to get ahead was clearly proscribed in this influential and representative text:

> Hast þow ay oppresset þy neghbour
> For to gete þe honour?
> Hast þou I-schend hys gode fame
> For to gete þe a gode name?

All of this could easily apply to the battle for reputation within one's own social group, but Mirk goes on to instruct the confessor to ask:

> Hast þou be prowde and hye of port
> For tryste of lady and eke of lord?[82]

Trying to impress one's social superiors in order to gain their trust is presented as folly, while the acquisition of a good name—whether described as troth, *fides*, esteem, or worship—among one's peers is understood to involve a good deal of competition, implying that there would be winners and losers. That this is recognized in such an influential text suggests a degree of ecclesiastical uneasiness about the inequalities of reputation upon which church government depended, although if so it was buried deep and never made its way into the documentation on inquests and visitations that will come under the microscope in the chapters that follow. Perhaps more significantly, what such critiques illustrate is the extent to which social elites had to play to different audiences in order to maintain their position. As Reemtsma has observed, 'to call oneself trustworthy means being trustworthy primarily for the social segment to which one identifies or is assigned'.[83] In the case of parish representatives in late medieval England, the performance of trustworthiness was made for the benefit of two 'segments' simultaneously: their neighbours in the parish, and the administrative hierarchy of the church. While this was an ambidexterity that brought with it the risks of sinful pride and exposure to criticism, it also brought enormous social capital that was unavailable to people whose calculations and feelings of trust were mostly *confined to* their fellow parishioners.

Face-to-face with the trustworthy men, the majority of people in late medieval England found their faith lacking. No matter how strong their belief in God, their innate honesty, or their reputation for fairness and reliability, there was always a group amongst them whom powerful people and institutions considered especially worthy of faith: the *fidedigni*. The hierarchy that this introduced into the web of words, concepts, and practices constituting the culture of faith did not, however, corrupt a social order that had hitherto been equitable: inequalities were already present, caused by shifts in the balance of a multitude of factors, sometimes operating alone, sometimes in tandem. But the trustworthiness attributed by bishops was a new and independent variable added into this mixture. At the structural level its impact was profound and in face-to-face interactions it made people keenly aware of the limitations of their *fides*.

PART IV

Bishops and a Church Built on Inequality and Faith, 1250–1500

GROWING INEQUALITY within the late medieval English parish occurred over the same period of time as the institutions of communal life, such as church-wardens and parish guilds, became more important, namely the fourteenth and fifteenth centuries. We can now add trustworthy men to the traditional picture of the parish, and put the churchwardens into context (for which see Chapter 7), and we can see how the communalism of parish life did not mean egalitarianism. There were meaningful inequalities in the way that parishes regulated their internal affairs and represented themselves to outside author-ity. Looking at the trustworthy men in their local context therefore rewrites the history of the parish but, as I said in the introduction, the history of the later medieval church cannot be written without considering the parish *and* the bishop. We have seen already (in Chapter 4) how the symbolic role of the *fidedigni* developed amidst the expansion in church power in the twelfth and thirteenth centuries; and I have alluded (in Chapter 5) to the fact that the English episcopacy showed especial affection for the term and for the role. The chapters in this final section of the book now put the bishop and his gov-ernance of the diocese centre stage, showing how a particular form of rela-tionship with the parish created what historians have habitually called the institutional church.

Bishops relied upon and exacerbated the inequalities of the parish in order to identify trustworthy men, and it was they who controlled the symbolic role. It was their language, and they deployed it for their own purposes. The rela-tionships of *fides* upon which institutional trusting depended (for which see Part I) were incorporated into a new epistemology by which knowledge could be confidently extracted from peasants and other laypeople. In the following chapters I will show how bishops commodified certain aspects of social rela-tionships, and built the church upon them. After all 'a church . . . is an orga-nization that has certain material requisites for its survival' and trustworthy men were one of the major resources utilized (and created) by late medieval English bishops for their own benefit.[1] They were useful not because they were honest, but because they had something to lose: possessing greater economic means and more cultural capital (in part derived from acting in representative roles) than the majority of their neighbours meant that they could lose their status if things went awry. Just as bishops wanted stability and constancy (see Chapter 5), so too did the trustworthy men.

Changes in church politics meant that bishops' need of trustworthy men grew considerably between about 1275 and the later fifteenth century, after which it seems to have faded. The period that saw an expanding role for the *fidedigni* was therefore also the period over which those men stood further and further apart from the rest of parish society, as discussed in Chapter 8. Although, as we shall see below, bishops used trustworthy men from the early thirteenth century onwards in the management of alms collectors and in-heritance (Chapter 11), it was when visitation became a means for regulating all manner of social relations and morality in the last quarter of that century that the need for trustworthy men became ubiquitous and reasonably regular (Chapter 13). Around the same time, between the issuing of the writ *Circumspecte agatis* in 1286 and the composition of the 'Articles of the Clerics' in 1316, the church courts also began to feel a little more secure in pressing their claims on various matters long disputed with the crown. Trustworthy men became more necessary here in contributing to inquests, but also in promoting secular confidence in the impartiality of ecclesiastical judgements as a whole; for there was always tension at the boundary of the two jurisdictions and many areas of shared or overlapping responsibility remained unresolved.[2] In addition to domestic competition for power, exertions of papal authority had been common between the mid-thirteenth and mid-fourteenth centuries as popes sought to control the filling of vacant benefices, but when Edward III put a stop to this in 1351, the papacy was reduced to flexing its muscles by providing dispensations for clerical study leave, illegitimate birth, and plurality (holding more than one ecclesiastical office simultaneously); these were all matters that bishops, in these cases delegated by the papacy with the task of gathering local information, settled through inquests of trustworthy men. In the early fifteenth century the frequency with which trustworthy men were used increased once more as they became the front line in the detection of heresy; in England this was an activity undertaken primarily by bishops, rather than by specially appointed inquisitors. If episcopal demand rose to significant levels in the late thirteenth century, and peaked in the early to mid-fifteenth, by 1500 it looks to have been in decline. Trustworthy men are mentioned less often in bishops' registers, and the business of the church courts was being eroded by a combination of legislative attacks from John Fyneux, chief justice of King's Bench, and a decline in aggregate demand amongst litigants.[3] But for most of the period between about 1275 and about 1495, bishops needed trustworthy men more and more.

In the remaining chapters I will show that bishops needed trustworthy men in order to persuade other people to trust episcopal judgements, and to think them authoritative and stable. This was an economy of circulating trust, carrying with it all the potential for devaluation and loss that affected the monetary economy, while also underpinning concrete activities and real power. Trust established a bishop's ability to govern a Christian society and to create Christian institutions such as dioceses and parishes. It was vital to the church's role in the circulation of money (including tithes, alms and testamentary bequests, discussed in Chapter 11), to the perpetual reshaping of the physical environment (in terms of landscape, buildings, and property rights, discussed in Chapter 12), and the definition of a criminal sphere of jurisdiction separate from that of secular authorities (discussed in Chapter 13). Together the assessment of what the 'trustworthy men' contributed to each of these areas over the three hundred years before the Reformation will amount to a reimagination of the history of the late medieval church. Particular beliefs and practices will not be absent from the discussion; they could not be since they were inseparable from the institutions and relationships in which they took place. But it is not my intention to write a new general history of the many varieties of the 'faith in which' people believed (for which concept see Chapter 1).[4]

As an institutional history my analysis will be distinctive in privileging the agency of many thousands of laypeople alongside the more commonly studied bishops, lawyers, preachers, and pastoral writers. The involvement of local men in the government of dioceses made possible the growth of the church as an institution, by permitting the social and material facts of everyday life themselves to become bearers and emanations of institutional power. Through the trustworthy men a bishop's authority was 'territorialized'; it became not just a distant source of power, but an actual component of social relations, of the built environment, and of the ethical universe. The growth of episcopal power to the point at which it could achieve this permeation of the world did not spring to life from a void the moment that the word *fidedigni* was first used. Bishops had wielded spiritual and political power since Roman times, but their exploitation of inquests massively increased their social reach between 1200 and 1500. As I will show in what follows, there was no linear progression or common phasing in the chronologies of the various activities where trustworthy men were put to work. Rather, changes in their role were contingent upon time, place, and events, including epidemic disease, papal policy, the legal framework, and the challenge of heresy, as described above.

The role played by trustworthy men in forming a relationship between the parish and the bishop was performed in inquests, convened in response to a particular complaint, and in visitations, which were regular tours of the diocese by a bishop during which the representatives of parishes reported on a number of matters.[5] In both scenarios the main role of the *fidedigni* was to provide testimony. Testimony has been called a 'fundamental source of knowledge', as basic as perception and memory in shaping human understanding.[6] We can define it as an assertion about the world communicated by one person to another, who may choose to accept or reject it. But what determines acceptance or rejection? Philosophers of science have taken a number of positions on this, which provide an interesting route into the consideration of medieval trust and institutions. They have variously argued that knowledge is a series of beliefs resting upon other beliefs in a self-contained cycle; that the acceptance of testimony depends upon an assessment of the trustworthiness of the person speaking; that we trust the symbols and culture projected by the speaker (the symbolic role discussed in Chapter 5 and elsewhere); that we calibrate our trust in testimony according to the extent of our existing knowledge and whether it can be corroborated by other means.[7] Although there is a great deal of disagreement between the proponents of these views, there is evidence from the material examined in the following chapters that such disparate attitudes to testimony were not incompatible with one another. In late medieval institutions it seems that there was no single epistemology at work. Practical action tends not to be governed by pure theoretical considerations because different needs and standards obtain at different moments.

Testimony can be framed so as to emphasize its congruence with established facts, in which case it is presented as adding to knowledge about the world; or it can involve an articulation of belief and opinion (more important in legal than in scientific matters), in which case it may combine statements about the world with claims about the speaker's knowledge and signals of his or her integrity and cooperation.[8] Recipients of testimony may then consciously or unconsciously tip the balance from opinion to fact as they use the information for their own purposes. As they modify meanings, the relationship between testimony and other sorts of evidence can be a determining factor, as we shall see in Chapter 10. It may be, as Glénisson argues with regards to the medieval administrative and judicial inquest, that other forms of knowledge—such as writing, oaths, confession, material proofs, and rational deduction or presumption—are treated as subordinate to testimony.[9] There are certainly plenty of late medieval examples of this, but we shall also encounter instances of testimony being thoroughly displaced by other forms of knowledge, as the trust accorded it crumbles. This phenomenon would fit very well Gambetta's observation that the key feature of trusting is that it is 'predicated not on evidence but on the lack of *contrary* evidence', which can make it vulnerable to the presentation of new information.[10]

In many real-world situations, including those addressed in this book, the acquisition of testimony is usually conditioned by thoughts about its future use. How will I deploy or rely upon this knowledge I have gained? Such considerations emphasize the practical dimension of knowledge acquisition alongside any purely epistemic concern with its truth.[11] Once again philosophy must give way to history if we wish to understand the world. A major concern always has to do with the time-consuming difficulty of capturing a clear message from the infinite noise and tumult of events and opinions. Many writers in the social sciences have concluded that deciding to accept knowledge on trust is a means of reducing this complexity, or lowering 'transaction costs', by ensuring that decision making is not snarled up in unfathomable detail and uncertainty.[12] We may be dubious about the truth of testimony, and we may also feel uncertain about the trustworthiness of our informant, which is equally costly to measure in terms of time and effort expended. Nevertheless, we usually have particular goals in mind, which shape our attitudes to truth and trust and lead to some form of calculative thinking about the risks or costs of getting things wrong. This problem will be addressed in Chapter 14.

It has been said that the search for trust happens 'in situations of transition from one institutional realm to another'.[13] In the later Middle Ages the parish and the episcopal palace were two such institutional realms: locals knew one thing, the bishop another, and trust was necessary to carry information across the divide. Trust and the attribution of trustworthiness affected how information was seen, how communication functioned, and how institutions like those of the later medieval church developed in order to deal with its demands and consequences. And in reverse, the structure of communication can be said to have determined the nature of trust in our period.[14]

Information was a valuable commodity in these centuries. But its diffusion bore no similarity to the trade in any sort of physical merchandise.[15] This means that before launching into the mass of episcopal documentation on the work of the *fidedigni* we need to highlight and query some of the common language and metaphor with which information is often described, namely 'production', 'collection', 'reception', and so on. Unlike the tithe crops or the wool from church estates that were traded on near and distant markets, information was a commodity that did not exist until it was called into being. It was 'produced' by a question. It changed in form and nature when it was 'collected' from the locals by officials, and again when it was received by a bishop. No single part of this chain could claim exclusive possession of it at any one time, and at every stage some new meaning and significance was being created around it. Although there were costs involved in its collection, and calculation was involved at every stage of its use, its value could not be tallied in money of account nor reckoned by physical weights and measures. Information was incorporeal, and its measure subjective. This is why trust was so necessary, and why the *zero-sum* language of production and collection must be treated with extreme care. Despite this subjectivity and the potential for meanings to multiply in unpredictable ways, such was the frequency of a bishop's need for information that his whole bureaucracy could be said to have been built upon trust. In this very real sense, faith made the church.

CHAPTER TEN

Practical Epistemology

AS WE SAW IN CHAPTER 4, the ideology of trustworthiness shifted considerably in the twelfth and thirteenth centuries, from being associated exclusively with scripture and the saints to being an acceptable way of describing peasant jurors and witnesses. Against a background of endemic distrust of the laity these new *fidedigni* had to be controlled, and the information that they provided had to be handled with care. In part this was achieved by the bishop's capacity for controlling the symbolic role, discussed in Chapter 5: he could attribute trustworthiness but also withdraw it as his needs dictated. Another major ingredient in ensuring the usefulness of information was to use men who constituted a recognized social elite within the very small kingdoms of their own parishes. Their position made them difficult to contradict. This meant that they might promote their own interests (for which see Chapter 7), but it also meant that the information they provided would serve the bishop's interests well. What sort of testimony did bishops want, and how did they control it?

Firm and Undisputed Judgements

When they used the language of trustworthiness, bishops were communicating on a number of levels with several different audiences, who will feature heavily in Chapters 11 to 13. These included anyone concerned with the market in benefices (posts in parish churches with income attached), notably the parish clergy, patrons among the gentry and nobility, and institutional rectors; also, people involved in the internal lives of parishes, including the parish clergy again, but also the laity at large. In their relationships with these audiences, bishops' principal aim was to settle disputes and magnify their own power, all of which rested upon their ability to make disputes go away. They hoped that when they gathered trustworthy testimony they would be able to come back years, or even decades, later and find that they got the same answers to the same questions. They did not want to have to return to a disagreement repeatedly. There were two reasons for this. First, inquests had to be managed, letters written and sent, agents rewarded or paid, all of which cost money. Second, disputes were like wounds. If left to fester they could spread infection to the surrounding body politic. Bishops preferred, if at all possible, to dress a wound once, see it heal, and not hear about it again. Because of this they valued stability of information above all else.

Bishops styled themselves as bringers of trust and certainty. They would seek to provide a definitive answer so that 'in the future [a judgement] remains firm and undisputed (*inconvulsa*)' or so that 'scandals or dissension . . . would not arise in the future'.[1] In 1242 the bishop of Worcester noted that his conclusion of a dispute about access rights to pasture land in Elmley should 'impose silence' upon the rector concerning his claim, and in 1331 the bishop of Winchester wrote that he was ordering an inquest of trustworthy men, 'wishing to bring to an end' a dispute about church bells.[2] Trustworthiness was deployed as a restraint against the 'convulsions' of rumbling disputes. Often it worked. In 1320 the bishop of Salisbury cited trustworthy testimony given in 1269 about the income of the vicar of Upavon in Wiltshire; he was able to use that historic inquest to insist that the vicarage not be diminished in its assets.[3] Fifty-one years was a long time for the word of trustworthy men to retain its power and to continue shaping local economic and political relationships, but it was not unusual. There were not, however, any guarantees, and many disputes had the potential to open up on new fronts, particularly when the protagonists changed.

If episcopal action based upon trustworthy testimony did not command consensus, a bishop could find himself returning to cases he had thought closed. For example, in 1444 John Kempe, the archbishop of York, received a petition from Thomas Aleby, the rector of Kirkby in Cleveland, complaining about the claim of the perpetual vicar of the parish, John Selby, that his income was insufficient and should be increased. The archdeacon of Cleveland had been told to inquire into the value of the vicar's income in a normal year, as well as his goods, through twelve sworn trustworthy local men, both clerics and laymen 'through whom the truth of the matter might be better known'. He had done this and reported to the archbishop that the vicarage was worth no more than a hundred shillings (five pounds) a year, but Thomas Aleby believed that it was worth at least ten marks a year (six pounds thirteen shillings eight pence) and asked the archbishop to order a 'better' inquest. So Kempe ordered the archdeacon to go back, cite the vicar and other interested parties, and inquire again into the value of the church through twelve 'impartial' (*indifferentes*) trustworthy men.[4] Two significant implications emerge from this, telling us a great deal about episcopal attitudes to testimony and truth. First, it might seem remarkable that the archbishop, having ordered one inquest through trustworthy men, consented to another just because someone did not like the result. One might think that to a prelate of the church such a demand would appear sour grapes at best, insubordination at worst. But Kempe relented without question. That he did so reveals what bishops wanted from trustworthy men: to produce information that could stand the test of time. For this to happen it had to command a degree of consensus. At Kirkby the rector's unhappiness was a recipe for instability, and it meant that the first inquest had not produced information to meet the episcopal standard of trustworthiness, whether or not it was true (which we cannot tell). The other point that jumps out of this letter is the description of the second group of trustworthy men as 'impartial'. There is no information about the case that would allow us to assess the likely bias of the first group. We don't know who they were. But in a way this doesn't matter. Because their information had been challengeable, they must—in the institutional mind—have been biased. The surest sign that the locals had been impartial and trustworthy would be an unchallenged judgement.

In order to buttress the alleged impartiality of inquests bishops might, as well as relying upon the social capital of parish elites, insist that they took place 'in full chapter' or 'in the presence of all interested parties'.[5] The typical example of Burlingthorp and Frisby in Lincolnshire is a case in point. In 1447 there was an inquest of trustworthy men into the poverty of these two churches and whether they could be joined together to create a viable benefice for a single rector. All interested parties were to be called to the hearing in a session of the local chapter, and Sir William, the patron of Burlingthorp, was singled out as someone whose presence was especially desired.[6] On such occasions the trustworthy men might be presented as 'unsuspected by either party', a standard against which they were sometimes measured by the protagonists.[7] At Hereford in 1346 the visitation representatives were to be 'unsuspected, chosen without fraud, disregarding all attachments or passions, whatever their status within the parish'.[8] In 1370 when the rector of Roche in Cornwall was rumoured to be sexually incontinent and unfit to serve his parish, the purpose of an inquest through 'trustworthy men . . . in no way suspected by him' was to reassure the rector that he was not being victimized and that his case would be dealt with fairly.[9] Being at the sharp end of episcopal government often put the clergy at risk of unpopularity or even violence, and so one of the functions of 'trustworthiness' in inquests was to arm them with defensible information. When, for example, the dean of Holderness was told to go and reprimand some parishioners of Preston for not attending their parish church in 1350, he would have wanted to know that he was doing so with some local support. The testimony of trustworthy men, gathered in an earlier inquest, was meant to give him this confidence.[10]

Relationships with other powerful people, in the church and among the secular elite, could be challenging for bishops. When the needs of a local church and its parishioners clashed with the interests of a major figure, bishops were often caught in the middle. If the situation demanded a soft touch, this could be achieved with reference to the impartial judgement of trustworthy men. For instance, trustworthy men mediated between the interests of the earl of Warwick (as patron) and the parishioners of Church Lench in Worcestershire when a question was raised about the value of the vicarage there in 1262; the archbishop of York called upon trustworthy men in 1280 to inquire into the 'intrusion' of William de Vescey, the lord of Alnwick, into the church at North Ferriby on the Humber; the bishop of Salisbury used an inquest in 1321 to deal with the vociferous demands of his absentee archdeacon of Berkshire relating to a notably small patch of land in North Moreton (now in Oxfordshire); when the Duke of Northumberland put forward his own son for a canonry at Chester-le-Street in 1352, local concern as to his suitability was forestalled by an inquest of trustworthy men.[11]

These examples are a typical selection from the hundreds of letters documenting the relationships between bishops and the gentry and nobility of late medieval England, many more of which will provide the evidence base for the discussion in Chapters 11 to 13. Sometimes bishops fell over themselves in their efforts to please powerful lords, but when the interests of the church were at stake they usually drew a clear line to remind landed families of the limits of their influence. In all of this bishops were able to claim impartiality because they were calling on the testimony of trustworthy men. Telling a lord that the information relevant to his case had come from a trustworthy source boosted confidence in the authority of the bishop, and it told everyone concerned that the judgement was more likely to be durable. Just like bishops, secular lords wanted to be able to rely upon such judgements. They were, after all, quite literally building a great deal upon them. To contemplate endless legal challenge and the reopening of costly local disputes was not in the least appealing.

The thing of real importance was the stability and durability of the information upon which bishops would determine how to act. They were pragmatists. Though they believed that truth was the highest standard of knowledge, they also recognized that it was hard to attain. For the purposes of day-to-day government second best was usually more than enough.[12] While they might sometimes ask for 'the truth', bishops were usually more than content with the 'best information' if it enabled them to act decisively.[13] The qualities ascribed to trustworthy men (see Chapter 5) were therefore meant to advertise the reliability of the information they generated, and we should not imagine they denoted actual virtues or even necessarily beliefs about virtues. Being able to trust had more to do with the acceptance of symbolic roles within a system of knowledge exchange than with innate honesty and trustworthiness (again see Chapter 5).

Despite the practical necessity that drove bishops to take testimony from trustworthy men, their residual and persistent distrust towards the common people meant that knowledge obtained in this way was never wholly secure. Bishops worked within an epistemological framework that valorised truth whilst simultaneously hedging its discovery about with caveats. How it was made as secure as possible, and what limitations it suffered, are therefore of some importance in understanding the place of trustworthy men within the church. Inquests and visitations were grounded in a practical epistemology which was as important to the formation of the medieval Christian church as anything discussed by theologians. Though related to the theology of faith and knowledge discussed in Chapter 1, it was focussed not on knowing God and professing religious belief, but on dealing with the problems inherent in knowing people, places, and histories. Its principal feature was the coexistence of a belief in absolute truth with considerable circumspection about the possibility of attaining it. This meant that there was a spectrum of standards for knowledge, ranging from gossip and hearsay at one end to putative certainty at the other.

Trustworthiness and trustworthy testimony came into play in two circumstances. They occupied an intermediate point on the spectrum of knowledge: not necessarily facts, but stronger than rumour. In this respect the word of trustworthy men was akin to Hugh of St Victor's definition of *fides*, first mentioned in Chapter 1, as something 'established beyond opinion and short of knowledge', which only the negligent would ignore.[14] This was not the whole story though, since trustworthiness could also be invoked at will according to need, in order to boost the truth-value of a particular piece of information, wherever it had originated. The hierarchy of knowledge was not a rigid order. In this chapter I will pursue these two circumstances by first examining how trustworthiness supported *fama* as an intermediate form of knowledge, and then asking how it was related to concepts of truth and belief.

'Fama' and Proof

As in the identification of the qualities desired in trustworthy men, for which see Chapter 5, when it comes to bishops' attitudes to testimony, the best place to begin is with the procedural rules of proof utilized in litigation. This is where we see a practical legal epistemology being put to work most explicitly, and it was applied by bishops not only in their ex officio judicial role, but also in their administrative work, because so much that they dealt with had the potential to be contested in court. As Bishop Grandisson said during his appropriation of Islington church to his new collegiate foundation at Ottery St Mary, it was always desirable to have 'complete information and credible proofs' when carrying out acts of church governance, just in case one was challenged in court.[15]

A 'full proof' in canonical criminal procedure could be achieved either by extracting a confession from the accused or by securing the testimony of two eyewitnesses.[16] Eyewitness testimony, or *oculata fide*—trusting in what you see—naturally became the gold standard of evidence adduced in support of all sorts of claims made about churches, legal processes, local customs, and so on. We see this right through our period, from the appropriation of a church in the late twelfth century to the confiscation of the rents of a hospital in the late fourteenth. In the latter case the facts had been established by the 'view and testimony of trustworthy persons' (*visum et testimonium . . . fidedigno-rum*), a formulation that echoed the inspection of royal rights embodied in the 'view of frankpledge' and the primacy of vision in the hierarchy of the senses (discussed in Chapter 3). The men of a church inquest were sometimes told to examine a place in person, 'subjecting it to the eye' (*oculis subiciens*).[17] There was a recurrent leitmotif of self-evident truth in such references to sense experience that, it seems likely, gave some practical affirmation to the 'reliabilist' approach to perception pursued by philosophers like Walter Chatton and William Ockham in the early fourteenth century.[18] Here is John Pontoise, bishop of Winchester, in 1300, on his knowledge of the flooding at Bermondsey Priory: it was plain to see, 'as the whole world cries out, as faith in our sight declares, and as the appearance of things clearly demonstrates' (*clamat mundi, fides oculata declarat et inevitabilis rei evidencia manifestat*).[19]

While eyewitnesses could tip the balance of a criminal case, the sense of sight was not usually thought strong enough to determine the outcome of a complex dispute with many potential winners and losers. Pontoise's claims about Bermondsey were the exception rather than the rule. If overused such claims might not be believed. They could also, perhaps obviously, only relate to things that *were* visible to the eye, like the physical state of church buildings or the location of a field. The legal status of a church or a field was, of course, another question, something more unseen like God (as discussed in Chapter 1), though not eternal, meaning that there may have been eyewitnesses to the acts and events that created that legal status.[20] In matters affecting the conduct of church services and the validity of the sacraments—such as the character and ordination of the clergy—sense perception was certainly deemed an inferior order of knowledge to faith in invisible things. Sight was therefore often coupled to some other form of proof or claim to knowledge. Church officers might refer, in the same breath, to what they had seen for themselves and what had been discovered through inquests of trustworthy men.[21] Eyewitnessing suffered from a somewhat ambiguous status. It fell short of the ineffable faith in God towards which all Christians were meant to strive, but it nonetheless conformed to a view of the world that was very easy to communicate. It was valuable, but on its own it could not convince everyone. Nor was it always easy to obtain.

When a witness in a 1291 marriage suit claimed to have been an eyewitness to a man and a woman having sex (*hoc vidit oculata fide*), he was making a claim that was meant to boost the significance of his testimony. But on his own he could not meet the canonical standard of proof, which demanded *two* witnesses who had seen or heard the events at issue.[22] In cases hinging on sexual activity this was an understandably rare occurrence. For some in the church, facing the huge challenge of separating the clergy from their wives and concubines in the wake of twelfth-century reform, the standard of proof was unacceptably high. In the succeeding generations canon lawyers began to assert new doctrines of proof that made it easier for the authorities to convict offenders.

The first major area of innovation in judicial process concerned the means by which prosecutions were initiated. Roman-canonical procedure had, until the twelfth century, permitted cases to be begun only by accusation (publicly and by a named accuser) or denunciation (in private by a named individual, following an attempt to correct the offender in person). In both instances the prosecution was the responsibility of the individual accuser or denouncer. Neither of these was a particularly attractive course of action. The person reporting the crime would have to expose him- or herself to a high level of judicial or social risk. Accusers whose reports of crime were left unproven were liable to be punished for the offence as if they were guilty of it themselves, while prospective denouncers might reasonably baulk at the correction of a criminal in person before reporting them to a judge.[23] The solution offered by canonists—as discussed above in Chapter 4—was that the judge should himself act as the prosecutor in an inquisitorial procedure. This route forked in two directions. The first led to summary procedure on the strength of notoriety, permitting a judge to punish someone whose crimes were scandalous and undisputed; the second to allowing *fama* or public fame to initiate a case (removing the need for a private prosecutor) after which the judge would double as the prosecutor. This was seen as an abuse of due process by some legal minds, but in other respects procedure by inquisition followed the usual rules of evidence and proof and it became the dominant mode of fact-finding in many European judicial systems.[24]

Both of these new routes to legal proof also became important in the pastoral and administrative work of the church over the ensuing centuries. In the case of notoriety this was despite its almost universal unpopularity with canon law commentators and the courts. Procedure by notoriety contravened so many accumulated notions of due process, especially the principle that guilt should be proven (and not merely taken for granted) before the offender was punished. Moreover the potential for judges to be suspected of political motivation in the prosecution of crime was liable to bring the whole judicial system of the church into disrepute.[25] But in the administration of dioceses, the rhetoric—if not the practical implications—of this legal revolution proved extremely popular and, we must presume, useful. Very often, for instance, the qualities of a candidate for a benefice or some other position were said to be 'undoubted', the faults of an errant priest or monk 'notorious' or 'manifest'.[26]

Trustworthy men were not typically needed when claims were being made about supposedly self-evident truths. A letter from the bishop of Lincoln in 1381 is a case in point. The archdeacons of Stow and Lincoln were warned that they should stop ordering inquisitions into already-vacant churches because 'it is true and well known that the right of presentation to vacant churches lies with the bishop, and the whole populous is witness to this'.[27] Given the claim that the bishop's rights were 'true and well-known' trustworthy men would not quite have provided the requisite rhetorical ballast. The rather more universal witness of the whole populous struck just the right note of disbelief that any-one would think otherwise.

The certainty of such claims was however highly politicized and at odds with the pervasive culture of doubt and circumspection that surrounded knowledge, something which we saw in Chapter 1 in the discussion of belief in God. While the certainty involved in calling something notorious might have been desirable, it was not wholly credible that knowledge could be so secure. More representative is the ambiguity conveyed in an instruction to a group of trustworthy compurgators at Barnard Castle (County Durham) in 1436, to provide 'certain and probable knowledge' (*certam et probabilem . . . noticiam*) of an offender's life and character.[28] Probable knowledge was, as we have seen, a philosophical concept developed in theology and the science of optics, but increasingly applied to the apprehension of sin and intention in pastoral the-ology and confessors' manuals. This was not so much doubt as a certainty about what could not be known.[29] In administrative matters as in the courts, bishops preferred to avoid notoriety and deal in 'public fame' or *fama*. Con-siderably less was claimed for *fama* in terms of its epistemology, and despite some early qualms the canon lawyers considered it to be in greater conformity with due process than cases dealt with summarily *per notorium*. In addition to this academic advantage *fama* commanded greater consensus. It connoted an inherent caution and was embedded in local knowledge. It was also very closely associated with trustworthy men.

Fama was the report of the locality, not one person's word but something that had been repeated by many people. It was suspicion amongst the 'good and serious' men of the neighbourhood, and it was thought sufficient to force a suspect to answer before a judge.[30] Popes and bishops were captivated by the possibility it offered them of seeming to side with public opinion against crim-inal churchmen who might otherwise go unpunished.[31] In England the first institution to harness *fama* to large-scale investigation was not the church, however, but the crown. The author of the treatise known as 'Bracton' drew extensively upon Tancred's *Judicial Procedure* and the Decretals for his in-structions to the justices in eyre, noting that *fama* was suspicion that arose 'amongst good and serious persons' and was repeated by more than one per-son.[32] Over the course of the thirteenth century English bishops adopted this concept and applied in their courts, visitations, and inquests. Although *fama* was generally conceived as the anonymous clamour of the country, and we see this in many vague allusions to 'trustworthy reports', it was not incompatible with testimony from named trustworthy men.

Merely reporting that something was *fama* was not enough to establish that it was common knowledge. It had to be proven that it was what everyone, at least everyone who mattered, believed. If witnesses claimed to know something on the strength of *fama* its basis would be investigated. In a case heard by the Court of Canterbury around 1270 for example, witnesses were asked whether their evidence came from sight, hearing, knowledge, belief, or *fama*; in the last instance what did they mean by *fama*, how many people had repeated it, where and with whom had it originated?[33] *Fama* could be chiselled away by lawyers if it was found to arise from only one person, if there was contrary fame, or if it had not often been repeated. This was where the invocation of trustworthy men became useful. To say that something had been reported by such people was to claim it as genuine *fama* and not just malicious rumour. This close connection between *fama* and trustworthiness comes sharply into focus if we consider for a moment a formula that was *not* widely adopted by churchmen. A mid-fourteenth century formulary book from Ely contains a model for a letter that a bishop or archdeacon might wish to use when pronouncing excommunication:

> Because it has been suggested to us by that trustworthy man I. de T., that certain utterly unknown sons of iniquity stole two horses from him, they therefore incur the sentence of excommunication *ipso facto*.[34]

In contrast to virtually all the references to reports from trustworthy men, in the plural, that I will describe in the following chapters, this letter refers to the submission of a single trustworthy man. This would have been inadequate for most purposes, since the word of one man was not proof and it was not even *fama*. It is striking and informative that this supposed model letter was not followed in any of the thousands of cases I have identified in my research for this book.

When their information fell short of the standards demanded by *fama*, late medieval English bishops grasped at whatever 'insinuations . . . and widespread rumours' they could, knowing that they had more work to do to build up a case.[35] Rumours would not force a person to defend themselves in court. *Fama*, however, would, and the offenders reported at visitation were often said to have been 'de-*famed*' by the trustworthy men.[36] Sometimes, however, it is hard to tell whether bishops were carefully describing the precise status of a piece of information, or in fact bending the rules to suit their own purposes. One often suspects that talk of *fama* was special pleading on behalf of some politically useful rumour. For example, when he wished to assert his right to visit Tavistock Abbey in 1338, the bishop of Exeter explained that he had heard about the faults of the house 'from the testimony of trustworthy men and the truthful clamour of public fame'; in 1436 another bishop of Exeter used the same phrase about discord in Bosham (Sussex), jurisdiction over whose chapel he disputed with the king.[37] But they would, wouldn't they? Whatever the truth in these cases, the bishops involved had aligned themselves with a category of knowledge that was more secure than gossip or rumour but whose veracity, like that of God, was approachable only with faith.[38] *Fama* was useful because it made action possible.

Besides innovations surrounding fame and the *initiation* of lawsuits, canon lawyers of the twelfth and thirteenth centuries were energetic in their search for solutions to the problems created by the tough criteria of proof in the *ordo judiciarius*. The gold standard of two eyewitnesses was now joined by the possibility of several half or partial proofs adding up to full proof. William Durandus (1231–96) listed six half-proofs that could add up to full proof: an accusation made on oath, a single witness, documents, flight from justice, false statements made by the accused, or (in civil cases only) common fame.[39] Like *fama*, some of these became important in the administrative inquests of the late medieval church, though the arithmetic of fractional proofs was never precisely adhered to outside the courts. The most important additional partial proof in inquests was the oath. But the epistemological status of oaths was problematic, as we saw in the discussion of *fides* in law and agreements in Chapter 2. What effect did they have upon claims to knowledge? Did an oath make a statement more or less reliable? Although they were sworn before God there were theological grounds for treating them with caution, and they raised questions of authority and jurisdiction that demanded careful management.

During the later Middle Ages, but particularly in the thirteenth century, the English church found itself fighting over oaths on several fronts. The right to compel oaths from subjects was jealously guarded as a sign of lordship, and there were significant ramifications attendant upon the act itself. In 1251 Henry III reproved Walter de Cantilupe, the bishop of Worcester, for 'travelling through his diocese taking inquisitions on oath from free men as much as villeins without a royal mandate, thus causing scandal and division'.[40] The king objected to the bishop's extraction of oaths from free men, which was a royal prerogative.[41] He may not have minded too much about the villeins, for they had few or no rights in his courts in any case. But manorial lords did mind, believing that only they could compel their unfree tenants to take oaths.[42] Two years before in 1249 Robert Grosseteste's 'new and uncustomary' use of sworn testimony in his visitations was said to have taken people away from the fields, harming their livelihoods.[43] This may have been true, but it should be seen as part of a royal backlash against increased church assertiveness in using sworn inquests. For its part, the church frequently complained about secular courts breaching a canonical prohibition on oath-swearing during Lent, and about secular courts with their 'public oaths' being conducted in churchyards.[44] All parties to these jurisdictional disputes feared that oath-taking could be used as grounds upon which to renegotiate legal status. Service on a common-law jury seems to have created a presumption of personal freedom while service on a manorial jury implied unfree status.[45] Service on a church inquest may have been seen as a way to escape the legal disabilities of villeinage. For this reason bishops were sometimes extremely cagey about how and when they insisted upon oaths. For example, when Archbishop Corbridge of York wanted to administer a will in 1302 he gave an instruction to gather sworn trustworthy witnesses from among the tenants of Meaux Abbey only 'if it pleased' their lord, the abbot.[46]

For the most part though, by the early fourteenth century most of the heat seems to have evaporated from this issue, and bishops were confident in requiring sworn inquests without fear of royal interference. The church courts had come to rely upon oaths in civil and criminal procedure. An important moment came when Edward I attempted to limit the power of the English church courts in 1285 by insisting that only the royal courts could oblige someone to swear an oath. The convocation of bishops and clergy issued an angry response:

> Because it is forbidden by the authority of the king for laymen to appear before an ecclesiastical judge to be examined upon oath, unless in testamentary or matrimonial cases, the sinews of ecclesiastical discipline are dissolved. People defamed of crimes are accustomed to purge themselves by their own oath and those of others, or to submit themselves to special inquests which, customarily conducted by the oaths of trustworthy persons, are completely prevented by this prohibition. And the same obstacle appears when prelates wish to inquire into the bounds of a parish or some other thing which they cannot decide without the trustworthy testimony of laymen.[47]

In addition court officers such as advocates and even summoners were made accountable with oaths, and witnesses swore to tell the truth.[48] This reliance was more than matched in common-law inquests, where oaths had been routine since Anglo-Saxon times, both in judicial procedure, where they have been called a form of ordeal 'which relied upon God's eventual rather than his immediate judgement', and in feudal relations, where the oaths of fealty and homage were essential public rituals.[49] In all these contexts oaths were public affirmations of an obligation: to tell the truth, to be loyal, to perform a particular act. Such a public declaration gave the receiver of the oath practical leverage over the swearer of the oath. Not only was God the eventual judge of oaths, but having sworn to do something, the swearer could be called upon to honour that promise.

The broad acceptance of oaths in church inquests during the fourteenth century was made possible by the steps that individual bishops had made, after Grosseteste, to *limit* their use in visitations.[50] Note that convocation's answer to Edward I in 1285 had specified 'special inquests' and omitted visitations. In this subcategory of inquest the initial reports of the trustworthy men were said to be *fama*, that is reports of what was widely believed in the neighbourhood, and not statements of fact to which they should swear, and for which they could be held responsible. Accountability and legal facts were introduced at a subsequent stage, once *fama* had been gathered in. People reported for offences and faults were called to answer the *fama* and separately to admit or deny the substantive charge. In 1291, for example, a couple accused of fornication in Brenzett, Kent, acknowledged that there was *fama* against them as well as admitting to the deed itself.[51] Some might attempt to deny the existence of *fama*, and then, of course, they would deny the deed as well. This could lead to purgation or a 'special inquisition' upon oath.[52] The lack of oaths in the preceding establishment of *fama* meant that no final judgements could, in theory, be made on the strength of the local reports alone.[53] Like secular juries of presentment, trustworthy men therefore exercised a 'licensed imprecision' in giving their testimony.[54] The findings of the different phases of visitation became known as *detecta* (things reported) and *comperta* (things confirmed), and the records regularly make this distinction between *fama* and fact, suspicion and guilt.[55] The distinction protected the trustworthy men from the dangers that awaited the ill-prepared or unlucky accuser whose allegations were not upheld. It also limited the occasions on which laymen might be required to swear to an authority other than their own lord, thus minimizing a potential arena of contestation between the church and lay lordship. It also dissociated trustworthiness from oaths, and facilitated a degree of invisibility for the trustworthy men who, to a certain extent and despite sometimes being named, became symbolic figures.

The relative peace of the fourteenth century was disturbed by the challenge to ecclesiastical jurisdiction, and in particular oaths, launched by John Wyclif and those who were influenced by him from the 1380s onwards, sometimes called lollards. Lollards and Wycliffites began from the same starting point as many of their contemporaries, regarding excessive or unnecessary swearing as sinful, and repeating the gospel injunction to be true to one's word. They did not, on the whole, reject oaths out of hand. Oaths made to God were permissible in certain circumstances, but oaths made upon 'creatures'—that is, objects, such as books—were unacceptable. Rather more significant than what lollards actually wrote or said was what people thought they stood for. There was an increasingly widespread feeling in the fifteenth century that disapproval of oaths was a heretical position. This was foreshadowed in the epilogue to 'The Man of Law's Tale' in the *Canterbury Tales*. The parson in Chaucer's pilgrimage party objects to innkeeper Harry Bailey swearing by God's bones. Bailey's riposte—'I smelle a Lollere in the wynd'—has the feel of a joke, but it does seem to have drawn upon a sense that oaths were once more a decidedly political issue.[56] In 1431 the bishop of Bath and Wells thought it necessary to explain that the constitutions of the church against false swearing were intended to prohibit perjury, not oaths tout court: 'We understand that an oath is not evil in itself, when it confirms the truth'.[57] In the right circumstances an oath could confirm the truth, but it could not make the truth.

Besides oaths, one of the most important partial proofs in the new canon law of the thirteenth century was documentary evidence.[58] A single witness together with a supporting charter was meant to be sufficient proof that an act had taken place. Obviously this was more common in some situations than others. Wills were frequently considered by the church courts, but Richard Helmholz has shown that in England, at least, other documents were brought as evidence only on rare occasions, much more seldom than in the common-law courts. In his commentary on the provincial constitutions of the English church the fifteenth-century canonist William Lyndwood even omitted any mention of the decretal 'On trust in documents' (*De fide instrumentorum*).[59]

In their pastoral and administrative work, however, English bishops were wedded to the consideration of written evidence but only as one potential proof amongst many. Writing was coming to be trusted more and more on its own account, but circumstances frequently arose when trust in people was invoked alongside documentary evidence. For example when Bishop Grandisson received a written complaint about the malfeasance of his sequestrator in 1328 he wrote to the accused officer saying that 'we do not wish to have faith in the aforesaid [report] in your absence and without consulting you, in whose faithfulness and discreet industry we have immeasurable confidence'.[60] On another occasion Grandisson referred to complaints that had come to him 'by the oral and written reports of many trustworthy persons and also by widely circulating public fame'.[61] His fifteenth-century successor Edmund Lacy once took up a case about the depreciation of the vicarage of Spreyton about which he had received 'lawful documents' *and* heard reports from trustworthy persons.[62]

Truth and Trust

Although its usual location within the practical epistemology of the church was in close proximity to *fama*, trustworthiness could be invoked at various points along the spectrum of knowledge, providing credibility and rhetorical momentum to information founded on hearsay, sworn statements, inquest verdicts, and documents. It made information seem true, and truth was the stated object of all church inquiries. Truth and trust were closely tied to one another, and they could indeed be seen as synonyms for God and faith: truth and God are the objects of human enquiry and perception, trust and faith the means by which the enquiry is carried out. Other props like perception, reason, and legal proofs played their part, but *fides* of one kind or another was necessary at some point. In this, as Alain Boreau has pointed out, Christian truth was paradoxical. It was at once objective—certain and enduring like God himself—but at the same time it was the product of belief: fragile and provisional.[63] There was always doubt. Yet, as with the act of faith in God, finding truth did not have to mean extinguishing all doubt. Doubt was after all at the heart of Christianity and its striving for knowledge.[64] Consequently the objective existence of truth was assumed and liberally asserted, while at the same time not being confined to the distant prospect of unassailable certainty. It is notable that late medieval categories of knowledge did not supersede one another in a zero-sum game, as illustrated by a letter sent to Pope Innocent IV in 1245 accompanying a dossier of evidence for miracles attributed to Edmund of Abingdon. The dossier was said to contain 'fama, truth, belief, opinion, and knowledge' gleaned from 'sight, hearing, hearsay, proofs, and experience'.[65] Truth did not make fama and opinion unnecessary, while hearsay was worth reporting alongside the evidence of documents and the senses. Truth, like God, was something in which one had to have faith, confident of its existence in some rather unlikely places.

Wherever it was found, and by whatever means, truth was considered a powerful influence upon people as well as upon the course of judicial proceedings or the results of inquests.[66] We can see this in the canonical presumption against those men and women who fled after being accused.[67] In 1378, for example, Elias of Newton was cited at the instance of Katerina Drew to appear before the bishop of Ely's consistory court on account of the betrothal that Katerina alleged they had made to each other in the presence of trustworthy persons. It was, she said, now public knowledge in the village and neighbouring places, but Elias had fled 'fearing the truth'. A year later the judge found that Katerina had been betrothed to Elias and they were told to marry.[68] Trustworthy men were expected to tell the truth, from which it follows that those who fled before it were not to be believed. In this case the objective truth of Katerina's claim was confirmed by both Elias's flight and the testimony of trustworthy men.

The connection between trustworthy testimony and truth was often spelt out in the instructions for visitation that bishops sent to their officers on the ground. In 1283 Archbishop Pecham wanted trustworthy men through whom he could 'best inquire into the truth'; in 1324 Bishop Orleton of Hereford wanted trustworthy men who would tell the truth 'in the proper way . . . about those things asked of them that demand to be caught in the net of correction'; also in 1324 Archbishop Melton of York asked for parishioners who would say 'what they know to be true concerning those things required of them'.[69] Upon receiving information they regarded as meeting these requirements bishops might claim that their evidence was based upon the 'testimony of trustworthy jurors [which] we fully accept to be true'.[70] Truth, in these formulations, was something to be accepted rather than known beyond doubt. The effect of trustworthy testimony was to pull information into the orbit of truth in a way that was hard to resist, especially when it corroborated other proofs such as flight or documents. In this sense the medieval regime of truth conforms somewhat to Thomas Kuhn's paradigmatic model of 'normal science': that we are more likely to accept statements that corroborate existing assumptions than those that contradict them.[71] In medieval Christianity as in modern science this is perfectly compatible with a belief in objective (divine or scientific) truth. So while it is true to say, following Michael Polanyi, that the 'attribution of truth ... is a fiduciary act', the recipient of information is rarely solely reliant upon trust.[72] They are able to assess the trustworthiness of information by assessing its conformity to existing knowledge, accepted beliefs, and evidence from other sources.[73]

Caution and Belief

The argument of this chapter has been that late medieval practical knowledge was founded upon a malleable hierarchy of assumptions and proofs. There was nothing rigid about the degrees of confidence that judges and bishops placed in witnesses, rumours, documents, oaths, and whatever other forms of evidence they could find. The order of knowledge was traversed and sometimes circumvented by the highly mobile concepts of truth and trustworthiness. Truth could be found in many places, and trustworthiness could be invoked to boost the credibility of all sorts of claims. But despite all this there was nonetheless a widespread assumption that some forms of knowledge were more provisional than others.

In Chapter 1 I sketched the outlines of high and late medieval concepts of faith and belief, following the use of words derived from the noun *fides* and the verb *credere*. There we found that when it came to knowing God, belief, in the sense of a willing assent, was a necessary and prior condition of understanding. It was the starting point of a Christian's relationship with God. Equally, in Chapters 2 and 3, I showed how the protestations of faith that were so essential to promise making and personal relationships were intended as statements of an absolute commitment, however insincere they might turn out to be in reality. However, when trustworthy men gave testimony before inquests and visitations, their assertions of belief were not even intended as absolute commitments, but as a limit placed upon their assurances. While this circumspection owed something to the fragility of human knowledge admitted in the Christian's placement of faith in God, it was defined by uncertainty rather than certainty. In other words, whereas the 'I believe' of the creed denoted someone's willingness to join a community of knowledge, the 'I believe' of the law drew a line beyond which the witness was not prepared to step. It was not 'thinking with assent' nor 'faith seeking understanding', but an end-point highlighting imperfect knowledge and a cautious desire to avoid legal reckoning.[74] The only common ground was the witnesses' acceptance of the limits of their understanding, and the implied submission to church authority, which stood a better chance of knowing God or the truth.

Assertions of belief were common in witness statements in the church courts, and in the reports of trustworthy men to visitations. The deposition book of the bishop of London's consistory court between 1467 and 1476 is, for example, littered with the phrase 'as he or she believes' (*ut credit*).[75] This short but ubiquitous phrase could resonate with some of the assuredness and confidence of the creed, but it also contained the grounds for its own cautious qualification. The deponents may well have felt their evidence to be true so far as they were concerned. They had confidence in their own judgement and perception.[76] But this was also a way of admitting the possibility of error and protecting oneself against the consequences of being proved wrong: the 'licensed imprecision' of jury testimony once more.[77] It was therefore possible for belief to be inferior to knowledge, and in contrast to theological belief, to lack certainty. The root of the difference lay in the fact that God was deemed certain while the world was thought changeable, something that will come into play in Chapter 12.

The trustworthy men reporting to several late medieval visitations adopted this strategy with regards to everything from commonplace sexual offences to politically tricky issues of authority. In Hereford diocese in 1397 the parish representatives of Norton had said that Sybil Gyfker fornicated with a clergyman called John Matthew or John Smith, 'or so they believed'. They did not know his name for certain, though they were prepared to say that he did live in Norton. Meanwhile the parishioners of Weobley said that Katherine Ondys was pregnant and it was not known (*nescitur*) by whom, but it was believed (*creditur*) to be the rector of Sarnesfield; the parishioners of Culmington in Shropshire reported two couples—Jankyn Tasger and Katherine 'whom he keeps as his wife', and Matthew Tailor and Philippa Bakon—for fornication because they *believed* both pairs were unmarried. They also reported Isabelle of Wales for fornicating with a Welshman whose name was not known, though they *believed* him to be Jankyn Tailor.[78] In Lichfield sometime in the 1460s the lay representatives of Stow Street and Tamworth Street said that they did not 'know' who had made Margaret Seyne pregnant, but they 'believed' that it had been William Harper; at Saddler Street they reported that the priest William Heyth had suspiciously gone to the house of Emmota Garnet with a woman called Helena Puella ('the girl'?). There, so they believed, he 'knew' her (*cognovit eam*). They were heard carousing and drinking later than was decent (*extra tempus honestum*).[79] In this carefully constructed report the closing of the brothel door set a seal upon the boundary between knowing and believing, but the level of detail suggests they were in no doubt themselves as to what had occurred. The submission to authority was there, as with theological belief, but a juror's belief about the facts was formed *before* it was scrutinized by a judge, and was not an obedient response to an authoritative statement of the faith.

Sometimes more subtle judgements were wrapped in the guarded language of belief, such as a report of watching for ghosts in a Gloucestershire graveyard in 1397, which will be discussed further in Chapter 13. The trustworthy men said that 'they believed' this to be a great scandal to the Christian faith, words that were both an assertion of their firm views on Christian propriety, and an acknowledgement that the bishop was the only person with the authority to decide whether this was really orthodox or not. They were not qualified to judge. Another matter of authority troubled the parish representatives of Waterdine, Shropshire, in the same year. They claimed that they were customarily served by a secular priest despite their church being appropriated to Wenlock Priory. But the prior had foisted a parish chaplain upon them, taking away their vicar and his portion 'without sufficient authority, as they believe'. They wanted the visiting bishop to demand that the prior show his authority. This was caution in the face of possible future documentary proof. The parishioners knew that documents were what secured rights in such matters: there should have been an episcopal 'ordination' for the vicarage at the time when the parish was first appropriated to Wenlock. Without a copy of the document, and recognizing that this was an area where custom and memory alone would not do, all they could do was assert their cautious belief.[80] In the North Riding of Yorkshire in 1428 the parish representatives of Farnham took a slightly different approach, but it amounted to the same thing. They said that William Smyth and Alice Verte had married and then separated because of his impotence, but they 'doubted' whether the separation was canonically sanctioned.[81] Canonical sanction was something that only a bishop or the pope could grant, and so the parishioners were right to express caution.

The men who represented parishes at visitation were aware of the huge power imbalances between them and their visitors. In this context belief was the perfect vehicle for expressing opinions and doubtful information. Belief brought with it huge implications of trust in authority and strength of judgement derived from faith in God. These men knew how to couch complaints so as to demand a bishop's attention. But assertions of belief also played on the weaknesses of human perception which, when coupled with the bishop's superior legal standing and the parishioners' subaltern status, became a way for a line to be drawn between what the locals were qualified to say and the establishment of fact and law by proper authorities.

In treading this line the representatives of both the parish and the institutional church were aware of an unwritten rule to which most visitation proceedings conformed. In spite of the official line that lay reports constituted mere *fama* or belief, upon which a judge would have to adjudicate, it was widely accepted that the articulation of these provisional forms of knowledge set in train a process whereby report became fact. In cases of 'continuous facts' amenable to collective remembrance, such as boundaries or ownership, *fama* had long been accorded great weight. We will see this at work in the many inquests into patronage and tithes discussed in Chapters 11 and 12. Gradually, between 1100 and 1250, *fama* also became admissible as a proof of more transient facts such as whether a marriage had been made.[82] This was in spite of the insistence of canon lawyers that *fama* should be distinguished from fact.[83] In practice the boundary was impossible to maintain. In 1328 the regent queen Isabella called for some trustworthy men to inform the exchequer of the extent of the devastation suffered by Egglestone Abbey at the hands of the Scots. The abbey was trying to wriggle out of paying a tenth of its annual income to meet the demands of a tax authorised by Parliament. The official of Richmond reported that according to trustworthy men the abbey had indeed suffered dreadfully in frequent Scottish raids to the extent that the abbot and monks could barely support themselves, and that he had, in fact, been unable to find anything there that the king could tax even if he wanted to. Once the results of this inquest by trustworthy men had been reported in writing they were a matter of record, and when this record was referred to one short year later, what had been local opinion was found elevated to a higher plane of knowledge. In 1329 Archbishop Melton called the abbey's poverty 'manifest and notorious', which was shorthand for *there is no need to run through the evidence since everyone knows it is true*.[84] As we have seen, notoriety that was merely asserted was widely mistrusted, but notoriety forged from the opinion of trustworthy men could be accepted as unchallengeable common knowledge.

The tendency for opinion to be converted into fact, and for judges to play only a minimal role, has also been noted by historians of the English common-law juries of presentment and trial. The common-law verdict (*veredictum*: a statement of the truth) was the untested report of a jury. It might be their collective answer to the articles in eyre or a determination of the facts at issue in a single case.[85] Despite the insistence of 'Glanvill' (late twelfth century) and 'Bracton' (ca. 1230) that jurors should merely be witnesses and not judges, indictment and judgement were blurred from the first. Jury presentments have been described as 'opinions approximating to verdicts on guilt or innocence' and jurors themselves have been said to have possessed 'a considerable say in who was prosecuted . . . and what happened to them'.[86] The exigencies of church governance meant that local knowledge was not only valuable; bishops would have been unwise to reject it. For the most part bishops accepted the reports of trustworthy men, and the sorts of withdrawals of trustworthy status mentioned in Chapter 5 were in fact incredibly rare. In this way, for all that they constituted 'mere' *fama* or belief, trustworthy testimony arrived with the weight of local knowledge behind it, propelling it strenuously down the path towards accepted facts, alleged certainty, and acknowledged truth.

{⚊⚊}

In the landscape of late medieval practical epistemology, positions were not fixed. Truth, like God, could be found anywhere, and human perception of it was always imperfect. This meant that the information required for church administration and pastoral care could not be evaluated in a mechanistic or precise way. Hierarchies of knowledge constituted a framework for expressing the degree of confidence that information should command. They were not a means for quantifying truth. Within this landscape trustworthiness was an immeasurably useful, and mobile, feature. We can catch glimpses of it in the company of oaths, documents, rumour, and *fama*. Everywhere it was meant to encourage readers and listeners, whoever they were, to give credence to the message; in other words, to believe.

We must remember, however, that it was the institution that ultimately controlled the written records from which we have drawn the foregoing examples and ideas. Even when the words are putatively those of the laity, the decision to record them, and the form and language in which this happened, were at the discretion of the bishop's household clerks. In this sense at least the institutional church controlled the truth-value, or knowledge status, of any given statement. But this was not the whole story. Set against a gloomy picture of the crushing power of the medieval church, it appears that the locals themselves possessed enormous adjudicatory power. While the institution might control the medium of recording, it did not have the resources to make frequent or substantial alterations to the statements of belief and *fama* that it received from trustworthy men; nor could it control how messages were received and understood. The location of power in relation to knowledge was not simple.

It was, nonetheless, foundational in shaping the institutions of diocesan government. Because bishops needed to use local testimony to acquire the knowledge that would permit them to resolve disputes and project their power, the management of that testimony was all important. They could not do without it, but they had some trouble accepting it. Forging a symbolic role, and working with local elites were two ways in which the uncertainties of lay testimony were mitigated, but in canon law commentaries on evidence and proof, and in the practice of inquests and visitations, patterns of institutional thought evolved that would further define the church's engagement with the laity. These were pragmatic attitudes based on harnessing lay testimony while keeping the actual laity at arm's length. The laity themselves participated in this paradoxical relationship, asserting their certainty with caution. As the following chapters will show, the practice of gathering lay testimony was so unavoidable and so arduous that it shaped the institutions of episcopal governance, and so potent that it strengthened the hand of the bishop enormously, making the late medieval church.

CHAPTER ELEVEN

Other People's Money

IN THE REFORMING SYNODS of the early thirteenth century and in the growing documentation of episcopal governance as the century wore on, one of the earliest things that we find bishops asking of 'trustworthy men' was to assist in safeguarding other people's money. The organs of the institutional church, principally the church courts and the personal authority of bishops, were becoming more and more central to all manner of economic dealings, some well-known to historians, others less so. Churches relied upon the collection of tithes, rents, and voluntary offerings; as agricultural producers they sold grain and livestock in regional and national markets; bishops and religious houses cooperated in the collection of royal taxes on the clergy; the church courts oversaw the administration of wills and adjudicated failed credit agreements. All these movements of money and wealth were transactions of one kind or another, and as such were in some way reliant on trust. Trust underpinned the acceptance of goods and payments as the satisfactory completion of a contract or understanding; trust in some future benefit—be it patronage or salvation— was itself a commodity traded in exchange for gifts and offerings; furthermore, higher officers had to trust that their subordinates were not deceiving them.

The role of trust and trustworthiness in the movement of money was an important element in the making of the late medieval church, and yet it is underappreciated how significant bishops were as economic 'institutions' in their own right.[1] While historians have devoted considerable attention to bishops' roles in the economies of their regions, polities, and the wider world as landowners, lords, tax collectors, consumers, and producers, far less historical attention has been given to their mediation of economic relationships in which they were not directly implicated. The extent to which a bishop's involvement with other people's money was a contributing factor in the formation and continuance of his status has not even been a question that historians have asked; yet it should be. Episcopal power derived not solely from landed wealth, social and legal status, or the ideology of apostolic succession, but also from the nature and quality of a bishop's interactions with a whole host of other individuals and groups.[2]

What did their entanglements in third-party economic transactions contribute to bishops' status and power, and how were trustworthy men implicated in them? This is the question that the present chapter will seek to answer. Bishops were major institutional players in the movement of money and wealth, partly by design and partly as a side effect of other aims, such as ensuring the provision of pastoral care. They were the agents of kings, the brokers of trade deals, the supervisors of charitable giving, and the providers of remedies for unfulfilled last wills and testaments. They did not, however, act alone. Much, although not all, of the work arising from these responsibilities could not have been completed without the participation of those laypersons identified as trustworthy. From the early thirteenth century trustworthy men were acting as passive witnesses and guarantors of land transactions and other financial agreements, before they became the regular suppliers of information in inquests and visitations that would define their role from the later 1200s onwards. In both scenarios trustworthiness was the language in which bishops communicated the reliability and constancy of these local elites. In this chapter I will examine the financial responsibilities undertaken by trustworthy men in conjunction with bishops, in order to assess the nature and purpose of the trust relationships involved, the effect that each activity had on episcopal governance, and the contribution made by both parties.[3] However, in order to define the scope of these activities more precisely it is helpful for us to begin with two situations in which trust was paramount, but which did not see the emergence of that alliance between bishops and lay trustworthy men. These are the collection of tithes and the collection of clerical subsidies. A brief glance at them will help clarify the role of the trustworthy men.

Tithes and Trust

Lay parishioners were, for the most part, unnecessary to the collection of the tithes that they paid to the rector of their parish church (one tenth of their produce).[4] Tithes were gathered in one of three ways: by a parish priest, by an institution that owned the revenues due to the priest, or by lessees who had bought the right to 'farm' the tithes of a parish. In the first case, of a parish priest collecting directly, there was a simple relationship between producer and recipient and therefore no need for any independent verification or supervision of the render. When the recipient was an institutional tithe owner or a tithe farmer, collection did need supervising but this could not be done by the parishioners because they had an incentive to defraud the collector and therefore could not be trusted. Institutional tithe owners such as bishops and religious houses employed salaried officers to oversee collection; these were usually mounted *equitatores*, sergeants, or proctors, often local gentry such as the knight Thomas of Wensley who worked for the canons of Lichfield in their Derbyshire parishes of Hope, Tideswell, and Bakewell in 1400.[5] When tithes were sold to 'farmers' or lessees collection would again be made either directly or by paid employees, obviating the need for local arbiters of trust. However, in these circumstances bishops and religious houses needed to trust that sufficient produce was being put aside for the vicars of churches. To this end they typically relied upon the bonds of *fidelitas* linking them to the lessees, often local men of substance whose desire to be in good standing with powerful churchmen was an imperfect but partial guard against fraud.[6] The only circumstance in which there may have been a need for an honest render to be guaranteed by local trustworthy men was when a collective of parishioners had taken on a lease from the tithe owner.[7] Although we have no direct evidence of this, they must have wanted some supervision of those of their neighbours who were not included in the consortium: how would they have done this? One can envisage a role for an independent group of parishioners, but this would not have been something recorded in episcopal or institutional records, so there is no documentary trace of any such putative trustworthy men.

Their absence is explained by the fact that this conjectural trust relationship was not one that affected the power of the record makers: the bishops. This chapter, by contrast, deals with those financial trust relationships that *were* recorded by bishops, because it was these that fed the capacity of bishops to play the role of regional arbiters of trust in the movement of money and wealth. Without this capacity bishops would not have been able to exercise much secular power at all, at least not beyond their own estates, and would have had to confine themselves to a purely exemplary spiritual role.

Monks, Trustworthiness, and Clerical Taxation

One of the most common financial situations where the language of trustworthiness was regularly deployed was nonetheless one that completely excluded lay parishioners. This was the collection of clerical subsidies. By thinking about this usage we can further delineate the circumstances in which bishops might deem laymen to be appropriate partners.

When a clerical subsidy was agreed by parliament or, after 1340, by convocation, bishops were sent mandates for collection. The exchequer needed reassurance that each diocese would make an honest return and, since they depended so much on royal patronage, it was natural that bishops were given the job. These mandates usually asked for collection by 'trustworthy men of the diocese' whom the bishop was to identify before writing back to the exchequer for approval.[8] As well as specifying trustworthy men, these mandates dripped with the lexicon of faith: they asked for 'trustworthy men in whom you have confidence', or 'wise, faithful and God-fearing suitable men' for example.[9]

The English crown may well have adopted this language from ecclesiastical formulas for tax collection, in papal and crusading levies for example, where trustworthy clerics and religious 'in whose conscientious piety and brilliant wisdom we have complete trust in God' were commonly called for.[10]

In response to royal demands bishops almost always appointed the heads of religious houses as collectors for their dioceses.[11] Abbots and priors were not necessarily seen as more honest and reliable than the bishop's own household, or his archdeacons. Rather, it is most likely that bishops passed on the responsibility for taxation because they wanted to avoid having the crown sanction them by seizing episcopal revenues. The wealthier religious houses also had extensive lands that could be seized as collateral if necessary, and this was clearly where considerations of trustworthiness lay: recalling the status of lay *fidedigni* as members of a peasant elite, the question was not 'who is honest' but 'who has something to lose'. Royal mandates stipulated that the collectors should be clerics from within the dioceses, and this was often what happened.[12] But it was also common for bishops to recruit from outside the diocese. This occurred with particular frequency in Hereford. In 1422 the crown objected to the appointment of Llanthony Priory since it was in Wales, and Bishop Spofford had to employ St Guthlac's in Hereford instead. Spofford was struggling to find houses with the resources to manage the collection from within his own diocese, and over the following fourteen years he looked again to Llanthony, besides Monmouth, Gloucester, Worcester, and Shrewsbury, each time pointing out that these houses had interests in many churches within his own diocese.[13] Clearly he was looking for collectors whom he could sanction if he had to. Such reasoning is made plain in a document of 1492 in which each collector's name is followed by the collateral that ensured their trustworthiness: thus, Avenbury church for the abbot and convent of Dore, Wenlock church for the prior and convent of Wenlock, and so on.[14]

The heads of religious houses were deemed suitable for this role because they could inspire confidence in kings and overawe the diocesan clergy.[15] No parishioners, however trustworthy they might prove in other circumstances, could have fulfilled these criteria.

Now that we have traced the outline of the space where they were not, and could not, be useful, we can see more clearly where lay trustworthy men were called for. First it had to be a transaction where a bishop's authority was relevant, necessitating a record that might describe the lay participants; second, the parochial peasant elite had to be capable of playing some supervisory or reassuring role. The particular arenas in which bishops found that their status as arbiters of financial trust depended upon the cooperation of trustworthy men were in the management of institutional alms collectors, the enforcement of last wills and testaments, the supervision of some institutional revenues, and the scrutiny of financial support for sick and disabled clergy.

Keepers of the Keys

In Chapter 4 we saw how the figure of the trustworthy man emerged in papal and episcopal documents amidst the febrile legal, theological, and institutional creativity of the late twelfth and early thirteenth centuries. Although the phrase was first attached to witnesses in lawsuits, especially in marriage cases, this was not a usage that took root in the formulas of English episcopal communication. Instead the concept of the trustworthy man was first put to use in describing the parishioners who might help bishops to regulate the activities of itinerant alms collectors.

Wandering alms collectors, sometimes called 'questors', 'questmongers', or *nuncii*, were agents who raised funds for enterprises like crusades and the construction of hospitals or shrines. Because they travelled and asked for money they were sometimes associated with the mendicant orders of friars (although alms collectors were mostly not members of a religious or clerical order), with the indulgence sellers sometimes called palmers or pardoners, and with vagrant beggars. A whiff of fraud and suspicion hung around the reputations of all these itinerant groups at one time or another, and so it is no surprise to find alms collectors similarly mistrusted.[16] In 1328 Bishop Grandisson of Exeter warned his flock that no trust (*fidem*) should be placed in false alms collectors, only in those whose letters of authorization had been inspected by him and which inspired 'complete trust' (*plenam fidem*). Fraudulent documentation haunted the episcopal imagination, and some contemporary forgeries are known to have existed.[17] That the word, or even the oath, of an alms collector was not to be trusted became axiomatic, as shown by its appearance as a fifteenth-century London street insult: 'thou false forsworon questmonger'.[18]

Concern about alms collecting had, however, begun much earlier. A constitution of Archbishop Stephen Langton for the diocese of Canterbury, drawn up between 1213 and 1214, was the first text to mention trustworthiness in connection with alms. Langton stipulated that alms collectors should not preach without a licence, and that any money they collected be put in the hands of the parish priest. The priest was to keep it safe under the watch of two 'trustworthy persons' until it could be collected by the bishop's own representative.[19] Langton's constitution was picked up and repeated by Richard Poore in his constitutions first for Salisbury diocese between 1217 and 1219 and then Durham between 1228 and 1236. Poore added only two details: the collectors should be able to explain clearly the cause for which they were raising money, and the *fidedigni* were explicitly recommended to be *viri*.[20]

The registers of English bishops in the thirteenth and fourteenth centuries provide evidence that these measures were thought practical enough to be implemented. In 1233 money for the repair of the Ouse bridge in York was to be guarded by two 'of the more faithful' parishioners before being handed over to the bridge wardens; in 1320 the collectors for the hospital of the Holy Spirit in Rome were to place their funds under the supervision of 'approved men'; in 1330 funds for a new chapel dedicated to St Thomas at Weare in Somerset were to be given to the vicar and 'two or more trustworthy parishioners', who were to count the money and see that it was used for its intended purpose; in 1331 'law-worthy men' were stipulated in Carlisle, and in 1335 'upright laymen' (*vite probate laycum*) were mandated in Worcestershire; in 1383 the preachers fund-raising for Bishop Despenser's ill-fated crusade to Flanders were told to gather 'persones dez pluis sufficiauntz' to assist them.[21] When bishops heard about actual fraud taking place they furthermore recorded the source of the information as 'reports from trustworthy men'.[22] Equally, inquiries into mis-appropriated funds also called on the services of these trustworthy men.[23] Whatever the language it is clear that bishops were keen to ensure money donated to pious causes reached its destination, and alms collectors were not trusted to do this alone.

For whom was this rhetoric of trust and probity intended? There were four audiences that bishops may have wanted to reach. First, the patrons of the hospitals, churches, and other projects funded by donations, who must have appreciated reassuring noises made about the security of their money (we saw how important patrons could be in the case-study of North Newton chapel in Chapter 8); second, the donors who would surely have wanted to know that their money was not being siphoned off by unscrupulous collectors; third, the parish clergy, who might have valued a third-party guarantee that took some of the responsibility and potential blame for lost revenue off their shoulders; fourth, and perhaps counterintuitively, the involvement of trustworthy men approved by the bishop might have insulated the collectors themselves from suspicion. However, in addition to the reassurance of these various audiences, one of the overriding purposes of a bishop's effort was the establishment his own authority in such matters. He was the person who could put trustworthi-ness to work.

But this is not the whole story. Safeguarding money in this way de-pended not just on a bishop's attribution of trustworthiness, but also on a well-established set of material security measures—namely chests, locks, and keys—and the people responsible for them. In religious houses it was com-mon practice for treasure (including documents, money, and valuables) to be kept in a triple-locked chest whose keys were held by three separate people. This was to insure against theft and corruption.[24] Parishes had similar chests and followed comparable practices. For example in 1335 the bishop of Worces-ter referred to new 'offertory chests' being placed in parish churches to hold donations for a crusade; two keys were held by clerics and a third by a lay parishioner.[25] When a collection had been completed a bishop might order the opening of all the chests and trunks in the parish churches, under the supervision of an archdeacon.[26] Another method was to have the 'keepers of the keys'—the clergy and the trustworthy laity—bring their chests to a cathedral church, as happened at Carlisle in 1310, where they would be opened in front of the bishop.[27] The centrality of chests, locks, and keys to proceedings speaks of the worry and necessity that governed a bishop's collaboration with trustworthy men. He could not do without them, but their involvement was not itself beyond reproach.

Enforcing Last Wills and Testaments

Following hard on the heels of 'trustworthy' supervision of alms collection, English bishops began to use the same rhetoric with regards to last wills and testaments from the mid-thirteenth century onwards. Responsibility for different aspects of inheritance was split between the church, royal, and manorial courts. However, the English church courts' control of probate (authenticating a will) gave them de facto control over most of the process of making, executing, and contesting wills. This was peculiar to England; elsewhere inheritance was mostly a secular matter.[28] The requirement for wills to be proved drew people into the church courts, willingly or not, but their capacity to enforce judgements in disputed cases may have been genuinely popular. Enforcement was achieved through a combination of the bishop's jurisdictional and even charismatic reach across his diocese (to say nothing of the wider scope of the Prerogative Court of Canterbury and the Exchequer Court of York, which dealt with the wills of people with property in more than one diocese), and the scrutiny that could be provided by panels of leading parishioners designated trustworthy men.

Bishops advertised the alliance between their courts and local testimony with much talk of faithfulness and trustworthy men. This may have been a conscious or unconscious reflection of the trust that individual testators expressed with regards to their family or executors. Although legally superfluous, such expressions speak of the uncertainty generated by the expectation of death.[29] In 1472, for example, Ralph Snaith, a merchant from Pontefract in Yorkshire, made his wife his executor putting his 'full trust' in her and hoping that her 'faithful life' would ensure her compliance with his bidding.[30] Bishops, for their part, instructed that inventories were to be made by 'faithful and industrious men'; estates were to be administered by 'trusted friends' or 'upright and faithful men'; executors were to swear on the gospels to make 'full and faithful' inventories; sureties or *fideiussores* who could 'pledge their faith' regarding the completion of the task were to stand behind the executors; property might be placed in legal trusts or *fidecommisi*.[31]

Besides the self-interest inherent in promoting their own courts, bishops also knew that churches of all kinds were major beneficiaries of many wills. As the pastors of their dioceses, bishops felt some responsibility towards all ecclesiastical institutions, whether formally in their care or not. For example in 1352 Bishop Grandisson of Exeter said that he had heard from trustworthy men that some people were holding on to property formerly belonging to Lady Margaret Dynham which she had bequeathed to the rector of Roche. Grandisson ordered local clergymen to investigate and to empanel further trustworthy men who had the 'greatest knowledge of the matter' to make an inventory.[32] Bishops were also constrained and guided in their actions by a long tradition that represented them as guarantors of order and of 'good faith'; they were, moreover, by instinct as much as office responsible for the memory of the Christian dead. This was perhaps the thing that required the greatest trust of all.

From the middle of the thirteenth century onwards (shortly after inheritance settled firmly into the ecclesiastical orbit around 1230) the presence of *fidedigni* at various moments of will making and inheritance was frequently stipulated. Their ostensible purpose was both to prevent fraud and to protect the other people involved—whether relatives and friends, executors, beneficiaries, debtors and creditors, the parish clergy, and even the bishop and his court—from suspicion of corruption. Often it is not clear which of these motivations was more important, preventing fraud or avoiding suspicion, and it is likely that they were both real goals. In 1258 Bishop William Bitton of Bath and Wells ordered that there should be no distribution of a testator's goods without the presence of trustworthy men, a ruling that was repeated by Bishop John Gervais of Winchester in the early 1260s. In 1268 the papal legate Ottobono added that a written inventory of the deceased's goods should be drawn up in the presence of trustworthy men who knew their measure. By 1287 the presence of trustworthy men was being recommended as necessary at the point of making a will as well.[33] Each of these enactments may well have been driven as much by fear of suspicion as by concern that fraud was actually taking place. Such ambiguity is particularly noticeable in canon 27 of the Second Council of Lyons, 1274, which ordered the presence of trustworthy men to ensure the compensation of debtors following the death of a usurer. If the debtor was not personally available, a bishop or parish priest was to receive the payment but, nevertheless, *fidedigni* were needed to inspire confidence in the proceedings.[34] Either the clergy were not to be trusted, or they needed to be protected from accusations of dishonesty.

The importance of trustworthiness to all parties is confirmed by the habit bishops made of mentioning the testimony of trustworthy men when justifying their involvement in disputed cases, and the way that rival litigants made claims about the trustworthiness of their witnesses.[35] But who was mistrusted so much as to make all this necessary? Landed families were certainly not shy of taking legal action against clergy they thought guilty of maladministration. In 1381 a priest of Great Torrington in Devon, acting as the feoffee and executor for one John Clay, was accused of putting the whole estate into the hands of Clay's second wife, leaving a daughter by his first marriage with nothing, against Clay's wishes. Bishop Brantyngham investigated through a panel of ten burgesses of the vill.[36] Equally there is evidence from litigation of lay executors falling under suspicion. In 1417 John Hopkins, a tailor, was reported at a visitation of Norwich for holding onto the goods of Thomas Westwyk, a weaver. The record states that Hopkins appeared 'with trustworthy witnesses' after which the will was proved and Hopkins drew up a full inventory of Westwyk's goods.[37] The image of the *fidedigni* strong-arming a tardy executor is hard to avoid. There is also a good deal of evidence that rival claimants to estates mistrusted each other. When Sir John Bluet died in 1316 there was a scramble among his family and associates to divide the estate, especially the moveable goods, without proper reference to his will. The bishop of Salisbury asked the rectors of Lacock and Bromham to publicize a decision to freeze Bluet's assets so that the will could be properly executed. The two rectors were to summon 'trustworthy men who knew the truth' for an inquiry into the location of Bluet's goods and the names of whoever was detaining them.[38] In instances such as this witnesses very likely drew on their experience in valuing goods and property in other contexts, some of which will be discussed in the following chapters. One of the main analogous fields of action was the 'inquisition post mortem', an investigation into the lands and property of deceased feudal tenants undertaken by crown officers in conjunction with local jurors from the 1230s onwards.[39]

While the synodal and conciliar constitutions describe an ideal world in which disputes are forestalled by the prescient gathering of trustworthy men, the records of litigation suggest that their involvement was often more restorative than preventative. Even at a very late stage though, anyone who was vulnerable to charges of fraud, or anyone who suspected it, must have valued the independent judgement made possible by a distant yet powerful bishop and the testimony of trustworthy men. Amongst all matters relating to last wills and testaments, the public power of bishops was most notably reliant upon their local collaborators in cases of intestacy. Where no will had been made a bishop could intervene using an inquiry by *fidedigni* to discover the value of the deceased's estate, the identity of any creditors and debtors, whether an active fraud was taking place, or whether there was in fact a will that no-one had known about.[40] That this was often done to make sure widows and orphans received their due gave to bishops and church courts an ethical purpose which contributed to the spiritual lustre of their institutional power.[41] They could not have done it without the trustworthy men.

Supervising Institutional Revenues

As with the enforcement of wills, the primary function of the trustworthy men in relation to institutional revenues was to demonstrate the authority or utility of a bishop or some other prelate. Of course, there was more to their work, but we can confidently refer to a 'primary function' in the eyes of the episcopate because it was (as we saw in Chapter 5) bishops who deployed this language of trustworthiness, and we may assume that they did so because it suited their purposes. Although many would have welcomed the bishop's authority, especially if it meant they received money that was due to them, others might have felt that their own rights were being denied. In particular cathedral chapters may have noticed that trustworthy men were often mentioned when capitular independence or income was being challenged.

Bishops and other churchmen had long sought local collaborators in the management of ecclesiastical revenues. There had never been a time when they had been able to rely solely upon appointed officials. In common with secular landowners, ecclesiastical lords relied a great deal upon their tenants in the management of their estates.[42] A distinctive feature of church lordship, however, was a tendency to blur the line between the administration of manors and of parishes. Take the use of visitations to audit and collect the revenues of church estates as well as to oversee church reform, a practice that persisted in England right through the twelfth and thirteenth centuries. For example, visitations of the Berkshire possessions of Salisbury cathedral in 1220 and 1222 were as much concerned with the revenues of manors as with the reform of the clergy. Lay informants were consulted as tenants rather than as parishioners. Similarly the visitations of churches belonging to St Paul's Cathedral in Essex, Hertfordshire, and Middlesex in 1181 and 1222 were inquiries into the value of church lands and rents. This was augmented in 1249–52 to include an oral account of payments made by the parishioners to the light funds or 'luminaria' of the churches. The information came from local juries as well as the clergy.[43] Visitations and inquests conducted by cathedral chapters retained this dual interest in revenues and reform into the early fourteenth century.[44] In all of this work, as with the church courts' jurisdiction over wills and testaments, the involvement of trustworthy locals was designed both to prevent fraud *and* to prevent suspicion of fraud falling on the local clergy. For example in 1328 two Cornish priests were commissioned to supervise Bishop Grandisson's woods in the county, selling the brush and dead wood. They were to work 'under the supervision (*visum et testimonium*) of four trustworthy men' from among the bishop's tenants in each place, in order that the bishop's 'advantage and profit be best and usefully served'.[45] Grandisson naturally wanted to make sure he was not swindled, but he may also have wished to limit any accusations of corruption against the two priests. In having their work overseen by local laymen the priests may have felt protected or punished, or both: all a historian can do is to tease out the probable parameters of any emotional imprint left by such action.

Grandisson's use of trustworthy men to supervise the collection of his own revenues was rather unusual however, standing out from the reservation of such language for occasions when a bishop was superintending the movement of other people's money. When thinking about their own income bishops naturally wanted to see results, but when considering their role in safeguarding someone else's finances bishops additionally wanted *to be seen* to be getting results. This is where the language of trustworthiness came into its own. As well as seeking to prevent fraud and protect reputations, when bishops called upon the aid of trustworthy men they were making claims about the nature of their own episcopal power. They were the custodians of *fides* who brought certainty in place of confusion. For example when, in 1385, Bishop Buckingham of Lincoln heard—from trustworthy men of course—that the deeds and charters of the hospital of St John the Baptist in Huntingdon had been lost, he commissioned an inquiry through further trustworthy men into how the hospital had been set up and endowed in the first place. Buckingham wanted to establish the will of the founders and to renew the financial viability of the hospital. In place of vanished documentary proofs he brought the reliable testimony of trustworthy men.[46]

In dealing with the canons or monks of their cathedral chapters and priories English bishops of the later Middle Ages often found that trust was in short supply. In 1402 Bishop Rede of Chichester was investigating suspected corruption in his cathedral; mistrustful of the Under Treasurer he made sure that two 'trustworthy persons' observed him each time he made a deposit in the cathedral treasury.[47] This was provocative, as the bishop's mistrust and his solution to it intruded episcopal authority where it could not be assured of a warm welcome. It had been a long time since bishops had personally seen to the governance of their cathedrals. The chapters of secular cathedrals had well-established deans and the priories of the monastic cathedrals had their priors. In this guise they asserted a great deal of independent power: until 1307 chapters had the right to elect each new bishop; bishops were bound to consult their cathedral clergy on important matters to do with church property and benefices; each community was a major source of patronage within and beyond the diocese, with responsibility for many parish churches; most had well-defined autonomous jurisdiction over their parishes or a territorial deanery; they were often the financial partners or even backers of hard-pressed bishops.[48] Even so, the cathedral was still the seat of the bishop's authority and the mother church of the diocese. There was no bishop who did not take any opportunity he could to remind his cathedral clergy of their theoretical subordination to him, whatever the reality. Although the trustworthy persons invoked by Bishop Rede were more likely to have been other canons than local laymen, his choice of rhetoric is telling: it was he—the bishop—who introduced trust into a body corrupted by dishonesty.

At other times bishops called upon the collaboration of leading lay parishioners in smoothing relations with their cathedral clergy. One of the biggest headaches for bishops in their dealings with the cathedrals was occasioned by the potential for those parishes possessed by the canons as 'prebends' to be exploited as cash cows while simultaneously neglected as communities requiring divine services and pastoral care. Bishops had to tread carefully in such cases, as prebends were not under their jurisdiction, but if they were drawn into a dispute they could feel compelled to act. In 1306, for example, Archbishop Greenfield of York issued a synodal constitution that required the executors of prebendaries to see that money for repairs to churches was put into the custody of two or three specially chosen local men. This was meant to ensure that the funds were used for a purpose that would benefit the parishioners as well as ease the financial burden on the incoming prebendary. Three years later Greenfield stepped into a dispute over just such an arrangement at Wetwang, where there was an archiepiscopal manor and a prebendal church. The chapter of York had levied a charge of 132 marks on the goods of the late prebendary, Thomas of Adderbury, for repairs to the rectory estate, but no payment had been received. The new incumbent was Raymond del Got, a nephew of Pope Clement V and, though a notable pluralist (holding more than one benefice simultaneously), someone to be placated rather than antagonized. That Del Got's interest in having repairs paid for coincided with those of the parish in seeing the repairs done enabled Greenfield to enter the fray as the backer of both parties. He ordered that whoever the initial 'specially chosen men' had been, they should now put the money into the hands of some 'trustworthy persons chosen from the parish'.[49] Such arrangements were never perfectly stable, but it was in the power of a bishop not only to impose a settlement, but to choose how to represent his intervention. These opportunities to advertise the bishop's restoration of trust where there had been only bad faith, contributed to the conduct and extent of his institutional power.

Managing the Market in Benefices

However important relations with his cathedral clergy were to a bishop, the business of overseeing parish churches entangled him in dealings with a much wider range of people and institutions. Indeed it could be argued that the status of the bishop in the later Middle Ages was principally dependent on how he managed the market in parochial benefices.

A benefice was both an office entailing certain duties and responsibilities, and a bundle of rights and revenues received in return for fulfilling that office.[50] Rectories, the main category of parochial benefice, had come into being gradually during the twelfth and early thirteenth centuries following the demise of private, heritable, churches and of Anglo-Saxon minsters. This new world was one of complex interactions and shared responsibilities at the centre of which the bishop stood supreme.[51] The possession of rectories was shared between an incumbent rector, a patron, and the bishop of the diocese, with no one of these being able to exercise total control over it. The incumbent holder of a benefice was called the rector, who might be the resident priest, but in many parishes the rector was a corporate body such as a religious house or a college. Rectors were able to manage the goods and property of a benefice as they saw fit while they were incumbent, but they could not sell or bequeath any immoveable property or church goods and the whole package had to be transferred (intact and with repairs made good) to their successor. Patrons possessed the right, known as the 'advowson', to appoint the rector. This right was treated as alienable property, capable of being sold or given away, and of being subdivided, in practice shared on rotation between several parties. An institutional rector would also usually be the patron. Despite this density of co-ownership and overlapping interests bishops retained significant rights over all benefices in their dioceses, being able to step in to confiscate ('sequester') the revenues of a church when it was being badly run, or when the incumbent was suspected of criminal behaviour.[52] Bishops were also the patrons of many churches themselves, in which case they had a direct interest in the integrity of the property. When, for example, Bishop Asserio of Winchester heard about the rector of Extone mortgaging church property as security for a loan, he was furious about the 'unreasonable claims' his church had been saddled with, seeing a future of litigation and debt that could have been avoided.[53]

As if this proprietorial complexity was not enough, the challenge that benefices posed for bishops was magnified by three further factors. There was, naturally, substantial demand from parishioners themselves for adequate pastoral care and a level of divine service that they deemed 'worthy' and respectable. This was often expressed at visitation, and bishops were bound to at least appear to be active in finding 'proper' and 'adequate' solutions when problems were reported.[54] Then, behind the many real patrons of churches there lurked a number of indirect patrons, such as the king, his ministers, and some religious houses, who often put pressure on actual patrons to nominate a particular candidate to a benefice. Church benefices were the main source of financial support for the men who staffed church, royal, and noble administrations.[55] Finally there was the mass of unbeneficed clergy and men unsatisfied with their current position, all eager for the income and status that a wealthy rectory would give them.[56] Rectors came and went. Many died in post but others arranged exchanges of their own church with another elsewhere in the country, and some resigned in order to take up other forms of clerical employment. Priests, clerks in secular service, and patrons alike would have taken a great interest in the availability and value of benefices in their local region, watching with eager attention for any change in circumstances: where are the oldest priests, which are likely to move on soon, which benefices have been under- or overvalued in the past?[57]

There was a great deal at stake when a rectory fell vacant, and trustworthy men played an important role. They were crucial to a bishop's ability to satisfy the various concerned parties that the economic value locked up in rectories

had been honestly assessed and would be transferred to its new owner without fraud. Furthermore, given that bishops did not have exclusive jurisdiction
over benefices as property—the royal courts had been providing their own
remedies for disputes since the late twelfth century—their inquests through
trustworthy men were not just attempts to inspire confidence in particular
outcomes, they were strident declarations in support of church jurisdiction
as a whole.[58]

The first thing bishops sought to establish was who had the right of patronage over a benefice. The interested parties had to agree on where the right
of advowson lay. Jurors, as in this example of a group of Nottinghamshire
parishes between 1444 and 1452, were asked: Is the church really vacant? How
was it left vacant? Who is the true patron? When was the last presentation?
What is the character of the candidate?[59] There was much here that local
clerics could easily have answered without lay participation, but the trustworthy men, with their capacity for defining locally accepted truth, specialised in remembering the history of their parish. On one exceptional occasion
this memory was incredibly precise: in June 1457 trustworthy men reported
that the church of Finghall in Yorkshire had been vacant since three o'clock in
the afternoon of 24 May.[60] But more often it was deeper memories that were
needed, and jurors recounted presentations of clergy by patrons in a line of
succession; this necessarily involved tracing the descent of manors within and
between landholding families.[61] Something of the complexity this involved
can be seen in the dispute over the advowson of Culmington in Shropshire in
1475 following the death of Sir John Talbot. Bishop Myllyng of Hereford called
on trustworthy clerics and laymen from the parish and surrounding area to
give evidence about two competing claims. The witnesses all agreed that patronage had long lain with the Talbot earls of Shrewsbury, but whereas some
concluded that the feoffees of Sir John's estate currently possessed the right,
others were adamant that the earl had sold the advowson, before he died, to
a priest called David ap Howell for twenty pounds, and that the Welshman
(Ap Howell) had already awarded the benefice to his brother. There were rumours about Ap Howell's documentation being forged, suspicions of simony
(the illegal sale of church office), and a good deal of confusion as to whether
the earl had changed his mind.[62] Where there was disagreement about the
facts, bishops had to do all they could to inspire trust in the judgements they
eventually reached. For the most part the laity was not involved in adjudicating disputes over the patronage of local churches. Bishops preferred to deal
with the clergy in these circumstances, often through a local meeting or 'chapter' arranged by a dean or an archdeacon.[63]

Lay participation was much more common in assessments of the value of
churches, with hundreds of examples littering the surviving records. There are
a number of reasons why this should have been so, underlying all of which was
the need to find an independent basis for the valuation. The judgement of any

neighbouring clerics in the market for a new benefice might have been compromised, and they could not be left to act alone. One mandate for a valuation, at Lillingstone (Buckinghamshire) in 1366, explicitly called for witnesses who were 'not suspected of any interest' in the benefice itself, although the most common solution was to summon a mixed jury of clergy and laymen.[64] Incumbent clergy, and by extension prospective candidates, generally wanted official valuations to be as low as possible so that their exposure to clerical taxation was minimized, despite their preference for benefices whose actual returns were high, and outgoings (from pensions or other payments) low. While it is impossible to say whether the 'trustworthy men' colluded with this in any way, the impression of impartiality was what mattered most to bishops, who wanted to maintain confidence levels in the marketplace of patrons and candidates. In addition to alleged impartiality, local lay witnesses were uniquely well-placed to report on the agricultural returns of a benefice averaged over a number of years or, as the trustworthy men of Acton Turville (Gloucestershire) reported in 1344, 'in normal years'.[65] Most inquests conducted by trustworthy men arose from proposals to unify two or more benefices into a single package, or from plans to appropriate a church to a religious house (meaning to place the revenues of its rectory into institutional ownership).

The proposal to unify one benefice with another typically occurred when changing circumstances meant it could no longer support a priest. Sometimes a whole parish could fall into penury, although the poverty of benefices also often resulted from historic divisions of rectories into 'portions', usually for the patron's financial gain. A complaint from Grayingham, Lincolnshire, in 1453, claimed that the division of the parish had resulted in one part becoming unviable given the costs of caring for the parishioners, a lack of tenants, poor cultivation and other reasons.[66] Although concern for pastoral care no doubt motivated lay witnesses, they, along with the priests and their patrons, were also motivated by a desire for economic stability and the attractiveness of service in a particular church. Trustworthy men were usually called upon to verify the poverty claimed in such petitions.[67]

Unions of benefices were sometimes the prelude to an appropriation.[68] If a religious house, hospital, or college wanted to appropriate the revenues of a church of which it was patron, bishops generally wanted to know whether it would be possible to pay for a vicar (literally a deputy) once the new institutional rector had taken the lion's share. This was very much in the interests of parishioners. Mandates for inquests frequently asked trustworthy men whether a church could support a vicar as well as a rector, and there are many examples of the results of such inquiries in the bishops' registers.[69] A positive answer could mean that the parishioners were happy, or that they could see no point in protesting, but there are some examples of resistance, perhaps motivated by fears of a diminution in the quality or quantity of attention that they would receive from a salaried, as opposed to a beneficed, priest. In 1344 for example, when they were asked for a valuation of their parish in preparation for the church's appropriation to Queen's Hall in Oxford, the trustworthy men of Brough in present-day Cumbria reported a *marked decline* in the revenues of their parish. It seems as though they were trying to make the benefice unattractive so that the appropriation would not happen. But they made mistakes. The valuation they made was in fact significantly *higher* than those reported in 1291 and 1318 so there was certainly no decline, as the bishop of Carlisle pointed out to them.[70] Parishioners, especially the wealthier among them, might also be worried about incurring costs themselves. In Somerset in 1449 the parishioners of Bradley and East Pennard were told to bear the cost of a chaplain's house themselves because even the soon-to-be united benefice of the two churches could not support it.[71]

Sometimes it seems as though the needs of the parishioners themselves came second to a desire for confidence in the market. Although lay communities in parishes could be strong and independent, they could not function as communities of the faithful without clergy to lead worship and administer the sacraments. An institutional rector, or one who was a servant of the church or crown and therefore not resident, was expected to support a vicar from the proceeds of the benefice. This put the economic interests of rectors and parishes at odds and frequently led to disappointment and conflict. These countervailing forces are particularly pronounced with inquests into the foundation of chapels and chantries in churches patronised by great lords. When, for example, the archbishop of York was dealing with the terms of Henry of Grosmont's will in 1361, the intention to found a chantry in Pontefract parish church to memorialize Thomas of Lancaster led to an inquest by trustworthy men into how much money was available for the new chapel from the revenues of the parish, and how the existing vicar would be affected.[72] Pontefract's Lancastrian patrons were important allies of any northern bishop, but the bishop had a responsibility for pastoral care too.

Real Property and Human Frailty

The very real concern of parishioners for the continuity of pastoral care and divine service was surely a major motivating factor in the cooperation of trustworthy men with episcopal authority. The two parties were natural allies in this much, even though the bishop's invocations of trustworthiness were made with other audiences in mind. One of the most common circumstances in which the financial well-being of a benefice intersected with the parishioners' needs was when a rector or vicar became so ill or infirm that he could not conduct services or manage the benefice properly.

Priests might be incapacitated by old age, illness, or the onset of a physical impairment such as deafness or blindness.[73] Worsening eyesight was in fact the most frequently cited reason for the appointment of a coadjutor in Exeter diocese between 1300 and about 1430, being mentioned in almost a quarter of cases.[74] As a degenerative condition of old age, blindness may really have been the most common problem, but cultural associations between loss of sight and pastoral or spiritual imperfection may also have played a part in the frequency of its reporting.[75] Parishioners often used visitations as a chance to alert their bishop to the changing health of their clergy. For example in 1286 the parishioners of Ledbury in Herefordshire reported the 'frenetic weakness and madness' of their vicar, and Bishop Swinfield responded by appointing an assistant.[76] Physical disability, chronic illness, or simply declining strength could make it impossible for a parish priest to conduct services, hear confessions, visit the sick, lead processions, or manage his household and his income. The remedy for this could entail the cleric's retirement on a pension paid from the proceeds of the benefice he resigned, or the appointment of an assistant (called a 'coadjutor') to help with the work while the incumbent soldiered on as best he could. Because the appointment of a coadjutor was not only meant to provide pastoral care during an elderly priest's final months or years, but also to ensure that the revenues of the benefice were kept intact until a permanent successor arrived, bishops wanted to broadcast the integrity of the process. They endeavoured to manufacture confidence by deploying the language of faith, and the bishop's authority, in attributing trustworthiness to male parish elites. Whether the coadjutor was a neighbouring cleric, an unbeneficed priest or a member of the bishop's staff, trustworthy men were nominated to supervise the creation of an inventory that listed the goods and revenues of the benefice.[77] For example, when William the vicar of Chitterne was appointed coadjutor for the incapacitated vicar of Netheravon, about ten miles away around the edge of Salisbury Plain, the bishop wrote that he trusted in William's faithfulness, but nonetheless ordered him to 'fully and faithfully' make an inventory on arrival under the watchful eye of trustworthy men.[78] It was not that bishops did not trust coadjutors; the language of faith was necessary because the process had to be seen to be scrupulous, and because it was a discourse that stimulated the nerve endings of a dense network of mutual trusting, reciprocity, and obligation in which the trustworthy men played an important part.

Sometimes the desire for confidence in the process required that the coadjutor swear an oath that the inventory was true, *as well as* having it overseen by trustworthy men.[79] There is also some evidence that particular clerics became experienced administrators of other people's benefices. For example Master Elias of Darley Dale in Derbyshire was appointed coadjutor to the old and weak rector of Duffield, further down the river Derwent, in 1327, and later he played the same role in his home parish where he was a 'portioner', that is the incumbent of a portion of a divided rectory. Upon his first appointment Bishop Northburgh of Coventry and Lichfield diocese wrote of the 'complete trust' that he had in Elias, but on both occasions trustworthy men were

nonetheless asked to supervise him while he made an inventory.[80] Overseeing the smooth transfer of resources from an ill or incompetent priest to an
assistant was just another way in which the trustworthy men were both the
practical enablers of financial continuity in the parishes, and the emblem by
which benefice-seeking clergy and their patrons might have confidence in the
bishop's ability to offer a trouble-free and profitable tenure.

As the scope and ambition of episcopal governance increased during the
thirteenth and fourteenth centuries bishops began to rely more and more
on so-called trustworthy men. That the first things they did, from the early
thirteenth century, involved the transfer of other people's money is telling. In
supervising the collection of alms, the making and execution of wills, or the
sound assessment and transfer of parochial revenues, trustworthy men helped
bishops to prevent fraud and to protect various third parties from suspicion
of fraud. Ecclesiastical trustworthiness was a commodity with a particular
character. It was achieved through a combination of the bishop's reputation
and resources with the testimony of very local elites (for whom see Chapter 6),
whose status meant that they could command fear as well as respect locally,
and whose concern for their own reputations would guarantee their cooperation. Within this relationship the language of faith played an important
role: while the trustworthy men might have made all sorts of mental connections between the *fides* placed in them and their role as representatives of
such places, services, and people as constituted 'the faith', the salient message
of episcopal invocations of trustworthiness was meant for other ears. To the
clergy and the patrons of churches, bishops proclaimed that they were the
bringers of certainty in place of confusion, and of trust in place of doubt. Although some of this activity—particularly in securing adequate provision for
vicars—was of clear benefit to the parishioners, the main effect of trustworthy
men upon church governance was to enhance the status of bishops.

CHAPTER TWELVE

The Material Church

IN THEIR SUPERVISION of other people's money trustworthy men were the hands-on custodians and symbolic guarantors of financial trust. They were the bishop's agents in mediating relationships with institutions, powerful laymen, churchmen, and their fellow parishioners. In the valuation of churches, however, we have seen that they also did something else. They provided the bishop with information. This, as we have seen (most particularly in Chapters 4, 5, and 10) was the characteristic form of their collaboration with authority and, indeed, their speciality. In this chapter and the next the passage of information, opinion, and judgement from trustworthy men to bishops will be examined in depth, and its effect upon a bishop's institutional and charismatic power described. In terms of institutions it is obvious to say that the bishop's need for testimony about local knowledge was mediated through the inquest, whose essential form arguably changed little over the centuries, and the visitation, which was much altered during the thirteenth century as the role of trustworthy men emerged.[1] It is a bracing thought to reflect upon the role of thousands of trustworthy men, the majority being elite peasants with a smattering of wealthier townsmen and gentlemen thrown in, in building up the power of the inquest and the visitation, two of the key elements in a bishop's institutional power: the means by which he governed his diocese. This in itself is a novel perspective brought about simply by changing the questions one asks of episcopal records. However, such organizational aspects of institutional history are only part of the story. As I have argued in the previous chapter, the nature of a bishop's power is best described in terms of what it could achieve, of its limitations, and of its operation. This brings me back to the rationale for the whole book: to find the nature of the institutional church not in the parish, nor in diocesan structures, but in the relationship between the two.

In this chapter I focus on how trustworthy men mediated information on the buildings, land, and divisions of space that together constituted what we might call the 'material church'. Bishops were understandably eager to be able to settle disputes and make authoritative statements about the physical things that constituted the world that Christians lived in. These things, whether they were church buildings, rectories, or parish boundaries, often had financial implications which attracted rival claims to possession, rights, and responsibilities. Bishops were sometimes directly implicated, on their own estates for example or in the parishes where they were the patrons of benefices, but they also had an interest in the orderly transfer of property and endurance of rights enjoyed by other parties. However, despite the material world being visible, its legal status was a human construct and as such invisible to the eye. Once again trust was necessary to establish knowledge of the unseen. In soliciting reports from trustworthy men, bishops were working hard to make the landscape legible to authority, and to appear ordered and permanent, a task that was never-ending because memories faded, disagreements came and went, and matter altered. In the rhetoric of their letters then, churchmen gave the impression that trustworthy men contributed to a stable and orderly world. The role of the *fidedigni* was never so functional and simple though. We cannot say that the trustworthy men always made the world appear unchanging. In some instances they surely did. They were, after all, figures of some parochial importance whose word had the power to shape locally agreed truths, whether through respect or fear. But their alliance with bishops was mostly in the latter's favour: theirs was a symbolic role brought into being by the dictates of episcopal governance. Consequently we need to pay close attention to the effect of all this work and effort upon bishops. Here I argue that episcopal attributions of trustworthiness enabled the bishop's authority to inhere in the material landscape, to become an immanent part of the lived environment, and to grow.

Material conceptions of the church were common in the medieval period and they have long been important to historical scholarship. To begin with the parish church was a potent physical embodiment and expression of a Christian community; it was a liturgical, ethical, and social space.[2] No matter the level of disharmony, private interest, or open conflict that might exist in a parish, the presence of holy objects and their use for salvific ritual made the church and its contents a powerful agent of socialization. As one archaeologist has recently put it 'the sacred geography of the parish church integrated the human body with . . . the Christian cosmos'.[3] Beyond the church the churchyard, while not a purely sacred space, was thought of as different from the wider landscape. Sports, markets, sex, and even agriculture may have taken place there, but it was nonetheless regarded as a special place where sermons were preached, the needy were lodged in almshouses, and—fundamentally—most of the parish's dead were buried.[4] Although both church and churchyard had to be consecrated by a bishop in order to receive burials, the holiness of the site was not static thereafter. We know that bones were often disturbed, sometimes in a clean sweep to create space for more bodies, which suggests that its holiness was retained more by the mixture of impressions, memories, and assumptions associated with it than through physical immutability.[5] And this is a very important point. The world of matter was coming to be conceived of in terms of mutability. Following the influence of Aristotle's *Physics* many scholastic thinkers of the thirteenth century held that matter was always changing, generating, and decaying; indeed change from one state to another was thought to define, or even constitute, matter as an ontological category.[6] Questions about the material world were often therefore, at root, questions about natural change of one sort or another. In this context the main quality of trustworthiness was to enable people and institutions to feel confident in the face of mutability: an unconscious echo perhaps of the fortitude in the face of change that the translator of the *Imitation of Christ*, cited in Chapter 3, attributed to the *fides* of the heart. Law dealt with this problem using the concept of 'continuous facts' about supposedly unchanging conditions like boundaries and long-held custom.[7] But such continuity was a fiction. However changeable things might be trustworthy opinion lent the fiction a degree of credibility.

As historians have come to think more and more in terms of the material world, the study of the parish church has been augmented and transformed by investigations of the body in Christianity, and the physical stuff through which belief was mediated. The body of Christ as both a symbol of and a challenge to faith in the later Middle Ages has become central to our understanding of the period: why did God become a man, how could believers relate to the suffering of Christ, what did people think about holy bodies in art?[8] In a book that gathers and reflects upon the richness of the 'material turn' in religious studies, Caroline Walker Bynum has described the later Middle Ages as a period 'characterized by intense awareness of the power of the material', in which 'holy matter' was considered to be animated by God. Painted images and statues of the saints might move, bleed, or weep because they were alive with divinity, while mechanical objects of devotion such as hinged altarpieces or models of the Virgin Mary that opened to reveal the three persons of the Trinity, were acknowledged as artificial aids to devotion. God was even visualized as physically present within the holy book. Much of this was popular and characteristic of the thirteenth to fifteenth centuries, but it was also controversial: blood relics attracted scepticism and criticism well before the Reformation, an image of Mary suggestively giving birth to God as well as Christ was theologically challenging, and heretics were depicted kicking God as he rose from an open Bible.[9] Physicality was not superstition or folklore though, but a medium for those cognitive and emotional workings of faith that I presented in Chapters 1 and 3. Sensory and spiritual vision required effort and commitment from the individual but it led towards, and was ultimately dependent upon, God: 'the iconography seems to be about seeing an unseen that is, although hidden, really there'.[10] Faith in the unseen was an act that took the believer on a journey from things material and present to the conceptual and the absent.

Themes of distance and absence are, coincidentally enough, also fundamental to the way in which landscape historians conceive of the material world: as people inhabit and move through the world their subjective understanding of one place is conditioned by knowledge of its physical and symbolic relationships to other places.[11] In this way the seen and the unseen are given meaning by their interdependence. Medieval Christianity was notable as a belief system that both imbued the physical landscape with spiritual qualities *and* made physical interventions which channelled those resonances. Some cultures with comparable attitudes to numinous space have made little or no impression upon the landscape.[12] However, in the Christian landscape 'natural' features such as hilltops, caves, woods, and streams were also suffused with religious meaning as often as built structures including wells, crosses, shrines and ruins.[13] Sometimes meaning derived from seeing a local landscape as if it were the Holy Land, making the distant proximate.[14] This may have been a mentality most developed among the literate, but more central to the lives of the majority was the intimate and visual web of connections between the parish church and the agricultural landscape: churches contained plough-lights and even ploughs, while the fields were dotted with wayside chapels, shrines, and lights. Blessings and prayers punctuated working hours as well as time spent in church.[15] Objects and places could be reminders of other, distant and unseen, phenomena, be it Jerusalem, heaven, or God.

These ways of thinking about holy matter and seeing divine meaning in the landscape are echoed in a facet of 'Christian materiality' that has not hitherto been defined in this way: the physical incarnation of episcopal authority in the parish. Authority was by no means separate from spirituality, and here I will explore the ways in which authority, like divinity, did not merely *attach* itself to physical objects. Objects and places did more than simply trigger 'material memories' of a bishop's actions;[16] in addition to this, episcopal authority came to inhere in the material in much the same way that Bynum has described for holy matter. Tom Johnson has recently expounded a theory of the materiality of law in the later Middle Ages that elaborates upon this idea. His main contention is that 'law was a quality of physical stuff: it resided in trees and boundary stones that divided land, in deer that belonged to the king, and even in shipwrecked detritus that washed up on shore'.[17] In saying that law 'resided in' material things, Johnson suggests that legal thought and actions actually helped make physical objects into the things they were perceived to be.[18] To take an example that I shall return to later in this chapter, a collection of barns, fields, and houses plus the chancel of the parish church could not be seen and understood as 'the rectory' without its legally framed parameters and the very idea of a rectory being understood as constitutive of the lands and buildings themselves.

The materiality of episcopal power has not been ignored by historians, but it has not been seen in quite this way. Maureen Miller's studies of bishops' palaces and elite clerical vestments have blazed the trail in many respects as outstanding investigations of the material culture that surrounded and 'articulated' episcopal power. The architecture of his dwellings, she argues, 'communicates and generates meaning' about the office of a bishop, while clothing can, in words quoted from the Second Lateran Council of 1139, 'exhibit holiness'.[19] Miller demonstrates how ornate vestments made by rich women between the tenth and twelfth centuries were reminders of a 'concealed relationship' that brought the donor closer to the altar and closer to the cause of church reform.[20] However, I think it is true to say that for Miller the concept of power and the stuff of power are categorically separate. Johnson's approach by contrast makes the concept of power a constituent element in the stuff of power. The present investigation assumes that material things were indeed reminders of unseen power, but that they were also the products, vestiges, and bearers of it.

Sometimes, of course, bishops were not absent; they were spectacularly present, conducting the confirmation of children or the ordination of priests en masse in impressive and memorable ceremonies. A bishop's presence was also required for the consecration of newly built churches or of sacred spaces defiled by blood, faeces, or semen. Consecrations were moments when the bishop's ritual power clearly became a part of what made a church a church. Similarly the visitation of parishes brought bishops out of their manor houses and cathedrals, making their judgements present in the parochial landscape through memories of the events.[21] The alliance between bishops and trustworthy men was partially conducted at visitation—a local occurrence—but it also took place at a distance when mandated officers dealt with particular cases. In both circumstances the bishop's ability to make his judgements inhere within a material church was mediated by the trust that he had to place in his informants. To give an example: wanting to act upon his responsibility for the consecration of the churches in his diocese, but unable to proceed without good local information, Bishop William Gray of Lincoln launched a grand general inquiry in 1431 into unconsecrated and deconsecrated churches, altars, and churchyards in Huntingdon and Bedford archdeaconries, to be carried out by sworn trustworthy men.[22] The physical churches and churchyards were visible to anyone, and were thus capable of prompting as many interpretations of their status as there were people with eyesight and an opinion. What the bishop's alliance with local elites did was to make the status of those familiar places subject to his special authority: inquests were thus moments when episcopal power was territorialized, its constitutive power to make a church a church renewed, and it was made to seem present within the material world.

Buildings

In the emerging parish landscape of thirteenth-century England, the bishop's guiding role was manifested in his installation of the parish clergy. Although most parish priests were nominated by lay and religious patrons, a bishop had to approve each rector or vicar and invest him with his rectory or vicarage. Although, technically, these two terms refer to a whole benefice (in the sense of a package of possessions, rights, and duties), we have come to apply them to the building in which a rector or vicar lived and they endure in many an 'Old Rectory' house name today. In the Middle Ages too, the physical components of the rectory or vicarage were important, but these amounted to more than the dwelling house, consisting besides of land and multiple buildings. The bishop's responsibility for the transfer of all this from one incumbent to the next made him a lynchpin of the parochial system, in just the way that he was the arbiter of other people's money, as described in Chapter 11. It also caused his authority to inhere in these the most visible local manifestations of the institutional church. Of course, it was not only a bishop's authority that constituted a rectory as a legal object, the actions of the rector himself and the power of the patron were also significant ingredients. But it was only a bishop who could record the 'trustworthiness' of processes connected with it.

When a rector died or moved on the estate could not simply be passed to his successor. First a central paradox of the late medieval attitudes to matter had to be addressed. A rectory was, on the one hand, an immutable item of real property arousing material expectations among soon-to-be rectors; on the other hand it was valuable only because it was active matter, capable of productive generation yet subject to change and decay over time. As Bynum has shown, this propensity to corruption was something that late medieval intellectuals sought to control by pointing to the role of God in the material world, setting natural limitations upon change so that decay did not mean transformation into a wholly different thing. God was certain, but his creation was changeable, up to a point. Outside the realm of scholastic thought something more than logical argument was needed in order to set limits upon decay. Regular repairs had to be made, and the costs allocated.[23] Here bishops drew upon the testimony of trustworthy men. These local peasant elites knew the buildings of a benefice, they could inspect the extent of dilapidations, remember when they had occurred, and understand the costs and skills needed to repair them. Undertaking such inquests when a benefice changed hands was one of the commonest purposes for which bishops used panels of trustworthy men between the late thirteenth and late fifteenth centuries.[24] Unlike the inquests into patronage discussed in the last chapter, where laymen were not routinely used, inquests into dilapidations were unthinkable without lay participation.

Property transactions were fraught with potential for conflict in the gap between expectation and reality. A departing rector, the executors of a deceased priest, or the lessees of a rectory were all liable to claims for depreciation in the physical estate. Just as the potential for material things to change was a 'mechanism of reproach and accusation' in Eucharistic miracles (which became vehicles for anti-Jewish hatred and casual allegations against women, servants, and thieves), so the dilapidation of rectories was a breeding ground for mistrust between the interested parties.[25] Contests over dilapidations could embroil a new rector in drawn-out and costly proceedings, which were made more complicated by the possibility of pursuing a case in either the church or the common-law courts.[26] Therefore, what bishops did and said in disputes about rectories was often conditioned by the reality or threat of litigation at common law. Bishops wanted to deal with cases not only because it was good business for the church courts but because settling such disputes was a way of projecting their authority, having it become a component of ecclesiastical matter in parishes across their dioceses. Each of the following cases is thus the articulation of an overarching jurisdictional claim as well as being a particular intervention. Trustworthiness—articulated by bishops and enacted by locals—was the linguistic and ethical glue that shored up fragile social relations, the conceptual counterpart of the work done by carpenters and tilers to repair the roof of the rectory barn. Although the principal players were rectors, lessees, and executors, and despite the fact that bishops gave a lot of humdrum administrative time to these issues, to pay for repairs was grandly claimed to 'recompense God, the church, and the parishioners'.[27] So important was the transfer of the physical benefice that it was presented as a splendid moral endeavour.

Although the majority of recorded cases relate to alleged defaults on obligations, there is some evidence of this ethic being honoured in the diligent maintenance of benefices. For example in 1475–76, Robert Skynner, the lessee of Wainfleet rectory in Lincolnshire (appropriated to the nuns at Stixwold), spent fifteen shillings two pence on repairs to the glazing and soldering on the chancel windows, to the doors of his tithe barn, and to the earth banks that kept the sea from encroaching on this low-lying coastal parish.[28] Annual expenditure was what prevented trouble of the kind encountered by a later rector of the same parish who was accused of laying waste to his lands, '*diggyng de le turphes* to the irredeemable detriment of the rectory'.[29] Occasionally a rector or lessee went beyond what was demanded in law, as in the few examples of an incoming cleric agreeing to bear the costs incurred by his predecessor: for instance in 1494 the new vicar at Chesham in Buckinghamshire stood surety for (*fideiussit*) the costs of repairs to the manse or vicarage. Whether he did so out of charity, generosity, or weary resignation at there being no other option, we cannot know.[30] He may have wanted to avoid litigation.

Where altruism did not prevail, minor disputes could be resolved if the parishioners reported on the physical state of churches in visitation. Many bishops' and archdeacons' records of visitation begin with a report on the fabric of the church building and its contents.[31] These were probably made by the parish representatives along with one of the parish clergy, walking the visitor around the church, pointing out faults and ascribing responsibility. Repairs to the chancel of the church and the provision of some liturgical paraphernalia fell to the rector, while the parishioners were charged with responsibility for the nave and some of the service books. Sometimes accountability could not be settled during a visitation hearing, and then bishops might arrange special inquests by trustworthy clerics and laymen to settle the matter. These could arise from negligence on the part of the parishioners, as at Paull in Yorkshire in 1353, or of the rector, as at Brampton in Derbyshire in 1324 where the dean of Lincoln was rector.[32] For the most part visitation reports of material decay tended to focus on the church building, although visitations of the parishes subject to Exeter cathedral regularly dealt with repairs to the whole rectory following the departure or death of a lessee.[33] One report arising from visitation (but requiring a further inquest by trustworthy men), at Swine in Yorkshire in 1308, was occasioned by doubt about responsibility for a new aisle or chapel with an altar, built in 'le North Crouche' of the church. Did the parishioners or the nuns with whom they shared the church have to pay for repairs?[34] While the condition of physical structures was easily ascertained, their unseen legal attributes were often subject to disagreement.

All the cases discussed here were necessary because the costs involved in maintaining the fabric of churches and rectories were considerable, and worth fighting over. Some were even taken to appeal at the archbishop of Canterbury's 'provincial court', known as the Court of Arches, in London.[35] If one's predecessor in a benefice had not kept it in good repair the profits of the estate could easily be eaten up for years to come. Such jeopardy is dramatically illustrated if we take a look at one of the more valuable rectories in England. Clifton Campville in Staffordshire had been the subject of dispute on more than one occasion in the later Middle Ages before an especially notable inquest in 1453.[36] A new rector called Robert Godibowore complained about the state in which his predecessor, William Duffield, had left the rectory. Summoned to conduct an inquest by the bishop of Coventry and Lichfield, local clergy and trustworthy laymen gave a highly detailed account of the repairs that were needed. They examined the rector's dwelling itself consisting of hall, louvre, parlour, and six other principal rooms together with a pantry and buttery; in addition they inspected a larder house, kitchen, bakery, brewhouse, malthouse, kilnhouse, granary, and stables arranged around a courtyard; and beyond this a tithe barn, dovecote, and nine further houses plus the chancel of the church. The total cost of repairs was pegged at a hundred and thirty-three pounds six shillings four pence and responsibility was allocated firmly to William Duffield's executors, who would have had to raise the capital by selling off Duffield's other assets, if he had any.[37] This adjudication may well have led to a compromise and a deal, as seems to have happened at Lanchester collegiate church in Durham in 1418. There the incoming dean believed that his three predecessors had neglected the church's estates. Trustworthy men reported on the condition of walls, roofs, timbers, kitchens, 'Le Kylnehouse', a bridge, and various tenanted houses, as well as identifying which trades would be needed to make good the problems. The total cost of forty-four pounds was split between the current dean (ten pounds), two former and still-living deans (ten pounds and five marks), and the executors of a deceased former dean (twenty pounds).[38]

The trustworthy men involved in such inquests had to be independent of either party. They were not commenting on repairs to the nave, which was their own responsibility as lay parishioners. They also had to have good memories of how and when particular buildings had decayed, which tells us that the leading parishioners took an almost proprietorial interest in the physical state of buildings which they might have lived alongside since childhood, while rectors and lessees came and went. They must also have had some expertise in estimating the extent and cost of problems, as the Lanchester and Clifton Campville assessments suggest. Expertise was something that bishops desired, as we saw in Chapter 5, and which real trustworthy men embodied, treated in Chapter 6. It is likely that some of the men charged with this responsibility had also at one time or another acted as supervisors of buildings and tenements in a manorial context.[39] Upon the completion of the repairs itemized in their reports, the trustworthy men would go on living in sight of these structures that embodied not only a rector's power but also a bishop's authority. Taking up Johnson's idea of law and judgement being constitutive of matter, it is not much of a leap of the imagination to think of these local men recalling the bishop's intervention and seeing his guiding hand in the enduring physical structures of the rectory. A new roof or a repaired wall might bear the stamp of episcopal action as long as memory fixed it there. Perhaps they even saw his authority in less prominent examples of the craftsman's work: a particular buttress against the chancel, the ties made of lead or wood holding broken masonry together, the bolts and new timber plating decayed beams, door and window fastenings, or even hidden features such as the underpinning of tottering walls, something unseen but of which one would like to be confident, no doubt.[40] Sometimes the books and ornaments that were the rector's responsibility were also mentioned in such inquests, and they too may have borne memories of the bishop's collaboration with trustworthy men.[41]

The actual inspection was carried out visually—sometimes an explicit requirement—but the jurors probably also consulted any written accounts kept by the rector or lessee. They might also be questioned individually to rule out collusion.[42] Such measures were infrequent, however, and speak of an unusually serious breakdown of trust. More often the report seems to have been a collective view, a pooling of local memory and written record. Two more or less identical tiny slips of parchment detailing the repairs and replacements necessary to the rectory of Ivychurch in Kent around 1293 could be evidence that assessments were made individually and then compared.[43] These checks were, like the very involvement of trustworthy men, measures designed to bolster the eventual judgement and the bishop's authority. It cannot have been all that uncommon for a rector to resent a judgement that went against him, as transpired in a 1373 dispute between Nicholas Monke, the lessee of Hurstbourne in Hampshire, and the executors of the remarkably named deceased rector, Saladin. Trustworthy men reported that money for repairs was already in Monke's hands, but Monke would not do anything about them and was called to explain himself before the bishop.[44]

Land

The productivity of the land was a seasonal and perennial reminder of the changeability of matter. The crops grew, animals were reared, trees were coppiced and felled. Temporary dearth could affect an individual parishioner's willingness to lose a tenth of his produce, but longer-term changes in the landscape and the way it was used created the conditions in which uncertainty and dissatisfaction could really thrive. Natural mutability thus affected how tithes were understood at any given time. Because of the strong link between the payment of tithes and membership of a parish, any changes in agricultural practice would have a profound effect upon the administrative landscape, creating tension between tithe payers and tithe owners, and between rival claimants to tithes. It is therefore notable that marshes, woodland, wastes, and commons were so frequently the objects of contestation in tithe disputes. It was here that changes in agricultural and industrial land use most often collided with customary practice or posed questions that had not arisen before. Because parish boundaries were not clearly demarcated in unproductive areas, it was uncertain to whom the tithes on newly cultivated land (known as 'assarts') were payable. Often it took a dispute just to establish such boundaries. Over the longer term, the value of tithes of grain declined in the fifteenth century while those of wool and livestock increased, meaning that the rectors (who most often took the 'great' tithes on grain) suffered and looked enviously at the vicars whose 'small' tithes on livestock and related produce had begun to grow in value. The shift to pastoral husbandry in many areas also aggravated questions about tithes on herds of animals that wandered across parish boundaries.[45]

Tithe disputes could also arise when a new rector arrived from a distant parish. He might bring with him particular expectations of tithing custom that clashed with what his new parishioners accepted as right and natural.

Local customs relating to tithes were deep-rooted because they governed how and when crops were collected, and they set a limit on the profitability of the land.[46] The new rector might find that the local situation could not easily be made to conform to his expectations. If he was wise he would settle for the 'relatively inefficient collection' of his tithes, accepting that his parishioners' compliance would always be tempered by their reluctance to pay and their considerable skill in the arts of evasion.[47] The records rarely reveal much of this. If a rector heard that his predecessors had received certain tithes 'quietly and peacefully', it would be wise to assume a certain amount of low-level resistance.[48] Furthermore, although custom was presented as immutable the arrival of a new rector, the appropriation of a church, or the leasing of tithes to third parties may well have been an occasion for a recalibration of memories.[49]

Despite, or perhaps because of, their changeability, memories of customs were part of the productive landscape that tithe owners had to negotiate and come to terms with. In just the way that Johnson has described for law, custom was also an element of the land, not something imposed upon it. This meant that latent uncertainty permeated any consideration of tithes, and that discontent could be diminished only by locally mediated agreements. The relative power that this memory-vested-in-land gave to local people has been well-studied by historians.[50] However, the imprint of outside authority has received less attention. There is good reason, as John Eldevik has suggested, for seeing tithes as 'a visible reminder . . . of the overlordship of the bishop', but we should also heed Luigi Provero's counsel that both the territory at issue and the projection of authority via tithing were uncertain and contestable.[51] Bishops sought to use their capacity for dispute settlement as a means to make their presence felt in a given locality both at the moment of payment and afterwards in a renewed conception of the very land itself. Although episcopal judgements valorized custom and depended upon the testimony of trustworthy men, bishops themselves were also necessary to 'shape material stuff into discrete objects of legal concern', making a waste into a field by the addition of episcopal power.[52]

Each dispute over tithes highlights a facet of agricultural production or economic life about which certainty was not possible, because of the changeability of the material world. Change opened up an unfamiliar scenario, a caesura in the knowable world, a challenge to the confidence necessary for everyday life. And an articulated trust was the ingredient thought necessary for the reestablishment of confidence in accepted rights and duties. With the testimony of trustworthy men, bishops sought to present the material world as fixed and stable, like God, even though it was subject to the natural laws of corruption and change. Trustworthiness, for example, established the 'usual' value of tithes in a 1228 dispute that was described by Bishop Thomas Blundeville of Norwich as 'seemingly interminable'.[53] Fluctuations from one harvest to another had sown discord between the monks of Colchester and the rector of Eriswell, and local knowledge about growing conditions, weather patterns, and market values was intended to make all of these sliding variables seem more steady and predictable. The value of tithes was being presented as a 'continuous fact', the fiction of this legal category. Whether the word of trustworthy men really did create such confidence and order in the legal status of the material world is hard to say. We should probably assume that it did have this effect some of the time, but the very disputes that demanded trustworthy testimony are themselves evidence of the difficulty entailed in making the world amenable to a bishop's authority. What is more certain, for historians, is the fact that every such dispute was an opportunity for bishops to augment their power by rhetorical, legal, and political means.

The great problems with tithes often arose from change and uncertainty to do with boundaries. The boundaries between parishes were not mapped until the sixteenth century, before when they existed in memory and social practice, which could change. Uncertain boundaries abounded, and trustworthy men were called upon to 'fix' them, at least for the time being. For example, in the jurisdiction of the dean of Durham cathedral, the limits of the parishes of Kellawe, Middleham, and St Oswald's required establishment beyond opinion in 1313.[54] The allocation of tithes between the parishes of Pilton and Barnstaple in Devon was called into doubt in 1435, and so trustworthy men were asked to testify. That they did so in great detail conjures images of them conferring in advance and perhaps walking the boundary together, disputing the line when their memories diverged.[55] The same could happen in suburban settings, as for example at Tottenham Magna in Middlesex (now Greater London) around 1470, where an account of the tithes and boundaries was recalled by a witness who had himself heard it from 'men in whom he had faith'.[56] Trust or faith was associated with 'certainty of the mind in things absent, established beyond opinion and short of knowledge', as Hugh of St Victor had said, and the changeability of the physical world made it highly amenable to this way of thinking.[57]

Where there had previously been no boundary, because land had lain uncultivated as forest or marsh, the absence of certain knowledge was most pronounced. Bringing new land into cultivation was an important feature of late medieval economic and landscape history, especially during the long period of demographic expansion from 1200 until the early fourteenth century. For example, trustworthy clerics and laymen were commissioned to inquire into the possession of assarts in the parishes of Chester-le-Street, Lanchester, and Bishop Auckland in 1312: How much are the tithes worth? Who has been receiving them?[58] Even in the aftermath of the famines of that decade conflicts over the parochial allocation of assarts and their tithes continued to arise.[59] In Nottinghamshire there were inquests through trustworthy men into assarted land at Norwood in 1324 and on 'Theveswelhill' between Treswell and Rampton in 1331. Both Norwood and Rampton were prebends of Southwell

Minster, whose canons generated a great deal of litigation in this period.[60] As well as the vast uplands of the Pennines and scraps of waste in Midland parishes, sure and identifiable demarcations of tithe were tricky to pin down in the fens of East Anglia. At Littleport in Cambridgeshire in 1385 'trustworthy witnesses' were examined on oath about the allocation of tithes from the reed beds, which were disputed by the hospital of St John the Baptist and Mary Magdalene in Ely and the vicar of the parish.[61] There were also sudden manifestations of uncertainty in urban environments. In 1303 doubt spread through Norwich about which parish John Weston should pay tithes to in respect of a new shop he had built on land previously owned by Jews. Jews did not pay tithes, and so this land had not hitherto been a 'discrete object of legal concern' for Christian courts. Here the bishop's efforts to introduce material certainty in place of doubt took on additional meaning as the *fides* of the trustworthy Christian witnesses replaced the perfidy of the former Jewish owners, now either exiled or forcibly converted. Whether or not the interest held by the prior and convent of St Faith at Horsham in one of the parishes concerned was read as a further layer of significance is impossible to say.[62] In all such cases an adjudicated settlement associated the advent of certainty with trustworthy locals and the bishop's authority, which became a facet of the landscape itself.

The other major challenge to the supposed universality and completeness of the parish system was lordship. Long after private churches had come under ecclesiastical control, lordship continued to determine the parochial allegiance of many people in a number of ways. One was the enduring existence and new foundation of chapels: churches with a lower, though indeterminate, status than parish churches. This will be dealt with further on in this chapter. Another was the tendency for tithing to follow tenancy rather than settlement, meaning that neighbours living side by side in the shadow of a parish church might nevertheless feel allegiance and pay tithes to different churches.[63] For example in 1302 the bishop of Hereford tried to clear up doubt that had arisen over the destination of tithes from the demesne lands of the lord of Bitterley in Shropshire. These had historically been detached from the parish, a situation that did not seem justifiable to a newly appointed prebendary, and a panel of trustworthy men were asked to report.[64] The desire of bishops to bring reason and conformity to such places was often expressed in terms of driving out uncertainty: a role specially reserved for faith or trust in late medieval thinking, as we saw in Chapter 1. When the archbishop of York was riding through north Nottinghamshire one day in 1402, he was petitioned about the poverty of the parishes of Boughton and Kneesall, neither of which could support a rector. If only they could be united as a single benefice, their patrons opined. When he came to investigate Archbishop Scrope found to his horror that the two parishes were 'hopelessly intermingled' (*multipliciter sunt permixta*) and because the boundaries were not well established there was great confusion, perplexity, doubt, and obscurity (*confusione et perplexitate, dubia et obscura*) about the collection of tithes and other dues, which had led to disputes and scandal between the two rectors. The confusion seems to have arisen because the tenants of the manor of Ollerton, who were parishioners of Kneesall by virtue of their tenancy, and the tenants of part of the honour of Tickhill (South Yorkshire), who were parishioners of Boughton by virtue of *their* tenancy, did not live in two distinct settlements but had lands and property across the two parishes. Lordship was here felt as a natural *ecclesiastical* allegiance. The solution was to unite the parishes and have them served at Kneesall church, abandoning any attempt to find a boundary between them.[65] It is hard to imagine the parishioners of Boughton being happy at losing their parochial identity for the sake of administrative expedience, but that was the price of certainty and confidence for the bishop and the patrons of the churches. However much the lingering episcopal presence in this redrawn landscape might present a picture of order and homogeneity, lived experience and the landscape itself were always changing, and so the bishop's efforts were never done.[66]

The biggest change in the human use of land during the later Middle Ages was the retreat from intensive cultivation in many lowland regions and a widespread turn towards pastoral farming. This change, whose implications for the work of trustworthy men have been discussed in detail in Chapter 8, was significant in the history of tithes because it had the potential to make rectors poorer and vicars wealthier. When the small tithes (including livestock) increased at the expense of the great tithes on grain, institutional or absentee rectors (priests who were possessors of ecclesiastical benefices) might look askance at the deals they had done to support the vicars (deputies paid a salary or supported from a smaller endowment) serving their churches and parishioners. But there appears to have been little they could do about it. Some of the late medieval attempts to revalue churches, examined in the previous chapter, may have been preludes to the reassignment of tithes, but the most common response to challenging economic conditions was for rectors to lease their tithes on a bigger and bigger scale. Only in exceptional circumstances, as when the vicar of Sheriff Hutton in North Yorkshire faced unexpected bills for rebuilding a chapel in 1319, were bishops prepared to revise an existing arrangement.[67] Part of the reason for inertia in the allocation of tithes was the very role played by trustworthy men in the original establishment, or 'ordination' (not to be confused with the ordination of a priest), of a vicar's material means of support. An ordination was drawn up when a rectory was taken over by an institution or used to support a cathedral canon or a member of the bishop's staff. Sheriff Hutton had been appropriated to Marton Priory in 1282, and like its revision in 1319, the original ordination had been based on an assessment of tithes and revenues conducted by local trustworthy men. In such cases the focus was usually on the small tithes. For example, when Wolford church in Warwickshire was appropriated to Merton College Oxford in 1322, the bishop of Worcester convoked 'fit and trustworthy persons' to provide 'exact information as to the value of the small tithe of all produce' there, so that he could carve out an adequate vicarage from the rectory estate. Perhaps as keen as the bishop to ensure the vicarage was viable, the jurors of Wolford reported in great detail on the value of the tithes.[68] Most vicarages were endowed with just enough resources to make them attractive, while leaving the greatest share of the glebe (agricultural estate) and the tithes to the rector, so 'adequacy' was often a parsimonious sufficiency. The capacity of trustworthy men to determine what their vicar should receive was thus strictly limited. Such constraints are conspicuous in the instructions given for an inquest into the value of the vicarage at Padbury in Buckinghamshire in 1274, where the vicar was to have two acres of land for his horses. Not the best land, mind you, nor the worst, but middling 'according to the opinion of trustworthy men' (*per considerationem fidedignorum*).[69] By the fifteenth century when trustworthy men were drawn from a much narrower segment of parish society than in the thirteenth (for which see Chapter 8), such considerations were being made by people who were very likely to have been the peers of tithe farmers (see Chapter 11), and there may even have been conflicts of interest. For bishops this would have meant that their institutional power was increasingly a component in the further enrichment and social dominance of this rising group. However, although rectors and tithe farmers too were watching closely to make sure vicars got no more than they needed, it was bishops, who controlled the whole process by being the central node in a small web of competing interests, whose authority was most augmented.

Routes and Boundaries

Between the twelfth century and the Reformation the landscape of local religion was fluid and labile, not static. So numerous were disputes over the relative rights of parish churches and chapels that we must reject the scholarly orthodoxy that holds this parochial landscape to have been 'frozen' by around 1200. The replacement of minsters and private churches with thousands of parish churches was not a once-and-for-all event and anomalies were not simply 'ironed out'.[70] There was certainly change at the normative level, with the parish church becoming the model unit of Christian belonging, economics, and pastoral care, important elements of which were the allocation of tithes and the centralization of burial in consecrated parish cemeteries.[71] And there is no disputing the very real changes to the landscape that occurred as a result: parish churches were built, tithes made people think harder about boundaries, and the establishment of rectories and vicarages introduced new power dynamics into the agricultural and built environment. But none of this, as we have seen, was fixed. The thirteenth century saw the replacement of one changeable situation, characterized by a small number of high-status minsters and a multitude of (poorly documented) low-status private churches, with another, in which a high number of well-documented medium-status parish churches have diverted attention from the continuity and mutability of chapels and other local sites of worship.

A neat hierarchy of parish churches with cure of souls and sacramental functions, and inferior churches having purely private or liturgical purposes, existed more in the bureaucratic mind than on the ground, where things were always complicated. Bishops sought to impose rational schemes of organization upon the parish but, in common with the efforts of authorities in many historical settings, they never wholly succeeded because of the dynamic forces generated by the messy business of living in a place.[72] A diverse reality coupled with a narrowly conceived official norm caused resentment in some communities, especially in regions of dispersed settlement, and also amongst lords whose formerly private churches had not attained parish status. Small churches attracted investments of identity, emotion, time, and money from parishioners of all sorts with as much intensity as larger ones. As well as this imperfect beginning, dissatisfaction with the parish was fostered by local demographic changes (whether caused by settlement growth and decline, famine, plague, or other factors), by the mutability of the natural environment, and by shifting religious aspirations. Separately or together these forces stimulated discontent amongst people whose main affective connection was not necessarily with a parish church.[73]

Sometimes the motivating force behind a rebellion against the parochial order was a widely shared communal ambition for recognition, but campaigns to protect or change the status of churches were also frequently driven by the claims of lordship. While the inhabitants of some seigneurial boroughs (towns or villages without any formal corporate governance) built their own churches in order to resolve the problems of using one in the lord's castle, other lords became the figureheads of campaigns to raise the status of a public chapel.[74] There were many disputes over the rights of non-parochial churches that became lawsuits in the episcopal and even papal courts.[75] Many more entailed petitions to the papacy, but legal action was expensive and bishops often arbitrated settlements helped by the testimony of local trustworthy men.[76] Such disputes usually combined economic issues, such as the payment of tithes and voluntary offerings, with feelings of belonging and exclusion arising from receipt of the sacraments. This was a potent mix. As in the other fields of action we have been considering, the purpose of a bishop's invocation of trustworthiness was twofold: to help settle a dispute and to reinforce episcopal authority. In the case of disputed church status the testimony of trustworthy men opened the way for a bishop's power to seep into the demarcation of the spatial relationships between churches.

Besides tithes, one of the most common bones of contention between churches was place of burial. Frustrations over this were typically expressed in terms of distance and journeys to the parish church. Conversely clashes over the allocation of tithes, as suggested above, or the costs of repairing the parish church more often focussed on the demarcation of the parish as a geographical unit. These distinctive spatial dynamics—journeys and boundaries—affected the interplay between trustworthy testimony and episcopal authority in subtly different ways. While neat boundaries and claims about inclusion tended to uphold the impression of a universal parish system, grievances expressed in terms of distance and journeys were apt to emphasize lived experience over administrative convenience. Although the bishop's aim was ostensibly to make an uncertain situation more stable, his association with trustworthy local witnesses was arguably tighter and more collaborative when demarcating bounded units of territory than it was when validating the lived experiences expressed in personal journeys.

On many occasions the reasons why a bishop commissioned an inquest by trustworthy men into the status of a church are not recorded.[77] At other times an unspecified complaint or incident seems to have sparked a general inquiry covering all contingencies. For example the 1324 inquest into the 'church or chapel' of Willey in Shropshire was asked to comment on whether the church was within the bounds or limits of any other, whether the sacraments were ministered there and on whose authority, who received the tithes and mortuaries (payments for burial), whether baptisms were carried out, whether there was a physical baptistery (and was this a sign of parochial status or a concession from a mother church?), who had cure of souls, was there an altar, and did the parishioners parade to another church on feast days as a sign of subjection?[78] When the bounds of a parish became an issue, money was generally the motive and settlement dispersion the cause. Often when a parish church was located in one of several settlements within the parish the inhabitants of other hamlets and farmsteads felt allegiance to a chapel closer to their homes. This frequently became an issue when the nave of the church needed repairing. Trustworthy men might be called on to determine whether an affective boundary qualified as a genuine parish boundary, although the result was usually a foregone conclusion in favour of the existing parish church.[79] In these cases trustworthy men territorialized episcopal authority by confirming the universality of the parish system.

Sometimes the inquest reported in great detail on the bounds of a parish, calling upon the memories of a large number of witnesses. At Witheridge in Devon in 1439, for example, the inhabitants of Templeton were claiming parochial status for a church in their village, which was about five miles away from Witheridge. They had lately had an Irish chaplain serving their church after an unknown cleric, claiming to be a bishop, had consecrated it. The first lay witness summoned was John Webber, a seventy-five-year-old freeman who had lived in Witheridge for sixty years. He commented on the patronage of Templeton and its status as a chapel, and on the burial of all parishioners—even villeins and infants—in Witheridge. Then, in order to show that Templeton was definitely within Witheridge parish, he recited his knowledge of the bounds: from the eastern end of the parish adjoining Tiverton they extended to the house of Henry atte Clyffe in the south, then to the hamlet of 'Erthrygge' in the southeast where it met Thelbridge parish; from there on to the vill of Drayford where the boundary was with East Worlington in the northwest, then to the house of Thomas Grendon where the northern part of Witheridge adjoined Rose Ash; from there on again to the houses of William Wylshethyng and Richard Hyaver where the parish bordered Rakenford and Creacombe in the northeast; finally he traced it on to the hamlet called Hylle and back to Templeton in the east. Webber had been called as a trustworthy man and he said that he had known all of this for as long as he could remember as well as having heard it from his elders in whom he had complete faith (*plenam fidem adhibuit*).[80] Webber's recitation seems well-practised, and his reference to houses and their named inhabitants served to make his evidence all the more credible.[81] But what was important for Bishop Lacy (besides trustworthiness) was the way that this account placed Witheridge within a clear geographical system of well-defined parishes bordering one another. Bureaucracy favours geographical clarity. Like the boundary itself, the testimony of elders was presented as if it were a continuous fact, immutable and certain.

Even so, the witness and the bishop were aware that other claims were being made about the truth of Templeton's status, and at some level they may also have been conscious that customs, memory, and even matter were liable to shift over time. After Webber had spoken John Palfreyman appeared and offered a different view of things. Palfreyman was seventy-two years old and had also lived in the parish most of his life. He began disarmingly enough by agreeing with everything that Webber had said about the bounds of the parish, but then he departed from the authorized script and went on a voyage of reminiscence into his own family history. He had heard from his parents, particularly his father, who had been a servant of the then rector, that in the first great pestilence of 1348 some of the rector's servants had taken bodies on a cart to be buried in Witheridge at night. The cart was so full that at 'Belbyford' one of the corpses fell off and a man was paid a penny to go and collect it the next day. Like the first witness, Palfreyman too claimed to have been told this 'by his elders in whom he had faith'. Then he told a further short story about journeys, ram-packed with meaning: the villeins of Templeton took their babies to be baptised in Witheridge, though the distance was such that if they feared for their child's life, they usually ran.[82]

Although Palfreyman did not demur from the view that Templeton was within the bounds of Witheridge, his description of these journeys, in which corpses and sickly unbaptised infants were put at risk on the way to the mother church, seems to have been designed to show that there was discontent in Templeton and that the boundaries that dominated John Webber's evidence were damaging to the lives of the parishioners. Every component of his story could have been calculated to cause disquiet. Burials at night were frowned upon, the sign of a disordered nature. At Birch St Thomas, Herefordshire, in 1397 for example, the burial of a body in the wrong cemetery was compounded by its being done furtively at night, transgressing both a spatial and a temporal boundary.[83] The fact that a corpse fell from the cart in Palfreyman's evidence, and lay on the ground all night, also spoke to the deep-seated late medieval fear of corporeal decay, which may have been greater than fear of death itself, as well as the hurt caused to the deceased's family and neighbours.[84] Complaints about the onset of putrefaction, because of the difficulty entailed in carrying the dead body from an outlying settlement to the parish church, were a common element in burial dispute testimonies. For instance at Haxby in Yorkshire trustworthy witnesses said in 1328 that if only they were allowed to bury corpses in their own churchyard and not have to carry them to Strensall church then 'scandalous and unseemly accidents' would not occur.[85] As if these evocations of decay were not enough Palfreyman had also conjured an image of distraught parents running with their ailing newborn babies to have a priest baptise them before it was too late.

All of the medieval stories told by parishioners about the need for local burial were configured around the narrative device of the bad journey: impeded by floods, mountains, and rivers, risking accidents to the living and the dead, it would have been better if we could have stayed at home. Many such tales were set in the upland parishes of Devon not so far from Witheridge where the landscape still serves today as a reminder that politically useful stories could nonetheless be true. In 1260 trustworthy men told of the 'excessive distance' travelled by the inhabitants of Babeny and Pizwell to attend their parish church at Lydford, twelve difficult miles away across Dartmoor. In 1426 trustworthy men inquired into the problems the people of coastal Buckland had travelling over the hills or up the Avon estuary to the parish church at Loddiswell.[86] Mountainous terrain elsewhere caused similar problems and fed comparable stories. Archbishop Zouche of York heard reports about the parishioners of Windermere struggling to carry their dead over the rocky Cumberland fells in stormy conditions during the plague year of 1348.[87] But low-lying areas could also be affected. In 1369 the parishioners of a chapel called St Edmund in the Marsh in Sutton, Lincolnshire, petitioned their bishop for burial rights with stories of arduous winter journeys across flooded land.[88]

The composition of stories about boundaries and journeys owed a great deal to witnesses' own memories of particular events and their evocations of a familiar and meaningful landscape, but they also framed their petitions in such a way as to conform with aspects of the institutional culture of canon law. As Bronach Kane has put it, 'the memories upon which parish boundaries depended were not the product of a hermetic vernacular culture . . . the influence of court officials not only shaped how these accounts were recorded, but structured the language used'.[89] Evidence about boundaries was especially formal, because it tended to reinforce territorial divisions that were 'legible' to government. But accounts of delayed burial also contained elements of canonical thought, such as references to 'scandal', defined as anything that hindered the proper function of the church. Nor were journeys absent from authorized forms of pious expression. If we think of the tower or spire of a church as 'essentially a landscape feature' it is easy to recalibrate our concept of Christian space to include routes, sightlines, and journeys as well as boundaries and territories.[90] Part of the evolution of the ecclesiastical landscape between the tenth and thirteenth centuries had been the localization of the 'ritual geography' of Christianity.[91] Parish churches were the focus for a liturgical life that included processions along the bounds of the parish and around the church, and they were the point of departure for processions to cathedrals and other major churches at Pentecost. Routes could take on 'specific meanings in relation to the places they connected' and the physical appearance of structures and landscapes encountered along the way. On pilgrimage routes in particular, wayside chapels and crosses in the middle of the road served to foster reflection upon the journey as much as on the destination.[92] There is a great deal of continuity between the way that real or imagined pilgrimage contributed to conceptualizations of a wider Christian landscape, and the way that walking and recalling burial routes fostered a sense of Christian ethics rooted in the local landscape. In many parish churches these dynamic and linear ways of thinking about Christian space combined in mural paintings of St Christopher, the patron saint of pilgrims, which faced the parishioner as she or he entered through the main south door. The church building was a bounded site, but the experience of it was shaped by journeys to and fro. On a larger scale the hilltop churches of St Giles, St James, and St Catherine surrounding Winchester, built sometime after 1100, were visible markers of routes away from the town, reminding the inhabitants that the city was the 'starting point of journeys through France to Spain, the Mediterranean, and the Holy Land'.[93]

Even so, personal journey stories did play a role in challenging the simplistic version of Christian belonging that vaunted parishes as the universal norm. What John Blair has written of the late Anglo-Saxon ecclesiastical landscape remained true in the later Middle Ages: the repertoire of 'routes, assembly-sites, powerful or dangerous places on the community's margins' was 'peasants' rather than a landlord's vocabulary of demarcation'.[94] The bad journey stories in burial petitions expressed just such a view of the parish from its margins, where the familiarity of chapels, shrines, and the rocks and tides encountered on the path were the touchstones of belonging. For Michel de Certeau stories about travel, especially walking, are 'makeshift things . . . composed with the world's debris'.[95] 'Debris' in our burial histories means events known to have happened to neighbours, in settings that could be vividly brought to mind.

Every demand for the separation of a chapel from a 'mother church' opened up a crack in the conceptual edifice of the universal parish system. It drew attention to the imperfect match between lived reality and the institutional church. Journeys and distance evoked a mobility and unpredictability that clashed with an institutional worldview in which stability and order were more highly prized, highlighting the political nature of trustworthy testimony: they were most often the servants of an institutional view of the world. Because journey narratives typically involved leaving 'home' and experiencing the dangers of 'away', they were vehicles for the imagination of alternative ways of being.[96] In the context of burial disputes this could be disruptive to the stability of parishes, but in other contexts, such as pilgrimage, it was something to be encouraged. And yet bishops knew they could not arrest the mutability of matter, nor control people's living use of space.

For this reason bishops deployed the rhetoric of trustworthiness as a means of bridging the gap between ideas about whole parishes and the assertiveness of their fragments. Church-chapel disputes were, from the bishop's point of view, settled either by creating a new parochial entity, or by enforcing the integrity of the existing unit; the latter option meant insisting on the inferior character of the local chapel (or fragment), limiting its sacramental functions, and instituting some sort of economic subordination. But the map was never completely tidied up because people continued to act in ways determined by landscape and custom even as they were shoehorned into a bureaucratic order. This meant the disgruntled laity had to be persuaded to accept the superior claims of the whole parish (and the totality of the parish system), while bishops had to accept that in real life the whole could not make the same affective claims upon people as were possible in the fragment. Trustworthy men stood in the middle of these pressures and incentives. How could the idea of wholeness and the reality of fragmentation be held together in such a way as to keep the peace and make the world governable? The practical answer lay in the ambidexterity of episcopal collaboration with trustworthy locals, but was also underpinned by some theological reasoning about unity and partition.

Because the bishop's arbitration could validate the route of a 'bad journey' as well as the official bounds of a parish, the parts and the whole were held together in a sort of dynamic equilibrium. Primarily this balancing act happened in the official documentation, and while it may also have shaped the popular imagination to some degree, new experiences, resistance, and the lapse of memory meant that fragments were always being chipped away from the episcopal version of reality. In this there was a significant echo of theological concerns about parts and wholes. The principle that material things could be divided and yet still whole was fundamental to doctrines such as the three persons of the Trinity (one and three at the same time), the real presence of Christ in the Eucharist (many thousands of wafers concurrently, all broken into small pieces, each containing the whole body of Christ) and the bodily integrity of saints in heaven (despite the fragmentation of their bones across the Christian world).[97] Maintaining orthodoxy on these tricky subjects required some management of the way people thought about the parts, which they might see, and the invisible whole: visible bread, unseen Christ; visible bones, unseen saint. A parishioner's focus on a particular piece of blessed bread lying in their own hands was thought liable to slide into superstition or heresy by emphasizing the division of holy matter without regard for the wholeness of the body of Christ. This is what churchmen worried about when laypeople stole Eucharistic wafers or venerated the divided matter rather than the divine whole that it contained. Similarly a parishioner's focus on his or her own particular journeys to the parish church, made under bad circumstances, stood to endorse a view of the parish as endlessly divisible and negotiable on the basis of personal need. The settlement of church-chapel disputes, based on the testimony of men called trustworthy by bishops, was intended to create the impression of an undivided community of faith, even while permitting worship and sacramental life in two different places. We saw in Chapter 1 how visible signs could be used as crutches for the leap of faith necessary for belief in God, and something similar was at work in the way that bishops wanted people to believe in the unity of the parish even though they experienced it as individuals.

{⚬⚬⚬⚬}

Just as 'animated' images of saints bridged the gap between the Christian believer and ineffable divinity, or as the wounds of Christ allowed Thomas to move beyond doubt and to believe in unseen divinity, so bishops mobilised trustworthiness to encourage people to believe in unseen rights, wholes, and authority.[98] The authority of bishops could be recalled and even seen (where it was accepted) via its presence in the material church, made up of rectory buildings, tithes of agricultural produce, and the routes and boundaries of parish life. And in the same way that *fides* (faith) was required to see God through a glass darkly, so *fides* (trust) was necessary in order to accept a bishop's settlement of a dispute about the material world. Of course to submit to a bishop's judgement was never the same as submitting one's will to God in an act of pious belief: it was always more politic and provisional than that. But in the rhetoric of episcopal government, and in the bishop's pragmatic alliance with 'trustworthy' parish elites, *fides* emanating from the institutions of the church could be made to seem secure and stable. Trustworthiness thus provided the conceptual bridge between the seen and the unseen, uncertainty and stability, expectation and reality, the contingent and the universal, fragmentation and unity. It was a provisional bridge, and one upon which a never-ending battle against forgetfulness and disagreement was fought, but the combined effect over time was the creation and perpetuation of a material church in which the bishop's right to judge matters was habitually assumed.

CHAPTER THIRTEEN

Subtle Judgements

THE PATTERN OF LOCAL ENGAGEMENT with episcopal power that was established in the thirteenth century persisted in its basic lineaments until the Reformation. But although the pattern was set, the volume of business increased, with more and more responsibility being heaped upon the so-called trustworthy men of the parishes. Already we have begun to see how the alliance with trustworthy men changed the church substantially, allowing it to act in a more interventionist manner in relation to local society than it ever had before, living up to some of the ambition expressed in the reforming councils and synods of the thirteenth century. In the previous two chapters I have shown how bishops became lynchpins in regional movements of money, and how their power entered into the physical matter of churches, rectories, and boundaries. I have emphasized the importance of trustworthiness (the testimony and the rhetoric) in allowing bishops to form relationships with parishes, patrons, and the clergy, and to communicate with other power-holders such as the crown and the papacy. The present chapter looks at another field of action where trustworthy testimony contributed to growth in bishops' governmental power, one defined by judgements that were more subtle and subjective than opinions on the cost of dilapidations or the value of benefices. It was a category that would prove even more transformational for the church, bringing a bishop's authority to bear upon less tangible but arguably more fundamental facets of experience concerned with subjectivity, feelings, and belief itself.

Trustworthy men were coming to be asked about the personal qualities of the clergy (their character, conduct, and learning), about sinfulness and criminal guilt, and about such secrets of the mind as mental illness and heresy. Precisely what this far-reaching endeavour contributed to the nature and development of the institutional church is, however, tricky to capture. Whereas in the last chapter we saw how a bishop's authority might come to inhere within those material features of the church that were subjected to trustworthy judgement, there is nothing so concrete about personality and sin onto which that authority might have latched. But that does not mean that bishops could find no purchase upon such things. Quite the contrary: through this category of trustworthy testimony, the bishop's authority became a constituent of nothing less than the ordinary act of making decisions about other people. What is more, because such subtle judgements were typically made about people known to the trustworthy men, episcopal power came to inhere within a plethora of local relationships. The bishop entered the parish through the word of trustworthy men.

As we have seen in Chapters 6 to 9 the late medieval parish was defined by its inequalities of gender, wealth, and status. Bishops relied upon these intersecting disparities to provide them with the men who could most easily fulfil the symbolic role of trustworthiness, providing 'firm and uncontested' judgements by virtue of their social position and influence. But in asking the trustworthy men to report not only upon other people's money but also upon other people themselves, bishops did not merely *rely upon* the relationships between trustworthy men and their fellow parishioners, they came to inhabit those relationships, to commodify them as a resource available to governance, and to change them.[1] We tend to think of the regulation of sin and the persecution of religious difference as the hallmarks of the late medieval church, for good or for ill, but historians have not hitherto appreciated how far these activities rested upon the alliance between bishops and parish elites. When trustworthy men collaborated with bishops they sometimes did so with compatible goals of moral reform in mind, while at other times acting upon self-interest. Whatever its motivation, had they not been willing to fulfil the symbolic role there would have been no institutional church capable of intervening in the ethical and mental universe.

Although bishops had long sought to involve themselves in the minutiae of local Christian life, this became much more of a realistic prospect in the thirteenth century when visitation developed significantly as a tool of episcopal government. Visitations were the primary vehicle for much of this deep intervention in the affairs of the mind and the heart. A great deal of the evidence in this chapter comes therefore from visitations as well as from inquests. By the last quarter of the thirteenth century visitations were commonly and regularly dealing with the quality of relationships between priests and their parishioners, with lay and clerical morality, and with matters of belief. This was the first period of rapid change in the way that bishops engaged with the local church, and it was followed by another in the early fifteenth century during which the detection of heresy came within the orbit of trustworthy men.[2]

Managing the Clergy from Above and Below

As we have seen in the previous two chapters the institution of clergy to benefices was one of the major responsibilities of late medieval bishops, and they used it as a means to build relationships with clerics and patrons. It was also an opportunity to insert their own power into the transactions and buildings that constituted rectories and vicarages. Here we can add another element of the system: the clergy themselves.

Canon law and episcopal rhetoric had long made it plain that bishops were responsible for guaranteeing the quality of the clergy they instituted.[3] But from the thirteenth century onwards, the episcopal interest in clerical reform was joined to that springing from the laity. Visitation records are crammed with complaints about priests who do not know their Latin, who cannot speak English (or Cornish or Welsh), who do not perform services or administer the sacraments appropriately, or who live immoral lives, all of which points to a great weight of lay expectation bearing down upon the parish clergy.[4] Long before Chaucer painted his portrait of an impossibly perfect parish priest, the Parson in the 'General Prologue' to the *Canterbury Tales*, the inevitable gap between expectation and reality was a driving force in the discourse of reform.[5] The clergy, according to numerous councils and synods, were to set a good example to their flock.[6] Stephen Langton's constitutions of Canterbury in 1213 suggested that 'the people of the lord', by which lay audiences would have understood themselves, were the victims of clerical sinfulness. Echoing this, Peter Quinel's constitutions for Exeter diocese in 1287 included the throwaway comment that the loss of church services through clerical negligence was 'an injury to God *and to man*'.[7] Quinel imagined the relationship between parish priests and their people as close, akin to that between a shepherd and his sheep: the sheep should be able to recognize their pastor's voice and he should live amongst them.[8] Naturally, such physical and social proximity in conjunction with high normative standards set the clergy up to fail, but the real driver of lay scrutiny of pastors came from the fact that theirs was an unequal relationship: the clergy were expected to live better lives than the people in their spiritual care, and this—rather unsurprisingly—encouraged the laity to adopt a watchful and critical attitude towards them.[9]

At the point of ordination bishops were expected to make rudimentary checks of clerical Latin, doctrinal knowledge, and past behaviour.[10] In addition, bishops frequently made further inquiries when a priest was the candidate for a particular benefice. This was to reassure the patron, the parishioners, and (between 1265 and 1351) the pope that episcopal responsibilities were being fulfilled.[11] At this point the assistance of local trustworthy men was frequently sought as a mechanism for dredging the reservoir of local knowledge about the character and reputation of candidates for benefices, as well as of schoolmasters, scholars, and diocesan officials.[12] Very occasionally such inquiries might be extended to lay 'farmers' of benefices as well.[13]

Whether a cleric was believed to be of good character was a matter of judgement and opinion, partly grounded in his actual behaviour, but also in a mass of social considerations. We do not know what trustworthy men truly thought when faced with requests for information, but we can reconstruct something of the social logic implied by the situation, to imagine a place for such questions as the following: Can I give my honest opinion of this man? Is the best course of action to report a favourable impression and avoid ill-feeling? How will our future relationship be affected? How will his patron react? In the surviving documents the closest we come to any of this is the recitation of the social basis for the witness's knowledge. Typical is John Agate, a sixty-year-old trustworthy man from Eaton Bray, Bedfordshire, who testified in 1307 that he had known the priest Elias Wiseard since birth and his parents since the time of their marriage. His personal knowledge of Elias's good character and honest living had been augmented by talking to his neighbours and other people living nearby.[14] All of this suggests that he took a degree of care to appear informed and astute. Occasionally the solemn mask of bureaucracy slips a little, as in the 1312 investigation of John Ockham who was presented as a suitable candidate for the benefice of Broadchalke in Wiltshire. Trustworthy men had reported him to be honest and of good behaviour 'so far as human weakness permits'.[15] Here we seem to be given a glimpse of the subtle ethical and social considerations involved—even if they remain ambiguous—but for the most part inquests into clerical character were routine, and only thoroughly positive answers were recorded.[16]

The social delicacy of inquests into clergy was usually effaced by a bureaucratic desire for clarity, something amply illustrated by inquiries into legitimate birth.[17] In fact questions of legitimacy depended upon local knowledge of the timing and propriety of the marriage between the cleric's parents, and this made them subject to similar social considerations as assessments of character. Trustworthy men had to think about how the individual in question would be affected by their answers, and how credible their report would appear to others who knew him. There were complex webs of subjective perception and social calculation at work here. What is more, when granting dispensations for self-confessed illegitimacy bishops were explicitly concerned with character, asking whether the priest in question was 'an imitator of his parents' vice'.[18] In such cases the trustworthy men were being asked to compare and contrast the sexual behaviour of fathers and sons, and to assess whether any sin was too egregious to ignore. Other apparently simple cases could also have hidden depths. For example bodily flaws were not permitted in the clergy, who were meant to mirror the perfection of Christ, but many men fell short. William Lorimer from Bishop Auckland was challenged about his physical deformity in 1313: he had been born with only one ear. An inquest established that he had not lost the ear as a punishment and the bishop of Durham had to decide whether to issue a dispensation allowing him to take holy orders and acquire a benefice.[19] In this case even the attestation of physical appearance involved an assessment of sinfulness.

Visitations were a forum in which parish representatives—in the guise of trustworthy men—could regularly make judgements about whether their clergy were living up to the standards established in synodal constitutions.[20] For example, Quinel's Exeter constitutions asked laymen

> to diligently inquire whether the parish priests fulfil their office as they are bound to do regarding the divine offices both during the day and the night, as set out in the general council and above [in the other constitutions]. . . . They are to inquire into the excesses of every cleric whose deeds, whether good or bad, may easily be copied by their subjects as an example.[21]

Many bishops—though not necessarily all—itemized the issues on which they expected lay parish representatives to report in series of visitation articles. Two influential texts give a flavour of what was expected. In 1253 Archbishop Boniface of Canterbury solicited information on the illiteracy of clergy, their sexual continence and marital status, whether they visited nuns or kept suspect persons in their houses, their morality in general, whether they carried arms, if they permitted their sons to inherit church property, if they accepted payments for penance or other sacraments, if they used vinegar instead of wine for the Eucharist, if they were resident in the parish, if they were studying or teaching secular law, if they performed services correctly, whether they attempted to serve more than one parish by celebrating twice in a day in different churches, whether vicars behaved as if rectors (collecting tithes due to the rector), whether any illegitimate priests were celebrating without dispensation, and finally whether they had been ordained and where (Ireland was thought a suspicious place of origin at the time).[22] In a much more summary fashion Archbishop Thoresby of York's visitation articles issued between 1353 and 1373 asked for reports on the residence of the parish clergy and on whether there were any sorcerers among them, about their deeds in taverns, any drunkenness, lechery, other bad behaviour or dishonesty, as well as their concubines, their goods and chattels, and whether they kept any women suspected of prostitution.[23] Most of these charges could be said to relate to 'factual' or visible things, but they also gave trustworthy men considerable latitude to determine how far their priests lived up to the clerical ethic. Whether the clergy were good was fundamentally a judgement about intangible intentions, attitude, respectability, and living up to expectations. Such instructions, and many others written in a similar vein throughout the later Middle Ages, therefore required of trustworthy men a high degree of independent moral and 'political' judgement. Their social position offered some much needed protection against the hostility they might encounter from the clergy.

The parish representatives were therefore more than just ciphers for episcopal policy. They applied their own standards and made selective choices about which clerics required correction and which offences were pardonable in their eyes. It is fair to assume that they reported only things that were of concern to them (and for the social politics of this see Chapter 7). They had no incentive to do otherwise. One might object that the parishioners' interest in clerical reform is often indistinguishable from the visitor's. This is certainly true in many cases. For example, during the visitation of Wingham in Kent in 1294 twenty-four reports (out of a total of seventy-three) record the parishioners' expectation that their clergy be resident, celibate, competent in saying divine service, and dutiful in giving alms: all in line with episcopal expectation. However, there was nothing in synodal constitutions about the clergy offering credit to laymen, but the representatives of Nonington, a church within Wingham's large parish, reported this nonetheless.[24] Equally, the protests made during the same visitation that the rector of Womenswold 'does not know that which a rector *ought* to know' or that the chaplain of Nonington 'has *too much* land and busies himself in secular affairs' are highly subjective and speak of a frustration arising from the long accumulation of expectation and grievance in a specifically local context.[25] These sorts of subjective judgements are repeated in all late medieval visitation records: a priest who 'does no good in the parish', a chaplain who is 'useless and inexperienced', and so on.[26]

Visitation reporting of clerical faults was integral to the episcopal management of benefices and pastoral care from the mid-thirteenth century to the Reformation and beyond. Clerics knew that they were being monitored from above and from below, and this was the most effective means available for regulating their behaviour. In some extraordinary cases, especially from the second half of the fourteenth century onwards, powerful groups of parishioners might force a legal 'performance bond' upon their parish priest, actionable in the royal courts if he breached its terms.[27] But this was far less common than the perennial dialogue, negotiation, and modification of expectation occasioned by regular visitation. Many cases were followed up from visitation in the church courts, and this was often signalled in bishops' registers by citing trustworthy men as the source of information about a nonresident or negligent priest.[28] At the point where a case was extracted from the usual round of visitations and presented to a diocesan court, trustworthy men might be called upon to provide further information, enabling the bishop to exert his personal judicial power. This seems to have happened most often where there was some doubt as to the facts of the case: Which rectors have failed to proceed to 'major orders' of priesthood within a year of their appointment? Have services in a chantry chapel been reduced, or was it always so? Has a particular friar *really* been soliciting money in return for confession? Are the reports of a vicar attempting to sell his office true? Has that vicar abandoned his parish, or is he still there?[29]

For all that it responded to lay demands from below, visitation reporting was an activity called into being by episcopal mandate. If a case of clerical discipline reached the bishop directly and unsolicited from a group of parishioners, in the form of litigation or a petition, they were unlikely to be described as 'trustworthy'.[30] Trustworthiness was the bishop's *imprimatur* upon lay participation in clerical regulation, and its invocation had the effect of inserting the bishop's authority into parish society. Specifically it became a component of the judgement exercised by trustworthy men, and of the relationships between them and the parish clergy. Their relationships became, in turn, commodities or social facts to be exploited in the service of episcopal governance.

Crime and Sin

Historians of confession have described how the clergy were taught to pay attention to the conscience and intentions of lay Christians. Pastoral and spiritual discernment was supposedly a clerical task.[31] But this perspective omits from historical attention the degree to which lay reports to inquests and visitations demanded comparable perspicacity in determining interior states. Every report from trustworthy men to do with behaviour, sin, and guilt relied upon multiple individual perceptions of other people, balanced against calculations about how local relationships would be affected by saying one thing rather than another. The business of confession—individual intention—was not at all confined to the 'penitential forum' separate from the public forum of the church courts. Canonists went to great efforts to distinguish—in theoretical terms at least—the realm of individual confession from that of public reports of crime, and some sins heard in confession, such as coveting another man's wife, would never come before a court. But if coveting was acted upon and became adultery, then judges as well as confessors were capable of dealing with it, opening the door to lay participation.[32] I would argue that in being more frequent and more socially implicated than confession, lay discernment was more important than confession in shaping the culture of interiority that has been seen as a keynote of European civilization since the twelfth century.

Many inquests of trustworthy men into crime were connected with matters of ambiguous or contested authority. Jurisdiction over wrong behaviour—its definition, identification, judging, and correction—was disputed between church and secular institutions. The second half of the thirteenth century saw some major milestones in the accommodation between royal and ecclesiastical justice in England. The conflict that had raged since at least the days of Henry II and Thomas Becket was settled to a great extent by the 1286 writ *Circumspecte agatis* (which we might translate as 'Tread carefully!') advising royal justices on which areas of criminal jurisdiction were rightly within the remit of church judges.[33] This greatly enhanced the power of ecclesiastical tribunals, which in some places now looked more and more like established law courts—with officials, discrete bodies of documentation, rules of practice, and regular sittings—and increased demand for lay witnesses and panels of trustworthy men providing information on request.[34]

One of the most important fields of action for the church courts—and the one that had caused the most friction with royal justice—was the criminal behaviour of the clergy, over which the church claimed exclusive jurisdiction. Trustworthy men were especially important in helping bishops to police the actions of the royal courts and to dissipate unease over ecclesiastical claims. When clerical suspects claimed 'benefit of clergy'—the right to be tried in a church court—there was often a great deal of bitterness. People thought that clerics were getting off lightly and the secular courts were jealous of the lost business. If the crown and the public at large had been regularly presented with an impression of gross injustice and scandalous acquittals, then benefit of clergy may not have survived as long as it did. In this context it is very interesting that so many of the records made about serious clerical crimes describe the involvement of trustworthy men.[35] They performed a politically important function.[36] By invoking trustworthiness bishops sent a message about the rigour and respectability of their justice. Panels of locals approximated secular presentment and trial juries, and their testimony was frequently recorded in terms that echoed the procedures and categories of the common law.[37] In these circumstances references to trustworthy men should be seen as an attempt to secure the claims of the church's criminal jurisdiction in toto as well as to resolve individual cases.

The particular advantage of trustworthy men was that they permitted a judge—as mentioned in Chapter 4—to vicariously 'descend to the place' where an event had happened, a contribution that was trumpeted in episcopal rhetoric. In 1287, for example, the dean of Ryedale was told to summon trustworthy men from places where a cleric suspected of theft was well known, and in 1302 neighbouring clerics and trustworthy laymen 'who best knew the truth of the matter' commented on the charge of murder against the rector of Clayworth in Yorkshire.[38] The idea of soliciting testimony from men who lived side by side with the accused was common to all medieval jurisdictions, and the distinctive reference to witnesses 'best able' to report the truth (or some similar form of words) was shared between canon law and English common law.[39] Bishops were careful to represent their justice as equal to that provided by the crown. A striking example of this occurs in the 1436 case of John Lage, a chaplain of Staverton in Devon who had killed a man and claimed benefit of clergy. The witnesses—four 'trustworthy parishioners' of Staverton with the 'fullest knowledge' of the events—told a detailed and vivid story. They said that on the feast of the nativity of the virgin John Lage had been drinking with John and Isabella Gayne in the house of Matthew Fremyngton in the parish of Dartington. Upon leaving for home and before they came to the narrow and high bridge over the river Dart, John Gayne began to abuse Lage for some unknown reason, and then midway across the bridge he struck him two or three times with a sword, whereupon Lage, fearing for his life, lethally stabbed John Gayne with his 'baselard' or dagger. They had heard all this confessed by John and Isabella Gayne themselves, after the attack and before John died of his wounds. They also said that John Gayne was a very tall, strong man and that he had insulted Lage greatly before attacking him. They also believed that if Lage had not defended himself then John Gayne would have thrown him into the Dart and killed him; Lage could not have fled to save his life because Isabella Gayne had held him back by his clothes, which she had admitted to other witnesses. All 'good and serious persons' in the neighbourhood agreed that Lage could not have saved his own life without taking that of Gayne. What they did not know firsthand they had heard from 'other trustworthy persons who had given their faith (*fidem adhibent*)' about these things. Lage himself had said that on the bridge he felt such fear as would sway a constant man.[40]

Whatever the veracity of their evidence, and whether or not the witnesses had described things in quite this way, the manner in which it was summarized by Bishop Lacy emphasized the congruity between canonical and common-law concepts. The trustworthy parishioners were the equivalent of a jury of presentment, local men who knew and had spoken to the protagonists, who had investigated the case themselves, and consulted other reputable witnesses. The 'good and serious persons' and trustworthy men of church rhetoric were akin to the 'lawful and upright men' who had already presented Lage's case before royal justices (we do not know the outcome of that first trial). Furthermore the detailed description of how Lage could not have done other than stab Gayne with his dagger was made to conform not only to the canonical concept of the 'constant man' (who did not anger easily and who would act only if he had no other option), but also to the common-law doctrine of pardonable homicide, defined by the impossibility of escape and reasonable fear for one's life.[41] In presenting his investigation in this way, Bishop Lacy was preparing the way for a proclamation of Lage's innocence, at pains to demonstrate that his justice was as good as the king's.[42]

Besides benefit of clergy, the other major intersection between canonical and secular criminal justice occurred when the perpetrators of crime fled to churches and claimed sanctuary. All churches (and some larger areas such as those surrounding Westminster Abbey or Ripon Minster) were sanctuaries at this time, where royal justices had no authority and from where criminals could not be extracted without offending the sanctity of the place.[43] At times bishops wanted to be seen to cooperate with secular justice, commissioning trustworthy men to investigate whether tales of flight to churches were in fact true.[44] But more often, after criminals had been forcibly extracted from sanctuary, they found themselves having to balance the fury of their own insistence upon church rights with the facts of a secular—often royal—fait accompli.[45] In such cases the use of trustworthy laymen rather than clerical officers in the pay of the bishop was designed to reassure the crown that ecclesiastical liberties were not being taken.

Trustworthy men were also deployed in handling cases of bloodshed in churches and churchyards, a fascinating example of which we encountered at the opening of Chapter 6. Formally such things were prosecuted as the 'pollution' of holy ground in which the facts of deconsecration (by the spilling of blood) had to be established before reconsecration could take place. But the frequency with which trustworthy rhetoric accompanied these carefully recorded cases suggests that they were also sensitive jurisdictional flashpoints. It is possible that many incidents reported as pollution were proxies for the prosecution of interpersonal violence, which was not normally an ecclesiastical competence. Bishops often asked trustworthy men to investigate what had happened, who had been involved, whether—and how much—blood had been spilled.[46] Pollution cases may have been reported to bishops because people were genuinely shocked by the sight of blood on holy ground, but it is also possible that there was disagreement about which jurisdiction—if any—was the appropriate one to deal with a case of personal violence. As with the navigation of church-crown relations surrounding benefit of clergy, bloodshed in churches required stories to be told in a particular way, though here the emphasis was on the factors that excluded secular involvement, namely the fact that it had happened inside rather than outside the churchyard. Such detail, combined with the designation of the witnesses as trustworthy, was intended to validate episcopal dominion over the clergy and sacred space, and in so doing the bishop caused his authority to enter into the determinations of the trustworthy men as well as the physical spaces concerned, making them the living guardians of the uneasy boundaries between secular and spiritual jurisdictions.

Behind those boundaries bishops, and other churchmen with judicial authority, were busy marking out an arena of uncontested activity. In visitations they pursued social regulation pertaining to spiritual and ethical matters, and trustworthy men were—between about 1270 and the Reformation—the supreme arbiters of lay morality, behaviour, and interaction. As with the management of clerical behaviour, a great deal of lay social regulation also took place in the church courts, some of whose business arose from visitation. Many visitation books, such as that for Hereford in 1397, make frequent mention of serious or delicate cases sent to the bishop's personal 'consistory' court.[47] Other cases mentioned in bishops' registers or court 'act books' may well have begun in visitation even though this is not mentioned in the record.[48] This business included sexual morality, since marriage was a sacrament and sex the vehicle by which original sin was transmitted across the generations, in addition to matters of reputation and good faith, such as various forms of verbal interaction amongst parishioners like gossip and insult.[49] Each of these major

spheres of activity required subtle judgements of trustworthy men: they had
to take a view on the likely guilt of an individual, often where the original act
or acts had taken place in private or been witnessed by only a few people, or
indirectly; estimations of degrees of ethical failure or local scandal would have
coloured their judgements; they also had to weigh up the personal and social
desirability of dealing with sexual and reputational issues in a quasi-judicial
setting.

In our sources, as medieval historians perennially lament, we can see precious little of the psychological difficulties such considerations would have
engendered, but we can sometimes nevertheless pierce the canonical jargon
of even the most terse visitation report to find evidence of how important the
subtle judgements about intention and subjectivity were. A very common element in lay reporting of conjugal and domestic problems is reference to a lack
of 'marital affection'. This was a staple of the canon law on lawful separation,
and was sometimes identified as the crucial difference between a marriage
and an illicit long-term domestic partnership.[50] Although the phrase was
formulaic, perhaps added on the suggestion of an advocate or the scribe, its
invocation had to command credibility amongst family and neighbours. The
proof that Roger Arnald of Much Marcle in Herefordshire was failing to treat
his wife with marital affection, in 1397, was the fact that he had denied her
food and clothing. In keeping with the operation of *fides*, the trustworthy men
had extrapolated from visible evidence to arrive at conclusions about unseen
motivation. It is such occasional departures from the usual formulas that indicate the exercise of lay judgement about interior states: in 1291 for example
a husband and wife in Kent were said to 'stand in fear of one another'.[51] Defamation was similarly defined in canon law with adjectives that made their
way into reports of real cases, where they were sometimes modified to reflect
the discernment of the parish representatives. For words to constitute defamation they had to have been uttered maliciously.[52] This in itself is evidence that
trustworthy men had to impute states of mind that were believable, but sometimes their words are still more revealing. In 1512, for example, a woman in
Dover was said to have been maliciously defamed by a fellow parishioner, 'the
whiche causithe the good woman to take great thought and hevynes'.[53] While
malice was an aspect of intention that came from canon law, an assessment
of how an insult had affected the victim's state of mind was not. We also find
attributions of malicious intent in reports of false indictments.[54]

Snatches of evidence such as these suggest that the reports of trustworthy
men included an element of judgement about the psychology of sin as well as
its commission. In considering what things were 'in need of correction' they
thought about intention as well as the act itself. They thought like confessors.
Certainly they should have had plenty of experience in seeing how confessors
approached similar questions. Reporting faults in another person's sexual and
social behaviour demanded that the trustworthy men knew the individual in

question, their reputation, family, social contacts, and activities; and it presumed that certain people had the right to criticize and correct others' behaviour. Episcopal scrutiny of Christian morality therefore depended upon a vast number of existing relationships and established roles which, as we have seen in Chapters 6 and 7, were predicated upon and contributed to the inequalities of late medieval life. Bishops commodified these relationships and roles, enhancing their own authority by attributing trustworthiness to one section of parish society, giving those men the right to make subtle judgements about acts and intentions. Episcopal authority came to inhere within that dubious social capital.

Character and Personal Information

The concern with reputation and character that is often implicit or veiled in formulaic visitation reports was explicit in the judicial ritual of compurgation. Compurgation was an old practice of 'oath helping', once common to many legal systems but by the thirteenth century significant only in the church. If a person was suspected of a crime but there was no-one willing to bring a formal accusation, or there was insufficient evidence for a judge to proceed ex officio, then the suspect could be given the opportunity to swear a public oath asserting his or her innocence, supported by the oaths of a number of the suspect's neighbours. The oath helpers were usually known as compurgators.[55] They would be asked to swear to the innocence of the suspect and to his or her good reputation and character. For the most part bishops and other judges did not comment on the qualities desirable in compurgators on a particular occasion, beyond tacitly accepting the canonical rule that they should not themselves be suspected of any crime, and perhaps stipulating that they should be of the same 'order' (clergy or laity, men or women) as the suspect: women were frequently told to find female compurgators, clerics to find other clerics, and so on (although this was not always adhered to).[56] However, in a large minority of cases, mandates permitting purgation specifically called for men who were 'trustworthy', alerting us to the likelihood that bishops were trying to defray potential criticism of this procedure.

One of the most notable things about the compurgation of clerics was the frequency with which the involvement of laymen was explicitly required, against the canonical norm. 'Trustworthy and unsuspected men' were called to assist in the purgation of suspected clerical thieves and killers in particular.[57] For example the 1408 purgation of Geoffrey Horsman, previously tried by royal justices for burglary at Masham in Yorkshire, was preceded by an inquest of 'trustworthy clerics and laymen' who came from the place where the crime had been committed and the place where Horsman had lived longest. They were examined individually about the truth of the allegation and about Horsman's character and reputation.[58] A similar pattern occurred in many other cases.[59]

Whoever was involved the purgation of a cleric rested upon the relationship that the compurgators had with the suspect and with the people of the locale. When, for example, in 1343, the bishop of Bath and Wells ordered an inquest into the alleged theft of a horse by a cleric from Bradford-on-Tone, the questions asked of the trustworthy jurors demanded an intimate knowledge of his social network. Was he defamed of stealing the horse, did any *fama* come from many people or just a few, was he indicted out of hatred? Finally they were asked to advise the bishop on whether purgation would be suitable.[60]

The compurgation of laypersons by trustworthy men arose from a wider range of circumstances, but all ones that required subtle judgements about relationships and reputation. Compurgators were to be 'good, law-worthy, and trustworthy neighbours who have knowledge of [the suspect's] status and behaviour'.[61] Alleged offences ranged from minor faults, such as attempting to wriggle out of a promise,[62] to major crimes, such as the treason alleged against Robert Fuller, a burgess of Plymouth, in 1450. Fuller was rumoured to have smuggled weapons to the French in wine casks, but he purged himself with 'a great multitude of his trustworthy neighbours' and his defamers were excommunicated.[63] The majority of purgations were, however, for sexual offences. Suspects were often presented with a choice of attempting to find compurgators or admitting the offence and undergoing some sort of penance. If purgation failed then penance, which usually meant being whipped in public, was inevitable.[64] Around 1469 Joan Clerk of Wisbech in Cambridgeshire was accused of defamation and ordered to purge herself with eight trustworthy women of her neighbourhood, but, perhaps in an admission of guilt, she instead opted to undergo public penance in the parish church.[65] The ease with which purgation could fail and tip into a humiliating and perhaps painful penance meant that an awful lot rested on the judgements of the compurgators. This much is acknowledged in a 1432 case arising from the alleged theft of a salmon from the vicar of Gainford in County Durham, that relied not only on the oaths of twelve 'upright' men, but also on the validation of their judgement by a second group of 'trustworthy men' appointed by the bishop of Durham to receive the purgation.[66] Such was the delicacy of involving the laity in assessments of guilt and innocence, such the potential for serious social and institutional consequences that the presiding judge often proceeded with great care and some trepidation. To act as a compurgator was to inhabit a role designated by judicial authority. And the authority of the judge or bishop made an instrumental commodity out of the relationships and judgements of these men, one that boosted episcopal authority and helped to delineate the criminal jurisdiction of the church.

Assessments of character and personal circumstances by trustworthy men took place in other situations too. For instance, before accepting the wish of a pious layperson to submit themselves to the testing spiritual life of an anchorite or hermit, bishops sometimes consulted trustworthy men as to their lifestyle, character, and suitability. Something similar could be ordered before permitting a lay pilgrim to collect the alms that would fund his onwards journey.[67] But perhaps the commonest inquests into the intimate details of life were those concerning the sexual past and family trees of people trapped by the rules surrounding marriage and inheritance. This had, after all, been the context in which the Fourth Lateran Council of 1215 had precociously recommended the use of *fidedigni*, as we saw in Chapter 4. The difficulties that people experienced in these matters came from two directions: the complexity of the rules and the willingness of other people to use them maliciously. These were murky waters in which bishops feared to tread without the guiding hand of local testimony. Such great malevolence seems to lurk behind the cases we read about that no wonder an injection of trust was deemed necessary! For example the intricate rules of consanguinity were exploited to the full in 1378 when someone objected to the future marriage of John Page and Margery Chapman of Shelford in Cambridgeshire.[68] It was claimed that in the past John had had sex with a woman who had since married a relative of Margery's. The local rector and three trustworthy witnesses, two of whom were women, investigated, but sadly we do not know either the outcome of their deliberations into this tenuous connection or what motivated the objection. Most often it seems that inheritance lay behind such disputes. Trustworthy men were often called to adjudicate in cases of uncertain parentage, where the rights of an heir were in question.[69] They were also asked to confirm local inheritance customs from time to time.[70]

Being rooted in the places where people were known and events remembered, and enjoying a social position that meant they could speak without too much fear of contradiction, was what enabled trustworthy men to provide 'firm and uncontested' judgements on such sensitive matters. The case of Geoffrey Kindersley and Amice L'Enveise, both members of the Bedfordshire gentry, in 1384, illustrates this very well. Geoffrey asked the bishop of Lincoln to launch an inquest into their marriage, which had taken place thirty-three years earlier. In 1383 the couple were trying to sell part of Amice's family lands but the manor in question appeared to have already been sold by someone called James de Beele, a merchant from Liège, who claimed that he, and not Geoffrey, was Amice's husband. There is no explanation of how this had come about, but the inquest launched by the bishop, calling upon the testimony of trustworthy men, contradicted Beele's claims with recollections of the marriage ceremony itself, the party afterwards, the gifts, a honeymoon or temporary home at a friend's house, and the lands and tenants they had acquired during their long marriage.[71] Above all of these things however, what the trustworthy men were judging was the character and honesty of Geoffrey and Amice evinced by the stability of their life together and the richness of local knowledge about them. Had there been any hint of success for Beele's claim we might expect him to have taken a leaf out of the handbook on vexatious marriage litigation and raised the spectre of consanguinity. The frequency with which trustworthy men were called upon to say whether a couple had known they were distantly related when they married suggests that tracing back family trees was a popular way to challenge the legitimacy of a marriage and its offspring.[72] Often it was not hard to find some shared ancestor within four generations, but in order to counter such impediments and secure a papal dispensation, couples, witnesses, and trustworthy men conspired to craft narratives of ignorance followed by surprise at some newfound piece of genealogical knowledge, always rounded off by humble supplication and a paean to the sanctity of marriage and the scandal of leaving children as bastards. The possible lack of sincerity in such cases was discussed in Chapter 5. Sincerity aside though, probing personal histories and navigating challenges to the integrity of families and identity was sensitive work. In addition to post hoc petitions for dispensation, trustworthy men adjudicated preemptive petitions relating to consanguinity, and appeals for separation or annulment on grounds of bigamy, impotence, and desertion.[73]

Secrets of the Mind

Lying behind the trustworthy testimony described in this chapter is the social character of all human judgements about other people. These judgements are not made by an isolated individual facing a generalized 'other'. Rather they are made by people whose own identity is informed by their relationships with others, and they are made about specific people similarly influenced by social interaction: dealings that may include connections to the very person making the judgement.[74] Navigating thorny relationships, being alive to the sensitivities at play in any given social situation, and handling information relating to fundamental aspects of existence or identity were all demanded by the various tasks of discernment that we have encountered here. But perhaps the most subtle judgements required of trustworthy men were those concerning things hidden in the mind of another.

Ascertaining how another person feels or thinks is always a subjective judgement. In the Middle Ages this was explicitly imagined to be the special province of faith and trust, as a manner of knowing not wholly reliant on sensory perception. In Chapter 1 we saw how having faith in God could be seen as analogous to the essential element in theory of mind: belief in the reality of another person's interior life. Both God and another's mind were said by Augustine of Hippo to be apprehensible only via a leap of faith—or a trusting acceptance—towards something that was unseen but whose effect on the world, and the subjects themselves, might be perceptible.[75] Augustine's failure to limit this cognitive ability to people of a certain status or level of education suggests that he thought it inherent to the human condition. And although they did not explain their rationale, in relying upon the judgement of trustworthy men to ascertain mental states and wrong belief, late medieval bishops implicitly aligned themselves with the view that everyone has the capacity to perceive things in the mind of another. They cannot, moreover, have been unaware of the innumerable mutual assessments of good faith that laypeople made of one another, in making marriages and doing deals, that I discussed in Chapters 2 and 3.

Nevertheless it is in many ways remarkable that the unequal expectations towards clergy and laity, learned and unlearned, discussed in Chapter 1, regarding faith in God should be so utterly overridden in episcopal information gathering. Bishops asked trustworthy men to report to them on such intangibles as intention, contrition, mental stability and strength, incorrect belief, and—in time—heresy. Almost every relevant recorded enactment is, however, untheorized. These were administrative acts just like thousands of others relating to money or the material world that I mentioned in the previous two chapters. We may have to work a little harder to appreciate exactly what was being asked of the local witnesses in the most subtle cases, but the implications of their actions were so significant that it is worth doing so.

Hearing confession, issuing penance, and granting absolution were sacramental acts that only a priest could perform. From the twelfth century onwards this had entailed a priest looking for and judging whether his subject was repentant or not. This remained so despite the noticeable shift towards lay participation in the rituals of the deathbed from the late fourteenth century onwards.[76] However, there are a few examples of lay trustworthy men being asked to read the signs of contrition that were a necessary condition of absolution. One such is the case of man called John Halton, who had died in prison in 1373. Halton had been arrested as an excommunicate having failed to appear before an ecclesiastical judge. Because his case never came to court and no priest was on hand to hear his confession, the bishop of Lincoln was left with a problem relating to burial. Excommunicated people who had not received absolution could not be given a Christian burial, and so the bishop needed to know whether Halton had been repentant. In this situation he asked trustworthy men to report whether there had been any signs of contrition in Halton before his death.[77] Presumably this meant asking whoever had been guarding him, rather than a group of parish representatives, but the unusual circumstances point to the fact that contrition was usually determined only by confessors. This exception, however, shows us that Augustine's belief in a universal human capacity to perceive the unseen interior world of other people was accepted in principle at least by churchmen. The main areas in which it was put to work were assessments of mental well-being and of right and wrong belief.

People who made wills were guided in their forms of expression by the notaries or priests who helped them put their wishes into writing. One of the commonest rhetorical elements of the preamble to a will was an assertion that the testator was 'of sound mind' and legally able to dispose of their property.[78] If it was not apparent to the witnesses that the testator was *compos mentis*, doubt might arise about the validity of the will. It is likely that this is what lay behind a written certificate stating that one of the archbishop of York's tenants had received the sacraments and was of sound mind when he died in 1304. The report came from the people who had been caring for him at the time 'and other trustworthy persons who visited his deathbed'.[79] While on that occasion it seems there was a will, many cases of intestacy also came before the church courts. Heirs anxious about their inheritances were often quick to make themselves known. A 1303 petition to the archbishop of York from the son of Margery Irnham of Tadcaster explained that according to trustworthy persons his mother had not been able to make a will because she was not of sound mind. This judgement then became the cue for the local dean to take Margery's estate into his own hands for safekeeping while the case was cleared up.[80]

The comprehensive claim to be 'of sound mind' is a piece of legal boilerplate bolted onto most wills, but if it was questioned then the men charged with making a definitive judgement would have had to be very careful of how they proceeded. There were some powerful interested parties to many cases, especially where substantial properties were at issue. In common-law tribunals, mental incapacity could be used to disqualify heirs in favour of other family members or of the crown, which had extensive rights of wardship. Coroners' juries were also sometimes called upon to determine whether a suicide was the result of mental instability. As in cases of homicide this could be an extenuating circumstance, and jury assessments of the subject's mental state are thought to have been entwined with considerations of how their culpability—or a denial of it—would impact upon their dependents.[81] There seems to have been some sensitivity towards the grief and shame of the surviving family, and the ameliorative potential of enabling a Christian burial. The subtlety of these judgements is suggested by the fact that juries employed a wide range of explanations for mental instability, including demonic possession, the mentally debilitating effects of physical illness, and other terms more descriptive of how the subject behaved: in a fury or frenzy, anguished, demented, and so on. They were also careful to distinguish between the person living with what we would call a cognitive disability (*idiotus*) and the person suffering a temporary loss of reason (*furiosus*), and to separate rage from mere anger, which was compatible with culpability.[82] Ecclesiastical juries of trustworthy men were likely to overlap with common-law juries in their personnel, and there was a shared legal culture between them relating to mental well-being.

As we have seen in Chapter 11 trustworthy men frequently reported on the incapacity of their clergy and then often supervised the transfer of the fiscal benefice to a curate or coadjutor. Although blindness was the most commonly adduced cause, mental ill-health was also sometimes mentioned. For example in 1440 the bishop of Exeter launched an inquiry into the physical *and mental* incapacity of the rector of Looe. Scandal and neglect were given as the reasons for the bishop's action, both of which terms relate the rector's health to a loss of divine service and the potential for a diminution in the faith. Employing *faith*-worthy men to investigate was his attempt to repair the community of faith for which he was responsible.[83] More secular concerns were likely at play in questions about mental instability in benefit of clergy cases, where any exculpation of the alleged criminal was a touchy subject. This may have been a factor in the 1312 case of Oliver Badley, suspected of murder in Wetherby (Yorkshire): trustworthy men inquired into his reputation and the story that he had been suffering from 'morbo frenesis' at the time of the offence.[84]

Spiritual considerations were to the fore when bishops asked trustworthy men to give their assessments of the state of mind in which pious laywomen decided to become anchorites. The Spartan material conditions and psychological challenges anchorites encountered demanded a high degree of fortitude and resilience. The fact that we have evidence of episcopal inquiries suggests that bad experiences were not unknown. Bishops would have wanted to avoid the doubts and scandal that might arise if a vow was broken and a spiritual example crumbled in what was—despite the spatial enclosure—nonetheless usually a publicly visible place beside a church. The diocese of York made particular use of trustworthy men in judging the state of mind of would-be anchorites. In 1408 Archbishop Bowet ordered an inquest into the life, character, and condition of Margaret Gyseley of St Saviour's parish in York, who had proclaimed herself mentally and physically prepared and firm in her will to live as a recluse. The inquest of trustworthy men was to pay particular attention to her 'constancy of mind' and the persistence of her desire to live in this way.[85] Constancy of mind was also the phrase used by Archbishop Kempe in an inquiry of 1448.[86] There were distinct echoes here of the firmness with which the laity were expected to hold to their faith (discussed in Chapter 1), suggesting a close conceptual connection between belief and mental well-being. Indeed, in 1409, Archbishop Bowet had explicitly placed trustworthiness, the perception of mental states, and religious faith side by side in his mandate for another inquiry into an anchorite. The prospective recluse Isabella German of Kingston-Upon-Hull was to be investigated by trustworthy men 'considering the attacks that the Devil makes upon such people'.[87] It is a pity that we do not have the jury's report on any of these cases, meaning that it is hard to know how the trustworthy men approached their task. Bowet's 1408 mandate does at least hint at what he expected them to do: in asking about the persistence of Margaret Gyseley's intentions he implied that they should ask her friends and neighbours whether she had planned this for some time. Other inquests imply links between behaviour and the life of the mind. Only rarely do we gain any deeper insight into their methods. For example in 1500 Bishop Fox of Durham recorded the judgement of trustworthy men about the infirmity of the warden of Sherburn hospital. He was much recovered, they said, so much so that he once more 'took pleasure in the light of day'.[88] This may be a colloquial phrase, and a highly impressionistic form of psychological assessment, but it seems to reflect an approach to mental illness that was at once empirical and sympathetic. In other words, such subtle judgements were humanistic and reflected a churchman's trust in peasant elites providing reliable verdicts.

The apprehension of interior states by observation, carried out by people who lived in close proximity to the subject, and paying heed to behaviour as an indicator of psychological processes was also a critical element in bishops' attempts to monitor and correct the faith of the laity. The involvement of trustworthy men in the assessment of right and wrong belief underwent a huge expansion during the course of the later Middle Ages, as changes to the way that heresy was investigated placed them at the heart of the disciplinary apparatus of the church.[89] This important shift happened in England in the early fifteenth century, but it rested upon earlier developments in miracle inquests and visitation reporting.

From the early thirteenth century the papacy had begun to exert control over the popular acclamation of saints, creating an inquisitorial process of local investigation under central authority. Such inquisitions were massive administrative undertakings and gave many laypeople the chance to influence a process of judgement concerning subtle matters of divine election and supernatural events. Yet the witnesses before such tribunals were not usually described as trustworthy men, as the inquisitors took testimony from whatever witnesses came forward, making no special claims for those with whom they dealt. The testimony could always be scrutinized at a later date and anything deemed unreliable weeded out.[90] Where trustworthy men were sometimes used was in the investigation of an existing unofficial cult, an element of Christian culture that continued despite the papacy's attempts to arrogate to itself the creation of saints. In the new world of legal inquiry and 'scientific' approval, popular acclamation was inherently suspicious and an inquest by trustworthy men was often used to stamp out excessive enthusiasm. For instance in 1361 Bishop Grandisson of Exeter became concerned about reports of miracles at the grave of the late rector of Whitestone (Cornwall). He wrote to his commissary:

> Because miracles can be attributed both to good and evil . . . we enjoin you to inquire diligently and shrewdly, through trustworthy sworn men having the fullest knowledge of these matters, into the persons who claim to have been cured, whether they are known or unknown and of what condition, into their infirmities and illnesses, what these were and for how long they endured them. And if you find that [these cures]

have not been fabricated by some art or device, and they are not natural, you should cite them . . . and witnesses through whom the truth may be clearly proved to appear before us.

The 'men of the inquest' (*inquisitores*) reported that a woman called Lavyna Stolloke was cured of an infirmity at the burial site and so she and some other witnesses were cited to the bishop's court. In addition it was said that the rector had performed ten miracles including cures for blindness, lameness, deformities of the feet and legs, paralysis, arthritis, and mental illness. One story that seems to have been particularly affecting concerned a woman from Northam who, 'raving mad and out of her mind' (*furiosa et mente alienata*), was restrained and bound and taken to the burial site. She had been so disturbed that she had tried to destroy candles and images in the church, but after about a year she was completely cured of the madness and came on pilgrimage to the site of her miracle in Whitestone.[91] This case is typical of many instances of unofficial sanctity and locally acclaimed miracles, even though it is richer in documentation than most. The role of the trustworthy men was to bring episcopal authority to bear upon local devotion, pitting an approved inquest against unsolicited witness stories, and trusted procedure against distrusted enthusiasm.[92] The role of authority in deciding sanctity was reaffirmed by the bishop acting through trustworthy men. A similar purpose could also be pursued in quite different circumstances. When Thomas of Lancaster sought to promote the canonization of the late archbishop of Canterbury, Robert of Winchelsey, in the 1320s, the project was resisted by Thomas's cousin Edward II and by some of the English bishops, who remembered Winchelsey as a thorn in the side of both crown and papacy. The bishops were asked to investigate the 'life, fame, habits, and miracles' of Winchelsey through well-known (*famosus*) and trustworthy men. Bishop Martival of Salisbury replied that having done so he could confirm that although the late archbishop was well-regarded in his diocese, no reports of miracles could be found.[93] In political terms these trustworthy men (in this instance of a somewhat higher status than usual, as indicated by the adjective *famosus*) were a bulwark against a political project their bishop disapproved of, but their immediate task was to voice an opinion on the truth of miracles.

These are significant examples, but isolated and infrequent. Much more common was the work of trustworthy men in monitoring and regulating the frontiers of Christian belief in their role as visitation representatives. Visitation records are teeming with reports of nonattendance at church as well as failure to receive the Eucharist or to make a confession. All such lapses in behaviour had two aspects: the seen and the unseen. On the one hand they might be no more than failures of action, bad habits picked up in the pursuit of some goal that made church attendance difficult, be it making a living or avoiding social conflict. On the other hand such lapses could be signs of dissenting or simply divergent beliefs. There was often no clear distinction between the two. This is plainly evident in some reports. At Ruardean in Gloucestershire in 1397, for example, Nicholas Cuthler was reported for keeping vigil at his father's grave, which, so the trustworthy men said, was a sign that he expected to meet his ghost there 'to the great scandal of the Christian faith'.[94] Sometimes explicit assertions of belief were reported to visitors, but only if they clearly transgressed unofficial as well as official concepts of doctrinal boundaries. At Kilpeck during the same visitation the parishioners said that one chaplain seemed to them infirm in his faith 'because he has often made boast that he goes about at night with imagined spirits'.[95] Because the chaplain had articulated ideas that might have remained unseen inside his mind, he made the job of the trustworthy men easy in one respect: they could report his own words. But it is also significant that they felt able to extrapolate from them to a conclusion about his *fides*. The chaplain had failed to meet even the basic requirement of faith: that it be stable and firm.

The extrapolation necessary, from actions or from words, was what made lay reports on such matters subtle judgements. They had to decide what deeds and talk were suspicious and why. Naturally these were subjective evaluations, requiring a leap from the tangible to the intangible, but they were also 'intersubjective', in being inextricable from the relationship between offender and reporter, and from the reputation that the offender had in his or her parish. For example, around 1405 at Dunham in Yorkshire, John Plasterer was reported at visitation because he 'did not receive communion at Easter like other Christians, but absented himself, setting a bad example to Christians'.[96] In making a comparison with the behaviour of others, and in commenting on the possibility that others still might learn from Plasterer's bad behaviour, the trustworthy men of Dunham indicated the essentially social character of both behaviour and belief on the one hand, and of their judgements on the other. Meanwhile bishops, and other visitors, by soliciting reports about deviant belief, were interposing their own authority into existing social bonds, making a useful bureaucratic commodity of human relations.

Lay parishioners had not been much involved in the detection of heresy in England during the thirteenth and fourteenth centuries. A rather gnomic instruction sent to the official of the archdeacon of Winchester in 1310 required him to investigate the Templars through twelve trustworthy men in each deanery, but it is not clear whether this refers to the charges of heresy against them or to the value of their lands and houses.[97] Even the advent of Wycliffism at Oxford in the 1370s and the race to track down Wyclif's most active academic followers in the 1380s and 1390s did not immediately lead to the widespread use of trustworthy men to tackle unorthodox belief. Although Bishop Brantyngham of Exeter twice referred to trustworthy men in the mid-1380s in relation to the pursuit of Wycliffites, such rhetoric was scarce among the wider English episcopate.[98] But after a generation or so of experiencing widespread heresy, the English church as a whole began to involve the laity systematically in the detection of heresy.

With political manoeuvres that echo the situation we have encountered so often in the past three chapters, ecclesiastical use of trustworthy men in the fight against heresy was part of a jurisdictional struggle with the royal courts. The crown made the first significant move. In 1406 Henry IV's chancellor Thomas Arundel, who was also archbishop of Canterbury, introduced a statute that gave all manner of royal justices and lesser officers the power to inquire into heresy. This was a challenge to the established balance of powers between church and crown. Up to that point a fairly clear distinction had been drawn between the arrest (crown) and judgement (church) of heretics, but the terms of the 1406 statute implied that secular officers would be exercising a good deal of discernment in cases of suspected heresy. The new powers were repeated and firmed up in 1414 in the wake of John Oldcastle's so-called 'lollard' revolt.[99] In the meantime, Bishop Repingdon of Lincoln—who had been a youthful follower of Wyclif—had made the first step in the church's response. In 1413 he saddled his regular visitation of the archdeaconry of Leicester, an area particularly known for lollardy, with the additional task of discovering heresy. Consequently, alongside the usual litany of sexual offences, clerical faults, crumbling buildings, and minor sins, we find a clutch of reports of heresy including several lengthy investigations. This approach meant that the parish representatives—the trustworthy men—were responsible for deciding who was suspected of heresy. And in a constitution for the province of Canterbury in 1416 *fidedigni* were called upon to man special inquisitions into heresy, although bishops generally responded by following Repingdon's model of heresy detection in ordinary visitations.[100]

But how were laymen to decide whether heresy lurked in their neighbours' hearts? As archbishop in 1407, Thomas Arundel had laid out the grounds upon which suspicion of heresy could legitimately be based. His constitutions ordered the citation of anyone defamed, detected, or vehemently suspected of any heretical acts or words, or of anyone preaching 'any article whatsoever sounding evilly against the catholic faith or good morals'.[101] In practice this meant that trustworthy men reported words 'sounding like lollardy', and persons who 'spoke certain words redolent of heresy'.[102] Actions were also thought to be indicators of belief, and it became common for bishops to ask visitation representatives to report 'anyone taking part in secret meetings, or anyone *differing in life and morals from the usual behaviour of the faithful* and the determinations of the church'.[103] The breadth of this formulation gave extraordinary latitude to the suspicions of trustworthy men, inviting them to find any deviation from ordinary behaviour reasonable cause for suspicion of heresy. But still we must ask how they would have decided what constituted suspicious difference. Of course it is impossible to know what thoughts went through their minds, but it was inevitably a judgement based on their own impression of the individual in question and their assessment of his or her reputation with others. 'Usual', when applied to life and morals, must have entailed a comparison with some assumed norm, a norm established by observing how one's own thoughts and behaviour seem to be corroborated by those of others. At times an inquisitor might hint at the connections they should make: for instance during an investigation at Bury St Edmunds in 1428 the bishop referred to suspects 'withdrawing' themselves from the faithful, which was a strong hint that the *fidedigni* should draw a link between nonattendance at church and possible heresy.[104] But even this encouragement to *look for* signs of heresy still left trustworthy men with a great deal of freedom to exercise their own judgement about a subtle question of belief.

The changes to the investigation of heresy that began in the first quarter of the fifteenth century augmented the considerable responsibility that trustworthy men already had for the discernment of things hidden in the minds of other people. By the early sixteenth century it was even possible for 'trustworthy men' to head off a heresy charge by their sworn word in a form of compurgation. In 1517 a suspect was released from the bishop of Lincoln's court because 'many trustworthy and venerable men' affirmed that he was a 'wholly catholic man'.[105] The ability of lay witnesses to make such judgements, and to be taken seriously, was rooted in the common social experience they shared with the people whom they judged. It was the intersubjective qualities of the relationships between neighbours that allowed them to make such subtle judgements: weighing the ineffable quality of a person's mental state or beliefs against a norm derived from self-examination and comparisons with other people.

{≈≈≈⊛W⊛≈≈≈}

Subtle judgements that relied upon the relationships between trustworthy men, their clergy, and their neighbours were enormously useful to bishops in entrenching their power and projecting their authority over their dioceses. Episcopal authority became a real element in decisions made at the level of the parish because it permitted laymen to conjure firm categories (heresy, madness, bad character, sin) out of the untidy indeterminacy of human emotion, motivation, and relationships. And it penetrated the very relationships within which those judgements were made, grounding institutional power in everyday social interaction and in the unequal relationships that defined the position of the trustworthy men. The alliance between bishops and their local collaborators gave uncertain matters of character and belief the appearance of cognizable facts. Subtle judgements rendered hidden things visible, knowable, and capable of being dealt with by the courts. This increased the volume of business that church courts had to deal with, augmenting their authority and that of the bishops and other churchmen who presided over them. But this is not the whole story of how trustworthy men made the medieval church, for the institutional power of bishops was not confined to the courts and tribunals, the written mandates and clerical subordinates, which constituted the organizational landscape of their dioceses. Rather it was located in the synapses of an expanding complex of relationships within the parish, and between the parish and those organizations. Going even further, we might say that the institutional power of the church resided in the culture of moral watchfulness that bishops promoted and trustworthy men enacted.

CHAPTER FOURTEEN

The Church Built on Trust

IN THE PRECEDING CHAPTERS we have seen that between the twelfth and thirteenth centuries, especially in England, bishops began to make more use than ever before of local panels in inquests and eventually by the 1270s in visitations, calling these people trustworthy men, the *fidedigni*. We have seen that this term was transformed from a way to describe the gospel authors to a plausible description of peasant witnesses. This was achieved in part by drawing upon preexisting discourses of theological belief, law and agreements, and the expression of identity, reputation, and sincerity, and in part by making it a symbolic role under the control of bishops. The actual trustworthy men were for the most part elite peasants in the rural parishes and the leading townsmen in urban parishes, with various regional differences of emphasis that were discussed in Chapter 8. We have seen how these trustworthy men used their social position to speak for their parishes, garnering social capital for themselves and providing bishops with the information on which episcopal governance was based.

All of this, but especially the foregoing discussion of what the *fidedigni* did for bishops and how it augmented episcopal power, means that we are now in a position to assess how the collection of testimony from trustworthy men shaped the institutional church. At a very deep level the challenges involved in gathering and conveying information determined the nature of the episcopal governance. It should be pointed out that I mean 'government' and 'institutions' both in the traditional sense of organizational structures, officers, bureaucratic procedures, and technologies of recording, as well as in the more expansive sense developed in the preceding chapters: institutional power was located in the trustworthy men, their words, social position, actions, and attitudes, as well as in all the things, people, transactions, and relationships implicated by their testimony. But the principal vector of all this was information.

There can be no doubt as to the scale of bishops' need for information and their ambition in acquiring it; but nor can we dismiss as minor problems the uncertainty, fragility, and transience of information taken on trust. Ways of thinking about knowledge (surveyed in Chapter 10) and the trustworthy men (addressed in Chapter 5) were part of bishops' response to this fragility, creating categories of knowledge and action that downplayed doubt, but the way in which they handled testimony and information was arguably the major component in ecclesiastical government. The movement of information in the late medieval church was, in simplified terms, a cycle animated by the idea of trustworthiness.[1] Testimony was collected from trustworthy men, becoming information that aided the church in the settlement of disputes and its management of benefices; this information circulated in modified forms among various interested parties; finally it might be used as the basis for an official intervention in the world of local knowledge, completing a cycle. Of course all of this happened within much broader and more complex flows of information, concerned with many matters and taking many forms, but the basic model provides a useful starting point for analysis. Something of this model is applicable to all governing institutions from the thirteenth century onwards, as I argued in Chapter 4, not just to the church. However, the nature of information founded explicitly upon *fides* (with all its connotations of good faith, personal reputation, commitment to God, and membership of 'the faith' as described in Chapters 1 to 3) was particular to the relationship between bishops and the *fidedigni*. One of these characteristics was a relative openness about uncertainty and doubt, the terrain delineated by talk about trust. In a church built on trust, the need for information, the ambition for truth, the uncertainty about *fama*, and the transience of meaning were part and parcel of the bishop's relationship with information and with trustworthy men, and they all contributed to the nature of episcopal power and the shape of the institutional church.

The Costs of Information

Finding things out by asking the locals came at a cost. Even though the financial burden of maintaining a diocesan administration cannot ever have been far from a bishop's mind, the costs in question here were not necessarily monetary: they could also involve the loss of certainty and the acceptance of such doubt as was necessary to make the world knowable and governable. We have already seen (in Chapter 10) that bishops were content to live with a degree of doubt, and that they tried to boost the stability of testimony with talk of trustworthiness, but negotiating the price of certainty also entailed certain institutional imperatives that are also worthy of historical attention.

At one level bishops had to deal with purely quantitative information problems: too much or too little. As we saw in Chapters 11 to 13, churches, patrons, parishioners, and others looked to their bishop as a provider of judgements. A great deal of power was concentrated in his hands, exemplified by the phenomenon of 'reserved cases' that only bishops could judge.[2] For such a hierarchical and nodal system to work effectively information had to reach bishops when they required it, something that is borne out by the fact that English bishops collected huge amounts of information in their registers, using them to record vast numbers of outgoing letters and instructions. What is more, all of that rested upon a world of ephemeral records that informed, preceded, and emanated from the registers, including visitation rolls and books.[3] If bishops were starved of testimony, they could not take the action that would fulfil their pastoral and governing roles. If officials at different levels failed to pass on messages as they were expected to, bottlenecks could be created. Even the supposedly characteristically modern condition of 'information overload' could affect medieval administrators.[4] Some historians have suggested that the Domesday Book of 1086 and Edward I's Hundred Rolls of 1279–80 contained so much information that they were not much used as a result, while visitation books and rolls contain many entries that do not appear to have been followed up.[5]

Geographical distance and the logistical trials of itinerant government added to the challenges posed by information. When a bishop or other visitor planned a tour of his jurisdiction, multiple groups of trustworthy men had to be organized to appear at particular times and places, each having submitted written reports in advance. Frequently these groups did not appear, or the information was not available all in one place, and so cases trailed along in the visitor's wake, dragging parishioners and litigants, letters and reports, from place to place. A great deal of ecclesiastical record keeping therefore bears the signs of a constant effort to make sure that information kept pace with itineraries, with visitation books being a case in point. These were typically composed of stub entries for each parish, written out in advance, to which the reports of trustworthy men were added on the day itself. If someone did not appear, or if the initial estimation of the space needed for each parish was insufficient, testimony and procedural notes might be interlineated or squeezed into the margin at a later date. The work of the registrar and his scribes was to capture the complex and amorphous world of local knowledge in simplified form as the visitor's party kept to their ordered schedule.[6] On occasion therefore, peripatetic tribunals may not have made for efficient decision making, but they did allow bishops to collapse the geographical distance separating them from their flocks, just as they travelled their estates in order to be a visible presence to the gentry and nobility living far from cathedral cities. There were calculations of cost and benefit here that went beyond those recorded in the documentation of household revenues and expenses.[7]

When the information needed to resolve a dispute was hard to locate, the costs of retrieving it could escalate, in terms of both money and doubt. For example, when in 1320 Andrew le Boteler claimed benefit of clergy after being charged with murder, the archbishop of York ordered an inquest into his life and character, his 'name and opinion', in his home region. The problem was that he had moved around a great deal and there was no question of sending a commissioner to empanel the trustworthy men of a single parish. Instead Archbishop Melton called for 'trustworthy clerics and laymen . . . from the places where he is most well-known', and these were scattered across Nottinghamshire and the East Riding. Somewhat unsurprisingly, nothing definitive emerged from these attenuated efforts, and the only option after six months was to advertise Andrew le Boteler's desire to undergo purgation and see if 'objectors' came forward.[8] This was an unsatisfactory and inferior means of testing for truth because the verdict would come from the suspect's friends and supporters rather than the trustworthy men, more easily presented as impartial. As an example of bureaucratic failure, this highlights the preference for stable collective testimony.

Nevertheless, quantitative problems were only the tip of an iceberg. More significant to administrative bureaucracies is the qualitative distance that can separate their various levels from one another. In the *Critique of the Philosophy of Right*, Karl Marx wrote that the apex of a bureaucracy 'entrusts the lower circles with insight into the individual while the lower circles leave insight into the universal to the apex, so they deceive each other reciprocally'.[9] Given what we have seen of theological attitudes towards lay belief, and of the episcopal need for local knowledge, it is easy to see how useful Marx's aphorism might be as a tool with which to think about the medieval church. To begin with, the mutual deception he describes need not be intentional. Just as bishops had to overcome powerful cultural tendencies towards distrust when asking the laity for information, so the trustworthy men might fail to understand what really mattered in the world of canon law and government. Each might simply misunderstand the other. To give just one example, in 1346 the bishop of Hereford ordered an inquest to discover who was the patron of Sibdon chapel in Shropshire. He commissioned local clerics to gather information from trustworthy men, but one or other of these groups either failed to understand precisely what was being asked of them, or had an agenda that was at odds with the bureaucratic needs of the moment. The trustworthy men reported that the chaplain had a customary duty to celebrate mass twice a day and bemoaned the fact that the chapel could be served only three days a week; they identified the current chaplain; they described how a previous lord of Sibdon had endowed the chapel. But they did not say who had last presented to the chapel, and so the patron remained unidentified. Because of this the inquest was deemed to have 'failed' and the bishop's official, a university graduate and experienced administrator, was sent to repeat the exercise.[10]

In this instance having to repeat an inquest could be said to have doubled the financial cost of information, but all interested parties also had to accept the prolongation of doubt, which they were trying to avoid. The solution pursued by Bishop Trillek, to send in a more educated officer, points to one of the significant ways in which information problems shaped the structure of the institutional church. If the bishop's agents—the men who carried the instructions of the bishop to the locality, and then reported the testimony of trustworthy men—were inexperienced or unversed in the cultures of law and administration, they might perform their tasks diligently, but in vain. Most of the time this problem was mitigated by pairing local clergy with members of the bishop's household in the hope that together they would be able to translate the universal into the local and vice versa. On other occasions parish priests who were themselves graduates, or who had experience in dealing with the wishes of their superiors, might perform the translation single-handedly. As a failed inquest the Sibdon case is in fact a rarity. Most reports of inquests kept costs of all kinds low by confining themselves to the matter at hand and carefully adhering to the wording of the bishop's original instructions, so that mutual deception was kept to a tolerable minimum and the complexity of the real (local) world was reduced so that it was legible to the bishop's administration.

The key to understanding such reductions in complexity is to observe the extent to which acceptable doubt conditioned episcopal information gathering. This can be illustrated with an inquest of trustworthy men held in 1309 to discover which rectors of parish churches in the deanery of Warwick had failed to become ordained priests within a year of their appointment.[11] It was not unusual for the politics of patronage to result in men who were not yet full priests being placed in benefices. Six rectors were reported on this occasion, of whom three went on to be ordained even though they did not have their papers in order. They merely had to swear that they had not been in their churches more than a year and the bishop allowed them to be ordained 'at their own risk'. That is, they had to accept that if their ordination was later discovered to have been illegal it would be their problem and not his. There must have been some doubt, but there was a limit to what the bishop could find out. What is more, in this case and many others like it we also do not know whether the inquiry exposed all offenders or merely those whose impropriety the trustworthy men found egregious. There was, after all, always some potential for parish representatives to privilege the mutual *fides* they owed to their community (as they saw it) over the good faith demanded by external authority. As Steven Justice has said in relation to manorial politics, the court 'depended on the *trewþe* tenants owed to the lord' but at the same time this left the lord 'at the mercy of the *trewþe* tenants owed to each other'.[12] But such resistance, if it occurred, did little to affect the power of bishops, who paid for the trust necessary to secure information with the shrugging acceptance that it might be incomplete or misleading.

There was a strong instrumental rationality driving bishops' actions in such cases and, thereby, shaping the institutional church. Trusting the locals despite the impossibility of knowing whether one had been fully informed, and accepting the word of delinquent priests despite a lack of strong evidence to exonerate them, were rational acts insofar as the benefits of trusting were soundly understood. In the Warwick case Bishop Reynolds had decided that to trust and accept doubt was better than to attempt a precise calculation of probabilities.[13] They were working within tolerable levels of uncertainty, echoing (albeit without directly engaging) scholastic notions of reliable and probable knowledge, tacitly understanding that to have pursued the truth remorselessly would have been both costly and counterproductive. At root this pragmatism arose from the potentially infinite cost of assessing the trustworthiness of local informants and, indeed, of the need to accept that fidelity to purely local priorities and to the mutual obligations of parochial *fides* might on occasion trump the duties implied by being labelled *fidedignus*. As we have seen in Chapter 5, the institutional view of trustworthiness held it to be a symbolic role rather than a measurable character trait, and the major reason for this was precisely these immaterial costs. Although they did not articulate this motivation, it does seem that medieval bishops were contemplating what Douglass North has identified as a common feature of economic transactions: third parties might possess desirable attributes to varying levels, but 'the measurement of these levels is too costly to be comprehensive or fully accurate'.[14] By trusting men whose position in their parishes was already marked by wealth or status, and by accepting doubt as to their actual trustworthiness, bishops could 'shift the problem into a realm where it [could] be mastered more effectively', namely finding men whose word would be unassailable in their communities.[15] There would always be considerable uncertainty, and since doubt and risk increase transaction costs, it was necessary to find a way of reducing them.[16] For Luhmann and many other commentators trust is a way of doing just that: 'the complexity of the future world is reduced by the act of trust'.[17] Late medieval bishops learnt to trust parish representatives because over time the information they provided was a better means of settling disputes than any other available method.

Accepting incomplete or flawed information did not make the church less powerful. It was done in the pursuit of power. In common with all governing institutions throughout history medieval bishops had an inexorable desire to render their subjects more predictable, more measurable, and more malleable, and the first rule of governance is to be willing to translate local into institutional knowledge. Local knowledge taken with a pinch of doubt brought power, whereas true local knowledge would have overwhelmed the institution with its unbounded variety, its illegibility, and its strangeness. Cases had to be made to fit the patterns by which the law operated.[18] Tolerating doubt was made possible by the inheritance of legal and theological understandings of *fides*, which lent to the *fidedigni* an air of assurance and fixity, helping to make local society seem more 'legible', permitting the creation of information that could be utilised for the purposes of episcopal administration.

Circulating Information

However important the extraction of information from trustworthy men was to episcopal governance, it was only one part of a much more complex cycle. Inquests and visitations were triggered with written mandates sent by bishops to one of their subordinates, and while visitations were theoretically regular occurrences, inquests were often responses to requests from an individual or an institution. Inquest mandates set out the terms of the information required, giving a deadline by which it was to be returned, and visitation mandates sometimes referred to written 'articles' or lists of questions, which may or may not have been circulated around the parishes. In all of this the transmission of written documents was accompanied and augmented by oral proclamations and explanations. Upon the completion of an inquest the bishop was to receive a report (known as a 'certification'), which might be entered in his general register, while visitation rolls and books were stored for as long as was deemed useful.[19] From these documents many 'pieces' of information could be passed to, and copied by, diverse officers and interested parties. Huge numbers of episcopal business letters (or *acta*), for instance, survive in the charter collections ('cartularies') kept by monastic houses.[20]

Acting upon information gathered from trustworthy men, a bishop might send out orders for court appearances, reciting the contents and source of the information, and these would pass through the hands of one or more messengers and scribes, reaching an archdeacon or rural dean, before finally being executed by a summoner or some other lowly officer. Several actions in this sequence might have generated their own certifications, sent to the bishop wherever he was in his diocese.[21] Such reports would frequently repeat or anticipate the bishop's fetish of trustworthiness, spreading this ideal far and wide.[22] From the later thirteenth century onwards, bishops, aping the practices of the English royal exchequer, began to store their records on a more or less formal basis, so that information could be retrieved when the need arose. It is also likely that many low-ranking clerics kept their own dossiers of letters received in the execution of diocesan business, and perhaps even copies of their outgoing correspondence, but very little evidence of this survives because such men did not usually have access to institutional archival storage.[23]

For the most part such activity has been taken for granted by historians. As I contended in the introduction, it has been frequently described, but less often analysed. Echoing Weber's ideal type of bureaucracy, an incredibly persistent assumption in the study of historical organizations has been that they were machines, functioning smoothly or poorly according to the quality of the design thought to be inherent in their structures.[24] The sociology of organizations has long rejected this naïve simplification. Individual agency and social interaction currently play much more prominent roles in explanations of institutional form, and human beings are no longer imagined to be 'caught in the toils of a complex machinery that they do not help to make'.[25] Even though medieval historians would also be quick to deny the applicability of so rigid a model when it comes to the study of the institutional church, the *metaphor* of the machine has cast a long shadow over our thinking.[26] It has long been the default mode for thinking about the movement of information in the late medieval church.[27] But the medieval church cannot be understood as a mechanical input and output system for the transmission of information. For one thing it was not a single organism (let alone a single machine), but a multi-institutional entity, and for another information was not transmitted in concrete 'pieces' like some physical produce, and so its meaning was not stable as it circulated, however much bishops sought to make it so by their rhetoric and their employment of trustworthy men.[28]

The need for information to travel between a plethora of institutions is amply illustrated by the example of the archbishops of York and their relationship with Ripon Minster. Ripon was a proudly independent church with important jurisdictional rights over that bustling small town and a limited area of the surrounding countryside. It was a sanctuary, which meant that men and women suspected of felonies could escape royal justice by taking refuge there. Wilfrid's bones, some of the holiest relics in the north of England, were housed in Ripon, and there had once even been a convention that pilgrims en route to St Wilfrid's shrine were under the protection of the minster.[29] The archbishops of York were outwardly respectful of this holiness and independence, while going to some lengths to nonetheless control the jurisdictional 'freedom' enjoyed by the smaller church. The York registers are full of carefully monitored permissions for Ripon to act in particularly sensitive cases, where in fact no permission was needed. They reveal the multi-institutional complexity of the church as a whole and the sensitivities involved in moving information through this complex and dynamic landscape. In 1293 Archbishop Romeyn insisted that the purgation of a Ripon man suspected of homicide and theft should be monitored by 'good and trustworthy persons' so that he could guarantee the rigour of the process to an understandably sceptical crown. In 1306 a canon of Ripon Minster was asked by the archbishop to inquire into the financial condition of a hospital in the town through 'unsuspected trustworthy men'. Around 1314 'trustworthy reports' were circulating that accused several former wardens of that institution of asset-stripping; Archbishop Greenfield asked the town bailiff to inquire. In 1356 the hospital warden was told to supply three priests for a chantry, a customary duty that had been confirmed by an inquest of trustworthy men. In 1372 an inquest into a vacant prebend was to be conducted through trustworthy clerics under the supervision of the chapter of Ripon, the archbishop's commissary general, and the rural dean of Ripon. In 1452 Archbishop Kempe related the trustworthy reports he had heard about the disrepair of Ripon Minster and ordered an inquest of trustworthy clerics and laymen. This final letter was prefaced with an unusual paean of praise for the beauty and importance of Ripon, 'resting place of St Wilfrid and home to so many holy men'.[30] The long-term consideration on the part of the archbishop was twofold. He wished to maintain good relations with several independent institutions—the crown, the borough of Ripon, the hospital, and the minster itself—while establishing links with so-called trustworthy men in Ripon whose testimony would allow him to penetrate a town ostensibly under the sole jurisdiction of the minster. The movement of information within the church happened in complex webs such as this, where bishops could not simply issue commands, but had to share information—frequently couched in talk about trust—with other institutions enjoying varying degrees of independence.

Many questions also cut across diocesan boundaries. Such situations demanded careful political mediation, which is where the rhetoric of trustworthiness came into its own. When a bishop received a letter from one of his counterparts elsewhere in the country, or from the papacy, asking for information on the life and character of someone who had lived or been born in his diocese, he might be asked to inquire through trustworthy men, or he might put his reply in similar terms. For example, in 1312 the pope sent a letter to the rector of Tibshelf in Derbyshire (Coventry and Lichfield diocese) permitting him, given the reports of trustworthy persons as to his merits, to hold a canonry in Exeter cathedral. The letter is preserved in an Exeter register.[31] In 1320 and 1321 the bishop of Salisbury requested the archdeacon of Berkshire to inquire into the value of Shinfield and Swallowfield churches through trustworthy men. In 1326 the renowned canonist William Paull, who was the rector of nearby Winkfield, was asked to find out the cost of repairs to the rectory buildings. These letters were copied into the register of the bishop of Hereford, who was the rector of Shinfield.[32] Bishop William Gray's Lincoln register contains the results of a 1431 inquest into the value and liabilities of Naseby church in Northamptonshire, which was about to be appropriated by the Cistercian abbey of Combe in Coventry and Lichfield diocese. Detailed information was provided by 'the closest' (viciniores) trustworthy men.[33] Similar cross-diocesan inquests were commonplace throughout the later Middle Ages, and the use of trustworthy men was symptomatic of the care needed when treading on someone else's toes.

The invocation of trustworthiness in these letters was an attempt to conquer distance, to mediate between multiple institutions, and to reduce the costs of information by encouraging all parties to accept its imperfections. These principles governed all information exchanges within the medieval church, even those involving laypeople. A case in point is the marriage of William Mull from Gloucestershire and Francisca Wichingham from Norfolk, which was certified in 1457 by the bishop of Coventry and Lichfield, in whose diocese it had taken place, following an inquest of trustworthy men. The bishop's letter explained that such a formal record was necessary 'lest the *distance* of the place of marriage from their homes leads to doubt and uncertainty in the future'.[34] But there would always be doubt. There always is. What matters in the generation of useful information is a realistic acceptance of uncertainty.

Intervening in Local Knowledge

One thing that has become apparent in the preceding discussion is that the church lived by local knowledge. The evidence of Chapters 11 to 13 has shown that its law was a 'craft of place'.[35] But testimonials about marital status, or the good character of a candidate for ordination, are examples of bishops' attempts to actively shape local knowledge as well as merely drawing upon it for bureaucratic purposes. They made many such interventions, often intended to affect someone's reputation. For example, following the successful purgation of a person previously suspected of a crime, a bishop would restore him or her to 'pristine good fame'. Obviously this cannot always have been effective. Local opinions about reputation were certainly in dialogue with official pronunciations, but they were not governed by them.[36] The challenges of gathering local knowledge were therefore more than matched by the challenges of intervening to shape social memory. Though it is probably one of the more persistent assumptions about the medieval church, the ability to tell people what to do and how to think cannot be taken for granted: it was a constant struggle to make the knowledge of the locals conform to the episcopal view of the world. The institutional church, with all its scribes and muniment chests, its endless oral instructions, and the vast number of recorded and unrecorded attempts to generate, discover, transmit, and understand local knowledge, was moulded by the nature of this struggle.

There are many ways of conveying information so as to have an impact upon local systems of belief and knowledge. In the partially literate culture of later medieval Europe, where some (but not all) of the clergy were able to read (but not necessarily to write), and where the number of laymen or laywomen possessing either skill was minute until the later fourteenth century, communication to large numbers of people or over substantial distances typically had a hybrid written-oral form.[37] Of course much of the church's communication with the laity took place in very intimate parochial settings where a multitude of media coalesced and subtle inferences were possible. Sermons were probably rare in this context, but liturgy and prayers conveyed simple theological, moral, and aesthetic ideas, complemented by the visual experience of church architecture, sculpture, and wall paintings. Through confession the clergy were supposed to instruct the adult laity in the articles of the faith and to correct their sins 'lest like dogs that do not bark they allow the wolf to ravage the Lord's flock'.[38] By the example of their lives and behaviour—good or bad— parish priests were also responsible for a channelling a never-ending stream of unconscious communication about clerical status and the Christian life.

At this intimate local level communication was probably strong. Interactions between the clergy and the laity were frequent and patterned in such a way as to inculcate a sense that the relationship between the instructor and the instructed was a given fact of life. However, intimacy also made the priest-parishioner relationship vulnerable to what economists call 'moral hazard' and 'adverse selection'. Moral hazard is the problem of principals not being able to supervise their agents, and in the case of late medieval bishops this meant the diocesan clergy; adverse selection refers to the problems arising from choosing the wrong agents in the first place.[39] Both were serious challenges to the effectiveness of local communication. The problem was not so much one of clerical dogs failing to bark at all, as one of their barking at all the wrong times and up the wrong trees. Priests might be thoroughly embedded in their communities (*might* being the operative word), but would they always do what bishops expected? The effect of a bad priest was not neutral. It was negative. Recognizing this, successive campaigns of communication between 1200 and 1500 were directed at the parish clergy in an attempt to mould their communications with parishioners. This was the context into which more direct episcopal interventions were made, so it is worth summarizing here.

Although gatherings of the English higher clergy had generated substantial bodies of instructive and exhortatory texts—constitutions—for centuries, the momentum created by the Council of Westminster in 1213 and the Fourth Lateran Council held in Rome in 1215 inaugurated a period of great communicative activity that evolved substantially over the ensuing three centuries. From the Council of Oxford in 1222 until the Council of London in 1342 episcopal intervention in the communication between priests and the people was dominated by large programmes of legatine, provincial, and diocesan constitutions.[40] Overlapping with this phase of activity, from 1281 until the end of the Middle Ages, more expansive and practical texts were produced that spelt out what the clergy should be telling the laity. At first these were in Latin, but from 1356 their translation into English initiated an explosion in copying and modification that saw manuals for priests become a significant genre of Middle English literature.[41] From the middle of the fourteenth century large all-encompassing legislative programmes were no longer promulgated, but the most influential provincial constitutions were copied into collections that became handbooks for church administrators and lawyers. The period of the church's legislative response to heresy, between 1407 and 1428, saw production of such collections peak, culminating in William Lyndwood's famous commentary on the provincial constitutions up to 1413.[42] New instructions for the clergy were by then, however, sent out as stand-alone statutes and mandates, while laypeople were barraged with long lists of offences that incurred automatic excommunication: the 'General Sentence'.

Whether in fact such texts filtered at all into the world of local knowledge is hard to verify. Even when, for example, notices were nailed to the doors of churches, they could be ignored or misunderstood.[43] It should be said that despite this bishops certainly assumed their communication of constitutions to be effective, since ignorance was inadmissible as a defence for breaking the law: the constitutions of many a council were to be proclaimed 'so that ignorance of them is not used as an excuse'.[44] In upholding a widow's right to a third of her husband's estate in 1315, Bishop Drokensford of Bath and Wells said this was something that 'our synodal constitution has made known to all in the diocese'.[45] In 1351 his successor Bishop Shrewsbury responded to reports of negligence in the publication of constitutions saying 'unless they are brought to the notice of our subjects [they] tend not to bind and draw them together'.[46] Perfect knowledge and the 'inviolable observation'[47] of constitutions were assumed to have been made real purely by the fact of promulgation. If we were to take such rhetoric at face value we should probably think that late medieval bishops were peculiarly, even wilfully, ignorant about the workings of knowledge and communication. But perhaps we should take these more as pronouncements on the universality of the law than as a realistic theory of communication and action. For bishops, as we have so often seen, were pragmatists.

At least, they could be. Constitutions and stand-alone mandates were used to alter knowledge and behaviour, but whether or not they were effective was determined by how much thought was given to the audience. There were many situations where bishops wanted to establish something in a locale, but they had not always used trustworthy men to do this. In the second quarter of the twelfth century Bishop Robert de Bethune of Hereford wanted to inform 'all his faithful parishioners' in Hatfield that he had consecrated their graveyard. But he addressed this only to the monks of Leominster Priory, within whose ancient *parochia* Hatfield sat and in whose cartulary this was recorded. No formal provision was made to tell the locals themselves, and this seems like a mistake, given the fact that the bishop wanted them to remember that their church only enjoyed the rights of a chapel and that Leominster was still their mother church.[48] This case is just one of thousands of potential examples. It was composed in the characteristic mode of episcopal communication before the age of the trustworthy men. Perhaps the archetypal document of that period was the charter, with its distinctive opening clause: 'To all the faithful in Christ to whom this present letter comes'.[49] A less discriminating form of communication is hard to imagine.

Some bishops, especially later in our period, used groups of 'trustworthy men' to hear official pronouncements, relay the gist of it to their neighbours, and to stand responsible for any future default or malfeasance. This practice, which was a significantly more focussed way of conveying information, must have arisen out of the experience of visitation, where the trustworthy were charged not only with reporting their parish's grievances and offences, but also with carrying back injunctions at the end of the day, and providing surety that they would be followed. Sometimes this is spelt out. At Boroughbridge in 1300 Archbishop Corbridge summoned additional trustworthy men from three parishes in order to hear the charges reported to his visitation. In 1373 the trustworthy men of the parishes in Winchester were told not only to report the truth but to 'accept what is right in these matters'.[50] The twelfth-century Herefordshire example above may be contrasted with arrangements for the dedication of Henstridge church and cemetery in Somerset in 1332. The bishop's action there was witnessed not by the whole parish but by twelve sworn parishioners who are named in the bishop's register.[51] This was to become a feature of episcopal efforts to actively shape local memory in the later Middle Ages.

By insisting on the presence of a group of trustworthy men to witness their interventions in local disputes, bishops were looking to create an institutionally sanctioned form of social memory, so as to achieve the stability that they so desired. As with royal justices, their interest lay in 'harnessing the prestige and knowledge' of local brokers, and from the analysis conducted in Chapters 6 and 7 we know that in the case of trustworthy men this prestige could come about in a number of ways, including personal status, frequency of service, age, family membership, and physical position within a settlement pattern.[52] In 1281 for example, not only was the inquest into a proposed increase in the revenues of the vicar of Blyth in Nottinghamshire informed by trustworthy men, but the proclamation of the 'ordination' made by the archbishop of York was also witnessed by trustworthy men. Presumably the archbishop wanted to guard against challenges by future abbots of Blyth's mother house, Holy Trinity in Rouen. Planting a hardy public knowledge of the settlement among the local laity may have been especially necessary in this case because the custom of Rouen was to place its monks at Blyth for just a few years at a time, undermining the usual long-term institutional memory incubated by religious houses.[53] If the monks were coming and going every few years, institutional knowledge might have been weak and periodic forgetfulness might have revived this dispute to everyone's annoyance.

Bishops used trustworthy men because they had a peculiarly close connection with *fama* and locally agreed truths, as we saw in Chapter 10. Since these were the men who acted as the voice of common knowledge, and whose local clout was the bishop's guarantee of 'firm and uncontested judgements', it was naturally through them that attempts to establish new facts were also best made.[54] In 1432 Philip Dumbleton lay old and dying in Bromyard, Herefordshire. On his deathbed he had heard that there had been an inquest into the course of the bishop's mill stream, and that 'certain ill-wishers' had objected to its passing by an orchard in Inchstone and a meadow known as Calford. Dumbleton, so his testimony relates, hobbled off to talk to the vicar of Bromyard and a notary 'and other trustworthy men of the town' because he was worried that a diversion of the stream would prejudice the bishop, and that to stay silent would be a danger to his soul and to those of his heirs. (How much of this tale and the alleged manner of its telling we believe is immaterial to the fact that, sycophancy aside, it was crafted so as to seem plausible.) Dumbleton told these trustworthy men that the current course of the mill stream had been agreed many years before and sealed with a one-off payment by the bishop to the lord of Inchstone. He told the notary to come and search among his lifetime's collection of papers and to show what evidence he found there to the bishop; he told the vicar to 'declare all of this in the church of Bromyard when the greatest number of people are present', so that no-one in the future would doubt the rights of the bishop. The notary explained things to the burgesses of Bromyard in an open letter:

> Because memory often becomes unreliable and clouded, and over long periods of time things that were clear become obscure to the future, it is right and proper to bear witness, therefore these things are presented to you in this open letter so that the things of memory are recorded in perpetuity.

Dumbleton's act had restored an almost-forgotten agreement to the status of common knowledge. But this had had to happen in stages. First he told the vicar, a notary, and a group of trustworthy men. The imprimatur of notarized testimony was a large component of stable knowledge in the period, but the contribution of trustworthy men was at least equally as important in this instance.[55] Because of their status and position trustworthy men could transmit consensus, or a locally indisputable version of the truth that was as good as consensus, upwards to a bishop. But they could also represent this 'downwards' to their fellow townsmen and parishioners.

Bishops used trustworthy men as witnesses whose local influence would dispel rumours and quell doubts. For example, in 1280 an elderly couple in the East Riding, Roger and Margaret Ayton, wanted to take vows of religion and live chastely for the remainder of their lives, and so the archbishop asked his archdeacon to check that their motivations were sound and their desire genuine. If all was as he had heard, Wickwane told the archdeacon, Margaret should be admitted into this new life 'before trustworthy men'.[56] Her husband's vow was not mentioned. A woman who wanted to change her status in this way, even while she continued to live amongst her former friends and neighbours, needed some formal social approval of her respectability. The bishop could not provide this by himself, nor could her husband. Only trustworthy men would do: they would carry the knowledge with them and make it real in the community that mattered, when it mattered. Similarly when Roger Conk of Leicester complained that he had been defamed as a lollard and heretic in 1526, his defamer was told to stand before the curate of St Martin's church 'and ten other trustworthy parishioners' and publicly seek Conk's forgiveness. At the same time a parishioner of Shakerstone who had defamed his priest of revealing things heard in confession had to seek forgiveness in front of eight or ten trustworthy parishioners.[57] Reputation was best repaired if it was vested in a select group made up of the habitual arbiters of *publica fama*.

Using supposedly trustworthy men to fix messages in local memory worked to the same rules of political language that governed the gathering of information from them. The virtues of the trustworthy did not matter; only their social position and their ability to fashion a locally agreed truth counted. Sometimes they were present in order to publicize consensus. The induction of Reginald Huse to a parish church by Archbishop Giffard of York in 1268 looked a little suspicious to onlookers: it had been made in the wake of a very short tenure by Leodegarius of Nottingham and, what is more, Huse was already a client of Giffard's. He was allegedly given the keys to the church 'peacefully in the presence of many trustworthy persons', even though the archdeacon's official had to fulminate a curse of excommunication against anyone who opposed his installation.[58] At other times they were present because credible social memory enabled future sanctions against clerical malfeasance. The foundation of a chantry in Yorkshire by John Wykeham in 1323 was allowed on the condition that any offerings made in the chapel would be immediately transferred to the local parish church. This stipulation was announced in a special ceremony 'in the presence of trustworthy persons of the parish'.[59] The chapel was on an old cult site, and these had a tendency to siphon funds away from established parish churches. In such examples of episcopal intervention in the world of local knowledge we see formal and written communication, instigated at a distance, interacting with semiformal oral communication and social memory. Combined, they may well have been the most effective and durable means of creating knowledge in the later Middle Ages.

Culture and Understanding

Effective communication was essential to the medieval church, but however shrewd the combination of official proclamations with a select audience, meaning did not arise simply from the act of sending a message. However much they might try to make the social world conform to their own view of things, bishops' efforts were hindered by a characteristic shared between information and trustworthiness: neither is a phenomenon that can be measured. Both rest upon claims that are socially constructed. Information consists of *agreed* facts, while trustworthiness is an *attributed* value.[60] Together they can prove strong, even determinative in shaping the world, but equally, being mutually constitutive, they can evaporate in the blink of an eye.[61] This was as true at the institutional and social levels as it was for the individual who experienced the 'metaphysical tailspins' and 'transcendental homelessness' discussed in Chapter 3. Moreover, the social character of knowledge means that in order to apprehend the movement of trust and information we must think about the generation of meaning in social interaction and in individual minds.

Information is produced not only when a message is sent. It is also produced when a message is received. This is now a widespread idea across the humanities and social sciences. For the twentieth-century literary scholars Wolfgang Iser and Hans Robert Jauss, all readers make sense of texts by referring to their current knowledge. They come to a text with a preexisting 'horizon of expectation'. Readers fill in the gaps of a text—the things left unsaid—for themselves and thus create their own meaning. This has become an enormously influential assumption among literary critics, shifting the ground of the subject away from authorial intention towards reader reception.[62] As Alan Bowman and Greg Woolf put it in their discussion of the ancient world, 'the power of authors and exegetes to impose an "authorised" reading is ranged against the power of readers to generate new interpretations'.[63] In what could be called a parallel development, neoclassical economic theory has been revolutionized by the concept of a 'bounded rationality' in which agents' horizons shape the interpretations they are able to place on any situation within a series of transactions.[64] The sociology of knowledge has likewise shifted far away from the study of how rules and instructions can be made clear and efficient *by the sender*. Under the powerful influence of Michel Foucault meanings are now generally understood to be 'always at the discretion of agents'.[65] Most of the 'agents' or 'recipients' I have presented in this book were probably unable to read, and so their generation of meaning came in response to oral proclamations and enquiries, and was closely bound up with how events and rights were remembered in their particular village or 'country'.[66]

Not only did bishops have to trust that the information they received from local men would command consensus and prove durable, when they transmitted a message to a parish they equally had to trust that local understanding of it would adhere to their intended meaning. It was unlikely to do so, at least not perfectly. In this way, what the local elites told the bishop, what the bishop told the local elites, and what all the other locals understood by all this were geometrical multiplications of 'knowledge'. This circulation and multiplication did not, however, lead to the harmonization of knowledge and beliefs. Michael Polanyi summed this up very well in his characterization of knowledge transfer between generations: 'submission to a consensus is always accompanied to some extent by the imposition of one's views on the consensus'. This is true, he goes on to say, even though agreement might at face value seem far less active a stance than dissent.[67] Steven Shapin echoes this point, arguing that whatever respected source we may trust, 'since each acceptance of authoritative knowledge at the same time modifies existing usage, trusting is an unending means for the extension and modification of knowledge'.[68] The process of modification is something that bishops, in their attempts to fix local knowledge at a given point in time, were battling against even as their information-gathering activity facilitated it. Like the battles against sinfulness (Chapter 13) and the changeability of matter (Chapter 12), it could never be completely won, but ostensibly at least the institutions of the church existed in order to place limits on the multiplication of meaning. Because many versions of reality could be in circulation at any given time, the stamp of authority (whether that of the bishop or that of trustworthy men) was what mattered most to the practice of governance.

The modification of knowledge by trustworthy parish witnesses (let alone by the wider population) completes the cycle of information that we have traced in this chapter, while at the same time making plain just how fissiparous and unquantifiable such things were in reality. The cycle is only a model, and the bishop's control of the symbolic role of the trustworthy man does not equate to his total control over knowledge and ideas. Episcopal injunctions aimed at altering local knowledge would themselves have been altered by their recipients even if they were faithfully learnt, remembered, and respected. It could not be otherwise. Every act of listening or reading was an act of translation and the creation of knowledge. Indeed for the bishop's words to have any meaning at all they had to be incorporated into a body of memories that were meaningful to the parishioners.[69] The mental world of most parishioners was far removed from that of a bishop and his household staff, and so their generation of meaning worked to different rules.[70] This conclusion allows us to nuance Marx's remark about the 'mutual deception' exercised by the upper and lower reaches of an institution. There may well often have been moments of wilful deception, as when parishioners deliberately undervalued their church with an eye on future taxation levels, but there were also more pervasive forms of unintentional deception. Since meaning and understanding are dependent upon individuals and their different social experiences, all meaning is to some degree subjective and all understanding contains within it some misunderstanding. The structures of the institutional church by which information was captured, circulated, stored, and transmitted—all the documentation and personnel of governance—were conditioned at a deep and causal level by the fragility of meaning and the utter dependence of the whole exhausting drive for legibility and control upon information that was useful before it was necessarily true. Trustworthy men were integral to all of this, and they made the institutional church. But they did not make a church in which all power accrued to the apex, and the bishop was never able to 'control' the parish. Trustworthy men made a church in which meaning was 'at the discretion of agents', and although everyone must have had slightly different impressions of the parish and its rights, the social capital gained by trustworthy men meant that it was their discretion that frequently carried the most weight, and this only added to their advantage. If bishops built a church upon trust, they also built it upon the inequalities that flowed from all of this.

CONCLUSION

OVER THE COURSE OF THIS BOOK I have argued that episcopal governance of the English church between 1200 and 1500 was more than a series of offices and organizations. The bishop's household, his subordinates, the diocesan clergy, the church courts, and visitations were all essential to this institutional church, but their existence is not a sufficient explanation of its operation or its power. The local world of the parish needs to be brought into consideration as well, while being substantially reconceptualized. Instead of seeing the parish merely as the object of episcopal action, or—as in many histories of the late medieval parish—as barely affected by power and rule, I have proposed that the institutional church resided in elements of parish life quite as much as it did in the work of a bishop's official or in the practices of record making.

Given the sheer weight of business that late medieval bishops were coming to transact, by accident or design, they could not rely upon the lustre of official letters and the obedience of subordinates. They needed an alliance with the localities, something that would bring them not only the local knowledge necessary to settle disputes, but also an impression of impartiality and a boost to confidence in their governance. This was the task performed by trustworthy men, both in the flesh and in the episcopal rhetoric that brought their role into being. Part III showed the effect of that role upon the parish, and Part IV its impact upon the development of episcopal governance between the middle of the thirteenth century and the Reformation. But this arrangement of the argument was really determined by the need for clarity and a certain depth of engagement with each of the issues in turn. In reality, as the discussion in the individual chapters made plain, the bishop was an ineluctable presence in the parish, and the institutional church was the product of myriad 'transactions' of *fides* conducted in, from, and between the parishes. Trustworthiness was the linguistic and ethical glue that bound parish to diocese; the trustworthy men were its embodiment; its greatest effect was to habituate lay Christians and clergy alike to the idea—probably unconsciously held for the most part—that the power of the church was natural and right, a part of the landscape (quite literally sometimes, as we saw in Chapter 12), and something to be taken for granted. The institutional church was therefore an agglomeration of roles, expectations, actions, reactions, values, feelings, and—yes—offices and organizational structures, with the trustworthy men at the dynamic centre.

However, the symbiosis of bishops and parishes was not a perfectly functional system, and in fact very few of its social and institutional effects were the result of conscious intention on the part of bishops. The strength and endurance of the 'social church' rested instead upon the interaction between three uncontrollable things: trust, information, and people themselves. Trust, faith, and belief, as we saw in Part I, were the basis for all strong relationships, whether those were with God, another person, a group of people, or oneself. And yet it was always under pressure from nagging doubt as well as the more dramatic 'metaphysical tailspins' discussed in Chapter 3. Trust is, after all, something that draws attention to our ignorance and uncertainty as much as providing a remedy for it. The potential instability of information arose, as I argued in Chapters 10 and 14, from its intimate relationship to trust. Testimony was both essential for knowledge of the world, and yet always compromised by its subjectivity. What is more, trusting testimony was 'an unending means for the extension and modification of knowledge'[1] so that no amount of effort to control it (and the evidence of this book illustrates the massive time and energy that went into the attempt) could ever totally succeed. The reception of information and its translation (both from language to language and from culture to culture) inevitably involved misinterpretation, subtle modifications of meaning, as well as a degree of forgetfulness and occasional outright deception.

The uncontrollability of the people, the trustworthy men, derived from the fact that their symbolic role was performed by real people. On the one hand the trustworthy men were anonymous mummers performing a symbolic role that had been called into existence by bishops, labelled with a term that bishops controlled, and made to act in ways that bishops determined. But looked at from another perspective, they were real (and often named) men whose value as performers was determined by their preexisting social and economic status, analysed in Chapters 6 and 7. John Law has argued that the history of power 'may be explained by referring to revolutions in [the] methods for creating loyal, mobile, yet otherwise passive agents'.[2] To some extent this is indeed what the arguments and evidence of this book have shown: how bishops sought to make the physical and social world legible through the controlled collection of local testimony, with the intention of augmenting their institutional power and extending their capacity to intrude upon the lives of the clergy and lay Christians. The trustworthy men were useful to bishops insofar as they fulfilled this role, but Law's characterization of useful agents as 'passive' does not quite hit the mark. As we have seen in Chapter 5 and elsewhere, trustworthiness was a symbolic role, and as such it could withstand the occasional act of overt defiance (to use another word in the *fides* lexicon, literally a renunciation of faith or loyalty, from the Latin *diffidentia*) and the absolutely universal fact that the trustworthy men were not passive: far from it. They often pursued their own interests ahead of those of their communities, and some of their acts (such as reporting to an episcopal visitor that all was well: *omnia bene*) could have the effect of holding a bishop's power at bay rather than letting it in. However, this was not a problem for bishops, since the great paradox of episcopal government through trustworthy men was that their very uncontrollability was precisely what made them so useful in the first place. Their pursuit of status within the parish meant that their word in matters of fact, law, and morality was protected from too much dissent by the dominant position they occupied. Whether through respect, agreement, deference, fear, or resignation, their judgements could be treated by bishops as 'firm and uncontested'.

The reliance of bishops upon active, rather than passive, agents meant that they depended upon inequality. Trust or faith was an inherently discriminating act, and in many cases discriminatory as well, for tangible distinctions between people reduce the incalculable complexity of working out who is genuinely trustworthy. The institutional church was located in the combination of respect, fear, deference, and envy with which the trustworthy men were viewed, for this was what made their testimony useful, and this is also what kept women, the poor, and those without good *fama* out of the late medieval public sphere. The effect that the ideology of ecclesiastical trustworthiness had upon the distribution of economic resources was considerable, but it was arguably even more significant in entrenching assumptions about masculinity and femininity, hardening attitudes against female participation in public life, and projecting the alliance between patriarchal institutions and male heads of household far into the future. This 'dark side' of trust, as Sheilagh Ogilvie has called it, is something that emerges more clearly from histories attuned to the breadth of social experience than from the more theoretical treatments of trust in economics and political science, where rationality and agency tend to be tacitly gendered male and treated as individual rather than social phenomena.[3] There is also, as I argued in the introduction to Part I, much to be gained from looking at historical examples of institutions considering how to trust the people, rather than vice versa.

As I have said, these negative social effects were not entirely intended by the bishops who relied upon the rhetoric and reality of trustworthy men. They were side effects of the drive to build governing institutions. Equally, bishops' reliance upon uncontrollable information and people did not mean that they could accommodate infinite disagreement. Quite the contrary, as the withdrawal of trustworthy status, the rejection of lay concerns, or—in extreme cases—prosecution for heresy demonstrate, they often acted consciously to enforce hierarchy as well. Bishops were, after all, able to impose spiritual and material sanctions upon anyone under their jurisdiction. The fact that their power rested upon lay cooperation increased, rather than lessened, their capacity for domination.

{⸎⸎⸎W⸎⸎⸎}

As David d'Avray has argued, principles and values are made durable by their 'embodiment in social action and institutional life', and for the medieval church faith and trust were embodied in parish elites and the relationships those men had with their neighbours.[4] The growing capacity for bishops to govern their dioceses, the clergy and churches within them, and the individual Christians who lived in the parishes was thereby founded upon the commodification of social identities and relationships, and it is notable that these were, in many respects, themselves founded upon faith. That is to say, they were founded upon the feeling of belonging to a 'community of the faith', being a Christian in 'the faith', being in good faith with one's neighbours, possessing sufficient *fides* or troth to be able to make promises and strike bargains, perceiving friendship and sincerity in the heart of another, and upon the emotional and mental struggles involved in the contemplation of an unseen God. It was from these other varieties of *fides* that the ideology surrounding the *fidedignus* drew so much of its meaning and viability, and yet its rise to prominence in the thirteenth century also impacted upon that wider culture. Primarily the elevation of the *fidedigni* (trustworthy) implied that the merely *fidelis* (faithful) were not to be trusted, an attitude that was not—of course—shared by all in the church, but one that was strengthened greatly by this innovation. Being *fidedignum* also disrupted the culture of interpersonal faith, since men called trustworthy by the church brought fragments of that institutional approval to bear in their relations with other people, tipping the popular understanding of *fides* and troth away from something shared and reciprocal, and making it more of a means to differentiate and discriminate. This was not the transformation from medieval to modern much vaunted in some of the historical and theoretical scholarship, but simply a reconfiguration of society and culture, of which there had been many hitherto and would be many more to come in succeeding centuries. Interpersonal trust was not swept away by this era of the trustworthy men, but it now took place in a more unequal social environment in which institutions were stronger than ever before.

{⸎⸎⸎W⸎⸎⸎}

Many of my findings in relation to the trustworthy men in the church could, with due consideration of cultural specificity, apply to the people who played similar roles in other contexts. The roles of local elites in enabling the growth of institutional power, and of institutions in stimulating the formation of local elites, are both eminently capable of comparative treatment. This study has also demonstrated the value of pursuing an integrated history, in defiance of increasing specialization in academia. I have shown that histories of churches and religion are enriched when they are also social histories, and equally, that the potential for social and economic histories to comprehend the nature of human action and cooperation is enhanced when culture (religion, values, and habits of thought) is taken into account.

Introduction

1. *Register of John de Grandisson*, 349–50. The mandate was addressed to the vicar of 'Poutone', which is a fourteenth-century variant of Pawton, the name of Bishop Grandisson's manor in the parish.

2. For Grandisson's career, see Audrey Erskine, 'Grandison, John (1292–1369)', *Oxford Dictionary of National Biography* (Oxford: Oxford University Press, 2004), http://www.oxforddnb.com/view/article/11238.

3. *Register of John de Grandisson*, 341. The rector, Walter de Cantilupe (not to be confused with the thirteenth-century bishop of Worcester of the same name), may have been studying at Stapledon Hall in Oxford, founded in 1314 by a former bishop of Exeter and later elevated to college status. The issue of mortuaries in English canon law is discussed in Richard H. Helmholz, *The* Ius Commune *in England: Four Studies* (Oxford: Oxford University Press, 2001), 135–86.

4. For discussion, see pp. 107–8.

5. The towering figures of the nineteenth and twentieth centuries, writing in English, were arguably William Stubbs and Christopher Cheney, for whom see James Campbell, 'Stubbs, William (1825–1901)', and Marjorie Chibnall, 'Cheney, Christopher Robert (1906–1987)', in *Oxford Dictionary of National Biography*; for context, see Henry Mayr-Harting, 'Ecclesiastical History', in Alan Deyermond (ed.), *A Century of British Medieval Studies* (Oxford: Oxford University Press, 2007), 131–57.

6. See, for example, Alexander Hamilton Thompson, *The English Clergy and Their Organization in the Later Middle Ages* (Oxford: Clarendon, 1947), 40–71; Christopher R. Cheney, *English Bishops' Chanceries 1100–1250* (Manchester: Manchester University Press, 1950); Robin L. Story, *Diocesan Administration in Fifteenth-Century England* (York: Borthwick Institute, 1959); Roy Martin Haines, *The Administration of the Diocese of Worcester in the First Half of the Fourteenth Century* (London: SPCK, 1965); Dorothy M. Owen, *Church and Society in Medieval Lincolnshire* (Lincoln: History of Lincolnshire, 1981), 20–36.

7. Peter Biller, 'Popular Religion in the Central and Later Middle Ages', in Michael Bentley (ed.), *Companion to Historiography* (Abingdon: Routledge, 1997), 221–46; John H. Arnold, 'Histories and Historiographies of Medieval Christianity', in John H. Arnold (ed.), *The Oxford Handbook of Medieval Christianity* (Oxford: Oxford University Press, 2014), 23–39.

8. This is a phrase coined by Sethina Watson and myself in 2006 to name an annual discussion group for medievalists, which ran until 2015. The group comprised historians of religion and the church interested in social analysis, and social historians interested in the explanatory potential of culture.

9. Barry Barnes, *The Elements of Social Theory* (London: Routledge, 1995); Avner Greif, *Institutions and the Path to the Modern Economy: Lessons from Medieval Trade* (Cambridge: Cambridge University Press, 2006); Douglass C. North, *Institutions, Institutional Change and Economic Performance* (Cambridge: Cambridge University Press, 1990); Judith M. Bennett, *History Matters: Patriarchy and the Challenge of Feminism* (Manchester: Manchester University Press, 2006). The application of sociological and economic models to the study of the medieval church is further discussed in Ian Forrest,

'Continuity and Change in the Institutional Church', in Arnold (ed.), *Oxford Handbook of Medieval Christianity*, 185–200.

10. Susan Reynolds, 'Social Mentalities and the Case of Medieval Scepticism', *Transactions of the Royal Historical Society*, sixth series 1 (1991), 21–41; John Van Engen, 'The Christian Middle Ages as an Historiographical Problem', *American Historical Review*, 91 (1986), 519–52; Biller, 'Popular Religion'; Arnold, 'Histories and Historiographies'.

11. A position criticized in Christine Caldwell Ames, 'Authentic, True, and Right: Inquisition and the Study of Medieval Popular Religion', in David C. Mengel and Lisa Wolverton (eds.), *Christianity and Culture in the Middle Ages: Essays to Honor John Van Engen* (Notre Dame, Ind.: University of Notre Dame Press, 2015), 87–119.

Part I: Late Medieval Cultures of Trust

1. Ferdinand Tönnies, *Gemeinschaft und Gesellschaft*, trans. Jose Hollis as *Community and Civil Society* (Cambridge: Cambridge University Press, 2001); Max Weber, *Wirtschaft und Gesellschaft*, trans. Günther Roth and Claus Wittich as *Economy and Society: An Outline of Interpretive Sociology* (Berkeley: University of California Press, 2013); Karl Polanyi, *The Great Transformation* (New York: Farrer and Rinehart, 1944); Émile Durkheim, *De la division du travail social* (Paris: Alcan, 1893).

2. Adam B. Seligman, *The Problem of Trust* (Princeton, N.J.: Princeton University Press, 1997), 73; Jan Philipp Reemtsma, *Trust and Violence: An Essay on a Modern Relationship* (Princeton, N.J.: Princeton University Press, 2012), 14–15, 35–46.

3. Barbara A. Misztal, *Trust in Modern Societies: The Search for the Bases of Social Order* (Cambridge: Polity, 1996), 9. Similarly Richard Sosis, 'Does Religion Promote Trust? The Role of Signaling, Reputation, and Punishment', *Interdisciplinary Journal of Research on Religion*, 1 (2005), 18–19, argues that trust is more necessary in modern societies because of individualism and lack of monitoring, though for the same reasons it is not more prevalent. Another version of this is the argument that modern societies experience 'generalized trust', whereas premodern societies knew only group-specific trust. Scholars who buy into the modernization narrative seek to explain how local and group-based trust expanded into general trust: Richard Tilly, 'Introduction', *Jahrbuch für Wirtschaftsgeschichte*, 46 (2005), 10–12.

4. Richard Smith, 'Modernization and the Corporate Village Community in England: Some Sceptical Reflections', in Alan R. H. Baker and Derek Gregory (eds.), *Explorations in Historical Geography: Interpretative Essays* (Cambridge: Cambridge University Press, 1984), 140–79; David Postles, 'Personal Pledging in Manorial Courts in the Later Middle Ages', *Bulletin of the John Rylands Library*, 75 (1993), 71–76; John Dagenais and Margaret R. Greer, 'Decolonizing the Middle Ages: Introduction', *Journal of Medieval and Early Modern Studies*, 30 (2000), 431–48; Clare Haru Crowston, 'Credit and the Metanarrative of Modernity', *French Historical Studies*, 34 (2011), 7–19; Carol Symes, 'When We Talk about Modernity', *American Historical Review*, 116 (2011), 715–26.

5. Geoffrey A. Hosking, *Trust: A History* (Oxford: Oxford University Press, 2014), 5. To an extent Hosking is himself locked in a developmental approach to the study of trust, identifying a 'broadening of the radius of trust' over time (48) and buying into accounts of growing tolerance and decreasing violence.

6. Sebastien Conrad, *What Is Global History?* (Princeton, N.J.: Princeton University Press, 2016), 53–61, succinctly describes the main critiques from postcolonial studies, while noting their lack of historical time depth. David Graeber, *Debt: The First 5000 Years* (New York: First Melville, 2011), 21–41, skewers one of the central myths of modernization as it relates to trust in economic exchange: barter.

7. Seligman, *Problem of Trust*, 49.

8. Encapsulated in the statement that religion deals in confidence, while law and government necessitate trust: Niklas Luhmann, 'Familiarity, Confidence, Trust: Problems and Alternatives', in Diego Gambetta (ed.), *Trust: Making and Breaking Cooperative Relations* (Oxford: Blackwell, 1988), 99–100.

9. Richard Firth Green, *A Crisis of Truth: Literature and Law in Ricardian England* (Philadelphia: University of Pennsylvania Press, 1999), 39–40; Robert C. Palmer, *English Law in the Age of the Black Death, 1348–1381: A Transformation of Governance and Law* (Chapel Hill: University of North Carolina Press, 1993), makes a case for 1350 being the crucial turning point in the adoption of contracts.

10. Craig Muldrew, *The Economy of Obligation: The Culture of Credit and Social Relations in Early Modern England* (Basingstoke: Macmillan, 1998), 15–59, 95–96, 149–50, 157–72.

11. Muldrew, *Economy of Obligation*, 133–34, 320.

12. Among the theorists of trust, see, for example, Piotr Sztompka, *Trust: A Sociological Theory* (Cambridge: Cambridge University Press, 1999), 119–38; Marek Kohn, *Trust: Self-Interest and the Common Good* (Oxford: Oxford University Press, 2008).

13. William Ouchi, 'Markets, Bureaucracies, and Clans', *Administrative Science Quarterly*, 25 (1980), 129–42; Niklas Luhmann, *Trust and Power: Two Works* (Chichester: John Wiley, 1979), 34–36; Diego Gambetta, 'Can We Trust Trust?', in Gambetta (ed.), *Trust*, 219; Sosis, 'Does Religion Promote Trust?', 7–8; Francis Fukuyama, *Trust: The Social Virtues and the Creation of Prosperity* (New York: Free Press, 1995), 224.

14. Sosis, 'Does Religion Promote Trust?', 13; Oliver Williamson, 'Calculativeness, Trust, and Economic Organization', *Journal of Law and Economics*, 36 (1993), 463, 483; Luhmann, *Trust and Power*, 20.

15. Charles Tilly, *Trust and Rule* (Cambridge: Cambridge University Press, 2005), 26. Tilly nonetheless assumed trust to be a universal human phenomenon, rather than something with different *meanings* in different cultures, and his co-option of numerous medieval and early modern case studies, including Eamon Duffy's account of parish organizations in sixteenth-century Morebath, does not give him access to the level of detail to be found in the present book: Tilly, 91, writes that 'neither Duffy nor his readers know to what extent these obviously important social organizations actually contained trust networks'. This is because to date historians have seldom asked such questions, let alone answered them in detail.

16. Bernard Williams, *Truth and Truthfulness: An Essay in Genealogy* (Princeton, N.J.: Princeton University Press, 2002), 93.

17. Dorothea Weltecke, 'Trust: Some Methodological Reflections', in Petra Schulte, Marco Mostert, and Irene van Renswoude (eds.), *Strategies of Writing: Studies on Text and Trust in the Middle Ages* (Turnhout: Brepols, 2008), 379–92.

18. Ernest Gellner, 'Trust, Cohesion, and the Social Order', in Gambetta (ed.), *Trust*, 143; Hosking, *Trust*, 43.

19. Martin Hollis, *Trust within Reason* (Cambridge: Cambridge University Press, 1998). Paul Seabright, *The Company of Strangers: A Natural History of Economic Life* (Princeton, N.J.: Princeton University Press, 2004), 58–61, argues that both the calculation and the reciprocity involved in trusting are evolutionary adaptations.

20. Works dealing substantially with trust include Steven Johnstone, *A History of Trust in Ancient Greece* (Chicago: University of Chicago Press, 2011); Teresa Morgan, *Roman Faith and Christian Faith: Pistis and Fides in the Early Roman Empire and Early Churches* (Oxford: Oxford University Press, 2015); Petra Schulte, *Scripturae publicae creditur: Das Vertrauen in Notariatsurkunden im kommunalen Italien des 12. und 13. Jahrhunderts*

(Tübingen: Max Niemeyer, 2003); Susan Reynolds, 'Trust in Medieval Society and Politics', in idem, *The Middle Ages without Feudalism* (Farnham: Ashgate Varorium, 2012); Steven Shapin, *A Social History of Truth: Civility and Science in Seventeenth-Century England* (Chicago: University of Chicago Press, 1994); Thierry Dutour, *Sous l'empire du bien: 'bonnes gens' et pacte social (XIIIe-XVe siècle)* (Paris: Classiques Garnier, 2015).

21. On guilds, see Sheilagh Ogilvie, *Institutions and European Trade: Merchant Guilds, 1000–1800* (Cambridge: Cambridge University Press, 2011), and Gervase Rosser, *The Art of Solidarity in the Middle Ages: Guilds in England 1250–1550* (Oxford: Oxford University Press, 2015); on credit, see Steven A. Epstein, 'Secrecy and Genoese Commercial Practices', *Journal of Medieval History*, 20 (1994), 313–25, Gabriele Signori, *Schuldenwirtschaft: Konsumenten- und Hypothekarkredite im spätmittelalterlichen Basel* (Munich: Universitätsverlag Konstanz, 2015), and Muldrew, *Economy of Obligation*; on networks and enforcement, see Ghislaine Lydon, *On Trans-Saharan Trails: Islamic Law, Trade Networks, and Cross-Cultural Exchange in Nineteenth-Century West Africa* (Cambridge: Cambridge University Press, 2009), Francesca Trivellato, *The Familiarity of Strangers: The Sephardic Diaspora, Livorno and Cross-Cultural Trade in the Early Modern Period* (New Haven, Conn.: Yale University Press, 2009); David Sebouh Aslanian, *From the Indian Ocean to the Mediterranean: The Global Trade Networks of Armenians from New Julfa* (Berkeley: University of California Press, 2010), and Jessica Goldberg, *Trade and Institutions in the Medieval Mediterranean: The Geniza Merchants and Their Business World* (Cambridge: Cambridge University Press, 2012); on the 'embeddedness' of trust, see Phillip I. Ackerman-Lieberman, *The Business of Identity: Jews, Muslims, and Economic Life in Medieval Egypt* (Stanford, Calif.: Stanford University Press, 2014), and in a more summary and comparative fashion, Ian Forrest and Anne Haour, 'Trust in Long Distance Relationships', in Catherine Holmes and Naomi Standen (eds.), *The Global Middle Ages* (forthcoming).

22. Dallas G. Denery II, *Seeing and Being Seen in the Later Medieval World: Optics, Theology, and Religious Life* (Cambridge: Cambridge University Press, 2005); Christophe Grellard, *Croire et savoir: les principes de la connaissance selon Nicolas d'Autrécourt* (Paris: Vrin, 2005); Sabina Flanagan, *Doubt in an Age of Faith: Uncertainty in the Long Twelfth Century* (Turnhout: Brepols, 2008); Dallas G. Denery II, Kantik Ghosh, and Nicolette Zeeman (eds.), *Uncertain Knowledge: Scepticism, Relativism, and Doubt in the Middle Ages* (Turnhout: Brepols, 2014); Frances Andrews, Charlotte Methuen, and Andrew Spicer (eds.), *Doubting Christianity: The Church and Doubt*, Studies in Church History, 52 (Cambridge: Cambridge University Press, 2016).

Chapter One: Theology

1. Morgan, *Roman Faith and Christian Faith*; Gérard Freyburger, *Fides: Étude sémantique et religieuse depuis les origines jusqu'à l'époque augustéenne* (Paris: Belles Lettres, 2009); Emile Benveniste, *Indo-European Language and Society*, trans. Elizabeth Palmer (London: Faber, 1973), 94–98.

2. Rodney Needham, *Belief, Language, and Experience* (Oxford: Blackwell, 1972), 5–7; Jean Wirth, 'La naissance du concept de croyance', *Bibliothèque d'humanisme et renaissance*, 45 (1983), 8.

3. Notable exceptions are John Van Engen, 'Faith as a Concept of Order in Medieval Christendom', in Thomas Kselman (ed.), *Belief in History: Innovative Approaches to European and American Religion* (Notre Dame, Ind.: University of Notre Dame Press, 1991), 38–47; Steven Justice, 'Did the Middle Ages Believe in their Miracles?', *Representations*, 103 (2008), 1–29. Eamon Duffy, *The Stripping of the Altars: Traditional Religion in England 1400–1580*, 2nd ed. (New Haven, Conn.: Yale University Press, 2005), 53–87, provides an

exemplary guide to 'how the ploughman learnt his paternoster' but focuses on the content of belief rather than the act of believing. Paul Hyams, 'Faith, Fealty and Jewish "infideles" in Twelfth-Century England', in Sarah Rees Jones and Sethina Watson (eds.), *Christians and Jews in Angevin England: The York Massacre of 1190, Narratives and Contexts* (Woodbridge: York Medieval Press, 2013), 125–47, is an exceptional study of faith talk by a social historian.

4. Michel de Certeau, 'Une pratique sociale de la différence: croire', in *Faire croire: modalités de la diffusion et de la réception des messages religieux du XIIe au XVe siècle* (Rome: École Française de Rome, 1981), 364–65, 373–75.

5. Jaroslav Pelikan, *Credo: Historical and Theological Guide to Creeds and Confessions of Faith in the Christian Tradition* (New Haven, Conn.: Yale University Press, 2003), 44; Benveniste, *Indo-European Language and Society*, 99–100; Needham, *Belief, Language, and Experience*, 40–50.

6. Cambridge University Library, EDR G/1/5, fos. 132v–133r. For similar examples, see Lincolnshire Archives, REG/20, fos. 13v, 62v; *Register of Thomas Rotherham*, 190.

7. Augustine, *De fide et symbolo*, ed. Joseph Zycha, CSEL 41 (Vindobonae: Tempsky, 1900), 1.1, trans. Michael G. Campbell in *The Works of Saint Augustine: On Christian Belief*, ed. Boniface Ramsey (New York: New York City Press, 2005), 155.

8. John Mirk, *Instructions for Parish Priests*, ed. Gillis Kristensson (Lund: CWK Gleerup, 1974), 90–91: 'I believe in our holy host / Father of heaven, god almighty, / That all therein made and wrought, / Heaven and earth and all from nought. / In Jesus Christ I believe also, / His only son, and no other . . .'.

9. A different, and intriguing, use of the lexicon of belief occurs in inquisitorial texts on heretics, where 'believers' were those who followed heretical preachers: Lucy Sackville, *Heresy and Heretics in the Thirteenth Century: The Textual Representations* (Woodbridge: York Medieval Press, 2011), 97–98, 117–21, 129.

10. Augustine, *De trinitate*, 13.2.5, ed. William John Mountain, 2 vols. CCSL 50, 50A (Turnhout: Brepols, 1968), 385–87; idem, *De fide et symbolo*, 1.1, trans. Campbell, 155–56.

11. Hugh of St Victor, *On the Sacraments of the Christian Faith*, trans. Roy J. Deferrari (Cambridge, Mass.: Medieval Academy of America, 1951), 168. This was an influential formulation, repeated in canon law commentaries, pastoral treatises, and sermons, for example Hostiensis, *Aurea summa* (Venice: Gratiosum Perchacinum, 1605), 1.1: *Quid est fides*; Ranulph Higden, *Speculum Curatorum (A Mirror for Curates), Book 1: The Commandments*, ed. Eugene Crook and Margaret Jennings (Paris: Peeters, 2012), 71; *A Repertorium of Middle English Prose Sermons*, ed. Veronica O'Mara and Suzanne Paul, 4 vols. (Turnhout: Brepols, 2007), 3.2089–91. Other theologians differed in how they defined knowledge and certainty, but many of their schemas amounted to much the same thing. In the later fifteenth century Reginald Pecock's argument that the faith of living Christians was 'opynyonal' as opposed to 'sciencial' was highly provocative because it seemed to go beyond the consensus on certainty and admit the validity of lay doubts: Mishtooni Bose, 'Vernacular Opinions', in Denery, Ghosh, and Zeeman (eds.), *Uncertain Knowledge*, 240, 253–56.

12. Pastoral texts often differentiated between accepting God's word as true and believing that he exists, in which there was no merit, and the more affective formation of a relationship of faith *in* God: Peter Lombard, *Libri quattuor Sententiarum*, PL 192, 3.23.4, trans. Giulio Silano, 4 vols. (Toronto: PIMS, 2008), 3.98–99; comparable points are made in Hugh of St Victor, *On the Sacraments of the Christian Faith*, 171–73; Joannes Balbus, *Catholicon* (Mainz, 1460: repr., Farnborough: Gregg International, 1971), unpaginated, s.v. *Fides*; Higden, *Speculum Curatorum*, 69, 71; William Lyndwood, *Provinciale seu constitutiones Angliae*, I.1 *Ignorantia sacerdotum*, s.v. *Credo in Deum* (Oxford: Hall, 1679), 2–3.

13. *Biblia Latina cum glossa ordinaria: Facsimile Reprint of the Editio Princeps Adolph Rusch of Strasburg 1480/81*, 4 vols. (Turnhout: Brepols, 1992), 4.443 (Hebrews 11.7).

14. *Repertorium of Middle English Prose Sermons*, 1.227–28. This theme is discussed in Frances Andrews, 'Doubting John?', in Andrews, Methuen, and Spicer (eds.), *Doubting Christianity*, 17–48.

15. Lombard, *Sentences*, 3.23.7, trans. Silano, 3.100–101; Hugh of St Victor, *On the Sacraments of the Christian Faith*, 168.

16. Higden, *Speculum Curatorum*, 69; *Fasciculus Morum: A Fourteenth-Century Preacher's Handbook*, ed. Siegfried Wenzel (University Park: Pennsylvania State University Press, 1989), 571–73.

17. Hugh of St Victor, *On the Sacraments of the Christian Faith*, 165–66; Bernard of Clairvaux, *De consideratione*, 5.3.6, in Jean Leclercq et al. (eds.), *Sancti Bernardi opera*, 8 vols. (Rome: Editiones Cisterciensis, 1957–77), 3.471.

18. Thomas Aquinas, *Summa theologiae*, 2a2ae. I, I, ed. Thomas Gilby et al., 60 vols. (London: Blackfriars, 1964–76), 31.9.

19. Richard W. Southern, *Saint Anselm and His Biographer: A Study of Monastic Life and Thought 1059–c.1130* (Cambridge: Cambridge University Press, 1966), 54–57, 346; Avery Dulles, *Assurance of Things Hoped For: A Theology of Christian Faith* (Oxford: Oxford University Press, 1994), 28–29.

20. While it is true that Abelard placed greater emphasis upon reason, it is a fallacy promoted by his Cistercian detractors—notably Bernard of Clairvaux (1090–1153) and William of St Thierry (ca. 1080–1148)—that he sought to replace the operation of faith with rational thought: Rik Van Nieuwenhove, *Introduction to Medieval Theology* (Cambridge: Cambridge University Press, 2012), 105–18; Michael Clanchy, *Abelard: A Medieval Life* (Oxford: Blackwell, 1997), 35–37.

21. Hugh of St Victor, *On the Sacraments of the Christian Faith*, 167, 169; Lombard, *Sentences*, 3.23.7, trans. Silano, 3.100–101. The *Ordinary Gloss* to Wisdom 3.9 explains that trust (*confidencia*) brings understanding, and without faith one cannot be part of the elect: *Biblia Latina cum glossa ordinaria*, 2.726.

22. Frederick Christian Bauerschmidt, *Thomas Aquinas: Faith, Reason and Following Christ* (Oxford: Oxford University Press, 2013), 143–48; William J. Courtenay, 'Nominalism and Late Medieval Religion', in Charles Trinkaus and Heiko A. Oberman (eds.), *The Pursuit of Holiness in Late Medieval and Renaissance Religion* (Leiden: Brill, 1974), 57; Alfred J. Freddoso, 'Ockham on Faith and Reason', in Paul Vincent Spade (ed.), *The Cambridge Companion to Ockham* (Cambridge: Cambridge University Press, 1999), 326–49. For Ockham natural reason was sufficient for enquiry within its own sphere of competence, namely the natural world, where knowing meant seeing. But the mysteries of theology lay beyond where reason could penetrate, and faith was what permitted the believer to accept the revealed truths of theology.

23. Heiko Augustinus Oberman, *The Harvest of Medieval Theology: Gabriel Biel and Late Medieval Nominalism* (Durham: Labyrinth Press, 1963), 68–84; Steven Ozment, *The Age of Reform 1250–1550: An Intellectual and Religious History of Late Medieval and Reformation Europe* (New Haven, Conn.: Yale University Press, 1980), 46, 61–62; Michael H. Shank, *Unless You Believe, You Shall Not Understand: Logic, University, and Society in Late Medieval Vienna* (Princeton, N.J.: Princeton University Press, 1988), 178–84; Berndt Hamm, *The Reformation of Faith in the Context of Late Medieval Theology and Piety: Essays* (Leiden: Brill, 2004), 163–78; Dulles, *Assurance of Things Hoped For*, 36–38.

24. Higden, *Speculum Curatorum*, 71. Faith was variously described as the strength given to those who believe in Him (2 Chronicles 16.9), the virtuous disposition with which the Holy Spirit flooded the soul (Peter Lombard), and the 'habit of mind, whereby eternal life is begun in us' (Thomas Aquinas): Lombard, *Sentences*, 3.23.8, trans. Silano, 3.102–3; Aquinas, *Summa theologiae*, 2a2ae. I, I.

25. Eileen C. Sweeney, 'New Standards for Certainty: Early Reception of Aristotle's *Posterior Analytics*', in Denery, Ghosh, and Zeeman (eds.), *Uncertain Knowledge*, 53–54, 57. The idea of a mutable universe set in motion by God had implications for concepts of property and knowledge, as discussed in Chapter 12.

26. Dulles, *Assurance of Things Hoped For*, 34; Bauerschmidt, *Thomas Aquinas*, 148–50.

27. Baldwin of Ford, *De commendatione fidei*, 13.1, ed. David N. Bell, CCCM 99 (Turnhout: Brepols, 1991), 361. Baldwin also made the same point as William of Auvergne, that knowledge of God was more certain than knowledge about the world: David N. Bell, '*Certitudo fidei*: Faith, Reason, and Authority in the Writings of Baldwin of Forde', in John R. Sommerfeldt (ed.), *Bernardus Magister* (Cîteaux: Cistercian, 1992), 249–75.

28. Mirk, *Instructions for Parish Priests*, 93.

29. John Acton, *Constitutiones legatinae*, in *Provinciale seu constitutiones Angliae* (Oxford: Hall, 1679), pt. 2, 3–4; Duffy, *Stripping of the Altars*, 53.

30. Cambridge, Trinity College, MS B.14.52, fos. 14r–17v, in *Repertorium of Middle English Prose Sermons*, 1.144–45.

31. Lateran, 1215 c. 1, in *Decrees of the Ecumenical Councils*, ed. Norman P. Tanner, 2 vols. (Washington, D.C.: Georgetown University Press, 1990), 1.230.

32. *Repertorium of Middle English Prose Sermons*, 1.144–45, 4.2536–38.

33. Hamm, *Reformation of Faith*, 156–57.

34. William Langland, *The Vision of Piers Plowman: A Critical Edition of the B-Text*, ed. A.V.C. Schmidt (London: Dent, 1978), passus XVII, lines 59–64.

35. 'Quinque verba', in John Shinners and William J. Dohar (eds.), *Pastors and the Care of Souls in Medieval England* (Notre Dame, Ind.: University of Notre Dame Press, 1998), 133. In this, late medieval Christianity had something in common with the first-century church: Morgan, *Roman Faith and Christian Faith*, 308–15.

36. John of Freiburg, *Summa confessorum* (Augsburg, 1476), book iii, cap. xxxiv, questio cciii; Higden, *Speculum Curatorum*, 79, 81; *Repertorium of Middle English Prose Sermons*, 2.1216–19.

37. Robert Grosseteste, *Templum Dei*, ed. Joseph Goering and F.A.C. Mantello (Toronto: PIMS, 1984), 39, 43–44, 51. For discussion of superfluity and scrupulosity, see Robert N. Swanson, '*Dubius est in fide fidelis est?* Doubt and Assurance in Late Medieval Catholicism', in Andrews, Methuen, and Spicer (eds.), *Doubting Christianity*, 186–202.

38. Mirk, *Instructions for Parish Priests*, 92–95, 116–17, 164; for similar enquiries in fifteenth-century English texts, see Amy Appleford, *Learning to Die in London, 1380–1540* (Philadelphia: University of Pennsylvania Press, 2015), 32, 35, 43.

39. *Memoriale credencium: A Late Middle English Manual of Theology for Lay People*, ed. J.H.L. Kengen (Nijmegen: Katholieke Universiteit Nijmegen, 1979), 200; John of Freiburg, *Summa confessorum*, book iii, cap. xxxiv, questio cciv.

40. *Councils and Synods with Other Documents Relating to the English Church*, II: *A.D. 1205–1313*, ed. F. M. Powicke and Christopher R. Cheney (Oxford: Clarendon, 1964), 2.1063.

41. *The Lay Folks Mass Book*, ed. T. F. Simmons, EETS 71 (1879), 105.

42. Higden, *Speculum Curatorum*, 73. Higden was picking up a similar point made by Augustine, though ultimately derived from Cicero, that *fides* derived from 'facere' (*fi*) and 'dicere' (*des*) 'because what is said is done': *St Augustine Letters Volume I (1–82)*, ed. Sister Wilfrid Parsons (Washington, D.C.: Catholic University of America Press, 1951), 409; M. Tulli Ciceronis, *De officiis*, ed. Michael Winterbottom (Oxford: Clarendon, 1994), 10 (1.7.23).

43. Augustine, *De fide et symbolo*, 1.1, trans. Campbell, 155.

44. 1 Timothy 1.5; *Biblia Latina cum glossa ordinaria*, 4.404–5; Lateran 1215 c. 1, in *Decrees of the Ecumenical Councils*, 1.230; Johannis Teutonicus and Vincentius Hispanis in *Constitutiones Concilii quarti Lateranensis una cum Commentariis glossatorum*, ed. Antonio García y García, Monumenta Iuris Canonici Series A: Corpus Glossatorum, 2 (Vatican: Biblioteca Apostolica, 1981), 187, 287; *Decretum* D. 23 c. 2; Glos. ord. to *Decretals* X 1.1.1 s.v. *Simpliciter*; 'The Athanasian Creed from the *Sarum Breviary*', in *Pastors and the Care of Souls*, 151–52.

45. *Speculum Vitae: A Reading Edition*, ed. Ralph Hanna and Venetia Somerset, 2 vols., EETS 331–32 (2008), 1.51; Higden, *Speculum Curatorum*, 73.

46. *A Late Fifteenth-Century Dominical Sermon Cycle*, ed. Stephen Morrison, 2 vols., EETS 337–38 (2012), 176; *A Macaronic Sermon Collection from Late Medieval England: Oxford, MS Bodley 649*, ed. Patrick J. Horner (Toronto: PIMS, 2006), 456.

47. Colossians, 1.23, in *The Holy Bible . . . Made from the Latin Vulgate by John Wycliffe and his Followers*, ed. Josiah Forshall and Frederic Madden, 4 vols. (Oxford: Oxford University Press, 1850), 4.431.

48. Matthew 8.23; James 1.6; *Repertorium of Middle English Prose Sermons*, 1.511–12, 3.1722, 1737.

49. A view primarily associated with Robert I. Moore's succinct and influential book *The Formation of a Persecuting Society: Power and Deviance in Western Europe, 950–1250* (Oxford: Blackwell, 1987).

50. Hugh of St Victor, *On the Sacraments of the Christian Faith*, 169–70.

51. Lombard, *Sentences*, 3.25.3, trans. Silano, 3.108–9; Hugh of St Victor, *On the Sacraments of the Christian Faith*, 173–74, 180; Higden, *Speculum Curatorum*, 73; Peter Biller, 'Intellectuals and the Masses: Oxen and She-asses in the Medieval Church', in Arnold (ed.), *Oxford Handbook of Medieval Christianity*, 328–29.

52. Christophe Grellard, 'How Is It Possible to Believe Falsely? John Buridan, the *Vetula*, and the Psychology of Error', in Denery, Ghosh, and Zeeman (eds.), *Uncertain Knowledge*, 93; Biller, 'Intellectuals and the Masses', 329.

53. Shank, *Unless You Believe, You Shall Not Understand*, 172; *Macaronic Sermon Collection from Late Medieval England*, 168. While the gospels might inveigh against riches and 'respect of persons', and praise the 'poor in this world, rich in faith', medieval commentaries turned such ideals into exhortations to give alms to the poor and to look beyond a man's riches to his inner qualities. (The implication being that the poor needed food not ideas, and it was only rich men whose inner qualities were worth probing.) They were not taken as injunctions to listen to the poor and the simple: James 2.1–2: *Biblia Latina cum glossa ordinaria*, 4.514. The clergy were likewise divided into those with cure of souls (who needed a clear and distinct knowledge) and those without, but the strongest division was nonetheless that between clergy and laity: Lyndwood, I.1 *Ignorantia sacerdotum*, s.v *Sciat*, in *Provinciale*, 1; John of Freiburg, *Summa confessorum*, book iii, cap. xxxiv, questio ccii.

54. Flanagan, *Doubt in an Age of Faith*, 118, has suggested that there was then a 'gradual increase' in what was expected of the laity in terms of understanding the faith, but this ignores the strong opposition to lay ambitions from many churchmen.

55. Vincent Gillespie, 'Vernacular Theology', in Paul Strohm (ed.), *Middle English* (Oxford: Oxford University Press, 2007), 401–20.

56. *Speculum Vitae*, 1.52–53: 'For all that come to that place / Shall see him there face to face / And that sight is their sovereign bliss'.

57. *Speculum Vitae*, 1.156, 2.302–3: 'the murkiness that holds back the day / And the mists of the morning'.

58. Kantik Ghosh, 'Logic, Scepticism, and "Heresy" in Early-Fifteenth Century Europe', in Denery, Ghosh, and Zeeman (eds.), *Uncertain Knowledge*, 261–79, contrasts the

responses of Reginald Pecock, who wanted to open the gates of academia, and Nicholas Fleming, the founder of Lincoln College, who wanted to close and guard them.

59. Flanagan, *Doubt in an Age of Faith*, 121; Bell, '*Certitudo fidei*', 259.

60. *Repertorium of Middle English Prose Sermons*, 2.1271, 2.1422–23, 3.1722, 3.2086–87, 4.2528–29; Higden, *Speculum Curatorum*, 69; *Fasciculus Morum*, 563.

61. 'Quinque verba', in *Pastors and the Care of Souls*, 134; Higden, *Speculum Curatorum*, 81.

62. Dorothea Weltecke, 'Doubts and the Absence of Faith', in Arnold (ed.), *Oxford Handbook of Medieval Christianity*, 364.

63. Dulles, *Assurance of Things Hoped For*, 36.

64. Weltecke, 'Doubts and the Absence of Faith', 358–59; John H. Arnold, *Belief and Unbelief in Medieval Europe* (London: Hodder Arnold, 2005), 225–26. See also Reynolds, 'Social Mentalities and the Case of Medieval Scepticism'.

65. Augustine, *De fide rerum invisibilium*, ed. M.P.J van den Hout, CCSL 46 (Turnhout: Brepols, 1969), 5.8, trans. Michael G. Campbell, in Ramsey (ed.), *Works of Saint Augustine*, 190–91; *Fasciculus Morum*, 569–71; Acton, *Constitutiones*, 3–4, citing *Decretum* C. 24 q. 3 c. 27, which is a letter of Augustine to Jerome on the nature of heresy.

66. Allan D. Fitzgerald (ed.), *Augustine through the Ages: An Encyclopedia* (Grand Rapids, Mich.: Eerdmans, 1999), 347–50; Hyams, 'Faith, Fealty and Jewish "infideles" in Twelfth-Century England', 137–38, stresses the ambiguities in attributions of *fides* to God and to people.

67. Augustine, *De fide rerum invisibilium*, 1.1–2.4, trans. Campbell, 183–86.

68. Balbus, *Catholicon*, s.v. *Fides*. Remarkably, Augustine's account of trust also found an echo in Georg Simmel's twentieth-century description of trust in economic exchange: 'Without the general trust that people have in each other, society itself would disintegrate, for very few relationships are based entirely upon what is known with certainty about another person, and very few relationships would endure if trust were not as strong as, or stronger than, rational proof or personal observation'. See *The Philosophy of Money* (London: Routledge, 1978), 178–79.

69. Langland, *Vision of Piers Plowman*, passus XVI, lines 262–63. On wed and borrow, see Frederick Pollock and Frederic William Maitland, *The History of English Law before the Time of Edward I*, 2 vols. (Cambridge: Cambridge University Press, 1968), 2.185–87.

70. Baruch 1.17; Mark 10.24; 2 Corinthians 1.9.

71. *Register of Simon de Montacute*, 249; *Repertorium of Middle English Prose Sermons*, 1.834–35; *Fasciculus Morum*, 561, 569–71. Faith would protect against the world, the flesh, and the devil: Jennifer Depold, 'Preaching the Name: The Influence of a Sermon on the Holy Name of Christ', *Journal of Medieval History*, 40 (2014), 195–208.

72. *Early English Versions of the Gesta Romanorum*, ed. Sidney J. H. Herrtage (London: Trübner, 1879), 41: 'As it is hard to pass a deep water without a bridge, so it is hard to be saved without faith. But there are many of us that will rather put their life and trust in the help of the world than the help of god'.

73. For example, see *Proverbia sententiaeque Latinitatis medii aevi*, ed. Hans Walther, 5 vols. (Göttingen: Vandenhoeck & Ruprecht, 1963–67), 2.114; Carleton Brown and Rossell Hope Robbins (eds.), *The Index of Middle English Verse* (New York: Columbia University Press, 1943), 678 (item 4224).

74. Higden, *Speculum Curatorum*, 69. See also Glos. ord. to *Decretals* X 1.1.1; Balbus, *Catholicon*, s.v. *Fides*.

75. 'Oculus Sacerdotis', in *Pastors and the Care of Souls*, 141, 146–47. This echoed Lateran 1215 c. 65, in *Decrees of the Ecumenical Councils*, 1.265, which stipulated that money paid to the church should be used 'faithfully' for the donor's intended purposes.

76. Lyndwood, V.5 *De haereticis*, s.v. *Fides*, in *Provinciale*, 289, 294. Compare to Higden, *Speculum Curatorum*, 87, where *fides* was said to be like the articles that, though already true, are proven in court.

77. *Decrees of the Ecumenical Councils*, 1.231, 245, 253; Vincent of Spain glossed the 'faithfully' of c. 21 as meaning 'in person and not by proxy', in *Constitutiones Concilii quarti Lateranensis*, 315.

78. *The Book of Sainte Foy*, trans. Pamela Sheingorn and Robert L. A. Clark (Philadelphia: University of Pennsylvania Press, 1995), 37.

79. Elisabeth F. Vodola, '*Fides et culpa*: The Use of Roman Law in Ecclesiastical Ideology', in Brian Tierney and Peter Linehan (eds.), *Authority and Power: Studies on Medieval Law and Government Presented to Walter Ullmann* (Cambridge: Cambridge University Press, 1980), 87–88, 91–92, 94–95.

80. Vodola, '*Fides et culpa*', 97.

81. See, for example, the use of this vocabulary in describing the covenant between God and the Jews: Judith 7.20; Job 13.15; Psalms 2.13, 7.2, 9.11, 15.1, 16.7, 33.23, 61.9; Jeremiah 39.18; Daniel 13.60. In other passages God's relationship with the Israelites was described in terms of a promise of protection (shield, refuge, and so on): 2 Samuel 22.3; Psalms 17.3, 35.8, 90.4. In later medieval England individual faith was occasionally linked to community by way of the ancient theme of covenant and refuge, as in this vernacular sermon: 'Thi feythe hathe made the safe. For Crist hathe delyuered vs out of the fendes power. If that we stedefastely beleue and loue hym . . . he made vs free to duell with hym euermore in the blis of heuen'. *Repertorium of Middle English Prose Sermons*, 3.1645–46.

82. Mark 4.40; Matthew 14.31, 16.8, 17.20.

83. Galatians 3.22–23; Romans 3.20–31; Ben C. Dunson, *Individual and Community in Paul's Letter to the Romans* (Tübingen: Mohr Siebeck, 2012), 123–26.

84. Morgan, *Roman Faith and Christian Faith*, 14; Dulles, *Assurance of Things Hoped For*, 17, argues that in the later books of the New Testament (Jude, Apocalypse, the Pastoral Letters) faith most often refers to doctrine, but Morgan, *Roman Faith and Christian Faith*, 345–46, refutes this.

85. 2 Corinthians 10.7; Augustine, *De trinitate*, 1.4.7; Lombard, *Sentences*, 3.23.6, trans. Silano, 3.100.

86. *Register of Walter Gray*, 149.

87. John Wyclif, *Trialogus*, trans. Stephen E. Lahey (Cambridge: Cambridge University Press, 2013), 116–17.

88. Lateran 1215 c. 1, in *Decrees of the Ecumenical Councils*, 1.230.

89. Hamm, *Reformation of Faith*, 155–56, 158–59.

90. The broadest possible use of *fides* in the Middle Ages was that which is most analogous to our modern sense of 'religion': a complex of beliefs, shared identity, cultural practices, and institutions. This seems to have been implicit in Paul's references to the people who are 'in the faith of Jesus Christ' (Romans 3.16; 1 Timothy 3.13). Peter Biller showed in 1985 how the words *fides*, *lex*, and *secta* were often used this way in the twelfth and thirteenth centuries, with *religio* having a quite different meaning (worship or devotion) before the Reformation: Peter Biller, 'Words and the Medieval Notion of "Religion"', *Journal of Ecclesiastical History*, 36 (1985), 351–69. For example the late twelfth-century bishop of Hereford, William de Vere, referred to the Knights Templar as an order that was 'perpetually fighting for the Christian faith against the enemies of the faith': *EEA 7: Hereford 1079–1234*, ed. Julia Barrow (Oxford: Oxford University Press, 1993), 175. There can be no doubt that the Templars were fighting to defend an idea of Christendom and real Christian people, as well as the notion of the faith as a set of ideas.

91. *Register of Ralph of Shrewsbury*, 527.

92. *EEA* 1: *Lincoln 1067–1185*, ed. David M. Smith (London: Oxford University Press, 1980), 167.

93. *Register of John le Romeyn*, 1.176. The connection between excommunication and the 'community of the faithful' was enshrined in canon law: see, for example, the 1298 General Sentence of Excommunication in *Councils and Synods*, 2.1192–96.

94. *Register of Edmund Lacy, Hereford*, 34.

95. De Certeau, 'Une pratique sociale de la différence', 373–75, 380–83.

Chapter Two: Law and Agreements

1. Augustine, *De fide rerum invisibilium*, 1.1–2.4, trans. Campbell, 183–86.

2. Hosking, *Trust*, 43.

3. Reemtsma, *Trust and Violence*, 19.

4. *Institutes* 4.6.28, in *Corpus iuris civilis*, ed. Paul Krüger and Theodor Mommsen, 3 vols. (Berlin: Weidmann, 1906–12), 1.51; *Digest* 50.16.109, in *Corpus iuris civilis*, 1.861; *Decretum* C. 23 q. 1 c. 3; Glos. ord. to *Decretals* X 1.1, s.v. *De summa trinitate*. For discussion of good faith in sales and contracts, see David Johnston, *Roman Law in Context* (Cambridge: Cambridge University Press, 1999), 81–82; Morgan, *Roman Faith and Christian Faith*, 104–8; Johnstone, *History of Trust in Ancient Greece*, 15–33.

5. Manlio Bellomo, *The Common Legal Past of Europe 1000–1800*, trans. Lydia G. Cochrane (Washington, D.C.: Catholic University of America, 1995).

6. *Register of John le Romeyn*, 1.230; *Register of Thomas de Cobham*, 15; *Register of John Trefnant*, 130; London Metropolitan Archives, DL/C/0205, fo. 41v; David Postles, 'Pledge of Faith in Transactions of Land', *Journal of the Society of Archivists*, 7 (1984), 295–98; *Register of Thomas Rotherham*, 202; Lincolnshire Archives, REG/3, fo. 34v.

7. Thinking with legal concepts outside the strictly legal sphere is known to anthropologists as 'legalism', for which see Paul Dresch and Hannah Skoda (eds.), *Legalism: Anthropology and History* (Oxford: Oxford University Press, 2012).

8. Seligman, *Problem of Trust*; Reemtsma, *Trust and Violence*; Misztal, *Trust in Modern Societies*; Luhmann, *Trust and Power*; Simmel, *Philosophy of Money*; Anthony Giddens, *The Consequences of Modernity* (Cambridge: Polity, 1990). For discussion, see the introduction to Part I.

9. Sosis, 'Does Religion Promote Trust?'; Fukuyama, *Trust*.

10. Green, *Crisis of Truth*, 39–40; Muldrew, *Economy of Obligation*, 133–34, 320; Muldrew's contention finds support among early modernists; for example, Michael Braddick, *State Formation in Early Modern England, c.1550–1700* (Cambridge: Cambridge University Press, 2000), 3, holds that at some point in the century and a half before 1650 there was a 'displacement of informal means of dispute resolution by the use of the law'.

11. Steven Justice, *Writing and Rebellion: England in 1381* (Berkeley: University of California Press, 1994), 138–39, 182–91.

12. Most of the real-life moments of trusting we know about are those that backfired and resulted in litigation. So, paradoxically, we have to rely on legal records to tell us something about life beyond the courts. These do not, of course, tell us everything we would like to know about trusting and promising: as Michael Clanchy put it in 'Law and Love in the Middle Ages', in John Bossy (ed.), *Disputes and Settlements: Law and Human Relations in the West* (Cambridge: Cambridge University Press, 1983), 52: 'all this parchment provides only a partial record'. There is a rich critical literature on the relationship between legal narratives and the fabric of everyday life, which is insightfully and trenchantly treated in Frances E. Dolan, *True Relations: Reading, Literature, and Evidence in Seventeenth-Century England* (Philadelphia: University of Pennsylvania Press, 2013), 111–53; Dolan

presents a scathing critique of historians who recognize the distinction between legal records and real conversations, yet nevertheless treat witness depositions as if they were verbatim reports of overheard words. My approach in these chapters is to treat witness statements as narratives crafted for a purpose, whilst also recognising that their crafting often began long before there was any hint of going to law; some legal narratives also highlight moments when in ordinary speech someone failed to use formal language, suggesting that it was indeed expected: see my discussion of 'heightened formality' at pp. 40–45.

13. Chris Briggs, *Credit and Village Society in Fourteenth-Century England* (Oxford: Oxford University Press, 2009), 12–18, 57–62, 146–48; James Davis, *Medieval Market Morality: Life, Law and Ethics in the English Marketplace, 1200–1500* (Cambridge: Cambridge University Press, 2012), 205–11, 348–68; examples in Dorset History Centre, Tarrant Gunville Manor D 151/1, rot. 6; Cambridge, King's College Archives, STP/3 (dorse); *The Early Records of Medieval Coventry*, ed. Peter R. Coss and Trevor John, Records of Social and Economic History, new series 11 (London: Oxford University Press, 1986), 77, 148, 156, 328–29. A Nottingham water carrier was charged in 1330 with failing to take water to a customer, whom he called 'false and unfaithful' for failing to pay: *Records of the Borough of Nottingham*, I: *King Henry II to King Richard II*, ed. William Henry Stevenson (London: Bernard Quaritch, 1882), 114–16. The form and appearance of these cases was determined by whether a particular court recognized the promise itself as the contentious issue, or whether litigation was permitted only on the performance of the obligation implied by the promise.

14. David Ibbetson, 'From Property to Contract: The Transformation of Sale in the Middle Ages', *Journal of Legal History*, 13 (1992), 12–13; this situation persisted despite the general acceptance of the importance of promise keeping in law: Morris S. Arnold, 'Fourteenth-Century Promises', *Cambridge Law Journal*, 35 (1976), 333; John H. Baker, *An Introduction to English Legal History*, 4th ed. (London: Reed Elsevier, 2002), 318.

15. The common law initially provided a remedy for unfulfilled covenants, meaning promises and agreements, but in a landmark case of 1321 the judge determined that a written agreement was necessary, making action on covenant impractical for small transactions conducted face-to-face. Actions on debt were feasible for low-value sales and agreements, because debt was thought of as the detention of someone else's property, and not a broken promise, but the routine lack of written contracts permitted defendants to 'wager law'—a process akin to compurgation in canon law—and escape responsibility: *Sources of English Legal History: Private Law to 1750*, ed. John H. Baker and S.F.C. Milsom (London: Butterworths, 1986), 229, 285–86; Arnold, 'Fourteenth-Century Promises', 323–30; Palmer, *English Law in the Age of the Black Death*, 64, 66; Baker, *Introduction to English Legal History*, 322–23. The statutes of Acton Burnell (1283) and Merchants (1285) enabled creditors to record debts in writing, but their restriction to debts above forty shillings kept the majority of promises, agreements, and small debts out of the central courts: Christopher McNall, 'The Business of Statutory Debt Registries, 1283–1307', in Phillipp R. Schofield and Nicholas J. Mayhew (eds.), *Credit and Debt in Medieval England c. 1180–c. 1350* (Oxford: Oxbow, 2002), 68–88. The closest that the common law came to an all-encompassing law of contracts was a knowing manipulation of the law on trespass—a wrong done to a person's property—which dressed up unfulfilled obligations as damage to property: for example, harm to a horse who died under the knife of an incompetent surgeon, or to goods lost through the inattention of a ferryman who let his boat sink: *Sources of English Legal History*, 358–60. Such actions could be initiated from the mid-fourteenth century onwards by a new writ of *assumpsit* (meaning 'he undertook'), and they regularly claimed that the defendant had 'faithfully promised' to do something (*fideliter promisit*). However, this dealt with poor or negligent fulfilment of a promise while leaving complete

nonperformance unremedied; no-one could be compelled to fulfil a promise, and the plaintiff could only be awarded damages: Baker, *Introduction to English Legal History*, 330; David Ibbetson, *Historical Introduction to the Law of Obligations* (Oxford: Oxford University Press, 1999), 38; Palmer, *English Law in the Age of the Black Death*, 139–40, 169.

16. Richard H. Helmholz, *The Oxford History of the Laws of England*, I: *Canon Law* (Oxford: University of Oxford Press, 2004), 358, 360–61; this was not the case in the fourteenth century, where Dorothy Owen has found much lower proportions (between 6 and 10 percent of cases): Dorothy M. Owen, 'Ecclesiastical Jurisdiction in England 1300–1500', in Derek Baker (ed.), *The Materials, Sources and Methods of Ecclesiastical History*, Studies in Church History, 11 (Oxford: Oxford University Press, 1975), 211.

17. London Metropolitan Archives, DL/C/B/043/MS09064/001, fo. 163v. This was the usual form for breach of faith actions on debt.

18. Robert N. Swanson, *Church and Society in Late Medieval England* (Oxford: Blackwell, 1989), 188; Helmholz, *Oxford History of the Laws of England*, 1.365. Plaintiffs were, of course, also attracted by the possibility of enforcing small debts, and by the additional publicity that public penance could achieve for their grievance.

19. *Register of William Greenfield*, 5.48.

20. James S. Coleman, *Foundations of Social Theory* (Cambridge, Mass.: Belknap, 1990), 98.

21. Graeber, *Debt*, 90–92, argues that the concept of debt encourages an instrumental view of social relations in which payment puts an end to relationships that in systems of reciprocity might endure over time; however, as I will show, the medieval evidence is that demands for repayment were often just punctuation marks in an ongoing relationship.

22. *The Paston Letters 1422–1509*, ed. James Gardiner, 6 vols. (London: Chatto and Windus, 1904), 5.293 (letter 916: Sir John Paston to Margaret Paston, 7 August 1477): 'I know not yet the means possible that I might pay by that day'. For examples of the typical form see Canterbury Cathedral Archives, Y.1.5, fos. 27v, 29r, 64r, 68v, 69v, 71v, 73v, 78v, 79v, 81v, 93r, 96v, 106r, 149v. For examples of perennial deferral of repayment in the church courts, see Worcester Record Office, BA 2636/11 43700, fo. 59r (*Moggys c. Burton*); 'Proceedings of the Ecclesiastical Courts in the Archdeaconry of Leicester, 1516–1535', ed. A. Percival Moore, *Associated Architectural and Archaeological Societies Reports and Papers*, 28 (1905–6), 645 (*Thompson c. Shoemaker*).

23. On the wholesale wool trade, see Adrian R. Bell, Chris Brooks, and Paul R. Dryburgh, *The English Wool Market, c.1230–1327* (Cambridge: Cambridge University Press, 2007).

24. Canterbury Cathedral Archives, X.1.1, fo. 108r.

25. London Metropolitan Archives, DL/C/B/043/MS09064/003, fo. 240v.

26. London Metropolitan Archives, DL/C/B/043/MS09064/001, fo. 42r (*Crakyngthorpe c. Rede*), and DL/C/B/043/MS09064/002, fos. 57r (*Jafferey c. Bruampton*), 118v (*Brays c. Barton*).

27. London Metropolitan Archives, DL/C/B/043/MS09064/003, fos. 110v, 136v. On gages see Briggs, *Credit and Village Society*, 82–84, 91–92; Paul Brand, 'Aspects of the Law of Debt, 1189–1307', in Schofield and Mayhew (eds.), *Credit and Debt in Medieval England*, 30–31.

28. Muldrew, *Economy of Obligation*, 97–98; Julie Claustre, 'Vivre à crédit dans une ville sans banque (Paris, XIVe–XVe siècle), *Le Moyen Âge: Revue d'histoire et de philologie*, 119 (2013), 567–96.

29. 'Some Late Thirteenth-Century Records of an Ecclesiastical Court in the Archdeaconry of Sudbury', ed. Antonia Gransden, *BIHR* 32 (1959), 66 (*Sturbot c. Len*); London Metropolitan Archives, DL/C/B/043/MS09064/004, fos. 152r (*Wright c. Smith*), 224r (*Brother William c. Laylond*).

30. London Metropolitan Archives, DL/C/B/043/MS09064/002, fo. 159r.

31. For example London Metropolitan Archives, DL/C/B/043/MS09064/004, fos. 161v (*Thirlthorpe c. Adamson*), 328r (*Andrew c. Cooper*); York, Borthwick Institute, CP E.241P (*Rishton c. Isabel*). A rare common law example is noted by Arnold 'Fourteenth-Century Promises', 322, in which an apprentice was called to honour an alleged undertaking to enter a master's service. After the Black Death the obligation to work, terms of service, and rates of pay were enforced under the Statute of Labourers, but all of these 'obligations' were tacit agreements at best, and at worst forced contracts affecting those without legal protection, especially single women: Chris Given-Wilson, 'The Problem of Labour in the Context of English Government, c. 1350–1450', in James Bothwell, P.J.P. Goldberg, and W. Mark Ormrod (eds.), *The Problem of Labour in Fourteenth-Century England* (Woodbridge: York Medieval Press, 2000); Judith M. Bennett, 'Compulsory Service in Late Medieval England', *Past & Present*, 209 (2010). Palmer, *English Law in the Age of the Black Death*, 139–40, argues that an unintended effect of the labour legislation was to incentivise the poor performance of work. Men and women obliged to work on unfavourable terms were hardly likely to do their best, he argues, suggesting that this prompted Chancery to craft the new action of *assumpsit* with occupational competency in mind.

32. York, Borthwick Institute, CP F.82.

33. London Metropolitan Archives, DL/C/B/043/MS09064/002, fo. 89r, and DL/C/B/043/MS09064/003, fos. 215v–216r.

34. London Metropolitan Archives, DL/C/B/043/MS09064/003, fo. 36v.

35. Swanson, *Church and Society*, 167–68.

36. Lichfield Record Office, D 30/9/3/2/11, m. 2r. For similar 'no express promise' cases, see London Metropolitan Archives, DL/C/B/043/MS09064/001, fo. 187v (*Hobbeson c. Chapman*), DL/C/B/043/MS09064/002, fo. 43v (*Jamys c. Smyth & Ordyng*), and DL/C/B/043/MS09064/005, fos. 86v (*Malverley c. fraternities of St Bartholomew, Sts Mary & John, St George, and St Christopher*), 111r (*Sympson c. Suthworth*), 146v (*Gilbert c. Alenby*).

37. Worcester Record Office, BA 2636/11 43700, fo. 11v.

38. London Metropolitan Archives, DL/C/B/043/MS09064/003, fo. 40r.

39. Worcester Record Office, BA 2636/11 43700, fo. 57r-v; London Metropolitan Archives, DL/C/B/043/MS09064/005, fo. 94r.

40. London Metropolitan Archives, DL/C/B/043/MS09064/003, fo. 127r.

41. *Lower Ecclesiastical Jurisdiction in Late-Medieval England: The Courts of the Dean and Chapter of Lincoln, 1336–1349 and the Deanery of Wisbech, 1458–1484*, ed. Lawrence R. Poos, Records of Social and Economic History, new series 32 (Oxford: Oxford University Press, 2001), 148; Lloyd Bonfield and Lawrence Raymond Poos, 'The Development of Death-bed Transfers in Medieval English Manor Courts', in Zvi Razi and Richard M. Smith (eds.), *Medieval Society and the Manor Court* (Oxford: Oxford University Press, 1996), 117–42.

42. London Metropolitan Archives, DL/C/B/043/MS09064/002, fos. 53r (*Smyth c. rector of St Olave*), 128v (*Smith c. rector of All Saints Staining*), 139r (*Smyth c. rector of St Peter Westcheap*), and DL/C/B/043/MS09064/005, fo. 6v (*Freeman c. Walsham*).

43. Moore, 'Proceedings of the Ecclesiastical Courts', 645–46.

44. *Lower Ecclesiastical Jurisdiction*, 285 (*Peryson c. Leverington parish*), 345 (*Blewyk & Blewyk c. Elm parish*); London Metropolitan Archives, DL/C/B/043/MS09064/002, fo. 102r (*Perse c. rector of St Alphage*), and DL/C/B/043/MS09064/003, fos. 73v (*Johnson c. Guild of St Michael*), 221r (*Washoldeuson c. Fraternity of St Barbara*).

45. *Lower Ecclesiastical Jurisdiction*, 360.

46. York, Borthwick Institute, CP E.144 (*Nevill c. Nevill*), CP F.294 (*Hutchinson c. Hodgson*); London Metropolitan Archives, DL/C/B/043/MS09064/001, fo. 129r (*Tailour c. Portelowche*), DL/C/B/043/MS09064/003, fo. 18v (*Appleby c. Stevens*), DL/C/B/043/

MS09064/005, fo. 106v (*Twhayt c. Latter*), and DL/C/B/043/MS09064/006, fo. 16v (*Scarlett c. Sindre*).

47. *Register of John le Romeyn*, 1.65, 1.266; *Register of John de Halton*, 1.178, 1.190.

48. Martin Pimsler, 'Solidarity in the Medieval Village? The Evidence of Personal Pledging at Elton, Huntingdonshire', *Journal of British Studies*, 17 (1977), 3.

49. *Register of Walter Gray*, 269; *An Episcopal Court Book for the Diocese of Lincoln 1514–1520*, ed. Margaret Bowker, Lincoln Record Society, 61 (1967), 9–10.

50. London Metropolitan Archives, DL/C/0205, fos. 17v, 26r–27r (*Arwam c. Deyndo*).

51. The law and rituals of marriage in late medieval England are discussed in Shannon McSheffrey, *Marriage, Sex, and Civic Culture in Late Medieval London* (Philadelphia: University of Pennsylvania Press, 2006).

52. Ibbetson, 'From Property to Contract', 4.

53. Mari Pakkala-Weckström, '*No botmeles bihestes*: Various Ways of Making Binding Promises in Middle English', in Andreas H. Jucker and Irma Taavitsainen (eds.), *Speech Acts in the History of English* (Amsterdam: Benjamin, 2008), 141.

54. Matthew 5.33–37; this text was cited by Gratian in his introduction to the problem of obedience within clerical hierarchies and the need for oaths: *Decretum d.a.* C. 22 q. 1. See also James 5.12.

55. Lesley Smith, *The Ten Commandments: Interpreting the Bible in the Medieval World* (Leiden: Brill, 2014), 95; see, for example, *Memoriale credencium*, 42.

56. *Fasciculus Morum*, 166; Robert Grosseteste, *De Decem Mandatis*, ed. Richard C. Dales and Edward B. King (Oxford: Oxford University Press, 1987), 27; Smith, *Ten Commandments*, 165–69; Vodola, '*Fides et culpa*'.

57. *Register of John Stafford*, 103–8; Grosseteste, *De Decem Mandatis*, 27. False swearers in assizes were condemned as excommunicates in almost all texts of the 'General Sentence of Excommunication' compiled during the fourteenth and fifteenth centuries: see, for example, British Library, MS Burney 356, fos. 53r–54v, and MS Harley 2383, fo. 47r; Lambeth Palace Library, MS 172, fo. 172v. Casual swearing (intensifying one's claims with an oath 'by God's bones' or some similar phrase) was said to be a particular vice of market traders, whom moralists accused of holding truth and speech to be cheap: see Davis, *Medieval Market Morality*, 68–73.

58. Smith, *Ten Commandments*, 170–71; *Register of Adam of Orleton, Hereford*, 310–11; on perjury in canon law, see Helmholz, *Oxford History of the Laws of England*, 1.363.

59. *Quattuor Sermones*, ed. Norman Francis Blake (Heidelberg: Carl Winter, 1975), 27; *Speculum Vitae*, 37.

60. Pollock and Maitland, *History of English Law*, 2.194, 197.

61. Helmholz, *Oxford History of the Laws of England*, 1.361–62, 364.

62. Pollock and Maitland, *History of English Law*, 2.195.

63. Canterbury Cathedral Archives, X.1.1, fo. 136r.

64. For example, ca. 1485 Matilda Martyn claimed that John Hale had delivered twenty cartloads of firewood worth two pounds six shillings eight pence to her on credit and without her giving faith: London Metropolitan Archives, DL/C/B/043/MS09064/002, fo. 2r.

65. Canterbury Cathedral Archives, X.10.1, fos. 121r, 130r.

66. For example *Lower Ecclesiastical Jurisdiction*, 102 (manure); London Metropolitan Archives, DL/C/B/043/MS09064/002, fo. 107r (books), DL/C/B/043/MS09064/004, fos. 32r (possibly tools), 250v (cloth), 263r (a gown).

67. London Metropolitan Archives, DL/C/0205, fos. 74r–v, 76v, 91v.

68. Helmholz, *Oxford History of the Laws of England*, 1.364.

69. York, Borthwick Institute, CP E.132; there is no surviving sentence in this case to show what the judge thought about an agreement concluded with bare words.

70. London Metropolitan Archives, DL/C/B/043/MS09064/005, fo. 66v.

71. Canterbury Cathedral Archives, Y.1.5, fo. 174r; *Register of Walter de Stapeldon*, 164; *Register of John de Stratford*, 128; *Lower Ecclesiastical Jurisdiction*, 188.

72. Helmholz, *Oxford History of the Laws of England*, 1.358-59, 361; *Select Cases from the Ecclesiastical Courts of the Province of Canterbury c. 1200-1301*, ed. Norma Adams and Charles Donahue Jr., Selden Society, 95 (1981), 17.

73. Canterbury Cathedral Archives, Y.1.5, the consistory act book for 1454-57, is highly unusual in referring to breach of faith suits as perjury throughout. Most cases do relate to explicit oaths, and only about a third refer to faith in any way, clearly reflecting a particular preference in this court at this time.

74. Pollock and Maitland, *History of English Law*, 2.189.

75. York, Borthwick Institute, CP F.23; see also *EEA 6: Norwich 1070-1214*, ed. Christopher Harper-Bill (Oxford: Oxford University Press, 1990), 169, 173.

76. *Lower Ecclesiastical Jurisdiction*, 482.

77. Canterbury Cathedral Archives, X.1.1, fo. 51v; at fo. 135v there is a similar elision of faith and oath from 1457.

78. London Metropolitan Archives, DL/C/B/043/MS09064/001, fo. 18r.

79. London Metropolitan Archives, DL/C/0206, fo. 89r.

80. Sometimes the pledge of faith was even described as a recitation (*recitavit*) by the witness or the scribe: London Metropolitan Archives, DL/C/0205, fo. 33r-v (*Pope c. Bragge*).

81. For example, *Select Cases from the Ecclesiastical Courts*, 104-5, 121-22, 129-30, 339-41; Canterbury Cathedral Archives, X.10.1, fos. 6v, 12r, 16v, 23v, 27v, 31r-32r, 33r, 35r, 40v, 44r, 48r-49r, 53r-54r, 68r, 87v, 91r, 99r, 95r-v, 98v, 107r-v, 114r, 121v, 132r, 133v-134r, 136v.

82. *Norwich Consistory Court Depositions, 1499-1512 and 1518-1530*, ed. E. D. Stone and B. Cozens-Hardy, Norfolk Record Society, 10 (1938), item 67.

83. For example York, Borthwick Institute, CP F.174 (*Lascelles c. Harman*), CP F.225 (*Deepdale c. Carthorpe*); London Metropolitan Archives, DL/C/B/043/MS09064/002, fo. 177r (*Elys c. Asswell*), DL/C/0205, fos. 94v-95r (*Grygge c. Parker*); *The Courts of the Archdeaconry of Buckingham 1483-1523*, ed. E. M. Elvey, Buckinghamshire Record Society, 19 (1975), 88 (*Kirkby c. Storey*).

84. Canterbury Cathedral Archives, X.10.1, fo. 115r.

85. Canterbury Cathedral Archives, X.10.1, fo. 100r.

86. Occasionally 'trothplight' was translated with the verb 'affidare': George Caspar Homans, *English Villagers of the Thirteenth Century* (Cambridge, Mass.: Harvard University Press, 1942), 164-65.

87. *Paston Letters 1422-1509*, 2.241-43 (letter 193: John Osbern to John Paston, 27 May 1451).

88. Pakkala-Weckström, 'No botmeles bihestes', 139-41, with emendations from Hans Kurath and Sherman M. Kuhn (eds.), *Middle English Dictionary* (Ann Arbor: University of Michigan, 1952-2001).

89. London Metropolitan Archives, DL/C/0205, fos. 56v, 57v, 217v, 224v. Betrothal was a promise made in what the canonists called 'words of future consent' because the action was uncompleted, whereas the marriage rite in the Use of Sarum, in *Manuale ad usum percelebris ecclesiae Sarisburiensis*, ed. A. Jeffries Collins, Henry Bradshaw Society, 91 (1960), 47-48, recommends the much plainer present-tense words 'I take the to my wedded wyf/housbonde'. On future consent, see Charles Donahue Jr., *Law, Marriage, and Society in the Later Middle Ages: Arguments about Marriage in Five Courts* (Cambridge: Cambridge University Press, 2007), 16-18.

90. Canterbury Cathedral Archives, Y.1.5, fo. 169v.

91. *Norwich Consistory Court Depositions*, item 19 (*Cooper c. Shardlowe*); London Metropolitan Archives, DL/C/0206, fo. 12v; *Courts of the Archdeaconry of Buckingham*, 302 (*Ball c. Hickman*).

92. Canterbury Cathedral Archives, X.10.1, fo. 45r–v (*Brabourn c. More*).

93. Moore, 'Proceedings of the Ecclesiastical Courts', 630; *EEA* 3: *Canterbury 1193–1205*, ed. C. R. Cheney and Eric John (Oxford: Oxford University Press, 1986), 81–83; *EEA* 6: *Norwich 1070–1214*, 94.

94. London Metropolitan Archives, DL/C/0205, fos. 253v, 266r–v, 275r–277r; there is no judgement recorded in this case.

95. Ibbetson, 'From Property to Contract', 6.

96. A view expressed in *Borough Customs*, ed. Mary Bateson, 2 vols., Selden Society, 18 and 21 (1904–6), 2.lxxx; Green, *Crisis of Truth*, 59; Ibbetson, 'From Property to Contract', 6–10.

97. For discussion of *main-foi*, see Jean-Luc Lefebvre, *Prud'hommes, serment curial et record de cour: la gestion locale des actes publics de Liège à l'Artois au Bas Moyen Âge* (Paris: Boccard, 2006), 159–72; clasped hands had been a common symbol for *fides* on Roman coins, medals, and gems, as well as in real rituals: Morgan, *Roman Faith and Christian Faith*, 83; Freyburger, *Fides*, 251. The kiss was a normal part of betrothals, but as a sign of faith rather than sexual licence as it often is, with some irony, today: London Metropolitan Archives, DL/C/0205, fos. 17v, 19v–20r, 23v, 42v, 45r, 57r, 64r, 104v, 112r, 115v, 179r, 199r, 213v, 228v, 222v, 257v, 272v, 291r; the kiss as a sign of reconciliation, peace, homage, respect, private affection and other relationships is discussed in John A. Burrow, *Gestures and Looks in Medieval Narrative* (Cambridge: Cambridge University Press, 2002), 50–57.

98. Marc Bloch, *Feudal Society*, trans. L. A. Manyon (London: Routledge, 1961), 145–46; bended knees and a kiss might also be involved: Burrow, *Gestures and Looks*, 11–12.

99. '*fide interposita in manu nostra firmavit*', in *EEA* 1: *Lincoln 1067–1185*, 117; c.f. *EEA* 6: *Norwich 1070–1214*, 121.

100. Pollock and Maitland, *History of English Law*, 2.189.

101. Canterbury Cathedral Archives, X.10.1, fo. 91v (*Garden c. Edmund*); *Episcopal Court Book for the Diocese of Lincoln*, 38, 56–57, 111.

102. *Bracton on the Laws and Customs of England*, trans. Samuel E. Thorne, 4 vols. (Cambridge, Mass.: Belknap, 1968–77), 2.405.

103. Chaucer, 'General Prologue', I (A) 783 in *Riverside Chaucer*, ed. Larry D. Benson (Oxford: Oxford University Press, 1988), 35; *Lancelot du Lac: The Non-Cyclic Old French Prose Romance*, ed. Elspeth Kennedy, 2 vols. (Oxford: Clarendon, 1980), 363.37–38, both cited in Burrow, *Gestures and Looks*, 13, 16.

104. Canterbury Cathedral Archives, X.10.1, fo. 23r.

105. Ibbetson, 'From Property to Contract', 5–6, and Pollock and Maitland, *History of English Law*, 2.185ff., assume the historical time depth of the handshake, but Burrow, *Gestures and Looks*, 35–38, refutes this. Ibbetson provides an example from late thirteenth-century Sweden in which the Latin is 'porrectum'—out-held—which would indicate a unilateral gesture rather than the 'joining of hands' he suggests.

106. Paul R. Hyams, 'Maitland and the Rest of Us', in John Hudson (ed.), *The History of English Law: Centenary Essays on 'Pollock and Maitland'*, Proceedings of the British Academy, 89 (Oxford: Oxford University Press, 1996), 240–41; idem, 'Faith, Fealty and Jewish "infideles" in Twelfth-Century England', 142–43.

107. Bill Laws and Bobbie Blackwell (eds.), *A Slap of the Hand: The History of Hereford Market* (Almeley: Logaston Press, 2007), 56 (sale of horses 'by hand'), 65 ('in those days a slap of the hand and that was the deal').

108. A handclasp to seal the sale of a horse for forty-three shillings four pence in Northumberland was described in 1535: *Depositions and Other Ecclesiastical Proceedings from the Courts of Durham*, ed. James Raine, Surtees Society, 21 (1845), 50.

109. Davis, *Medieval Market Morality*, 201, 205.

110. Chaucer, 'The Wife of Bath's Tale', III (D) 1009, and 'The Franklin's Tale', V (F) 1327–28 in *Riverside Chaucer*, 118, 185; Pakkala-Weckström, '*No botmeles bihestes*', 142, 146, 156; Burrow, *Gestures and Looks*, 14–15.

111. For example Lichfield Record Office, D 30/9/3/1, fo. 6r; Canterbury Cathedral Archives, X.1.1, fos. 19r–v, 30v–31v, 40v, 42r–v, 102v, 112v.

112. Eleanor Standley, *Trinkets and Charms: The Use, Meaning and Significance of Dress Accessories 1300–1700* (Oxford: Oxford University School of Archaeology, 2013), 35.

113. London Metropolitan Archives, DL/C/0205, fo. 61r (*Greve c. Knyff*).

114. McSheffrey, *Marriage, Sex, and Civic Culture*, 121–34.

115. The 1247 statutes for Winchester diocese prohibited betrothals in taverns or at festive 'ales' (*puplicis potationibus*), but a further set dating from 1262–65 permitted betrothals in taverns so long as they were conducted in the presence of 'trustworthy persons' who could provide testimony if necessary: *Councils and Synods*, 2.411, 707.

116. Lichfield Record Office, D 30/9/3/1, fo. 24v.

117. London Metropolitan Archives, DL/C/B/043/MS09064/004a, fo. 19r (*Preston c. Martyn*).

118. For example, *Select Cases from the Ecclesiastical Courts*, 540; Homans, *English Villagers*, 171; London Metropolitan Archives, DL/C/0205, fos. 47r, 112r: Alan Macfarlane, *Marriage and Love in England: Modes of Reproduction 1300–1840* (Oxford: Blackwell, 1986), 300, lists some of the more unusual objects, and the subject is given thorough and subtle treatment in Anna Boeles Rowland, 'Material Mnemonics and Social Relationships in the Diocese of London 1467–1524' (D.Phil. thesis, University of Oxford, 2018).

119. Ibbetson, 'From Property to Contract', 7.

120. David Ibbetson, 'Sale of Goods in the Fourteenth Century', *Law Quarterly Review*, 107 (1991), 484–90; Davis, *Medieval Market Morality*, 199.

121. In 1370 the betrothal of Robert Beresford and Elizabeth Miltecombe was followed by drinking in the cemetery: Lincolnshire Archives, REG/12, fos. 91r–92r; witnesses to the betrothal of Robert Forster and Katherine Pokke in London in 1468 recalled the words, the kiss, the ring, and the beer: London Metropolitan Archives, DL/C/0205, fos. 7r, 10v; drinks to seal a bargain in Ibbetson, 'From Property to Contract', 7–8; Davis, *Medieval Market Morality*, 199.

122. Canterbury Cathedral Archives, X.1.1, fos. 40v–41r (*Stonour c. Fox*).

123. York, Borthwick Institute, CP E.130 (*Topcliff c. Sualbe, Baron and Tees*).

124. Canterbury Cathedral Archives, X.10.1, fos. 5r–6r (*Godeman c. Garden*), and X.1.1, fos. 22v (*Vyrle c. Adam*), 94v (*Wyndham c. Borman*).

125. See, for example, London Metropolitan Archives, DL/C/0205, fos. 5r–6r (*Blacman c. Young*). The magical formula 'by my faith' could accompany quite unsuitable protestations of *fides*; for instance, in 1490 Margaret Baker brought an action for breach of faith against a man who had stolen her coral rosary beads and then offered—by his faith—to return them if she came to his room: London Metropolitan Archives, DL/C/B/043/MS09064/004, fo. 129r. Similar cases are discussed in Sara Butler, '*I Will Never Consent to Be Wedded with You!* Coerced Marriage in the Courts of Medieval England', *Canadian Journal of History*, 39 (2004), 247–70.

126. He also sent Archbishop Romeyn's staff on what was possibly a wild goose chase to find Matilda Langwath, with whom there was precontract, in the deanery of Holland: *Register of John le Romeyn*, 1.70–71.

127. James Buchanan Given, *Society and Homicide in Thirteenth-Century England* (Stanford, Calif.: Stanford University Press, 1977), 201.

128. Seabright, *Company of Strangers*, 57.

129. Lichfield Record Office, D 30/9/3/1, fo. 11r; London Metropolitan Archives, DL/C/B/043/MS09064/002, fo. 15v.

130. Canterbury Cathedral Archives, DCc/ChChLet/11/55 (*Smyth c. Bartelot*).

131. Cambridge University Library, EDR D/2/1, fo. 93v.

132. Clanchy, 'Law and Love', 47, 50, refers to 'bonds of affection', but love as a mode of dispute resolution may not have involved any positive emotion.

133. For discussion, see Chapter 4.

134. Coleman, *Foundations of Social Theory*, 180–85; Hyams, 'Faith, Fealty and Jewish "infideles" in Twelfth-Century England', 142–43.

135. Pimsler, 'Solidarity in the Medieval Village?', 3; Postles, 'Personal Pledging in Manorial Courts', 65.

136. For examples of the latter types, see Lichfield Record Office, D 30/9/3/1, fo. 21Ar (*Visitor c. Coke*) and London Metropolitan Archives, DL/C/B/043/MS09064/002, fo. 5v (*Russell c. Bennys*).

137. Chris Briggs and Mark Koyama, 'Pledging and Credit Markets in Medieval England', Cambridge Working Papers in Economic and Social History, 5 (2013), 16–18.

138. Lichfield Record Office, D 30/9/3/1, fo. 15r (*Mogge c. Depyng*). The plaintiff in this case was one of the lay representatives for his street at the bishop's 1466 visitation.

139. Canterbury Cathedral Archives, Y.1.5, fo. 14r (*Osborne c. Smyth*).

140. *Lower Ecclesiastical Jurisdiction*, 270 (*Artor c. Freeman*); London Metropolitan Archives, DL/C/B/043/MS09064/001, fo. 162v (*Reygate c. Gill*).

141. See, for example, London Metropolitan Archives, DL/C/0205, fo. 261v (*Clyve c. Plummer*), an action for breach of faith ca. 1470 in which the pledge for a loan was indemnified by the lender against any liability once the debt had been paid: 'I promitte by my feith and so helpe me god atte holy dome þat I, nor no man for me, shall aske no maner of dewte or dette þat is dew vnto me by John Walker yf it be so þat Joan Plummer pays to me xs'.

142. *EEA 9: Winchester 1205–1238*, ed. Nicholas Vincent (Oxford: Oxford University Press, 1994), 3.

143. There are two models: the objective outsider, for which see Georg Simmel, 'The Stranger', in Kurt H. Wolff (ed.), *The Sociology of Georg Simmel* (London: Collier, 1950), 402–8, and the equal citizens in a civil society, ubiquitous in the literature but see Sztompka, *Trust*, 105–7, and Mark Jurdjevic, 'Trust in Renaissance Electoral Politics', *Journal of Interdisciplinary History*, 34 (2004), for two different approaches; James C. Scott, *Two Cheers for Anarchism: Six Easy Pieces on Autonomy, Dignity, and Meaningful Work and Play* (Princeton, N.J.: Princeton University Press, 2012), 79–80, gives a succinct critique.

144. Members of religious orders were discouraged from acting as pledges because of the blurred lines between individual and corporate liability. For three northern English examples, see *Register of John le Romeyn*, 1.199; *Register of William Greenfield*, 3.257; *Register of Henry of Newark*, 284.

145. Justice, *Writing and Rebellion*.

146. Briggs and Koyama, 'Pledging and Credit Markets', 22, citing Prabal Roy Chowdhury, 'Group-Lending: Sequential Financing, Lender Monitoring and Joint Liability', *Journal of Development Economics*, 77 (2005), 415–39.

147. Canterbury Cathedral Archives, X.10.1, fo. 69v. It may be that Atte Stapul was deemed an appropriate *fideiussor* because he was a man of means. Besides having a surname that suggests mercantile interests, he was the farmer of a reasonably valuable benefice,

worth eleven pounds six shillings eight pence in 1291: *Taxatio ecclesiastica Angliae et Walliae auctoritate P. Nicholai IV circa A.D. 1291* (London: HMSO, 1802), 2.

148. Canterbury Cathedral Archives, X.10.1, fo. 65r.

149. Briggs and Koyama, 'Pledging and Credit Markets', 22–24; Maryanne Kowaleski's description of them, in *Local Markets and Regional Trade in Medieval Exeter* (Cambridge: Cambridge University Press, 1995), 208–10, as 'embryonic firms' was getting at a similar point, though before the study of group lending and microcredit had really taken off. The insurance function seems to be salient in a case heard at Hartlebury in Worcestershire in 1412, in which the holy water clerk was told to find sufficient *fideiussores* for the goods of the church: Worcester Record Office, BA 2636/11 43700, fo. 15v.

150. Edwin Brezette DeWindt, *Land and People in Holywell-cum-Needingworth: Structures of Tenure and Patterns of Social Organization in an East Midlands Village 1252–1457* (Toronto: PIMS, 1972), 244–62.

151. Pimsler, 'Solidarity in the Medieval Village?', 5–11; Postles, 'Personal Pledging in Manorial Courts', 68–70, 75–76; Kowaleski, *Local Markets and Regional Trade*, 208–9. Pledging within the family, Pimsler argues, was also not quite what DeWindt thought, since it most often entailed husbands pledging for their wives: a solution for (and arguably the cause of) women's lack of legal status, rather than a privatization of trust.

152. London Metropolitan Archives, DL/C/B/043/MS09064/005, fo. 147r (*Sauson c. Grey*).

153. Northallerton, North Yorkshire Record Office, ZBA/17/2/3: '. . . if they hinder, vex, accuse, or annoy any man for such a reason as might remove the said tenure or any part thereof from the said lord, or from his heirs, then he shall forfeit to the said lord and to his heirs forty shillings, and that it shall be lawful for the said lord and his heirs to distrain the said Hugh and his pledges to the value of forty shillings from all of their goods until it is fully paid and quit'.

154. For comparable ideas about sanctioning communities, see Coleman, *Foundations of Social Theory*, 185; Goldberg, *Trade and Institutions*, 37.

155. Edward Powell, *Kingship, Law, and Society: Criminal Justice in the Reign of Henry V* (Oxford: Clarendon, 1989), 93.

156. London Metropolitan Archives, DL/C/B/043/MS09064/002, fos. 6v (*Peny & Everton c. Bardolf*), 31v (*Eughs & Mariot c. Hilton*), 146r (*Sonym & Petit c. Cowper*), DL/C/B/043/MS09064/003, fo. 30v (*Nevell c. Martyn*), DL/C/B/043/MS09064/004, fos. 108r (*Recognizance of Gunton and Executors of Mayler*), 131r (*Maidewell and Lubsed c. Watson*), and DL/C/B/043/MS09064/005, fo. 67v (*Malpas c. Yngill*). In some cases of failed arbitration the faith said to have been broken was that between the parties to the original agreement: London Metropolitan Archives, DL/C/B/043/MS09064/002, fos. 16r (*Farby c. Brown*), 111v (*Spenser c. Clerke*), and DL/C/B/043/MS09064/004, fo. 148r (*Rector of St Michael's c. Norfolk*).

157. Palmer, *English Law in the Age of the Black Death*, 96–99.

158. Powell, *Kingship, Law, and Society*, 104.

159. London Metropolitan Archives, DL/C/B/043/MS09064/003, fo. 72r (*Cole & Standon c. Shrewsbury*); Robert C. Palmer, *Selling the Church: The English Parish in Law, Commerce, and Religion, 1350–1550* (Chapel Hill: University of North Carolina Press, 2002), 51, describes a 1387 case in which damages were awarded and a penal bond imposed upon a chaplain by the father of a girl with whom he had been having sex.

160. *Lower Ecclesiastical Jurisdiction*, 297.

161. Clanchy, 'Law and Love', 48, 64.

162. Powell, *Kingship, Law, and Society*, 107; this suggests an additional category of resistance to the 'predation' by authorities discussed in Tilly, *Trust and Rule*, 84–99.

163. Green, *Crisis of Truth*, 178–80.

164. *Courts of the Archdeaconry of Buckingham*, 220.

165. Aylesbury, Centre for Buckinghamshire Studies, D/BASM/15/8a–c, 9a, 9b (dorse); *The Certificate of Musters for Buckinghamshire in 1522*, ed. Arthur Charles Chibnall (London: HMSO, 1973), 255.

166. For discussion, see Chapters 6 to 9.

167. Rosser, *Art of Solidarity*, 58–62.

168. *Records of the Borough of Leicester, 1103–1327*, ed. Mary Bateson (London: Clay and Sons, 1899), 12–35, 86; *Lower Ecclesiastical Jurisdiction*, 407–8.

169. Norwich, Norfolk Record Office, DCN 67/6, rot. 3. In such cases the breach of faith was said to be against the 'aldermen and brothers of the guild' or some similar form of words: *Lower Ecclesiastical Jurisdiction*, 278 (*Guild of St Mary Magdalen c. Bukk*); London Metropolitan Archives, DL/C/B/043/MS09064/002, fos. 169r (*Fraternity of St Katherine c. Cobeler*), 182v (*Fraternity of the Holy Saviour c. Russell*), 259r (*Guild of Marbelers c. Mott*), and DL/C/B/043/MS09064/004, fo. 137v (*Guild of Cappers c. Christopher*). See also *English Gilds*, ed. Joshua Toulmin Smith and Lucy Toulmin Smith, EETS 40 (1870), 63, on the Gild of St Peter in Lynn: 'quo-so enter into this gyld, he schal makyn feythe to the aldermen'. Other guilds used oaths: ibid., 316–19 (Tailors' Guild, Exeter); or eschewed oaths and faith altogether, preferring the 'bond of charity' (Corpus Christi, York), which amounts to a reiteration of the gospel injunction to live by one's words.

170. Lichfield Record Office, D 30/9/3/1, fo. 16r.

171. York, Borthwick Institute, CP E.199.

172. Canterbury Cathedral Archives, X.1.1, fo. 67r; although summoners (or apparitors) were ubiquitous as employees of bishops and courts, they were insufficiently numerous or effective to ensure that litigants and witnesses turned up: Richard Wunderli, 'Pre-Reformation London Summoners and the Murder of Richard Hunne', *Journal of Ecclesiastical History*, 33 (1982), 211–13; Ian Forrest, 'The Summoner', in Stephen H. Rigby (ed.), *Historians on Chaucer: The 'General Prologue' to the Canterbury Tales* (Oxford: Oxford University Press, 2014), 432–36.

173. Winchester, Hampshire Record Office, 21M65/B/1/1, fo. 47r.

174. Worcester Record Office, BA 2636/11 43700, fos. 9v, 11r, 12v, 13r–v.

175. Canterbury Cathedral Archives, X.10.1, fo. 23r.

176. Gambetta, 'Can We Trust Trust?'. See S.F.C. Milsom, *Historical Foundations of the Common Law*, 2nd ed. (London: Butterworths, 1981), 247–48, on good faith and mercantile trade; the prevalence of trust without the law has also been noted in a number of different premodern trading situations: Epstein, 'Secrecy and Genoese Commercial Practices', 170–71.

177. *Advance Contracts for the Sale of Wool c. 1200–c. 1327*, ed. Adrian Bell, Chris Brooks, and Paul Dryburgh, List and Index Society, 315 (Kew: TNA, 2006); for further discussion of the balance between institutions and social relations in trade, see Forrest and Haour, 'Trust in Long Distance Relationships'.

178. Canterbury Cathedral Archives, Y.1.5, fos. 74r (*Huvet c. Gavyn*), 112r (*Wolman c. Stone*), 130v (*Rector of Ore c. Kene*). The same phrase appears in cases at fos. 75v, 78v, 79r, 80r, 83r, 91r, 104r, 107r, 108v, 116v, 119r, 121r, 122r, 123v, 124v, 125r, 128v, 134r–v, 139r, 140v, 143v, 144r, 149r–v, 152r, 154r, 156v, 161r, 163v, 164v.

179. *Lower Ecclesiastical Jurisdiction*, 550 (*William c. Bocher*); Moore, 'Proceedings of the Ecclesiastical Courts', 625 (*Prior of Land c. Smith & Walton*).

180. London Metropolitan Archives, DL/C/B/043/MS09064/002, fo. 201v (*Whichell, Manners & Mathew c. Knaplock*), DL/C/B/043/MS09064/003, fo. 252v (*Anin c. Matthew*).

181. Arnold, 'Fourteenth-Century Promises', 322.

182. London Metropolitan Archives, DL/C/B/043/MS09064/001, fo. 162r (*Loveson c. Benett*).

183. *EEA* 1: *Lincoln 1067–1185*, 150 (*Ou c. Hardwick*); London Metropolitan Archives, DL/C/B/043/MS09064/001, fo. 99v (*Smyth c. Payntar*).

184. Pollock and Maitland, *History of English Law*, 2.204, and Baker, *Introduction to the History of English Law*, 334–35, suggest that undetermined actions on the plea rolls performed the same function; Briggs, *Credit and Village Society*, 37, notes a similar function for manor court rolls; Richard H. Helmholz, 'Assumpsit and *fidei laesio*', *Law Quarterly Review*, 91 (1975), 407, and *Oxford History of the Laws of England*, 1.360, is sceptical as to whether more than a handful of cases in the church courts can be unofficial recognizances. In the early sixteenth century the archbishop's court of York began keeping 'registers of condemnations', which were essentially books of recognizances: Swanson, *Church and Society*, 167.

185. *Lower Ecclesiastical Jurisdiction*, 323.

186. Lincolnshire Archives, REG/17, fos. 174r–v.

Chapter Three: Identity and Emotion

1. Augustine, *De fide rerum invisibilium*, 1.1–2.4, trans. Campbell, 183–86.

2. Karen Jones, 'Trust as an Affective Attitude', *Ethics*, 107 (1996), 4–25.

3. Luhmann, *Trust and Power*, 62; Sosis, 'Does Religion Promote Trust?', 22; David Good, 'Individuals, Interpersonal Relations and Trust', in Gambetta (ed.), *Trust*, 38.

4. Weltecke, 'Trust', 382.

5. A good introduction to the debate is contained in Nicole Eustace et al., 'Conversation: The Historical Study of Emotions', *American Historical Review*, 117 (2012), 1487–1531.

6. Lichfield Record Office, D 30/9/3/2/8d.

7. London Metropolitan Archives, DL/C/0205, fo. 124v.

8. London Metropolitan Archives, DL/C/0205, fos. 227r–228r.

9. Reemtsma, *Trust and Violence*, 21; see pp. 83–87 for discussion.

10. Canterbury Cathedral Archives, X.10.1, fo. 45r–v.

11. Green, *Crisis of Truth*, 20–31; for 'trewthe' as vested in communal relationships rather than objectivity see Justice, *Writing and Rebellion*, 184–85, and Phillip R. Schofield, *Peasant and Community in Medieval England 1200–1500* (Basingstoke: Palgrave Macmillan, 2003), 168–69.

12. Barbara H. Rosenwein, *Emotional Communities in the Early Middle Ages* (Ithaca, N.Y.: Cornell University Press, 2006), refers to precise words and phrases as constituting an emotional script that, when integrated with the other lines of script, amount to emotional styles, regimes, or communities. The expression of emotions and the way in which they were reported were social and linguistic performances, however sincere; they were conventions that arose from expected gender and status roles. For the most part, however, the expressions of *fides* in this chapter cannot be differentiated between men and women, rich and poor, since in this discourse at least *fides* seems to have occupied an agreed and shared role in the culture of trusting.

13. On emotions and the heart, see, for example, Chaucer, 'The Man of Law's Tale', II (B) 660, 1056, 1065–67, and 'The Pardoner's Tale', VI (C) 317, in *Riverside Chaucer*, 96, 102, 194. For the beginnings of a purely physiological understanding of the heart in the seventeenth century, see Heather Webb, *The Medieval Heart* (New Haven, Conn.: Yale University Press, 2010).

14. *Paston Letters 1422–1509*, 5.267 (letter 897: Margery Brews to John Paston, February 1477), emphasis added; Gairdner's edition presents this as verse, but this is not apparent in the manuscript: British Library, MS Add. 43490, fo. 23.

15. British Library, MS Harley 4011, fo. 163v. 'My owne dere hert I grete you well / yevyn as hit ys my mynde / in your loue trustyng for to dwell / and lovyng you to fynde / Wherefore old loue to renewe / now to you wrytt y / herin trustyng to contynewe / Wntyll þat I shall dye'.

16. *Paston Letters 1422–1509*, 6.68, item 988 (no author or date; punctuation added to aid comprehension).

17. Eric Jager, *The Book of the Heart* (Chicago: University of Chicago Press, 2000), 69–70, 109.

18. Jager, *Book of the Heart*, 50–51, 85, 113–19.

19. The image of the heart bursting with love and/or death is common in medieval literature. See, for example, *The Romance of Sir Degrevant*, ed. L. F. Casson, EETS 221 (1949), 91, l.1525.

20. 'The Franklin's Tale', V (F) 758–59, 1327–28, in *Riverside Chaucer*, 179, 185.

21. Dorigen believes that love should be free and not bound by 'mastery'; she is also said to be someone who thinks she knows better than God how the world should have been created (namely to provide a landscape that would complement her own emotions): 'The Franklin's Tale', V (F) 767–70, 865–75, in *Riverside Chaucer*, 179–80.

22. London Metropolitan Archives, DL/C/0205, fos. 44r (*Palgrave c. Taylour*), 111r–v; *Episcopal Court Book for the Diocese of Lincoln*, 8–9.

23. London Metropolitan Archives, DL/C/0205, fo. 96v: 'If you may find it in your heart to have me as your wife, by my troth and by the faith of my body there is not that man alive that I will have before you'.

24. Pastoral texts sometimes glossed the faith of betrothal as pertaining to sexual fidelity, for example 'Quinque verba', in *Pastors and the Care of Souls*, 138.

25. Philippa Maddern, '*Best Trusted Friends*: Concepts and Practices of Friendship among Fifteenth-Century Norfolk Gentry', in Nicholas Rogers (ed.), *England in the Fifteenth Century* (Stamford: Watkins, 1994), 105.

26. *Paston Letters 1422–1509*, 5.27 (letter 713: Richard Calle to Margery Paston, 1469).

27. *Kingsford's Stonor Letters and Papers*, ed. Christine Carpenter (Cambridge: Cambridge University Press, 1996), 266–67 (letter 69: Elizabeth Stonor to William Stonor, 12 September 1476).

28. *Paston Letters 1422–1509*, 2.55–56 (letter 47: Margaret Paston to John Paston, 28 September 1443).

29. *Paston Letters 1422–1509*, 3.303 (letter 478: Clement Paston to John Paston, 25 August 1461).

30. *Paston Letters 1422–1509*, 4.12 (letter 495: Anon. to John Paston, December 1461?).

31. Lombard, *Sentences*, 3.23.7, trans. Silano, 3.100; Balbus, *Catholicon*, unpaginated, s.v. *Fides*.

32. The Wycliffite translation of Daniel 13.35, in *The Holy Bible*, ed. Forshall and Maddern, 3.664; compare 'The Man of Law's Tale', II (B) 476, in *Riverside Chaucer*, 94, for God in the heart.

33. *Macaronic Sermon Collection from Late Medieval England*, 450–52.

34. *The Doctrine of the Hert: A Critical Edition with Introduction and Commentary*, ed. Christiana Whitehead, Denis Reveney, and Anne Mouron (Exeter: Exeter University Press, 2010), 5–6.

35. *The Chastising of God's Children and the Treatise of Perfection of the Sons of God*, ed. Joyce Bazire and Eric Colledge (Oxford: Basil Blackwell, 1957), 155 (lines 13–15).

36. 'The Man of Law's Tale', II (B) 167–68, in *Riverside Chaucer*, 89.

37. *Jacob's Well: An English Treatise on the Cleansing of Man's Conscience*, ed. Arthur Brandeis, EETS 115 (1900), 288.

38. *The Earliest English Translations of the De Imitatione Christi*, ed. John K. Ingram, EETS extra series 63 (1893), 14, emphasis added.

39. *The Orcherd of Syon*, ed. Phyllis Hodgson and Gabriel M. Liegey, EETS 258 (1966), 74, emphasis added: 'The mercy of the holy spirit certified and made sure this true doctrine, and strengthened the hearts and the souls of his disciples to trust as to his truthfulness/good faith and to show this way, that is to say, the doctrine of Christ'.

40. Webb, *Medieval Heart*, 52, discusses circulation and the heart with reference to the information of the senses.

41. Mary Carruthers, *The Craft of Thought: Meditation, Rhetoric, and the Making of Images, 400–1200* (Cambridge: Cambridge University Press, 1998), 103, 105, describes the use of *compunctio cordis*, the compunction of the heart, or literally the piercing of the heart, as an emotional spur to prayer in the monastic and meditative traditions; but it could also be a feeling induced by carefully considered mental and physical effort. This was echoed in vernacular texts such as the *Pricke of Conscience*.

42. 'The Second Nun's Tale', VIII (G) 249–52, in *Riverside Chaucer*, 265.

43. Although the heart was the most common corporeal site of inner change, the kidneys are occasionally mentioned, as in *The Earliest Complete English Prose Psalter*, ed. K. D. Bülbring, EETS 97 (1891), 88 (psalm 72 [73], line 21): 'For myn hert is enflamned, & myn kidnares ben chaunged'.

44. Swanson, *Church and Society*, 271; Jager, *Book of the Heart*, 113–19.

45. John 20.29, Wycliffite translation in *The Holy Bible*, ed. Forshall and Maddern, 4.295.

46. Augustine, *Epistula* 76.1, ed. Klaus D. Daur, CCSL 31A (Turnhout: Brepols, 2005), 77.

47. Hugh of St Victor, *On the Sacraments of the Christian Faith*, 167; there are also clear echoes here of Augustine's explanation of belief in God by analogy with human knowledge of one's own mind and other people's trust, for which see Chapter 1; Matthew R. Lootens, 'Augustine', in Paul L. Gavrilyuk and Sarah Coakley (eds.), *The Spiritual Senses: Perceiving God in Western Christianity* (Cambridge: Cambridge University Press, 2011), 56–70.

48. *Augustinus Hipponensis Epistulae*, PL 44, col. 274, trans. Eno and Parsons, 3.171–72; Ephesians 1.18: 'with the eyes of your heart enlightened you may know what is the hope to which he has called you'.

49. Augustine, *Sermon* 159.4, in PL 38, col. 869; discussed in Lootens, 'Augustine', 62.

50. On fraternal correction, see Edwin Craun, *Ethics and Power in Medieval English Reformist Writing* (Cambridge: Cambridge University Press, 2010), 15; for discussion of the original controversy, see Jennifer Ebbeler, *Disciplining Christians: Correction and Community in Augustine's Letters* (Oxford: Oxford University Press, 2012), 103–6.

51. Augustine, *Epistula* 40.7, ed. Klaus D. Daur, CCSL 31 (Turnhout: Brepols, 2004), 163–64; see also *De trinitate*, 13.1.3, in CCSL 50A, 383.

52. Sara Lipton, *Dark Mirror: The Medieval Origins of Anti-Jewish Iconography* (New York: Metropolitan Books, 2014), 64–71.

53. T. K. Johansen, *Aristotle on the Sense-Organs* (Cambridge: Cambridge University Press, 1997), 78–80.

54. Augustine, *De decem chordis*, X: 'Sicut lucet aurum ad oculos corporis, sic lucet fides ad oculos cordis', cited in Southern, *Saint Anselm and His Biographer*, 56; Hugh of St Victor, *On the Sacraments of the Christian Faith*, 167; Abbot John the German of St Victor similarly held that redemption depended upon 'seeing' with faith and not with any eyes: Paris, Bibliotèque National de France, MS. lat. 14525, fo. 104v (with thanks to Sara Lipton for drawing this reference to my attention).

55. The Barnwell Chronicler, cited in Christopher M. Woolgar, *The Senses in Late Medieval England* (New Haven, Conn.: Yale University Press, 2006), 177; see also Webb, *Medieval Heart*, 61–70.

56. *Fifteenth-Century English Translations of Alain Chartier's Le Traite de l'Esperance and Le Quadrilogue Invectif*, ed. Margaret S. Blayney, EETS 270 (1974), 79.

57. Reputation has long been recognized as a variable in economic transactions: for discussion, see Avner Greif, 'Reputations and Coalitions in Medieval Trade: Evidence on the Maghribi Traders', *Journal of Economic History*, 49 (1989), 857–82; Partha Dasgupta, 'Trust as a Commodity', in Gambetta (ed.), *Trust*, 53; Goldberg, *Trade and Institutions*, 27; Catherine Casson, 'Reputation and Responsibility in Medieval English Towns: Civic Concerns with the Regulation of Trade', *Urban History*, 39 (2012), 387–408. On the crucial importance of *fama*, see, as well as Chapter 10, Thelma Fenster and Daniel Lord Smail (eds.), *Fama: The Politics of Talk and Reputation in Medieval Europe* (Ithaca, N.Y.: Cornell University Press, 2003).

58. *Register of John de Stratford*, 133.

59. The standard overview of procedures is the introduction to *Select Cases on Defamation to 1600*, ed. Richard H. Helmholz, Selden Society, 101 (1985), but see also James A. Brundage, *Medieval Canon Law* (London: Longman, 1995), 91–92, and Ian Forrest, 'Defamation, Heresy, and Late Medieval Social Life', in Linda Clark, Maureen Jurkowski and Colin Richmond (eds.), *Image, Text and Church, 1380–1600: Essays Presented to Margaret Aston* (Toronto: PIMS, 2009), 142–61.

60. Forrest, 'Defamation', 144–45.

61. Good, 'Individuals, Interpersonal Relations and Trust', 38, 40.

62. The presence of mere insults or 'defects' in complaints of defamation before the church courts is interesting because they were not strictly actionable in law: *Select Cases on Defamation*, xxvi–xxx. Several church tribunals recorded testimony on insults and slurs as well as strict imputations of crimes.

63. *Registers of John de Sandale and Rigaud de Asserio*, 19.

64. London Metropolitan Archives, DL/C/B/043/MS09064/001, fo. 164v.

65. Gambetta, 'Can We Trust Trust?', 234.

66. London Metropolitan Archives, DL/C/B/043/MS09064/001, fo. 87r.

67. *Norwich Consistory Court Depositions*, item 167.

68. Ralph Houlbrooke, *Church Courts and the People during the English Reformation 1520–1570* (Oxford: Oxford University Press, 1979), 79–80; James Sharpe, *Defamation and Sexual Slander in Early Modern England: The Church Courts at York* (York: Borthwick Institute, 1980), 10; Martin Ingram, *Church Courts, Sex and Marriage in England, 1570–1640* (Cambridge: Cambridge University Press, 1987), 297–98; Lawrence R. Poos, *A Rural Society after the Black Death: Essex 1350–1525* (Cambridge: Cambridge University Press, 1991), 84–85; Laura Gowing, *Domestic Dangers: Women, Words and Sex in Early Modern London* (Oxford: Clarendon, 1996), 59–67; Ruth Mazo Karras, 'Two Models, Two Standards: Moral Teaching and Sexual Mores', in Barbara A. Hanawalt and David Wallace (eds.), *Bodies and Disciplines: Intersections of Literature and History in Late Medieval England* (Minneapolis: University of Minnesota Press, 1996), 123–38; David Cressy, *Dangerous Talk: Scandalous, Seditious and Treasonable Speech in Pre-Modern England* (Oxford: Oxford University Press, 2010), 23–24.

69. *Norwich Consistory Court Depositions*, item 26.

70. London Metropolitan Archives, DL/C/B/043/MS09064/003, fo. 224v (*Flete c. Weston*), and DL/C/B/043/MS09064/001, fo. 47r (*Lynley c. Strengar*).

71. Shannon McSheffrey, 'Whoring Priests and Godly Citizens: Law, Morality, and Sexual Misconduct in Late Medieval London', in Norman L. Jones and Daniel Woolf (eds.), *Local Identities in Late Medieval and Early Modern England* (Basingstoke: Palgrave Macmillan, 2007), 50–70; Derek G. Neal, *The Masculine Self in Late Medieval England* (Chicago: University of Chicago Press, 2008), 25–36.

72. London Metropolitan Archives, DL/C/B/043/MS09064/001, fo. 33v (*Scheffe c. Brokun*).

73. *Register of Henry Woodlock*, 473.

74. Derek Pearsall, 'Strangers in Late-Fourteenth Century London', in F.R.P. Akehurst and Stephanie Cain Van D'Elden (eds.), *The Stranger in Medieval Society* (Minneapolis: University of Minnesota Press, 1997), 50–52.

75. *Register of John de Halton*, 1.117.

76. R. Rees Davies, *The First English Empire: Power and Identities in the British Isles 1093–1343* (Oxford: Oxford University Press, 2000), 129–30.

77. Wyclif, *Trialogus*, trans. Lahey, 120.

78. *Register of Richard Fox*, 29.

79. London Metropolitan Archives, DL/C/B/043/MS09064/001, fo. 181v (*Halltina c. Lymyngton*), DL/C/B/043/MS09064/003, fos. 36r (*Dryver c. Patrick*), 241v (*Berwick & Berwick c. Norman & Norman*), and DL/C/B/043/MS09064/005, fo. 76v.

80. London Metropolitan Archives, DL/C/B/043/MS09064/002, fo. 132v: 'I defy thee such as thou art. There is no man who knows from whence thou came'. It is notable that all these cases suggest an eastern England Scottish trade diaspora.

81. *Norwich Consistory Court Depositions*, items 317, 333.

82. Norfolk Record Office, DCN 67/6, rot. 1.

83. Arlette Farge, *The Allure of the Archives* (New Haven, Conn.: Yale University Press, 2013), 80–81, notes this as a widespread feature of witness depositions in criminal trials.

84. London Metropolitan Archives, DL/C/0205, fos. 79v–80v.

85. *Select Cases from the Ecclesiastical Courts*, 122 (*Atte Bury c. De la Leye*).

86. London Metropolitan Archives, DL/C/0205, fos. 195r–v (*Thorness c. Richemond*); 285v (*Hay c. Reygate*); 299r (*Fauconer c. Golston*), 305r.

87. London Metropolitan Archives, DL/C/0205, fos. 51r–52r.

88. Reemtsma, *Trust and Violence*, 21.

89. Kathryn Reyerson, 'The Merchants of the Mediterranean: Merchants as Strangers', in Akehurst and Van D'Elden (eds.), *Stranger in Medieval Society*, 1.

90. Canterbury Cathedral Archives, DCc/ChAnt/Y/56.

91. *Proverbia sententiaeque Latinitatis medii aevi*, 2.114. The word of God was reassuringly said not to be far away across the sea, but nearer to home in the mouth and in the heart: Deuteronomy 30.14.

92. There is huge scope for more research into the trust practices of medieval merchants. The Cairo Geniza has been at the centre of some notable recent contributions, including Goldberg, *Trade and Institutions*, who addresses the classic economic sociology problem of principal-agent relationships, and Ackerman-Lieberman, *Business of Identity*, who takes a more cultural approach. Quentin van Doosselaere, *Commercial Agreements and Social Dynamics in Medieval Genoa* (Cambridge: Cambridge University Press, 2009), poses similar questions of a rich body of Italian evidence, while Greif, *Institutions and the Path to the Modern Economy*, compares Italian and Geniza material. Some of the potential is outlined in Forrest and Haour, 'Trust in Long Distance Relationships'. The *lex mercatoria* was widely recognized, and there was a high degree of confluence between the jurisprudence of municipal courts in port towns across Europe, but merchants still relied upon their own standing and that of their rulers to secure favourable treatment: Edda Frankot, *Of Laws of Ships and Shipmen: Medieval Maritime Law and Its Practice in Urban Northern Europe* (Edinburgh: Edinburgh University Press, 2012), 9–26.

93. Sir Thomas Wyatt, *The Complete Poems*, ed. Ronald A. Rebholz (New Haven, Conn.: Yale University Press, 1981), 301, item CCXLV.

94. *The Works of Sir Thomas Malory*, ed. Eugène Vinaver, 3 vols. (Oxford, 1947), 3.1240.

95. Ibid., 3.1254.

96. *Early English Versions of the Gesta Romanorum*, 50.

97. 'Troilus and Criseyde', book 5, lines 1247–48, 1259, in *Riverside Chaucer*, 576.

98. Shapin, *Social History of Truth*, 35.

99. The spread of risk and the construction of information are discussed in Chapter 14.

100. London Metropolitan Archives, DL/C/B/043/MS09064/002, fo. 190v.

101. Canterbury Cathedral Archives, DCc/ChChLet/2/218 (*failure to appear at visitation cited as a violation of faith, 1293*), and X.1.1, fo. 22v (*Vyrle c. Adam, 1450*); Norfolk Record Office, DCN 67/2, rots. 1 (*Benne c. Wakeman, 1419*), 2 (*Boson c. Deynes, 1419*).

102. Canterbury Cathedral Archives, Y.1.5, fos. 40r–41v, 54r.

103. Good, 'Individuals, Interpersonal Relations and Trust', 32, referring to student-participant experiments of Harold Garfinkel reported in his *Studies in Ethnomethodology* (Englewood Cliffs, N.J.: Prentice Hall, 1967), 49–53; for further discussion, see Shapin, *Social History of Truth*, 34–36.

104. *Register of Lewis Charlton*, 50. For discussion of episcopal attitudes towards trustworthiness and their persistent distrust of the laity, see Chapters 4 and 5.

105. Canterbury Cathedral Archives, X.10.1, fo. 83r; same phrase in similar context at fos. 86v, 100v, 101v.

106. 'ducam te in uxorem quam citius ero homo in statu quod possum uxorem ducere, ita quod permittas me totum carnaliter comisseri, et ad hoc do tibi fidem meam': *Lower Ecclesiastical Jurisdiction*, 226.

107. Cited in Richard Whitford, *The Werke for Housholders*, in *A dayly exercyse and experyence of dethe, gathered and set forth, by a brother of Syon Rycharde Whytforde* (London: Wynkyn de Worde, 1537; Short Title Catalogue 25414), no pagination.

108. Robert Mannyng of Brunne, *Handlyng Synne*, ed. Idelle Sullens (Binghampton: State University of New York, 1983), 211, lines 8398–8400.

Part II: Identifying the Trustworthy Men

1. Luhmann, *Trust and Power*, 39–46, 48–58, 68–69. Luhmann was influenced by the seminal Simmel, *Philosophy of Money*. See also Giddens, *Consequences of Modernity*, 21–27, 79–85; Tilly, 'Introduction', 9–14. Crucially, Luhmann points out, trust in institutions is in fact a form of generalized trust in other people's assumed trust: if we were to examine the basis of our trust in banks, we would find that it lies in our confidence that other people have confidence in banks. If we thought they did not, we would lose confidence, and the institution would lose public trust.

2. Morgan, *Roman Faith and Christian Faith*, 86.

3. A classic treatment of this by a historian is Ute Frevert, *Vertrauensfragen: eine Obsession der Moderne* (Munich: Beck, 2013); see also Coleman, *Foundations of Social Theory*, 193–96; Fukuyama, *Trust*, 269–321.

4. Martin Daunton, *Trusting Leviathan: The Politics of Taxation in Britain 1799–1914* (Cambridge: Cambridge University Press, 2001), 10–12.

5. Shmuel Noah Eisenstadt and Luis Roniger, *Patrons, Clients and Friends: Interpersonal Relations and the Structure of Trust in Society* (Cambridge: Cambridge University Press, 1984).

6. Paul Hyams, *Rancor and Reconciliation in Medieval England* (Ithaca, N.Y.: Cornell University Press, 2003), 21–33, on the politics of friendship; Rosser, *Art of Solidarity*, on fraternity; Gerd Althoff, *Spielregeln der Politik im Mittelalter. Kommunikation in Frieden und Fehden* (Darmstadt: Primus Verlag, 1997), on symbolic communication between rulers and counsellors.

7. Seligman, *Problem of Trust*, 23–27, 35, 58, 70; Luhmann, *Trust and Power*, 29.

8. Shapin, *Social History of Truth*, xxv.

9. For discussion see Chapter 4.

10. 'Trustworthy' is also accepted as the proper translation of the noun *fidedignus* and adjective *fidedignum* in the standard medieval Latin dictionary: *Dictionary of Medieval Latin from British and Irish Sources*, http://www.dmlbs.ox.ac.uk (consulted 29 July 2016).

Chapter Four: The Emergence of the Trustworthy Men

1. Robert I. Moore, *The First European Revolution c.970–1215* (Oxford: Blackwell, 2000), 127.

2. Moore, *First European Revolution*; Michael Clanchy, *From Memory to Written Record: England 1066–1307*, 3rd ed. (Oxford: Blackwell, 2013).

3. W. Mark Ormrod and János Barta, 'The Feudal Structure and the Beginnings of State Finance', in Richard Bonney (ed.), *Economic Systems and State Finance* (Oxford: Clarendon, 1995), 53–79; Wolfgang Reinhard, 'Power Elites, State Servants, Ruling Classes, and the Growth of State Power', in Wolfgang Reinhard (ed.), *Power Elites and State Building* (Oxford: Clarendon, 1996), 1–18; W. Mark Ormrod, 'England in the Middle Ages', in Richard Bonney (ed.), *The Rise of the Fiscal State in Europe, c. 1200–1815* (Oxford: Oxford University Press, 1999), 19–52; Georges Duby, *The Early Growth of the European Economy: Warriors and Peasants from the Seventh to the Twelfth Century* (Ithaca, N.Y.: Cornell University Press, 1974); Richard Britnell, *Britain and Ireland, 1050–1530: Economy and Society* (Oxford: Oxford University Press, 2004).

4. John Hudson, *The Oxford History of the Laws of England*, II: *871–1216* (Oxford: Oxford University Press, 2012), 506–7, 516–17; William Chester Jordan, *Louis IX and the Challenge of the Crusade: A Study in Rulership* (Princeton, N.J.: Princeton University Press, 1979), 51–61. Gellner, 'Trust, Cohesion, and the Social Order', 156, wrote that 'cohesion and trust contribute not merely towards the establishment of a social order as such, but also towards the establishment of checks on government'.

5. Jean Glénisson, 'Les enquêtes administratives en Europe occidentale aux XIIIe et XIVe siècles', in Werner Paravicini and Karl Ferdinand Werner (eds.), *Histoire comparée de l'administration: IVᵉ–XVIIIᵉ siècles* (Munich: Verlag, 1980), 17–25; Mike Macnair, 'Vicinage and the Antecedents of the Jury', *Law and History Review*, 17 (1999), 537–90. Glénisson's survey is conceptually valuable, but his chronology is open to question: he asserts that inquests of correction and reformation are common from the thirteenth century, and inquests designed to gather information appear only in the fourteenth, both of which place crucial developments rather later than they in fact occurred. The Carolingian use of inquests in place of partisan oath helpers is discussed by Janet L. Nelson, 'Dispute Settlement in Carolingian West Francia', and Chris Wickham, 'Land Disputes and Their Social Framework in Lombard-Carolingian Italy, 700–900', both in Wendy Davies and Paul Fouracre (eds.), *The Settlement of Disputes in Early Medieval Europe* (Cambridge: Cambridge University Press, 1986), 45–64, 105–24.

6. Jerry R. Craddock, 'La pesquisa en Castilla y Aragón: un caso curioso del "Libre dels Feyts" de Jaume I', *Anuario de Estudios Medievales*, 27 (1997), 369–79; Evelyn S. Proctor, *The Judicial Use of Pesquisa in León and Castille 1157–1369* (London: Longmans, 1966).

7. Wilfred Lewis Warren, *The Governance of Norman and Angevin England 1086–1272* (London: Edward Arnold, 1987), 106.

8. Thomas N. Bisson, *The Crisis of the Twelfth Century: Power, Lordship, and the Origins of European Government* (Princeton, N.J.: Princeton University Press, 2009), 318, 423.

9. Glénisson, 'Les enquêtes administratives', 19.

10. John Sabapathy, *Officers and Accountability in Medieval England 1170–1300* (Oxford: Oxford University Press, 2014), 13–19.

11. Bisson, *Crisis of the Twelfth Century*, 321, 369.

12. Notable exceptions are Lefebvre, *Prud'hommes, serment curial*; Jean-Pierre Jessenne and François Menant (eds.), *Les élites rurales dans l'Europe médiévale et moderne* (Toulouse: Presses Universitaire du Mirail, 2007); James Masschaele, *Jury, State, and Society in Medieval England* (Basingstoke: Macmillan, 2008); Philippe Jansen, 'La participation des communautés et de leurs représentants à l'enquête comtale de 1332–1333', in Thierry Pécout (ed.), *Quand gouverner c'est enquêter: les pratiques politiques de l'enquête princière (occident, XIIIᵉ–XIVᵉ siècles)* (Paris: Boccard, 2010), 397–419; Ian Forrest, 'Power and the People in Thirteenth-Century England', in Janet Burton, Phillipp Schofield, and Björn Weiler (eds.), *Thirteenth Century England XV: Authority and Resistance in the Age of Magna Carta* (Woodbridge: Boydell, 2015); Dutour, *Sous l'empire du bien*.

13. Sabapathy, *Officers and Accountability*, 236, summarizes the links between 'institutional growth, scholastic rationalization, and public power's self-consciousness', while Sabina Flanagan, *Doubt in an Age of Faith*, 51, characterises twelfth-century legal changes as making the resolution of uncertainty a public and institutional, rather than a private, act.

14. Lotte Kéry, 'Canon Law and Criminal Law: The Results of a New Study', in Uta-Renate Blumenthal, Kenneth Pennington, and Atria A. Larson (eds.), *Proceedings of the Twelfth International Congress of Medieval Canon Law* (Vatican: Biblioteca Apostolica, 2008), 414; Yves Sassier, 'L'utilisation du concept de *res publica* en France du nord aux Xe, XIe et XIIe siècles', in Jacques Krynen and Albert Rigaudiere (eds.), *Droits savants et pratiques francaises du pouvoir (XIᵉ–XVᵉ siècles)* (Bordeaux: Presses Universitaire de Bordeaux, 1992), 79–97; Matthew Kempshall, *The Common Good in Late Medieval Political Thought* (Oxford: Oxford University Press, 1999), 9; David L. d'Avray, *Medieval Religious Rationalities: A Weberian Analysis* (Cambridge: Cambridge University Press, 2010), 150–56.

15. Richard M. Fraher, 'The Theoretical Justification for the New Criminal Law of the High Middle Ages: *Rei publicae interest, ne crimina remaneant impunita*', *University of Illinois Law Review*, 3 (1984), 577–95; Moore, *Formation of a Persecuting Society*, 9–11; Sackville, *Heresy and Heretics*, 121–35; Mario Sbriccoli, 'Legislation, Justice and Political Power in Italian Cities, 1200–1400', in Antonio Padoa-Schioppa (ed.), *Legislation and Justice* (Oxford: Clarendon, 1997), 48–52. Massimo Vallerani, *Medieval Public Justice* (Washington, D.C.: Catholic University of America Press, 2012), chaps. 5–6, chart the uneven way in which inquisitorial procedure joined accusation in the courts of Perugia and Bologna in the twelfth and thirteenth centuries.

16. Alberto Gandino, *Tractatus de maleficiis*, in Vallerani, *Medieval Public Justice*, 230–31.

17. Brian Tierney, *Foundations of the Conciliar Theory* (Cambridge: Cambridge University Press, 1955), 87–95; Kenneth Pennington, *The Prince and the Law 1200–1600: Sovereignty and Rights in the Western Legal Tradition* (Berkeley: University of California Press, 1993), 44–47.

18. Bisson, *Crisis of the Twelfth Century*, 401.

19. Craddock, 'La pesquisa en Castilla y Aragón'.

20. John Baldwin, 'The Intellectual Preparation for the Canon of 1215 against Ordeals', *Speculum*, 36 (1961), 613–36, makes the case for a general pessimism in epistemology around 1200, though this has lately been cautioned against by Hyams, 'Faith, Fealty and Jewish "infideles" in Twelfth-Century England', 146.

21. '*ex vicinitate praesumitur notitia facti loci vicini*': Decretals X 2.23.7.

22. *Decretum* C. 23 q. 1 c. 2; Glos. ord. to *Decretals* X 5.1.24.

23. *Joannis Tevtonici apparatvs in concilivm qvartvm Lateranense*, in *Constitutiones Concilii quarti Lateranensis*, 191–92, 198, citing *Decretum* C. 24 q.1 c. 33; C. 2 q. 1 c. 20; C. 23 q. 1 c. 2; *Decretals* X 2.23.7. See also *Decretals* X 1.6.3; Glos. ord. ad *Decretals* X 5.1.24; Hostiensis, *Aurea summa*, Book 5, *De inquisitionibus* §6.

24. Historians of the English common law tend to assume that the jury was an exceptional institution, distinct from continental inquisitorial procedure and from ecclesiastical practice in general: see Susan Reynolds, 'The Emergence of Professional Law in the Long Twelfth Century', *Law and History Review*, 21 (2003), 363–64; Paul Brand, 'The English Difference: The Application of Bureaucratic Norms within a Legal System', *Law and History Review*, 21 (2003), 387; Roger de Groot, 'The Jury of Presentment before 1215', *American Journal of Legal History*, 1 (1982), 1–2; Raoul C. von Caenegem, 'Public Prosecution of Crime in Twelfth-Century England', in C.N.L. Brooke et al. (eds.), *Church and Government in the Middle Ages: Essays Presented to C. R. Cheney* (Cambridge: Cambridge University Press, 1976), 42. This point is brushed aside by Bruno Lemesle, 'L'ênquete contre les épreuves: les enquêtes dans la région Angevine (XIIe-debut XIIIe siècle)', in Claude Gauvard (ed.), *L'enquête au Moyen âge* (Rome: École Française de Rome, 2008), 60–67, who describes the 'porosity' and 'contagion' between jurisdictions in the late twelfth and early thirteenth centuries. Glénisson, 'Les enquêtes administratives', 20–21, argues that Louis IX's inquests in the mid-thirteenth century were directly influenced by canon law inquisition; Winfried Trusen, 'Der Inquisitionsprozess: seine historischen Grundlagen und frühen Formen', *Zeitschrift der Savigny-Stiftung für Rechtsgeschichte*, 105 (1988), 230, traces the connections between secular and church inquisitorial procedures, and Kéry, 'Canon Law and Criminal Law', 412–13, provides a revised account of their relationship; Ian Forrest, 'The Transformation of Visitation in Thirteenth Century England', *Past & Present*, 221 (2013), 3–38, examines the symbiosis between secular juries and visitation panels. As will become clear in what follows, the church clearly *did* make extensive use of the 'secular' or 'Norman' jury-like inquest.

25. The category of coercion does not stand up to scrutiny, since the encounter between local witness and powerful institutions *always* combined freedom of action with implicit or explicit threat of sanction. The elision of testimony and judgement in some circumstances will be discussed in Chapter 10.

26. Robin Fleming, 'Oral Testimony and the Domesday Inquest', *Anglo-Norman Studies*, 17 (1995), 105–6; David Roffe, *Domesday: The Inquest and the Book* (Oxford: Oxford University Press, 2000), 50–51.

27. All definitions from the *Dictionary of Medieval Latin from British and Irish Sources*, http://www.dmlbs.ox.ac.uk (consulted 29 July 2016).

28. The early history is detailed in Karin Nehlsen-von Stryk, *Die boni homines des frühen Mittelalters: unter besonderer Berücksichtigung der fränkischen Quellen* (Berlin: Duncker & Humblot, 1981).

29. Thomas Szabó, 'Zur Geschichte der *boni homines*', in Duccio Balestracci et al. (eds.), *Uomini paesaggi storie* (Siena: Salvietti e Barabuffi, 2012), 305; Pere Benito i Monclús, 'Marché foncier et besoin d'expertise dans la Catalogne des Xe–XIIe siècles: le rôle des *boni homines* comme estimateurs de biens', in Claude Denjean and Laurent Feller (eds.), *Expertise et valeur des choses au Moyen Âge. I: Le besoin d'expertise* (Madrid: Casa de Velázquez, 2013), 153–65; Davies and Fouracre (eds.), *Settlement of Disputes*, 269–70.

30. Piero Brancoli Busdraghi, '*Masnada* und *boni homines* als Mittel der Herrschaftsausübung der ländlichen Herrschaften in der Toskana (11.-13. Jahrhundert)', in Gerhard Dilcher and Cinzio Violante (eds.), *Strukturen und Wandlungen der ländlichen Herrschaftsformen vom 10. Zum 13. Jahrhundert: Deutschland und Italien im Vergleich* (Berlin: Duncker & Humblot, 2000), 391–404; Szabó, 'Geschichte der *boni homines*', 319–20; Chris

Wickham, *Medieval Rome: Stability and Crisis of a City, 900–1150* (Oxford: Oxford University Press, 2015), 48.

31. Monique Bourin, *Villages médiévaux en Bas-Languedoc: genèse d'une sociabilité (Xᵉ–XIVᵉ siècle)*, 2 vols. (Paris: Editions l'Harmattan, 1987), 1.316; Mark Pegg, 'Heresy, Good Men, and Nomenclature', in Michael Frassetto (ed.), *Heresy and the Persecuting Society in the Middle Ages: Essays on the Work of R.I. Moore* (Leiden: Brill, 2006), 227–39, interprets such *bon oms* as a distinctive religious status group, above and beyond any recognition of their social standing, but this is treated sceptically by Claire Taylor, 'Looking for the "Good Men" in the Languedoc: An Alternative to Cathars?', in Antonio Sennis (ed.), *Cathars in Question* (Woodbridge: York Medieval Press, 2016), 242–56.

32. Carl Stephenson, *Mediaeval Institutions: Selected Essays* (Ithaca, N.Y.: Cornell University Press, 1954), 42; Alice Taylor, *The Shape of the State in Medieval Scotland, 1124–1290* (Oxford: Oxford University Press, 2016), 293. In Scotland from the mid-thirteenth century a royal inquest on a particular matter could be sought by a petitioner. The process was to request a 'retourable brieve': a sheriff was instructed to carry out an inquest and report his findings to the king.

33. Morgan, *Roman Faith and Christian Faith*, 51–52, 55, 77–85, 113; Stefan Esders, 'Faithful Believers: Oaths of Allegiance in Post-Roman Societies as Evidence for Eastern and Western "Visions of Community"', in Walter Pohl, Clemens Gantner, and Richard Payne (eds.), *Visions of Community in the Post-Roman World: The West, Byzantium, and the Islamic World 300–1100* (Farnham: Ashgate, 2012), 357–74.

34. Bisson, *Crisis of the Twelfth Century*, 51–53; Hyams, 'Faith, Fealty and Jewish "infideles" in Twelfth-Century England', 126–27, 129–32; Gerd Althoff, 'Establishing Bonds: Fiefs, Homage and Other Means to Create Trust', in Sverre Bagge et al. (eds.), *Feudalism: New Landscapes of Debate* (Turnhout: Brepols, 2011), 103–4, 113–14; Kenneth Pennington, 'Feudal Oath of Fidelity and Homage', in Pennington and Melodie Harris Eichbauer (eds.), *Law as Profession and Practice in Medieval Europe* (Farnham: Ashgate, 2011), 93–115. On medieval jurisprudential disagreement about the meanings of *fidelitas*, see Magnus Ryan, 'The Oath of Fealty and the Lawyers', in Joseph Canning and Otto Gerhard Oexle (eds.), *Political Thought and the Realities of Power in the Middle Ages* (Göttingen: Vandenhoeck & Ruprecht, 1998), 211–28. Pennington unfairly characterises Ryan's essay as describing canonistic 'confusion', but in fact it notes real differences of opinion, usefully highlighting the political nature of all discussions of *fidelitas*.

35. Benveniste, *Indo-European Language and Society*, 97–98; Frederic L. Cheyette, *Ermengard of Narbonne and the World of the Troubadours* (Ithaca, N.Y.: Cornell University Press, 2001), 191, echoes this, contrasting the impression of 'trust beyond suspicion, support without stinting' created by *fides* language, with the reality that feudal oaths were 'bleak promises' merely to not harm the other party.

36. Freyburger, *Fides*, 218–22; Ferdinando Treggiari, 'La *fides* dell'unico teste', in Paolo Prodi (ed.), *La fiducia secondo i linguaggi del potere* (Bologna: Mulino, 2007), 53–72; Hyams, 'Faith, Fealty and Jewish "infideles" in Twelfth-Century England'; Vodola, '*Fides et culpa*'.

37. Thomas N. Bisson, *Medieval France and Her Pyrenean Neighbours* (London: Hambledon, 1989), 13–15, 35; Lemesle, 'L'ênquete contre les épreuves', 61; Jansen, 'La participation des communautés', 401; Bourin, *Villages médiévaux* , 1.323–24; idem, 'Les *boni homines* de l'an mil', in *La justice en l'an mil* (Paris: La Documentation Française, 2003), 53–66.

38. Taylor, *Shape of the State*, 302. Taylor translates *fidelis* as sworn, but faithful or loyal are equally plausible. I would like to thank her for discussing the Latin with me.

39. Jean-Luc Lefebvre, '*Prud'hommes* et *bonnes gens* dans les sources flamandes et wallonnes du Moyen Âge tardif ou l'éligibilité dans la fonction publique médiévale', *Le Moyen Age*, 108 (2002), 253–300; idem, *Prud'hommes, serment curial*. 'Prodome' and 'prozome'

occasionally substituted for 'bon oms' in the heresy trials of the thirteenth-century Laura-gais: Pegg, 'Heresy, Good Men, and Nomenclature', 230–32, although see Bourin, *Villages médiévaux*, 1.323–24, for the difference in emphasis.

40. *Records of the Borough of Leicester*, 165, 168; *The Oak Book of Southampton of c. A.D. 1300*, ed. Paul Studer, 3 vols., Southampton Record Society, 10–12 (1910–11), 1.45; *The Records of the City of Norwich*, ed. William Hudson and John Cottingham Tingey, 2 vols. (Norwich: Jarrold & Sons, 1906), 1.66–93, 1.230.

41. *Select Charters and Other Illustrations of English Constitutional History*, ed. William Stubbs, 9th ed. (Oxford: Clarendon, 1913), 170, 179; John W. Baldwin, *The Government of Philip Augustus: Foundations of French Royal Power in the Middle Ages* (Berkeley: University of California Press, 1986), 141–41, 248–49. There were notable precursors, such as the 'lawful men' (*legitimi viri*) attesting donations to the abbey of Caen in the 1070s: Sally Harvey, *Domesday: Book of Judgement* (Oxford: Oxford University Press, 2014), 77.

42. *Bracton on the Laws and Customs of England*, 2.328.

43. *Select Cases of Procedure without Writ under Henry III*, ed. Henry G. Richardson and George O. Sayles, Selden Society, 60 (1941), 33.

44. For example, TNA, C 60/9, m.5, 14 June 1218, a petition of Richard son of Simon son of Richard, seeking an inquest by 'trustworthy' (*probos*) and lawful men of Buckworth in Huntingdonshire, to discover whether his grandfather had established legal title to the advowson of the church of Buckworth. The translation of *probi* as trustworthy comes from the *Calendar of the Fine Rolls of the Reign of Henry III 1216–1234*, ed. Paul Dryburgh and Beth Hartland, 3 vols. (Woodbridge: Boydell, 2007–9), 1.28; *Bracton on the Laws and Customs of England*, 2.346–47; for the 1225 tax, see *Calendar of Patent Rolls 1216–1225*, ed. Henry Churchill Maxwell Lyte (London: HMSO, 1901), 560–61.

45. Sandra Raban, *A Second Domesday? The Hundred Rolls of 1279–80* (Oxford: Oxford University Press, 2004), 68–71, 191.

46. *EEA 1: Lincoln 1067–1185*, 137; *EEA 9: Winchester 1205–1238*, 49.

47. For examples of bishops using *probus* and *legalis* in dealing with the stewards of their estates, see *Register of William Wickwane*, 224–26, 253; York, Borthwick Institute, Register 10, fos. 294r, 295v, and Register 19, fos. 139v–140r, 153v–154r; Cambridge University Library, EDR G/1/5, fo. 21r.

48. *EEA 2: Canterbury 1162–1190*, ed. Christopher R. Cheney and Bridgett E. A. Jones (London: Oxford University Press, 1986), 45–46.

49. Hubert Walter to the prior of Dover c.1195, in *EEA 3: Canterbury 1193–1205*, 101.

50. Lateran 1215 cc. 3, 6, 26, 47, in *Decrees of the Ecumenical Councils*, 1.235–36, 240, 248, 252 (*Decretals* X 5.7.13, X 5.1.25, X 1.6.44, X 5.39.48). What is more the Ordinary Gloss's discussion of witnesses, Glos. ord. to *Decretals* X 2.20.1, uses the word 'idonei', suggesting that suitability could be established in court. *Idoneus* was used to describe witnesses and representatives in Italian documents up to the early eleventh century: Szabó, 'Geschichte der *boni homines*', 315, 318.

51. Lateran 1215 cc. 10, 11, 27, 38, in *Decrees of the Ecumenical Councils*, 1.240, 248, 252 (*Decretals* X 1.13.15, X 5.5.4, X 1.14.14, X 2.19.11).

52. Passive witnesses in *The Letters and Charters of Gilbert Foliot*, ed. Z. N. Brooke, Adrian Morey, and C.N.L. Brooke (Cambridge: Cambridge University Press, 1967), 201; *EEA 2: Canterbury 1162–1190*, 59–60, 62–63, 64–66. Active witnesses in *EEA 7: Hereford 1079–1234*, 177–79; *EEA 3: Canterbury 1193–1205*, 192; *Magna vita sancti Hugonis: The Life of St Hugh of Lincoln*, ed. Decima L. Douie and Hugh Farmer, 2 vols. (London: Nelson, 1961), 2.41; *EEA 2: Canterbury 1162–1190*, 258–59, though this last is probably a forgery.

53. Further work comparing the findings of the present book with the records of episcopal administration in other regions would yield a more comprehensive picture, but it does look as though the continental *fidedignus* was more often either a rhetorical figure

('we have heard from trustworthy men') or a passive witness, rather than a juror speaking on behalf of his parish in an inquest or visitation; some of the other terms described above substitute for *fidedigni*. For example, *Actes des princes-évêques de Liège Hugues de Pierrepont 1200–1229*, ed. Edouard Poncelet (Brussels: Palais des Académies, 1941), 27, refers to inquest jurors as 'viris prudentibus'; *Un formulari i un registre del bisbe de València En Jaume d'Aragó*, ed. Milagros Cárcel Ortí (València: Universitat de València, 2005), 163, 223, 226, 278, 281, 285, 288, 290, uses *fidedigni* as a rhetorical figure, and elsewhere records visitation representatives as 'probi homines' or 'prohomens'; *Lettres patentes des évêques de France recueillies dans les registres du pape Clément VI (1342–1352)*, ed. Élie Griffe (Paris: Auguste Picard, 1933), 72, 86, are purely rhetorical references to *fidedigni* as sources of information; *The Register Notule Communium 14 of the Diocese of Barcelona (1345–1348)*, ed. J. N. Hillgarth and Giulio Silano (Toronto: PIMS, 1983), 243, is a rare instance of inquiry through a single trustworthy person; *Le registre de l'officialité de l'abbaye de Cerisy*, ed. Gustave Dupont (Caen, 1880), 273, is a single trustworthy witness; *Protocollum visitationis archidiaconatus Pragensis annis 1379–1382 per Paulum de Janowicz archidiaconum Pragensem factae*, ed. Ivan Hlaváček and Zdeňka Hledíková (Prague: Academia, 1973), 40, is a summary of visitation practice that describes witnesses as 'iurati', while 'Manuale incultum visitatorum ecclesiarum: ein bisher unbekannter Visitationstraktat aus dem späten 15. Jahrhundert', ed. Peter Thaddäus Lang, *Zeitschrift für schweizerische Kirchengeschichte*, 79 (1985), 159, notes visitation representatives described as the 'better and more honest of the parish' rather than *fidedigni*. This is only a small sample, proving the need for further research more than anything else, but it is possible that the English church used *fidedigni* as a way of reassuring the English crown that oaths were not being required of the king's free subjects (for discussion of which see Chapter 10).

54. The tendency for kings to refer to *fidedigni* when addressing churchmen suggests that the close association between church inquests and *fides* was noticed by others: *Registers of Roger Martival*, 1.9; *Register of Simon de Montacute*, 250; Lincolnshire Archives, REG/6, fo. 9v.

55. Augustine, *De vera religione*, PL 34, col. 142, *Confessionum*, PL 32, col. 723, *De civitate dei contra paganos*, PL 41, col. 719, and *De trinitate*, 14.8.11 and 14.15.21, in CCSL 50A, 437, 449–50.

56. Jerome, *Commentariorum in epistolam ad Titum*, PL 26, col. 569; see also Anon., *Explanatio in epistolam Pauli ad Titum*, PL 100, col. 1015. Being *fide dignum* was a new way to describe scripture in the patristic period: Morgan, *Roman Faith and Christian Faith*, 410–12, discusses the wider lexicon of trusting the word of God in the Greek, Roman, and Jewish scriptures.

57. Theodoretus Cyrensis, *Philotheus*, PL 74, col. 797; Bede, *Super acta apostolorum expositio*, PL 92, col. 939.

58. Morgan, *Roman Faith and Christian Faith*, 381–91.

59. *Biblia Latina cum glossa ordinaria*, 4.442–43; Hugh of St Victor, *On the Sacraments of the Christian Faith*, 168; Lombard, *Sentences*, 3.23.8, trans. Silano, 3.101; Augustine, *De fide rerum invisibilium*, 4.7, trans. Campbell, 189; Augustine, *De trinitate*, 13.1.2, in CCSL 50A, 382.

60. Augustine, *De civitate dei contra paganos*, PL 41, col. 758; Pope Julius I (d. 352) in *Epistola Julii ad Antiochenos*, PL 8, col 884; Sedulius Scottus, *De rectoribus Christianis*, trans. Robert W. Dyson (Woodbridge: Boydell, 2010), 93. The latter repeated the use of *fide dignum* in the Pseudo-Isidorian decretals: *Decretalium collectio*, PL 130, col. 62 (attributed to Pope Anacletus).

61. Rabanus Maurus, *Enarrationum in epistolas beati Pauli*, PL 112, col. 668; Hervé de Bourgdieu, *Commentaria in epistolas divi Pauli*, PL 181, col. 1485. Hrabanus's trust in historical witnesses to Christ conforms to his general theme of attaining knowledge of the

unseen from observation of the visible: Toby Burrows, 'Holy Information: A New Look at Raban Maur's *De naturis rerum*', *Parergon*, 5 (1987), 28–37. Hervé's faith in true utterances was consonant with his stress on the unity of Old and New Testaments, which together constituted the truth of faith: Ian Levy, '*Fides quae per caritatem operatur*: Love as the Hermeneutical Key in Medieval Galatians Commentaries', *Cistercian Studies Quarterly*, 43 (2008), 56–57.

62. Peter the Venerable, *Adversus nefandam haeresim sive sectam Saracenorum*, PL 189, col. 688. On *communis opinio* as trustworthy see the two commentaries on the *Sentences* of Peter Lombard by the greatest Dominican and Franciscan masters of the thirteenth century: Albertus Magnus, *Commentarii in secundum librum Sententiarum*, ed. Auguste Borgnet (Paris: Ludovicum Vivès, 1893), 514, and Bonaventure, *Opera Omnia*, ed. Collegii a S. Bonaventura (Florence: Quaracchi, 1897), 894. Their attribution of trustworthiness to 'common opinion' rested on Augustine's efforts to establish the authority of consensus, and on the formation of an authoritative patristic canon by Carolingian monks: Éric Rebillard, 'A New Style of Argument in Christian Polemic: Augustine and the Use of Patristic Citations', *Journal of Early Christian Studies*, 8 (2000), 559–78; Bernice Kaczynski, 'The Authority of the Fathers: Patristic Texts in Early Medieval Libraries and Scriptoria', *Journal of Medieval Latin*, 16 (2006), 1–27.

63. Some of this descended from Tertullian's (160–ca. 230) reference to ideas common to pagan and Christian authors being *fide dignum*: *De anima adversus philosophos*, PL 2, col. 689. On Tertullian's 'common ideas' see *Christian and Pagan in the Roman Empire: The Witness of Tertullian*, ed. Robert Sider (Washington, D.C.: Catholic University of America Press, 2001), 78n.

64. Baldwin of Ford, *De commendatione fidei*, 391; Petrus Alphonsi, *Ex Judaeo Christiani*, PL 157, col. 601; William of Malmesbury, *Gesta regum Anglorum: The History of the English Kings*, ed. R.A.B. Mynors, Rodney M. Thomson and Michael Winterbottom, 2 vols. (Oxford: Clarendon, 1998–99), 1.74; Hugh of St Victor, *De sacramentis Christiane fidei*, PL 176, cols. 278, 330; *Hincmari Laudunensis episcopi opuscula et epistolae*, PL 124, col. 1049.

65. Relying on living people as trustworthy depended in part upon accepting the evidence of their sensory perception. This was a common theme in medieval discussions of faith, as we saw in Chapter 1, and was approached with great caution. It was, for instance, only when pushed to respond to Manichaean 'heretics' that Augustine allowed that sensory evidence of the divine *could be* trustworthy: it was insufficient, but not—as the dualists argued—wholly corrupted. Warnings about sensory perception being trustworthy resounded through scholastic theology. Both Peter Abelard and Bartholomew of Exeter thought that while it may seem so to us, that very seeming could be dangerous given how imperfect was the mind and how unreliable the senses: Augustine, *Retractionum libri duo*, PL 32, col. 607; Peter Abelard, *Sic et non: A Critical Edition*, ed. Blanche B. Boyer and Richard McKeon (Chicago: University of Chicago Press, 1976), 125; Bartholomaeus Exoniensis, *Contra fatalitatis errorem*, ed. David N. Bell, CCCM 157 (Turnhout: Brepols, 1996), 67. For discussion, see Constant Mews, 'Man's Knowledge of God According to Peter Abelard', in Christian Wenin (ed.), *L'homme et son univers au moyen âge*, 2 vols. (Louvain-le-Neuve: Institut supérieur de philosophie, 1986), 1.419–26.

66. Cassiodorus, *Historia ecclesiastica tripartita*, PL 69, cols. 928, 953 (referring to his predecessor Eusebius); on Bede, see Matthew Kempshall, *Rhetoric and the Writing of History, 400–1500* (Manchester: Manchester University Press, 2011), 392. Testimony as a form of knowledge is discussed below in the introduction to Part IV, as well as in Chapter 10.

67. William of Malmesbury, *Gesta regum Anglorum*, 1.16–17, 2.797; Willelmi Tyrensis Archiepiscopi, *Chronicon*, ed. R.B.C. Huygens, CCCM 63 (Turnhout: Brepols, 1986), 414–15; Chris Given-Wilson, *Chronicles: The Writing of History in Medieval England* (Ham-

bledon: Continuum, 2004), 6, cites a late fourteenth-century Cistercian chronicler on his acquisition of information from *fidedigni*.

68. Peter the Venerable, *De miraculis libri duo*, ed. Dyonisia Bouthillier, CCCM 83 (Turnhout: Brepols, 1987), 93; Marie-Anne Polo de Beaulieu, 'L'émergence de l'auteur et son rapport à l'autorité dans les recueils d'*exempla* (XIIᵉ–XVᵉ siècle)', in Michel Zimmermann (ed.), *Auctor et auctoritas: invention et conformisme dans l'écriture médiévale* (Paris: École des Chartes, 2001), 175–200, shows how Peter the Venerable and other authors of miracle collections constructed authority and witness testimony.

69. *The Letters of Peter the Venerable*, ed. Giles Constable, 2 vols. (Cambridge, Mass.: Harvard University Press, 1967), 1.313, 348.

70. *Alexandri III pontificis Romani epistolae et privilegia*, PL 200, col. 726. From the later thirteenth century onwards it became rare for a monk to be described as *fidedignus*. In an example of the diametric oscillation that can sometimes take place in the history of a concept, trustworthiness went from being more or less only applicable to the religious to being pretty much exclusively applied to the laity.

71. For example Adrian I to Charlemagne in 780: *Epistolae pontificum Romanorum*, PL 98, col. 327; Honorius II to the bishop of Bayeux in 1127: *Honorii II pontificis Romani epistolae et privilegia*, PL 166, col. 1275.

72. *Codex* 1.4.34, in *Corpus iuris civilis*, 2.49: 'neque defunctoriam inquisitionem faciant, sed et testes fide dignos audiant et nihil ad earundam veritatem praetermittant'.

73. Authorship of the *Decretum* (or *Concordance of Discordant Canons* as it was formally titled) is disputed, with the current accepted view being that of Anders Winroth, *The Making of Gratian's* Decretum (Cambridge: Cambridge University Press, 2000).

74. *Decretum* C. 4 q. 2 & 3 c.3. The absence of the *fide dignus* from the *Decretum* is attested by Timothy Reuter and Gabriel Silagi (eds.), *Wortkonkordanz zum Decretum Gratiani*, 5 vols. (Munich: Monumenta Germaniae Historica, 1990), 2.1867–89.

75. *Pillii, Tancredi, Gratiae libri de iudiciorum ordine*, ed. Friedrich C. Bergmann (Göttingen: Vandenhoeck & Ruprecht, 1842), 65, 237, 251; *Bernardi Papiensis summa decretalium*, ed. E.A.T. Laspeyres (Regensburg, 1860), 46, 96, 302, 305. The technical meanings of *fama* will be described in Chapter 10.

76. *Pillii, Tancredi, Gratiae libri de iudiciorum ordine*, 244–48.

77. *Councils and Synods*, 2.33–34 (c. 51). For further discussion and context, see Chapter 11.

78. *Decretals* X 1.6.42, X 2.20.47.

79. Lateran 1215 cc. 24, 52, in *Decrees of the Ecumenical Councils*, 1.246, 259; *Decretals* X 2.20.47, with Glos. ord.; *Constitutiones Concilii quarti Lateranensis*, passim; *Johannis Teutonici Apparatus glossarum in Compilationem tertiam*, ed. Kenneth Pennington, Monumenta Iuris Canonici Series A: Corpus Glossatorum, 3 (Vatican: Biblioteca Apostolica, 1981), 242–65.

80. The permeability of legal learning across ecclesiastical and secular jurisdictions meant that the church's favoured term also occasionally appeared in royal and civic contexts. For example, Bracton wrote of compurgators as 'faithful men of good reputation' (*fideles . . . et bonae opinionis*) and jurors as 'wise and trustworthy persons' (*providis et fide dignis*). The late thirteenth-century custumal of Norwich urged the appointment of a few 'of the stronger and more trustworthy' (*potencioribus et fide dignioribus*) men from each craft to conduct inquiries into fraudulent practices: *Bracton on the Laws and Customs of England*, 2.403–4, 3.276; *Records of the City of Norwich*, 1.193. A further example indicates how exceptional such cases were: in 1279 the jurors of Bread Street ward in London, answering to Edward I's 'hundred' inquiries, were referred to as *fidedigni*. The commission itself had asked for twelve *probos et legales homines* in each hundred, and most returns reflected this language, but this particular hearing took place in the bishop of London's

hall at St Paul's, and some of the commissioners were clerics, so terminological drift is not surprising: Raban, *Second Domesday?*, 68–69.

81. *Decretals* X 2.19.12; *EEA* 9: *Winchester 1205–1238*, 6. The Honorius letter reflects a tendency to use 'trustworthiness' in situations where weak evidence or testimony needed strengthening, for example *Decretals* X 3.32.20, Gregory IX's letter to the nuns of Plauda, telling them that five sworn trustworthy witnesses were needed when a married woman wished to enter a convent; VI 5.2.3, Alexander IV's letter (1254–61) to inquisitors clarifying that the sons or heirs of convicted heretics could not give evidence on behalf of their own or their family's interests, but only in support of other witnesses, who must be trustworthy and zealots for the faith.

82. Paul Freedman, *Images of the Medieval Peasant* (Stanford, Calif.: Stanford University Press, 1999), 133–56.

83. *Tela aranearum studiose texitur, flatu venti dissipatur. Sic quidquod hypocrita exudat favoris aura tollit*: Job 8.14 with *Biblia Latina cum glossa ordinaria*, 2.393–94.

84. 'A Sermon on the Anniversary of the Death of Thomas Beauchamp, Earl of Warwick', ed. Patrick J. Horner, *Traditio*, 34 (1978), 381–401. My thanks to Jenn Depold for this reference.

85. *Register of Thomas de Cobham*, 190; John XXII warned Philippe IV of France against petitioners who claimed to represent the *vox populi* in 1317 (http://apps.brepolis.net/litpa/Search.aspx); he may have been echoing Alcuin's address to Charlemagne in the same terms. It is notable that praise for trustworthy testimony in practical documents was not underpinned by any positive theory of lay action in canon law, where laypeople seem of interest only when they impinged upon church liberties or were in need of correction. The only substantial study to date is that of Ronald J Cox, *A Study of the Juridic Status of Laymen in the Writing of the Medieval Canonists* (Washington, D.C.: Catholic University of America Press, 1959), which finds plenty to say about laymen usurping jurisdiction, holding church office and about proprietary churches, but nothing about what the twentieth-century Catholic church would call 'lay action'.

86. *Book of Sainte Foy*, 39, emphasis added. This was echoed in some thirteenth-century thinkers, such as Roger Bacon, for whom consensus and common opinion were unsatisfactory and should be swept aside by mathematical demonstration of philosophical truths: Sweeney, 'New Standards for Certainty', 38–49.

87. George Ashby, 'Active Policy of a Prince', in *George Ashby's Poems*, ed. M. Bateson, EETS extra series 76 (1899; reprint 1965), 40, lines 870–71.

88. More or less this point is made in Reemtsma, *Trust and Violence*, 16: 'One can't speak of trust until there exists a practice of distrust'.

Chapter Five: Bishops Describe Trustworthiness

1. Women were generally prohibited from testifying in criminal and testamentary matters in the church courts: see Tancred's procedural comments in *Pillii, Tancredi, Gratiae libri de iudiciorum ordine*, 223; for discussion of instances in which they did act, see P.J.P. Goldberg, 'Gender and Matrimonial Litigation in the Church Courts in the Later Middle Ages: The Evidence of the Court of York', *Gender and History*, 19 (2007), 43–59, and Elisabeth van Houts, 'Gender and Authority of Oral Witnesses in Europe (800–1300)', *Transactions of the Royal Historical Society*, 9 (1999), 201–20.

2. *Decretals* X 4.15.7; the Glossa ordinaria to the *Decretals* explained that the trustworthiness of these women depended upon their being unrelated to the couple at the heart of the case.

3. *Register of Henry Woodlock*, 378–79; Lincolnshire Archives, REG/17, fos. 172v, 179r.

4. *Select Cases from the Ecclesiastical Courts*, 270–73, 279, 284–91, 328. In court Nevill claimed that Picheford's witnesses had perjured themselves when they said they were all free men, because three of them were in fact serfs. Geoffrey Sampson was said to be a 'villein of servile condition' who could be bought and sold along with the glebe land of the parish church 'as if he were an ox or an ass'; nor was his oath accepted in the assizes or the king's courts. Nevill also argued that his case was the stronger because he had brought sixteen witnesses and Picheford only five.

5. *An Anthology of Chancery English*, ed. Jane L. Fisher, John H. Fisher, and Malcolm Richardson (Knoxville: University of Tennessee Press, 1984), 233.

6. Green, *Crisis of Truth*, 63, takes the phrase 'worthi of trouthe' to refer to oaths, but bearing in mind the distinction between oaths and *fides* discussed in Chapter 2, and seeing how literal a translation of *fidedignum* the phrase looks to be, this seems unlikely.

7. *Norwich Consistory Court Depositions*, item 126.

8. Lemesle, 'L'ênquete contre les épreuves', 66–67, describes the classic attributes of 'hommes dignes de foi' as being that 'n'ayant pas été dans le passé convaincus d'infamie, et résidant sur le lieu concerné par l'enquête ou à proximité'. Lemesle also draws attention to the significant similarities and overlap between instances when collective testimony or the interrogation of individual witnesses was used.

9. Rita Copeland, 'Living with Uncertainty: Reactions to Aristotle's *Rhetoric* in the Later Middle Ages', in Denery, Ghosh, and Zeeman (eds.), *Uncertain Knowledge*, 125–26.

10. Richard H. Helmholz, *Marriage Litigation in Medieval England* (Cambridge: Cambridge University Press, 1974), 130.

11. London Metropolitan Archives, DL/C/0205, fos. 129r, 130r.

12. Christopher Fletcher, *Richard II: Manhood, Youth, and Politics, 1377–99* (Oxford: Oxford University Press, 2008), 60–73, discusses the prevailing moral and medical theories of the late Middle Ages that linked constancy closely with masculinity.

13. *Register of John Waltham*, 7, drawing on *Decretals* X 5.34.7; *Register of John Gilbert*, 78–79. See *Register of Lewis Charlton*, 7–8, for the form of this mandate. For similar phrases, see *Register of Simon de Montacute*, 204; Cambridge University Library, EDR G/1/5, fos. 39v–40v.

14. *Register of Robert Mascall*, 74–75.

15. *Register of John Waltham*, 208, emphasis added.

16. *Register of Thomas Langley*, 4.47–48, emphasis added. For a similar phrase used in 1436, see ibid., 4.209–10.

17. Lincolnshire Archives, REG/20, fo. 15v.

18. *Register of John Peckham*, 2.512–14; Lichfield Record Office, B/A/1/3, fo. 8v.

19. *Register of Ralph of Shrewsbury*, 596. As polemic it may have been particularly stinging because the neighbour was more usually contrasted with the stranger, the vagrant, or the outsider than with the 'community of the town': 'Some Late Thirteenth-Century Records of an Ecclesiastical Court', 68; *Select Cases from the Ecclesiastical Courts*, 551.

20. *Register of John de Drokensford*, 60; *Register of Henry Woodlock*, 543; *Lower Ecclesiastical Jurisdiction*, 70.

21. *Register of William Greenfield*, 1.68.

22. *Registers of Roger Martival*, 4.120. For discussion of compurgation see pp. 318–19.

23. *Register of John Waltham*, 208; York, Borthwick Institute, Register 19, fo. 90r–v.

24. Lincolnshire Archives, Dean and Chapter, Dij/64/2/18, item 6.

25. *Register of Thomas of Corbridge*, 1.144. The same phrase occurs in Alexander Nevill's York register in 1374 (York, Borthwick Institute, Register 12, fo. 90v.), suggesting this was a piece of house style.

26. *Register of William Melton*, 5.136.

27. *Registers of Roger Martival*, 2.300–302; *Register of John de Grandisson*, 684.

28. *Register of John le Romeyn*, 1.366, 372–74, 381.

29. On the power of categorization and choices, see Steven Lukes, *Power: A Radical View*, 2nd ed. (Basingstoke: Palgrave Macmillan, 2005), 25–29; Henri Tajfel, *Human Groups and Social Categories: Studies in Social Psychology* (Cambridge: Cambridge University Press, 1981).

30. *Select Cases from the Ecclesiastical Courts*, 222–23; *Register of William Wykeham*, 2.155.

31. *Register of Robert Winchelsey*, 226.

32. *Register of Robert Mascall*, 44.

33. *Register of John Waltham*, 133, 142, 146, 149; further examples from the parishes of Fonthill Bishop, Chilmark, and West Knoyle at 152.

34. *Register of John Waltham*, 135, 155–56. The substance of the offence in canon law was the use of the churchyard for secular purposes, but it was reported in the way a public nuisance might come before a municipal court.

35. *Register of John Waltham*, 167. For further discussion of the Gillingham men and their social status, see p. 198.

36. Coleman, *Foundations of Social Theory*, 106–7.

37. *The Metropolitan Visitations of William Courtenay, Archbishop of Canterbury, 1381–1396*, ed. Joseph Henry Dahmus (Urbana: University of Illinois Press, 1950), 171.

38. Chris Sparks, *Heresy, Inquisition and Life Cycle in Medieval Languedoc* (Woodbridge: York Medieval Press, 2014), 22–23.

39. *Register of John de Grandisson*, 1147–49, 1180.

40. *Registers of John de Sandale and Rigaud de Asserio*, 234–53; York, Borthwick Institute, Register 11, fo. 21v; *Register of Robert Rede*, 140–41; Cambridge University Library, EDR G/1/5, fo. 96v; London Metropolitan Archives, DL/C/B/043/MS09064/003, fo. 79v.

41. See, for example, Lichfield Record Office, B/A/1/9, fos. 143r, 157v, 162v, 168r.

42. *Register of Wolstan de Bransford*, 122.

43. Spreading rumours about consanguinity was explosive stuff and regularly treated as defamatory: London Metropolitan Archives, DL/C/B/043/MS09064/002, fos. 234r, 263v, and DL/C/B/043/MS09064/004, fo. 199r; Hereford Cathedral Archives, 1779, fo. 3v.

44. *Register of Walter Gray*, 163–64. In the register Guisborough is referred to by its old name 'Gisburn', but it should not be confused with Gisburn-in-Craven, Lancashire.

45. *Register of Walter Bronscombe*, 2.27.

46. Cambridge University Library, EDR G/1/5, fos. 31r–32v; Cambridgeshire Archives, R52/12/1/3, rot. 3.

47. Hannah Skoda, 'Violent Discipline or Disciplining Violence?', *Cultural and Social History*, 6 (2009); Goldberg, 'Gender and Matrimonial Litigation'; Sara Butler, 'Runaway Wives: Husband Desertion in Medieval England', *Journal of Social History*, 40 (2006).

48. York, Borthwick Institute, CP E.46; *Register of John Kirkby and John Ross*, 1.135–37; *Calendar of Inquisitions Post Mortem*, VIII: *10–20 Edward III*, ed. J.E.E.S. Sharp, E. G. Atkinson, and J. J. O'Reilly (London: HMSO, 1913), 24–25.

49. Alice Kirkbride was not the only woman who would have had cause to think the institutional rhetoric of trustworthiness an empty shell. In 1307 the Nottinghamshire landowner Sir William Sampson was ordered to do penance after committing incest with his daughters and adultery with another man's wife. However, once Archbishop Greenfield had been informed by trustworthy persons that Sampson had begun his penance, he postponed the remaining bulk of it indefinitely: *Register of William Greenfield*, 4.14. The egregious knight was placated with lenient treatment and talk of trustworthy reports.

50. *Register of Gilbert Welton*, 64.

Chapter Six: Very Local Elites

1. 'The Register of the Archdeaconry of Richmond, 1442–1477', ed. Alexander Hamilton Thompson, *Yorkshire Archaeological Journal*, 30 (1930–31), 82; public penance demanded witnesses, and it was a visual occasion. We should imagine a gathering of parishioners, perhaps some people from neighbouring Sedbergh and the few isolated settlements of Dent Dale and the surrounding hills. Many details of the ritual cannot be recovered. Was the flogging intended to cause pain or to draw blood, or was it the show of contrition that mattered most? Who raised the whip or birch? Were the penitents shamefaced, or did they brazen it out? For discussion of penitential rituals, see Mary C. Mansfield, *The Humiliation of Sinners: Public Penance in Thirteenth-Century France* (Ithaca, N.Y.: Cornell University Press, 1995).

2. Because we can identify only six of the twelve trustworthy men, no definitive conclusions can be drawn about the exclusiveness or openness of that group. The four men of the inquest who cannot be identified from any surviving record are John Coupestake, William Couestake of Alanhous, Christopher of Burton, and William of Stokdale. Two more—Henry Hogeson and Nicholas Garnet—were related to better-documented men, but as individuals they remain in the shadows. A William Garnet was a juror in the 1451 inquest into the patronage of Sedbergh church: 'Register of the Archdeaconry of Richmond, 1442–1477', 101.

3. North Yorkshire Record Office, ZJX/3/2/69, ZJX/3/2/75, ZJX/3/2/91, and ZJX/3/2/95; Colchester, Essex Record Office, D/DL M108; 'Register of the Archdeaconry of Richmond, 1442–1477', 101.

4. North Yorkshire Record Office, ZJX/3/2/69, fo. 3r, ZJX/3/2/91 m. 1r, ZJX/3/2/93, m. 1r, ZDX, rot. 4, and ZBA/17/2/3; Essex Record Office, D/DL M108, rots. 2, 7. For the terminology of *borh* or 'borrow', see Pollock and Maitland, *History of English Law*, 2.185–87, and for the practice of pledging see pp. 53–56.

5. There is another example of this in the Hutte family of Wigston Magna, Leicestershire, where the father reported the son for heresy in 1413: Ian Forrest, *The Detection of Heresy in Late Medieval England* (Oxford: Oxford University Press, 2005), 223.

6. The presence of lower-status peasants on inquests contrasts with the Southern European experience of the *boni homines* or *prudhommes*, discussed in p. 101.

7. Hereford Cathedral Archives, 1462; this original mandate was sent to the summoner of Ludlow deanery, but it is likely to have followed the pattern of orders given to other clergy.

8. *Register of John de Trillek*, 105–6.

9. Christopher Dyer, *Standards of Living in the Later Middle Ages: Social Change in England c.1200–1520* (Cambridge: Cambridge University Press, 1989), 119–20; Britnell, *Britain and Ireland*, 172–79, 297–98; Bruce M. S. Campbell, 'The Land', in Rosemary Horrox and W. Mark Ormrod (eds.), *A Social History of England, 1200–1500* (Cambridge: Cambridge University Press, 2006), 230; Giuliano Pinto, 'Bourgeoisie de village et différenciations sociales dans les campagnes de l'Italie communale (XIIIe–XVe siècle)', in Jessenne and Menant (eds.), *Les élites rurales*, 91–110; Frederic Aparisi and Vicent Royo (eds.), *Beyond Lords and Peasants: Rural Elites and Economic Differentiation in Pre-Modern Europe* (València: Universitat de València, 2014).

10. Matthew Holford, 'Thrifty Men of the Country? The Jurors and their Role', in Michael Hicks (ed.), *The Fifteenth-Century Inquisitions Post Mortem: A Companion* (Woodbridge: Boydell, 2012), 214–15, uses the term while noting its unhelpfulness, while the editors' introduction to Jonathan Barry and Christopher Brooks (eds.), *The Middling Sort of People: Culture, Society and Politics in England, 1550–1800* (Basingstoke: Macmillan,

1984), argues that this is a 'less analytic' terminology than that of class. One work that takes a critical view of the imprecision afforded by 'the middling sort' and other roughly contemporary phrases is Francesca Bumpus, 'The "Middling Sort" in the Lordship of Blakemere, Shropshire, c. 1380–c. 1420', in Tim Thornton (ed.), *Social Attitudes and Political Structures in the Fifteenth Century* (Stroud: Sutton, 2000), 202–19.

11. Amartya Sen, *On Economic Inequality* (Oxford: Oxford University Press, 1973), 48–63; for further discussion, see the introduction to Part III.

12. Lincolnshire Archives, Dean and Chapter, A/1/14, p. 140, item 100.

13. *The Miracles of Simon de Montfort*, ed. James Orchard Halliwell-Phillipps, Camden Society, 15 (1840), 85, 89.

14. Lichfield Record Office, B/C/1/1, fo. 140v; Worcester Record Office, BA 2636/11 43700, fo. 55v.

15. Kathryn Reyerson, 'Le témoignage des femmes, d'après quelques enquêtes montpelliéraines du XIVe siècle', in Gauvard (ed.), *L'enquête au moyen âge*, 153–68, discusses a case from Montpellier in which male and female witnesses framed their answers in very different ways, even when asked the same question: women tended to speak about their experiences and firsthand knowledge, while men spoke of general principles that they 'knew'.

16. York, Borthwick Institute, Register 19, fos. 92r, 101r, 108v–110r.

17. For the qualities bishops desired in the *information* they received from trustworthy men, see Chapter 10.

18. Andy Wood, *The Memory of the People: Custom and Popular Senses of the Past in Early Modern England* (Cambridge: Cambridge University Press, 2013), 57–65; Clanchy, *From Memory to Written Record*, 296–300.

19. *Register of Adam of Orleton, Hereford*, 348. Was one portion, quite literally, a sinecure (without cure of souls)?

20. *Register of Thomas Langley*, 4.200–201.

21. *Register of Walter Giffard, York*, 34.

22. *Register of Richard de Kellawe*, 1.297–98.

23. *Register of Edmund Lacy, Exeter*, 2.259–63; London Metropolitan Archives, DL/C/0206, fo. 90r.

24. Terence Ranger, 'The Invention of Tradition in Colonial Africa', in Eric Hobsbawm and Terence Ranger (eds.), *The Invention of Tradition* (Cambridge: Cambridge University Press, 1983), 254–57.

25. Shulamith Shahar, *Growing Old in the Middle Ages: 'Winter Clothes Us in Shadow and Pain'* (London: Routledge, 1997), 15–17.

26. *Register of Edmund Lacy, Exeter*, 2.259–63.

27. Lincolnshire Archives, REG/2, fos. 177r–178r.

28. Joel T. Rosenthal, *Telling Tales: Sources and Narration in Late Medieval England* (University Park: Pennsylvania State University Press, 2003), 7.

29. Of the skeletal remains recovered from the 'catastrophe' sites of the Smithfield and Hereford plague pits, the Mary Rose ship, and Towton battlefield, only 3 percent were over forty-six: Roberta Gilchrist, *Medieval Life: Archaeology and the Life Course* (Woodbridge: Boydell, 2012), 255–56; Darlene Weston, Alan Ogden, and Anthea Boyleston, *Excavations for the Mappa Mundi Museum at Hereford Cathedral 1993: Draft Report on the Human Skeletal Remains* (University of Bradford, unpublished, n.d.), 21–30. The Hereford data on adults over forty-six are comparatively high (24 percent in the 'normal' burials, 10 percent in the plague burials), which raises the averages for both. These figures cast significant doubt upon the representativeness of the London merchants studied by Sylvia Thrupp, of whom about half died aged fifty or older: Sylvia Thrupp, *The Merchant Class of Medieval London* (Ann Arbor: University of Michigan Press, 1976), 194.

30. It may be thought remarkable that inequalities of liberty, which some might say defined medieval society, had perhaps the least importance in institutional attributions of trust. Genuine freedom—to pursue personal goals and function as a member of society—was more closely bound up with other variables both hard (e.g., wealth) and soft (e.g., reputation).

31. John Hatcher and Mark Bailey, *Modelling the Middle Ages: The History and Theory of England's Economic Development* (Oxford: Oxford University Press, 2001), 99; Stephen H. Rigby, *English Society in the Later Middle Ages: Class, Gender, and Status* (Basingstoke: Macmillan, 1995), 40–45.

32. Paul R. Hyams, *Kings, Lords and Peasants in Medieval England: The Common Law of Villeinage in the Twelfth and Thirteenth Centuries* (Oxford: Clarendon, 1980).

33. *Register of John Waltham*, 164; Wimborne St Giles, St Giles House, Shaftesbury Archives, M3, rots. 1, 2, 2d, and M5, rots. 1, 4d.

34. *Register of Henry Woodlock*, 478–79; Hampshire Record Office, 11M59/B1/57, rots. 19, 19d; 11M59/B1/59, rot. 29; 11M59/B1/60, rot. 19d; 11M59/B1/61, rot. 18; 11M59/B1/62, rots. 32, 32d; 11M59/B1/63, rot. 20d; 11M59/B1/64, rot. 19d; 11M59/B1/65, rots. 22, 22d; 11M59/B1/66, rot. 23; 11M59/B1/67, rots. 31d, 32; 11M59/B1/68, rot. 29; 11M59/B1/69, rot. 42; 11M59/B1/70, rot. 26; 11M59/B1/71, rots. 37, 37d; 11M59/B1/72, rot. 27; 11M59/B1/74, rots. 6d, 7; 11M59/B1/75, rot. 15d; *The Pipe Roll of the Bishopric of Winchester 1301-2*, ed. Mark Page, Hampshire Record Series, 14 (1996), 268–69, 275. The wealth of these men is discussed at greater length at pp. 141–42.

35. Zvi Razi, *Life, Marriage and Death in a Medieval Parish: Economy, Society and Demography in Halesowen 1270-1400* (Cambridge: Cambridge University Press, 1980), 122–23; Cicely Howell, *Land, Family and Inheritance in Transition: Kibworth Harcourt 1280-1700* (Cambridge: Cambridge University Press, 1983), 30; Schofield, *Peasant and Community*, 167–68.

36. J. Ambrose Raftis, *Warboys: Two Hundred Years in the Life of an English Mediaeval Village* (Toronto: PIMS, 1974), 229, even refers to the 'genetic qualities of leadership', the 'highest level' of which were 'manifested by involvement in a wide variety of responsibility in the village'. Sheri Olson, 'Jurors of the Village Court: Local Leadership Before and After the Plague in Ellington, Huntingdonshire', *Journal of British Studies*, 30 (1991), 244, assumes that jurors were selected by 'public scrutiny'; she pursues a rather circular argument about jurors dominating the court because they were the best qualified men of the village, with their actions as jurors 'inspiring trust in their character' (255).

37. Exeter Cathedral, MS 2857, m. 2d. John is described as 'son of Henry atte Thorne'.

38. *Register of John Waltham*, 164.

39. Ibid., 165; TNA, DL 30/57/704, mm. 1, 2.

40. *Register of Thomas Myllyng*, 20–25; *Register of John de Trillek*, 103–4; TNA, SC 2/197/97, m. 3, and SC 12/14/21; Worcester Record Office, BA 2636/11 43700, passim.

41. Eccles. 36.28.

42. Exeter Cathedral, MS 3673, p. 38; Hampshire Record Office, 11M59/B1/68, rot. 29; 11M59/B1/70, rot. 26; *Register of Henry Woodlock*, 478–79. These surnames were very likely inherited, in common with most occupational names by the late thirteenth century. As an example consider Walter 'le Cowherd' of Leominster, who in 1332 admitted he owed the bishop of Hereford thirteen pounds for the lease of New Radnor church: some cowherd! *Register of Thomas Charlton*, 18–19.

43. See Chapter 7 for further discussion of these men.

44. *Register of John de Grandisson*, 360; Davis, *Medieval Market Morality*, 34–136.

45. *Register of John Waltham*, 165, 209–10; *The Poll Taxes of 1377, 1379 and 1381*, I: *Bedfordshire-Leicestershire*, ed. Carolyn C. Fenwick (Oxford: Oxford University Press, 1998), 151.

46. Norfolk Record Office, DCN/85/2–3; *Register of John Waltham*, 165; *Poll Taxes* I, 151.

47. *Register of Edmund Lacy, Exeter*, 2.392–93, 396–97, 400–402. For discussion of inquests into dilapidation and repair, see Chapter 12.

48. Masschaele, *Jury, State, and Society*, 157–97.

49. *Registers of John de Sandale and Rigaud de Asserio*, 142–46; William Page (ed.), *The Victoria History of Hampshire and the Isle of Wight*, 5 vols. (London: Institute of Historical Research, 1973), 4.150.

50. Canterbury Cathedral Archives, DCc/VR/6; British Library, MS Add. 29794, mm. 3, 3d; *The Survey of Archbishop Pecham's Kentish Manors 1283–85*, ed. and trans. Kenneth Witney, Kent Records, 28 (2000), 56.

51. *Register of John Waltham*, 165; TNA, DL 29/682/11049, m. 2, and DL 29/682/11045, mm. 1, 1d; Dorchester, Dorset History Centre, D/BKL/CK/1/1, rot. 1, D/BKL/CK/1/2, rots. 1–7, 3d, 7d, D/BKL/CK/1/3, rots. 1, 2, and D/BKL/CK/3/1, m. 1.

52. The leet was a court where the king's right to keep the peace ('view of frankpledge') had been franchised out to a lord who combined it with his manorial administration.

53. Cambridge University Library, EDR G/1/5, fos. 31r–32v; Cambridgeshire Archives, R52/12/1/3, rots. 1–8, 5d.

54. Norfolk Record Office, DCN/85/2–3.

55. Davis, *Medieval Market Morality*, 189–96.

56. *Lower Ecclesiastical Jurisdiction*,70–71; *Early Taxation Returns: Taxation of Personal Property in 1332 and Later*, ed. Albert Charles Chibnall, Buckinghamshire Record Society, 14 (1966), 24.

57. TNA, E179/135/25, rots. 2, 4, 7d, 11.

58. Exeter Cathedral, MS 2857, mm. 2d, 3; *Poll Taxes* I, 131, and III, 466.

59. Although free tenants did use the courts, and were sometimes obliged to, the unfree predominated. Even amongst the unfree, those who did not cause trouble or transact land, rents, or credit during the sample period were unlikely to be named. For the present study the sample period has been defined as twenty-five years either side of the list of trustworthy men. At the outer limits of this range, where the identification of individuals by name alone becomes less certain, only those men for whom continuous presence or activity is documented have been included in the analysis.

60. Hatcher and Bailey, *Modelling the Middle Ages*, 43–49; Richard M. Smith, 'Demographic Developments in Rural England, 1300–48: A Survey', in Bruce M. S. Campbell (ed.), *Before the Black Death: Studies in the 'Crisis' of the Early Fourteenth Century* (Manchester: Manchester University Press, 1991), 25–77.

61. *Register of Henry Woodlock*, 478–79; Hampshire Record Office, 11M59/B1/57, rots. 19, 19d; 11M59/B1/59, rot. 29; 11M59/B1/60, rot. 19d; 11M59/B1/61, rot. 18; 11M59/B1/62, rots. 32, 32d; 11M59/B1/63, rot. 20d; 11M59/B1/64, rot. 19d; 11M59/B1/65, rots. 22, 22d; 11M59/B1/66, rot. 23; 11M59/B1/67, rots. 31d, 32; 11M59/B1/68, rot. 29; 11M59/B1/69, rot. 42; 11M59/B1/70, rot. 26; 11M59/B1/71, rots. 37, 37d; 11M59/B1/72, rot. 27; 11M59/B1/74, rots. 6d, 7; 11M59/B1/75, rot. 15d; *Pipe Roll of the Bishopric of Winchester 1301–2*, 268–69, 275. Besides the Boles and Le Sedares, the Crowde and Trewe families were major tenants who provided trustworthy men in 1310.

62. For discussion, see James H. Landman, 'The Doom of Reason: Accommodating Lay Interpretation in Late Medieval England', in Barbara A. Hanawalt and David Wallace (eds.), *Medieval Crime and Social Control* (Minneapolis: University of Minnesota Press, 1999), 95–103.

63. *Carte Nativorum: A Peterborough Abbey Cartulary of the Fourteenth Century*, ed. Christopher N. L. Brooke and Michael M. Postan, Northamptonshire Record Society, 20 (1960), 123, 125; *The White Book of Peterborough: The Registers of Abbot William of Wood-*

ford, 1295–99 and Abbot Godfrey of Crowland, 1299–1321, ed. Sandra Raban, Northampton-shire Record Society, 41 (2001), 119–20; Edmund King, *Peterborough Abbey 1086–1310: A Study in the Land Market* (Cambridge: Cambridge University Press, 1973), 120–22, 153–57; Northamptonshire Record Office, F (M) 2389, m. 23v; TNA, E179/155/31, mm. 39–41; *Chronicon Petroburgense*, ed. Thomas Stapleton, Camden Society, 47 (1849), 82.

64. Canterbury Cathedral Archives, DCc/VR/6; F.R.H Du Boulay, *The Lordship of Canterbury: An Essay on Medieval Society* (London: Nelson, 1966), 49, 59, 196, 384–90; *Survey of Archbishop Pecham*, xiii–xiv; *Register of John Pecham*, 1.58–64; Brian L. Woodcock, *Medieval Ecclesiastical Courts in the Diocese of Canterbury* (Oxford: Oxford University Press, 1952), 21–25. The 1283–85 survey simplified what was a highly complex tenurial situation of divided holdings and subletting, and so some tenants are inevitably not named. It does however permit the identification of the archbishop's most important tenants, and those smallholders owing portions of significant revenues or services. It is possible that the fourteen unidentifiable parish representatives were unimportant smallholders, but they may equally have been tenants, small or large, of other lords.

65. Ros Faith, *The English Peasantry and the Growth of Lordship* (Leicester: Leicester University Press, 1997), 135, 207.

66. *Survey of Archbishop Pecham*, lxxiii.

67. *Survey of Archbishop Pecham*, 12, 14–15; Du Boulay, *Lordship of Canterbury*, 60.

68. *Survey of Archbishop Pecham*, 21; *Register of John Pecham*, 1.8; British Library, MS Add. 29794, m. 3d.

69. *Survey of Archbishop Pecham*, li, lxxii.

70. *Survey of Archbishop Pecham*, 6–7.

71. John Aleyn of Womenswold personally held 20.75 acres, and he had a third interest in a further 20 acres; Henry at Mollond of Ash held 8 acres himself and a further 28.5 acres with his two brothers; Theobald the tanner of Wingham held 17 acres; the Nethersole family of Womenswold together held between 30 and 40 acres; the Clerk family in Ash held at least 37.5 acres: *Survey of Archbishop Pecham*, 12–13, 17–19, 33, 35–37.

72. For further discussion of the conjunction between economic growth, social stratification, and local office-holding, see Forrest, 'Power and the People', 30–33.

73. *The Cartulary of Blyth Priory*, ed. Reginald Thomas Timson (London: HMSO, 1973), 400–406; Hampshire Record Office, 5M50/83; Nottingham, UNMSC, Mi 6/174/1. Other rentals matching lists of trustworthy men can be found, but those in which fewer than 50 percent of the trustworthy men can be identified have not been used. It is impossible to construct a general model of where the missing men would sit within the visible yet 'truncated' distribution. Rentals separated from the census date by more than twenty-five years have been excluded.

74. Some people paying high rents may have struggled with them and achieved very slim profit margins. Others paying lower rents might have had more profitable holdings and therefore have been wealthier. A more significant problem, the extent of which is unknown, is the effect of bureaucratic simplification. Rentals were made to facilitate the easy collection of rents, not to assess personal wealth, and so only the primary tenants are listed. In addition, some rents are recorded for a property, rather than for an individual tenant. It may be that some of the property held by the individuals we are interested in has been hidden from view: Evgenii Alekseevich Kosminsky, *Studies in the Agrarian History of England in the Thirteenth Century* (Oxford: Blackwell, 1955), 207. For example in the 1396 rental for Southwick some of the highest rents, including an enormous four pounds seven shillings and one of one pound six shillings eight pence, were due from properties and not tenants. These properties were probably subdivided and the tenants too numerous to list. They have consequently been excluded from the following quantitative analysis.

75. The analysis that follows was conducted with the assistance of Francisco Beltran Tapia, using Stata software.

76. Because different rentals list quite different numbers of tenants, comparison between the places has been facilitated by grouping the tenants of each manor into five bands. The analysis was done twice: once using banded class intervals and again using the original data. There were no significant deviations arising from the two techniques, but using bands permits comparison more easily and these are the figures used. One feature of the raw data on rents that has the potential to skew the analysis is the presence of outliers: that is, rents that were so much higher than the next nearest as to affect the correlation. If the highest rent paid was more than 1.25 times the second rent paid, as at Blyth where the highest was nineteen shillings and the second thirteen shillings six pence, the correlation and the probability have been calculated twice; once including the outlier, and once excluding it.

77. The Gini index is a figure between 0 and 100, where 0 indicates perfect equality: for our purposes a hypothetical situation in which everyone paid the same rent. The tenants and their rents were divided into five equal ranked bands and the online Peter Rosenmai Lorenz curve and Gini index calculator was used to arrive at the figures for each place: http://www.peterrosenmai.com/lorenz-curve-graphing-tool-and-gini-coefficient-calculator.

78. Because it is unlikely that other manors in the same parishes had radically different distributions of rent (similar economies, similar tenants, and similar tenancies), we can reasonably assume that this reflects the social structure of each whole parish.

79. Bruce M. S. Campbell and Ken Bartley, *England on the Eve of the Black Death: An Atlas of Lay Lordship, Land and Wealth, 1300–49* (Manchester: Manchester University Press, 2006), Map 18.16 (before p. 195). In this tripartite classification of lay wealth and taxpayers, Campbell and Bartley summarise their main findings by sub-county region (not to level of parishes); where £ = wealth, p = per, t = taxpayer, m = mile. Campbell and Bartley calculate regional mean wealth per taxpayer (£.p.t.) from the lay subsidy assessments of 1327, 1332, and 1334, and they characterize it—based on national trends—as being 'very high' (above £2.3), 'high' (above £1.9), 'low' (below £1.9), or 'very low' (below £1.5). In addition they calculate landed wealth per square mile (£.p.m.) using inquisitions post mortem of the same period, and the number of taxpayers per square mile (t.p.m.) from the lay subsidy assessments.

80. We can be fairly confident that these results would not be much different if we had complete information on the trustworthy men: *Register of William Wickwane*, 77–78; *Cartulary of Blyth Priory*, 308–9, 374, 386, 388, 437; TNA, C 241/23/20. There is a possibility that two of the trustworthy men paid lower rents that would affect the correlation, but it is equally possible that they were just as well-off as the other five, perhaps as tenants of one of the other manors within the parish. It is assumed that these unknown values would have a neutral effect on the correlation.

81. Hert's lands were dispersed in many small chunks after his death (before 1406), while Abbot's were returned to the lord and rented out again in half-virgate plots after his death in 1412: *Register of John Waltham*, 164; Nottingham, UNMSC, Mi 6/174/1, mm. 1, 2, Mi 6/170/4, Mi 5/164/37/2, and Mi M/151, m. 2.

82. Although six of the trustworthy men of 1379 cannot be found in the 1396 rental, we can still be reasonably confident about the results. There had been great deal of stability in the structure of rents in Southwick since the mid-fourteenth century: five of the trustworthy men (Nicholas Grym, John Bocher, Andrew Hurt, Roger Taylour, and Richard Prat) paid the same rents in in 1396 as they had in 1352: Hampshire Record Office, 5M50/83, m. 1.

83. We have evidence of landholding in the neighbouring manors, and of rents in Southwick not accounted for in the rental. Andrew Hurt (who paid sixteen pence rent in

1396) held land from John Ulvedale worth eight shillings a year in 1401. William atte Halle (who paid six shillings one pence rent in 1396) held a tiny plot of land in Belney manor in 1381, and in 1401 he paid a rent of nine shillings to John Ulvedale. Valentine atte Mede (who is not recorded as a tenant of Southwick in 1396) was nonetheless a powerful man, whose influence in the local area will be the subject of further discussion in Chapter 7: suffice to say he possessed enough land to be able to grant away a plot worth ten shillings a year in 1391. The rents and properties of Hurt, Atte Mede, and Atte Hall suggest they were major players in the area. Much of their land was probably held as sub-tenancies, joint-tenancies, leases, and gages, none of which would show up in the rental: Hampshire Record Office, 5M50/26, 5M50/81, m. 1, 5M50/83, mm. 1, 2, and 5M50/84; North Yorkshire Record Office, ZJX/3/10/1, rots. 2, 2d, 3, 4, 4d.

84. Brian K. Roberts and Stuart Wrathmell, *An Atlas of Rural Settlement in England*, corrected reprint ed. (London: English Heritage, 2003), online datasets used in conjunction with Google Earth at http://www.english-heritage.org.uk/professional/research/archaeology /atlas-of-rural-settlement-gis/; Joan Thirsk (ed.), *The Agrarian History of England and Wales*, V: *1640–1750*, I: *Regional Farming Systems* (Cambridge: Cambridge University Press, 1984), 91, 131, 161, 318, 360; John Throsby, *Thoroton's History of Nottinghamshire: Volume 3. Republished with large additions* (London: Burbage, 1796), 424–29; *Cartulary of Blyth Priory*; William Page (ed.), *The Victoria History of the County of Nottingham* (London: Archibald Constable, 1910), 83–88; *Calendar of Inquisitions Post Mortem*, XVII: *15–23 Richard II*, ed. Michael Charles Burdett Dawes et al. (London: HMSO, 1988), 457; *Calendar of Inquisitions Post Mortem*, XVIII, *1–6 Henry IV (1399–1405)*, ed. J. L. Kirby (London: HMSO, 1987), 358.

85. How the relative inclusivity of Southwick's trustworthy inquest translated, if at all, into a sense of broad community participation in the affairs of the parish is discussed at pp. 197–99.

86. Campbell and Bartley, *England on the Eve of the Black Death*; for problems, see Stephen Rigby, 'Urban Society in Early Fourteenth-Century England: The Evidence of the Lay Subsidies', *Bulletin of the John Rylands Library*, 72 (1990), 171.

87. Kathleen Biddick, 'Missing Links: Taxable Wealth, Markets, and Stratification among Medieval English Peasants', *Journal of Interdisciplinary History*, 18 (1987), 277–98; Miri Rubin, *Charity and Community in Medieval Cambridge* (Cambridge: Cambridge University Press, 1987), 41–47; Rigby, 'Urban Society', 169–84; Derek Keene, *Survey of Medieval Winchester*, 2 vols. (Oxford: Clarendon, 1985), 2.402–28; Terry R. Slater, 'The Urban Hierarchy in Medieval Staffordshire', *Journal of Historical Geography*, 11 (1985), 115–37.

88. W. Mark Ormrod, 'Poverty and Privilege: The Fiscal Burden in England (XIIIth–XVth Centuries)', in Simonetta Cavaciocchi (ed.), *La Fiscalità nell'Economia Europea Secc. XIII–XVIII* (Florence: Firenze University Press, 2008), 641, suggests that lords used 'a whole range of ruses' to reduce their burden, including claiming nonresidence in the place of assessment, intimidating collectors, and cajoling taxpayers; Paul D. A. Harvey, *A Medieval Oxfordshire Village: Cuxham 1240 to 1400* (Oxford: Oxford University Press, 1965), 105, notes an itemization of the cost of bribing the tax assessors in the manorial accounts of Cuxham in Oxfordshire, while at Henstridge in Somerset the Earl Warenne was assessed to pay just eight pence more than his wealthiest tenant: TNA, E 179/169/6, rot. 22.

89. In the late thirteenth century Suffolk set the taxable limit at six shillings eight pence, which was enough to buy just one cow or ox 'or a poor specimen of a horse': Edward Miller and John Hatcher, *Medieval England: Rural Society and Economic Change 1086–1348* (London: Longman, 1978), 154.

90. *The Lay Subsidy of 1334*, ed. Robin E. Glasscock, Records of Social and Economic History, new series 2 (Oxford: Oxford University Press, 1975), xxv–xxvi; James Field Willard,

Parliamentary Taxes on Personal Property 1290 to 1334: A Study in Mediaeval English Financial Administration (Cambridge, Mass.: Medieval Academy of America, 1934), 73–81; Stuart Jenks, 'The Lay Subsidies and the State of the English Economy, 1275–1334', *Vierteljahrschrift für Sozial- und Wirtschaftsgeschichte*, 85 (1998), 29; Biddick, 'Missing Links', 280, 283–84; Pamela Nightingale, 'The Lay Subsidies and the Distribution of Wealth in Medieval England, 1275–1334', *Economic History Review*, 57 (2004), 6–7. In some regions livestock was given a standard valuation regardless of condition or market value: J. F. Hadwin, 'The Medieval Lay Subsidies and Economic History', *Economic History Review*, second series 36 (1983), 203–4.

91. Lincolnshire Archives, Dean and Chapter, Dij/64/2/18, item 6; TNA, E 179/135/11, rot. 26. Although the tax list is twenty-five years later than the visitation, three of the seven trustworthy men were still alive, while three other taxpayers can be identified as close relatives (in one case the widow) of other trustworthy men.

92. Lincolnshire Archives, REG/3, fo. 119r; *Two Bedfordshire Subsidy Lists. 1309 and 1332*, ed. S.H.A. Hervey (Bury St Edmunds: Suffolk Green Books, 1925).

93. *Register of Adam de Orleton, Worcester*, 172–74; *The Lay Subsidy Roll for Warwickshire of 6 Edward III (1332)*, ed. William Fowler Carter (London: Dugdale Society, 1926), 76.

94. *Register of Ralph of Shrewsbury*, 96–97; 'Exchequer Lay Subsidies 169/5 which is a Tax Roll for Somerset for the First Year of Edward the 3rd', ed. F. H. Dickinson, Somerset Record Society, 3 (1889), 218–19.

95. *Lower Ecclesiastical Jurisdiction*, 42, 66, 78, 94, 102, 140, 157, 164, 180, 184, 193, 199, 224, 233, 246; TNA, E 179/135/15, rot. 15. Wellingore was also assessed for the twentieth in 1327 (TNA, E 179/135/10, rot. 11d), but this tax list includes fewer of the trustworthy men than that for 1332.

96. The Spearman rank correlation coefficient has been calculated twice if there is an obvious outlier in the amount of tax assessed. In two cases, at Eaton Bray and Snitterfield, the lord is identifiable as the outlier.

97. A column giving the mean total assessed wealth per taxpayer in the period 1327–34 has been added. This was calculated by taking the average tax burden for 1327, 1332, and 1334 (where all three are available) and dividing by the number of taxpayers (averaging the figures for 1327 and 1332). Values from 'Very High' to 'Very Low' are given according to the Campbell and Bartley classifications described above. This figure can thereby be compared with Campbell and Bartley's data on regional wealth, allowing us to see whether or not the parishes were in line with their local region.

98. This conclusion will be challenged by the analysis presented in Chapter 7.

99. C.R.J. Currie and Robert W. Dunning (eds.), *A History of the County of Somerset: Volume 7: Bruton, Horethorne and Norton Ferris Hundreds* (London: Institute of Historical Research, 1999), 108–19.

100. Northamptonshire Record Office, F (M) 2388, m. 20d; F (M) 2389, m. 17; King, *Peterborough Abbey*, 136, 150–51.

101. For the collapse in agricultural prices, see David L. Farmer, 'Prices and Wages: Statistical Supplement', in Edward Miller (ed.), *The Agrarian History of England and Wales*, III: *1348–1500* (Cambridge: Cambridge University Press, 1991), 502–3.

102. *Poll Taxes* I, xiv. For discussion see Rigby, *English Society in the Later Middle Ages*, 120–24.

103. The problems attendant upon calculations of total population from the 1377 poll tax assessments are discussed in John Hatcher, *Plague, Population and the English Economy 1348–1530* (London: Macmillan, 1977), 13–14, and in Miller and Hatcher, *Medieval England*, 28–29; the characteristics of rural and urban occupational structures are ad-

dressed in P.J.P. Goldberg, 'Urban Identity and the Poll Taxes of 1377, 1379 and 1381', *Economic History Review*, second series 43 (1990), 194–216; the relative strength of the farming, fishing, and forestry 'sectors' is investigated by Gregory Clark, '1381 and the Malthus Delusion', *Explorations in Economic History*, 50 (2013), 4–15.

104. *Poll Taxes* I, xiv–xvi.

105. *Poll Taxes* I, xvi–xvii.

106. *Poll Taxes* I, 158–59.

107. *Poll Taxes* I, xxvi.

108. The likely extent of evasion is discussed in *Poll Taxes* I, xxiii–xvi; for reassessment in Gloucestershire, see Rodney H. Hilton, 'Some Social and Economic Evidence in Late Medieval English Tax Returns', in Hilton, *Class, Conflict and the Crisis of Feudalism* (London: Hambledon, 1985), 261–63.

109. TNA, C 143/287/28, C 143/350/5, and DL 30/89/1202; *Calendar of Inquisitions Post Mortem*, XVII, 457.

110. TNA, DL 30/57/704, mm. 1–2, 2d; *Poll Taxes* I, 151.

111. Cambridge, King's College Archives, STP/3 dorse, STP/4–6, STP/83. John Tarry is the only trustworthy man not identifiable in the manorial records. In 1380 he was assessed to pay the standard two-shillings poll tax, but this merely tells us he was not among the poorest: *Poll Taxes* I, 158–59.

112. Britnell, *Britain and Ireland*, 175–76; Razi, *Life, Marriage and Death*, 83–85, 139–50.

Part III: Trustworthiness and Inequality in the Parish

1. Amartya Sen, *Inequality Re-examined* (Oxford: Oxford University Press, 1995), 15.

2. Perhaps the most influential study of this phenomenon is in Kimberlé Crenshaw, 'Demarginalizing the Intersection of Race and Sex: A Black Feminist Critique of Antidiscrimination Doctrine, Feminist Theory and Antiracist Politics', *University of Chicago Legal Forum*, 140 (1989), 139–67. Biddick's comment in 'Missing Links', 278, that stratification in medieval society has to be studied as a 'multi-focal problem', is based on similar assumptions. The phrase 'axes of inequality' comes from Frank Parkin, *Class Inequality and Political Order* (London: Paladin, 1972), 14–15, and was picked up by Rigby, *English Society in the Later Middle Ages*, 283. Philippe Jarnoux, 'Entre pouvoir et paraître. Pratiques de distribution et d'affirmation dans le monde rural', in Jessenne and Menant (eds.), *Les élites rurales*, 132–33, discusses these phenomena in a rural medieval context.

3. Sztompka, *Trust*, 8–9; Seabright, *Company of Strangers*, 65; Fukuyama, *Trust*, 26–27; Coleman, *Foundations of Social Theory*, 300–307; Robert D. Putnam, *Bowling Alone: The Collapse and Revival of American Community* (New York: Simon & Schuster, 2000); Manuel DeLanda, *A New Philosophy of Society: Assemblage Theory and Social Complexity* (London: Continuum, 2006), 33–36.

4. I will not pursue the idea that in-group trust is 'transitive' and capable of spreading throughout society: see Robert D. Putnam et al., *Making Democracy Work: Civic Traditions in Modern Italy* (Princeton, N.J.: Princeton University Press, 1993), 167–71; Sztompka, *Trust*, 5, 105–7, 114–15, 130. This assumption is intuitive and cannot be empirically verified, nor has any mechanism for the spread of trust from closed groups to wider society been identified. For criticisms, see Sheilagh Ogilvie, 'The Use and Abuse of Trust: Social Capital and Its Deployment by Early Modern Guilds', *Jahrbuch für Wirtschaftsgeschichte*, 46 (2005), 46–47, and for examples of generalized *distrust* sitting alongside strong in-group trust, see Dale Kent, *Friendship, Love and Trust in Renaissance Florence* (Cambridge, Mass.: Harvard University Press, 2009), 157–61, and Jurdjevic, 'Trust in Renaissance Electoral Politics', 601–14.

5. Seligman, *Problem of Trust*, 80–92; Muldrew, *Economy of Obligation*, 332. To a great extent this view rests upon a 'Jeffersonian' caricature of the male, free, independent, substantial householders on whom modern democracy is supposedly based: Scott, *Two Cheers for Anarchism*, 79–80.

6. Sheilagh Ogilvie, 'How Does Social Capital Affect Women?', *American Historical Review*, 109 (2004), 325–59; Geoffrey Hawthorn, 'Three Ironies in Trust', in Gambetta (ed.), *Trust*, 118. Luhmann, *Trust and Power*, 14, argued that social differentiation allows some people to manipulate the perceptions of others.

7. Johnstone, *History of Trust in Ancient Greece*, 143; Morgan, *Roman Faith and Christian Faith*, 52–54; Chris Wickham, *Community and Clientele in Twelfth-Century Tuscany: The Origins of the Rural Commune in the Plain of Lucca* (Oxford: Clarendon, 1998).

Chapter Seven: Representing the Community?

1. The importance of the passage of time and repeated experiences to the reproduction of inequality is discussed in Pedro Ramos Pinto, 'Why Inequalities Matter', in Rémi Genevey, Rajendra K. Pachauri, and Laurence Tubiana (eds.), *Reducing Inequalities: A Sustainable Development Challenge* (New Delhi: TERI, 2013), 23.

2. Charles Tilly, *Durable Inequality* (Berkeley: University of California Press, 1998), 155, 158.

3. Christopher Dyer, 'Costs and Benefits of English Direct Taxation, 1275–1525', in Simonetta Cavaciocchi (ed.), *La Fiscalità nell'Economia Europea Secc. XIII–XVIII* (Florence: Firenze University Press, 2008), 915–16.

4. Beat Kümin, *The Shaping of a Community: The Rise and Reformation of the English Parish, c. 1400–1560* (Aldershot: Scolar, 1996), 100–101; Swanson, *Church and Society*, 217; see also George Bernard, *The Late Medieval English Church: Vitality and Vulnerability before the Break with Rome* (New Haven, Conn.: Yale University Press, 2012), 117–18; Palmer, *Selling the Church*, 13–14. The alternative view is expressed trenchantly in Clive Burgess, 'Pre-Reformation Churchwardens' Accounts and Parish Government: Lessons from London and Bristol', *English Historical Review*, 117 (2002), 312.

5. The terminology is surveyed in Charles Drew, *Early Parochial Organization in England: The Origins of the Office of Churchwarden* (London: St Anthony's Press, 1954), 6; Katherine L. French, *The People of the Parish: Community Life in a Late Medieval Diocese* (Philadelphia: University of Pennsylvania Press, 2001), 70; Kümin, *Shaping of a Community*, 22 (which also provides European comparisons); Owen, *Church and Society in Medieval Lincolnshire*, 116.

6. Burgess, 'Pre-Reformation Churchwardens' Accounts', 322–25; we see something similar in a London court case of 1512 involving the alleged embezzlement of fraternity funds. The court heard that when the fraternity warden read his annual account 'some of the more honest and trustworthy parishioners', not including the rector or the churchwardens, were formally present to hear it: London Metropolitan Archives, DL/C/0206, fo. 177v. Kümin, *Shaping of a Community*, 21, accepts that before the Black Death, at least, there were complex hierarchies of office-holding in many parishes. He cites the 1287 constitutions of Exeter diocese which stipulated that the *custodes* of the church should read their account before the rector, vicar or chaplain plus five or six of the trustworthy parishioners chosen by the clergy. Kümin acknowledges that these 'fabric wardens' were subordinate to the panel of clergy and trustworthy men, though he regards this as a situation that only applied in the earlier period.

7. *Register of Richard de Kellawe*, 1.176.

8. Margaret Harvey, *Lay Religious Life in Late Medieval Durham* (Woodbridge: Boydell, 2006), 42.

9. *Lower Ecclesiastical Jurisdiction*, 8; Owen, *Church and Society in Medieval Lincolnshire*, 106.

10. Drew, *Early Parochial Organization*, 25–26; Kümin, *Shaping of a Community*, 241n; Eamon Duffy, *The Voices of Morebath: Reformation and Rebellion in an English Village* (New Haven, Conn.: Yale University Press, 2001), 29–31, 114. For urban parallels, see Susan Reynolds, *An Introduction to the History of Medieval English Towns* (Oxford: Clarendon, 1977), 172–77.

11. Kümin, *Shaping of a Community*, 33.

12. In his pioneering study of churchwardens, *Early Parochial Organization*, 24–25, Drew assumed that it was they who had always been the representatives of the parishes in episcopal visitations. French, *People of the Parish*, 11, 31, 72, has gone so far as to say that visitation records cannot be used to study collective parish life and decision-making processes, for which view see also Owen, *Church and Society in Medieval Lincolnshire*, 121–22; Swanson, *Church and Society*, 165–66.

13. Swanson, *Church and Society*, 165; Kümin, *Shaping of a Community*, 226–27, notes that thirteenth-century parish representatives were called *fidedigni*, but because he is not directly concerned with visitation and its records, he assumes that the fifteenth century saw a simple replacement of poorly defined 'trustworthy men' by office-holding churchwardens.

14. Hereford Cathedral Archives, 1050a (Hope under Dinmore, Pudleston, and Eye); Lincolnshire Archives, Dean and Chapter, A/1/14, p. 29, item 97 (Lyndon); Canterbury Cathedral Archives, DCc/VR/4 (Well, Ickham, Adisham and Worth). During visitations and in litigation 'the parishioners' (*parochiani*) is a phrase used to describe the select group of trustworthy men, not the population of the parish as a whole.

15. Canterbury Cathedral Archives, DCc/VR/15 (Kent in 1291); *Register of John Waltham*, 125 (Berkshire in 1391); Canterbury Cathedral Archives, Y.1.5, fo. 19v (Kent in 1454).

16. Kümin, *Shaping of a Community*, 239–40.

17. *Lower Ecclesiastical Jurisdiction*, 270–560.

18. These comments are based upon an analysis of parish office holders between 1475 and 1480 when the records are fullest: Worcester Record Office, BA 2636/11 43700, fos. 53r–63r.

19. Hampshire Record Office, 21M65/B/1/1, fo. 47r (1517), and 21M65/B/1/2, fo. 2v (1520). Despite this real change the distinction between churchwardens and trustworthy men (or other parish representatives with wider responsibilities) continued in some places into the late sixteenth and seventeenth centuries: 'Some Elizabethan Visitations of the Churches belonging to the Peculiar of the Dean of York', ed. T.M. Fallow, *Yorkshire Archaeological Journal*, 18 (1905–6), 197–232, 313–41; Houlbrooke, *Church Courts and the People*, 29–30.

20. Worcester Record Office, BA 2636/11 43700, fos. 47v, 50r. In a similar vein the 1538 churchwardens of St Botolph's Aldersgate in London were 'chosen . . . in the presence of the parisshoners beyng present at the seid accompt', while in 1546 the 'whole parish' elected its churchwardens: cited in Kümin, *Shaping of a Community*, 28.

21. French, *People of the Parish*, 68.

22. Miri Rubin, 'Small Groups: Identity and Solidarity in the Late Middle Ages', in Jenny Kermode, (ed.), *Enterprise and Individuals in Fifteenth Century England* (Stroud: Sutton, 1991), 132–50; Gervase Rosser, 'Going to the Fraternity Feast: Commensality and Social Relations in Late Medieval England', *Journal of British Studies*, 33 (1994), 430–46.

23. Ellen K. Rentz, *Imagining the Parish in Late Medieval England* (Columbus: Ohio State University Press, 2015).

24. Kümin, *Shaping of a Community*, 28–29; Duffy, *Stripping of the Altars*, 153–54.

25. Worcester Record Office, BA 2636/11 43700, fo. 8v; *Register of Thomas Rotherham*, 68-69, 114, 122, 128.

26. York, Borthwick Institute, Register 16, fo. 171r; *Register of Thomas Rotherham*, 74, 115, 121.

27. Kümin, *Shaping of a Community*, 232-37, 260-61. His most recent articulation of this point of view can be found in *The Communal Age in Western Europe, c.1100-1800* (Basingstoke: Palgrave Macmillan, 2013), 40-52.

28. *Lower Ecclesiastical Jurisdiction*, ed. Poos, xxi-xxiv; the tribunals are at 5-248.

29. The inquest lists for Glentham have been augmented with the names of those who served on two special inquests into tithes in 1340 and 1341.

30. TNA, E179/135/25, rot. 1, m. 2.

31. In Glentham the 1340 sub-taxers were again men who served on the inquest, but in contrast with the Friesthorpe men the sub-taxers were only *inquisitores* on one, four and five occasions each: TNA, E179/135/25, rot. 4 (Simon Walsh, Robert son of Petronilla, Henry of Ounby).

32. For the seven parishes minus Friesthorpe the number of households is expressed as upper and lower limits in order to reflect uncertainty about extrapolation from the lay subsidy assessments. The number of householders has been estimated using a maximum multiplier of x3 (supported by W. Mark Ormrod, 'The Crown and the English Economy, 1290-1348', in Campbell (ed.), *Before the Black Death*, 156), and minimum multiplier of x2 (supported by Dyer, *Standards of Living*, 130, 138). The lower and upper figures for each parish were Skillington (26, 39); Scredington (30, 45); Hainton (44, 66); Searby, with Owmby (52, 78); Strubby with Woodthorpe (66, 99); Wellingore (90, 135); Glentham (130, 195).

33. Unfortunately it is not possible, except in the case of Wellingore which featured in Chapter 6, to identify more than a handful of the dozens of men who served on these Lincolnshire inquests in the records of the 1327 and 1332 tax assessments. Why this should be the case is not clear. Some *inquisitores* may have arrived in the parishes since the assessments had been made; other may have been assessed in other, neighbouring vills (but they could not be easily identified here either, especially since many names repeat and/or vary between places within a region). We are, however, able to use the raw numbers of taxpayers in 1327 and 1332 to calculate the rough proportion of taxpayers who could expect to serve on the inquest in each parish. This is not possible for Friesthorpe, for which no lay subsidy returns at all survive.

34. The total population has been estimated by applying Titow's and Hallam's conservative estimate of 4.5 persons per household to the lower and upper estimated numbers of households. Jan Zbigniew Titow, *English Rural Society 1200-1350* (London: George Allen and Unwin, 1969), 89; Herbert Enoch Hallam, 'Some Thirteenth-Century Censuses', *Economic History Review*, 10 (1958), 340-61. The lower and upper figures for each parish were Skillington (117, 176); Scredington (135, 203); Hainton (198, 297); Searby, with Owmby (234, 351); Strubby, with Woodthorpe (297, 446); Wellingore (405, 608); Glentham (585, 878).

35. There are problems with the evidence, but these are minimal and do not affect the overall conclusions. A small number of individuals were hard to identify from one year to the next. This is because the scribe changed several times over the decade, and he was, in any case, an outsider unfamiliar with the local names. Some guesses were necessary: for example it seems likely that the recorded names John Stoures, John Sturus, John Stures, and John Steres in Friesthorpe refer to the same man.

36. In part this distribution could be affected by the inclusion of observations from two special inquisitions, but since these drew on the same pool of men, it was thought legitimate to include them.

37. Exeter Cathedral, MS 3673, pp. 19, 35, 38, 40, 42, 48.

38. *Lay Subsidy of 1334*: this tax was a fifteenth on moveable property. See comments above at p. 148 on exemptions and the limitations of the data. The amounts due for each vill have been multiplied by fifteen to reach the assessed value of taxable property in each vill. According to Campbell and Bartley, *England on the Eve of the Black Death*, 322, the mean assessed wealth of vills in England in 1334 was just under £39.58; the modal value was between £15 and £20.

39. Remembering that tax liability is only an indirect measure of wealth.

40. Roberts and Wrathmell, *Atlas of Rural Settlement in England*; Graham Platt, *Land and People in Medieval Lincolnshire* (Lincoln: History of Lincolnshire, 1985); King, *Peterborough Abbey*; Joan Thirsk, *English Peasant Farming: The Agrarian History of Lincolnshire from Tudor to Recent Times* (London: Methuen, 1957); Herbert Arthur Doubleday and William Page (eds.), *The Victoria History of the County of Bedford: Volume Three* (Westminster: Archibald Constable, 1912), 369–75; Philip Styles (ed.), *The Victoria History of the County of Warwick: Volume Three* (London: Institute of Historical Research, 1945), 167–72; Thirsk (ed.), *The Agrarian History of England and Wales*, 5.91, 131, 161, 318, 360; William Page (ed.), *The Victoria History of the County of Lincoln: Volume Two* (London: Archibald Constable, 1906), 188–91, 210–13; *Calendar of Close Rolls, Edward II: Volume 2, 1313–18*, ed. Henry Churchill Maxwell Lyte (London: HMSO, 1893), 373; *Lower Ecclesiastical Jurisdiction*, ed. Poos, xxi–xxiii; TNA, C 143/287/28 and DL 30/89/1202; *Lay Subsidy of 1334*; Campbell and Bartley, *England on the Eve of the Black Death*, 332.

41. Samantha Letters, *Gazetteer of Markets and Fairs in England and Wales to 1516* (Kew: TNA, 2003).

42. Christopher Dyer, 'Small Places with Large Consequences: The Importance of Small Towns in England 1000–1540', *Historical Research*, 75 (2002), 1–24.

43. TNA, E179/135/11, rot. 25d. Eaton Bray in Bedforshire is comparable.

44. Duffy, *Voices of Morebath*, 31.

45. *Worcestershire Taxes in the 1520s: The Military Survey and Forced Loans of 1522–3 and the Lay Subsidy of 1524–7*, ed. Michael A. Faraday, Worcestershire Historical Society, new series 19 (2003), 200.

46. Duffy, *Voices of Morebath*, 28–30.

47. *Register of William Greenfield*, 1.176.

48. French, *People of the Parish*, 77–78.

49. *Lower Ecclesiastical Jurisdiction*, 48, 70.

50. Clive Burgess has argued, in relation to churchwardens, that parish government depended not solely upon 'consecutive sets of agents acting in pairs for brief spells' but on 'a broader and more stable elite of self-selecting accomplishment and proven talent': 'Pre-Reformation Churchwardens' Accounts', 330.

51. French, *People of the Parish*, 81–82.

52. *Lower Ecclesiastical Jurisdiction*, 195, 198.

53. Worcester Record Office, BA 2636/11 43700, fo. 12v.

54. Ibid., fos. 53r–63r.

55. These figures were arrived at by taking the numbers of householders assessed in the 1524 and 1525 lay subsidies (51 and 63) to be 15 percent of the total adult population; a more or less level population between 1480 and 1524 is assumed: *Worcestershire Taxes in the 1520s*, 103, 108, 200; see xxxi for discussion of the multiplier used in this calculation.

56. The Gini index generated by this distribution of office-holding is 29.52, which reflects a lesser degree of inequality within the trustworthy men than we saw in all the Lincolnshire parishes bar Skillington.

57. Cambridgeshire Archives, R52/12/1/3.

58. Olson, 'Jurors of the Village Court', 237–56; Anne Reiber DeWindt and Edwin Brezette DeWindt, *Ramsey: The Lives of an English Fenland Town, 1200–1600* (Washington,
D.C.: Catholic University of America Press, 2006), 102, assert the 'truly representative'
character of manorial and leet court jurors, who were not ambitious or self-seeking, nor
were they 'set apart from the community'.

59. *Register of Lewis Charlton*, 7–8; *Register of John Gilbert*, 78–79; *Register of Richard
Mayew*, 165–66. For nomination, see *Lower Ecclesiastical Jurisdiction*, 26 (Glentham).

60. *Register of John le Romeyn*, 1.365; *Register of John Kirkby and John Ross*, 1.95;
Lincolnshire Archives, REG/12, fo. 19v.

61. *Register of Simon of Ghent*, 127–28.

62. *Register of Thomas Langley*, 3.181–82; the rhetoric of truth and the 'better able' will
be discussed at p. 260.

63. *Lower Ecclesiastical Jurisdiction*, 26; Hereford Cathedral Archives, 1462.

64. *Register of Wolstan de Bransford*, 18.

65. *Register of William Wickwane*, 77–78. The name of the seventh is only partially
recorded in the register. The rents paid by these men were discussed at pp. 145–47; for the
valuation of churches, see Chapters 11 and 12.

66. Nottingham, UNMSC, Cl/M/85; Throsby, *Thoroton's History of Nottinghamshire*,
424–29; Page (ed.), *Victoria History of the County of Nottingham*, 83–88.

67. *Cartulary of Blyth Priory*, 21–22, 88, 101–2, 319–20, 363, 376, 404.

68. *Chronicon Petroburgense*, 81–82; there is no mention of the dispute in Sutton's
register. In practice bishops are likely to have frequently turned a blind eye to the packing
of inquests and visitation panels by local secular and religious landlords. As with common-
law juries, which lords frequently packed with their own tenants in order to secure the
'right' result, such behaviour was generally considered corrupt only by the party who had
lost out. When the boot was on the other foot, no impassioned defender of the impartiality
of the law was above such ruses and stratagems: Christine Carpenter, *Locality and Polity:
A Study of Warwickshire Landed Society, 1401–1499* (Cambridge: Cambridge University
Press, 1992), chap. 8.

69. *Register of Nicholas Bubwith*, 380; Taunton, Somerset Heritage Centre, DD/WY/
B3a/2, 17, 21, 76.

70. Tilly, *Durable Inequality*, 94: 'Elites typically *become* elites and maintain themselves as elites by controlling valuable resources'. Historians might be able to identify processes of strengthening and weakening of elites, but rarely their beginnings. Even in the
early Anglo-Saxon settlement period, for example, there is evidence for disparities between
households predating the emergence of intensive lordship: Faith, *English Peasantry and
the Growth of Lordship*, 5; Kosminsky, *Studies in Agrarian History*, 207.

71. 'Richard II: Parliament of January 1390, Text and Translation', in *The Parliament
Rolls of Medieval England*, ed. C. Given-Wilson et al., Internet version, http://www.sd
-editions.com/PROME (Leicester: Scholarly Digital Editions, 2005).

72. *Register of John Waltham*, 165; Dorchester, Dorset History Centre, Tarrant Gunville Manor D 151/1, rots. 5, 6, 8, 9, 9d, 10, 11, 12d, 13, D 151/2, rots. 1, 2, 2d, 3, 4, 8, and
D 151/9, m. 1.

73. Kosminsky, *Studies in Agrarian History*, 208.

74. TNA, DL 30/57/704, m. 2 (and dorse); *Register of John Waltham*, 165. For a statistical analysis of the Blandford trustworthy, see pp. 153–55.

75. Britnell, *Britain and Ireland*, 175.

76. *Calendar of Inquisitions Post Mortem*, XVII, 127; *Calendar of Inquisitions Post
Mortem*, XVIII, 212–13; Nottingham, UNMSC, Mi 6/174/1, m.1, Mi 6/170/2, m. 2, and Mi
M/150, mm. 1, 3.

77. St Giles House, Shaftesbury Archives, M64, rot. 1, M65, rots. 3–3d, and M67, rots. 1, 2.

78. Similar strategies may have been behind the actions of another trustworthy man in 1460s Cambridgeshire. Richard Madingly was a manorial presentment juror and 'trustworthy man' in Kingston, who used his lord's court to defend himself against defamations, and who was reported for attempting to train a hobby—the bird of prey—without a licence. Hunting rights were both severely socially restricted and highly desirable to the upwardly mobile. Madingly's action was therefore highly symbolic and likely to be seen as a challenge to local lordship: Cambridgeshire Archives, R52/12/1/3, rot. 8.

79. St Giles House, Shaftesbury Archives, M65, rots. 1, 2, 3, and M67, rot. 1d; Nottingham, UNMSC, Mi 6/174/6.

80. St Giles House, Shaftesbury Archives, M64, rots. 1, 2, M66, rot. 1, and M70, rots. 5–5d.

81. St Giles House, Shaftesbury Archives, M63, and M65, rot. 3d.

82. St Giles House, Shaftesbury Archives, M66, rots. 2, 3; Nottingham, UNMSC, Mi 5/164/3, rot. 9.

83. Christopher Dyer, 'The Experience of Being Poor in Late Medieval England', in Anne M. Scott (ed.), *Experiences of Poverty in Late Medieval and Early Modern England and France* (Farnham: Ashgate, 2012), 29–30.

84. *Register of John Waltham*, 165; St Giles House, Shaftesbury Archives, M63, M64, rot. 3, M67, rots. 2d, 3, M68, rot. 1, M70 rots. 1, 5, 6 (and attached slip), and M71 (attached slip).

85. St Giles House, Shaftesbury Archives, M64, rots. 1, 1d, M69, rot. 4, and M70, rot. 1.

86. Judith M. Bennett, *Ale, Beer, and Brewsters in England: Women's Work in a Changing World, 1300–1600* (Oxford: Oxford University Press, 1996), 159–63.

87. Davis, *Medieval Market Morality*, 189–96; excommunication for using false weights and measures was commonplace, for example, British Library, MS Arundel 130, fo. 118r, and MS Harley 2383, fo. 48r; Lambeth Palace Library, MS 172, fo. 173r; Oxford, Bodleian Library, MS Douce 60, fo. 161r.

88. St Giles House, Shaftesbury Archives, M63, M64, rot. 3, and M68, rot. 1; Nottingham, UNMSC, Mi 5/164/1, and Mi 6/174/4.

89. St Giles House, Shaftesbury Archives, M65, rots. 1, 3, 3d, and M67, rot. 1.

90. St Giles House, Shaftesbury Archives, Deeds T239–242, and M65, rots. 1, 3; *Calendar of Inquisitions Post Mortem*, XVII, 423; *Calendar of Inquisitions Post Mortem*, XIX: 7–14 Henry IV, ed. J. L. Kirby (London: HMSO, 1992), 84–85.

91. Another example, from nearby Chalbury, is Richard Wiltshire. He was one of four visitation representatives in 1394, and an important tenant whose wealth was based on sheep rearing; he bridled at the lord's insistence that he should perform his customary obligations: *Register of John Waltham*, 164; St Giles House, Shaftesbury Archives, M3, rots. 1, 2, 2d, and M5, rot. 1.

92. Schofield, *Peasant and Community*, 71.

93. *Register of John le Romeyn*, 2.75–76.

94. Christopher Dyer, *An Age of Transition? Economy and Society in England in the Later Middle Ages* (Oxford: Oxford University Press, 2007), 245.

95. At Nonington in Kent there was an expectation that the clergy of Ash should lend from the profits of the rectory: Canterbury Cathedral Archives, DCc/VR/6, m. 2.

96. Thomas the chaplain of Nonington held 11 acres in 1283–85, putting him amongst the upper half of peasant society: Canterbury Cathedral Archives, DCc/VR/6, mm. 1d, 2; *Survey of Archbishop Pecham*, 40.

97. Canterbury Cathedral Archives, DCc/VR/6, m. 1d; *Survey of Archbishop Pecham*, 35–37.

98. John Aleyn of Womenswold personally held 20.75 acres, and he had a third interest in a further 20 acres; Henry at Mollond of Ash held 8 acres himself and a further 28.5 acres with his two brothers; Theobald the tanner of Wingham held 17 acres: *Survey of Archbishop Pecham*, 17–19, 33, 36. The Nethersole family of Womenswold together held between 30 and 40 acres; the Clerk family in Ash held at least 37.5 acres: *Survey of Archbishop Pecham*, 12–13, 35–37.

99. *Register of Godfrey Giffard*, 90; Hereford Cathedral Archives, 1050a; *Register of Robert Winchelsey*, 87.

100. Lichfield Record Office, B/A/1/12, fo. 141v.

101. Moore, *First European Revolution*, 65–111. See pp. 316–18 for further discussion.

102. Canterbury Cathedral Archives, DCc/VR/6, mm. 2, 2d. Janelle Werner, 'Promiscuous Priests and Vicarage Children: Clerical Sexuality and Masculinity in Late Medieval England', in Jennifer D. Thibodeaux (ed.), *Negotiating Clerical Identities: Priests, Monks and Masculinity in the Middle Ages* (Basingstoke: Macmillan, 2010), 159–84; Marie A. Kelleher, 'Like Man and Wife: Clerics' Concubines in the Diocese of Barcelona', *Journal of Medieval History*, 28 (2002), 349–60; Ruth Mazo Karras, *Unmarriages: Women, Men, and Sexual Unions in the Middle Ages* (Philadelphia: University of Pennsylvania Press, 2012), 148.

103. Canterbury Cathedral Archives, DCc/VR/6, m. 1; *Survey of Archbishop Pecham*, 16–17. On shiremen see p. 143.

104. Canterbury Cathedral Archives, DCc/VR/6, mm. 1, 1d, 2.

105. McSheffrey, *Marriage, Sex, and Civic Culture*, 135–89; Neal, *Masculine Self*, 36–55. Visitation records offer the potential for much more detailed work than has hitherto been done on the relationship between the control of sexuality and the pursuit of other social goals; there is especially great scope for new insights through quantitative modelling.

106. *Register of William Wykeham*, 2.305. On *fama* see pp. 251–58.

107. There is a chance that the clergy of Boarhunt were struggling financially in 1379 because the revenues of the church had been confiscated by the bishop in 1376: *Register of William Wykeham*, 2.259.

108. His main residence and holdings may have been in Bramdean, to the north, while he was mentioned twice as a tenant in Belney in 1381: *Poll Taxes* III, 481; *The Cartularies of Southwick Priory*, ed. Katharine A. Hanna, Hampshire Record Series, 9–10 (1988–89), 1.229–33; North Yorkshire Record Office, ZJX/3/10/1, rot. 2. Though the 1396 rental for Southwick has him paying just ten pence in rent there, we know that this did not reflect the total extent of his landholdings. For example, he was subletting two properties built against the corner of Southwick parish church in 1401: Hampshire Record Office, 5M50/83–84.

109. Hampshire Record Office, 5M50/81, m. 3; *Cartularies of Southwick Priory*, 1.257; he was also a witness to a gift of land between local families in 1354: Hampshire Record Office, 5M50/19.

110. Valentine sublet some of his land to Nicholas Waythe, while in 1374 he had witnessed a land grant made by another man of the inquest: Andrew Hurt. In 1383 and 1391 Simon and Valentine atte Mede, Nicholas Wayte, Walter Knygt, and John atte Hulle together witnessed some leases made to the priory: Hampshire Record Office, 5M50/26; *Cartularies of Southwick Priory*, 1.288, 2.430–31.

111. *Cartularies of Southwick Priory*, 1.229–33, 235–37, 246–49, 292; TNA, C 143/351/5; Hampshire Record Office, 4M53/6, 4M53A1–5; *Register of William Wykeham*, 1.349.

112. *Cartularies of Southwick Priory*, 1.254.

113. Hampshire Record Office, 5M50/44, m. 2, and 5M50/22; *Cartularies of Southwick Priory*, 1.219. Simon atte Mede was paid ten pounds for some land in 1391 by John Cook, who was an agent of the priory: Hampshire Record Office, 5M50/44, m. 1; 5M50/45, m. 3.

114. Hampshire Record Office, 5M50/43–46; *Cartularies of Southwick Priory*, 1.254–55, 2.54–55, 2.92, 2.190, 2.382.

115. For the 'more trustworthy' men of Gillingham, see pp. 121–22.

116. *Register of John Waltham*, 167–68.

117. *Poll Taxes* I, 160; Dorchester, Dorset History Centre, D/FAN court rolls 1–20 Ric. II. One John Cresben was a juror in 1382 and the bailiff of Gillingham in 1394; an undated chancery petition (TNA, C 1/16/181, in English, addressed to the archbishop and chancellor) names him as the late farmer of the royal manor of Gillingham. Someone called William Cresben was a regular creditor, witness, pledge, and purchaser of land in the town between 1380 and 1398.

118. The exceptions are John Graunt, reported for adultery in 1394, who sued Nicholas Bennet for the recovery of debt in 1396, and John Cley, reported for fornication, who was a well-connected attorney.

119. *Register of John Waltham*, 167–68; Dorchester, Dorset History Centre, D/FAN court rolls 1–20 Ric. II. These court rolls have not yet been fully catalogued and I am immensely grateful to Dr Mark Forrest of the Dorset History Centre for making available to me his database of property transfers and debt litigation based on the Gillingham rolls.

120. Tilly, *Durable Inequality*, 158.

Chapter Eight: Time, Place, and the Limits of Trustworthy Status

1. Coleman, *Foundations of Social Theory*, 192: 'the implications of population composition for the placement of trust, and thus for the content of judgements and evaluations, provide a valuable avenue for research'.

2. Britnell, *Britain and Ireland*, 172–79, 297–98; for further discussion see Forrest, 'Power and the People'.

3. Hatcher and Bailey, *Modelling the Middle Ages*, 30–49, 52–65, provide a good discussion of the debate.

4. Christopher Dyer, *Making a Living in the Middle Ages: The People of Britain 850–1520* (New Haven, Conn.: Yale University Press, 2002), 160–78; P.J.P. Goldberg, *Medieval England: A Social History 1250–1550* (London: Arnold, 2004), 147–60.

5. Ian Kershaw, 'The Great Famine and the Agrarian Crisis in England, 1315–1322', *Past & Present*, 59 (1973), 3–50; Philip Slavin, 'The Great Bovine Pestilence and Its Economic and Environmental Consequences in England and Wales, 1318–1350', *Economic History Review*, 65 (2012), 1239–66. Changes in the fourteenth-century economy have now been recast, in a comprehensive new interpretation, as a transition to a new 'socio-ecological regime' in Bruce M. S. Campbell, *The Great Transition: Climate, Disease and Society in the Late-Medieval World* (Cambridge: Cambridge University Press, 2016).

6. Razi, *Life, Marriage and Death*, 79–81; Mark Bailey, *Medieval Suffolk: An Economic and Social History, 1200–1500* (Woodbridge: Boydell, 2007), 59–60; Dyer, *Making a Living*, 232. Recent work by Philip Slavin has shown that winning and losing was determined by various forms of market failure, some of which were beyond any individual's control, while others—such as hoarding—resulted from producers attempting to profit from general misery: 'Market Failure during the Great Famine in England and Wales (1315–1317)', *Past & Present*, 222 (2014), 9–49.

7. Stephen Broadberry et al., *British Economic Growth, 1270–1870* (Cambridge: Cambridge University Press, 2015), 20–21.

8. Goldberg, *Medieval England*, 170.

9. Simon A. C. Penn and Christopher Dyer, 'Wages and Earnings in Late Medieval England: Evidence from the Enforcement of the Labour Laws', *Economic History Review*, 43 (1990), 356–76; Samuel K. Cohn, 'After the Black Death: Labour Legislation and Attitudes towards Labour in Late-Medieval Western Europe', *Economic History Review*, 60 (2007), 457–85; Bennett, 'Compulsory Service in Late Medieval England'.

10. Broadberry et al., *British Economic Growth*, 308–9; Schofield, *Peasant and Community*, 122; Zvi Razi, 'The Myth of the Immutable English Family', *Past & Present*, 140 (1993), 3–44.

11. *Register of William Wykeham*, 2.121–22.

12. Richard H. Britnell, *Growth and Decline in Colchester, 1300–1525* (Cambridge: Cambridge University Press, 1986), 110; Olson, 'Jurors of the Village Court', 240; Peter Larson, *Conflict and Compromise in the Late Medieval Countryside: Lords and Peasants in Durham, 1349–1400* (London: Routledge, 2014), 220.

13. York, Borthwick Institute, Register 10, fos. 29r, 59r–v, 148r, 171r, Register 11, fos. 13v, 34r, 113v, 152r, 161r, 165r, 235v, 252r, Register 12, fo. 14v, and Register 15, fo. 6r; Lincolnshire Archives, REG/12, fos. 21r, 25r, 60v, 94r, 178r, 321r–v; Cambridge University Library, EDR G/1/2, fos. 33r, 41v–42r; *Register of Ralph of Shrewsbury*, 694, 719; *Register of Robert de Stretton*, 98; *Register of William Wykeham*, 2.21, 2.125, 2.352–53, 2.374, 2.383; 2.453, 2.459; *Register of Lewis Charlton*, 50; *Register of Thomas de Brantyngham*, 273–74, 311, 316, 321, 333, 359, 437, 466, 471, 489, 526, 528, 534–35, 590, 593, 599, 606–7, 610, 626, 630, 640, 642, 648, 703.

14. Before the Black Death this formulation was used on average 1.5 times in each register. But between 1350 and 1374 the average rises to 3.1 uses per register, and between 1375 and 1399 there were 2.6 instances per register. These are admittedly rough-and-ready figures, but the difference separating the half century after the Black Death from the rest of the late Middle Ages is worthy of comment.

15. William J. Dohar, *The Black Death and Pastoral Leadership: The Diocese of Hereford in the Fourteenth Century* (Philadelphia: University of Pennsylvania Press, 1995).

16. Dyer, *Making a Living*, 346–62; Bailey, *Medieval Suffolk*, 246.

17. Schofield, *Peasant and Community*, 75–76.

18. Bailey, *Medieval Suffolk*, 61; Olson, 'Jurors of the Village Court', 248, suggests that before 1350 the jurors of Ellington regulated their inferiors, while after the plague they regulated each other.

19. Dyer, *Age of Transition?*, 195.

20. For bullion shortage, see Peter Spufford, *Money and Its Uses in Medieval Europe* (Cambridge: Cambridge University Press, 1988), 339–62. The monetarist hypothesis proposed in Pamela Nightingale, 'Gold, Credit, and Mortality: Distinguishing Deflationary Pressures on the Late Medieval English Economy', *Economic History Review*, 63 (2010), 1081–1104, linking a retraction of credit to scarcity of coin has recently been confirmed in Matthew Stevens's analysis: 'London Creditors and the Fifteenth-Century Depression', *Economic History Review*, 69 (2016), 1083–1107.

21. *Register of Nicholas Bubwith*, 312; *Registers of Robert Stillington and Richard Fox*, 76, 162–63; *Register of Edmund Lacy, Hereford*, 47–50; *Register of Edmund Lacy, Exeter*, 2.173; 'Register of the Archdeaconry of Richmond, 1442–1477', 76, 101, 119; Lichfield Record Office, B/A/1/11, fos. 50r, 55r, 67r.

22. *Register of Nicholas Bubwith*, 329, 406; *Register of John Stafford*, 5–7.

23. In 1428 Thomas Mitchell was co-parcener of one-fourth knight's fee in 'Boure', of one-half knight's fee in 'Cleyhull', and sole possessor of one-half knight's fee in 'Wemedon':

Inquisitions and Assessments Relating to Feudal Aids with Other Analogous Documents Preserved in the Public Record Office, A.D. 1284–1431, 6 vols. (London: HMSO, 1899–1920), 4.364. Sir John's wife Elizabeth had held land jointly with Richard Wyryng *alias* Mordcok who had been the chantry chaplain some time in Henry V's reign: Somerset Heritage Centre, A/AHT/172/3.

24. Sir Thomas was co-parcener of a knight's fee in 'Wolmerston' and 'Huntworth' in 1428: *Inquisitions and Assessments Relating to Feudal Aids*, 4.364. In 1358 a John Payn of North Petherton had granted 36 acres of land to the vicar of the parish; in 1382 he granted a cottage and one acre of land to someone else, which could be extended into the 'moor' at Edington; this was confirmed in 1399 by his wife, which suggests this may have been the father and mother of our John Payn; the John Payn of this inquest sold a messuage and fourteen acres in 1449: Somerset Heritage Centre, A/AHT/172/2, and A/AHT/172/4. Godehyne part held one-half knight's fee in 'Donwer' in 1428: *Inquisitions and Assessments Relating to Feudal Aids*, 4.364.

25. Somerset Heritage Centre, DD/H1/115, un-numbered charter.

26. In 1403 John Godehyne and Hugh Skathelok were witnesses together to property sales in North Petherton: Somerset Heritage Centre, A/AHT/172/3. In 1404 Thomas Mitchell was a witness to a land sale in North Petherton between Robert Bertelot (the chaplain presented to Newton that same year) and John Ellis: TNA, E 210/4258; Somerset Heritage Centre, DD/S/WH/64. In 1404 John son of John Ellis (ours must be this younger John) and his wife Joan bought three acres of land and rents worth thirteen shillings five pence a year from John Churchey and Robert Bertelot; among the witnesses were trustworthy men Simon and Thomas Mitchell: TNA, E 210/4258. In 1429 Robert Parle bought all the lands belonging to Nicholas Ebbeworth and William Godehyne in three parishes in Somerset; the grant was witnessed by Sir Thomas Popham, William Poulet (who held the advowson in 1425, as well as various knights' fees in the locality) and Thomas Mitchell: Somerset Heritage Centre, A/AHT/172/4; *Inquisitions and Assessments Relating to Feudal Aids*, 4.365.

27. John A. F. Thomson, *The Early Tudor Church and Society, 1485–1529* (London: Longman, 1993), 265–74; Duffy, *Stripping of the Altars*, 131–32.

28. Dyer, *Age of Transition?*, 196–210; Broadberry et al., *British Economic Growth*, 307–8, 419–20.

29. Bailey, *Medieval Suffolk*, 248, is worth comparison with Schofield, *Peasant and Community*, 151: 'the wealthy peasant landholder or gentleman-farmer as he was fast becoming'.

30. See discussion at p. 165.

31. John S. Beckerman, 'Procedural Innovation and Institutional Change in Medieval English Manorial Courts', *Law and History Review*, 10 (1992); Schofield, *Peasant and Community*, 167.

32. Marjorie Keniston McIntosh, *Controlling Misbehavior in England, 1370–1600* (Cambridge: Cambridge University Press, 1998).

33. Angus J. L. Winchester, *Landscape and Society in Medieval Cumbria* (Edinburgh: John Donald, 1987), 1, opens with the comment that upland England comprised a series of regions in which 'the physical environment produced a different set of constraints and offered a different range of opportunities to the medieval community'. Britnell, *Britain and Ireland*, 206–17, summarizes the practice and impact of pastoral farming.

34. Schofield, *Peasant and Community*, 136, 155.

35. Winchester, *Landscape and Society*, 22.

36. *Councils and Synods*, 2.794–95.

37. Harold Fox, *Dartmoor's Alluring Uplands: Transhumance and Pastoral Management in the Middle Ages* (Exeter: Exeter University Press, 2012), 29–37, 155–56, 205. Place

names with 'scale', 'set', and 'shiel' elements denote seasonal structures, while the 'maiden' element is suggestive of extensive female responsibility for summering.

38. Fernand Braudel, *The Mediterranean and the Mediterranean World in the Age of Philip II*, 2 vols., trans. Siân Reynolds (London: Collins, 1972–73), 1.25–53; James C. Scott, *The Art of Not Being Governed: An Anarchist History of Upland South-East Asia* (New Haven, Conn.: Yale University Press, 2009); important developments of Braudel's ideas by medieval historians include Chris Wickham, *The Mountains and the City: The Tuscan Apennines in the Early Middle Ages* (Oxford: Oxford University Press, 1988); Samuel K. Cohn, *Creating the Florentine State: Peasants and Rebellion, 1348–1434* (Cambridge: Cambridge University Press, 1999); Peregrine Horden and Nicholas Purcell, *The Corrupting Sea: A Study of Mediterranean History* (Oxford: Blackwell, 2000); Benoît Cursente summarizes recent research trends in 'Les montagnes des médiévistes', in *Montagnes médiévales* (Paris: Sorbonne, 2004), 419–21.

39. Gellner, 'Trust, Cohesion, and the Social Order', 144.

40. *Register of William Melton*, 1.25–27, 1.33.

41. Rosalind M. T. Hill, *The Labourer in the Vineyard: The Visitations of Archbishop Melton in the Archdeaconry of Richmond* (York: St Anthony's Press, 1968), 14; 'The Registers of the Archdeaconry of Richmond, 1361–1442', ed. Alexander Hamilton Thompson, *Yorkshire Archaeological Journal*, 25 (1920), 151–52, 161; Winchester, *Landscape and Society*, 5.

42. Similar contrasts between alluvial lands and mountain regions, with pronounced inequalities in the former, have been noted in other regions of Europe, for example Vicent Baydal Sala and Ferran Esquilache Martí, 'Exploitation and Differentiation: Economic and Social Stratification in the Rural Muslim Communities of the Kingdom of Valencia, 13th–16th Centuries', in Aparisi and Royo (eds.), *Beyond Lords and Peasants*, 37–67.

43. Winchester, *Landscape and Society*, 5–6, 22, 44–51.

44. *Register of William Melton*, 1.104–6. See also Year Books report on a parallel suit in the court of common pleas: http://www.bu.edu/phpbin/lawyearbooks/display.php ?id=7235. Given the litigation in two courts, it seems likely that Dalston had remained profitable in the face of regional decline.

45. *Register of William Melton*, 1.63–64.

46. Higden, *Speculum Curatorum*, 101–3; Catherine Rider, *Magic and Religion in Medieval England* (London: Reaktion Books, 2012), 48–51; Flanagan, *Doubt in an Age of Faith*, 22–23. In 1316 the bishop of Salisbury used trustworthy men to investigate a report of a soothsayer using divination to discover stolen goods, a proscribed act that had 'damned men of good fame': *Registers of Roger Martival*, 2.106.

47. An example of a thorough inquest by trustworthy men, fitting the dominant lowland pattern, occurred at Dent on the border of Yorkshire and Westmorland in 1444, as described in detail at pp. 129–31; but although the inquest took place, it was not respected in the same way that we have seen in innumerable lowland examples. The vicar-general of York commissioned the inquest and trustworthy men came forward, but penances were not awarded in line with what they reported. This suggests a different sort of disjuncture between parish society and episcopal authority in upland regions, but a disjuncture nonetheless.

48. Miller and Hatcher, *Medieval England*, 110.

49. Braudel, *Mediterranean*, 1.38.

50. French, *People of the Parish*, 114.

51. Christopher Dyer and Terry R. Slater, 'The Midlands', in David Palliser (ed.), *The Cambridge Urban History of Britain*, I: *600–1540* (Cambridge: Cambridge University Press, 2000), 625, 627.

52. A fair and market were granted in 1215: Letters, *Gazetteer of Markets and Fairs*.

53. York, Borthwick Institute, Register 10, fos. 128v, 130v.

54. York, Borthwick Institute, Register 12, fo. 82r.

55. York, Borthwick Institute, Register 16, fos. 87v–88v.

56. York, Borthwick Institute, Register 19, fos. 208v–209r. Ferrour's endowment further specified that repairs to the chantry's fabric should be commissioned by the priest 'under the supervision of trustworthy persons'.

57. Rosser, *Art of Solidarity*, 194–207; Kümin, *Shaping of a Community*, 152; Duffy, *Stripping of the Altars*, 151–54; Dyer, 'Small Places with Large Consequences', 11–12; Mark Bailey, 'Self-Government in the Small Towns of Late-Medieval England', in Ben Dodds and Christian Liddy (eds.), *Commercial Activity, Markets and Entrepreneurs in the Middle Ages: Essays in Honour of Richard Britnell* (Woodbridge: Boydell, 2011), 107–28.

58. York, Borthwick Institute, Register 19, fo. 144v.

59. York, Borthwick Institute, Register 22, fo. 271r.

60. York, Borthwick Institute, Register 11, fos. 249v, 250v, 251v, 273r, Register 12, fos. 72v, 76v, 83v, 84v, Register 14, fos. 25v, 47v, Register 15, fo. 7v, Register 16, fos. 78v, 80v–81r, 84r, 87v–88v, 89r, 91v, 93r, 98v, Register 18, fos. 206r, 231r, 251v, 256r, 261r, 263r, Register 20, fos. 81v, 85r, 86v, 91v, 92r, 95r, 98r, 104r, Register 21, fo. 28v, Register 22, fos. 271r, 272v, 273v, 275r, and Register 23, fos. 32v, 54v, 55v; *Register of Thomas Rotherham*, 73, 90–91, 157, 161, 166, 171–72.

61. Alan Dyer, 'Ranking Lists of English Medieval Towns', in Palliser (ed.), *Cambridge Urban History*, I: 758; female guild members in York, Borthwick Institute, Register 10, fos. 149r, 150r.

62. York, Borthwick Institute, Register 19, fos. 208v–209r.

63. Duffy, *Stripping of the Altars*, 33.

64. York, Borthwick Institute, Register 10, fo. 128v, Register 16, fos. 87v–88v, Register 20, fo. 92r, and Register 22, fo. 271v.

65. *Register of John Waltham*, 209–10.

66. *Registers of Walter Giffard and Henry Bowet*, 60–61; *English Gilds*, 46; *The Making of King's Lynn: A Documentary Survey*, ed. Dorothy M. Owen, Records of Social and Economic History, new series 9 (London: Oxford University Press, 1984), 391–92.

67. *Metropolitan Visitations of William Courtenay*, 164–66.

68. *Records of the Borough of Leicester*, 132, 156, 165, 203, 206, 408–10, 448, 461 (Clerk); 93, 131, 137, 139, 158, 173–74, 177–78, 191, 447, 461 (Belgrave); Burgh was also a member of the guild merchant; he is recorded as a 'barker' or tanner in 1365 and an ironmonger in 1376: ibid., 137, 156.

69. *Register of Simon de Montacute*, 170–72, 181–86; *Register of Wolstan de Bransford*, 126–27; Roy Martin Haines, *Archbishop John Stratford: Political Revolutionary and Champion of the Liberties of the English Church c.1275/80—1348* (Toronto: PIMS, 1986), 368–81. In the 1332 lay subsidy assessment Adam Steventon was described as 'litteratus' despite being one of the lesser taxpayers, and he, along with Clinton and various other knightly members of the archbishop's circle, was deeply involved in the multiple transfers of land to endow the chapel: *Lay Subsidy Roll for Warwickshire*, 5–6, 95–96; Christopher Dyer, 'Medieval Stratford: A Successful Small Town', in Robert Bearman (ed.), *The History of an English Borough: Stratford-upon-Avon 1196–1996* (Stroud: Sutton, 1997), 43–61; Rodney H. Hilton, *The English Peasantry in the Later Middle Ages* (Oxford: Clarendon, 1975), 93–94.

70. It is possible that this disparity contributed in some small way to English constructions of Scottish infidelity, for which see pp. 79–81.

71. For an example of a papal letter citing trustworthy men see *Registrum episcopatus Aberdonensis*, ed. Cosmo Innes, 2 vols. (Edinburgh: Spalding Club, 1845), 1.22. For 'reports of trustworthy men', see *Llandaff Episcopal Acta 1140-1287*, ed. David Crouch (Cardiff:

South Wales Record Society), 92; *The Episcopal Registers of the Diocese of St David's 1397–1518*, ed. Robert Fraser Isaacson, 2 vols. (London: Honourable Society of Cymmrodorion, 1917), 322, 474–76, 480; *The Register of Nicholas Fleming Archbishop of Armagh 1404–1416*, ed. Brendan Smith (Dublin: Irish Manuscripts Commission, 2003), 53, 257; *Registrum episcopatus Aberdonensis*, 1.70, 1.75.

72. *Registrum episcopatus Glasguensis*, ed. Cosmo Innes (Edinburgh: Maitland Club, 1843), 97–99; *Registrum episcopatus Moraviensis*, ed. Cosmo Innes (Edinburgh: Bannatyne Club, 1837), 341.

73. *The Register of Milo Sweteman Archbishop of Armagh 1361–1380*, ed. Brendan Smith (Dublin: Irish Manuscripts Commission, 1996), 161, 204–5, 202–3, 210–11, 214, 221, 237, 240; *Register of Nicholas Fleming*, 34–35, 80–82, 99–100, 184–86, 207, 237–38, 250.

74. *Llandaff Episcopal Acta*, 87–88; *Registrum episcopatus Aberdonensis*, 1.167; *Episcopal Registers of the Diocese of St David's*, 168, 500.

75. *Episcopal Registers of the Diocese of St David's*, 538–46.

76. *St David's Episcopal Acta 1085–1280*, ed. Julia Barrow (Cardiff: South Wales Record Society, 1998), 151; *Episcopal Registers of the Diocese of St David's*, 146, 526.

77. *Register of Nicholas Fleming*, 10–11; *Register of Milo Sweteman*, 79–80; *Episcopal Registers of the Diocese of St David's*, 322–24.

78. *Registrum episcopatus Glasguensis*, ed. Cosmo Innes (Edinburgh: Maitland Club, 1843), 88–89.

79. *Register of Milo Sweteman*, 4.

80. *Registrum episcopatus Aberdonensis*, 1.26, 1.177, 1.201.

81. *Registrum episcopatus Aberdonensis*, 1.244–45.

82. *Registrum episcopatus Moraviensis*, 29, 84, 100, 205.

83. *Episcopal Registers of the Diocese of St David's*, 176, 268.

84. *Registrum episcopatus Aberdonensis*, 1.163.

85. *Registrum episcopatus Aberdonensis*, 1.60.

86. *Llandaff Episcopal Acta*, 71.

Chapter Nine: Face-to-Face with the Trustworthy Men

1. Alain Corbin, *The Life of an Unknown: The Rediscovered World of a Clog Maker in Nineteenth-Century France*, trans. Arthur Goldhammer (New York: Columbia University Press, 2001), 21; although Corbin writes about a much later period, he captures something essential about the apprehension of status in a world defined primarily by localism.

2. David d'Avray, *Rationalities in History: A Weberian Essay in Comparison* (Cambridge: Cambridge University Press, 2010), 75–77.

3. Luke 16.11; the twelfth-century ordinary gloss to this verse, in *Biblia Latina cum glossa ordinaria*, 4.198, interpreted it as an injunction against those who do not share with their 'brothers' what God has created for all, hinting at an assumption of reciprocity in economic exchange.

4. *Wimbledon's Sermon Redde rationem villicationis tue: A Middle English Sermon of the Fourteenth Century*, ed. Ione Kemp Knight (Pittsburgh: Duquesne, 1967).

5. *Norwich Consistory Court Depositions*, item 17; Pollock and Maitland, *History of English Common Law*, 2.190. Pledges of 'religion' do not make the same direct connection, since that word did not carry all the meanings of faith as it would in the early modern period. Rather someone who *fidei sue religionem interposuit* pledged their conscientiousness or duty: *EEA 1: Lincoln 1067–1185*, 173; on religion see Biller, 'Words and the Medieval Notion of "Religion"'.

6. *Lower Ecclesiastical Jurisdiction*, 118, 146–47.

7. *Register of Richard Swinfield*, 18-19.

8. York, Borthwick Institute, CP F.225 (*Deepdale c. Carthorp*); see CP F.126 and F.216 for same formula concluding the positions and articles.

9. London Metropolitan Archives, DL/C/0206, fos. 87r, 90r, 91v-92r, 128r-138v.

10. York, Borthwick Institute, Register 10, fo. 19v; Canterbury Cathedral Archives, X.1.1, fos. 40v-41r, 96v, and Y.1.5, fo. 62r; Cambridge University Library, EDR D/2/1, fos. 35r-v, 39r, 44r, 48r, 55Bv (this case transcribed in Helmholz, *Marriage Litigation*, 213-14), 56Ar, 57r, 71r, 78r, 98v; Lincolnshire Archives, REG/13, fo. 25r; Lichfield Record Office, B/A/1/12, fos. 158r-159v; London Metropolitan Archives, DL/C/0205, fos. 89r, 203r-204v, DL/C/0206, fos. 1r-v, 4v, 61r, 105r, 106r, 123r, DL/C/B/043/MS09064/005, fo. 111v, and DL/C/B/043/MS09064/006, fos. 18v, 28v, 38v; *Register of Edmund Lacy, Exeter*, 2.20; *Lower Ecclesiastical Jurisdiction*, 323-24, 376, 486; *Courts of the Archdeaconry of Buckingham*, 272.

11. Canterbury Cathedral Archives, X.1.1, fo. 87v.

12. Hampshire Record Office, 21M65/B/1/2, fo. 60r.

13. London Metropolitan Archives, DL/C/B/043/MS09064/003, fos. 64v, 68r, and DL/C/0205, fo. 37v; Canterbury Cathedral Archives, X.10.1, fo. 102v; *Lower Ecclesiastical Jurisdiction*, 332; Neal, *Masculine Self*, 38-41, 97.

14. Tilly, *Trust and Rule*, 4, 33, 50-51; interestingly Tilly did not appreciate how closely this applied to the European Middle Ages, despite drawing upon a very wide reading in medieval history for case studies to support his argument.

15. Sheilagh Ogilvie, 'Use and Abuse of Trust', 47; see also Ogilvie, 'How Does Social Capital Affect Women?' Ogilvie has studied this primarily with regard to the exclusion of women from early modern guilds, but the dark side of trust is visible from any perspective. She is arguing against a broad consensus across sociology, economics, and political science that particular trust within closed groups (social capital) generates a more 'generalized' trust throughout society, despite no explanation for this transference being offered.

16. Schofield, *Peasant and Community*, 146, 155; Jarnoux, 'Entre pouvoir et paraître', 138-42. This does not mean that poorer peasants were confined to their villages, just that their wealthier neighbours had visibly wider horizons, a point made in J. Ambrose Raftis, *Tenure and Mobility: Studies in the Social History of the Mediaeval English Village* (Toronto: PIMS, 1964), 129-30, and idem, *Peasant Economic Development within the English Manorial System* (Montreal: McGill-Queens, 1996), 99-117.

17. Briggs, *Credit and Village Society*, 128-29, finds that credit relationships linking Cambridge to its surrounding villages were confined to wealthier peasants and townsmen, while poorer peasants participated in more local credit networks.

18. Biddick, 'Missing Links'.

19. For Towker, see *Register of John Waltham*, 165; TNA, DL 30/57/704, m. 1.

20. French, *People of the Parish*, 134.

21. St Giles House, Shaftesbury Archives, T219; Nottingham, UNMSC, Mi 5/164/37/2.

22. London Metropolitan Archives, DL/C/0205, fos. 248r-249r.

23. French, *People of the Parish*, 162.

24. French, *People of the Parish*, 168-70; idem, 'Women in the Late Medieval English Parish', in Mary C. Erler and Maryanne Kowaleski (eds.), *Gendering the Master Narrative: Women and Power in the Middle Ages* (Ithaca, N.Y.: Cornell University Press, 2003), 163-64; Sandy Bardsley, *Venomous Tongues: Speech and Gender in Late Medieval England* (Philadelphia: University of Pennsylvania Press, 2006), 51-58; Susan E. Phillips, *Transforming Talk: The Problem with Gossip in Late Medieval England* (University Park: Pennsylvania State University Press, 2007), 13-15, 21.

25. Hereford Cathedral Archives, 1779, fo. 18v.

26. London Metropolitan Archives, DL/C/B/043/MS09064/002, fos. 163v, 237v; Lincolnshire Archives, REG/3, fos. 248r–v.

27. On all these developments, see Maryanne Kowaleski, 'A Consumer Economy', in Horrox and Ormrod (eds.), *Social History of England*, 238–59; Jarnoux, 'Entre pouvoir et paraître'; Raymond van Uytven, 'Showing Off One's Rank in the Middle Ages', in Wim Blockmans and Antheun Janse (eds.), *Showing Status: Representation of Social Positions in the Late Middle Ages* (Turnhout: Brepols, 1999), 19–34; Christopher Dyer, 'The Material World of English Peasants, 1200–1540: Archaeological Perspectives on Rural Economy and Welfare', *Agricultural History Review*, 62 (2014), 15–22; Gilchrist, *Medieval Life*, 114–34. Specifically on food, see Christopher M. Woolgar, 'Meat and Dairy Products in Late Medieval England', in C. M. Woolgar, Dale Serjeantson, and Tony Waldron (eds.), *Food in Medieval England: Diet and Nutrition* (Oxford: Oxford University Press, 2006), 88–101; Miriam Müller, 'Food, Hierarchy, and Class Conflict', in Richard Goddard, John Langdon, and Miriam Müller (eds.), *Survival and Discord in Medieval Society: Essays in Honour of Christopher Dyer* (Turnhout: Brepols, 2010), 231–48. On pre-plague concern with mainly elite and clerical dress, see Frédérique Lachaud, 'Dress and Social Status in England before the Sumptuary Laws', in Peter Coss and Maurice Keen (eds.), *Heraldry, Pageantry and Social Display in Medieval England* (Woodbridge: Boydell Press, 2002), 105–23. On housing, see Christopher Dyer, 'Living in Peasant Houses in Late Medieval England', *Vernacular Architecture*, 44 (2013), 19–27.

28. *Statutes of the Realm*, 11 vols. (London: HMSO, 1810–28), 1.380–82; *The Complete Works of John Gower*, ed. George Campbell Macaulay, 4 vols. (Oxford: Clarendon, 1902), 4.218; Chaucer, 'The Miller's Tale', I (A) 3188, in *Riverside Chaucer*, 68.

29. Sally V. Smith, 'Materializing Resistant Identities Among the Medieval Peasantry: An Examination of Dress Accessories from English Rural Settlement Sites', *Journal of Material Culture*, 14 (2009), 309–32, argues that relatively high-value dress accessories made from iron and copper-alloy were worn by the peasantry in aspirational defiance of the ordered model of society. There may be a good deal of truth in this, and the social meaning of small finds is a fascinating and fertile new avenue of archaeological interpretation, but given what we know about the importance of stratification within peasant society for social relations and economic change, it seems likely that the politics of dress made a louder statement about hierarchy separating village elites from their poorer neighbours, than they did about peasant-lord relations.

30. The rectors of churches controlled lands and rents that effectively made them lords of small manors; they lived in substantial houses and often had family links to the regional gentry: Palmer, *Selling the Church*, 40; Swanson, *Church and Society*, 206–7; idem, 'Standards of Livings: Parochial Revenues in Pre-Reformation England', in Christopher Harper-Bill (ed.), *Religious Belief and Ecclesiastical Careers in Late Medieval England* (Woodbridge: Boydell, 1991), 151–96.

31. Clanchy, *From Memory to Written Record*, 53.

32. *Register of Walter Giffard, York*, 53.

33. *Register of Robert Hallum*, 133.

34. Rodney H. Hilton, 'Reasons for Inequality among Medieval Peasants', *Journal of Peasant Studies*, 5 (1978), 273–74.

35. London Metropolitan Archives, DL/C/B/043/MS09064/005, fos. 32v, 47r.

36. London Metropolitan Archives, DL/C/B/043/MS09064/001, fos. 81r, 87r, 89r, 90v; Briggs, *Credit and Village Society*, 112–16.

37. London Metropolitan Archives, DL/C/B/043/MS09064/001, fos. 120v, 127r, 133r.

38. Isabelle Scarlet may have been married to Thomas Scarlet, a regular money lender (London Metropolitan Archives, DL/C/B/043/MS09064/001, fos. 120v, 127r), suggesting

a partnership in which both husband and wife called people to be faithful to their promises. Married female creditors and debtors were rare in the manor court litigation studied
by Briggs, *Credit and Village Society*, 114.

39. Gratian *d.p.c. Decretum* C. 33 q. 5 c. 20. On the space available to women for independent action, see Cordelia Beattie, *Medieval Single Women: The Politics of Social Classification in Late Medieval England* (Oxford: Oxford University Press, 2007).

40. Judith M. Bennett, *Women in the Medieval English Countryside: Gender and
Household in Brigstock before the Plague* (Oxford: Oxford University Press, 1987), 198. This
contrasts with an absence of women litigating on their own behalves in the Lincolnshire
manors studied by Louise Wilkinson, *Women in Thirteenth-Century Lincolnshire* (Woodbridge: Boydell, 2007), 138–41.

41. Goldberg, 'Gender and Matrimonial Litigation', 46.

42. Katherine L. French, 'Women Churchwardens in Late Medieval England', in Clive
Burgess and Eamon Duffy (eds.), *The Parish in Late Medieval England* (Donington: Shaun
Tyas, 2006), 302–21.

43. *Register of Edmund Stafford*, 227–29.

44. Dyan Elliott, 'Gender and the Christian Traditions', and Katharine Park, 'Medicine
and Natural Philosophy: Naturalistic Traditions', in Judith M. Bennett and Ruth Mazo
Karras (eds.), *The Oxford Handbook of Women and Gender in Medieval Europe* (Oxford:
Oxford University Press, 2013), 21–35, 84–100, provide excellent summaries of the crucial
concepts.

45. John Lydgate, *Lydgate's Troy Book, A. D. 1412-20*, Part 1, ed. Henry Bergen, EETS
97 (1907), 67, lines 1845–51: For who was ever yet so mad or foolish / To give faith or,
hastily, credence / To any woman without experience, / In whom is neither trust nor stead-
fastness? / They are so two-faced and full of brittleness, / That it is hard to be sure of
them.

46. *The Early English Carols*, ed. Richard Leighton Greene (Oxford: Clarendon, 1935),
269.

47. Cambridge University Library, EDR D/2/1, fos. 85r, 95v, 111v: *Mirabile est quod
mulieres ita variant; si fuisset fideles fuisset uxore mea*. The priest went ahead with the
marriage even though he had discussed the objection raised by Fish. For this he was prosecuted by the bishop of Ely, who upheld the precontract between Brid and Fish and forced
them to marry a year later.

48. *Select Cases from the Ecclesiastical Courts*, 131, 136. The weight placed upon the
number of witnesses on each side in this and other cases casts doubt on the assertion in
Helmholz, *Marriage Litigation*, 128, that producing multiple witnesses to repeat the same
information was 'useless'.

49. Cambridge University Library, EDR D/2/1, fo. 9r; for compurgation, see pp. 318–20.

50. Goldberg, 'Gender and Matrimonial Litigation'; Bronach Kane, *Impotence and Virginity in the Late Medieval Ecclesiastical Court of York* (York: Borthwick Papers, 2008);
idem, 'Social Representations of Memory and Gender in Later Medieval England', *Integrative Psychological and Behavioural Science*, 46 (2012), 554–55; Monica H. Green, *Making Women's Medicine Masculine: The Rise of Male Authority in Pre-modern Gynaecology*
(Oxford: Oxford University Press, 2008), 18–21.

51. *Register of William Greenfield*, 1.136.

52. *Depositions and Other Ecclesiastical Proceedings from the Courts of Durham*, 27.

53. 'Register of the Archdeaconry of Richmond, 1442–1477', 134–35.

54. Hampshire Record Office, 21M65/B/1/2, fo. 31r.

55. Katherine L. French, *The Good Women of the Parish: Gender and Religion after the
Black Death* (Philadelphia: University of Pennsylvania Press, 2008), 126–32.

56. Phillips, *Transforming Talk*, 147–202, discusses the importance of bonds formed between women during all-female occasions such as childbirth, and the contexts of women-only speech.

57. Ruth Mazo Karras, *Common Women: Prostitution and Sexuality in Medieval England* (Oxford: Oxford University Press, 1996), 138; on insults, see Gowing, *Domestic Dangers*, 63–64.

58. See the example given in Marjorie Keniston McIntosh, *Working Women in English Society 1300–1620* (Cambridge: Cambridge University Press, 2005), 204, of an inn at Northallerton called 'the Backsyde', which attracted the attention of the authorities around 1500 on account of the Scots and prostitutes working there.

59. Canterbury Cathedral Archives, X.1.1, fo. 7v; London Metropolitan Archives, DL/C/B/043/MS09064/001, fo. 114r.

60. *The Canterbury Tales: Fifteenth-Century Continuations and Additions*, ed. John M. Bowers (Kalamazoo: Western Michigan University, 1992), 77, lines 653–55.

61. London Metropolitan Archives, DL/C/B/043/MS09064/003, fo. 254r.

62. Canterbury Cathedral Archives, X.10.1, fo. 16r.

63. Kathryn Gravdal, *Vilain and Courtois: Transgressive Parody in French Literature of the Twelfth and Thirteenth Centuries* (Lincoln: University of Nebraska Press, 1989), 77–80.

64. Bardsley, *Venomous Tongues*, 82–89, 141–42.

65. London Metropolitan Archives, DL/C/B/043/MS09064/004a, fo. 8v; Chaucer, 'The General Prologue', I (A) 501–4, in *Riverside Chaucer*, 31.

66. Rosser, *Art of Solidarity*, 40–44.

67. Rubin, *Charity and Community*, 82–98, summarizes the main strands of clerical instruction on poverty, wealth, charity, work, and idleness; see also idem, 'The Poor', in Rosemary Horrox (ed.), *Fifteenth Century Attitudes: Perceptions of Society in Late Medieval England* (Cambridge: Cambridge University Press, 1994), 169–82; David Aers, *Community, Gender, and Individual Identity: English Writing 1360–1430* (London: Routledge, 1988), 20–33.

68. Marjorie Keniston McIntosh, *Poor Relief in England, 1350–1600* (Cambridge: Cambridge University Press, 2012), 112, argues that there is 'little sign that late medieval parishes defined themselves as institutional centers for the provision of aid to needy people', but this does not take into account the widespread expectation that parish priests should distribute alms, noted in Rubin, *Charity and Community*, 237–45. On churchwardens and charity, see Kümin, *Shaping of a Community*, 276–315.

69. *Councils and Synods*, 2.910 (Lambeth 1281 c. 15).

70. McIntosh, *Poor Relief*, 107–9.

71. Dyer, *Age of Transition?*, 185.

72. Rubin, *Charity and Community*, 84; Briggs, *Credit and Village Society*, 113; Davis, *Medieval Market Morality*, 367; Muldrew, *Economy of Obligation*, 160.

73. Lincolnshire Archives, REG/3, charter inserted after fo. 102r.

74. *Register of Robert de Stretton*, 113.

75. Christopher Dyer, 'Poverty and Its Relief in Late Medieval England', *Past & Present*, 216 (2012), 57.

76. Steve Hindle, *On the Parish? The Micro-politics of Poor Relief in Rural England c.1550–1750* (Oxford: Clarendon, 2004), 257.

77. The effect that this had on the institutions of diocesan governance will be discussed in Chapter 13.

78. *Register of William Wykeham*, 2.417.

79. *Lower Ecclesiastical Jurisdiction*, 146.

80. On the 'objectification' of social categories during litigation, see Kane, 'Social Representations', 547-51.

81. Bodleian Library, MS eMus.180, fos. 157r–v, with thanks to Jenn Depold for the reference.

82. Mirk, *Instructions for Parish Priests*, 126-27, lines 999-1003, 1013-14: 'Have you ever oppressed your neighbour / For to get yourself honour? / Have you denigrated his good fame / for to get yourself a good name? / Have you been proud and haughty in demeanour / For trust of ladies and also of lords?'

83. Reemtsma, *Trust and Violence*, 40.

Part IV: Bishops and a Church Built on Inequality and Faith, 1250–1500

1. Randall Collins, *Weberian Sociological Theory* (Cambridge: Cambridge University Press, 1986), 8.

2. Swanson, *Church and Society*, 141-42; William R. Jones, 'Relations of the Two Jurisdictions: Conflict and Cooperation in England during the Thirteenth and Fourteenth Centuries', *Studies in Medieval and Renaissance History*, 7 (1970), 77-210; Helmholz, *Oxford History of the Laws of England*, 1.118-20.

3. For changes in the mid-fourteenth century, see W. Mark Ormrod, *Edward III* (New Haven, Conn.: Yale University Press, 2011), 367-68, and Chapter 13, note 11; in the 1490s Fyneux made it easier for litigants to bring cases of debt, defamation, tithes, breach of faith, execution of wills, and various issues to do with church property at common law, and litigants seemed to value the enforcement possibilities of the royal courts: Palmer, *Selling the Church*, 4-6, 23-27, 63-69; Swanson, *Church and Society*, 188-89; Helmholz, *Oxford History of the Laws of England*, 1.366-68; Houlbrooke, *Church Courts and the People*, 8-11, 39; Baker, *Introduction to English Legal History*, 338.

4. The implications of the new social and institutional history of the church that I am attempting to build could fruitfully be applied to the study of personal, local, and temporally specific expressions of religious faith, but that is not the task of this book.

5. For the development and process of visitation, see Forrest, 'Transformation of Visitation'; Ian Forrest and Christopher Whittick, 'The Thirteenth-Century Visitation Records of the Diocese of Hereford', *English Historical Review*, 131 (2016), 737-62.

6. Paul Faulkner, *Knowledge on Trust* (Oxford: Oxford University Press, 2011), 2-3.

7. Donald Davidson, 'A Coherence Theory of Truth and Knowledge', in Davidson, *Subjective, Intersubjective, Objective* (Oxford: Oxford University Press, 2001), 141; John Hardwig, 'The Role of Trust in Knowledge', *Journal of Philosophy*, 88 (1991), 693-708; Shapin, *Social History of Truth*; Paul L. Harris, 'Checking Our Sources: The Origins of Trust in Testimony', *Studies in the History and Philosophy of Science*, 33 (2002), 315-33; Jonathan Adler, 'Testimony, Trust, Knowing', *Journal of Philosophy*, 91 (1994), 264-75.

8. Williams, *Truth and Truthfulness*, 96-100.

9. Glénisson, 'Les enquêtes administratives', 18.

10. Gambetta, 'Can We Trust Trust?', 234.

11. Faulkner, *Knowledge on Trust*, 3. Faulkner does little to explore practical considerations except in the most artificial terms; his trust theory of knowledge ultimately draws such a stark distinction between 'believing a speaker' and 'getting to know things' (198) that there is no room for knowledge that could be described as 'social facts'. In most of the situations discussed in the present book, the knowledge sought by bishops had to do with people, relationships, and matters like boundaries where human categorization was a large part of the 'truth', therefore Faulkner's 'speakers' are often components of the 'things' a bishop sought to know.

12. Luhmann, *Trust and Power*, 20, 24–30; Kenneth J. Arrow, *The Limits of Organization* (New York: Norton, 1974), 23; Misztal, *Trust in Modern Societies*, 120–39; Brian Uzzi, 'Social Structure and Competition in Interfirm Networks: The Paradox of Embeddedness', in Mark Granovetter and Richard Swedberg (eds.), *The Sociology of Economic Life*, 2nd ed. (Boulder, Colo.: Westview, 2001), 214–15; Good, 'Individuals, Interpersonal Relations and Trust', 42.

13. Eisenstadt and Roniger, *Patrons, Clients and Friends*, 40.

14. Coleman, *Foundations of Social Theory*, 189–90.

15. Economists would call both information and trust 'externalities': important yet unquantifiable elements in a system of exchange.

Chapter Ten: Practical Epistemology

1. *EEA* 2: *Canterbury 1162–1190*, 143; *EEA* 21: *Norwich 1215–1243*, ed. Christopher Harper-Bill (Oxford: Oxford University Press, 2000), 26.

2. *EEA* 13: *Worcester 1218–1268*, ed. Philippa M. Hoskin (Oxford: Oxford University Press, 1997), 60; *Register of John de Stratford*, 190.

3. *Registers of Roger Martival*, 4.69. The institutional rector was the abbey of St Wandrille in Normandy.

4. York, Borthwick Institute, Register 19, fo. 90r–v.

5. See, for example, *Registers of John de Sandale and Rigaud de Asserio*, 476; *Register of John le Romeyn*, 1.89; *Register of John de Stratford*, 57; Canterbury Cathedral Archives, SVSB/2/160/1.

6. Lincolnshire Archives, REG/18, fo. 70r.

7. *Register of Richard de Kellawe*, 1.353–54; *Register of John de Grandisson*, 350; *Register of John de Stratford*, 161.

8. *Register of John de Trillek*, 30–31.

9. *Register of Thomas de Brantyngham*, 226.

10. York, Borthwick Institute, Register 10, fo. 205r.

11. *EEA* 13: *Worcester 1218–1268*, 52–53; *Register of William Wickwane*, 101–4; *Registers of Roger Martival*, 2.356, 362–63; York, Borthwick Institute, Register 10, fo. 210v.

12. Simon Blackburn, *Truth: A Guide for the Perplexed* (London: Penguin, 2005), 105, suggests that 'in many circumstances an adaptive illusion will do just as well as truth'. Blackburn is using adaptive in an evolutionary sense to mean beneficial or useful.

13. *Register of William Melton*, 5.71; *Register of John Stafford*, 53.

14. Hugh of St Victor, *On the Sacraments of the Christian Faith*, 168.

15. *Register of John de Grandisson*, 136. Compare Lichfield Record Office, B/A/1/9, fos. 150r–v, 155r, 164v–165r, where papal dispensations could be granted only upon presentation of 'lawful proofs' or 'sufficient proof'.

16. James A. Brundage, 'Proof in Canonical Criminal Law', *Continuity and Change*, 11 (1996), 331.

17. *EEA* 2: *Canterbury 1162–1190*, 231; *Register of William Wykeham*, 2.49; *Register of John de Stratford*, 56–57, 70; one of these cases involved a search for blood in a churchyard, another an inspection of the church fabric. On the view of frankpledge, see Helen M. Jewell, *English Local Administration in the Middle Ages* (New York: Barnes & Noble, 1972), 162–65.

18. Dominik Perler, 'Can We Trust Our Senses? Fourteenth-Century Debates on Sensory Illusions', in Denery, Ghosh, and Zeeman (eds.), *Uncertain Knowledge*, 65–86. Ockham believed that it was reasonable to trust the senses because God was a rational creator and our senses were created in order to perceive his creation.

19. *Register of John Pontoise*, 96.

20. On fields as a legal entity, see Tom Johnson, 'Medieval Law and Materiality: Ship-wrecks, Finders, and Property on the Suffolk Coast, ca. 1380–1410', *American Historical Review*, 120 (2015), 407–32, and discussion in Chapter 12.

21. *Register of Richard Swinfield*, 116; *Register of Thomas de Brantyngham*, 379; *Register of John Pontoise*, 124.

22. *Select Cases from the Ecclesiastical Courts*, 357.

23. Brundage, *Medieval Canon Law*, 142–43.

24. Richard M. Fraher, 'Preventing Crime in the High Middle Ages: The Medieval Lawyers' Search for Deterrence', in James R. Sweeny and Stanley Chodorow (eds.), *Popes, Teachers and Canon Law in the Middle Ages* (Ithaca, N.Y.: Cornell University Press, 1989), 212–33; Julien Théry, '*Fama*: l'opinion publique comme preuve judiciaire aperçu sur la révolution médiévale de l'inquisitoire (XIIᵉ–XIVᵉ siècle)', in Bruno Lemesle (ed.), *La Preuve en justice de l' Antiquité à nos jours* (Rennes: Presses Universitaires de Rennes, 2003), 119–47; Brundage, 'Proof in Canonical Criminal Law', 332–34.

25. Brundage, 'Proof in Canonical Criminal Law', 330–33.

26. *Registers of John de Sandale and Rigaud de Asserio*, 485, 528; *Register of Edmund Lacy, Exeter*, 3.111; Lichfield Record Office, B/A/1/3, fo. 17v.

27. Lincolnshire Archives, REG/12, fo. 246v.

28. *Register of Thomas Langley*, 5.3–4.

29. Denery, *Seeing and Being Seen*, 39–74.

30. *Decretum* C. 4. 2–3 c. 3; Hostiensis, *Aurea Summa*, Book 5, *De inquisitionibus* §6; Richard M. Fraher, 'Conviction According to Conscience: The Medieval Jurists' Debate Concerning Judicial Discretion and the Law of Proof', *Law and History Review*, 7 (1989); Chris Wickham, '*Fama* and the Law in Twelfth-Century Tuscany', in Fenster and Smail (eds.), *Fama*.

31. Théry, '*Fama*', 130–36.

32. *Bracton on the Laws and Customs of England*, 2.327–34, 403–5. Compare with Tancred, *Ordo iudiciarius*, in *Pillii, Tancredi, Gratiae libri de iudiciorum ordine*, 153; for discussion, see De Groot, 'Jury of Presentment', 5–6, 8–13.

33. *Select Cases from the Ecclesiastical Courts*, 270–73.

34. *Vetus Liber Archidiaconatus Eliensis*, ed. Charles Lett Feltoe and Ellis H. Minns (Cambridge: Cambridge Antiquarian Society, 1917), 177.

35. *Register of Edmund Lacy, Exeter*, 2.41.

36. Hereford Cathedral Archives, 1050a; Lichfield Record Office, D30/9/3/2/2–3; Canterbury Cathedral Archives, DCc/VR/4, /VR/6, and /VR/9/1; DCc/SB/A/16.

37. *Register of Edmund Lacy, Exeter*, 2.4.

38. Théry, '*Fama*', 139–40, argues that *fama* was assigned a 'subaltern' status in the cognitive hierarchy; it was something that required verification by competent authorities.

39. Brundage, 'Proof in Canonical Criminal Law', 335.

40. *Calendar of Close Rolls, Henry III: Volume 6, 1247–1251*, ed. Henry Churchill Maxwell Lyte (London: HMSO, 1922), 554; *EEA 13: Worcester 1218–1268*, xxx; similar examples in *Register of Godfrey Giffard*, 172, and Durham Cathedral Archives, 2.2.Arch.Dunelm.17n.

41. Macnair, 'Vicinage and the Antecedents of the Jury', 579.

42. *Register of John Pecham*, 1.230.

43. *Councils and Synods*, 2.265; *Calendar of Close Rolls, Henry III: Volume 5, 1242–1247*, ed. Henry Churchill Maxwell Lyte (London: HMSO, 1916), 543; *Calendar of Close Rolls 1247–1251*, 221–22, 554; *Calendar of Close Rolls, Henry III: Volume 7, 1251–3*, ed. Alfred Edward Stamp (London: HMSO, 1927), 224, 226; *Annales monastici*, ed. Henry Richard Luard, 5 vols. (London: Longman, 1864–69), 4.579–80, 5.256–57.

44. Christopher R. Cheney, *A Handbook of Dates for Students of British History* (London: Royal Historical Society, 1955), 66; *Register of William Greenfield*, 1.150–51; 'Documents Relating to Visitations of the Diocese and Province of York', ed. Alexander Hamilton Thompson, in *Miscellanea*, II, Surtees Society, 127 (1916), 221.

45. Masschaele, *Jury, State, and Society*, 135–36; Beckerman, 'Procedural Innovation and Institutional Change', 229, 233; Statute of Marlborough (52 Hen. III), c. 22, in *Statutes of the Realm*, 1.24.

46. *Register of Thomas of Corbridge*, 1.172.

47. *Councils and Synods*, 2.971.

48. Helmholz, *Oxford History of the Laws of England*, 1.334–36; for summoners' oaths, see *Councils and Synods*, 2.609, and Lichfield Record Office, B/A/1/2, fo. 2v, and B/A/1/11, fo. 86v; on witnesses and oaths, see Charles Donahue Jr., 'Proof by Witness in the Church Courts of Medieval England: An Imperfect Reception of the Learned Law', in Morris S. Arnold et al. (eds.), *On the Laws and Customs of England: Essays in Honor of Samuel E. Thorne* (Chapel Hill: University of North Carolina Press, 1981), 130.

49. On common-law inquests, see Hudson, *Oxford History of the Laws of England*, 2.321–25; the remark about oaths as ordeals is from Robert Bartlett, *Trial by Fire and Water: The Medieval Judicial Ordeal* (Oxford: Clarendon, 1986), 30; on oaths in feudal relations, see Cheyette, *Ermengard of Narbonne*, 187–92, and Susan Reynolds, *Fiefs and Vassals: The Medieval Evidence Reinterpreted* (Oxford: Oxford University Press, 1994), 210–14 (the papacy), 261–62 (France), 370–73 (England).

50. Elsewhere in Europe oaths were commonplace in visitation proceedings.

51. Canterbury Cathedral Archives, DCc/VR/15.

52. Canterbury Cathedral Archives, DCc/VR/11 and 13 (cases of Godfrey Aleyn and John Wylminton).

53. Donahue, 'Proof by Witness', 131.

54. Hyams, *Rancor and Reconciliation in Medieval England*, 160.

55. Haines, *Administration of the Diocese of Worcester*, 157; *Register of Walter Giffard, York*, 324, 326; *Register of Robert Winchelsey*, 101–2.

56. Chaucer, 'Epilogue to the Man of Law's Tale', II [B1], 1172–73, in *Riverside Chaucer*, 104. For discussion, see Anne Hudson, *The Premature Reformation: Wycliffite Texts and Lollard History* (Oxford: Oxford University Press, 1988), 371–74.

57. *Register of John Stafford*, 103–8, 171–72.

58. Similar trends were changing judicial practice in the English common-law and manorial courts too: Fraher, 'Conviction According to Conscience'; Beckerman, 'Procedural Innovation and Institutional Change'; Clanchy, *From Memory to Written Record*, 274–80.

59. Helmholz, *Oxford History of the Laws of England*, 1.333.

60. *Register of John de Grandisson*, 411.

61. *Register of John de Grandisson*, 670.

62. *Register of Edmund Lacy, Exeter*, 2.105.

63. Alain Boreau, 'Introduction', in Gauvard (ed.), *L'enquête au Moyen âge*, 9–10. Boreau suggests that in medieval society there were three regimes of truth: first, the idea of an eternal and universal divine truth; second, the presumptive knowledge that may be gained by human effort; and third, the pervasive concept that truth was inaccessible to humanity.

64. See Andrews, Methuen, and Spicer (eds.), *Doubting Christianity*, passim.

65. *EEA 22: Chichester 1215–1253*, ed. Philippa M. Hoskin (Oxford: Oxford University Press, 2001), 130.

66. The importance of truth in secular inquests is noted in Laure Verdon, 'Le roi, la loi, l'enquête et l'officier: procédure et enquêteurs en Provence sous le règne de Charles II

(1285–1309)', and Olivier Mattéoni, 'Enquêtes, pouvoir et contrôle des hommes dans les territoires des ducs de Bourbon', both in Gauvard (ed.), *L'enquête au moyen âge*, 325, 363.

67. Brundage, 'Proof in Canonical Criminal Law', 335.

68. Cambridge University Library, EDR D/2/1, fos. 95r, 123v. Katerina was herself cited at the instance of another man called John Pope, who alleged that he and Katerina had also been contracted to marry. Pope admitted that they had not in fact been able to marry because they were related. It is probable that her claim against Elias was made in order to counter John Pope's suit.

69. *Register of John Pontoise*, 278–79; *Register of Adam of Orleton, Hereford*, 287; *Register of William Melton*, 1.134–35. For other examples, see *Register of John de Grandisson*, 639, 1021, 1215.

70. *Register of Hamo de Hethe*, 173–74; similar at 174–75.

71. Thomas Kuhn, *The Structure of Scientific Revolutions*, 4th ed. (Chicago: University of Chicago Press, 2012), 43–51; see also Aron Gurevich, *Categories of Medieval Culture* (London: Routledge, 1985), 178, who argues for the 'medieval mind' having a particular propensity to judge truth by adherence to norms; d'Avray, *Rationalities in History*, 75–77, argues that the values in a system of thought gain 'mutual protection' from one another.

72. Michael Polanyi, *Personal Knowledge: Towards a Post-critical Philosophy* (London: Routledge, 1958), 294.

73. Adler, 'Testimony, Trust, Knowing'; Massimo Vallerani, 'Modelli di verità: le prove nei processi inquisitori', in Gauvard (ed.), *L'enquête au Moyen âge*, 123–42, argues that truth was something that could be discovered, but also something already known that is confirmed by investigation.

74. The civil law commentator Pillius (1169–1207) and the canonist Tancred (ca. 1185–1236) stressed the importance of distinguishing clearly between what was known and what was merely believed: *Pillii, Tancredi, Gratiae libri de iudiciorum ordine*, 46, 237–38.

75. London Metropolitan Archives DL/C/0205, passim.

76. Polanyi, *Personal Knowledge*, 267, argued that all claims to knowledge must rest on certain unexamined assumptions, whether they concern God or an individual's belief about him- or herself.

77. It is hard to discern exactly where bishops, courts, or witnesses thought the line between knowledge and belief should be drawn. Statements of the type 'I believe' and 'I know' may well, in fact, do more to describe the feelings of the witness or the scribe than the status of the evidence they were giving. Needless to say, such ambiguities must have given lawyers many opportunities to challenge witnesses' statements.

78. Hereford Cathedral Archives, 1779, fos. 2v, 3v, 22r.

79. Lichfield Record Office, D 30/9/3/1, fos. 23r, 26r.

80. Hereford Cathedral Archives, 1779, fos. 6v, 24v.

81. York, Borthwick Institute, Register 19, fos. 211v–213r.

82. *Decretals* X 2.19.13; X 2.23.11; X 4.14.2; *Acta Stephani Langton Cantuariensis Archiepiscopi A.D. 1207–1228*, ed. Kathleen Major, C&Y 50 (1950), 14–17; *EEA 6: Norwich 1070–1214*, 310–13; *The Domesday of St Paul's of the Year MCCXXII*, ed. William H. Hale, Camden Society, first series 69 (1858), passim; Canterbury Cathedral Archives, DCc/ChAnt/D/119; *Select Cases from the Ecclesiastical Courts*, 3–4, 8–12, 104–14; *Register of Robert Winchelsey*, 111; Donahue, 'Proof by Witness', 136–40.

83. Donahue, 'Proof by Witness', 131.

84. *Register of William Melton*, 1.37–38, 1.40, 1.45.

85. For a recent discussion, see John H. Langbein, 'Jury Influence on Conceptions of the Judiciary', in Paul Brand and Joshua Getzler (eds.), *Judges and Judging in the History of the Common Law and Civil Law: From Antiquity to Modern Times* (Cambridge:

Cambridge University Press, 2012), 69–72. Bishops sometimes borrowed common-law terminology and described the information of trustworthy men as verdicts. For example in 1385 the bishop of Hereford said of reports about clerical nonresidence that 'we have grasped and understood the implications of the infamy brought to our attention by the relation of the verdicts (*veredica*) of trustworthy persons': *Register of John Gilbert*, 80.

86. De Groot, 'Jury of Presentment', 1; Paul R. Hyams, 'What Did Edwardian Villagers Understand by "Law"?', in Razi and Smith (eds.), *Medieval Society and the Manor Court*, 77, 79. For further comment see Paul R. Hyams, 'Trial by Ordeal: The Key to Proof in the Early Common Law', in Arnold et al. (eds.), *On the Laws and Customs of England*; Macnair, 'Vicinage and the Antecedents of the Jury', 547, 589–90; Morris S. Arnold, 'Law and Fact in the Medieval Jury Trial: Out of Sight, Out of Mind', *American Journal of Legal History*, 18 (1974), 278; Brand, 'English Difference', 387; Thomas A. Green, *Verdict According to Conscience: Perspectives on the English Criminal Trial Jury 1200–1800* (Chicago: University of Chicago Press, 1985), 4, 17; Beckerman, 'Procedural Innovation and Institutional Change', 238.

Chapter Eleven: Other People's Money

1. Overviews of several aspects of episcopal engagement with economic matters are provided by George Dameron, 'The Church as Lord', in Arnold (ed.), *Oxford Handbook of Medieval Christianity*, 457–72; Olivia F. Robinson, 'Bishops and Bankers', in Pennington and Eichbauer (eds.), *Law as Profession*, 11–26; Malte Prietzel, 'Canonistes et gens de finances: les officiers de l'évêque de Tournai au XVe siècle', in Jean-Marie Cauchies (ed.), *Finances et financiers des princes et des villes à l'époque bourguignonne* (Turnhout: Brepols, 2004), 121–31; Robert N. Swanson, 'Episcopal Income from Spiritualities in Later Medieval England: The Evidence for the Diocese of Coventry and Lichfield', *Midland History*, 13 (1988), 1–20.

2. Bishops' interactions with their cathedral clergy, household staff, archdeacons, and diocesan clergy, as well as with kings, popes, and councils, are very well studied. See, for example, Philippa Hoskin, 'Diocesan Politics in the See of Worcester, 1218–1266', *Journal of Ecclesiastical History*, 54 (2003), 422–40; Charles Vulliez, 'L'évêque de Paris Etienne Tempier (1268–1279) et son entourage ecclésiastique', in Cédric Giraud (ed.), *Notre-Dame de Paris 1163–2013* (Turnhout: Brepols, 2013), 217–33; Cheney, *English Bishops' Chanceries*; Storey, *Diocesan Administration*; Michael Burger, *Bishops, Clerks, and Diocesan Governance in Thirteenth-Century England: Reward and Punishment* (Cambridge: Cambridge University Press, 2012).

3. It should be noted that the use of inquests to protect the revenues of parishes, rights to and exemptions from taxation, and other fiscal interests was not a novelty in the thirteenth century but an intensification of a common Carolingian practice, itself rooted in Roman law: Stefan Esders, 'Die römischen Wurzeln der fiskalischen *Inquisitio* de Karolingerzeit', in Gauvard (ed.), *L'enquête au Moyen âge*, 13–28.

4. The role of trustworthiness in the settlement of tithe disputes was, however, significant, and will be discussed in Chapter 12. A rare example of tithes collected by a trustworthy man (singular) in 1270 was, notably, an interim measure while a dispute was settled: *Register of Walter Giffard, York*, 55. Panels of locals were also important to the collection of lay subsidies from the later thirteenth century onwards, for which see Forrest, 'Power and the People'.

5. Ben Dodds, 'Managing Tithes in the Late Middle Ages', *Agricultural History Review*, 53 (2005), 125–40, at 125–29; Robert N. Swanson, 'Economic Survival in Late Medieval Derbyshire: The Spirituality Income of the Dean and Chapter of Lichfield, c. 1400–c. 1535',

in Richard Goddard, John Langdon, and Miriam Müller (eds.), *Survival and Discord in Medieval Society: Essays in Honour of Christopher Dyer* (Turnhout: Brepols, 2010), 93.

6. John Eldevik, *Episcopal Power and Ecclesiastical Reform in the German Empire: Tithes, Lordship, and Community, 950–1150* (Cambridge: Cambridge University Press, 2012), 80–83, 153–58; Swanson, 'Economic Survival', 104; Ben Dodds, *Peasants and Production in the Medieval North-East: The Evidence from Tithes 1270–1536* (Woodbridge: Boydell, 2007), 139–43.

7. Dodds, *Peasants and Production*, 166, suggests that when some cultivators bought the rights to tithe collection in their own parish, the costs of collection were eliminated, but I am not so sure. It is hard to imagine the render being willing and honest just because it was made to one's richer neighbours.

8. *Register of John de Grandisson*, 67; *Register of Robert Mascall*, 17, 107, 112, 115, 121.

9. Cambridge University Library, EDR G/1/1, fo. 75r; *Register of William Wykeham*, 2.111.

10. The quotation is Bishop Gilbert of Hereford's characterization of the Franciscan David Hay, in *Register of John Gilbert*, 101. For papal levies calling for trustworthy men, see *Register of Walter Giffard, York*, 275; *Register of Simon of Ghent*, 224; Cambridge University Library, EDR G/1/2, fo. 9v.

11. Alison K. McHardy, 'Clerical Taxation in Fifteenth-Century England: The Clergy as Agents of the Crown', in Barrie Dobson (ed.), *The Church, Politics and Patronage in the Fifteenth Century* (Gloucester: Sutton, 1984), 171–72.

12. Sample mandates in Cambridge University Library, EDR G/1/2, fos. 3v, 81r, 89r, 105v, 113r, 114r, and EDR G/1/6, fo. 165r; *Register of John Gilbert*, 74, 85, 103, 108; *Registers of Walter Giffard and Henry Bowet*, 38, 51 (1404); Lichfield Record Office, B/A/1/7, fos. 149v, 155r, 159r. Sample confirmations that collectors were appointed from within the diocese in *Register of Ralph of Shrewsbury*, 338; Lichfield Record Office, B/A/1/3, fos. 111r, 116r.

13. *Register of Thomas Spofford*, 21–22, 88–89, 123, 128–29, 214. See similar in 1470s regarding Tintern Abbey and its Hereford possessions: *Register of Thomas Myllyng*, 4–5, 13–14.

14. *Register of Thomas Myllyng*, 148–49.

15. Frances Andrews, 'Living Like the Laity? The Negotiation of Religious Status in the Cities of Late Medieval Italy', *Transactions of the Royal Historical Society*, 20 (2010), 27–55, and idem '*Ut inde melius fiat*: The Commune of Parma and its Religious Personnel', in Frances Andrews and Maria Agata Pincelli (eds.), *Churchmen and Government in Late Medieval Italy c. 1200–c. 1450: Cases and Contexts* (Cambridge: Cambridge University Press, 2013), 45–66, has shown that Italian communes employed monks and friars as collectors and auditors because they were seen as independent of civic politics and therefore more trustworthy.

16. On mistrust of mendicants, see Guy Geltner, *The Making of Medieval Antifraternalism: Polemic, Violence, Deviance, and Remembrance* (Oxford: Oxford University Press, 2012); on pardoners, see Robert N. Swanson, *Indulgences in Late Medieval England: Passports to Paradise* (Cambridge: Cambridge University Press, 2007), 179–99; on vagrants, see McIntosh, *Controlling Misbehavior*, 88–93.

17. *Register of John de Grandisson*, 345; Karl Borchardt, 'Two Forged Thirteenth-Century Alms-Raising Letters Used by the Hospitallers in Franconia', in Malcolm Barber (ed.), *The Military Orders: Fighting for the Faith and Caring for the Sick* (Aldershot: Ashgate, 1994), 52–56; Swanson, *Indulgences in Late Medieval England*, 455–61, describes fraud but notes its rarity.

18. London Metropolitan Archives, DL/C/B/043/MS09064/004, fo. 36v.

19. *Councils and Synods*, 2.33–34 (c. 51); these provisions were influenced both by Bishop Eudes de Sully, whose synod of Paris in 1208 had warned parishes not to admit unlicensed preachers for fear of heresy, and by Robert Courson's constitutions issued as papal legate in 1213, which had called on bishops not to permit alms collectors to preach. Courson's text began in much the same way as Langton's, but did not express any disquiet about the probity of collectors where money was concerned; this seems to have been a peculiarly English concern: *Les statuts de Paris et le synodal de l'ouest (XIIIᵉ)*, ed. Odette Pontal (Paris: Bibliotèque Nationale, 1971), 86 (c. 92); *Sacrorum conciliorum nova et amplissima collectio*, ed. Giovanni Domenico Mansi, 31 vols. (Florence: Zatta, 1759–98), xxii. col. 846 (c. 9).

20. *Councils and Synods*, 2.85, 201 (Salisbury I, c. 76). It was also repeated in Hugh Foliot's constitutions for Hereford between 1225 and 1230, and in measures for the isolated churches of Durham within the diocese of York in the 1240s: *Councils and Synods*, 2.194 (Hereford, c. 79), and 443 (Durham peculiars, c. 48).

21. *Register of Walter Gray*, 60–61; *Register of John de Drokensford*, 141; *Register of Ralph of Shrewsbury*, 69; *Register of John Kirkby and John Ross*, 1.9; *Register of Simon de Montacute*, 224–25; *Knighton's Chronicle*, ed. Geoffrey H. Martin (Oxford: Clarendon, 1995), 333.

22. York, Borthwick Institute, Register 10, fo. 271r; *Register of Nicholas Bubwith*, 209.

23. *Register of Ralph of Shrewsbury*, 267–68.

24. See, for example, the measures taken by the nuns of Chester in 1456: Lichfield Record Office, B/A/1/11, fo. 81v.

25. *Register of Simon de Montacute*, 224–25.

26. See collections for the Hospitallers in 1309 and 1312: *Register of Henry Woodlock*, 365, 584–85.

27. *Register of William Greenfield*, 4.284–85.

28. Helmholz, *Oxford History of the Laws of England*, 1.396–98; Brian Edwin Ferme, *Canon Law in Late Medieval England: A Study of William Lyndwood's* Provinciale *with Particular Reference to Testamentary Law* (Rome: Libreria Ateneo Salesiano, 1995), 56; Palmer, *Selling the Church*, 56.

29. See p. 22 for the question of deathbed faith.

30. *Testamenta Eboracensia*, ed. James Raine, 6 vols., Surtees Society, 4, 30, 45, 53, 79, 106 (1836–1902), 3.203.

31. *Register of John le Romeyn*, 1.20; *Register of William Melton*, 2.168–69; *Register of Hamo de Hethe*, 202–4; *Lower Ecclesiastical Jurisdiction*, 122; *Vetus Liber Archidiaconatus Eliensis*, 178. Maurizio Lupoi, 'La *confidentia* è il *trust*', in Prodi (ed.), *La fiducia secondo i linguaggi del potere*, 27–39, discusses the role of legal trusts in creating trust.

32. *Register of John de Grandisson*, 1114.

33. *Councils and Synods*, 2.619 (c. 65), 716 (c. 71), 764–65 (c. 14), 1046 (c. 50).

34. *Decrees of the Ecumenical Councils*, 329; this was incorporated into the *Liber Sextus* of Boniface VIII in 1298 as *Quanquam usurarii* (*Decretals* VI 5.5.2).

35. *Registers of John de Sandale and Rigaud de Asserio*, 12; *Register of Thomas de Brantyngham*, 634; *Register of Richard de Kellawe*, 1.133–35, 1.628–29.

36. *Register of Thomas de Brantyngham*, 449.

37. Norfolk Record Office, DCN 67/1, rot. 5, m. 1. After 1285 executors were limited to dealing with the deceased's moveable goods and debts: Ferme, *Canon Law in Late Medieval England*, 69.

38. *Registers of Roger Martival*, 2.113–15.

39. Holford, 'Thrifty Men of the Country?', 201–21. The inspection or 'view' of property by trustworthy men was also sometimes referred to in disputes over *inter vivos* grants of

land, for example Canterbury Cathedral Archives, DCc/ChAnt/S/29; also in the formation of credit agreements, for example *Lower Ecclesiastical Jurisdiction*, 364. For further discussion of trust and credit, see Chapter 2.

40. *Register of Henry Woodlock*, 619; *Register of William Melton*, 5.17–18; Lichfield Record Office, B/A/1/3, fo. 145r; York, Borthwick Institute, Register 11, fo. 34r-v; Lincolnshire Archives, REG/8, fos. 146v–147r, and REG/12, fo. 21r.

41. Lichfield Record Office, B/A/1/3, fo. 134v; York, Borthwick Institute, Register 10, fo. 57v; *Register of Richard de Kellawe*, 1.369–70.

42. Ralph Evans, 'Whose Was the Manor Court?', in Ralph Evans (ed.), *Lordship and Learning: Studies in Memory of Trevor Aston* (Woodbridge: Boydell, 2004), 155–68; Jean Birrell, 'Manorial Custumals Reconsidered', *Past & Present*, 224 (2014), 3–37.

43. *Vetus Registrum Sarisberiense alias dictum Registrum S. Osmundi Episcopi*, ed. William Henry Rich Jones, Rolls Series, 2 vols. (1883–84), 1.275–314; *The Domesday of St Paul's*; *Visitations of Churches Belonging to St Paul's Cathedral 1249-1252*, ed. William Sparrow Simpson, Camden Society, second series 53 (1895).

44. See, for example, Exeter Cathedral, MS 3673, pp. 17–51, a visitation book dealing with manors and parish churches; Lincolnshire Archives, REG/2, 14v, a note on the involvement of trustworthy men in valuing the property of a chantry in Lincoln as well as being present at the examination of chaplains in the cathedral chapter house; Canterbury Cathedral Archives, DCc/ChAnt/S/429, for the use of trustworthy men to value the goods of a parish priest owing to a member of the royal household. Swanson, *Church and Society*, 198–99 discusses the manorial income of churches in general terms.

45. *Register of John de Grandisson*, 430.

46. Lincolnshire Archives, REG/12, fo. 309r. On the importance of the founder's will to hospitals (as sites for institutionalized almsgiving), see Sethina Watson, 'The Origins of the English Hospital', *Transactions of the Royal Historical Society*, sixth series 16 (2006), 83–87.

47. *Register of Robert Rede*, 121.

48. Katherine Harvey, *Episcopal Appointments in England, c. 1214-1344: From Election to Papal Provision* (Farnham: Ashgate, 2014), 158–61; Kathleen Edwards, *The English Secular Cathedrals in the Middle Ages: A Constitutional Study with Special Reference to the Fourteenth Century*, 2nd ed. (Manchester: Manchester University Press, 1967), 97–101; Lawrence G. Duggan, *Bishop and Chapter: The Governance of the Bishopric of Speyer to 1552* (New Brunswick, N.J.: Rutgers, 1978), 87–90; David Lepine, *A Brotherhood of Canons Serving God: English Secular Cathedrals in the Later Middle Ages* (Woodbridge: Boydell, 1995), 180–91.

49. *Councils and Synods*, 2.497–98 (c. 44); *Register of William Greenfield*, 1.130, 2.69. Repairs will be dealt with at greater length in the following chapter.

50. William Abel Pantin, *The English Church in the Fourteenth Century* (Cambridge: Cambridge University Press, 1955), 35–36; Burger, *Bishops, Clerks, and Diocesan Governance*, 24–25.

51. Hugh M. Thomas, *The Secular Clergy in England, 1066-1216* (Oxford: Oxford University Press, 2014), 114–16; John Blair, *The Church in Anglo-Saxon Society* (Oxford: Oxford University Press, 2005), chap. 8.

52. Haines, *Administration of the Diocese of Worcester*, 197–204.

53. Hamilton Thompson, *English Parish Clergy*, 102–31; *Registers of John de Sandale and Rigaud de Asserio*, 475.

54. The importance of the issue can be gauged from nineteen complaints in a single visitation book, Bishop Trefnant's 1397 visitation of Hereford diocese: Hereford Cathedral Archives, 1779, fos. 2 (Peterchurch), 3 (Mansell Gamage), 3v (Weobley), 5 (Llanrothal

and Welsh Newton), 5v (Goodrich Castle), 6 (Ganerew), 8 (Woolaston), 8v (Hewelsfield), 11 (Munsley), 11v (Coddington), 12v (Stretton), 14 (Hope-under-Dinmore), 15 (Docklow), 18 (Cussop), 19 (Kington), 21v (Bucknell), 23v (Wentnor), 24 (Clunbury). For episcopal action on nonresident clergy and poorly supported vicars, arising from visitations, see *Register of Thomas Spofford*, 98–99; *Register of Thomas Bekynton*, 22–25, 67–68.

55. Pantin, *English Church in the Fourteenth Century*, 34–35, 44.

56. Burger, *Bishops, Clerks, and Diocesan Governance*, 30–31, 33–37.

57. For discussion of the market in benefices, see Peter Heath, *The English Parish Clergy on the Eve of the Reformation* (London: Routledge, 1969), 27–36; Swanson, *Church and Society*, 40–58; Thomas, *Secular Clergy in England*, 88–90; Virginia Davis, 'Preparation for Service in the Late Medieval English Church', in Anne Curry and Elizabeth Matthew (eds.), *The Fifteenth Century*, I: *Concepts and Patterns of Service in the Later Middle Ages* (Woodbridge: Boydell, 2000), 38–51.

58. Henry Mayr-Harting, *Religion, Politics and Society in Britain 1066-1272* (Harlow: Pearson, 2011), 103–12; Palmer, *Selling the Church*, 17–23; idem, *English Law in the Age of the Black Death*, 28–56; Helmholz, *Oxford History of the Laws of England*, 1.477–91.

59. York, Borthwick Institute, Register 19, fos. 54v, 57r, 65r-v, 67r-v, 70v, 73r, 76r, 153r.

60. 'Register of the Archdeaconry of Richmond, 1442-1477', 118–19.

61. For example Ingram (Durham) in 1428: *Register of Thomas Langley*, 3.122–24.

62. *Register of Thomas Myllyng*, 20–25.

63. Haines, *Administration of the Diocese of Worcester*, 55–56. For examples from dioceses of York in 1388, Ely in 1406, and Durham in 1413, see York, Borthwick Institute, Register 14, fo. 4v; Cambridge University Library, EDR G/1/3, fo. 96v; *Register of Thomas Langley*, 2.39–40.

64. Lincolnshire Archives, REG/12, fos. 40r-v.

65. *Register of Wolstan de Bransford*, 306–8.

66. Lincolnshire Archives, REG/20, fos. 7r-v, 66r-v.

67. For example Lincolnshire Archives, REG/3, fo. 414v, and REG/18, fo. 53r; *Registers of Roger Martival*, 2.122; York, Borthwick Institute, Register 14, fo. 3r-v.

68. For example St Peter's Northampton in 1346: Lincolnshire Archives, REG/7, fo. 82r.

69. Mandates: Lichfield Record Office, B/A/1/3, fo. 28v; *Register of John de Stratford*, 225; Cambridge University Library, EDR G/1/1, fo. 32v; York, Borthwick Institute, Register 11, fos. 34v, 111r-v, 125r, and Register 12, fo. 40r. Responses: York, Borthwick Institute, Register 11, fo. 261r-v, and Register 12, fos. 77r, 80v; Lincolnshire Archives, REG/12, fo. 446r, and REG/20, fos. 40v, 41v.

70. *Register of John Kirkby and John Ross*, 1.156–57.

71. *Register of John Waltham*, 196–97; *Register of Thomas Bekynton*, 119–20.

72. York, Borthwick Institute, Register 11, fo. 109r.

73. 'Physical weakness': Lichfield Record Office, B/A/1/2, fo. 19v. Blindness: Lincolnshire Archives, REG/3, fo. 34r; *Register of John Waltham*, 23. For discussion, see Irina Metzler, *A Social History of Disability in the Middle Ages: Cultural Consideration of Physical Impairment* (Abingdon: Routledge, 2013), 142–44; Joel T. Rosenthal, *Old Age in Late Medieval England* (Philadelphia: University of Pennsylvania Press, 1996), 111–12.

74. Nicholas Orme, 'Sufferings of the Clergy: Illness and Old Age in Exeter Diocese, 1300-1540', in Margaret Pelling and Richard M. Smith (eds.), *Life, Death and the Elderly: Historical Perspectives* (London: Routledge, 1991), 71. After this date pensions replaced coadjutors almost completely.

75. Irina Metzler, *Disability in Medieval Europe: Thinking about Physical Impairment during the High Middle Ages, c. 1100-1400* (Abingdon: Routledge, 2006), 40–48.

76. *Register of Richard Swinfield*, 116. The visitation that precipitated Swinfield's action was lost in the Herefordshire Record Office sometime after 1978, but has been edited from a typescript in Forrest and Whittick, 'Thirteenth-Century Visitation Records', 756–58. Another example of mental illness creating the need for a coadjutor may be found in *Register of Wolstan de Bransford*, 9.

77. Lincolnshire Archives, REG/3, fos. 19v, 107v, 156v, 158v; *Registers of Roger Martival*, 2.149; Lichfield Record Office, B/A/1/2, fos. 27r, 75v, 137v; *Register of John de Stratford*, 62.

78. *Registers of Roger Martival*, 2.79.

79. *Register of William Gainsborough*, 172–73.

80. Lichfield Record Office, B/A/1/2, fos. 66r, 82v.

Chapter Twelve: The Material Church

1. Forrest, 'Transformation of Visitation', for a full discussion.

2. French, *People of the Parish*, chaps. 5 and 6.

3. Gilchrist, *Medieval Life*, 169.

4. Gervase Rosser, 'Religious Practice on the Margins', in John Blair and Carol Pyrah (eds.), *Church Archaeology: Research Directions for the Future* (York: Council for British Archaeology, 1996), 79–81; David Dymond, 'Gods' Disputed Acre', *Journal of Ecclesiastical History*, 50 (1999), 464–97.

5. Caroline Walker Bynum, *The Resurrection of the Body in Western Christianity, 200–1336* (New York: Columbia University Press, 1995), 203–8; Ian Forrest, 'The Politics of Burial in Late Medieval Hereford', *English Historical Review*, 125 (2010), 1116.

6. Nicolette Zeeman, 'Philosophy in Parts: Jean de Meun, Chaucer, and Lydgate', in Denery, Ghosh, and Zeeman (eds.), *Uncertain Knowledge*, 217–18; Caroline Walker Bynum, *Christian Materiality: An Essay on Religion in Late Medieval Europe* (New York: Zone Books, 2011), 30–32, 234–37.

7. Forrest, 'Transformation of Visitation', 13.

8. Caroline Walker Bynum, *Holy Feast and Holy Fast: The Religious Significance of Food to Medieval Women* (Berkeley: University of California Press, 1987); Sarah Beckwith, *Christ's Body: Identity, Culture and Society in Late Medieval Writings* (London: Routledge, 1993); Sarah Kay and Miri Rubin (eds.), *Framing Medieval Bodies* (Manchester: Manchester University Press, 1994); Jean-Claude Schmitt, *Le corps des images: essais sur la culture visuelle au moyen âge* (Paris: Gallimard, 2002).

9. Bynum, *Christian Materiality*, 18–22, 87–88, 125; on the presence of God within the Bible, see Margaret Aston, 'Devotional Literacy', in Aston, *Lollards and Reformers: Images and Literacy in Late Medieval Religion* (London: Hambledon, 1984), 110–13.

10. Bynum, *Christian Materiality*, 66.

11. Nicola Whyte, *Inhabiting the Landscape: Place, Custom and Memory, 1500–1800* (Oxford: Oxbow, 2009), 29–31.

12. Sam Turner, *Making a Christian Landscape: The Countryside in Early Medieval Cornwall, Devon and Wessex* (Exeter: University of Exeter Press, 2006), 4–5; Whyte, *Inhabiting the Landscape*, 32–39.

13. Stephen Mileson, 'The South Oxfordshire Project: Perceptions of Landscape, Settlement and Society, c. 500–1650', *Landscape History*, 33 (2012), 83–98, at 89; Alexandra Walsham, *The Reformation of the Landscape: Religion, Identity, and Memory in Early Modern Britain and Ireland* (Oxford: Oxford University Press, 2011), chap. 1.

14. Diane Watt, 'Faith in the Landscape: Overseas Pilgrimage in the *Book of Margery Kempe*', in Clare A. Lees and Gillian R. Overing (eds.), *A Place to Believe In: Locating Medieval Landscapes* (University Park: Pennsylvania State University Press, 2006), 170–87;

Anthony Bale, 'God's Cell: Christ as Prisoner and Pilgrimage to the Prison of Christ', *Speculum*, 91 (2016), 1–35.

15. Rosser, 'Religious Practice on the Margins', 75–79, 82–83; Blair, *Church in Anglo-Saxon Society*, 472–79; Whyte, *Inhabiting the Landscape*, 25, 39–40.

16. Ann Rosalind Jones and Peter Stallybrass, *Renaissance Clothing and the Materials of Memory* (Cambridge: Cambridge University Press, 2000), 2; on memories of authority triggered by landmarks, see Bronach Kane, 'Custom, Memory and Knowledge in the Medieval English Church Courts', in Rosemary C. E. Hayes and William J. Sheils (eds.), *Clergy, Church and Society in England and Wales c. 1200–1800* (York: Borthwick Institute, 2013), 71.

17. Johnson, 'Medieval Law and Materiality', 407–8.

18. Ibid., 431–32.

19. Maureen Miller, *The Bishop's Palace: Architecture and Authority in Medieval Italy* (Ithaca, N.Y.: Cornell University Press, 2000), 13; idem, *Clothing the Clergy: Virtue and Power in Medieval Europe, c. 800–1200* (Ithaca, N.Y.: Cornell University Press, 2014), 11, 36–38.

20. Miller, *Clothing the Clergy*, 162–76.

21. Forrest, 'Transformation of Visitation', 36.

22. Lincolnshire Archives, REG/17, fo. 89r–v.

23. Bynum, *Christian Materiality*, 240–41; Richard Morris, *Churches in the Landscape* (London: Dent, 1989), 316–49.

24. *Register of John le Romeyn*, 1.290; *Register of Thomas of Corbridge*, 1.36; *Register of William Greenfield*, 4.26; *Register of Henry Woodlock*, 486; *Register of Richard de Kellawe*, 1.101–2, 1.117–78, 1.245; *Registers of John de Sandale and Rigaud de Asserio*, 5–6, 122–23; *Registers of Roger Martival*, 2.370–71; Lichfield Record Office, B/A/1/3, fos. 7r, 130v, and B/A/1/12, fo. 124r; *Register of John de Stratford*, 105; *Register of John de Grandisson*, 349, 356, 379, 465; *Register of Ralph of Shrewsbury*, 137–38; *Register of John Kirkby and John Ross*, 1.29; Lincolnshire Archives, REG/7, fos. 12v–13r, and REG/12, fo. 2r; *Register of Richard d'Aungerville*, 50–51; *Register of John de Trillek*, 109; York, Borthwick Institute, Register 11, fo. 29v, Register 12, fo. 68v, and Register 19, fos. 91v, 95r; *Register of Thomas de Brantyngham*, 308; *Register of William Wykeham*, 2.35, 2.37; *Register of Edmund Lacy, Hereford*, 62, 96; *Register of Thomas Polton*, 6; *Register of Thomas Spofford*, 15; *Register of Thomas Langley*, 3.33, 3.83, 3.125, 3.155, 4.14, 4.26, 4.46, 4.126–27; *Register of Edmund Lacy, Exeter*, 1.117, 2.107; Cambridge University Library, EDR G/1/5, fo. 10v; *Register of Richard Fox*, 13.

25. Bynum, *Christian Materiality*, 171.

26. Although the benefice was a spiritual good, it was also real property where the law of possession or *seisin* was pertinent. Both jurisdictions claimed an interest: Palmer, *Selling the Church*, 48–49; Helmholz, *Oxford History of the Laws of England*, 1.498–501.

27. *Register of Gilbert Welton*, 59.

28. 'Accounts for the Rectory of Wainfleet St Mary for the Year 2 February 1475 to 1 February 1476', ed. Dorothy M. Owen, *Lincolnshire History and Archaeology*, 30 (1995), 53–54.

29. *Visitations in the Diocese of Lincoln, 1517–1531*, ed. Alexander Hamilton Thompson, 3 vols., Lincoln Record Society, 33, 35, 37 (1940–47), 1.79.

30. *Courts of the Archdeaconry of Buckingham*, 145.

31. See, for example, Bodleian Library, Norfolk Rolls 17, m. 2; Durham Cathedral, Dean and Chapter, 1.9.Pont.9; York, Borthwick Institute, MD 26; Hereford Cathedral Archives, 1779, fo. 2v; Canterbury Cathedral Archives, SVSB/III/354–55, Z.3.1, fo. 50, and Z.3.2, fo. 16; Lincolnshire Archives, Dean and Chapter, Dij/62/3/23; *Visitations in the Diocese of*

Lincoln, 1.12; *Kentish Visitations of Archbishop William Warham and His Deputies, 1511–12*, ed. Kathleen L. Wood-Legh, Kent Records, 24 (1984), 86–87.

32. York, Borthwick Institute, Register 11, fo. 13r; Lichfield Record Office, B/A/1/3, fo. 14v.

33. Exeter Cathedral, MS 2857. These visitations also dealt with the dean and chapter's manorial holdings.

34. *Register of William Greenfield*, 3.134–35, 5.232–33. In Middle English a 'Crouche' could be a cross or a crook, suggesting a lean-to structure against a wall or in a corner.

35. For example, the 1367 case of North Molton in Devon: *Register of Thomas de Brantyngham*, 261–63, 267–70.

36. Swanson, *Church and Society*, 212.

37. Lichfield Record Office, B/A/1/11, fos. 45r–46r; a summary of the survey and commission is given in R. Hutchinson and Nigel J. Tringham, 'A Medieval Rectory House at Clifton Campville, Staffordshire', *South Staffordshire Archaeological and Historical Society Transactions*, 32 (1990–91), 83–84.

38. *Register of Thomas Langley*, 2.164–66, 5.101–2.

39. See for comparison the discussions of expertise in Provencal and northern French financial *enquêtes* of the fourteenth century by John Drendel, 'Le recours aux experts sur des questions économiques dans deux enquêtes provençales au XIVe siècle', in Denjean and Feller (eds.), *Expertise et valeur des choses au Moyen Âge*, 65–72, and Lefebvre, *Prud'hommes, serment curial*, 136.

40. H. B. Sharp, 'Some Mid-Fifteenth Century Small-Scale Building Repairs', *Vernacular Architecture*, 12 (1981), 20–29; Warwick Rodwell, *The Archaeology of Churches* (Stroud: Amberley, 2012), 136–37.

41. *Register of Walter Reynolds*, 17; *Register of Richard de Kellawe*, 1.72–73, 1.106–7, 1.116–17, 1.144, 1.212–17; York, Borthwick Institute, Register 14, fo. 1v.

42. At Rampton in Nottinghamshire, a prebend of Southwell Minster, the jurors in an inquest of 1374 were told to inspect the defects visually for themselves, after which they were examined on oath individually: York, Borthwick Institute, Register 12, fo. 1r.

43. Canterbury Cathedral Archives, SVSB/2/189/3 and 5.

44. *Register of William Wykeham*, 2.183.

45. Paula Simpson, 'The Continuum of Resistance to Tithe, c. 1400–1600', in Rob Lutton and Elisabeth Salter (eds.), *Pieties in Transition: Religious Practices and Experiences, c.1400–1600* (Aldershot: Ashgate, 2007), 100; Kane, 'Custom, Memory and Knowledge', 71; Swanson, *Church and Society*, 211–15.

46. Palmer, *Selling the Church*, 32, 38; Kane, 'Custom, Memory and Knowledge', 66–74; Swanson, *Church and Society*, 211.

47. Dodds, *Peasants and Production*, 139–43; Simpson, 'Continuum of Resistance to Tithe', 103–4.

48. Canterbury Cathedral Archives, X.10.1, fo. 9r. For further examples, see Simpson, 'Continuum of Resistance to Tithe', 101.

49. James Fentress and Chris Wickham, *Social Memory* (Oxford: Blackwell, 1992), 41–51.

50. For instance, Wood, *Memory of the People*, 219–36.

51. Eldevik, *Episcopal Power and Ecclesiastical Reform*, 220; Luigi Provero, 'Les dîmes dans la territorialité incertaine des Campagnes du XIIIe siècle', in Michel Lauwers (ed.), *La dîme, l'Église et la société féodale* (Turnhout: Brepols, 2012), 309. Provero discusses the territorial authority of tithe owners, but we can extend the thrust of his analysis to bishops as the adjudicators of tithe disputes.

52. Johnson, 'Medieval Law and Materiality', 431–32.

53. *EEA* 21: *Norwich 1215–1243*, 45.

54. *Register of Richard de Kellawe*, 1.407–8.

55. *Register of Edmund Lacy, Exeter*, 1.309–14.

56. London Metropolitan Archives, DL/C/0205, fo. 185v.

57. Hugh of St Victor, *On the Sacraments of the Christian Faith*, 168.

58. *Register of Richard de Kellawe*, 1.161. Britnell, *Britain and Ireland*, 14, 15, 166, maps some of the parishes and wastes of County Durham.

59. The concentration of tithe disputes in the period 1290–1330 has been noted for other regions, for example South West France: Noël Coulet, 'Paroisse, œuvre et communauté d'habitants en Provence (le diocèse d'Aix dans la première moitié du XIVe s.)', in *La paroisse en Languedoc (XIIIᵉ–XIVᵉ s.)*, Cahiers de Fanjeaux, 25 (Toulouse: Privat, 1990), 228.

60. *Register of William Melton*, 4.150–51, 5.57.

61. Cambridge University Library, EDR G/1/2, fo. 50r–v.

62. Norfolk Record Office, DCN/85/2–3.

63. Morris, *Churches in the Landscape*, 229.

64. *Register of Richard Swinfield*, 386–87.

65. York, Borthwick Institute, Register 16, fos. 93r–94v.

66. Provero, 'Les dîmes dans la territorialité incertaine', 332–34.

67. *Register of William Melton*, 2.53–56, 2.151.

68. *Register of Thomas de Cobham*, 135–37.

69. *Register of Richard Gravesend*, 251.

70. For examples of 'frozen', see Kümin, *Shaping of a Community*, 16; Whyte, *Inhabiting the Landscape*, 20; the phrase 'ironed out' comes from Morris, *Churches in the Landscape*, 229.

71. Blair, *Church in Anglo-Saxon Society*, 463; Dominique Iogna-Prat, 'Churches in the Landscape', in Thomas F. X. Noble and Julia M. H. Smith (eds.), *The Cambridge History of Christianity*, 3: *Early Medieval Christianities, c. 600–c. 1100* (Cambridge: Cambridge University Press, 2008), 363–79; Elisabeth Zadora-Rio, 'The Making of Churchyards and Parish Territories in the Early-Medieval Landscape of France and England in the 7th–12th Centuries: A Reconsideration', *Medieval Archaeology*, 47 (2003), 1–19.

72. Michel de Certeau, *The Practice of Everyday Life*, trans. Steven Rendall (Berkeley: University of California Press, 1988), 94–95; for the variety of functions performed by chapels, see French, *People of the Parish*, 5; on the unreality of the canonical distinction between parish church and chapel, see Blair, *Church in Anglo-Saxon Society*, 393.

73. Gervase Rosser, 'Parochial Conformity and Voluntary Religion in Late-Medieval England', *Transactions of the Royal Historical Society*, sixth series 1 (1991), 173–89.

74. For seigneurial boroughs, see Morris, *Churches in the Landscape*, 262. Successive Rous lords of Baynton in the Wiltshire village of Edington roused their neighbours to the defence of their parish church in 1336, 1361, and 1428, representing a matter of family honour and personal income as a communal concern: Chippenham, Wiltshire and Swindon Record Office, MS D1 2/9, fos. 32r–33v; *The Edington Cartulary*, ed. Janet H. Stevenson, Wiltshire Record Society, 42 (1987), 12, 17–19, 165–69. On each occasion the lord used the status of Baynton church as a symbol to unite rebellions that had rather diffuse origins. The church in Baynton was a parish church, if you believed the lord, and a dependent chapel, if you believed the canons of Edington priory. An armed uprising in 1336 gave way to a long-running lawsuit from the 1360s onwards, culminating in 1428 in a conspiracy to withhold payments for the sacraments. This was a dispute over lordship conducted through the medium of popular communalism.

75. Christine Lutgens, 'The Case of Waghen vs. Sutton: Conflict over Burial Rights in Late Medieval England', *Mediaeval Studies*, 38 (1976), 145–84; Robert N. Swanson, 'Paro-

chialism and Particularism: The Dispute over the Status of Ditchford Frary, Warwickshire in the Early Fifteenth Century', in Michael J. Franklin and Christopher Harper-Bill (eds.), *Medieval Ecclesiastical Studies in Honour of Dorothy M. Owen* (Woodbridge: Boydell, 1995), 241–57; Forrest, 'Politics of Burial', 1127–34.

76. Between 1360 and 1509, at least 110 English chapels petitioned the pope about their status: French, *People of the Parish*, 26n.

77. *Register of Ralph of Shrewsbury*, 627–28; *Register of John Stafford*, 143; Lincoln-shire Archives, REG/12, fo. 166v.

78. *Register of Adam of Orleton, Hereford*, 272, 278–79, 281–83.

79. *Register of William Greenfield*, 2.6; York, Borthwick Institute, Register 12, fo. 54v.

80. *Register of Edmund Lacy, Exeter*, 2.150, 175, 211–22.

81. Witnesses frequently referred to landmarks in accounts of spatial boundaries: Kane, 'Custom, Memory and Knowledge', 71.

82. *Register of Edmund Lacy, Exeter*, 2.217–18.

83. Hereford Cathedral Archives, 1779, fo. 4v. Night is discussed as a frontier ordering behaviour and categories in similar ways to spatial boundaries by Murray Melbin, 'Night as Frontier', *American Sociological Review*, 43 (1978), 3–22.

84. Bynum, *Christian Materiality*, 186.

85. *Register of William Melton*, 5.83–84. See also the case of Abingdon in 1391, in Rosser, *Art of Solidarity*, 196.

86. *Register of Walter Bronscombe*, 1.99; *Register of Edmund Lacy, Exeter*, 1.176.

87. York, Borthwick Institute, Register 10, fo. 71r.

88. Lincolnshire Archives, REG/12, fo. 71v.

89. Kane, 'Social Representations', 550.

90. Morris, *Churches in the Landscape*, 299.

91. Blair, *Church in Anglo-Saxon Society*, 459.

92. Whyte, *Inhabiting the Landscape*, 29–31.

93. Keene, *Survey of Medieval Winchester*, 1.112–13.

94. Blair, *Church in Anglo-Saxon Society*, 488–89.

95. De Certeau, *Practice of Everyday Life*, 107.

96. Ibid., 105–7.

97. Bynum, *Christian Materiality*, 180–85.

98. Ibid., 66.

Chapter Thirteen: Subtle Judgements

1. Compare Justice, *Writing and Rebellion*, 185, who argues that manorial lords 'insinu-ated their power into the relations of their villagers, using the self-interest of each to lever them all against each other'.

2. These phases of rapid change are discussed in more detail in Forrest, 'Transfor-mation of Visitation', and idem, 'English Provincial Constitutions and Inquisition into Lollardy', in Mary C. Flannery and Katie L. Walter (eds.), *The Culture of Inquisition in Medieval England* (Woodbridge: Boydell, 2013), 45–59.

3. Sarah Hamilton, *Church and People in the Medieval West, 900–1200* (Harlow: Pear-son, 2013), 60–77.

4. The use of visitations to monitor the clergy quickly superseded the somewhat un-realistic practice of 'fraternal correction', by which laypeople were allowed to admonish a cleric in person and then report them to their superior: Craun, *Ethics and Power*, 15–23.

5. David Lepine, 'The Parson', in Rigby (ed.), *Historians on Chaucer*, 334–51.

6. *Councils and Synods*, 2.26 (Canterbury 1213x14, c.8), 62 (Salisbury 1217x19, c. 6), 603 (Wells 1258, c. 24), 710 (Winchester 1262x65, c. 42).

7. *Decretum* C. 30 q. 1 cc. 8–10; *Councils and Synods*, 2.26 (Canterbury 1213x14, c. 6), 464 (Chichester 1245x52, c. 60), 1018–20 (Exeter 1287, c. 21).

8. *Councils and Synods*, 2.1016–17 (Exeter 1287, c. 19).

9. *Councils and Synods*, 2.1084 (Chichester 1289, c. 8).

10. Although there was a deep cultural expectation that clergy should be Latinate, the extent to which this was actually tested is hard to tell until more detailed records appear, from time to time, in the late fifteenth and early sixteenth centuries: Mayr-Harting, *Religion, Politics and Society*, 121; Thomas, *Secular Clergy in England*, 290; Heath, *English Parish Clergy*, 73–75; Swanson, *Church and Society*, 58–59. This was supposed to be done by the bishop or his representative in person, but very occasionally lay testimony was explicitly sought prior to ordination: Cambridge University Library, EDR G/1/3, fo. 184r, is a 1395 licence to proceed to holy orders, following reports from trustworthy persons as to character and lifestyle.

11. From the late thirteenth to the middle of the fourteenth century many of the inquests into legitimacy and character were carried out on behalf of the papacy. In 1265 the pope had reserved to himself the right to appoint ('provide') to all benefices in England, both vacant and not-yet-vacant. A candidate would petition the pope asking to be considered for a benefice, and the pope, knowing nothing about him, had to find out whether he was suitable and acceptable to the interested parties. Papal claims to entitlement escalated around 1300, but English patrons fought back with complaints about intrusion into the churches their ancestors had founded, and bishops sometimes protested about the 'capricious and difficult' (*variis et arduis*) job of arranging the inquests: Cambridge University Library, EDR G/1/1, fo. 27v. This culminated in Edward III's Statute of Provisors of 1351, which ended the pope's right to 'provide' candidates to benefices. From 1351 onwards papal provision was rare and the pope's influence in English church affairs was limited to granting dispensations for study leave, plurality, and illegitimacy: Pantin, *English Church in the Fourteenth Century*, 48–53; Haines, *Administration of the Diocese of Worcester*, 213. See, for example, *Register of John de Grandisson*, 330; Lincolnshire Archives, REG/13, fos. 24r, 48v, 49r; *Register of Edmund Lacy, Exeter*, 1.149; Lichfield Record Office, B/A/1/1, fo. 151v.

12. *Lower Ecclesiastical Jurisdiction*, 19; Cambridge University Library, EDR G/1/4, fo. 7v; *Vetus Liber Archidiaconatus Eliensis*, 202; *Registers of Walter Giffard and Henry Bowet*, 27, 44; *Register of Walter de Stapeldon*, 138; Lichfield Record Office, B/A/1/2, fo. 2v. Many more such mandates do not mention trustworthy men, but since the normal discourses of canon law effaced almost all lay participation in the administration of the church, this should not surprise us. The large minority of examples that do mention them can be taken as indicative of a practice that was habitual and therefore not always recorded.

13. *Register of Henry Woodlock*, 288.

14. Lincolnshire Archives, REG/3, fo. 119 (an inserted original mandate).

15. *Register of Simon of Ghent*, 790.

16. *Register of John le Romeyn*, 1.272; *Register of Simon of Ghent*, 586; *Register of John Pontoise*, 149, 576–77; Lincolnshire Archives, REG/2, fos. 33r–v, 102v, 196v, 256v; *Register of Thomas de Cobham*, 200; *Register of Adam de Orleton, Worcester*, 92; *Register of John de Grandisson*, 385, 518–19; *Register of Thomas de Brantyngham*, 353; *Register of Robert Rede*, 29; *Register of Thomas Langley*, 6.2–3.

17. *Register of Walter Gray*, 79; *Register of William Wickwane*, 51; Lincolnshire Archives, REG/3, fo. 26v; *Register of Henry Woodlock*, 187–88; *Registers of Roger Martival*, 2.144; *Register of Simon de Montacute*, 14, 19; *Register of Gilbert Welton*, 46.

18. *Register of John de Halton*, 1.214; *Register of Walter Bronscombe*, 1.15; *Registers of John de Sandale and Rigaud de Asserio*, 407; *Register of John Kirkby and John Ross*, 1.127.

19. *Register of Richard de Kellawe*, 1.346–47; the bishop's decision is not recorded.

20. On the link between constitutions and visitations, see Odette Pontal, *Les Statuts Synodaux* (Turnhout: Brepols, 1975), 17.

21. *Councils and Synods*, 2.1034–36 (Exeter 1287, c. 40).

22. *Annales monastici*, 1.307–10.

23. York, Borthwick Institute, Register 11, fo. 396v.

24. Canterbury Cathedral Archives, DCc/VR/6, m. 2. For clergy as lenders, see Pamela Nightingale, 'The English Parochial Clergy as Investors and Creditors in the First Half of the Fourteenth Century', in Phillipp R. Schofield and Nicholas J. Mayhew (eds.), *Credit and Debt in Medieval England c.1180–c.1350* (Oxford: Oxbow, 2002), 89–105.

25. Canterbury Cathedral Archives, DCc/VR/6, mm. 1d, 2. Emphases added.

26. Canterbury Cathedral Archives, DCc/VR/6, m. 2d; Hereford Cathedral Archives, 1779, fo. 5r.

27. Palmer, *Selling the Church*, 53. Palmer's analysis focuses on the central courts, but there are occasional examples of clergy being disciplined in the local courts, for example in the hundred court of Upwimborne, Dorset, in 1394, where one of the visitation representatives of Wimborne All Saints was told to produce the vicar of Gussage St Michael: St Giles House, Shaftesbury Archives, M63. Personal oaths were also administered by bishops on recalcitrant clergy, for example the 1292 case of a rector forced to resign his benefice without argument having been defamed of adultery with the wife of one of his parishioners: *Register of Richard Swinfield*, 282.

28. *Register of Henry Woodlock*, 190; *Register of John de Stratford*, 65, 112; *Register of Thomas de Brantyngham*, 563; 'Register of the Archdeaconry of Richmond, 1442–1477', 80 (*fidedigna . . . insinuacione*).

29. *Register of Walter Reynolds*, 4–5; *Register of John de Stratford*, 164; *Register of Thomas de Brantyngham*, 167, 428; Lichfield Record Office, B/A/1/11, fo. 66r.

30. See, for example, the suit brought simply by 'the parishioners' of Kingston in Cambridgeshire in 1378 against their negligent rector: Cambridge University Library, EDR D/2/1, fos. 106v–107r. Some cases, such as that arising from the 'clamour of trustworthy persons' at Sherburn-in-Elmet in 1313, concerning their vicar's drunkenness, sexual immorality, fighting, and penchant for watching plays, may well have bypassed visitation, such was their notoriety: *Register of William Greenfield*, 1.68–69.

31. Joseph Goering, 'The Internal Forum and the Literature of Penance and Confession', in Wilfried Hartmann and Kenneth Pennington (eds.), *The History of Medieval Canon Law in the Classical Period, 1140–1234: From Gratian to the Decretals of Pope Gregory IX* (Washington, D.C.: Catholic University of America Press, 2008), 379–428; Alexander Murray, *Conscience and Authority in the Medieval Church* (Oxford: Oxford University Press, 2015); Thomas Izbicki, 'Sin and Pastoral Care', in Robert N. Swanson (ed.), *The Routledge History of Medieval Christianity 1050–1500* (London: Routledge, 2015), 147–58; Peter Biller, 'Confession in the Middle Ages', in Peter Biller and Alasdair J. Minnis (eds.), *Handling Sin: Confession in the Middle Ages* (Woodbridge: York Medieval Press, 1998), 3–33.

32. *Decretals* X 5.1.17, 18; *Constitutiones Concilii quarti Lateranensis*, 191–92, 198–99; *EEA 23: Chichester 1254–1305*, ed. Philippa M. Hoskin (Oxford: Oxford University Press, 2001), 214–15; Goering, 'Internal Forum'; Christopher R. Cheney, *Episcopal Visitation of Monasteries in the Thirteenth Century* (Manchester: Manchester University Press, 1931), 93–94, 137; Mary C. Flannery and Katie L. Walter, '*Vttirle Onknowe?* Modes of Inquiry and the Dynamics of Interiority in Vernacular Literature', in Flannery and Walter (eds.), *The Culture of Inquisition*, 77–93.

33. *Councils and Synods*, 2.974–75; Paul R. Hyams, 'Deans and Their Doings: The Norwich Inquiry of 1286', in Stephen Kuttner and Kenneth Pennington (eds.), *Proceedings*

of the Sixth International Congress of Medieval Canon Law (Vatican: Biblioteca Apostolica, 1985), 619–46.

34. James A. Brundage, *The Medieval Origins of the Legal Profession: Canonists, Civilians, and Courts* (Chicago: University of Chicago Press, 2008), 126–63.

35. For example *Register of Richard de Kellawe*, 3.86–87; York, Borthwick Institute, Register 11, fo. 49r; *Register of William Melton*, 4.122.

36. Occasionally this was in response to a direct question from the crown—was this man really a cleric?—but usually it looks to have been a preemptive expression of good faith: Lincolnshire Archives, REG/8, fo. 81r.

37. Donahue, 'Proof by Witness', 156.

38. *Register of John le Romeyn*, 2.54; *Register of Thomas of Corbridge*, 1.223–24.

39. For examples of 'best able' phrases, see *Select Cases of Procedure without Writ*, 35; Masschaele, *Jury, State, and Society*, 28–29; Macnair, 'Vicinage and the Antecedents of the Jury', 577. Common law had adopted the phrase from the procedural canon law writers in the late twelfth and early thirteenth centuries, for which see *The Treatise on the Laws and Customs of the Realm of England Commonly Called Glanvill*, ed. George Derek Gordon Hall (London: Nelson, 1965), 30; *Bracton on the Laws and Customs of England*, 2.346–47, 403. For further discussion, see p. 100.

40. *Register of Edmund Lacy, Exeter*, 2.17–22.

41. On constancy, see Helmholz, *Marriage Litigation*, 91; on informal jury discretion in homicide cases, see Naomi D. Hurnard, *The King's Pardon for Homicide before AD 1307* (Oxford: Clarendon, 1969), 75–79; Given, *Society and Homicide*, 91–105. Anthony Musson, *Medieval Law in Context: The Growth of Legal Consciousness from Magna Carta to the Peasants' Revolt* (Manchester: Manchester University Press, 2001), 114–16, suggests the phenomenon may also be explained by jury ignorance of the letter of the law, but this interpretation cannot be substantiated.

42. For other examples of trustworthy men describing violence against clerics in such a way as to reassure secular justice, see *Registers of John de Sandale and Rigaud de Asserio*, 76; *Register of John de Grandisson*, 481; *Register of Hamo de Hethe*, 243–44; Lincolnshire Archives, REG/8, fo. 78v; *Register of William Wykeham*, 2.102; *Register of Thomas de Brantyngham*, 169–70, 505.

43. Helmholz, Ius Commune *in England*, 16–81; Shannon McSheffrey, 'Sanctuary and the Legal Topography of Pre-Reformation London', *Law and History Review*, 27 (2009), 483–514; Thomas B. Lambert, 'Spiritual Protection and Secular Power: The Evolution of Sanctuary and Legal Privilege in Ripon and Beverley, 900–1300', in Thomas B. Lambert and David Rollason (eds.), *Peace and Protection in the Middle Ages* (Toronto: PIMS, 2009), 121–40.

44. For example, in the case of the escape of convicted clerics from Newark Castle to Southwell Minster, Nottinghamshire, in 1328: *Register of William Melton*, 4.122.

45. *Register of Simon of Ghent*, 281; *Registers of Roger Martival*, 2.125; *Register of John de Trillek*, 115.

46. *Register of John de Grandisson*, 769; *Register of Henry of Newark*, 281; Cambridge University Library, EDR G/1/1, fo. 60r–v; Lincolnshire Archives, REG/8, fo. 46v, REG/18, fo. 69r, and REG/20, fos. 87r, 92v–93r; *Register of Thomas de Brantyngham*, 168; *Register of Edmund Lacy, Exeter*, 1.111, 157. While violent crimes committed by clerics fell to the church courts to judge, violence between laypeople was usually a matter for common law or the manorial courts.

47. Hereford Cathedral Archives, 1779, fos. 1r (Brinsop), 3r (Mansell Lacy), 3v (Yazor), 4r (Llanwarne), 9r (Westbury), 21v (Bucknell), 26r (Hyssington).

48. See, for example, the case of Margery Bawe's forced separation from her husband in 1331: *Register of John de Stratford*, 207–8.

49. Kelleher, 'Like Man and Wife'; Bardsley, *Venomous Tongues*; McSheffrey, *Marriage, Sex, and Civic Culture*; Neal, *Masculine Self*; Werner, 'Promiscuous Priests and Vicarage Children'.

50. Kelleher, 'Like Man and Wife', 357; Helmholz, *Marriage Litigation*, 101–2; for examples see Hereford Cathedral Archives, 1779, fos. 1r, 2r, 6r, 12r, 19r, 19v, 22v, 23r.

51. Hereford Cathedral Archives, 1779, fo. 12r (such cases may have been reported so as to achieve a legal separation, or to enforce better treatment); Canterbury Cathedral Archives, DCc/VR/14.

52. *Select Cases on Defamation*, xxxii–xxxiv; for examples see Hereford Cathedral Archives, 1779, fos. 3v, 14v. Malice is mentioned in Archbishop Thoresby's visitation articles for the province of York (between 1353 and 1373) in relation to defamation and raising false impediments to marriage: York, Borthwick Institute, Register 11, fo. 396v.

53. *Kentish Visitations*, 133.

54. Lincolnshire Archives, MS Vj/3, fo. 2r; Hereford Cathedral Archives, 1779, fo. 26v.

55. Richard H. Helmholz, 'Crime, Compurgation and the Courts of the Medieval Church', *Law and History Review*, 1 (1983), 1–26.

56. Helmholz, *Oxford History of the Laws of England*, 1.615. For examples of clerics purging clerics, see *Register of Thomas of Corbridge*, 1.241–42; *Register of John de Grandisson*, 529–30.

57. *Register of Richard de Kellawe*, 1.58–59; *Register of Thomas de Cobham*, 105, 110–11; *Register of Adam of Orleton, Hereford*, 302–3, 313; *Register of John Kirkby and John Ross*, 1.89; *Register of John de Trillek*, 81–82; *Register of William Wykeham*, 2.5–6; *Register of Robert Mascall*, 47; York, Borthwick Institute, Register 18, fo. 8r.

58. York, Borthwick Institute, Register 18, fo. 3r. Note that the trustworthy men are here treated as witnesses, examined individually, rather than as jurors, deposing collectively; for the distinction, see p. 100.

59. *Register of Henry of Newark*, 331; *Register of Richard de Kellawe*, 1.462–64; York, Borthwick Institute, Register 16, fos. 123v–124r, 124r–v; *Register of Thomas Langley*, 5.125–26, 5.150–52; *Register of John de Grandisson*, 42.

60. *Register of Ralph of Shrewsbury*, 470–71. For *fama* see Chapter 10.

61. *Register of John de Grandisson*, 758.

62. Richard Odam had supposedly promised to join a guild in 1468: *Lower Ecclesiastical Jurisdiction*, 483.

63. *Register of Edmund Lacy, Exeter*, 3.76.

64. *Register of Thomas of Corbridge*, 1.286; Lichfield Record Office, D/30/2/1/2, fo. 34r.

65. *Lower Ecclesiastical Jurisdiction*, 490. This was one of only a handful of written references to trustworthy *women*; for further examples see pp. 133–34.

66. *Register of Thomas Langley*, 4.63.

67. *Register of William Greenfield*, 2.185, 4.138, 4.198.

68. Cambridge University Library, EDR D/2/1, fo. 113r.

69. Lincolnshire Archives, REG/3, fos. 137v, 167v; *Registers of Roger Martival*, 2.147; *Register of Thomas Charlton*, 42–43; *Register of Simon de Montacute*, 243–44; Cambridge University Library, EDR G/1/1, fo. 77r; York, Borthwick Institute, Register 10, fo. 75v; *Register of Gilbert Welton*, 80–81, 159; *Register of William Wykeham*, 2.372.

70. *Lower Ecclesiastical Jurisdiction*, 133.

71. Lincolnshire Archives, REG/12, fos. 280v–281r; William Page, Granville Proby, and Sidney Inskip (eds.), *The Victoria County History of Huntingdon*, 3 vols. (London: Institute of Historical Research, 1926–38), 3.35–38.

72. *Register of William Melton*, 4.101; Lincolnshire Archives, REG/12, fos. 61v, 377r; Lincolnshire Archives, REG/17, fo. 103r; Lichfield Record Office, B/A/1/6, fos. 80v, 83r–v,

98v, 99r, 101r, 107r, 112v, and B/A/1/7, fos. 157r, 175v, 178r, 179r, 185r, 190v; *Register of Thomas Langley*, 1.42, 1.173, 3.94.

73. York, Borthwick Institute, Register 18, fo. 332v, and Cambridge University Library, EDR D/2/1, fo. 11v (impediment prior to marriage); Lincolnshire Archives, REG/3, fos. 2v (bigamy), 32r (desertion); Lincolnshire Archives, REG/7, fo. 78r (desertion); 'Documents Relating to Visitations of the Diocese and Province of York', 217 (impotence).

74. For discussion in relation to medieval social life, and the debt to continental philosophy, particularly phenomenology, see Rosser, *Art of Solidarity*, 30–32.

75. Ramsey (ed.), *Works of Saint Augustine*, 183–84. For a critical survey of modern philosophical approaches to the question, see Anita Avramides, *Other Minds* (London: Routledge, 2001), who describes this as an issue of philosophical perplexity and denies that there is a genuine epistemological problem in knowing whether other people have minds; Alec Hyslop, 'Other Minds', in Edward N. Zalta (ed.), *The Stanford Encyclopedia of Philosophy* (Spring 2016 ed.), http://plato.stanford.edu/archives/spr2016/entries/other-minds/, gives a fair summary of other approaches, but does believe there to be an epistemological question. Augustine would side with Avramides, in some things.

76. Alexander Murray, 'Confession as a Historical Source in the Thirteenth Century', in Ralph H. C. Davis and John Michael Wallace-Hadrill (eds.), *The Writing of History in the Middle Ages: Essays Presented to R. W. Southern* (Oxford: Oxford University Press, 1981). On the deathbed, see Appleford, *Learning to Die*.

77. Lincolnshire Archives, REG/12, fo. 124v.

78. Helmholz, *Oxford History of the Laws of England*, 1.402–3.

79. *Register of Thomas of Corbridge*, 1.111–12.

80. Ibid., 1.85.

81. Alexander Murray, *Suicide in the Middle Ages*, 2 vols. (Oxford: Oxford University Press, 1998–2000), 1.166–75; Eliza Buhrer, ' "But What Is to Be Said of a Fool?" Intellectual Disability in Medieval Thought and Culture', in Albrecht Classen (ed.), *Mental Health, Spirituality, and Religion in the Middle Ages and Early Modern Age* (Berlin: De Gruyter, 2014), 314–43, 339–43; Wendy Turner, 'Mental Incapacity and the Financing of War in Medieval England', in L. J. Andrew Villalon and Donald J. Kagay (eds.), *The Hundred Years War (Part II): Different Vistas* (Leiden: Brill, 2008), 393–94.

82. Sara Butler, 'Degrees of Culpability: Suicide Verdicts, Mercy, and the Jury in Medieval England', *Journal of Medieval and Early Modern Studies*, 36 (2006), 263–90, 270–73; Buhrer, ' "But What Is to Be Said of a Fool?" ', 341–43, argues that distinguishing between idiocy and temporary insanity developed as a legal stratagem because it was easier to gain control of the property of an idiot.

83. *Register of Edmund Lacy, Exeter*, 2.200.

84. *Register of William Greenfield*, 2.116.

85. York, Borthwick Institute, Register 18, fo. 3v.

86. York, Borthwick Institute, Register 19, fo. 24v.

87. York, Borthwick Institute, Register 18, fo. 290v.

88. *Register of Richard Fox*, 141.

89. Forrest, *Detection of Heresy*, 49–52, 74–75; Diane Vincent, 'The Contest over the Public Imagination of Inquisition, 1380–1430', in Flannery and Walter (eds.), *Culture of Inquisition*, 60–76.

90. The prolixity and procedural scrutiny of canonization proceedings is particularly noted in Dyan Elliott, *Proving Woman: Female Spirituality and Inquisitional Culture in the Later Middle Ages* (Princeton, N.J.: Princeton University Press, 2004), 127–38, and André Vauchez, *Sainthood in the Later Middle Ages*, trans. Jean Birrell (Cambridge: Cambridge University Press, 1997), 33–84.

91. *Register of John de Grandisson*, 1231–34.

92. See comments on lay acclamation of saints made in the eleventh century by Bernard of Angers, at p. 110.

93. *Registers of Roger Martival*, 2.300–302, 318–20; Jeffrey H. Denton, 'Winchelsey, Robert (c.1240–1313)', in *Oxford Dictionary of National Biography*.

94. Hereford Cathedral Archives, 1779, fo. 6v.

95. Hereford Cathedral Archives, 1779, fo. 4v.

96. York, Borthwick Institute, MD 26.

97. *Register of Henry Woodlock*, 491. On the investigation of the English Templars, see *The Proceedings against the Templars in the British Isles*, ed. Helen Nicholson, 2 vols. (Farnham: Ashgate, 2011).

98. Sometime in the mid-1380s he wrote that Laurence Bedeman, an Oxford follower of Wyclif, had been examined before himself, several doctors of theology and law, and 'other trustworthy men of the church, both religious and seculars'; in 1384 he commissioned his officials to inquire into the truth of reports about a doctor of canon law preaching things 'harmful to the pope, the king and the bishops of England' by empanelling sworn trustworthy men 'who possess the fullest knowledge of these matters': *Register of Thomas de Brantyngham*, 158, 160.

99. Maureen Jurkowski, 'The Arrest of William Thorpe in Shrewsbury and the Anti-Lollard Statute of 1406', *Historical Research*, 75 (2002), 273–95; Forrest, *Detection of Heresy*, 41, 44–46.

100. *Register of Henry Chichele*, 3.18; *Kentish Visitations*, 17, 22, 40, 174, 232; Forrest, *Detection of Heresy*, 47–52, 207–30.

101. Lambeth Palace Library, Register of Thomas Arundel, vol. ii, fo. 12v.

102. *Register of Nicholas Bubwith*, 1.284; *Visitations in the Diocese of Lincoln*, 1.113.

103. Worcester Record Office, Register of Philip Morgan, p. 87.

104. Norfolk Record Office, MS DN Reg/5/9, fo. 108v.

105. *Episcopal Court Book for the Diocese of Lincoln*, 33.

Chapter Fourteen: The Church Built on Trust

1. Trustworthiness was more fundamental in the *cycle* of information than either memory or writing, the two things that have been most studied in relation to medieval forms of practical knowledge: Clanchy, *From Memory to Written Record*, 295–328; Richard Britnell (ed.), *Pragmatic Literacy: East and West, 1200–1330* (Woodbridge: Boydell, 1997); Arnved Nedkvitne, *The Social Consequences of Literacy in Medieval Scandinavia* (Turnhout: Brepols, 2004); Mary Carruthers, *The Book of Memory: A Study of Memory in Medieval Culture* (Cambridge: Cambridge University Press, 1990). Although all governing institutions came to rely upon writing, and upon trust in writing, to a much greater extent from the thirteenth century onwards, and although memory was important to testimony, behind every document there was an inquest or a group of witnesses in whose relationship to power trustworthiness was paramount. Trusting was thereby an inherent element in the testimony that relied on memory and was recorded in writing: it was not a separate variable, but rather the fundamental dynamo within the other two, and the end to which they strove. See essays in Schulte, Mostert, and van Renswoude (eds.), *Strategies of Writing*, for discussion of trust in writing.

2. British Library, MS Royal 11 A XIV, fos. 149–50 (William Durandus, *Repertorium*); *Concilia magnae Britanniae et Hiberniae*, ed. David Wilkins, 4 vols. (London, 1737), 3.72 (Constitutions of York, 1367); *Councils and Synods*, 2.73–74 (Constitutions of Salisbury, 1217–19, c. 41), 113 (Constitutions of Oxford, 1222, c. 25).

3. Ian Forrest, 'The Archive of the Official of Stow and the "Machinery" of Church Government in the Late-Thirteenth Century', *Historical Research*, 84 (2011); Forrest and Whittick, 'Thirteenth-Century Visitation Records'.

4. Barnes, *Elements of Social Theory*, 200, 204.

5. There is no consensus on the much-studied Domesday Book, but the case for its utility over its symbolism has not been proven: David Roffe, 'Domesday Now', *Anglo-Norman Studies* 28 (2006), 168–87; Raban, *Second Domesday?*

6. See, for example, the case of Monmouth in 1397, in Hereford Cathedral Archives, 1779, fos. 6r–v, whose business could not be contained within the space and time allocated to it, spilling into the margins and requiring an additional entry headed 'item Monemuth' following the business of nearby Duxton.

7. Forrest and Whittick, 'Thirteenth-Century Visitation Records'.

8. *Register of William Melton*, 4.35–36, 42–43, 63–65.

9. Karl Marx, *Selected Writings*, ed. David McLellan, 2nd ed. (Oxford: Oxford University Press, 2000), 37.

10. *Register of John de Trillek*, 39; the need for technical knowledge and precise adherence to rules figured as part of Weber's ideal type of bureaucratic administration, particularly associated with officials appointed by superior powers: Max Weber, 'Bureaucracy', in Hans H. Gerth and C. Wright Mills (eds.), *From Max Weber: Essays in Sociology* (London: Routledge, 1991), 196–244, at 201.

11. *Register of Walter Reynolds*, 4–5, 9, 32–33. Gambetta, 'Can We Trust Trust?', 218–19, argues that trust always implies a degree of ignorance and the potential for being deceived or disappointed.

12. Justice, *Writing and Rebellion*, 185.

13. Luhmann, *Trust and Power*, 26, 88; the instrumental rationality on display here is consonant with the ends-means reasoning described by d'Avray, *Rationalities in History*, 59–65 and passim; d'Avray argues that institutions frequently work to a hierarchy of values in which the overt value rationality (in this case the value placed upon trust) can seem to be contradicted by instrumental reasoning; yet if one attends to the ends that the instrumental actions are serving, a higher set of values can be discerned. In this case the 'ends' served by lip service to trustworthy testimony were the dignity of the clerical estate and the smooth functioning of church administration.

14. North, *Institutions*, 29; see also Good, 'Individuals, Interpersonal Relations and Trust', 42.

15. Luhmann, *Trust and Power*, 37.

16. Kenneth Arrow, 'Gifts and Exchanges', in Edmund S. Phelps (ed.), *Morality, Altruism and Economic Theory* (New York: Russell Sage Foundation, 1975), 24; Dasgupta, 'Trust as a Commodity', 64; John Dunn, 'Trust and Political Agency', in Gambetta (ed.), *Trust*, 73; Oliver Williamson, 'The New Institutional Economics: Taking Stock, Looking Ahead', *Journal of Economic Literature*, 38 (2000); idem, 'Calculativeness, Trust, and Economic Organization'.

17. Luhmann, *Trust and Power*, 20, 24–30.

18. Scott, *Art of Not Being Governed*; James C. Scott, *Seeing Like a State: How Certain Schemes to Improve the Human Condition Have Failed* (New Haven, Conn.: Yale University Press, 1998), 64–73; John Law, 'Power/Knowledge and the Dissolution of the Sociology of Knowledge' in Law (ed.), *Power, Action and Belief: A New Sociology of Knowledge?* (London: Routledge, 1986), 10.

19. On episcopal registers, see David M. Smith, *Guide to the Bishops' Registers of England and Wales: A Survey from the Middle Ages to the Abolition of Episcopacy in 1646* (London: Royal Historical Society, 1981), introduction; on visitation records, see Noël

Coulet, *Les visites pastorales* (Turnhout: Brepols, 1977), and Ian Forrest, 'The Survival of Medieval Visitation Records', *Archives*, 37 (2013).

20. On cartularies, see Adam J. Kosto and Anders Winroth (eds.), *Charters, Cartularies, and Archives: The Preservation and Transmission of Documents in the Medieval West* (Toronto: PIMS, 2002); Michael Spence, 'Cartularies of Fountains Abbey: Archival Systems and Practices', *Cîteaux*, 61 (2010), 185–205. On episcopal *acta*, see Christopher N. L. Brooke, 'English Episcopal *acta* of the Twelfth and Thirteenth Centuries', in Michael J. Franklin and Christopher Harper-Bill (eds.), *Medieval Ecclesiastical Studies in Honour of Dorothy M. Owen* (Woodbridge: Boydell, 1995), 41–56.

21. Jean Scammell, 'The Rural Chapter in England from the Eleventh to the Fourteenth Century', *English Historical Review*, 86 (1971), 1–21; Forrest, 'Archive of the Official of Stow'; Wunderli, 'Pre-Reformation London Summoners', 210–11; Forrest, 'The Summoner'.

22. For example, a certification sent to the archbishop of York by the archdeacon of Richmond in 1312: *Register of William Greenfield*, 4.217.

23. David M. Smith, 'Thomas Cantilupe's Register: The Administration of the Diocese of Hereford 1275–1282', in Meryl Jancy (ed.), *St Thomas Cantilupe Bishop of Hereford: Essays in his Honour* (Hereford: Hereford Cathedral, 1982), 85–86; Clanchy, *From Memory to Written Record*, 156–73. Lincolnshire Archives, Dean and Chapter, A/1/14, pp. 71–108, is the correspondence of Richard Stretton, who was official to the archdeacon of Stow between 1301 and 1304, which must have been deposited by him amongst the papers of the dean and chapter.

24. 'The fully developed bureaucratic mechanism compares with other organizations exactly as does the machine with the non-mechanical modes of production': Weber, 'Bureaucracy', 214.

25. Mary Douglas, *How Institutions Think* (Syracuse, N.Y.: Syracuse University Press, 1986), 32; Barnes, *Elements of Social Theory*, 193–222. See pp. 97–98 for discussion of the new institutional history, exemplified in Sabapathy's work on accountability.

26. D'Avray, *Medieval Religious Rationalities*, 154; for further discussion, see Forrest, 'Continuity and Change in the Institutional Church'.

27. Jane Gibbs and Marion Lang, *Bishops and Reform* (London: Oxford University Press, 1934), 143; Hamilton Thompson, *English Parish Clergy*, 70; Cheney, *English Bishops' Chanceries*, 3; Margaret Bowker, *The Secular Clergy in the Diocese of Lincoln* (Cambridge: Cambridge University Press, 1968), 22; Swanson, *Church and Society*, 1–8; Sophie Menache, *The Vox Dei: Communication in the Middle Ages* (Oxford: Oxford University Press, 1990), 51–71; Andrew Brown, *Church and Society in England, 1000–1500* (Basingstoke: Palgrave Macmillan, 2003), 50; Magdalena Satora, 'The Social Reception of the Templar Trial in Early Fourteenth-Century France', in Jochen Burgtorf, Paul F. Crawford, and Helen J. Nicholson (eds.), *The Debate on the Trial of the Templars* (Farnham: Ashgate, 2010), 162–63, 168.

28. The best survey of the multi-institutional situation in England is Swanson, *Church and Society*, 16–26.

29. Lambert, 'Spiritual Protection and Secular Power'.

30. *Register of John le Romeyn*, 2.72; *Register of William Greenfield*, 1.178, 1.261–62; *Memorials of the Church of SS. Peter and Wilfrid, Ripon*, ed. Joseph Thomas Fowler, 4 vols., Surtees Society, 78 (1882–1908), 2.53; York, Borthwick Institute, Register 11, fos. 35r, 74r, and Register 19, fos. 149r–v.

31. *Register of Walter de Stapeldon*, 389.

32. *Register of Adam of Orleton, Hereford*, 149–50, 158–61, 181–82, 318–19, 348–49. The case was especially sensitive because in the end the income of Shinfield had to be confiscated by the bishop of Salisbury.

33. Lincolnshire Archives, REG/17, fos. 168v-169r.

34. Lichfield Record Office, B/A/1/11, fos. 87v-88r, emphasis added.

35. Clifford Geertz, *Local Knowledge: Further Essays in Interpretative Anthropology*, 2nd ed. (New York: Basic Books, 1983), 167.

36. Francesco Migliorino, *Fama e infamia: problemi della società medievale nel pensiero giuridico nei secoli XII e XIII* (Catania: Editrice Giannotta, 1985), 73-83; Forrest, *Detection of Heresy*, 197-99; Thomas Kuehn, '*Fama* as Legal Status in Renaissance Florence', in Fenster and Smail (eds.), *Fama*, argues for a distinction between social and legal *fama*, but nonetheless provides examples of their mutual porosity.

37. Clanchy, *From Memory to Written Record*, 255-80; Colin Richmond, 'Hand and Mouth: Information Gathering and Use in England in the Later Middle Ages', *Journal of Historical Sociology*, 1 (1988), 233-52.

38. *Councils and Synods*, 2.593-94.

39. For an introductory account of these problems, see Inés Macho-Stadler and J. David Pérez-Castrillo, *An Introduction to the Economics of Information: Incentives and Contracts* (Oxford: Oxford University Press, 1997), 9-12; in *Foundations of Social Theory*, 100, James Coleman usefully parallels the economists' conception of moral hazard in describing 'actions that increase one's vulnerability to another whose behavior is not under one's control'.

40. Christopher R. Cheney, 'Legislation of the Medieval English Church', *English Historical Review*, 50 (1935); Norman Tanner and Sethina Watson, 'The Least of the Laity: The Minimum Requirements for a Medieval Christian', *Journal of Medieval History*, 32 (2006).

41. The preeminent (and still-unpublished) contribution to this field is Leonard E. Boyle, 'A Study of the Works Attributed to William of Pagula with Special Reference to the *Oculus Sacerdotis* and *Summa Summarum*' (D.Phil. thesis, University of Oxford, 1956). Some of Boyle's ideas were developed in the papers collected as *Pastoral Care, Clerical Education and Canon Law* (London: Varorium, 1981). On the Latin text tradition, see Joseph Goering and Daniel S. Talyor, 'The *Summulae* of Bishops Walter de Cantilupe (1240) and Peter Quinel (1287)', *Speculum*, 67 (1992), 576-94. On the incipient English text tradition of the fourteenth century, see Moira Fitzgibbons, 'Deceptive Simplicity: Gaytryge's Translation of Archbishop Thoresby's *Injunctions*', in Renate Blumenfeld-Kosinski, Duncan Robertson, and Nancy Bradley Warren (eds.), *The Vernacular Spirit: Essays on Medieval Religious Literature* (New York: Palgrave, 2002), 39-58.

42. Forrest, 'English Provincial Constitutions and Inquisition into Lollardy'.

43. 'Register of the Archdeaconry of Richmond, 1442-1477', 88-89.

44. See, for example, *Councils and Synods*, 2.782-83, 850-51; *Register of John de Trillek*, 179; *Registers of Roger Martival*, 2.598-99.

45. *Register of John de Drokensford*, 98.

46. *Register of Ralph of Shrewsbury*, 667.

47. *Councils and Synods*, 2.466-67.

48. *EEA* 7: *Hereford 1079-1234*, 30.

49. Sometimes, but only rarely, the witnesses to charters had been described as trustworthy men: *EEA* 23: *Chichester 1254-1305*, 288 (1291); Canterbury Cathedral Archives, DCc/ChAnt/C/1047 (1297), and DCc/ChAnt/M/16 (1322).

50. *Register of Thomas of Corbridge*, 1.287-88; *Register of William Wykeham*, 2.189. See also Hampshire Record Office, 21M65/B/1/1; Canterbury Cathedral Archives, DCc/VR/5.

51. *Register of Ralph of Shrewsbury*, 96-97; their social profile was examined in detail at p. 151.

52. Green, *Verdict According to Conscience*, 10.

53. *Register of William Wickwane*, 77–78; *Register of John le Romeyn*, 1.298; TNA, SC 1/8/95 is a letter from the dean and chapter of Rouen about a dispute over provision of a chaplain for Blyth parish church, ca. 1279.

54. This is analogous to the argument made in Shapin, *Social History of Truth*, xxv (with explication at 65–125), with regard to the establishment of truth in early modern England: scientific knowledge, he argues, was accepted as factual because it was generated and transmitted through gentlemanly learned societies, not because there were any agreed standards of proof: 'knowledge of what the world is like draws on knowledge about other people'.

55. *Register of Thomas Spofford*, 146–47.

56. *Register of William Wickwane*, 50.

57. Moore, 'Proceedings of the Ecclesiastical Courts', 629–30, 649.

58. *Register of Walter Giffard, York*, 77, 79–81, 111.

59. *Register of William Melton*, 2.92.

60. On information, see Peter Burke, *A Social History of Knowledge from Gutenberg to Diderot* (Cambridge: Polity Press, 2000); on attributed trust, see Chapter 5.

61. 'The structure of communication that confronts potential trustors may have an important effect on the expansion *and contraction* of trust': Coleman, *Foundations of Social Theory*, 189, emphasis added; Seabright, *Company of Strangers*, 194; Good, 'Individuals, Interpersonal Relations and Trust', 32.

62. Wolfgang Iser, *Prospecting: From Reader Response to Literary Anthropology* (Baltimore: Johns Hopkins University Press, 1989), 3–30; Hans Robert Jauss, *Literaturgeschichte als Provokation* (Frankfurt: Suhrkamp, 1970), 144–207. The extent to which this approach has influenced medieval studies (Jauss was himself a medievalist) is shown by the opening of Marion Turner's invaluable *Handbook of Middle English Studies* (Oxford: Wiley-Blackwell, 2013), 1: 'it is readers, however unsatisfactory they might be, who make meaning'; see also Elisabeth Salter, *Popular Reading in English c. 1400-1600* (Manchester: Manchester University Press, 2012), 79: 'A reader is constantly . . . bringing his or her own meanings to a piece of text'.

63. Alan Bowman and Greg Woolf, 'Introduction', in Bowman and Woolf (eds.), *Literacy and Power in the Ancient World* (Cambridge: Cambridge University Press, 1994), 7.

64. Ronald Coase, 'The Nature of the Firm', *Economica*, 4 (1937), 386–405; Oliver Williamson, *The Economic Institutions of Capitalism: Firms, Markets, Relational Contracting* (New York: Free Press, 1985).

65. Law, 'Power/Knowledge', 15. Even where information has been naïvely thought measurable, its creation at the point of reception as well as transmission is almost always assumed: for instance, Fritz Machlup, *Knowledge. Its Creation, Distribution, and Economic Significance, I: Knowledge and Knowledge Production* (Princeton, N.J.: Princeton University Press, 1980), 190–91.

66. Wood, *Memory of the People*, 94–111; making a similar observation on the reading experience, Salter, *Popular Reading in English*, 53, characterizes the reader's imagination as 'operating at the interface between the various elements of the physical page and the stored knowledge and experience of his or her imagination'. The creation of 'unintended receptions and contradictory appropriations' of official communication are wonderfully illuminated for a more literate and urban culture in Filippo de Vivo, *Information and Communication in Venice: Rethinking Early Modern Politics* (Oxford: Oxford University Press, 2007), 238–48.

67. Polanyi, *Personal Knowledge*, 208–9.

68. Shapin, *Social History of Truth*, 25.

69. Individuals, Karl Deutsch wrote, generate meaning not just from received messages, but from the 'continued stream of information about [their] own peculiar responses to the present': *Nationalism and Social Communication: An Inquiry into the Foundations of Nationality*, 2nd ed. (Cambridge, Mass.: Harvard University Press, 1966), 117.

70. Barnes, *Elements of Social Theory*, 199–200.

Conclusion

1. Shapin, *Social History of Truth*, 25.
2. Law, 'Power/Knowledge', 17.
3. Ogilvie, 'Use and Abuse of Trust'.
4. D'Avray, *Rationalities in History*, 91.

BIBLIOGRAPHY

ABBREVIATIONS

BIHR	*Bulletin of the Institute of Historical Research*
CCCM	Corpus Christianorum Continuatio Mediaevalis
CCSL	Corpus Christianorum Series Latina
CSEL	Corpus Scriptorum Ecclesiasticorum Latinorum
C&Y	Canterbury and York Society
EEA	*English Episcopal Acta*
EETS	Early English Text Society
Glos. ord.	Glossa ordinaria to the *Decretum* and *Decretals*
HMSO	His Majesty's Stationary Office
PL	*Patrologiae cursus completus, series latina,* ed. Jacques-Paul Migne, 221 vols. (Paris, 1844–64)
TNA	The National Archives, Kew
UNMSC	University of Nottingham Manuscripts and Special Collections

MANUSCRIPTS AND ARCHIVES

Aylesbury

CENTRE FOR BUCKINGHAMSHIRE STUDIES
D/BASM/15/8–9 (court rolls of Chalfont St Peter)

Cambridge

CAMBRIDGESHIRE ARCHIVES
R52/12/1/3 (court rolls of Kingston)

CAMBRIDGE UNIVERSITY LIBRARY
EDR D/2/1 (Ely consistory court 1372–81)
EDR G/1/1 (registers of Bishops Montacute and De Lisle)
EDR G/1/2 (register of Bishop Arundel)
EDR G/1/3 (register of Bishop Fordham)
EDR G/1/4 (register of Bishop Bourgchier)
EDR G/1/5 (register of Bishop Grey)

KING'S COLLEGE ARCHIVES
STP/3–6 (court rolls of Stour Provost)
STP/83 (rental of Stour Provost)

Canterbury

CANTERBURY CATHEDRAL ARCHIVES
DCc/ChAnt (Chartae antiquae)
DCc/ChChLet (Christ Church Letters)

DCc/VR/1–19 (visitation rolls, 1277–1328)
SVSB (*sede vacante* scrap books)
X.1.1 (consistory court act book, 1449–57)
X.10.1 (consistory court act book, 1410–21)
Y.1.5 (consistory court act book, 1454–57)
Z.3.1 (visitation book, 1499)
Z.3.2 (visitation book, 1501–8)

Chippenham

WILTSHIRE AND SWINDON RECORD OFFICE

MS D1 2/9 (register of Bishop Nevill)

Colchester

ESSEX RECORD OFFICE

D/DL M108 (court roll of Dent)

Dorchester

DORSET HISTORY CENTRE

D/BKL/CK/1/1–3 (court rolls of Shapwick)
D/BKL/CK/3/1 (account roll for Shapwick)
D/FAN court rolls 1–20 Richard II (court rolls of Gillingham)
Tarrant Gunville Manor D 151/1, 2, 9 (court rolls of Tarrant Gunville)

Durham

DURHAM CATHEDRAL ARCHIVES

2.2.Arch.Dunelm.17n (visitation roll)
Dean and Chapter, 1.9.Pont.9 (visitation roll)

Exeter

EXETER CATHEDRAL

MS 2857 (visitation book, 1381)
MS 3673 (visitation book, 1301–7)

Hereford

HEREFORD CATHEDRAL ARCHIVES

1050a (visitation roll, 1284)
1462 (visitation mandate, 1536)
1779 (visitation book, 1397)

Kew

THE NATIONAL ARCHIVES

C 1/16/181 (Chancery petition, Gillingham)

C 143/287/28 (inquisition *ad quod dampnum*, 1347, Strubby)
C 143/350/5 (inquisition *ad quod dampnum*, 1363, Blandford Forum)
C 241/23/20 (certificate of Statute Merchant, 1292, Blyth)
DL 29/682/11045, 11049 (court rolls of Shapwick)
DL 30/57/704 (court rolls of Blandford Forum)
DL 30/89/1202 (court rolls of Strubby)
E 179/135/10, 11, 15, 25 (lay subsidy rolls, Lincolnshire)
E 179/155/31(lay subsidy roll, Northamptonshire)
E 179/169/6 (lay subsidy roll, Somerset)
E 210/4258 (charter, North Petherton)
SC 2/197/97 (court rolls of Culmington)
SC 12/14/21 (court rolls of Culmington)

Lichfield

LICHFIELD RECORD OFFICE

B/A/1/2 (register of Bishop Northburgh)
B/A/1/3 (register of Bishop Northburgh)
B/A/1/6 (register of Bishop Scrope)
B/A/1/7 (register of Bishop Burghill)
B/A/1/9 (register of Bishop Heyworth)
B/A/1/11 (register of Bishop Boulers)
B/A/1/12 (register of Bishop Hales)
B/C/1/1 (consistory court act book, 1464–71)
D/30/2/1/2 (chapter act book)
D/30/9/3/1 (visitation book, 1460s)
D/30/9/3/2/2 (visitation roll, 1288)
D/30/9/3/2/3 (visitation roll, 1292)
D/30/9/3/2/8 (visitation roll, 1316)
D/30/9/3/2/11 (visitation roll, 1347)

Lincoln

LINCOLNSHIRE ARCHIVES

Dean and Chapter, A/1/14 (visitations and miscellaneous *acta*, 1299–1304)
Dean and Chapter, Dij/62/3/23 (visitations, 1289)
Dean and Chapter, Dij/64/2/18 (visitation, 1302)
MS Vj/3 (visitation book, 1469–70)
REG/2 (register of Bishop Dalderby)
REG/3 (register of Bishop Dalderby)
REG/6 (register of Bishop Bek)
REG/7 (register of Bishop Bek)
REG/8 (register of Bishop Gynwell)
REG/12 (register of Bishop Buckingham)
REG/13 (register of Bishop Beaufort)
REG/17 (register of Bishop Gray)
REG/18 (register of Bishop Alnwick)
REG/20 (register of Bishop Chedworth)

London

THE BRITISH LIBRARY

MS Add. 29794 (survey of Wingham)
MS Burney 356 (contains General Sentence of Excommunication)
MS Harley 2383 (contains General Sentence of Excommunication)
MS Harley 4011 (*miscellanea*)
MS Royal 11 A XIV (contains William Durandus, *Reportorium*)

LAMBETH PALACE LIBRARY

MS 172 (contains General Sentence of Excommunication)
Register of Thomas Arundel

LONDON METROPOLITAN ARCHIVES

DL/C/0205–0206 (consistory court deposition books, 1467–76 and 1509–16)
DL/C/B/043/MS09064/001–006 (commissary court act books, 1470–96)

Northallerton

NORTH YORKSHIRE RECORD OFFICE

ZBA/17/2/3 (court roll for Fitzhugh estate)
ZDX (court rolls of Sedbergh)
ZJX/3/2/69 (bailiffs' and collectors' account rolls of Fitzhugh estate)
ZJX/3/2/75 (reeves' account roll of Fitzhugh estate)
ZJX/3/2/91 (receiver's account roll of Fitzhugh estate)
ZJX/3/2/93 (receiver's account roll of Fitzhugh estate)
ZJX/3/2/95 (collector's account roll for Dent)
ZJX/3/10/1 (court rolls of Belney, Southwick)

Northampton

NORTHAMPTONSHIRE RECORD OFFICE

F (M) 2388 (account roll of Peterborough Abbey)
F (M) 2389 (account roll of Peterborough Abbey)

Norwich

NORFOLK RECORD OFFICE

DCN/67/1–11 ('inquisitions', 1416–37)
DCN/85/2–3 (archidiaconal *acta*, 1301)
MS DN Reg/5/9 (register of Bishop Alnwick)

Nottingham

UNIVERSITY OF NOTTINGHAM MANUSCRIPTS
AND SPECIAL COLLECTIONS

Cl/M/85 (rental for Hodsock and Oldcotes, Blyth)
Mi 5/164/1 and 3 (hundred court rolls of Knowlton)
Mi 5/164/37/2 (manor and hundred court rolls of Woodlands)
Mi 6/170/2 and 4 (reeve's account roll of Woodlands)
Mi 6/174/1 (rental for Woodlands)

Mi 6/174/4 and 6 (hundred court rolls of Upwimborne)
Mi M/150–151 (reeve's account roll of Woodlands)

Oxford

BODLEIAN LIBRARY

MS Douce 60 (contains General Sentence of Excommunication)
MS eMus.180 (sermons)
Norfolk Rolls 17 (visitation roll, 1331)

Taunton

SOMERSET HERITAGE CENTRE

A/AHT/172/2–4 (court rolls of Newton Plecy)
DD/H1/115 (Newton Plecy deed)
DD/S/WH/64 (Newton Plecy deed)
DD/WY/B3a/2, 17, 21, 76 (Beercrocombe deeds)

Wimborne St Giles

ST GILES HOUSE, SHAFTESBURY ARCHIVES

T219, T239–242 (Upwimborne deeds)
M3–M5 (court rolls of Didlington, Chalbury)
M63–71 (manor and hundred court rolls of Upwimborne)

Winchester

HAMPSHIRE RECORD OFFICE

11M59/B1/57–75 (Winchester pipe rolls)
21M65/B/1/1 (visitation book, 1517)
21M65/B/1/2 (visitation book, 1520)
4M53/6, 4M53A1–5 (Boarhunt Herberd deeds)
5M50/19 and 22 (Southwick deeds)
5M50/23 (sheriff's receipt for Boarhunt Herberd)
5M50/26 (Southwick deed)
5M50/43–46 (bailiff's account roll of Southwick Priory)
5M50/81, 83 (rentals for Southwick)
5M50/84 (Ulvedale rental, Southwick)

Worcester

WORCESTER RECORD OFFICE

BA 2636/11 43700 (Hartlebury Court Book)
Register of Bishop Morgan

York

BORTHWICK INSTITUTE

CP E and F (archbishop's consistory court Cause Papers)
MD 26 (visitation roll, ca. 1405)

Register 10 (register of Archbishop Zouche)
Register 11 (register of Archbishop Thoresby)
Register 12 (register of Archbishop A. Neville)
Register 14 (register of Archbishop Arundel)
Register 15 (register of Archbishop Waldby)
Register 16 (register of Archbishop Scrope)
Register 18 (register of Archbishop Bowet)
Register 19 (register of Archbishop Kempe)
Register 20 (register of Archbishop W. Booth)
Register 21 (register of Archbishop G. Neville)
Register 22 (register of Archbishop L. Booth)
Register 23 (register of Archbishop Rotherham)

PRINTED PRIMARY SOURCES

Note on the citation of printed bishops' registers: All printed registers of English bishops are listed as *Register of . . .* and arranged alphabetically by the first name of the bishop. Where the same individual had more than one episcopate, the name of the diocese is also given.

Abelard, Peter, *Sic et non: A Critical Edition*, ed. Blanche B. Boyer and Richard McKeon (Chicago: University of Chicago Press, 1976).

'Accounts for the Rectory of Wainfleet St Mary for the Year 2 February 1475 to 1 February 1476', ed. Dorothy M. Owen, *Lincolnshire History and Archaeology*, 30 (1995).

Acta Stephani Langton Cantuariensis Archiepiscopi A.D. 1207-1228, ed. Kathleen Major, C&Y 50 (1950).

Actes des princes-évêques de Liège Hugues de Pierrepont 1200-1229, ed. Edouard Poncelet (Brussels: Palais des Académies, 1941).

Acton, John, *Constitutiones legatinae*, in *Provinciale seu constitutiones Angliae* (Oxford: Hall, 1679), pt. 2.

Advance Contracts for the Sale of Wool c. 1200—c. 1327, ed. Adrian Bell, Chris Brooks, and Paul Dryburgh, List and Index Society, 315 (Kew: TNA, 2006).

Albertus Magnus, *Commentarii in secundum librum Sententiarum*, ed. Auguste Borgnet (Paris: Ludovicum Vivès, 1893).

Alexandri III pontificis Romani epistolae et privilegia, PL 200.

Annales monastici, ed. Henry Richard Luard, 5 vols. (London: Longman, 1864-69).

Anon., *Explanatio in epistolam Pauli ad Titum*, PL 100.

An Anthology of Chancery English, ed. Jane L. Fisher, John H. Fisher, and Malcolm Richardson (Knoxville: University of Tennessee Press, 1984).

Aquinas, Thomas, *Summa theologiae*, ed. Thomas Gilby et al., 60 vols. (London: Blackfriars, 1964-76).

Ashby, George, *George Ashby's Poems*, ed. M. Bateson, EETS extra series 76 (1899; repr., 1965).

Augustine of Hippo, *Confessionum*, PL 32.

———, *De civitate dei contra paganos*, PL 41.

———, *De fide et symbolo*, ed. Joseph Zycha, CSEL 41 (Vindobonae: Tempsky, 1900); trans. Michael G. Campbell in *The Works of Saint Augustine: On Christian Belief*, ed. Boniface Ramsey.

————, *De fide rerum invisibilium*, ed. M.P.J. van den Hout, CCSL 46 (Turnhout: Brepols, 1969), 1–19; trans. Michael G. Campbell in *The Works of Saint Augustine: On Christian Belief*, ed. Boniface Ramsey.

————, *De trinitate*, ed. William John Mountain, 2 vols., CCSL 50, 50A (Turnhout: Brepols, 1968).

————, *De vera religione*, PL 34.

————, *Enchiridion*, ed. M.P.J. van den Hout, CCSL 46 (Turnhout: Brepols, 1969); trans. Bruce Harbert in *The Works of Saint Augustine: On Christian Belief*, ed. Boniface Ramsey.

————, *Epistulae I–LV*, ed. Klaus D. Daur, CCSL 31 (Turnhout: Brepols, 2004), *Epistulae LVI–C*, ed. Klaus D. Daur, CCSL 31A (Turnhout: Brepols, 2005), *Epistulae CI–CXXXIX*, ed. Klaus D. Daur, CCSL 31B (Turnhout: Brepols, 2009), trans. Robert B. Eno and Wilfrid Parsons, *Letters*, 6 vols. (Washington: Catholic University of America Press, 1951–89).

————, *Retractionum libri duo*, PL 32.

————, *Sermones*, PL 38.

————, *The Works of Saint Augustine: On Christian Belief*, ed. Boniface Ramsey (New York: New City Press, 2005).

Balbus, Joannes, *Catholicon* (Mainz, 1460: repr., Farnborough: Gregg International, 1971).

Baldwin of Ford, *De commendatione fidei*, ed. David N. Bell, CCCM 99 (Turnhout: Brepols, 1991).

Bartholomaeus Exoniensis, *Contra fatalitatis errorem*, ed. David N. Bell, CCCM 157 (Turnhout: Brepols, 1996).

Bede, *Super acta apostolorum expositio*, PL 92.

Bernard of Clairvaux, *De consideratione*, in Jean Leclercq et al. (eds.), *Sancti Bernardi opera*, 8 vols. (Rome: Editiones Cisterciensis, 1957–77).

Bernardi Papiensis summa decretalium, ed. E.A.T. Laspeyres (Regensburg, 1860).

Biblia Latina cum glossa ordinaria: Facsimile Reprint of the Editio Princeps Adolph Rusch of Strasburg 1480/81, 4 vols. (Turnhout: Brepols, 1992).

Bonaventure, *Opera Omnia*, ed. Collegii a S. Bonaventura (Florence: Quaracchi, 1897).

The Book of Sainte Foy, trans. Pamela Sheingorn and Robert L. A. Clark (Philadelphia: University of Pennsylvania Press, 1995).

Borough Customs, ed. Mary Bateson, 2 vols., Selden Society, 18 and 21 (1904–6).

Bracton on the Laws and Customs of England, trans. Samuel E. Thorne, 4 vols. (Cambridge, Mass.: Belknap, 1968–77).

Calendar of Close Rolls, Edward II: Volume 2, 1313–18, ed. Henry Churchill Maxwell Lyte (London: HMSO, 1893).

Calendar of Close Rolls, Henry III: Volume 5, 1242–1247, ed. Henry Churchill Maxwell Lyte (London: HMSO, 1916).

Calendar of Close Rolls, Henry III: Volume 6, 1247–1251, ed. Henry Churchill Maxwell Lyte (London: HMSO, 1922).

Calendar of Close Rolls, Henry III: Volume 7, 1251–3, ed. Alfred Edward Stamp (London: HMSO, 1927).

Calendar of the Fine Rolls of the Reign of Henry III 1216–1234, ed. Paul Dryburgh and Beth Hartland, 3 vols. (Woodbridge: Boydell, 2007–9).

Calendar of Inquisitions Post Mortem, VIII: *10–20 Edward III*, ed. J.E.E.S. Sharp, E. G. Atkinson, and J. J. O'Reilly (London: HMSO, 1913).

Calendar of Inquisitions Post Mortem, XVII: *15–23 Richard II*, ed. Michael Charles Burdett Dawes et al. (London: HMSO, 1988).

Calendar of Inquisitions Post Mortem, XVIII, *1–6 Henry IV (1399–1405),* ed. J. L. Kirby (London: HMSO, 1987).

Calendar of Inquisitions Post Mortem, XIX: *7–14 Henry IV,* ed. J. L. Kirby (London: HMSO, 1992).

Calendar of Patent Rolls 1216–1225, ed. Henry Churchill Maxwell Lyte (London: HMSO, 1901).

The Canterbury Tales: Fifteenth-Century Continuations and Additions, ed. John M. Bowers (Kalamazoo, Mich.: Western Michigan University, 1992).

Carte Nativorum: A Peterborough Abbey Cartulary of the Fourteenth Century, ed. Christopher N. L. Brooke and Michael M. Postan, Northamptonshire Record Society, 20 (1960).

The Cartularies of Southwick Priory, ed. Katharine A. Hanna, Hampshire Record Series, 9–10 (1988–89).

The Cartulary of Blyth Priory, ed. Reginald Thomas Timson (London: HMSO, 1973).

Cassiodorus, *Historia ecclesiastica tripartita,* PL 69.

The Certificate of Musters for Buckinghamshire in 1522, ed. Arthur Charles Chibnall (London: HMSO, 1973).

The Chastising of God's Children and the Treatise of Perfection of the Sons of God, ed. Joyce Bazire and Eric Colledge (Oxford: Basil Blackwell, 1957).

Chaucer, Geoffrey, *The Riverside Chaucer,* ed. Larry D. Benson (Oxford: Oxford University Press, 1988).

Chronicon Petroburgense, ed. Thomas Stapleton, Camden Society, 47 (1849).

Ciceronis, M. Tulli, *De officiis,* ed. Michael Winterbottom (Oxford: Clarendon, 1994).

Concilia magnae Britanniae et Hiberniae, ed. David Wilkins, 4 vols. (London, 1737).

Constitutiones Concilii quarti Lateranensis una cum Commentariis glossatorum, ed. Antonio García y García, Monumenta Iuris Canonici Series A: Corpus Glossatorum, 2 (Vatican: Biblioteca Apostolica, 1981).

Corpus iuris civilis, ed. Paul Krüger and Theodor Mommsen, 3 vols. (Berlin: Weidmann, 1906–12).

Councils and Synods with Other Documents Relating to the English Church, II: *A.D. 1205–1313,* ed. F. M. Powicke and Christopher R. Cheney (Oxford: Clarendon, 1964).

The Courts of the Archdeaconry of Buckingham 1483–1523, ed. E. M. Elvey, Buckinghamshire Record Society, 19 (1975).

Decrees of the Ecumenical Councils, ed. Norman P. Tanner, 2 vols. (Washington, D.C.: Georgetown University Press, 1990).

[*Decretals*] of Gregory IX, in *Corpus iuris canonici,* ed. Emil Friedberg and Aemilius Ludwig Richter, 2 vols. (Lipsiae: Tauchnitz, 1879–81), vol. 2.

[*Decretum*] of Gratian, in *Corpus iuris canonici,* ed. Emil Friedberg and Aemilius Ludwig Richter, 2 vols. (Lipsiae: Tauchnitz, 1879–81), vol. 1.

Depositions and Other Ecclesiastical Proceedings from the Courts of Durham, ed. James Raine, Surtees Society, 21 (1845).

The Doctrine of the Hert: A Critical Edition with Introduction and Commentary, ed. Christiana Whitehead, Denis Reveney, and Anne Mouron (Exeter: Exeter University Press, 2010).

'Documents Relating to Visitations of the Diocese and Province of York', ed. Alexander Hamilton Thompson, in *Miscellanea,* II, Surtees Society, 127 (1916).

The Domesday of St Paul's of the Year MCCXXII, ed. William H. Hale, Camden Society, first series 69 (1858).

The Earliest Complete English Prose Psalter, ed. K. D. Bülbring, EETS 97 (1891).

The Earliest English Translations of the De Imitatione Christi, ed. John K. Ingram, EETS extra series 63 (1893).

The Early English Carols, ed. Richard Leighton Greene (Oxford: Clarendon, 1935).

Early English Versions of the Gesta Romanorum, ed. Sidney J. H. Herrtage (London: Trübner, 1879).

The Early Records of Medieval Coventry, ed. Peter R. Coss and Trevor John, Records of Social and Economic History, new series 11 (London: Oxford University Press, 1986).

Early Taxation Returns: Taxation of Personal Property in 1332 and Later, ed. Albert Charles Chibnall, Buckinghamshire Record Society, 14 (1966).

The Edington Cartulary, ed. Janet H. Stevenson, Wiltshire Record Society, 42 (1987).

EEA 1: *Lincoln 1067–1185*, ed. David M. Smith (London: Oxford University Press, 1980).

EEA 2: *Canterbury 1162–1190*, ed. Christopher R. Cheney and Bridgett E. A. Jones (London: Oxford University Press, 1986).

EEA 3: *Canterbury 1193–1205*, ed. C. R. Cheney and Eric John (Oxford: Oxford University Press, 1986).

EEA 6: *Norwich 1070–1214*, ed. Christopher Harper-Bill (Oxford: Oxford University Press, 1990).

EEA 7: *Hereford 1079–1234*, ed. Julia Barrow (Oxford: Oxford University Press, 1993).

EEA 9: *Winchester 1205–1238*, ed. Nicholas Vincent (Oxford: Oxford University Press, 1994).

EEA 13: *Worcester 1218–1268*, ed. Philippa M. Hoskin (Oxford: Oxford University Press, 1997).

EEA 21: *Norwich 1215–1243*, ed. Christopher Harper-Bill (Oxford: Oxford University Press, 2000).

EEA 22: *Chichester 1215–1253*, ed. Philippa M. Hoskin (Oxford: Oxford University Press, 2001).

EEA 23: *Chichester 1254–1305*, ed. Philippa M. Hoskin (Oxford: Oxford University Press, 2001).

English Gilds, ed. Joshua Toulmin Smith and Lucy Toulmin Smith, EETS 40 (1870).

An Episcopal Court Book for the Diocese of Lincoln 1514–1520, ed. Margaret Bowker, Lincoln Record Society, 61 (1967).

The Episcopal Registers of the Diocese of St David's 1397–1518, ed. Robert Fraser Isaacson, 2 vols. (London: Honourable Society of Cymmrodorion, 1917).

Epistolae pontificum Romanorum, PL 98.

'Exchequer Lay Subsidies 169/5 Which Is a Tax Roll for Somerset for the First Year of Edward the 3rd', ed. F. H. Dickinson, *Somerset Record Society: Miscellanea*, 3 (1889).

Fasciculus Morum: A Fourteenth-Century Preacher's Handbook, ed. Siegfried Wenzel (University Park: Pennsylvania State University Press, 1989).

Fifteenth-Century English Translations of Alain Chartier's Le Traite de l'Esperance and Le Quadrilogue Invectif, ed. Margaret S. Blayney, EETS 270 (1974).

Gower, John, *The Complete Works of John Gower*, ed. George Campbell Macaulay, 4 vols. (Oxford: Clarendon, 1902).

Grosseteste, Robert, *De Decem Mandatis*, ed. Richard C. Dales and Edward B. King (Oxford: Oxford University Press, 1987).

———, *Templum Dei*, ed. Joseph Goering and F.A.C. Mantello (Toronto: PIMS, 1984).

Hervé de Bourgdieu, *Commentaria in epistolas divi Pauli*, PL 181.

Higden, Ranulph, *Speculum Curatorum (A Mirror for Curates), Book 1: The Commandments*, ed. Eugene Crook and Margaret Jennings (Paris: Peeters, 2012).

Hincmar of Laon, *Hincmari Laudunensis episcopi opuscula et epistolae*, PL 124.

The Holy Bible . . . Made from the Latin Vulgate by John Wycliffe and His Followers, ed. Josiah Forshall and Frederic Madden, 4 vols. (Oxford: Oxford University Press, 1850).

Honorii II pontificis Romani epistolae et privilegia, PL 166.

[Hostiensis] Henrici à Segusio, *Aurea summa* (Venice: Gratiosum Perchacinum, 1605).

Hugh of St Victor, *On the Sacraments of the Christian Faith*, trans. Roy J. Deferrari (Cambridge, Mass.: Medieval Academy of America, 1951).

Inquisitions and Assessments Relating to Feudal Aids with Other Analogous Documents Preserved in the Public Record Office, A.D. 1284–1431, 6 vols. (London: HMSO, 1899–1920).

Jacob's Well: An English Treatise on the Cleansing of Man's Conscience, ed. Arthur Brandeis, EETS 115 (1900).

Jerome, *Commentariorum in epistolam ad Titum*, PL 26.

Johannis Teutonici Apparatus glossarum in Compilationem tertiam, ed. Kenneth Pennington, Monumenta Iuris Canonici Series A: Corpus Glossatorum, 3 (Vatican: Biblioteca Apostolica, 1981).

[John of Freiburg] Joannes Friburgensis, *Summa confessorum* (Augsburg, 1476).

Kentish Visitations of Archbishop William Warham and His Deputies, 1511–12, ed. Kathleen L. Wood-Legh, Kent Records, 24 (1984).

Kingsford's Stonor Letters and Papers, ed. Christine Carpenter (Cambridge: Cambridge University Press, 1996).

Knighton's Chronicle, ed. Geoffrey H. Martin (Oxford: Clarendon, 1995).

Lancelot du Lac: The Non-Cyclic Old French Prose Romance, ed. Elspeth Kennedy, 2 vols. (Oxford: Clarendon, 1980).

Langland, William, *The Vision of Piers Plowman: A Critical Edition of the B-Text*, ed. A.V.C. Schmidt (London: Dent, 1978).

A Late Fifteenth-Century Dominical Sermon Cycle, ed. Stephen Morrison, 2 vols., EETS 337–38 (2012).

The Lay Folks Mass Book, ed. T. F. Simmons, EETS 71 (1879).

The Lay Subsidy of 1334, ed. Robin E. Glasscock, Records of Social and Economic History, new series 2 (Oxford: Oxford University Press, 1975).

The Lay Subsidy Roll for Warwickshire of 6 Edward III (1332), ed. William Fowler Carter (London: Dugdale Society, 1926).

Le registre de l'officialité de l'abbaye de Cerisy, ed. Gustave Dupont (Caen, 1880).

Les statuts de Paris et le synodal de l'ouest (XIIIᵉ), ed. Odette Pontal (Paris: Bibliotèque Nationale, 1971).

The Letters and Charters of Gilbert Foliot, ed. Z. N. Brooke, Adrian Morey, and C.N.L. Brooke (Cambridge: Cambridge University Press, 1967).

Lettres patentes des évêques de France recueillies dans les registres du pape Clément VI (1342–1352), ed. Élie Griffe (Paris: Auguste Picard, 1933).

Llandaff Episcopal Acta 1140–1287, ed. David Crouch (Cardiff: South Wales Record Society).

Lombard, Peter, *Libri quattuor Sententiarum*, PL 192; trans. Giulio Silano, 4 vols. (Toronto: PIMS, 2008).

Lower Ecclesiastical Jurisdiction in Late-Medieval England: The Courts of the Dean and Chapter of Lincoln, 1336–1349 and the Deanery of Wisbech, 1458–1484, ed. Lawrence R. Poos, Records of Social and Economic History, new series 32 (Oxford: Oxford University Press, 2001).

Lydgate, John, *Lydgate's Troy Book, A. D. 1412–20*, pt. 1, ed. Henry Bergen, EETS 97 (1907).

Lyndwood, William, *Provinciale seu constitutiones Angliae* (Oxford: Hall, 1679).

A Macaronic Sermon Collection from Late Medieval England: Oxford, MS Bodley 649, ed. Patrick J. Horner (Toronto: PIMS, 2006).

Magna vita sancti Hugonis: The Life of St Hugh of Lincoln, ed. Decima L. Douie and Hugh Farmer, 2 vols. (London: Nelson, 1961).

The Making of King's Lynn: A Documentary Survey, ed. Dorothy M. Owen, Records of Social and Economic History, new series 9 (London: Oxford University Press, 1984).

Malory, Thomas, *The Works of Sir Thomas Malory*, ed. Eugène Vinaver, 3 vols. (Oxford, 1947).

Mannyng of Brunne, Robert, *Handlyng Synne*, ed. Idelle Sullens (Binghampton: State University of New York, 1983).

Manuale ad usum percelebris ecclesiae Sarisburiensis, ed. A. Jeffries Collins, Henry Bradshaw Society, 91 (1960).

'Manuale incultum visitatorum ecclesiarum: ein bisher unbekannter Visitationstraktat aus dem späten 15. Jahrhundert', ed. Peter Thaddäus Lang, *Zeitschrift für schweizerische Kirchengeschichte*, 79 (1985).

Maurus, Rabanus, *Enarrationum in epistolas beati Pauli*, PL 112.

Memoriale credencium: A Late Middle English Manual of Theology for Lay People, ed. J.H.L. Kengen (Nijmegen: Katholieke Universiteit Nijmegen, 1979).

Memorials of the Church of SS. Peter and Wilfrid, Ripon, ed. Joseph Thomas Fowler, 4 vols., Surtees Society, 78 (1882–1908).

The Metropolitan Visitations of William Courtenay, Archbishop of Canterbury, 1381–1396, ed. Joseph Henry Dahmus (Urbana: University of Illinois Press, 1950).

The Miracles of Simon de Montfort, ed. James Orchard Halliwell-Phillipps, Camden Society, 15 (1840).

Mirk, John, *Instructions for Parish Priests*, ed. Gillis Kristensson (Lund: CWK Gleerup, 1974).

Norwich Consistory Court Depositions, 1499–1512 and 1518–1530, ed. E. D. Stone and B. Cozens-Hardy, Norfolk Record Society, 10 (1938).

The Oak Book of Southampton of c. A.D. 1300, ed. Paul Studer, 3 vols., Southampton Record Society, 10–12 (1910–11).

The Orcherd of Syon, ed. Phyllis Hodgson and Gabriel M. Liegey, EETS 258 (1966).

The Parliament Rolls of Medieval England, ed. C. Given-Wilson et al., Internet version, http://www.sd-editions.com/PROME (Leicester: Scholarly Digital Editions, 2005).

The Paston Letters 1422–1509, ed. James Gardiner, 6 vols. (London: Chatto and Windus, 1904.

Pastors and the Care of Souls in Medieval England, ed. John Shinners and William J. Dohar (Notre Dame, Ind.: University of Notre Dame Press, 1998).

Peter the Venerable, *Adversus nefandam haeresim sive sectam Saracenorum*, PL 189.

———, *De miraculis libri duo*, ed. Dyonisia Bouthillier, CCCM 83 (Turnhout: Brepols, 1987).

———, *The Letters of Peter the Venerable*, ed. Giles Constable, 2 vols. (Cambridge, Mass.: Harvard University Press, 1967).

Petrus Alphonsi, *Ex Judaeo Christiani*, PL 157.

Pillii, Tancredi, Gratiae libri de iudiciorum ordine, ed. Friedrich C. Bergmann (Göttingen: Vandenhoeck & Ruprecht, 1842).

The Pipe Roll of the Bishopric of Winchester 1301-2, ed. Mark Page, Hampshire Record Series, 14 (1996).

The Poll Taxes of 1377, 1379 and 1381, ed. Carolyn C. Fenwick, 3 vols. (Oxford: Oxford University Press, 1998).

Pope Julius, *Epistola Julii ad Antiochenos*, PL 8.

The Proceedings against the Templars in the British Isles, ed. Helen Nicholson, 2 vols. (Farnham: Ashgate, 2011).

'Proceedings of the Ecclesiastical Courts in the Archdeaconry of Leicester, 1516–1535', ed. A. Percival Moore, *Associated Architectural and Archaeological Societies Reports and Papers*, 28 (1905-6).

Protocollum visitationis archidiaconatus Pragensis annis 1379-1382 per Paulum de Jano-wicz archidiaconum Pragensem factae, ed. Ivan Hlaváček and Zdeňka Hledíková (Prague: Academia, 1973).

Proverbia sententiaeque Latinitatis medii aevi, ed. Hans Walther, 5 vols. (Göttingen: Vandenhoeck & Ruprecht, 1963-67).

Pseudo-Isidore, *Decretalium collectio*, PL 130.

Quattuor Sermones, ed. Norman Francis Blake (Heidelberg: Carl Winter, 1975).

Records of the Borough of Leicester, 1103-1327, ed. Mary Bateson (London: Clay and Sons, 1899).

Records of the Borough of Nottingham, I: *King Henry II to King Richard II*, ed. William Henry Stevenson (London: Bernard Quaritch, 1882).

The Records of the City of Norwich, ed. William Hudson and John Cottingham Tingey, 2 vols. (Norwich: Jarrold & Sons, 1906).

The Register Notule Communium *14 of the Diocese of Barcelona (1345-1348)*, ed. J. N. Hillgarth and Giulio Silano (Toronto: PIMS, 1983).

[*Register of Adam of Orleton, Hereford*] *Registrum Ade de Orleton episcopi Herefordensis, A.D. MCCCXVII-MCCCXXVII*, ed. Arthur Thomas Bannister, C&Y 5 (1908).

[*Register of Adam de Orleton, Worcester*] *Calendar of the Register of Adam de Orleton Bishop of Worcester 1327-1333*, ed. Roy Martin Haines, Worcester Historical Society, new series 10 (1979).

'The Register of the Archdeaconry of Richmond, 1442-1477', ed. Alexander Hamilton Thompson, *Yorkshire Archaeological Journal*, 30 (1930-31).

[*Register of Edmund Lacy, Exeter*] *The Register of Edmund Lacy Bishop of Exeter, 1420-1455*, ed. Gordon Reginald Dunstan, 5 vols., Devon and Cornwall Record Society, new series 7, 10, 13, 16, 18 (1963-72).

[*Register of Edmund Lacy, Hereford*] *Registrum Edmundi Lacy, episcopi Herefordensis A.D. MCCCCXVII-MCCCCXX*, ed. Joseph Henry Parry, C&Y 22 (1918).

[*Register of Edmund Stafford*] *The Register of Edmund Stafford, (A.D. 1395-1419)*, ed. Frances Charles Hingeston-Randolph (London, 1886).

[*Register of Gilbert Welton*] *The Register of Gilbert Welton Bishop of Carlisle 1353-1362*, ed. Robin L. Storey, C&Y 88 (1999).

[*Register of Godfrey Giffard*] *Episcopal Registers, Diocese of Worcester. Register of Bishop Godfrey Giffard*, ed. John William Willis Bund (Oxford: Worcestershire Historical Society, 1902).

[*Register of Hamo de Hethe*] *Registrum Hamonis Hethe, diocesis Roffensis, A.D. 1319-1352*, ed. Charles Johnson, 2 vols., C&Y 48-49 (1948).

[*Register of Henry Chichele*] *The Register of Henry Chichele, Archbishop of Canterbury 1414-1443*, 4 vols., ed. Ernest F. Jacob, C&Y 44-47 (1941-45).

[*Register of Henry of Newark*] *The Register of Archbishop Henry of Newark*, ed. William Brown, Surtees Society, 128 (1916).

[*Register of Henry Woodlock*] *Registrum Henrici Woodlock, Diocesis Wintoniensis, A.D. 1305-1316*, ed. Arthur Worthington Goodman, 2 vols., C&Y 43-44 (1940-41).

[*Register of John de Drokensford*] *Calendar of the Register of John de Drokensford, Bishop of Bath and Wells (A.D. 1309-1329)*, ed. Edmund Hobhouse, Somerset Record Society, 1 (1887).

[*Register of John de Grandisson*] *The Register of John de Grandisson, Bishop of Exeter (A.D. 1327-1369)*, ed. Frances Charles Hingeston-Randolph, 3 vols. (London, 1894-99).

[*Register of John de Halton*] *The Register of John de Halton, Bishop of Carlisle, A.D. 1292-1324*, ed. William Nicholson Thompson and Thomas Frederick Tout, 2 vols., C&Y 12-13 (1913).

[*Register of John de Stratford*] *The Register of John de Stratford, Bishop of Winchester, 1323–1333*, ed. Roy Martin Haines, 2 vols., Surrey Record Society, 42–43 (2010–11).

[*Register of John de Trillek*] *Registrum Johannis de Trillek, episcopi Herefordensis, A.D. MCCCXLIV-MCCCLXI*, ed. Joseph Henry Parry, C&Y 8 (1907).

[*Register of John Gilbert*] *Registrum Johannis Gilbert episcopi Herefordensis, A.D. MCCCLXXV-MCCCLXXXIX*, ed. Joseph Henry Parry, C&Y 18 (1915).

[*Register of John Kirkby and John Ross*] *The Register of John Kirkby Bishop of Carlisle 1332–1352 and the Register of John Ross Bishop of Carlisle, 1325–32*, ed. Robin L. Storey, 2 vols., C&Y 79, 81 (1993–95).

[*Register of John le Romeyn*] *The Register of John le Romeyn, Lord Archbishop of York 1286–1296*, ed. William Brown, 2 vols., Surtees Society, 123, 128 (1913–16).

[*Register of John Pecham*] *Diocesis Cantuariensis, registrum Johannis Pecham*, ed. Frances Neville Davis et al. (vol. 1) and Decima L. Douie (vol. 2), C&Y 64–65 (1908–67).

[*Register of John Peckham*] *Registrum epistolarum Fratris Johannis Peckham, Archiepiscopi Cantuariensis*, ed. C. Trice Martin, 3 vols. Rolls Series, 77 (1882–85).

[*Register of John Pontoise*] *Registrum Johannis de Pontissara episcopi Wyntoniensis A.D. MCCLXXXII-MCCCIV*, ed. Cecil Deedes, 2 vols., C&Y 19, 30 (1915–24).

[*Register of John Stafford*] *The Register of John Stafford, Bishop of Bath and Wells, 1425–1443*, ed. Thomas Scott Holmes, 2 vols., Somerset Record Society, 31, 32 (1915–16).

[*Register of John Trefnant*] *Registrum Johannis Trefnant, episcopi Herefordensis A.D. 1389–1404*, ed. William Wolfe Capes, C&Y 20 (1916).

[*Register of John Waltham*] *The Register of John Waltham Bishop of Salisbury 1388–1395*, ed. T.C.B. Timmins, C&Y 80 (1994).

[*Register of Lewis Charlton*] *Registrum Ludowici de Charltone episcopi Herefordensis A.D. MCCCLXI-MCCCLXX*, ed. Joseph Henry Parry, C&Y 14 (1914).

The Register of Milo Sweteman Archbishop of Armagh 1361–1380, ed. Brendan Smith (Dublin: Irish Manuscripts Commission, 1996).

[*Register of Nicholas Bubwith*] *The Register of Nicholas Bubwith, Bishop of Bath and Wells, 1407–1424*, ed. Thomas Scott Holmes, 2 vols., Somerset Record Society, 29–30 (1914).

The Register of Nicholas Fleming Archbishop of Armagh 1404–1416, ed. Brendan Smith (Dublin: Irish Manuscripts Commission, 2003).

[*Register of Ralph of Shrewsbury*] *The Register of Ralph of Shrewsbury, Bishop of Bath and Wells, 1329–1363*, ed. Thomas Scott Holmes, 2 vols., Somerset Record Society, 9–10 (1896).

[*Register of Richard d'Aungerville*] *Richard d'Aungerville of Bury: Fragments of his Register and Other Documents*, ed. George William Kitchin, Surtees Society, 119 (1910).

[*Register of Richard de Kellawe*] *Registrum palatinum Dunelmense. The Register of Richard de Kellawe, Lord Palatine and Bishop of Durham, 1311–1316*, ed. Thomas Duffus Hardy, Rolls Series, 4 vols. (1873–78).

[*Register of Richard Fox*] *The Register of Richard Fox Lord Bishop of Durham 1494–1501*, ed. Marjorie Peers Howden, Surtees Society, 147 (1932).

[*Register of Richard Gravesend*] *Rotuli Ricardi Gravesend diocesis Lincolniensis*, ed. Frances Neville Davis, C&Y 31 (1925).

[*Register of Richard Mayew*] *Registrum Ricardi Mayew, episcopi Herefordensis. A.D. MDIV-MDXVI*, ed. Arthur Thomas Bannister, C&Y 27 (1921).

[*Register of Richard Swinfield*] *Registrum Ricardi de Swinfield episcopi Herefordensis, 1283–1317*, ed. William Wolfe Capes, C&Y 6 (1909).

[*Register of Robert de Stretton*] *The Registers or Act Books of the Bishops of Coventry and Lichfield, V: The Second Register of Bishop Robert de Stretton, 1360–1385*, ed. Rowland

Alwyn Wilson, William Salt Archaeological Society: Collections for a History of Staffordshire, 8 (1905).

[*Register of Robert Hallum*] *The Register of Robert Hallum Bishop of Salisbury 1407-17*, ed. Joyce M. Horn, C&Y 72 (1982).

[*Register of Robert Mascall*] *Registrum Roberti Mascall, episcopi Herefordensis A.D. MCCCCIV-MCCCCXVI*, ed. Joseph Henry Parry, C&Y 21 (1917).

[*Register of Robert Rede*] *The Episcopal Register of Robert Rede, Ordinis Predicatorum, Lord Bishop of Chichester, 1397-1415*, ed. Cecil Deedes, 2 vols., Sussex Record Society, 8, 11 (1908-10).

[*Register of Robert Winchelsey*] *Registrum Roberti Winchelsey Cantuariensis Archiepiscopi*, ed. Rose Graham, 2 vols., C&Y 51-2 (1952-56).

[*Register of Simon de Montacute*] *Calendar of the Register of Simon de Montacute, Bishop of Worcester, 1334-1337*, ed. Roy Martin Haines, Worcestershire Historical Society, new series 15 (1996).

[*Register of Simon of Ghent*] *Registrum Simonis de Gandavo diocesis Saresbiriensis A.D. 1297-1315*, ed. Cyril Thomas Flower and Michael Charles Burdett Dawes, 2 vols., C&Y 40-1 (1934).

[*Register of Thomas Bekynton*] *The Register of Thomas Bekynton Bishop of Bath and Wells 1443-1465*, ed. Henry Churchill Maxwell Lyte and Michael Charles Burdett Dawes, 2 vols., Somerset Record Society, 49-50 (1934-35).

[*Register of Thomas Charlton*] *Registrum Thome de Charlton, episcopi Herefordensis, AD MCCCXXVII-MCCCXLIV*, ed. William Wolfe Capes, C&Y 9 (1908).

[*Register of Thomas of Corbridge*] *The Register of Thomas of Corbridge, Lord Archbishop of York, 1300-1304*, ed. William Brown, 2 vols., Surtees Society, 138, 141 (1925-28).

[*Register of Thomas de Brantyngham*] *The Register of Thomas de Brantyngham, Bishop of Exeter (A.D. 1370-1394)*, ed. Frances Charles Hingeston-Randolph, 2 vols. (London, 1901-6).

[*Register of Thomas de Cobham*] *The Register of Thomas de Cobham Bishop of Worcester 1317-1327*, ed. Ernest Harold Pearce, Worcestershire Historical Society, 38 (1930).

[*Register of Thomas Langley*] *The Register of Thomas Langley Bishop of Durham 1406-1437*, ed. Robin L. Storey, 6 vols., Surtees Society 164, 166, 169, 170, 177, 182 (1956-70).

[*Register of Thomas Myllyng*] *Registrum Thome Myllyng, episcopi Herefordensis. A.D. MCCCCLXXIV-MCCCCXCII*, ed. Arthur Thomas Bannister, C&Y 26 (1920).

[*Register of Thomas Polton*] *Registrum Thome Poltone, episcopi Herefordensis A.D. MCCCCXX-MCCCCXXII*, ed. William Wolfe Capes, C&Y 22 (1918).

[*Register of Thomas Rotherham*] *The Register of Thomas Rotherham, Archbishop of York 1480-1500*, ed. Eric E. Barker, C&Y 69 (1976).

[*Register of Thomas Spofford*] *Registrum Thome Spofford, Episcopi Herefordensis. A.D. MCCCCXXII-MCCCCXLVIII*, ed. Arthur Thomas Bannister, C&Y 23 (1919).

[*Register of Walter Bronscombe*] *The Register of Walter Bronscombe Bishop of Exeter 1258-1280*, ed. Olivia F. Robinson, 3 vols., C&Y 82, 87, 94 (1995-2003).

[*Register of Walter de Stapeldon*] *The Register of Walter de Stapeldon, Bishop of Exeter (A.D. 1307-1326)*, ed. Frances Charles Hingeston-Randolph (London, 1892).

[*Register of Walter Giffard, York*] *The Register of Walter Giffard, Lord Archbishop of York 1266-1279*, ed. William Brown, Surtees Society, 109 (1904).

[*Register of Walter Gray*] *The Register, or Rolls, of Walter Gray, Lord Archbishop of York*, ed. James Raine, Surtees Society, 56 (1872).

[*Register of Walter Reynolds*] *The Register of Walter Reynolds Bishop of Worcester 1308-1313*, ed. Rowland Alwyn Wilson, Dugdale Society Publications, 9 (1928).

[*Register of William Gainsborough*] *Register of Bishop William Gainsborough, 1303 to 1307*, ed. John William Willis Bund (Oxford: Worcestershire Historical Society, 1907).

[*Register of William Greenfield*] *The Register of William Greenfield Lord Archbishop of York 1306–1315*, ed. William Brown and Alexander Hamilton Thompson, 5 vols., Surtees Society, 145, 149, 151, 152, 153 (1931–40).

[*Register of William Melton*] *The Register of William Melton Archbishop of York 1317–1340*, ed. Rosalind M. T. Hill, David Robinson, Reginald Brocklesby and T.C.B. Timmins, 5 vols., C&Y 70, 71, 76, 85, 93 (1977–2002).

[*Register of William Wickwane*] *The Register of William Wickwane, Lord Archbishop of York 1279–1285*, ed. William Brown, Surtees Society, 114 (1908).

[*Register of William Wykeham*] *Wykeham's Register*, ed. Thomas Frederick Kirby, 2 vols., (London, 1896–99).

[*Register of Wolstan de Bransford*] *A Calendar of the Register of Wolstan de Bransford Bishop of Worcester 1339–49*, ed. Roy Martin Haines (London: HMSO, 1966).

'The Registers of the Archdeaconry of Richmond, 1361–1442', ed. Alexander Hamilton Thompson, *Yorkshire Archaeological Journal*, 25 (1920).

[*Registers of John de Sandale and Rigaud de Asserio*] *The Registers of John de Sandale and Rigaud de Asserio, Bishops of Winchester (A.D. 1316–1323)*, ed. Frances Joseph Baigent (London, 1897).

[*Registers of Robert Stillington and Richard Fox*] *The Registers of Robert Stillington Bishop of Bath and Wells 1466–1491 and Richard Fox Bishop of Bath and Wells 1492–1494*, ed. Henry Churchill Maxwell Lyte, Somerset Record Society, 52 (1937).

[*Registers of Roger Martival*] *The Registers of Roger Martival, Bishop of Salisbury, 1315–1330*, ed. Kathleen Edwards, Christopher Robin Elrington, Susan Reynolds, and Dorothy M. Owen, 4 vols., C&Y 55, 56, 57, 58, 68 (1959–75).

[*Registers of Walter Giffard and Henry Bowet*] *The Registers of Walter Giffard, Bishop of Bath and Wells, 1265–6, and of Henry Bowet, Bishop of Bath and Wells, 1401–7*, ed. Thomas Scott Holmes, Somerset Record Society, 13 (1899).

Registrum episcopatus Aberdonensis, ed. Cosmo Innes, 2 vols. (Edinburgh: Spalding Club, 1845).

Registrum episcopatus Glasguensis, ed. Cosmo Innes (Edinburgh: Maitland Club, 1843).

Registrum episcopatus Moraviensis, ed. Cosmo Innes (Edinburgh: Bannatyne Club, 1837).

A Repertorium of Middle English Prose Sermons, ed. Veronica O'Mara and Suzanne Paul, 4 vols. (Turnhout: Brepols, 2007).

The Romance of Sir Degrevant, ed. L. F. Casson, EETS 221 (1949).

Sacrorum conciliorum nova et amplissima collectio, ed. Giovanni Domenico Mansi, 31 vols. (Florence: Zatta, 1759–98).

Scottus, Sedulius, *De rectoribus Christianis*, trans. Robert W. Dyson (Woodbridge: Boydell, 2010).

Select Cases from the Ecclesiastical Courts of the Province of Canterbury c. 1200–1301, ed. Norma Adams and Charles Donahue Jr., Selden Society, 95 (1981).

Select Cases of Procedure without Writ under Henry III, ed. Henry G. Richardson and George O. Sayles, Selden Society, 60 (1941).

Select Cases on Defamation to 1600, ed. Richard H. Helmholz, Selden Society, 101 (1985).

Select Charters and Other Illustrations of English Constitutional History, ed. William Stubbs, 9th ed. (Oxford: Clarendon, 1913).

'A Sermon on the Anniversary of the Death of Thomas Beauchamp, Earl of Warwick', ed. Patrick J. Horner, *Traditio*, 34 (1978).

'Some Elizabethan Visitations of the Churches Belonging to the Peculiar of the Dean of York', ed. T. M. Fallow, *Yorkshire Archaeological Journal*, 18 (1905–6).

'Some Late Thirteenth-Century Records of an Ecclesiastical Court in the Archdeaconry of Sudbury', ed. Antonia Gransden, *BIHR* 32 (1959).

Sources of English Legal History: Private Law to 1750, ed. John H. Baker and S.F.C. Milsom (London: Butterworths, 1986).

Speculum Vitae: A Reading Edition, ed. Ralph Hanna and Venetia Somerset, 2 vols., EETS 331-32 (2008).

St David's Episcopal Acta 1085-1280, ed. Julia Barrow (Cardiff: South Wales Record Society, 1998).

Statutes of the Realm, 11 vols. (London: HMSO, 1810-28).

The Survey of Archbishop Pecham's Kentish Manors 1283-85, ed. and trans. Kenneth Witney, Kent Records, 28 (2000).

Taxatio ecclesiastica Angliae et Walliae auctoritate P. Nicholai IV circa A.D. 1291 (London: HMSO, 1802).

Tertullian, *Christian and Pagan in the Roman Empire: The Witness of Tertullian*, ed. Robert Sider (Washington, D.C.: Catholic University of America Press, 2001).

———, *De anima adversus philosophos*, PL 2.

Testamenta Eboracensia, ed. James Raine, 6 vols., Surtees Society, 4, 30, 45, 53, 79, 106 (1836-1902).

Theodoretus Cyrensis, *Philotheus*, PL 74.

The Treatise on the Laws and Customs of the Realm of England Commonly Called Glanvill, ed. George Derek Gordon Hall (London: Nelson, 1965).

Two Bedfordshire Subsidy Lists. 1309 and 1332, ed. S.H.A. Hervey (Bury St Edmunds: Suffolk Green Books, 1925).

Un formulari i un registre del bisbe de València En Jaume d'Aragó, ed. Milagros Cárcel Ortí (València: Universitat de València, 2005).

Vetus Liber Archidiaconatus Eliensis, ed. Charles Lett Feltoe and Ellis H. Minns (Cambridge: Cambridge Antiquarian Society, 1917).

Vetus Registrum Sarisberiense alias dictum Registrum S. Osmundi Episcopi, ed. William Henry Rich Jones, Rolls Series, 2 vols. (1883-84).

Visitations in the Diocese of Lincoln, 1517-1531, ed. Alexander Hamilton Thompson, 3 vols., Lincoln Record Society, 33, 35, 37 (1940-47).

Visitations of Churches Belonging to St Paul's Cathedral 1249-1252, ed. William Sparrow Simpson, Camden Society, second series 53 (1895).

The White Book of Peterborough: The Registers of Abbot William of Woodford, 1295-99 and Abbot Godfrey of Crowland, 1299-1321, ed. Sandra Raban, Northamptonshire Record Society, 41 (2001).

Whitford, Richard, *A dayly exercyse and experyence of dethe, gathered and set forth, by a brother of Syon Rycharde Whytforde* (London: Wynkyn de Worde, 1537).

Willelmi Tyrensis Archiepiscopi, Chronicon, ed. R.B.C. Huygens, CCCM 63 (Turnhout: Brepols, 1986).

William of Malmesbury, *Gesta regum Anglorum: The History of the English Kings*, ed. R.A.B. Mynors, Rodney M. Thomson, and Michael Winterbottom, 2 vols. (Oxford: Clarendon, 1998-99).

Wimbledon's Sermon Redde rationem villicationis tue: A Middle English Sermon of the Fourteenth Century, ed. Ione Kemp Knight (Pittsburgh: Duquesne, 1967).

Worcestershire Taxes in the 1520s: The Military Survey and Forced Loans of 1522-3 and the Lay Subsidy of 1524-7, ed. Michael A. Faraday, Worcestershire Historical Society, new series 19 (2003).

Wyatt, Sir Thomas, *The Complete Poems*, ed. Ronald A. Rebholz (New Haven, Conn.: Yale University Press, 1981).

Wyclif, John, *Trialogus*, trans. Stephen E. Lahey (Cambridge: Cambridge University Press, 2013).

SECONDARY WORKS

Ackerman-Lieberman, Phillip I., *The Business of Identity: Jews, Muslims, and Economic Life in Medieval Egypt* (Stanford, Calif.: Stanford University Press, 2014).

Adler, Jonathan, 'Testimony, Trust, Knowing', *Journal of Philosophy*, 91 (1994).

Aers, David, *Community, Gender, and Individual Identity: English Writing 1360–1430* (London: Routledge, 1988).

Althoff, Gerd, 'Establishing Bonds: Fiefs, Homage and Other Means to Create Trust', in Sverre Bagge et al. (eds.), *Feudalism: New Landscapes of Debate* (Turnhout: Brepols, 2011).

——, *Spielregeln der Politik im Mittelalter. Kommunikation in Frieden und Fehden* (Darmstadt: Primus Verlag, 1997).

Ames, Christine Caldwell, 'Authentic, True, and Right: Inquisition and the Study of Medieval Popular Religion', in David C. Mengel and Lisa Wolverton (eds.), *Christianity and Culture in the Middle Ages: Essays to Honor John Van Engen* (Notre Dame, Ind.: University of Notre Dame Press, 2015).

Andrews, Frances, 'Doubting John?', in Andrews, Methuen, and Spicer (eds.), *Doubting Christianity*.

——, 'Living Like the Laity? The Negotiation of Religious Status in the Cities of Late Medieval Italy', *Transactions of the Royal Historical Society*, 20 (2010).

——, '*Ut inde melius fiat*: The Commune of Parma and its Religious Personnel', in Frances Andrews and Maria Agata Pincelli (eds.), *Churchmen and Government in Late Medieval Italy c. 1200–c. 1450: Cases and Contexts* (Cambridge: Cambridge University Press, 2013).

Andrews, Frances, Charlotte Methuen, and Andrew Spicer (eds.), *Doubting Christianity: The Church and Doubt*, Studies in Church History, 52 (Cambridge: Cambridge University Press, 2016).

Aparisi, Frederic, and Vicent Royo (eds.), *Beyond Lords and Peasants: Rural Elites and Economic Differentiation in Pre-modern Europe* (València: Universitat de València, 2014).

Appleford, Amy, *Learning to Die in London, 1380–1540* (Philadelphia: University of Pennsylvania Press, 2015).

Arnold, John H., *Belief and Unbelief in Medieval Europe* (London: Hodder Arnold, 2005).

——, 'Histories and Historiographies of Medieval Christianity', in Arnold (ed.), *Oxford Handbook of Medieval Christianity*.

—— (ed.), *The Oxford Handbook of Medieval Christianity* (Oxford: Oxford University Press, 2014).

Arnold, Morris S., 'Fourteenth-Century Promises', *Cambridge Law Journal*, 35 (1976).

——, 'Law and Fact in the Medieval Jury Trial: Out of Sight, Out of Mind', *American Journal of Legal History*, 18 (1974).

Arrow, Kenneth, 'Gifts and Exchanges', in Edmund S. Phelps (ed.), *Morality, Altruism and Economic Theory* (New York: Russell Sage Foundation, 1975).

——, *The Limits of Organization* (New York: Norton, 1974).

Aslanian, David Sebouh, *From the Indian Ocean to the Mediterranean: The Global Trade Networks of Armenians from New Julfa* (Berkeley: University of California Press, 2010).

Aston, Margaret, 'Devotional Literacy', in Aston, *Lollards and Reformers: Images and Literacy in Late Medieval Religion* (London: Hambledon, 1984).

Avramides, Anita, *Other Minds* (London: Routledge, 2001).

Bailey, Mark, *Medieval Suffolk: An Economic and Social History, 1200–1500* (Woodbridge: Boydell, 2007).

———, 'Self-Government in the Small Towns of Late-Medieval England', in Ben Dodds and Christian Liddy (eds.), *Commercial Activity, Markets and Entrepreneurs in the Middle Ages: Essays in Honour of Richard Britnell* (Woodbridge: Boydell, 2011).

Baker, John H., *An Introduction to English Legal History*, 4th ed. (London: Reed Elsevier, 2002).

Baldwin, John W., *The Government of Philip Augustus: Foundations of French Royal Power in the Middle Ages* (Berkeley: University of California Press, 1986).

———, 'The Intellectual Preparation for the Canon of 1215 against Ordeals', *Speculum*, 36 (1961).

Bale, Anthony, 'God's Cell: Christ as Prisoner and Pilgrimage to the Prison of Christ', *Speculum*, 91 (2016).

Bardsley, Sandy, *Venomous Tongues: Speech and Gender in Late Medieval England* (Philadelphia: University of Pennsylvania Press, 2006).

Barnes, Barry, *The Elements of Social Theory* (London: Routledge, 1995).

Barry, Jonathan, and Christopher Brooks (eds.), *The Middling Sort of People: Culture, Society and Politics in England, 1550–1800* (Basingstoke: Macmillan, 1984).

Bartlett, Robert, *Trial by Fire and Water: The Medieval Judicial Ordeal* (Oxford: Clarendon, 1986).

Bauerschmidt, Frederick Christian, *Thomas Aquinas: Faith, Reason and Following Christ* (Oxford: Oxford University Press, 2013).

Baydal Sala, Vicent, and Ferran Esquilache Martí, 'Exploitation and Differentiation: Economic and Social Stratification in the Rural Muslim Communities of the Kingdom of Valencia, 13th–16th Centuries', in Aparisi and Royo (eds.), *Beyond Lords and Peasants*.

Beattie, Cordelia, *Medieval Single Women: The Politics of Social Classification in Late Medieval England* (Oxford: Oxford University Press, 2007).

Beckerman, John S., 'Procedural Innovation and Institutional Change in Medieval English Manorial Courts', *Law and History Review*, 10 (1992).

Beckwith, Sarah, *Christ's Body: Identity, Culture and Society in Late Medieval Writings* (London: Routledge, 1993).

Bell, Adrian R., Chris Brooks, and Paul R. Dryburgh, *The English Wool Market, c.1230–1327* (Cambridge: Cambridge University Press, 2007).

Bell, David N., '*Certitudo fidei*: Faith, Reason, and Authority in the Writings of Baldwin of Forde', in John R. Sommerfeldt (ed.), *Bernardus Magister* (Cîteaux: Cistercian, 1992).

Bellomo, Manlio, *The Common Legal Past of Europe 1000–1800*, trans. Lydia G. Cochrane (Washington, D.C.: Catholic University of America, 1995).

Bennett, Judith M., *Ale, Beer, and Brewsters in England: Women's Work in a Changing World, 1300–1600* (Oxford: Oxford University Press, 1996).

———, 'Compulsory Service in Late Medieval England', *Past & Present*, 209 (2010).

———, *History Matters: Patriarchy and the Challenge of Feminism* (Manchester: Manchester University Press, 2006).

———, *Women in the Medieval English Countryside: Gender and Household in Brigstock before the Plague* (Oxford: Oxford University Press, 1987).

Bennett, Judith M., and Ruth Mazo Karras (eds.), *The Oxford Handbook of Women and Gender in Medieval Europe* (Oxford: Oxford University Press, 2013).

Benveniste, Emile, *Indo-European Language and Society*, trans. Elizabeth Palmer (London: Faber, 1973).

Bernard, George, *The Late Medieval English Church: Vitality and Vulnerability before the Break with Rome* (New Haven, Conn.: Yale University Press, 2012).

Biddick, Kathleen, 'Missing Links: Taxable Wealth, Markets, and Stratification among Medieval English Peasants', *Journal of Interdisciplinary History*, 18 (1987).

Biller, Peter, 'Confession in the Middle Ages', in Peter Biller and Alasdair J. Minnis (eds.), *Handling Sin: Confession in the Middle Ages* (Woodbridge: York Medieval Press, 1998).

———, 'Intellectuals and the Masses: Oxen and She-asses in the Medieval Church', in Arnold (ed.), *Oxford Handbook of Medieval Christianity*.

———, 'Popular Religion in the Central and Later Middle Ages', in Michael Bentley (ed.), *Companion to Historiography* (Abingdon: Routledge, 1997).

———, 'Words and the Medieval Notion of "Religion"', *Journal of Ecclesiastical History*, 36 (1985).

Birrell, Jean, 'Manorial Custumals Reconsidered', *Past & Present*, 224 (2014).

Bisson, Thomas N., *The Crisis of the Twelfth Century: Power, Lordship, and the Origins of European Government* (Princeton, N.J.: Princeton University Press, 2009).

———, *Medieval France and Her Pyrenean Neighbours* (London: Hambledon, 1989).

Blackburn, Simon, *Truth: A Guide for the Perplexed* (London: Penguin, 2005).

Blair, John, *The Church in Anglo-Saxon Society* (Oxford: Oxford University Press, 2005).

Bloch, Marc, *Feudal Society*, trans. L. A. Manyon (London: Routledge, 1961).

Boeles Rowland, Anna, 'Material Mnemonics and Social Relationships in the Diocese of London 1467–1524' (D.Phil. thesis, University of Oxford, 2018).

Bonfield, Lloyd, and Lawrence Raymond Poos, 'The Development of Deathbed Transfers in Medieval English Manor Courts', in Zvi Razi and Richard M. Smith (eds.), *Medieval Society and the Manor Court* (Oxford: Oxford University Press, 1996).

Borchardt, Karl, 'Two Forged Thirteenth-Century Alms-Raising Letters Used by the Hospitallers in Franconia', in Malcolm Barber (ed.), *The Military Orders: Fighting for the Faith and Caring for the Sick* (Aldershot: Ashgate, 1994).

Boreau, Alain, 'Introduction', in Gauvard (ed.), *L'enquête au Moyen âge*.

Bose, Mishtooni, 'Vernacular Opinions', in Denery, Ghosh, and Zeeman (eds.), *Uncertain Knowledge*.

Bourin, Monique, 'Les *boni homines* de l'an mil', in *La justice en l'an mil* (Paris: La Documentation Française, 2003).

———, *Villages médiévaux en Bas-Languedoc: genèse d'une sociabilité (Xᵉ–XIVᵉ siècle)*, 2 vols. (Paris: Editions l'Harmattan, 1987).

Bowker, Margaret, *The Secular Clergy in the Diocese of Lincoln* (Cambridge: Cambridge University Press, 1968).

Bowman, Alan, and Greg Woolf, 'Introduction', in Alan Bowman and Greg Woolf (eds.), *Literacy and Power in the Ancient World* (Cambridge: Cambridge University Press, 1994).

Boyle, Leonard E., *Pastoral Care, Clerical Education and Canon Law* (London: Varorium, 1981).

———, 'A Study of the Works Attributed to William of Pagula with Special Reference to the *Oculus Sacerdotis* and *Summa Summarum*' (D.Phil. thesis, University of Oxford, 1956).

Braddick, Michael, *State Formation in Early Modern England, c.1550–1700* (Cambridge: Cambridge University Press, 2000).

Brand, Paul, 'Aspects of the Law of Debt, 1189–1307', in Phillipp R. Schofield and Nicholas J. Mayhew (eds.), *Credit and Debt in Medieval England, c.1180–c.1350* (Oxford: Oxbow, 2002).

————, 'The English Difference: The Application of Bureaucratic Norms within a Legal System', *Law and History Review*, 21 (2003).

Braudel, Fernand, *The Mediterranean and the Mediterranean World in the Age of Philip II*, 2 vols., trans. Siân Reynolds (London: Collins, 1972–73).

Briggs, Chris, *Credit and Village Society in Fourteenth-Century England* (Oxford: Oxford University Press, 2009).

Briggs, Chris, and Mark Koyama, 'Pledging and Credit Markets in Medieval England', Cambridge Working Papers in Economic and Social History, 5 (2013).

Britnell, Richard, *Britain and Ireland, 1050–1530: Economy and Society* (Oxford: Oxford University Press, 2004).

————, *Growth and Decline in Colchester, 1300–1525* (Cambridge: Cambridge University Press, 1986).

———— (ed.), *Pragmatic Literacy: East and West, 1200–1330* (Woodbridge: Boydell, 1997).

Broadberry, Stephen, et al., *British Economic Growth, 1270–1870* (Cambridge: Cambridge University Press, 2015).

Brooke, Christopher N. L., 'English Episcopal *acta* of the Twelfth and Thirteenth Centuries', in Michael J. Franklin and Christopher Harper-Bill (eds.), *Medieval Ecclesiastical Studies in Honour of Dorothy M. Owen* (Woodbridge: Boydell, 1995).

Brown, Andrew, *Church and Society in England, 1000–1500* (Basingstoke: Palgrave Macmillan, 2003).

Brown, Carleton, and Rossell Hope Robbins (eds.), *The Index of Middle English Verse* (New York: Columbia University Press, 1943).

Brundage, James A., *Medieval Canon Law* (London: Longman, 1995).

————, *The Medieval Origins of the Legal Profession: Canonists, Civilians, and Courts* (Chicago: University of Chicago Press, 2008).

————, 'Proof in Canonical Criminal Law', *Continuity and Change*, 11 (1996).

Buhrer, Eliza, '"But What Is to Be Said of a Fool?" Intellectual Disability in Medieval Thought and Culture', in Albrecht Classen (ed.), *Mental Health, Spirituality, and Religion in the Middle Ages and Early Modern Age* (Berlin: De Gruyter, 2014).

Bumpus, Francesca, 'The "Middling Sort" in the Lordship of Blakemere, Shropshire, c. 1380–c. 1420', in Tim Thornton (ed.), *Social Attitudes and Political Structures in the Fifteenth Century* (Stroud: Sutton, 2000).

Burger, Michael, *Bishops, Clerks, and Diocesan Governance in Thirteenth-Century England: Reward and Punishment* (Cambridge: Cambridge University Press, 2012).

Burgess, Clive, 'Pre-Reformation Churchwardens' Accounts and Parish Government: Lessons from London and Bristol', *English Historical Review*, 117 (2002).

Burke, Peter, *A Social History of Knowledge from Gutenberg to Diderot* (Cambridge: Polity Press, 2000).

Burrow, John A., *Gestures and Looks in Medieval Narrative* (Cambridge: Cambridge University Press, 2002).

Burrows, Toby, 'Holy Information: A New Look at Raban Maur's *De naturis rerum*', *Parergon*, 5 (1987).

Busdraghi, Piero Brancoli, '*Masnada* und *boni homines* als Mittel der Herrschaftsausübung der ländlichen Herrschaften in der Toskana (11.–13. Jahrhundert)', in Gerhard Dilcher and Cinzio Violante (eds.), *Strukturen und Wandlungen der ländlichen Herrschaftsformen vom 10. Zum 13. Jahrhundert: Deutschland und Italien im Vergleich* (Berlin: Duncker & Humblot, 2000).

Butler, Sara, 'Degrees of Culpability: Suicide Verdicts, Mercy, and the Jury in Medieval England', *Journal of Medieval and Early Modern Studies*, 36 (2006).

———, 'I Will Never Consent to Be Wedded with You! Coerced Marriage in the Courts of Medieval England', *Canadian Journal of History*, 39 (2004).

———, 'Runaway Wives: Husband Desertion in Medieval England', *Journal of Social History*, 40 (2006).

Bynum, Caroline Walker, *Christian Materiality: An Essay on Religion in Late Medieval Europe* (New York: Zone Books, 2011).

———, *Holy Feast and Holy Fast: The Religious Significance of Food to Medieval Women* (Berkeley: University of California Press, 1987).

———, *The Resurrection of the Body in Western Christianity, 200–1336* (New York: Columbia University Press, 1995).

Campbell, Bruce M. S. (ed.), *Before the Black Death: Studies in the 'Crisis' of the Early Fourteenth Century* (Manchester: Manchester University Press, 1991).

———, *The Great Transition: Climate, Disease and Society in the Late-Medieval World* (Cambridge: Cambridge University Press, 2016).

———, 'The Land', in Rosemary Horrox and W. Mark Ormrod (eds.), *A Social History of England, 1200–1500* (Cambridge: Cambridge University Press, 2006).

Campbell, Bruce M. S., and Ken Bartley, *England on the Eve of the Black Death: An Atlas of Lay Lordship, Land and Wealth, 1300–49* (Manchester: Manchester University Press, 2006).

Carpenter, Christine, *Locality and Polity: A Study of Warwickshire Landed Society, 1401–1499* (Cambridge: Cambridge University Press, 1992).

Carruthers, Mary, *The Book of Memory: A Study of Memory in Medieval Culture* (Cambridge: Cambridge University Press, 1990).

———, *The Craft of Thought: Meditation, Rhetoric, and the Making of Images, 400–1200* (Cambridge: Cambridge University Press, 1998).

Casson, Catherine, 'Reputation and Responsibility in Medieval English Towns: Civic Concerns with the Regulation of Trade', *Urban History*, 39 (2012).

Cheney, Christopher R., *English Bishops' Chanceries 1100–1250* (Manchester: Manchester University Press, 1950).

———, *Episcopal Visitation of Monasteries in the Thirteenth Century* (Manchester: Manchester University Press, 1931).

———, *A Handbook of Dates for Students of British History* (London: Royal Historical Society, 1955).

———, 'Legislation of the Medieval English Church', *English Historical Review*, 50 (1935).

Cheyette, Frederic L., *Ermengard of Narbonne and the World of the Troubadours* (Ithaca, N.Y.: Cornell University Press, 2001).

Chowdhury, Prabal Roy, 'Group-Lending: Sequential Financing, Lender Monitoring and Joint Liability', *Journal of Development Economics*, 77 (2005).

Clanchy, Michael, *Abelard: A Medieval Life* (Oxford: Blackwell, 1997).

———, *From Memory to Written Record: England 1066–1307*, 3rd ed. (Oxford: Blackwell, 2013).

———, 'Law and Love in the Middle Ages', in John Bossy (ed.), *Disputes and Settlements: Law and Human Relations in the West* (Cambridge: Cambridge University Press, 1983).

Clark, Gregory, '1381 and the Malthus Delusion', *Explorations in Economic History*, 50 (2013).

Claustre, Julie, 'Vivre à crédit dans une ville sans banque (Paris, XIVe–XVe siècle), *Le Moyen Âge: Revue d'histoire et de philologie*, 119 (2013).

Coase, Ronald, 'The Nature of the Firm', *Economica*, 4 (1937).

Cohn, Samuel K., 'After the Black Death: Labour Legislation and Attitudes towards Labour in Late-Medieval Western Europe', *Economic History Review*, 60 (2007).

———, *Creating the Florentine State: Peasants and Rebellion, 1348–1434* (Cambridge: Cambridge University Press, 1999).

Coleman, James S., *Foundations of Social Theory* (Cambridge, Mass.: Belknap, 1990).

Collins, Randall, *Weberian Sociological Theory* (Cambridge: Cambridge University Press, 1986).

Conrad, Sebastien, *What Is Global History?* (Princeton, N.J.: Princeton University Press, 2016).

Copeland, Rita, 'Living with Uncertainty: Reactions to Aristotle's *Rhetoric* in the Later Middle Ages', in Denery, Ghosh, and Zeeman (eds.), *Uncertain Knowledge*.

Corbin, Alain, *The Life of an Unknown: The Rediscovered World of a Clog Maker in Nineteenth-Century France*, trans. Arthur Goldhammer (New York: Columbia University Press, 2001).

Coulet, Noël, *Les visites pastorales* (Turnhout: Brepols, 1977).

———, 'Paroisse, œuvre et communauté d'habitants en Provence (le diocèse d'Aix dans la première moitié du XIVe s.)', in *La paroisse en Languedoc (XIIIᵉ–XIVᵉ s.)*, Cahiers de Fanjeaux, 25 (Toulouse: Privat, 1990).

Courtenay, William J., 'Nominalism and Late Medieval Religion', in Charles Trinkaus and Heiko A. Oberman (eds.), *The Pursuit of Holiness in Late Medieval and Renaissance Religion* (Leiden: Brill, 1974).

Cox, Ronald J, *A Study of the Juridic Status of Laymen in the Writing of the Medieval Canonists* (Washington, D.C.: Catholic University of America Press, 1959).

Craddock, Jerry R., 'La pesquisa en Castilla y Aragón: un caso curioso del "Libre dels Feyts" de Jaume I', *Anuario de Estudios Medievales*, 27 (1997).

Craun, Edwin, *Ethics and Power in Medieval English Reformist Writing* (Cambridge: Cambridge University Press, 2010).

Crenshaw, Kimberlé, 'Demarginalizing the Intersection of Race and Sex: A Black Feminist Critique of Antidiscrimination Doctrine, Feminist Theory and Antiracist Politics', *University of Chicago Legal Forum*, 140 (1989).

Cressy, David, *Dangerous Talk: Scandalous, Seditious and Treasonable Speech in Pre-modern England* (Oxford: Oxford University Press, 2010).

Crowston, Clare Haru, 'Credit and the Metanarrative of Modernity', *French Historical Studies*, 34 (2011).

Currie, C.R.J., and Robert W. Dunning (eds.), *A History of the County of Somerset: Volume 7: Bruton, Horethorne and Norton Ferris Hundreds* (London: Institute of Historical Research, 1999).

Cursente, Benoît, 'Les montagnes des médiévistes', in *Montagnes médiévales* (Paris: Sorbonne, 2004).

Dagenais, John, and Margaret R. Greer, 'Decolonizing the Middle Ages: Introduction', *Journal of Medieval and Early Modern Studies*, 30 (2000).

Dameron, George, 'The Church as Lord', in Arnold (ed.), *Oxford Handbook of Medieval Christianity*.

Dasgupta, Partha, 'Trust as a Commodity', in Gambetta (ed.), *Trust*.

Daunton, Martin, *Trusting Leviathan: The Politics of Taxation in Britain 1799–1914* (Cambridge: Cambridge University Press, 2001).

Davidson, Donald, 'A Coherence Theory of Truth and Knowledge', in Davidson, *Subjective, Intersubjective, Objective* (Oxford: Oxford University Press, 2001).

Davies, R. Rees, *The First English Empire: Power and Identities in the British Isles 1093–1343* (Oxford: Oxford University Press, 2000).

Davis, James, *Medieval Market Morality: Life, Law and Ethics in the English Marketplace, 1200–1500* (Cambridge: Cambridge University Press, 2012).

Davis, Virginia, 'Preparation for Service in the Late Medieval English Church', in Anne Curry and Elizabeth Matthew (eds.), *The Fifteenth Century*, I: *Concepts and Patterns of Service in the Later Middle Ages* (Woodbridge: Boydell, 2000).

d'Avray, David L., *Medieval Religious Rationalities: A Weberian Analysis* (Cambridge: Cambridge University Press, 2010).

——, *Rationalities in History: A Weberian Essay in Comparison* (Cambridge: Cambridge University Press, 2010).

de Certeau, Michel, *The Practice of Everyday Life*, trans. Steven Rendall (Berkeley: University of California Press, 1988).

——, 'Une pratique sociale de la différence: croire', in *Faire croire: modalités de la diffusion et de la réception des messages religieux du XIIe au XVe siècle* (Rome: École Française de Rome, 1981).

de Groot, Roger, 'The Jury of Presentment before 1215', *American Journal of Legal History*, 1 (1982).

DeLanda, Manuel, *A New Philosophy of Society: Assemblage Theory and Social Complexity* (London: Continuum, 2006).

Denery, Dallas G., II, *Seeing and Being Seen in the Later Medieval World: Optics, Theology, and Religious Life* (Cambridge: Cambridge University Press, 2005).

Denery, Dallas G., II, Kantik Ghosh, and Nicolette Zeeman (eds.), *Uncertain Knowledge: Scepticism, Relativism, and Doubt in the Middle Ages* (Turnhout: Brepols, 2014).

Depold, Jennifer, 'Preaching the Name: The Influence of a Sermon on the Holy Name of Christ', *Journal of Medieval History*, 40 (2014).

Deutsch, Karl, *Nationalism and Social Communication: An Inquiry into the Foundations of Nationality*, 2nd ed. (Cambridge, Mass.: Harvard University Press, 1966).

de Vivo, Filippo, *Information and Communication in Venice: Rethinking Early Modern Politics* (Oxford: Oxford University Press, 2007).

DeWindt, Anne Reiber, and Edwin Brezette DeWindt, *Ramsey: The Lives of an English Fenland Town, 1200–1600* (Washington D.C.: Catholic University of America Press, 2006).

DeWindt, Edwin Brezette, *Land and People in Holywell-cum-Needingworth: Structures of Tenure and Patterns of Social Organization in an East Midlands Village 1252–1457* (Toronto: PIMS, 1972).

Dictionary of Medieval Latin from British and Irish Sources, http://www.dmlbs.ox.ac.uk.

Dodds, Ben, 'Managing Tithes in the Late Middle Ages', *Agricultural History Review*, 53 (2005).

——, *Peasants and Production in the Medieval North-East: The Evidence from Tithes 1270–1536* (Woodbridge: Boydell, 2007).

Dohar, William J., *The Black Death and Pastoral Leadership: The Diocese of Hereford in the Fourteenth Century* (Philadelphia: University of Pennsylvania Press, 1995).

Dolan, Frances E., *True Relations: Reading, Literature, and Evidence in Seventeenth-Century England* (Philadelphia: University of Pennsylvania Press, 2013).

Donahue, Charles, Jr., *Law, Marriage, and Society in the Later Middle Ages: Arguments about Marriage in Five Courts* (Cambridge: Cambridge University Press, 2007).

——, 'Proof by Witness in the Church Courts of Medieval England: An Imperfect Reception of the Learned Law', in Morris S. Arnold et al. (eds.), *On the Laws and Customs of England: Essays in Honor of Samuel E. Thorne* (Chapel Hill: University of North Carolina Press, 1981).

Doubleday, Herbert Arthur, and William Page (eds.), *Victoria History of the County of Bedford: Volume Three* (Westminster: Archibald Constable, 1912).

Douglas, Mary, *How Institutions Think* (Syracuse, N.Y.: Syracuse University Press, 1986).

Drendel, John, 'Le recours aux experts sur des questions économiques dans deux enquêtes provençales au XIVe siècle', in Claude Denjean and Laurent Feller (eds.), *Expertise et valeur des choses au Moyen Âge. I: Le besoin d'expertise* (Madrid: Casa de Velázquez, 2013).

Dresch, Paul, and Hannah Skoda (eds.), *Legalism: Anthropology and History* (Oxford: Oxford University Press, 2012).

Drew, Charles, *Early Parochial Organization in England: The Origins of the Office of Church-warden* (London: St Anthony's Press, 1954).

Du Boulay, F.R.H., *The Lordship of Canterbury: An Essay on Medieval Society* (London: Nelson, 1966).

Duby, Georges, *The Early Growth of the European Economy: Warriors and Peasants from the Seventh to the Twelfth Century* (Ithaca, N.Y.: Cornell University Press, 1974).

Duffy, Eamon, *The Stripping of the Altars: Traditional Religion in England 1400–1580*, 2nd ed. (New Haven, Conn.: Yale University Press, 2005).

——, *The Voices of Morebath: Reformation and Rebellion in an English Village* (New Haven, Conn.: Yale University Press, 2001).

Duggan, Lawrence G., *Bishop and Chapter: The Governance of the Bishopric of Speyer to 1552* (New Brunswick, N.J.: Rutgers University Press, 1978).

Dulles, Avery, *Assurance of Things Hoped For: A Theology of Christian Faith* (Oxford: Oxford University Press, 1994).

Dunn, John, 'Trust and Political Agency', in Gambetta (ed.), *Trust*.

Dunson, Ben C., *Individual and Community in Paul's Letter to the Romans* (Tübingen: Mohr Siebeck, 2012).

Durkheim, Émile, *De la division du travail social* (Paris: Alcan, 1893).

Dutour, Thierry, *Sous l'empire du bien: 'bonnes gens' et pacte social (XIIIᵉ–XVᵉ siècle)* (Paris: Classiques Garnier, 2015).

Dyer, Alan, 'Ranking Lists of English Medieval Towns', in David Palliser (ed.), *Cambridge Urban History of Britain*, I: *600–1540* (Cambridge: Cambridge University Press, 2000).

Dyer, Christopher, *An Age of Transition? Economy and Society in England in the Later Middle Ages* (Oxford: Oxford University Press, 2007).

——, 'Costs and Benefits of English Direct Taxation, 1275–1525', in Simonetta Cavaciocchi (ed.), *La Fiscalità nell'Economia Europea Secc. XIII–XVIII* (Florence: Firenze University Press, 2008).

——, 'The Experience of Being Poor in Late Medieval England', in Anne M. Scott (ed.), *Experiences of Poverty in Late Medieval and Early Modern England and France* (Farnham: Ashgate, 2012).

——, 'Living in Peasant Houses in Late Medieval England', *Vernacular Architecture*, 44 (2013).

——, *Making a Living in the Middle Ages: The People of Britain 850–1520* (New Haven, Conn.: Yale University Press, 2002).

——, 'The Material World of English Peasants, 1200–1540: Archaeological Perspectives on Rural Economy and Welfare', *Agricultural History Review*, 62 (2014).

——, 'Medieval Stratford: A Successful Small Town', in Robert Bearman (ed.), *The History of an English Borough: Stratford-upon-Avon 1196–1996* (Stroud: Sutton, 1997).

——, 'Poverty and Its Relief in Late Medieval England', *Past & Present*, 216 (2012).

——, 'Small Places with Large Consequences: The Importance of Small Towns in England 1000–1540', *Historical Research*, 75 (2002).

——, *Standards of Living in the Later Middle Ages: Social Change in England c.1200–1520* (Cambridge: Cambridge University Press, 1989).

Dyer, Christopher, and Terry R. Slater, 'The Midlands', in David Palliser (ed.), *The Cambridge Urban History of Britain, I: 600–1540* (Cambridge: Cambridge University Press, 2000).

Dymond, David, 'Gods' Disputed Acre', *Journal of Ecclesiastical History*, 50 (1999).

Ebbeler, Jennifer, *Disciplining Christians: Correction and Community in Augustine's Letters* (Oxford: Oxford University Press, 2012).

Edwards, Kathleen, *The English Secular Cathedrals in the Middle Ages: A Constitutional Study with Special Reference to the Fourteenth Century*, 2nd ed. (Manchester: Manchester University Press, 1967).

Eisenstadt, Shmuel Noah, and Luis Roniger, *Patrons, Clients and Friends: Interpersonal Relations and the Structure of Trust in Society* (Cambridge: Cambridge University Press, 1984).

Eldevik, John, *Episcopal Power and Ecclesiastical Reform in the German Empire: Tithes, Lordship, and Community, 950–1150* (Cambridge: Cambridge University Press, 2012).

Elliott, Dyan, 'Gender and the Christian Traditions', in Bennett and Karras (eds.), *Oxford Handbook of Women and Gender.*

———, *Proving Woman: Female Spirituality and Inquisitional Culture in the Later Middle Ages* (Princeton, N.J.: Princeton University Press, 2004).

Epstein, Steven A., 'Secrecy and Genoese Commercial Practices', *Journal of Medieval History*, 20 (1994).

Esders, Stefan, 'Die römischen Wurzeln der fiskalischen *Inquisitio* de Karolingerzeit', in Gauvard (ed.), *L'enquête au Moyen âge.*

———, 'Faithful Believers: Oaths of Allegiance in Post-Roman Societies as Evidence for Eastern and Western "Visions of Community"', in Walter Pohl, Clemens Gantner, and Richard Payne (eds.), *Visions of Community in the Post-Roman World: The West, Byzantium, and the Islamic World 300–1100* (Farnham: Ashgate, 2012).

Eustace, Nicole et al., 'Conversation: The Historical Study of Emotions', *American Historical Review*, 117 (2012).

Evans, Ralph, 'Whose Was the Manor Court?', in Ralph Evans (ed.), *Lordship and Learning: Studies in Memory of Trevor Aston* (Woodbridge: Boydell, 2004).

Faith, Ros, *The English Peasantry and the Growth of Lordship* (Leicester: Leicester University Press, 1997).

Farge, Arlette, *The Allure of the Archives* (New Haven, Conn.: Yale University Press, 2013).

Farmer, David L., 'Prices and Wages: Statistical Supplement', in Edward Miller (ed.), *The Agrarian History of England and Wales, III: 1348–1500* (Cambridge: Cambridge University Press, 1991).

Faulkner, Paul, *Knowledge on Trust* (Oxford: Oxford University Press, 2011).

Fenster, Thelma, and Daniel Lord Smail (eds.), *Fama: The Politics of Talk and Reputation in Medieval Europe* (Ithaca, N.Y.: Cornell University Press, 2003).

Fentress, James, and Chris Wickham, *Social Memory* (Oxford: Blackwell, 1992).

Ferme, Brian Edwin, *Canon Law in Late Medieval England: A Study of William Lyndwood's Provinciale with Particular Reference to Testamentary Law* (Rome: Libreria Ateneo Salesiano, 1995).

Fitzgerald, Allan D. (ed.), *Augustine through the Ages: An Encyclopedia* (Grand Rapids, Mich.: Eerdmans, 1999).

Fitzgibbons, Moira, 'Deceptive Simplicity: Gaytryge's Translation of Archbishop Thoresby's *Injunctions*', in Renate Blumenfeld-Kosinski, Duncan Robertson, and Nancy Bradley Warren (eds.), *The Vernacular Spirit: Essays on Medieval Religious Literature* (New York: Palgrave, 2002).

Flanagan, Sabina, *Doubt in an Age of Faith: Uncertainty in the Long Twelfth Century* (Turnhout: Brepols, 2008).

Flannery, Mary C., and Katie L. Walter (eds.), *The Culture of Inquisition in Medieval England* (Woodbridge: Boydell, 2013).

———, '*Vttirle Onknowe?* Modes of Inquiry and the Dynamics of Interiority in Vernacular Literature', in Flannery and Walter (eds.), *Culture of Inquisition*.

Fleming, Robin, 'Oral Testimony and the Domesday Inquest', *Anglo-Norman Studies*, 17 (1995).

Fletcher, Christopher, *Richard II: Manhood, Youth, and Politics, 1377–99* (Oxford: Oxford University Press, 2008).

Forrest, Ian, 'The Archive of the Official of Stow and the "Machinery" of Church Government in the Late-Thirteenth Century', *Historical Research*, 84 (2011).

———, 'Continuity and Change in the Institutional Church', in Arnold (ed.), *Oxford Handbook of Medieval Christianity*.

———, 'Defamation, Heresy, and Late Medieval Social Life', in Linda Clark, Maureen Jurkowski, and Colin Richmond (eds.), *Image, Text and Church, 1380–1600: Essays Presented to Margaret Aston* (Toronto: PIMS, 2009).

———, *The Detection of Heresy in Late Medieval England* (Oxford: Oxford University Press, 2005).

———, 'English Provincial Constitutions and Inquisition into Lollardy', in Flannery and Walter (eds.), *Culture of Inquisition*.

———, 'The Politics of Burial in Late Medieval Hereford', *English Historical Review*, 125 (2010).

———, 'Power and the People in Thirteenth-Century England', in Janet Burton, Phillipp Schofield, and Björn Weiler (eds.), *Thirteenth Century England XV: Authority and Resistance in the Age of Magna Carta* (Woodbridge: Boydell, 2015).

———, 'The Summoner', in Stephen H. Rigby (ed.), *Historians on Chaucer: The 'General Prologue' to the Canterbury Tales* (Oxford: Oxford University Press, 2014).

———, 'The Survival of Medieval Visitation Records', *Archives*, 37 (2013).

———, 'The Transformation of Visitation in Thirteenth Century England', *Past & Present*, 221 (2013).

Forrest, Ian, and Anne Haour, 'Trust in Long Distance Relationships', in Catherine Holmes and Naomi Standen (eds.), *The Global Middle Ages* (forthcoming).

Forrest, Ian, and Christopher Whittick, 'The Thirteenth-Century Visitation Records of the Diocese of Hereford', *English Historical Review*, 131 (2016).

Fox, Harold, *Dartmoor's Alluring Uplands: Transhumance and Pastoral Management in the Middle Ages* (Exeter: Exeter University Press, 2012).

Fraher, Richard M., 'Conviction According to Conscience: The Medieval Jurists' Debate Concerning Judicial Discretion and the Law of Proof', *Law and History Review*, 7 (1989).

———, 'Preventing Crime in the High Middle Ages: The Medieval Lawyers' Search for Deterrence', in James R. Sweeny and Stanley Chodorow (eds.), *Popes, Teachers and Canon Law in the Middle Ages* (Ithaca, N.Y.: Cornell University Press, 1989).

———, 'The Theoretical Justification for the New Criminal Law of the High Middle Ages: *Rei publicae interest, ne crimina remaneant impunita*', *University of Illinois Law Review*, 3 (1984).

Frankot, Edda, *Of Laws of Ships and Shipmen: Medieval Maritime Law and Its Practice in Urban Northern Europe* (Edinburgh: Edinburgh University Press, 2012).

Freddoso, Alfred J., 'Ockham on Faith and Reason', in Paul Vincent Spade (ed.), *The Cambridge Companion to Ockham* (Cambridge: Cambridge University Press, 1999).

Freedman, Paul, *Images of the Medieval Peasant* (Stanford, Calif.: Stanford University Press, 1999).

French, Katherine L., *The Good Women of the Parish: Gender and Religion after the Black Death* (Philadelphia: University of Pennsylvania Press, 2008).

———, *The People of the Parish: Community Life in a Late Medieval Diocese* (Philadelphia: University of Pennsylvania Press, 2001).

———, 'Women Churchwardens in Late Medieval England', in Clive Burgess and Eamon Duffy (eds.), *The Parish in Late Medieval England* (Donington: Shaun Tyas, 2006).

———, 'Women in the Late Medieval English Parish', in Mary C. Erler and Maryanne Kowaleski (eds.), *Gendering the Master Narrative: Women and Power in the Middle Ages* (Ithaca, N.Y.: Cornell University Press, 2003).

Frevert, Ute, *Vertrauensfragen: eine Obsession der Moderne* (Munich: Beck, 2013).

Freyburger, Gérard, *Fides: Étude sémantique et religieuse depuis les origines jusqu'à l'époque augustéenne* (Paris: Belles Lettres, 2009).

Fukuyama, Francis, *Trust: The Social Virtues and the Creation of Prosperity* (New York: Free Press, 1995).

Gambetta, Diego, 'Can We Trust Trust?', in Gambetta (ed.), *Trust*.

——— (ed.), *Trust: Making and Breaking Cooperative Relations* (Oxford: Blackwell, 1988).

Garfinkel, Harold, *Studies in Ethnomethodology* (Englewood Cliffs, N.J.: Prentice Hall, 1967).

Gauvard, Claude (ed.), *L'enquête au Moyen âge* (Rome: École Française de Rome, 2008).

Geertz, Clifford, *Local Knowledge: Further Essays in Interpretative Anthropology*, 2nd ed. (New York: Basic Books, 1983).

Gellner, Ernest, 'Trust, Cohesion, and the Social Order' in Gambetta (ed.), *Trust*.

Geltner, Guy, *The Making of Medieval Antifraternalism: Polemic, Violence, Deviance, and Remembrance* (Oxford: Oxford University Press, 2012).

Ghosh, Kantik, 'Logic, Scepticism, and "Heresy" in Early-Fifteenth Century Europe', in Denery, Ghosh, and Zeeman (eds.), *Uncertain Knowledge*.

Gibbs, Jane, and Marion Lang, *Bishops and Reform* (London: Oxford University Press, 1934).

Giddens, Anthony, *The Consequences of Modernity* (Cambridge: Polity, 1990).

Gilchrist, Roberta, *Medieval Life: Archaeology and the Life Course* (Woodbridge: Boydell, 2012).

Gillespie, Vincent, 'Vernacular Theology', in Paul Strohm (ed.), *Middle English* (Oxford: Oxford University Press, 2007).

Given, James Buchanan, *Society and Homicide in Thirteenth-Century England* (Stanford, Calif.: Stanford University Press, 1977).

Given-Wilson, Chris, *Chronicles: The Writing of History in Medieval England* (Hambledon: Continuum, 2004).

———, 'The Problem of Labour in the Context of English Government, c. 1350–1450', in James Bothwell, P.J.P. Goldberg, and W. Mark Ormrod (eds.), *The Problem of Labour in Fourteenth-Century England* (Woodbridge: York Medieval Press, 2000).

Glénisson, Jean, 'Les enquêtes administratives en Europe occidentale aux XIIIe et XIVe siècles', in Werner Paravicini and Karl Ferdinand Werner (eds.), *Histoire comparée de l'administration: IVᵉ–XVIIIᵉ siècles* (Munich: Verlag, 1980).

Goering, Joseph, 'The Internal Forum and the Literature of Penance and Confession', in Wilfried Hartmann and Kenneth Pennington (eds.), *The History of Medieval Canon Law in the Classical Period, 1140–1234: From Gratian to the Decretals of Pope Gregory IX* (Washington, D.C.: Catholic University of America Press, 2008).

Goering, Joseph, and Daniel S. Talyor, 'The *Summulae* of Bishops Walter de Cantilupe (1240) and Peter Quinel (1287)', *Speculum*, 67 (1992).

Goldberg, Jessica, *Trade and Institutions in the Medieval Mediterranean: The Geniza Merchants and Their Business World* (Cambridge: Cambridge University Press, 2012).

Goldberg, P.J.P., 'Gender and Matrimonial Litigation in the Church Courts in the Later Middle Ages: The Evidence of the Court of York', *Gender and History*, 19 (2007).

——, *Medieval England: A Social History 1250–1550* (London: Arnold, 2004).

——, 'Urban Identity and the Poll Taxes of 1377, 1379 and 1381', *Economic History Review*, second series 43 (1990).

Good, David, 'Individuals, Interpersonal Relations and Trust', in Gambetta (ed.), *Trust*.

Gowing, Laura, *Domestic Dangers: Women, Words and Sex in Early Modern London* (Oxford: Clarendon, 1996).

Graeber, David, *Debt: The First 5000 Years* (New York: First Melville, 2011).

Gravdal, Kathryn, *Vilain and Courtois: Transgressive Parody in French Literature of the Twelfth and Thirteenth Centuries* (Lincoln: University of Nebraska Press, 1989).

Green, Monica H., *Making Women's Medicine Masculine: The Rise of Male Authority in Pre-modern Gynaecology* (Oxford: Oxford University Press, 2008).

Green, Richard Firth, *A Crisis of Truth: Literature and Law in Ricardian England* (Philadelphia: University of Pennsylvania Press, 1999).

Green, Thomas A., *Verdict According to Conscience: Perspectives on the English Criminal Trial Jury 1200–1800* (Chicago: University of Chicago Press, 1985).

Greif, Avner, *Institutions and the Path to the Modern Economy: Lessons from Medieval Trade* (Cambridge: Cambridge University Press, 2006).

——, 'Reputations and Coalitions in Medieval Trade: Evidence on the Maghribi Traders', *Journal of Economic History*, 49 (1989).

Grellard, Christophe, *Croire et savoir: les principes de la connaissance selon Nicolas d'Autrécourt* (Paris: Vrin, 2005).

——, 'How Is It Possible to Believe Falsely? John Buridan, the *Vetula*, and the Psychology of Error', in Denery, Ghosh, and Zeeman (eds.), *Uncertain Knowledge*.

Gurevich, Aron, *Categories of Medieval Culture* (London: Routledge, 1985).

Hadwin, J. F., 'The Medieval Lay Subsidies and Economic History', *Economic History Review*, second series 36 (1983).

Haines, Roy Martin, *The Administration of the Diocese of Worcester in the First Half of the Fourteenth Century* (London: SPCK, 1965).

——, *Archbishop John Stratford: Political Revolutionary and Champion of the Liberties of the English Church c.1275/80–1348* (Toronto: PIMS, 1986).

Hallam, Herbert Enoch, 'Some Thirteenth-Century Censuses', *Economic History Review*, 10 (1958).

Hamilton, Sarah, *Church and People in the Medieval West, 900–1200* (Harlow: Pearson, 2013).

Hamilton Thompson, Alexander, *The English Clergy and Their Organization in the Later Middle Ages* (Oxford: Clarendon, 1947).

Hamm, Berndt, *The Reformation of Faith in the Context of Late Medieval Theology and Piety: Essays* (Leiden: Brill, 2004).

Hardwig, John, 'The Role of Trust in Knowledge', *Journal of Philosophy*, 88 (1991).

Harris, Paul L., 'Checking Our Sources: The Origins of Trust in Testimony', *Studies in the History and Philosophy of Science*, 33 (2002).

Harvey, Katherine, *Episcopal Appointments in England, c. 1214–1344: From Election to Papal Provision* (Farnham: Ashgate, 2014).

Harvey, Margaret, *Lay Religious Life in Late Medieval Durham* (Woodbridge: Boydell, 2006).

Harvey, Paul D. A., *A Medieval Oxfordshire Village: Cuxham 1240 to 1400* (Oxford: Oxford University Press, 1965).

Harvey, Sally, *Domesday: Book of Judgement* (Oxford: Oxford University Press, 2014).

Hatcher, John, *Plague, Population and the English Economy 1348–1530* (London: Macmillan, 1977).

Hatcher, John, and Mark Bailey, *Modelling the Middle Ages: The History and Theory of England's Economic Development* (Oxford: Oxford University Press, 2001).

Hawthorn, Geoffrey, 'Three Ironies in Trust', in Gambetta (ed.), *Trust.*

Heath, Peter, *The English Parish Clergy on the Eve of the Reformation* (London: Routledge, 1969).

Helmholz, Richard H., 'Assumpsit and *fidei laesio*', *Law Quarterly Review*, 91 (1975).

———, 'Crime, Compurgation and the Courts of the Medieval Church', *Law and History Review*, 1 (1983).

———, *The* Ius Commune *in England: Four Studies* (Oxford: Oxford University Press, 2001).

———, *Marriage Litigation in Medieval England* (Cambridge: Cambridge University Press, 1974).

———, *The Oxford History of the Laws of England*, I: *Canon Law* (Oxford: University of Oxford Press, 2004).

Hill, Rosalind M. T., *The Labourer in the Vineyard: The Visitations of Archbishop Melton in the Archdeaconry of Richmond* (York: St Anthony's Press, 1968).

Hilton, Rodney H., *The English Peasantry in the Later Middle Ages* (Oxford: Clarendon, 1975).

———, 'Reasons for Inequality among Medieval Peasants', *Journal of Peasant Studies*, 5 (1978).

———, 'Some Social and Economic Evidence in Late Medieval English Tax Returns', in Hilton, *Class, Conflict and the Crisis of Feudalism* (London: Hambledon, 1985).

Hindle, Steve, *On the Parish? The Micro-politics of Poor Relief in Rural England c.1550–1750* (Oxford: Clarendon, 2004).

Holford, Matthew, 'Thrifty Men of the Country? The Jurors and their Role', in Michael Hicks (ed.), *The Fifteenth-Century Inquisitions* Post Mortem*: A Companion* (Woodbridge: Boydell, 2012).

Hollis, Martin, *Trust within Reason* (Cambridge: Cambridge University Press, 1998).

Homans, George Caspar, *English Villagers of the Thirteenth Century* (Cambridge, Mass.: Harvard University Press, 1942).

Horden, Peregrine, and Nicholas Purcell, *The Corrupting Sea: A Study of Mediterranean History* (Oxford: Blackwell, 2000).

Hoskin, Philippa, 'Diocesan Politics in the See of Worcester, 1218–1266', *Journal of Ecclesiastical History*, 54 (2003).

Hosking, Geoffrey A., *Trust: A History* (Oxford: Oxford University Press, 2014).

Houlbrooke, Ralph, *Church Courts and the People during the English Reformation 1520–1570* (Oxford: Oxford University Press, 1979).

Howell, Cicely, *Land, Family and Inheritance in Transition: Kibworth Harcourt 1280–1700* (Cambridge: Cambridge University Press, 1983).

Hudson, Anne, *The Premature Reformation: Wycliffite Texts and Lollard History* (Oxford: Oxford University Press, 1988).

Hudson, John, *Oxford History of the Laws of England*, II: *871–1216* (Oxford: Oxford University Press, 2012).

Hurnard, Naomi D., *The King's Pardon for Homicide before AD 1307* (Oxford: Clarendon, 1969).

Hutchinson, R., and Nigel J. Tringham, 'A Medieval Rectory House at Clifton Campville, Staffordshire', *South Staffordshire Archaeological and Historical Society Transactions*, 32 (1990–91).

Hyams, Paul R., 'Deans and Their Doings: The Norwich Inquiry of 1286', in Stephen Kuttner and Kenneth Pennington (eds.), *Proceedings of the Sixth International Congress
of Medieval Canon Law* (Vatican: Biblioteca Apostolica, 1985).

——, 'Faith, Fealty and Jewish "infideles" in Twelfth-Century England', in Sarah Rees
Jones and Sethina Watson (eds.), *Christians and Jews in Angevin England: The York
Massacre of 1190, Narratives and Contexts* (Woodbridge: York Medieval Press, 2013).

——, *Kings, Lords and Peasants in Medieval England: The Common Law of Villeinage
in the Twelfth and Thirteenth Centuries* (Oxford: Clarendon, 1980).

——, 'Maitland and the Rest of Us', in John Hudson (ed.), *The History of English Law:
Centenary Essays on 'Pollock and Maitland'*, Proceedings of the British Academy, 89
(Oxford: Oxford University Press, 1996).

——, *Rancor and Reconciliation in Medieval England* (Ithaca, N.Y.: Cornell University
Press, 2003).

——, 'Trial by Ordeal: The Key to Proof in the Early Common Law', in Morris S. Arnold
et al. (eds.), *On the Laws and Customs of England: Essays in Honor of Samuel E. Thorne*
(Chapel Hill: University of North Carolina Press, 1981).

——, 'What Did Edwardian Villagers Understand by "Law"?', in Zvi Razi and Richard M. Smith (eds.), *Medieval Society and the Manor Court* (Oxford: Oxford University
Press, 1996).

Hyslop, Alec, 'Other Minds', in Edward N. Zalta (ed.), *The Stanford Encyclopedia of Philosophy* (Spring 2016 ed.), http://plato.stanford.edu/archives/spr2016/entries/other
-minds/.

Ibbetson, David, 'From Property to Contract: The Transformation of Sale in the Middle
Ages', *Journal of Legal History*, 13 (1992).

——, *Historical Introduction to the Law of Obligations* (Oxford: Oxford University Press,
1999).

——, 'Sale of Goods in the Fourteenth Century', *Law Quarterly Review*, 107 (1991).

Ingram, Martin, *Church Courts, Sex and Marriage in England, 1570–1640* (Cambridge:
Cambridge University Press, 1987).

Iogna-Prat, Dominique, 'Churches in the Landscape', in Thomas F. X. Noble and Julia M. H.
Smith (eds.), *The Cambridge History of Christianity*, 3: *Early Medieval Christianities,
c. 600–c. 1100* (Cambridge: Cambridge University Press, 2008).

Iser, Wolfgang, *Prospecting: From Reader Response to Literary Anthropology* (Baltimore:
Johns Hopkins University Press, 1989).

Izbicki, Thomas, 'Sin and Pastoral Care', in Robert N. Swanson (ed.), *The Routledge History
of Medieval Christianity 1050–1500* (London: Routledge, 2015).

Jager, Eric, *The Book of the Heart* (Chicago: University of Chicago Press, 2000).

Jansen, Philippe, 'La participation des communautés et de leurs représentants à l'enquête
comtale de 1332–1333', in Thierry Pécout (ed.), *Quand gouverner c'est enquêter: les pratiques politiques de l'enquête princière (occident, XIIIᵉ–XIVᵉ siècles)* (Paris: Boccard,
2010).

Jarnoux, Philippe, 'Entre pouvoir et paraître. Pratiques de distribution et d'affirmation
dans le monde rural', in Jessenne and Menant (eds.), *Les élites rurales*.

Jauss, Hans Robert, *Literaturgeschichte als Provokation* (Frankfurt: Suhrkamp, 1970).

Jenks, Stuart, 'The Lay Subsidies and the State of the English Economy, 1275–1334', *Vierteljahrschrift für Sozial- und Wirtschaftsgeschichte*, 85 (1998).

Jessenne, Jean-Pierre, and François Menant (eds.), *Les élites rurales dans l'Europe médiévale et moderne* (Toulouse: Presses Universitaire du Mirail, 2007).

Jewell, Helen M., *English Local Administration in the Middle Ages* (New York: Barnes &
Noble, 1972).

Johansen, T. K., *Aristotle on the Sense-Organs* (Cambridge: Cambridge University Press, 1997).

Johnson, Tom, 'Medieval Law and Materiality: Shipwrecks, Finders, and Property on the Suffolk Coast, ca. 1380–1410', *American Historical Review*, 120 (2015).

Johnston, David, *Roman Law in Context* (Cambridge: Cambridge University Press, 1999).

Johnstone, Steven, *A History of Trust in Ancient Greece* (Chicago: University of Chicago Press, 2011).

Jones, Ann Rosalind, and Peter Stallybrass, *Renaissance Clothing and the Materials of Memory* (Cambridge: Cambridge University Press, 2000).

Jones, Karen, 'Trust as an Affective Attitude', *Ethics*, 107 (1996).

Jones, William R., 'Relations of the Two Jurisdictions: Conflict and Cooperation in England during the Thirteenth and Fourteenth Centuries', *Studies in Medieval and Renaissance History*, 7 (1970).

Jordan, William Chester, *Louis IX and the Challenge of the Crusade: A Study in Rulership* (Princeton, N.J.: Princeton University Press, 1979).

Jurdjevic, Mark, 'Trust in Renaissance Electoral Politics', *Journal of Interdisciplinary History*, 34 (2004).

Jurkowski, Maureen, 'The Arrest of William Thorpe in Shrewsbury and the Anti-Lollard Statute of 1406', *Historical Research*, 75 (2002).

Justice, Steven, 'Did the Middle Ages Believe in Their Miracles?', *Representations*, 103 (2008).

———, *Writing and Rebellion: England in 1381* (Berkeley: University of California Press, 1994).

Kaczynski, Bernice 'The Authority of the Fathers: Patristic Texts in Early Medieval Libraries and Scriptoria', *Journal of Medieval Latin*, 16 (2006).

Kane, Bronach, 'Custom, Memory and Knowledge in the Medieval English Church Courts', in Rosemary C. E. Hayes and William J. Sheils (eds.), *Clergy, Church and Society in England and Wales c. 1200–1800* (York: Borthwick Institute, 2013).

———, *Impotence and Virginity in the Late Medieval Ecclesiastical Court of York* (York: Borthwick Papers, 2008).

———, 'Social Representations of Memory and Gender in Later Medieval England', *Integrative Psychological and Behavioural Science*, 46 (2012).

Karras, Ruth Mazo, *Common Women: Prostitution and Sexuality in Medieval England* (Oxford: Oxford University Press, 1996).

———, 'Two Models, Two Standards: Moral Teaching and Sexual Mores', in Barbara A. Hanawalt and David Wallace (eds.), *Bodies and Disciplines: Intersections of Literature and History in Late Medieval England* (Minneapolis: University of Minnesota Press, 1996).

———, *Unmarriages: Women, Men, and Sexual Unions in the Middle Ages* (Philadelphia: University of Pennsylvania Press, 2012).

Kay, Sarah, and Miri Rubin (eds.), *Framing Medieval Bodies* (Manchester: Manchester University Press, 1994).

Keene, Derek, *Survey of Medieval Winchester*, 2 vols. (Oxford: Clarendon, 1985).

Kelleher, Marie A., 'Like Man and Wife: Clerics' Concubines in the Diocese of Barcelona', *Journal of Medieval History*, 28 (2002).

Kempshall, Matthew, *The Common Good in Late Medieval Political Thought* (Oxford: Oxford University Press, 1999).

———, *Rhetoric and the Writing of History, 400–1500* (Manchester: Manchester University Press, 2011).

Kent, Dale, *Friendship, Love and Trust in Renaissance Florence* (Cambridge, Mass.: Harvard University Press, 2009).

Kershaw, Ian, 'The Great Famine and the Agrarian Crisis in England, 1315–1322', *Past & Present*, 59 (1973).

Kéry, Lotte, 'Canon Law and Criminal Law: The Results of a New Study', in Uta-Renate Blumenthal, Kenneth Pennington, and Atria A. Larson (eds.), *Proceedings of the Twelfth International Congress of Medieval Canon Law* (Vatican: Biblioteca Apostolica, 2008).

King, Edmund, *Peterborough Abbey 1086–1310: A Study in the Land Market* (Cambridge: Cambridge University Press, 1973).

Kohn, Marek, *Trust: Self-Interest and the Common Good* (Oxford: Oxford University Press, 2008).

Kosminsky, Evgenii Alekseevich, *Studies in the Agrarian History of England in the Thirteenth Century* (Oxford: Blackwell, 1955).

Kosto, Adam J., and Anders Winroth (eds.), *Charters, Cartularies, and Archives: The Preservation and Transmission of Documents in the Medieval West* (Toronto: PIMS, 2002).

Kowaleski, Maryanne, 'A Consumer Economy', in Rosemary Horrox and W. Mark Ormrod (eds.), *A Social History of England, 1200–1500* (Cambridge: Cambridge University Press, 2006).

———, *Local Markets and Regional Trade in Medieval Exeter* (Cambridge: Cambridge University Press, 1995).

Kuehn, Thomas, '*Fama* as Legal Status in Renaissance Florence', in Fenster and Smail (eds.), *Fama*.

Kuhn, Thomas, *The Structure of Scientific Revolutions*, 4th ed. (Chicago: University of Chicago Press, 2012).

Kümin, Beat, *The Communal Age in Western Europe, c.1100–1800* (Basingstoke: Palgrave Macmillan, 2013).

———, *The Shaping of a Community: The Rise and Reformation of the English Parish, c. 1400–1560* (Aldershot: Scolar, 1996).

Lachaud, Frédérique, 'Dress and Social Status in England before the Sumptuary Laws', in Peter Coss and Maurice Keen (eds.), *Heraldry, Pageantry and Social Display in Medieval England* (Woodbridge: Boydell, 2002).

Lambert, Thomas B., 'Spiritual Protection and Secular Power: The Evolution of Sanctuary and Legal Privilege in Ripon and Beverley, 900–1300', in Thomas B. Lambert and David Rollason (eds.), *Peace and Protection in the Middle Ages* (Toronto: PIMS, 2009).

Landman, James H., 'The Doom of Reason: Accommodating Lay Interpretation in Late Medieval England', in Barbara A. Hanawalt and David Wallace (eds.), *Medieval Crime and Social Control* (Minneapolis: University of Minnesota Press, 1999).

Langbein, John H., 'Jury Influence on Conceptions of the Judiciary', in Paul Brand and Joshua Getzler (eds.), *Judges and Judging in the History of the Common Law and Civil Law: From Antiquity to Modern Times* (Cambridge: Cambridge University Press, 2012).

Larson, Peter, *Conflict and Compromise in the Late Medieval Countryside: Lords and Peasants in Durham, 1349–1400* (London: Routledge, 2014).

Law, John, 'Power/Knowledge and the Dissolution of the Sociology of Knowledge', in John Law (ed.), *Power, Action and Belief: A New Sociology of Knowledge?* (London: Routledge, 1986).

Laws, Bill, and Bobbie Blackwell (eds.), *A Slap of the Hand: The History of Hereford Market* (Almeley: Logaston Press, 2007).

Lefebvre, Jean-Luc, '*Prud'hommes* et *bonnes gens* dans les sources flamandes et wallonnes du Moyen Âge tardif ou l'éligibilité dans la fonction publique médiévale', *Le Moyen Age*, 108 (2002).

————, *Prud'hommes, serment curial et record de cour: la gestion locale des actes publics de Liège à l'Artois au Bas Moyen Âge* (Paris: Boccard, 2006).

Lemesle, Bruno, 'L'ênquete contre les épreuves: les enquêtes dans la région Angevine (XIIe-debut XIIIᵉ siècle)', in Gauvard (ed.), *L'enquête au Moyen âge*.

Lepine, David, *A Brotherhood of Canons Serving God: English Secular Cathedrals in the Later Middle Ages* (Woodbridge: Boydell, 1995).

————, 'The Parson', in Stephen H. Rigby (ed.), *Historians on Chaucer: The 'General Prologue' to the* Canterbury Tales (Oxford: Oxford University Press, 2014).

Letters, Samantha, *Gazetteer of Markets and Fairs in England and Wales to 1516* (Kew: TNA, 2003).

Levy, Ian, *'Fides quae per caritatem operatur*: Love as the Hermeneutical Key in Medieval Galatians Commentaries', *Cistercian Studies Quarterly*, 43 (2008).

Lipton, Sara, *Dark Mirror: The Medieval Origins of Anti-Jewish Iconography* (New York: Metropolitan Books, 2014).

Lootens, Matthew R., 'Augustine', in Paul L. Gavrilyuk and Sarah Coakley (eds.), *The Spiritual Senses: Perceiving God in Western Christianity* (Cambridge: Cambridge University Press, 2011).

Luhmann, Niklas, 'Familiarity, Confidence, Trust: Problems and Alternatives', in Gambetta (ed.), *Trust*.

————, *Trust and Power: Two Works* (Chichester: John Wiley, 1979).

Lukes, Steven, *Power: A Radical View*, 2nd ed. (Basingstoke: Palgrave Macmillan, 2005).

Lupoi, Maurizio, 'La *confidentia* è il *trust*', in Prodi (ed.), *La fiducia secondo i linguaggi del potere*.

Lutgens, Christine, 'The Case of Waghen vs. Sutton: Conflict over Burial Rights in Late Medieval England', *Mediaeval Studies*, 38 (1976).

Lydon, Ghislaine, *On Trans-Saharan Trails: Islamic Law, Trade Networks, and Cross-Cultural Exchange in Nineteenth-Century West Africa* (Cambridge: Cambridge University Press, 2009).

Macfarlane, Alan, *Marriage and Love in England: Modes of Reproduction 1300–1840* (Oxford: Blackwell, 1986).

Machlup, Fritz, *Knowledge. Its Creation, Distribution, and Economic Significance, I: Knowledge and Knowledge Production* (Princeton, N.J.: Princeton University Press, 1980).

Macho-Stadler, Inés, and J. David Pérez-Castrillo, *An Introduction to the Economics of Information: Incentives and Contracts* (Oxford: Oxford University Press, 1997).

Macnair, Mike, 'Vicinage and the Antecedents of the Jury', *Law and History Review*, 17 (1999).

Maddern, Philippa, *'Best Trusted Friends*: Concepts and Practices of Friendship among Fifteenth-Century Norfolk Gentry', in Nicholas Rogers (ed.), *England in the Fifteenth Century* (Stamford: Watkins, 1994).

Mansfield, Mary C., *The Humiliation of Sinners: Public Penance in Thirteenth-Century France* (Ithaca, N.Y.: Cornell University Press, 1995).

Marx, Karl, *Selected Writings*, ed. David McLellan, 2nd ed. (Oxford: Oxford University Press, 2000).

Masschaele, James, *Jury, State, and Society in Medieval England* (Basingstoke: Macmillan, 2008).

Mattéoni, Olivier, 'Enquêtes, pouvoir et contrôle des hommes dans les territoires des ducs de Bourbon', in Gauvard (ed.), *L'enquête au moyen âge*.

Mayr-Harting, Henry, 'Ecclesiastical History', in Alan Deyermond (ed.), *A Century of British Medieval Studies* (Oxford: Oxford University Press, 2007).

————, *Religion, Politics and Society in Britain 1066–1272* (Harlow: Pearson, 2011).

McHardy, Alison K., 'Clerical Taxation in Fifteenth-Century England: The Clergy as Agents of the Crown', in Barrie Dobson (ed.), *The Church, Politics and Patronage in the Fifteenth Century* (Gloucester: Sutton, 1984).

McIntosh, Marjorie Keniston, *Controlling Misbehavior in England, 1370–1600* (Cambridge: Cambridge University Press, 1998).

———, *Poor Relief in England, 1350–1600* (Cambridge: Cambridge University Press, 2012).

———, *Working Women in English Society 1300–1620* (Cambridge: Cambridge University Press, 2005).

McNall, Christopher, 'The Business of Statutory Debt Registries, 1283–1307', in Phillipp R. Schofield and Nicholas J. Mayhew (eds.), *Credit and Debt in Medieval England c. 1180–c. 1350* (Oxford: Oxbow, 2002).

McSheffrey, Shannon, *Marriage, Sex, and Civic Culture in Late Medieval London* (Philadelphia: University of Pennsylvania Press, 2006).

———, 'Sanctuary and the Legal Topography of Pre-Reformation London', *Law and History Review* 27 (2009).

———, 'Whoring Priests and Godly Citizens: Law, Morality, and Sexual Misconduct in Late Medieval London', in Norman L. Jones and Daniel Woolf (eds.), *Local Identities in Late Medieval and Early Modern England* (Basingstoke: Palgrave Macmillan, 2007).

Melbin, Murray, 'Night as Frontier', *American Sociological Review*, 43 (1978).

Menache, Sophie, *The Vox Dei: Communication in the Middle Ages* (Oxford: Oxford University Press, 1990).

Metzler, Irina, *Disability in Medieval Europe: Thinking about Physical Impairment during the High Middle Ages, c. 1100–1400* (Abingdon: Routledge, 2006).

———, *A Social History of Disability in the Middle Ages: Cultural Consideration of Physical Impairment* (Abingdon: Routledge, 2013).

Mews, Constant, 'Man's Knowledge of God according to Peter Abelard', in Christian Wenin (ed.), *L'homme et son univers au moyen âge*, 2 vols. (Louvain-le-Neuve: Institut supérieur de philosophie, 1986).

Middle English Dictionary, ed. Hans Kurath and Sherman M. Kuhn (Ann Arbor: University of Michigan, 1952–2001).

Migliorino, Francesco, *Fama e infamia: problemi della società medievale nel pensiero giuridico nei secoli XII e XIII* (Catania: Editrice Giannotta, 1985).

Mileson, Stephen, 'The South Oxfordshire Project: Perceptions of Landscape, Settlement and Society, c. 500–1650', *Landscape History*, 33 (2012).

Miller, Edward, and John Hatcher, *Medieval England: Rural Society and Economic Change 1086–1348* (London: Longman, 1978).

Miller, Maureen, *The Bishop's Palace: Architecture and Authority in Medieval Italy* (Ithaca, N.Y.: Cornell University Press, 2000).

———, *Clothing the Clergy: Virtue and Power in Medieval Europe, c. 800–1200* (Ithaca, N.Y.: Cornell University Press, 2014).

Milsom, S.F.C., *Historical Foundations of the Common Law*, 2nd ed. (London: Butterworths, 1981).

Misztal, Barbara A., *Trust in Modern Societies: The Search for the Bases of Social Order* (Cambridge: Polity, 1996).

Monclús, Pere Benito i, 'Marché foncier et besoin d'expertise dans la Catalogne des Xe–XIIe siècles: le rôle des *boni homines* comme estimateurs de biens', in Claude Denjean and Laurent Feller (eds.), *Expertise et valeur des choses au Moyen Âge. I: Le besoin d'expertise* (Madrid: Casa de Velázquez, 2013).

Moore, Robert I., *The First European Revolution c.970–1215* (Oxford: Blackwell, 2000).

————, *The Formation of a Persecuting Society: Power and Deviance in Western Europe, 950–1250* (Oxford: Blackwell, 1987).

Morgan, Teresa, *Roman Faith and Christian Faith:* Pistis and Fides *in the Early Roman Empire and Early Churches* (Oxford: Oxford University Press, 2015).

Morris, Richard, *Churches in the Landscape* (London: Dent, 1989).

Muldrew, Craig, *The Economy of Obligation: The Culture of Credit and Social Relations in Early Modern England* (Basingstoke: Macmillan, 1998).

Müller, Miriam, 'Food, Hierarchy, and Class Conflict', in Richard Goddard, John Langdon, and Miriam Müller (eds.), *Survival and Discord in Medieval Society: Essays in Honour of Christopher Dyer* (Turnhout: Brepols, 2010).

Murray, Alexander, 'Confession as a Historical Source in the Thirteenth Century', in Ralph H. C. Davis and John Michael Wallace-Hadrill (eds.), *The Writing of History in the Middle Ages: Essays Presented to R. W. Southern* (Oxford: Oxford University Press, 1981).

————, *Conscience and Authority in the Medieval Church* (Oxford: Oxford University Press, 2015).

————, *Suicide in the Middle Ages*, 2 vols. (Oxford: Oxford University Press, 1998–2000).

Musson, Anthony, *Medieval Law in Context: The Growth of Legal Consciousness from Magna Carta to the Peasants' Revolt* (Manchester: Manchester University Press, 2001).

Neal, Derek G., *The Masculine Self in Late Medieval England* (Chicago: University of Chicago Press, 2008).

Nedkvitne, Arnved, *The Social Consequences of Literacy in Medieval Scandinavia* (Turnhout: Brepols, 2004).

Needham, Rodney, *Belief, Language, and Experience* (Oxford: Blackwell, 1972).

Nehlsen-von Stryk, Karin, *Die boni homines des frühen Mittelalters: unter besonderer Berücksichtigung der fränkischen Quellen* (Berlin: Duncker & Humblot, 1981).

Nelson, Janet L., 'Dispute Settlement in Carolingian West Francia', in Wendy Davies and Paul Fouracre (eds.), *The Settlement of Disputes in Early Medieval Europe* (Cambridge: Cambridge University Press, 1986).

Nicolette Zeeman, 'Philosophy in Parts: Jean de Meun, Chaucer, and Lydgate', in Denery, Ghosh, and Zeeman (eds.), *Uncertain Knowledge*.

Nightingale, Pamela, 'The English Parochial Clergy as Investors and Creditors in the First Half of the Fourteenth Century', in Phillipp R. Schofield and Nicholas J. Mayhew (eds.), *Credit and Debt in Medieval England c.1180–c.1350* (Oxford: Oxbow, 2002).

————, 'Gold, Credit, and Mortality: Distinguishing Deflationary Pressures on the Late Medieval English Economy', *Economic History Review*, 63 (2010).

————, 'The Lay Subsidies and the Distribution of Wealth in Medieval England, 1275–1334', *Economic History Review*, 57 (2004).

North, Douglass C., *Institutions, Institutional Change and Economic Performance* (Cambridge: Cambridge University Press, 1990).

Oberman, Heiko Augustinus, *The Harvest of Medieval Theology: Gabriel Biel and Late Medieval Nominalism* (Durham: Labyrinth Press, 1963).

Ogilvie, Sheilagh, 'How Does Social Capital Affect Women?', *American Historical Review*, 109 (2004).

————, *Institutions and European Trade: Merchant Guilds, 1000–1800* (Cambridge: Cambridge University Press, 2011).

————, 'The Use and Abuse of Trust: Social Capital and Its Deployment by Early Modern Guilds', *Jahrbuch für Wirtschaftsgeschichte*, 46 (2005).

Olson, Sheri, 'Jurors of the Village Court: Local Leadership Before and After the Plague in Ellington, Huntingdonshire', *Journal of British Studies*, 30 (1991).

Orme, Nicholas, 'Sufferings of the Clergy: Illness and Old Age in Exeter Diocese, 1300–1540', in Margaret Pelling and Richard M. Smith (eds.), *Life, Death and the Elderly: Historical Perspectives* (London: Routledge, 1991).

Ormrod, W. Mark, 'The Crown and the English Economy, 1290–1348', in Campbell (ed.), *Before the Black Death.*

——, *Edward III* (New Haven, Conn.: Yale University Press, 2011).

——, 'England in the Middle Ages', in Richard Bonney (ed.), *The Rise of the Fiscal State in Europe, c. 1200–1815* (Oxford: Oxford University Press, 1999).

——, 'Poverty and Privilege: The Fiscal Burden in England (XIIIth–XVth Centuries)', in Simonetta Cavaciocchi (ed.), *La Fiscalità nell'Economia Europea Secc. XIII–XVIII* (Florence: Firenze University Press, 2008).

Ormrod, W. Mark, and János Barta, 'The Feudal Structure and the Beginnings of State Finance', in Richard Bonney (ed.), *Economic Systems and State Finance* (Oxford: Clarendon, 1995).

Ouchi, William, 'Markets, Bureaucracies, and Clans', *Administrative Science Quarterly*, 25 (1980).

Owen, Dorothy M., *Church and Society in Medieval Lincolnshire* (Lincoln: History of Lincolnshire, 1971).

——, 'Ecclesiastical Jurisdiction in England 1300–1500', in Derek Baker (ed.), *The Materials, Sources and Methods of Ecclesiastical History*, Studies in Church History, 11 (Oxford: Oxford University Press, 1975).

Oxford Dictionary of National Biography (Oxford: Oxford University Press, 2004), http://www.oxforddnb.com.

Ozment, Steven, *The Age of Reform 1250–1550: An Intellectual and Religious History of Late Medieval and Reformation Europe* (New Haven, Conn.: Yale University Press, 1980).

Page, William (ed.), *The Victoria History of the County of Lincoln* (London: Archibald Constable, 1906).

—— (ed.), *The Victoria History of the County of Nottingham* (London: Archibald Constable, 1910).

—— (ed.), *The Victoria History of Hampshire and the Isle of Wight*, 5 vols. (London: Institute of Historical Research, 1973).

Page, William, Granville Proby, and Sidney Inskip (eds.), *The Victoria County History of Huntingdon*, 3 vols. (London: Institute of Historical Research, 1926–38).

Pakkala-Weckström, Mari, 'No botmeles bihestes: Various Ways of Making Binding Promises in Middle English', in Andreas H. Jucker and Irma Taavitsainen (eds.), *Speech Acts in the History of English* (Amsterdam: Benjamin, 2008).

Palmer, Robert C., *English Law in the Age of the Black Death, 1348–1381: A Transformation of Governance and Law* (Chapel Hill: University of North Carolina Press, 1993).

——, *Selling the Church: The English Parish in Law, Commerce, and Religion, 1350–1550* (Chapel Hill: University of North Carolina Press, 2002).

Pantin, William Abel, *The English Church in the Fourteenth Century* (Cambridge: Cambridge University Press, 1955).

Park, Katharine, 'Medicine and Natural Philosophy: Naturalistic Traditions', in Bennett and Karras (eds.), *Oxford Handbook of Women and Gender.*

Parkin, Frank, *Class Inequality and Political Order* (London: Paladin, 1972).

Pearsall, Derek, 'Strangers in Late-Fourteenth Century London', in F.R.P. Akehurst and Stephanie Cain Van D'Elden (eds.), *The Stranger in Medieval Society* (Minneapolis: University of Minnesota Press, 1997).

Pegg, Mark, 'Heresy, Good Men, and Nomenclature', in Michael Frassetto (ed.), *Heresy and the Persecuting Society in the Middle Ages: Essays on the Work of R.I. Moore* (Leiden: Brill, 2006).

Pelikan, Jaroslav, *Credo: Historical and Theological Guide to Creeds and Confessions of Faith in the Christian Tradition* (New Haven, Conn.: Yale University Press, 2003).

Penn, Simon A. C., and Christopher Dyer, 'Wages and Earnings in Late Medieval England: Evidence from the Enforcement of the Labour Laws', *Economic History Review*, 43 (1990).

Pennington, Kenneth, 'Feudal Oath of Fidelity and Homage', in Kenneth Pennington and Melodie Harris Eichbauer (eds.), *Law as Profession and Practice in Medieval Europe* (Farnham: Ashgate, 2011).

———, *The Prince and the Law 1200–1600: Sovereignty and Rights in the Western Legal Tradition* (Berkeley: University of California Press, 1993).

Perler, Dominik, 'Can We Trust Our Senses? Fourteenth-Century Debates on Sensory Illusions', in Denery, Ghosh, and Zeeman (eds.), *Uncertain Knowledge*.

Phillips, Susan E., *Transforming Talk: The Problem with Gossip in Late Medieval England* (University Park: Pennsylvania State University Press, 2007).

Pimsler, Martin, 'Solidarity in the Medieval Village? The Evidence of Personal Pledging at Elton, Huntingdonshire', *Journal of British Studies*, 17 (1977).

Pinto, Giuliano, 'Bourgeoisie de village et différenciations sociales dans les campagnes de l'Italie communale (XIIIe–XVe siècle)', in Jessenne and Menant (eds.), *Les élites rurales*.

Platt, Graham, *Land and People in Medieval Lincolnshire* (Lincoln: History of Lincolnshire, 1985).

Polanyi, Karl, *The Great Transformation* (New York: Farrer and Rinehart, 1944).

Polanyi, Michael, *Personal Knowledge: Towards a Post-critical Philosophy* (London: Routledge, 1958).

Pollock, Frederick, and Frederic William Maitland, *The History of English Law before the Time of Edward I*, 2 vols. (Cambridge: Cambridge University Press, 1968).

Polo de Beaulieu, Marie-Anne, 'L'émergence de l'auteur et son rapport à l'autorité dans les recueils d'*exempla* (XIIe–XVe siècle)', in Michel Zimmermann (ed.), *Auctor et auctoritas: invention et conformisme dans l'écriture médiévale* (Paris: École des Chartes, 2001).

Pontal, Odette, *Les Statuts Synodaux* (Turnhout: Brepols, 1975).

Poos, Lawrence R., *A Rural Society after the Black Death: Essex 1350–1525* (Cambridge: Cambridge University Press, 1991).

Postles, David, 'Personal Pledging in Manorial Courts in the Later Middle Ages', *Bulletin of the John Rylands Library*, 75 (1993).

———, 'Pledge of Faith in Transactions of Land', *Journal of the Society of Archivists*, 7 (1984).

Powell, Edward, *Kingship, Law, and Society: Criminal Justice in the Reign of Henry V* (Oxford: Clarendon, 1989).

Prietzel, Malte, 'Canonistes et gens de finances: les officiers de l'évêque de Tournai au XVe siècle', in Jean-Marie Cauchies (ed.), *Finances et financiers des princes et des villes à l'époque bourguignonne* (Turnhout: Brepols, 2004).

Proctor, Evelyn S., *The Judicial Use of Pesquisa in León and Castille 1157–1369* (London: Longmans, 1966).

Prodi, Paolo (ed.), *La fiducia secondo i linguaggi del potere* (Bologna: Mulino, 2007).

Provero, Luigi, 'Les dîmes dans la territorialité incertaine des Campagnes du XIIIe siècle', in Michel Lauwers (ed.), *La dîme, l'Église et la société féodale* (Turnhout: Brepols, 2012).

Putnam, Robert D., *Bowling Alone: The Collapse and Revival of American Community* (New York: Simon & Schuster, 2000).

Putnam, Robert D., et al., *Making Democracy Work: Civic Traditions in Modern Italy* (Princeton, N.J.: Princeton University Press, 1993).

Raban, Sandra, *A Second Domesday? The Hundred Rolls of 1279–80* (Oxford: Oxford University Press, 2004).

Raftis, J. Ambrose, *Peasant Economic Development within the English Manorial System* (Montreal: McGill-Queens, 1996).

———, *Tenure and Mobility: Studies in the Social History of the Mediaeval English Village* (Toronto: PIMS, 1964).

———, *Warboys: Two Hundred Years in the Life of an English Mediaeval Village* (Toronto: PIMS, 1974).

Ramos Pinto, Pedro, 'Why Inequalities Matter', in Rémi Genevey, Rajendra K. Pachauri, and Laurence Tubiana (eds.), *Reducing Inequalities: A Sustainable Development Challenge* (New Delhi: TERI, 2013).

Ranger, Terence, 'The Invention of Tradition in Colonial Africa', in Eric Hobsbawm and Terence Ranger (eds.), *The Invention of Tradition* (Cambridge: Cambridge University Press, 1983).

Razi, Zvi, *Life, Marriage and Death in a Medieval Parish: Economy, Society and Demography in Halesowen 1270–1400* (Cambridge: Cambridge University Press, 1980).

———, 'The Myth of the Immutable English Family', *Past & Present*, 140 (1993).

Rebillard, Éric, 'A New Style of Argument in Christian Polemic: Augustine and the Use of Patristic Citations', *Journal of Early Christian Studies*, 8 (2000).

Reemtsma, Jan Philipp, *Trust and Violence: An Essay on a Modern Relationship* (Princeton, N.J.: Princeton University Press, 2012).

Reinhard, Wolfgang, 'Power Elites, State Servants, Ruling Classes, and the Growth of State Power', in Wolfgang Reinhard (ed.), *Power Elites and State Building* (Oxford: Clarendon, 1996).

Rentz, Ellen K., *Imagining the Parish in Late Medieval England* (Columbus: Ohio State University Press, 2015).

Reuter, Timothy, and Gabriel Silagi (eds.), *Wortkonkordanz zum Decretum Gratiani*, 5 vols. (Munich: Monumenta Germaniae Historica, 1990).

Reyerson, Kathryn, 'Le témoignage des femmes, d'après quelques enquêtes montpelliéraines du XIVᵉ siècle', in Gauvard (ed.), *L'enquête au moyen âge*.

———, 'The Merchants of the Mediterranean: Merchants as Strangers', in F.R.P. Akehurst and Stephanie Cain Van D'Elden (eds.), *The Stranger in Medieval Society* (Minneapolis: University of Minnesota Press, 1997).

Reynolds, Susan, 'The Emergence of Professional Law in the Long Twelfth Century', *Law and History Review*, 21 (2003).

———, *Fiefs and Vassals: The Medieval Evidence Reinterpreted* (Oxford: Oxford University Press, 1994).

———, *An Introduction to the History of Medieval English Towns* (Oxford: Clarendon, 1977).

———, 'Social Mentalities and the Case of Medieval Scepticism', *Transactions of the Royal Historical Society*, sixth series 1 (1991).

———, 'Trust in Medieval Society and Politics', in Reynolds, *The Middle Ages without Feudalism* (Farnham: Ashgate Varorium, 2012).

Richmond, Colin, 'Hand and Mouth: Information Gathering and Use in England in the Later Middle Ages', *Journal of Historical Sociology*, 1 (1988).

Rider, Catherine, *Magic and Religion in Medieval England* (London: Reaktion Books, 2012).

Rigby, Stephen H., *English Society in the Later Middle Ages: Class, Gender, and Status* (Basingstoke: Macmillan, 1995).

———, 'Urban Society in Early Fourteenth-Century England: The Evidence of the Lay Subsidies', *Bulletin of the John Rylands Library*, 72 (1990).

Roberts, Brian K., and Stuart Wrathmell, *An Atlas of Rural Settlement in England*, corrected reprint ed. (London: English Heritage, 2003).

Robinson, Olivia F., 'Bishops and Bankers', in Kenneth Pennington and Melodie Harris Eichbauer (eds.), *Law as Profession and Practice in Medieval Europe* (Farnham: Ashgate, 2011).

Rodwell, Warwick, *The Archaeology of Churches* (Stroud: Amberley, 2012).

Roffe, David, *Domesday: The Inquest and the Book* (Oxford: Oxford University Press, 2000).

———, 'Domesday Now', *Anglo-Norman Studies* 28 (2006).

Rosenthal, Joel T., *Old Age in Late Medieval England* (Philadelphia: University of Pennsylvania Press, 1996).

———, *Telling Tales: Sources and Narration in Late Medieval England* (University Park: Pennsylvania State University Press, 2003).

Rosenwein, Barbara H., *Emotional Communities in the Early Middle Ages* (Ithaca, N.Y.: Cornell University Press, 2006).

Rosser, Gervase, *The Art of Solidarity in the Middle Ages: Guilds in England 1250–1550* (Oxford: Oxford University Press, 2015).

———, 'Going to the Fraternity Feast: Commensality and Social Relations in Late Medieval England', *Journal of British Studies*, 33 (1994).

———, 'Parochial Conformity and Voluntary Religion in Late-Medieval England', *Transactions of the Royal Historical Society*, sixth series 1 (1991).

———, 'Religious Practice on the Margins', in John Blair and Carol Pyrah (eds.), *Church Archaeology: Research Directions for the Future* (York: Council for British Archaeology, 1996).

Rubin, Miri, *Charity and Community in Medieval Cambridge* (Cambridge: Cambridge University Press, 1987).

———, 'The Poor', in Rosemary Horrox (ed.), *Fifteenth Century Attitudes: Perceptions of Society in Late Medieval England* (Cambridge: Cambridge University Press, 1994).

———, 'Small Groups: Identity and Solidarity in the Late Middle Ages', in Jenny Kermode (ed.), *Enterprise and Individuals in Fifteenth Century England* (Stroud: Sutton, 1991).

Ryan, Magnus, 'The Oath of Fealty and the Lawyers', in Joseph Canning and Otto Gerhard Oexle (eds.), *Political Thought and the Realities of Power in the Middle Ages* (Göttingen: Vandenhoeck & Ruprecht, 1998).

Sabapathy, John, *Officers and Accountability in Medieval England 1170–1300* (Oxford: Oxford University Press, 2014).

Sackville, Lucy, *Heresy and Heretics in the Thirteenth Century: The Textual Representations* (Woodbridge: York Medieval Press, 2011).

Salter, Elisabeth, *Popular Reading in English c. 1400–1600* (Manchester: Manchester University Press, 2012).

Sassier, Yves, 'L'utilisation du concept de *res publica* en France du nord aux Xe, XIe et XIIe siècles', in Jacques Krynen and Albert Rigaudiere (eds.), *Droits savants et pratiques francaises du pouvoir (XIe–XVe siècles)* (Bordeaux: Presses Universitaire de Bordeaux, 1992).

Satora, Magdalena, 'The Social Reception of the Templar Trial in Early Fourteenth-Century France', in Jochen Burgtorf, Paul F. Crawford, and Helen J. Nicholson (eds.), *The Debate on the Trial of the Templars* (Farnham: Ashgate, 2010).

Sbriccoli, Mario, 'Legislation, Justice and Political Power in Italian Cities, 1200–1400', in Antonio Padoa-Schioppa (ed.), *Legislation and Justice* (Oxford: Clarendon, 1997).

Scammell, Jean, 'The Rural Chapter in England from the Eleventh to the Fourteenth Century', *English Historical Review*, 86 (1971).

Schmitt, Jean-Claude, *Le corps des images: essais sur la culture visuelle au moyen âge* (Paris: Gallimard, 2002).

Schofield, Phillipp R., *Peasant and Community in Medieval England 1200–1500* (Basingstoke: Palgrave Macmillan, 2003).

Schulte, Petra, *Scripturae publicae creditur: Das Vertrauen in Notariatsurkunden im kommunalen Italien des 12. und 13. Jahrhunderts* (Tübingen: Max Niemeyer, 2003).

Schulte, Petra, Marco Mostert, and Irene van Renswoude (eds.), *Strategies of Writing: Studies on Text and Trust in the Middle Ages* (Turnhout: Brepols, 2008).

Scott, James C., *The Art of Not Being Governed: An Anarchist History of Upland South-East Asia* (New Haven, Conn.: Yale University Press, 2009).

———, *Seeing Like a State: How Certain Schemes to Improve the Human Condition Have Failed* (New Haven, Conn.: Yale University Press, 1998).

———, *Two Cheers for Anarchism: Six Easy Pieces on Autonomy, Dignity, and Meaningful Work and Play* (Princeton, N.J.: Princeton University Press, 2012).

Seabright, Paul, *The Company of Strangers: A Natural History of Economic Life* (Princeton, N.J.: Princeton University Press, 2004).

Seligman, Adam B., *The Problem of Trust* (Princeton, N.J.: Princeton University Press, 1997).

Sen, Amartya, *Inequality Re-examined* (Oxford: Oxford University Press, 1995).

———, *On Economic Inequality* (Oxford: Oxford University Press, 1973).

Shahar, Shulamith, *Growing Old in the Middle Ages: 'Winter Clothes Us in Shadow and Pain'* (London: Routledge, 1997).

Shank, Michael H., *Unless You Believe, You Shall Not Understand: Logic, University, and Society in Late Medieval Vienna* (Princeton, N.J.: Princeton University Press, 1988).

Shapin, Steven, *A Social History of Truth: Civility and Science in Seventeenth-Century England* (Chicago: University of Chicago Press, 1994).

Sharp, H. B., 'Some Mid-Fifteenth Century Small-Scale Building Repairs', *Vernacular Architecture*, 12 (1981).

Sharpe, James, *Defamation and Sexual Slander in Early Modern England: The Church Courts at York* (York: Borthwick Institute, 1980).

Signori, Gabriele, *Schuldenwirtschaft: Konsumenten- und Hypothekarkredite im spätmittelalterlichen Basel* (Munich: Universitätsverlag Konstanz, 2015).

Simmel, Georg, *The Philosophy of Money* (London: Routledge, 1978).

———, 'The Stranger', in Kurt H. Wolff (ed.), *The Sociology of Georg Simmel* (London: Collier, 1950).

Simpson, Paula, 'The Continuum of Resistance to Tithe, c. 1400–1600', in Rob Lutton and Elisabeth Salter (eds.), *Pieties in Transition: Religious Practices and Experiences, c.1400–1600* (Aldershot: Ashgate, 2007).

Skoda, Hannah, 'Violent Discipline or Disciplining Violence?', *Cultural and Social History*, 6 (2009).

Slater, Terry R., 'The Urban Hierarchy in Medieval Staffordshire', *Journal of Historical Geography*, 11 (1985).

Slavin, Philip, 'The Great Bovine Pestilence and its Economic and Environmental Consequences in England and Wales, 1318–1350', *Economic History Review*, 65 (2012).

———, 'Market Failure during the Great Famine in England and Wales (1315–1317)', *Past & Present*, 222 (2014).

Smith, David M., *Guide to the Bishops' Registers of England and Wales: A Survey from the Middle Ages to the Abolition of Episcopacy in 1646* (London: Royal Historical Society, 1981).

———, 'Thomas Cantilupe's Register: The Administration of the Diocese of Hereford 1275–1282', in Meryl Jancy (ed.), *St Thomas Cantilupe Bishop of Hereford: Essays in His Honour* (Hereford: Hereford Cathedral, 1982).

Smith, Lesley, *The Ten Commandments: Interpreting the Bible in the Medieval World* (Leiden: Brill, 2014).

Smith, Richard M., 'Demographic Developments in Rural England, 1300–48: A Survey', in Campbell (ed.), *Before the Black Death*.

———, 'Modernization and the Corporate Village Community in England: Some Sceptical Reflections', in Alan R. H. Baker and Derek Gregory (eds.), *Explorations in Historical Geography: Interpretative Essays* (Cambridge: Cambridge University Press, 1984).

Smith, Sally V., 'Materializing Resistant Identities among the Medieval Peasantry: An Examination of Dress Accessories from English Rural Settlement Sites', *Journal of Material Culture*, 14 (2009).

Sosis, Richard, 'Does Religion Promote Trust? The Role of Signaling, Reputation, and Punishment', *Interdisciplinary Journal of Research on Religion*, 1 (2005).

Southern, Richard W., *Saint Anselm and His Biographer: A Study of Monastic Life and Thought 1059–c.1130* (Cambridge: Cambridge University Press, 1966).

Sparks, Chris, *Heresy, Inquisition and Life Cycle in Medieval Languedoc* (Woodbridge: York Medieval Press, 2014).

Spence, Michael, 'Cartularies of Fountains Abbey: Archival Systems and Practices', *Cîteaux*, 61 (2010).

Spufford, Peter, *Money and Its Uses in Medieval Europe* (Cambridge: Cambridge University Press, 1988).

Standley, Eleanor, *Trinkets and Charms: The Use, Meaning and Significance of Dress Accessories 1300–1700* (Oxford: Oxford University School of Archaeology, 2013).

Stephenson, Carl, *Mediaeval Institutions: Selected Essays* (Ithaca, N.Y.: Cornell University Press, 1954).

Stevens, Matthew, 'London Creditors and the Fifteenth-Century Depression', *Economic History Review*, 69 (2016).

Storey, Robin L., *Diocesan Administration in Fifteenth-Century England* (York: Borthwick Institute, 1959).

Styles, Philip (ed.), *Victoria History of the County of Warwick*, vol. 3 (London: Institute of Historical Research, 1945).

Swanson, Robert N., *Church and Society in Late Medieval England* (Oxford: Blackwell, 1989).

———, '*Dubius est in fide fidelis est?* Doubt and Assurance in Late Medieval Catholicism', in Frances Andrews, Charlotte Methuen, and Andrew Spicer (eds.), *Doubting Christianity: The Church and Doubt*, Studies in Church History 52 (Cambridge: Cambridge University Press, 2016).

———, 'Economic Survival in Late Medieval Derbyshire: The Spirituality Income of the Dean and Chapter of Lichfield, c. 1400–c. 1535', in Richard Goddard, John Langdon, and Miriam Müller (eds.), *Survival and Discord in Medieval Society: Essays in Honour of Christopher Dyer* (Turnhout: Brepols, 2010).

———, 'Episcopal Income from Spiritualities in Later Medieval England: The Evidence for the Diocese of Coventry and Lichfield', *Midland History*, 13 (1988).

———, *Indulgences in Late Medieval England: Passports to Paradise* (Cambridge: Cambridge University Press, 2007).

———, 'Parochialism and Particularism: The Dispute over the Status of Ditchford Frary, Warwickshire in the Early Fifteenth Century', in Michael J. Franklin and Christopher Harper-Bill (eds.), *Medieval Ecclesiastical Studies in Honour of Dorothy M. Owen* (Woodbridge: Boydell, 1995).

———, 'Standards of Livings: Parochial Revenues in Pre-Reformation England', in Christopher Harper-Bill (ed.), *Religious Belief and Ecclesiastical Careers in Late Medieval England* (Woodbridge: Boydell, 1991).

Sweeney, Eileen C., 'New Standards for Certainty: Early Reception of Aristotle's *Posterior Analytics*', in Denery, Ghosh, and Zeeman (eds.), *Uncertain Knowledge*.

Symes, Carol, 'When We Talk about Modernity', *American Historical Review*, 116 (2011).

Szabó, Thomas, 'Zur Geschichte der *boni homines*', in Duccio Balestracci et al. (eds.), *Uomini paesaggi storie* (Siena: Salvietti e Barabuffi, 2012).

Sztompka, Piotr, *Trust: A Sociological Theory* (Cambridge: Cambridge University Press, 1999).

Tachau, Katherine, *Vision and Certitude in the Age of Ockham: Optics, Epistemology and the Foundations of Semantics 1250–1345* (Leiden: Brill, 1988).

Tajfel, Henri, *Human Groups and Social Categories: Studies in Social Psychology* (Cambridge: Cambridge University Press, 1981).

Tanner, Norman, and Sethina Watson, 'The Least of the Laity: The Minimum Requirements for a Medieval Christian', *Journal of Medieval History*, 32 (2006).

Taylor, Alice, *The Shape of the State in Medieval Scotland, 1124–1290* (Oxford: Oxford University Press, 2016).

Taylor, Claire, 'Looking for the "Good Men" in the Languedoc: An Alternative to Cathars?', in Antonio Sennis (ed.), *Cathars in Question* (Woodbridge: York Medieval Press, 2016).

Théry, Julien, '*Fama*: l'opinion publique comme preuve judiciaire aperçu sur la révolution médiévale de l'inquisitoire (XIIe–XIVe siècle)', in Bruno Lemesle (ed.), *La Preuve en justice de l' Antiquité à nos jours* (Rennes: Presses Universitaires de Rennes, 2003).

Thirsk, Joan (ed.), *The Agrarian History of England and Wales*, V: *1640–1750*, I: *Regional Farming Systems* (Cambridge: Cambridge University Press, 1984).

———, *English Peasant Farming: The Agrarian History of Lincolnshire from Tudor to Recent Times* (London: Methuen, 1957).

Thomas, Hugh M., *The Secular Clergy in England, 1066–1216* (Oxford: Oxford University Press, 2014).

Thomson, John A. F., *The Early Tudor Church and Society, 1485–1529* (London: Longman, 1993).

Throsby, John, *Thoroton's History of Nottinghamshire: Volume 3. Republished with Large Additions* (London: Burbage, 1796).

Thrupp, Sylvia, *The Merchant Class of Medieval London* (Ann Arbor: University of Michigan Press, 1976).

Tierney, Brian, *Foundations of the Conciliar Theory* (Cambridge: Cambridge University Press, 1955).

Tilly, Charles, *Durable Inequality* (Berkeley: University of California Press, 1998).

———, *Trust and Rule* (Cambridge: Cambridge University Press, 2005).

Tilly, Richard, 'Introduction', *Jahrbuch für Wirtschaftsgeschichte*, 46 (2005).

Titow, Jan Zbigniew, *English Rural Society 1200–1350* (London: George Allen and Unwin, 1969).

Tönnies, Ferdinand, *Gemeinschaft und Gesellschaft*, trans. Jose Hollis as *Community and Civil Society* (Cambridge: Cambridge University Press, 2001).

Treggiari, Ferdinando, 'La *fides* dell'unico teste', in Prodi (ed.), *La fiducia secondo i linguaggi del potere*.

Trivellato, Francesca, *The Familiarity of Strangers: The Sephardic Diaspora, Livorno and Cross-Cultural Trade in the Early Modern Period* (New Haven, Conn.: Yale University Press, 2009).

Trusen, Winfried, 'Der Inquisitionsprozess: seine historischen Grundlagen und frühen Formen', *Zeitschrift der Savigny-Stiftung für Rechtsgeschichte*, 105 (1988).

Turner, Marion, *Handbook of Middle English Studies* (Oxford: Wiley-Blackwell, 2013).

Turner, Sam, *Making a Christian Landscape: The Countryside in Early Medieval Cornwall, Devon and Wessex* (Exeter: University of Exeter Press, 2006).

Turner, Wendy, 'Mental Incapacity and the Financing of War in Medieval England', in L. J. Andrew Villalon and Donald J. Kagay (eds.), *The Hundred Years War (Part II): Different Vistas* (Leiden: Brill, 2008).

Uzzi, Brian, 'Social Structure and Competition in Interfirm Networks: The Paradox of Embeddedness', in Mark Granovetter and Richard Swedberg (eds.), *The Sociology of Economic Life*, 2nd ed. (Boulder, Colo.: Westview, 2001).

Vallerani, Massimo, *Medieval Public Justice* (Washington, D.C.: Catholic University of America Press, 2012).

————, 'Modelli di verità: le prove nei processi inquisitori', in Gauvard (ed.), *L'enquête au Moyen âge*.

Van Doosselaere, Quentin, *Commercial Agreements and Social Dynamics in Medieval Genoa* (Cambridge: Cambridge University Press, 2009).

Van Engen, John, 'The Christian Middle Ages as an Historiographical Problem', *American Historical Review*, 91 (1986).

————, 'Faith as a Concept of Order in Medieval Christendom', in Thomas Kselman (ed.), *Belief in History: Innovative Approaches to European and American Religion* (Notre Dame, Ind.: University of Notre Dame Press, 1991).

Van Houts, Elisabeth, 'Gender and Authority of Oral Witnesses in Europe (800–1300)', *Transactions of the Royal Historical Society*, 9 (1999).

Van Nieuwenhove, Rik, *Introduction to Medieval Theology* (Cambridge: Cambridge University Press, 2012).

Van Uytven, Raymond, 'Showing Off One's Rank in the Middle Ages', in Wim Blockmans and Antheun Janse (eds.), *Showing Status: Representation of Social Positions in the Late Middle Ages* (Turnhout: Brepols, 1999).

Vauchez, André, *Sainthood in the Later Middle Ages*, trans. Jean Birrell (Cambridge: Cambridge University Press, 1997).

Verdon, Laure, 'Le roi, la loi, l'enquête et l'officier: procédure et enquêteurs en Provence sous le règne de Charles II (1285–1309)', in Gauvard (ed.), *L'enquête au Moyen âge*

Vincent, Diane 'The Contest over the Public Imagination of Inquisition, 1380–1430', in Flannery and Walter (eds.), *Culture of Inquisition*.

Vodola, Elisabeth F., '*Fides et culpa*: The Use of Roman Law in Ecclesiastical Ideology', in Brian Tierney and Peter Linehan (eds.), *Authority and Power: Studies on Medieval Law and Government Presented to Walter Ullmann* (Cambridge: Cambridge University Press, 1980).

Von Caenegem, Raoul C., 'Public Prosecution of Crime in Twelfth-Century England', in C.N.L. Brooke et al. (eds.), *Church and Government in the Middle Ages: Essays Presented to C. R. Cheney* (Cambridge: Cambridge University Press, 1976).

Vulliez, Charles, 'L'évêque de Paris Etienne Tempier (1268–1279) et son entourage ecclésiastique', in Cédric Giraud (ed.), *Notre-Dame de Paris 1163–2013* (Turnhout: Brepols, 2013).

Walsham, Alexandra, *The Reformation of the Landscape: Religion, Identity, and Memory in Early Modern Britain and Ireland* (Oxford: Oxford University Press, 2011).

Warren, Wilfred Lewis, *The Governance of Norman and Angevin England 1086–1272* (London: Edward Arnold, 1987).

Watson, Sethina, 'The Origins of the English Hospital', *Transactions of the Royal Historical Society*, sixth series 16 (2006).

Watt, Diane, 'Faith in the Landscape: Overseas Pilgrimage in the *Book of Margery Kempe*', in Clare A. Lees and Gillian R. Overing (eds.), *A Place to Believe In: Locating Medieval Landscapes* (University Park: Pennsylvania State University Press, 2006).

Webb, Heather, *The Medieval Heart* (New Haven, Conn.: Yale University Press, 2010).

Weber, Max, 'Bureaucracy', in Hans H. Gerth and C. Wright Mills (eds.), *From Max Weber: Essays in Sociology* (London: Routledge, 1991).

——, *Wirtschaft und Gesellschaft*, trans. Günther Roth and Claus Wittich as *Economy and Society: An Outline of Interpretive Sociology* (Berkeley: University of California Press, 2013).

Weltecke, Dorothea, 'Doubts and the Absence of Faith', in Arnold (ed.), *Oxford Handbook of Medieval Christianity*.

——, 'Trust: Some Methodological Reflections', in Schulte, Mostert, and van Renswoude (eds.), *Strategies of Writing*.

Werner, Janelle, 'Promiscuous Priests and Vicarage Children: Clerical Sexuality and Masculinity in Late Medieval England', in Jennifer D. Thibodeaux (ed.), *Negotiating Clerical Identities: Priests, Monks and Masculinity in the Middle Ages* (Basingstoke: Macmillan, 2010).

Weston, Darlene, Alan Ogden, and Anthea Boyleston, *Excavations for the Mappa Mundi Museum at Hereford Cathedral 1993: Draft Report on the Human Skeletal Remains* (University of Bradford, unpublished, n.d.).

Whyte, Nicola, *Inhabiting the Landscape: Place, Custom and Memory, 1500–1800* (Oxford: Oxbow, 2009).

Wickham, Chris, *Community and Clientele in Twelfth-Century Tuscany: The Origins of the Rural Commune in the Plain of Lucca* (Oxford: Clarendon, 1998).

——, '*Fama* and the Law in Twelfth-Century Tuscany', in Fenster and Smail (eds.), *Fama*.

——, 'Land Disputes and Their Social Framework in Lombard-Carolingian Italy, 700–900', in Wendy Davies and Paul Fouracre (eds.), *The Settlement of Disputes in Early Medieval Europe* (Cambridge: Cambridge University Press, 1986).

——, *Medieval Rome: Stability and Crisis of a City, 900–1150* (Oxford: Oxford University Press, 2015).

——, *The Mountains and the City: The Tuscan Apennines in the Early Middle Ages* (Oxford: Oxford University Press, 1988).

Wilkinson, Louise, *Women in Thirteenth-Century Lincolnshire* (Woodbridge: Boydell, 2007).

Willard, James Field, *Parliamentary Taxes on Personal Property 1290 to 1334: A Study in Mediaeval English Financial Administration* (Cambridge, Mass.: Medieval Academy of America, 1934).

Williams, Bernard, *Truth and Truthfulness: An Essay in Genealogy* (Princeton, N.J.: Princeton University Press, 2002).

Williamson, Oliver, 'Calculativeness, Trust, and Economic Organization', *Journal of Law and Economics*, 36 (1993).

——, *The Economic Institutions of Capitalism: Firms, Markets, Relational Contracting* (New York: Free Press, 1985).

——, 'The New Institutional Economics: Taking Stock, Looking Ahead', *Journal of Economic Literature*, 38 (2000).

Winchester, Angus J. L., *Landscape and Society in Medieval Cumbria* (Edinburgh: John Donald, 1987).

Winroth, Anders, *The Making of Gratian's* Decretum (Cambridge: Cambridge University Press, 2000).

Wirth, Jean, 'La naissance du concept de croyance', *Bibliothèque d'humanisme et renaissance*, 45 (1983).

Wood, Andy, *The Memory of the People: Custom and Popular Senses of the Past in Early Modern England* (Cambridge: Cambridge University Press, 2013).

Woodcock, Brian L., *Medieval Ecclesiastical Courts in the Diocese of Canterbury* (Oxford: Oxford University Press, 1952).

Woolgar, Christopher M., 'Meat and Dairy Products in Late Medieval England', in Christopher M. Woolgar, Dale Serjeantson, and Tony Waldron (eds.), *Food in Medieval England: Diet and Nutrition* (Oxford: Oxford University Press, 2006).

———, *The Senses in Late Medieval England* (New Haven, Conn.: Yale University Press, 2006).

Wunderli, Richard, 'Pre-Reformation London Summoners and the Murder of Richard Hunne', *Journal of Ecclesiastical History*, 33 (1982).

Zadora-Rio, Elisabeth, 'The Making of Churchyards and Parish Territories in the Early-Medieval Landscape of France and England in the 7th–12th Centuries: A Reconsideration', *Medieval Archaeology*, 47 (2003).

A NOTE ON THE TYPE

{≈≈≈≈≈}

THIS BOOK has been composed in Miller, a Scotch Roman typeface designed by Matthew Carter and first released by Font Bureau in 1997. It resembles Monticello, the typeface developed for The Papers of Thomas Jefferson in the 1940s by C. H. Griffith and P. J. Conkwright and reinterpreted in digital form by Carter in 2003.

Pleasant Jefferson ("P. J.") Conkwright (1905–1986) was Typographer at Princeton University Press from 1939 to 1970. He was an acclaimed book designer and AIGA Medalist.

The ornament used throughout this book was designed by Pierre Simon Fournier (1712–1768) and was a favorite of Conkwright's, used in his design of the *Princeton University Library Chronicle*.